# INTRODUCTION TO CORRECTIONS

# INTRODUCTION TO CORRECTIONS

## THIRD EDITION

Vernon Fox

*Florida State University*

Prentice-Hall, Inc., Englewood Cliffs, New Jersey 07632

*Library of Congress Cataloging in Publication Data*

FOX, VERNON BRITTAIN
    Introduction to corrections.

    Bibliography: p.
    Includes index.
    1. Corrections.  I. Title.
HV8665.F725 1985      364.6′0973      83-24428
ISBN  0-13-480484-8

364.6
F794i
1985

Editorial/production supervision and interior design: Eve Mossman
Cover design: Wanda Lubelska Design
Manufacturing buyer: Ed O'Dougherty

Printed in the United States of America

10  9  8  7  6  5  4

ISBN 0-13-480484-8 01

Prentice-Hall International, Inc., *London*
Prentice-Hall of Australia Pty. Limited, *Sydney*
Editora Prentice-Hall do Brasil, Ltda., *Rio de Janeiro*
Prentice-Hall Canada Inc., *Toronto*
Prentice-Hall of India Private Limited, *New Delhi*
Prentice-Hall of Japan, Inc., *Tokyo*
Prentice-Hall of Southeast Asia Pte. Ltd., *Singapore*
Whitehall Books Limited, *Wellington, New Zealand*

*Dedicated to Dr. Coyle E. Moore*
*who helped me make the transition*
*from prison administration to the university*

# CONTENTS

# 5
## PROBATION  122

# 6
## PRISONS AND CORRECTIONAL INSTITUTIONS  143

# 7
## INSTITUTIONAL PROCEDURES—CUSTODY  179

# 8

## INSTITUTIONAL PROCEDURES—TREATMENT   203

# 9

## THE EFFECTS OF INSTITUTIONAL LIFE   228

# 10

## COMMUNITY-BASED CORRECTIONS  253

# 11

## SPECIAL AREAS IN CORRECTIONS  278

# 12

## PAROLE AND OTHER RELEASE PROCEDURES  315

# 13

## TREATMENT APPROACHES IN CORRECTIONS   340

# 14

## JUVENILE CORRECTIONS   366

# 15

## PRIVATE CORRECTIONS   393

# FOREWORD

For many years there has been little interest in improving correctional services. Public apathy resulted in meager budgets, which provided limited personnel, inadequate salaries, and often submarginal buildings and equipment.

Unfortunately, crisis is frequently the major catalytic agent in stimulating social progress. Fear of crime in the streets and of economic loss to businesspeople and others has awakened public concern to the importance of improving the criminal justice system. The role of corrections and its importance in the reduction and control of crime are now being recognized. For the first time, federal funds have been made available for improving correctional services, including the training of personnel.

The increased concern and funding are resulting in better salaries and greater diversity of personnel needs. Correctional service is an emerging profession, and more and better educational programs are needed.

This book by Dr. Vernon Fox is a timely contribution to the literature of the field. The author provides a brief history of corrections, a description of the "state of the art," and a projection of potentials for development in the future. The major facets of correctional service are well covered, and their functions within the field as a whole are clearly defined. This introductory text gives the student interested in career potentials an overview of the field. It aids the correctional employee in understanding his role and the relationship of the service in which he is employed to the total continuum of corrections.

This book is easy to read, its contents are interesting, and it will undoubtedly make a contribution as a text for students and a reference book for all who are interested in corrections.

THE LATE E. PRESTON SHARP, PH.D.

# INTRODUCTION

A book on corrections that would satisfy everyone in the field is impossible to write. The various views of corrections prevailing in different parts of the country and among the different specialties within the field result in divergent interpretations of correctional objectives and the means by which those objectives should be achieved and implemented. Even the President's Commission on Law Enforcement and Administration of Justice has been criticized privately by some correctional administrators and practitioners because its cover report, *The Challenge of Crime in a Free Society,* and the accompanying *Task Force Report* series published in 1967, was largely the work of lawyers and academic researchers, none well acquainted with everyday correctional tasks. While several competent correctional career persons were involved, there were not enough of them to satisfy some in the correctional field.

Visits to correctional programs throughout the United States and participation in regional and national conferences further point up the differences in viewpoints as to what corrections comprises. Some outstanding national organizations tend to emphasize adult prisons and correctional institutions. Others emphasize probation, parole, and juvenile court services. Some correctional administrators maintain that the jail is not and cannot be a correctional institution, while others hold that the jail has the greatest potential of all to be helpful in this field. Some administrators think that the police have no business in corrections, while others think that the voluntary police supervision of juveniles can have a great impact on the field.

In 1968 and 1969, regional meetings of outstanding practitioners and educators in corrections were called preparatory to the development of a curriculum in corrections. The thrusts that came from the Western meeting in Los Angeles, the Southern meeting in St. Petersburg, the Midwestern meeting in Chicago, and the Eastern meeting in Hershey were divergent in emphases. Occupational workshop meetings focusing on curriculum development in New York and Kansas City further demonstrated the differences. A meeting of national leaders in the correctional field in Williamsburg, Virginia, in 1969 helped to blend some of the similarities and to clarify some of the differences. Some of the areas emphasized in different parts of the country and by different people were treatment, custody, education, due process in trial procedure, prevention through police and school cooperation, social work and psychological services, and upgrading of personnel through in-service training. The advocacy and the rejection of some of these emphases by some participants are equally intense. Similarities in viewpoint were almost consistently in the area of objectives rather than in practice.

Consequently, the preparation of a book that covers all phases of the field of corrections must attempt to reflect a balance of regional and practitioner viewpoints. Any such blending must be a compromise of viewpoints. This book reflects the correctional field as seen by one who has had many years of experience in juvenile, youth, and adult corrections, both in practice and in education. It is hoped that the blend of emphases reflects in balance the total correctional field.

It takes considerable cooperation and effort on the part of many people to synthesize a subject area as diverse as the field of corrections. Any credit for the synthesis in this book goes to the many persons who contributed to it in the regional meetings, to those who provided special advice on frequent occasions, and to the persons mentioned above who helped to put the manuscript together. The weaknesses and deficiencies must be attributed to the author.

VERNON FOX
*Florida State University*

# 1

# THE DEVELOPMENT OF CORRECTIONS

Corrections is the part of society's agencies of social control that attempts to rehabilitate or neutralize the deviant behavior of adult criminals and juvenile delinquents. It functions with social and legal authority after the criminal court has held an adult to be guilty of a violation of law, or when the juvenile court acts in a child's interests after a complaint or referral has been made alleging a delinquent act. In practice, some correctional functions precede the formal assumption of responsibility by agencies for the administration of justice. For example, welfare departments have protective services for juveniles with behavioral problems, and most police departments have juvenile aid bureaus or a juvenile officer who works with children and adolescents. These agencies often function long before young offenders are referred to juvenile court and most frequently are able to avoid any court referral. Consequently, the correctional function may be assumed informally by society. Court action precedes formal beginnings of the correctional process.

Criminology is the body of knowledge from which the practical application of corrections emerges. It is an interdisciplinary science or system that seeks to comprehend the causes, dimensions, and implications of the multifaceted social disorders called crime and delinquency. The theoretical conceptualizations of criminology may find practical expression in the field of corrections. Theory and practice are functionally related. Good theory emerges from observation and study of good practice. Conversely, good practice can be guided by good theory. Theory is the rationale behind practice. Practice without theory is just as sterile as theory without practice. Consequently, some knowledge of criminology is essential to the practice of corrections.

The theory and practice of social control that is so necessary to orderly society emerges from and relates to the pattern and complexity of the society it serves. At each stage in society's evolution, the social patterns and the problems relating to them have become increasingly complex. The methods of social control, of law enforcement and corrections, and the theory behind them, have changed with the times. Early human beings had no law. On the other hand, the modern American urban human being has all phases of life and living conditions regulated. From early times to modern times, the controls grew functionally, as needed, to fit the society in which people lived. Delinquency and crime differ in definitions and in society's response according to the development of the society, its advance in civilization, its complexity, social conditions, and cultural values. There is no crime at all among the primitive Ifugao in northern Luzon. A study has pointed out variations in deliquency and its treatment in Boston, in San Antonio, and among Mexican nationals in Mexico.[1] Crime and delinquency, then, emerge from the cultural values and social problems in a society. They represent the dysfunctional relationship between the individual and the society, which corrections attempts to correct.

There are various methods of social control that hold individuals to the expected norms of behavior in any society. They range all the way from public opinion and disapproval to force and death. All organized societies include mechanisms for social control. Everybody will get along and will get along in the manner prescribed by these mechanisms.

The earth is approximately four and one-half billion years old. Man of some sort has probably existed for 1.3 million years. Modern humankind has existed for 240,000 years in some stage, while the *homo* genus of some sort has existed for 500,000 years. Anthropologists agree that the existence of various kinds of artifacts, such as chipped stone flakes, indicate that the people who made them could talk and transmit information. Such tools were developed in the Mousterian culture between 100,000 and 35,000 B.C., with increased development apparent around 50,000 B.C.[2] The development of language is important to organized society because it provides the basis for a culture. It is a vocal system by which human beings, as members of and participants in a culture, may interact and communicate. Human culture developed because people talk about what they do and what happens to them. Organized society, together with its rules and regulations, becomes culture. Religion provided the first political unity beyond that provided by family and kinship ties.

Spoken language gave rise to abstract thinking and symbolic interaction, which, in turn, gave rise to values, concepts of right and wrong, and

[1] Carl M. Rosenquist and Edwin I. Megargee, *Delinquency in Three Cultures* (Austin: University of Texas Press, 1969).

[2] Editors of *Life* magazine, *The Epic of Man* (New York: Time-Life Books, 1961), p. 18.

acceptable and unacceptable behaviors. Neanderthal man is generally credited with beginning spoken communication about 100,000 B.C. and the first primitive religion about 60,000 B.C., according to evidence found at the Shandilar Cave in the rugged Zagros Mountains in contemporary Northern Iraq.[3] Religion—not any specific religion, but religion in general—delineated the ethical systems from which the ancient codes and more modern laws were derived. These religious tenets were written into codes of behavior as soon as writing was available. Consequently, spoken language, religion, and writing all contributed to the development of criminal justice and corrections for modern man.

Writing by pictures emerged around 4000 B.C. Writing with symbols began around 3000 B.C., although there were some beginnings of written communication as early as 6000 B.C. Primitive language was without past, future, and subjective tenses. The Sumerian language, in which humanity's first code was written, ceased to be spoken around 1500 B.C. The earliest languages that really communicated were called the classical languages. Hebrew, Greek, and Latin are the classical languages in Western civilization. The earliest monuments in Hebrew were in the ninth or tenth century B.C., having developed as a mixture of several Semitic languages. Egyptian documents from the sixteenth century B.C. have revealed Semitic words. Inscriptions in Greek engraved on stones found in Greece date back to the eighth century B.C., and they become numerous in the fifth and later centuries. The oldest records of Latin date from 600 B.C., although some of its preceding languages date back to the Etruscan invasion of Italy in the eighth century B.C. All evidence indicates that sophisticated culture even in Western civilization has been developing for only a few thousand years. The value system and methods of social control to protect the social system take a long time to develop.

## PRIMITIVE LAW

The earliest behavioral norms were developed by groups of people as folkways and customs. They were only habitual ways of doing things. Many primitive peoples today have no organs of political government but live in what might be called anarchy. Some examples are the Papuans of New Guinea, the Veddahs of Ceylon, and the Tierra del Fuegians of Argentina and Chile. More advanced primitive peoples, such as the American Plains Indians, developed stronger systems and some political organization, but no judicial organs. Yet these people were governed by custom. If such behavior as murder, rape, and kidnapping were not considered to be crimes, they might be seen as affronts to individual families. An expedient for ad-

---

[3] George Constable, *The Neanderthals,* in *The Emergence of Man* series (New York: Time-Life Books, 1973), p. 7. "Intelligence, Language, and the Human Mind," Chapter 8 in Richard E. Leakey and Roger Lewin, *Origins* (London: Macdonald and Jane's, 1977), pp. 179–205.

justment of social ills among primitive peoples was the blood feud, in which one family avenged the wrongs wrought upon its members by assaulting or killing the offender or members of another family. Primitive man had no conception of "crime" or of "private property." He did know *when* his brother had been killed, but he did not rely on expert witnesses or rational proof. In case of doubt, he relied on oaths and ordeals. Primitive man was a slave to custom but recognized an obligation as binding only when he had received equivalence—a basis of the civil law of primitive society.[4]

Although deviations from these folkways and customs were not illegal, they did produce concern among other persons in the group whose anticipations and predictions of expected behavior had been violated. As people progressed further into civilization, they began to attach emotional values to some of these customs, and they became "right" and "wrong." With the development of organized primitive religion, conceivably around 25,000 B.C., creeds emerged to control the interaction between people within the social formation. The creeds controlled social behavior and were more complex and refined than the early folkways and customs.

Breach of exogamy and sorcery were the most prevalent primitive crimes. Incest or endogamy is taboo in all societies, the royal families of ancient Hawaii, Peru, and Egypt being notable exceptions. Exogamy, the custom of marrying only outside one's own tribe or clan, was often the inviolable custom of primitive society. Sorcery exposed the entire community to dark and sinister forces. Among the Plains Indians, it was illegal or a taboo to scare away the buffalo, while among the Eskimos, it was illegal to harm the seals.

Primitive African tribes today have courts and the organs of justice. Some of their legal transactions compare favorably with those of ancient Babylon. The transition from custom to law is easy to understand but takes a long time to accomplish.

The matrix of all law is the blood feud.[5] Primitive society intervened in the blood feud when too many persons were involved in it and the practice threatened the very existence of the society. Even though murder and theft, as well as other behavior now defined as "crime," were not considered to be very important, the resulting blood feuds became most important. While there are some "good riddance" actions by primitive peoples such as the Eskimo, the Chukchee, the Akamba, and the Bantu, the blood feuds in primitive societies of the past were carrying the concept too far for the welfare of the tribes. The total movement resulted in the tribe's or a political entity's taking more and more responsibility for individual crimes as civilization progressed. There was a shift from the idea that the political community was based on blood kinship to the idea that local contiguity could serve as the basis of common political action. The unity of kindred groups

---

[4] See Bronislaw Malinowski, *Crime and Custom in Savage Society* (New York: Harcourt, Brace & World, 1932).

[5] William Seagle, *The History of Law* (New York: Tudor, 1946), p. 36.

for the welfare of all among several tribes in an area resulted in agreements, such as those common among the more advanced American Indians a century and more ago.

In summary, it takes a long time for people to develop methods to control behavior of groups. Primitive people used custom as a control. After a period of time, they attached emotional meanings to that custom and it became "right" or "wrong," becoming what the sociologist calls *mores.* The next step in the development of social controls was the institutionalization of behavior in the culture. Then it became law. An example might be the emergence of monogamous marriage. In early times it was "customary" for one man and one woman to stay together because that arrangement avoided considerable conflict. Then, it became "right." After more time, it became a sacrament in the church. Then it became law. Primitive man lived by custom. Ancient man lived by mores and codes. Man in the Middle Ages lived by social institutions, primarily through the Church. Modern man lives by law. It takes a long time to move this far.

## ANCIENT CODES

After the development of writing, the tribal taboos were set down in codes. The first pleadings were in Sumer about 3500 B.C., but were fragmented, rather than being a true "code," and dealt with pleadings and land transactions. Some have referred to these as the Sumerian Code, but the first real code was the Code of Hammurabi in Babylon (about 1750 B.C.). Persia established the first known code created by a political state,[6] in which the usual punishment was execution, but mutilation and banishment were also used. Relatively few offenses were specified. The Law of Moses, developed between 1500 B.C. and 900 B.C., and lesser codes put together by other lawgivers in the ancient world were further refinements of the ethical principles of social interaction being forged from the experience of socialized people.

One of the most influential of the ancient codes was the Twelve Tables of wood on which were engraved or painted the earliest codification of Roman law. Two were added to the original ten for a total of twelve. Prepared in 451–450 B.C., the Twelve Tables show unmistakable influence of Greek law, particularly Athenian law. The need for them was practical: The patrician magistrates could not easily cope with the plebian litigants and needed some guidelines. The origins of the Twelve Tables are clouded in conflicting narrative, and the text of the codes, surprisingly, is gone, but the practice based upon them molded Roman law for several centuries. When the Roman Empire was formulated by Augustus, the Twelve Tables were functioning in stabilizing the society. Their influence extended into

[6] William Bain, "A History of Corrections," ed. Charle O'Neil, unpublished paper, 1975, p. 1.

the fifth century A.D., and much of them became part of the Justinian Code.

The Sermon on the Mount by Jesus was probably the epitome of the early formulations, which were really refinements of social experience in a society growing more civilized. Many of these codes were organized into a unitary code under commission by Emperor Justinian of the Byzantine Empire in A.D. 529–565 and became known as the Justinian Code. The Roman Empire in the West had fallen in 476 A.D. and had become the province of German kings, with Odoacer replacing the last Roman emperor, Romulus Augustus. This rule of the Byzantine Empire lasted until the fall of Constantinople in 1453.

Ancient Greece contributed law, as it is known today, to the world, as well as the practice of law. This is why lawyers and legislators are sometimes called Solons, a reference to an Athenian statesman (638?–558 B.C.). Rome gave civilization the most refined practice of law known to that time, a level of practice not achieved again until the great revolutions of the late 1700s.

It is important to remember that these formulations were codes, not laws. Functionally, the system of social control was much simpler than an imposed code might be. The earliest form of social control on an everyday, practical basis, was the interaction between the offender and his victim or the victim's family. In Western civilization, the procedure began in the formalized trial by combat in ancient England, a form of control which had been much less formalized among primitive peoples.

As civilized people moved into agriculture, land became valuable. A pastoral economy, based primarily on raising sheep, began around 10,000 B.C. Agriculture gave rise to cities, the first called Jericho, around 9,000 B.C. Cultivation of the land probably began a little earlier than 6000 B.C. with cereal cultivation, and 5000 B.C. with wheat and barley. The earliest plows portrayed on Egyptian tombs and Mesopotamian seals appeared around 3000 B.C. Land as a valuable commodity and agriculture as the basis of an economy necessitated permanent residence. The ancient feudal system began to emerge. The best organizer in an area claimed the land, and the other people worked for him in exchange for managerial services, both economic and in terms of security. As these feudal lords grew, they expanded their holdings by making war and capturing the land and people in neighboring domains. The ancient empires were thus developed. The strongest feudal lord became the king in that area. Modern Ethiopia evolved in this way, and Haile Selassie was known as the "King of Kings."

The consequences of the blood feud has forced society to take cognizance of wrongs between individuals such as murder, rape, kidnapping, and theft. This distinction made judicial process necessary. As a result, the ancient feudal lords established arbitration courts, which originally were voluntary but which were available and, after some persuasion, were used increasingly. Soon, people were compelled to go to court. The first known court was depicted on the shield of Achilles in Homer's *Iliad*. It probably existed around 2000 B.C. and was shown as being located at the gates of the city. The suggestion is that the offender was returned to the city or expelled from it, depending upon the verdict of the court. The decisions of the court generally involved an indemnity to the victim or the victim's family for two or three years. The offender may have been indentured to work for the victim or his family until the debt was paid or for life if it was not paid. The dispositions of these courts were (1) compensation and restitution; (2) bondage to the victim or his family until restitution was completed or for a number of years, including life; (3) assignment to the public works, like the quarry, building roads, buildings, or other service; or (4) vengeance by death or exile. A slave who committed another offense could be sold to gladiator school. This system developed a society of free people and slaves, which was described by Plato in *The Republic* and which forms the base of modern works about ancient society with slavery as a theme, such as *Spartacus*. This societal system pervaded the ancient feudal era as well as the medieval feudal era, and remained for centuries. The slaves who constituted the labor force were made up of offenders, debtors, and prisoners of war. At the time of Plato, for example, approximately one out of ten citizens was free and could vote as a citizen. Superimposed over that social structure were the lords and nobility of ancient and medieval times, who made up the ruling class. It might be noted here that Plato, in his *De Legibus*, suggested three prisons: one for the safe-keeping of persons awaiting trial and sentence; one for disorderly persons and vagrants; and a third to be situated away from the city for the punishment of felons. Jerusalem had places of detention as early as the sixth century B.C., although the concept of jails and prisons in the modern sense was centuries away.

## MEDIEVAL JUSTICE

The Justinian Code was the last formulation of law between the ancient Roman Empire and the social chaos that was the Middle Ages. When Justinian assumed the throne of the Eastern Roman Empire in Constantinople in 518 A.D., he commissioned ten commissioners to go through all existing constitutions and codes and to select the valuable sections and render them useful to the Empire. The resulting code was promulgated in 529. In the years that followed, until his death in 565, more revisions were made to the code. Four books were finally produced, and they became the standard of law throughout Europe during the Middle Ages in the absence of any other standard. The common law as it is known today, both English and Continental, is basically derived from the code of Justinian courts.

As the feudal fiefs developed into empires, all subjected peoples and slaves were forced to go to the courts for redress of wrongs. In many areas, free citizens could manage their own affairs through trial by combat or other individual efforts. Ancient and medieval noblemen were "above the law" and did not need to use the courts, and conflicts with neighboring lords were settled by arms.

With the downfall of the Roman Empire in 476 A.D., Europe was in chaos. The organized church developed as a political entity. The Church maintained control of territories and the peoples. Canon law was enforced by the arm of the Church. Ecclesiastical prisons were constructed to supplement the places of confinement of the time, which were mainly the gatehouses of the abbeys. The last ecclesiastical prison was constructed in Paris in the sixteenth century. A good example of the old confinement facility still remains in Provins, a town of northern France. The "prisoner's tower" serves as a belfry to the church of St. Quiriace, which was built in the twelfth century. The base now is surrounded by a thick mound of masonry added by the English in the fifteenth century when they held that territory.

Any secular ruler in Western civilization had to have the blessings of the pope. Charlemagne, around 800 A.D., began to organize secular control in Europe. The Holy Roman Empire, established around 1200 A.D., incorporated the entire Justinian Code and operated under the blessings of the pope. Referring to Joseph Stalin's comment—"How many divisions does the pope have?"—the pope *did* have divisions, which participated in the local wars on the Italian Peninsula. He was also effective in the diplomatic area throughout the world.

The Church was an important agent of social control, including crime, from the fourth century through the eighteenth century. The height of ecclesiastical jurisdiction was reached in the late Middle Ages in the Holy Roman Empire. Based on Matthew 18:15–18, the Church assumed the sanction of excommunication as spiritual coercive authority. After the Council of Nicaea in 325 A.D., at which the relationship of Christ to God was settled for Christians by a close majority (in favor of his being divine as opposed to being only a prophet), major developments occurred on the criminal side of church law and enforcement. The issue was so emotion-laden and the vote was so close that the victors pressed their advantage harshly, zealously punishing and eliminating their opposition. Heresy became a major crime. Christianity ceased to be a sect of Judaism and became an independent religion. Episcopal provincial synod sentences of excommunication could be appealed in the church hierarchy. The secular arm of the system of justice supported the decrees of the Church. The practice of adding banishment by the emperor to synodical condemnation strengthened the controls even further. The third and fourth ecumenical synods in the fifth century were really trials for heresy of Nestorius and Dioscorus, who occupied the thrones of Constantinople and Alexandria. The fifth ecumenical council came close to becoming a trial for the pope.

The system developed in which an ecclesiastical offense would be handled by the bishop. If a clergyman were accused of a secular crime, the bishop would have original jurisdiction and might or might not refer the case to secular courts. By the tenth century in England, the two were generally mixed in the same case, the bishop enforcing secular laws by ecclesiastical censure and the alderman enforcing ecclesiastical laws with secular punishment. On the Continent, Charlemagne empowered the bishops to act as real judges and provided that secular matters could be taken to the bishop's tribunal.

By the eleventh century, the tribunals or courts were church-operated and a class of church lawyers had emerged. The king did not hear complaints and accusations, but referred them to the bishops, who appointed the "vicar-general" or "chancellor" to hear them. While the feudal and spiritual courts were kept separate, the influence of the Church was unmistakable. In England, the Constitutions of Clarendon in the twelfth century gave the convicted person power to appeal to the king, which really meant a rehearing by an archbishop.

In the late Middle Ages, the ecclesiastical courts had jurisdiction over most issues, civil and criminal, except those involving real property. Some clerks in the ecclesiastical courts became an issue because of the way they handled criminal cases. Rising criticism resulted in the Constitutions of Clarendon in 1166 A.D., in which Henry II attempted to restore the power of the Crown over the church courts. For example, benefit of clergy was afforded everyone (not merely clergymen) who was able to read; thus these people were relatively safe from serious penalties for rape, burglary, homicide, or almost any crime, at least for the first offense. On the Continent, the history of courts was almost congruous with the history of the Roman Catholic Church.

Penalties were divided into (1) punishments and (2) censures. For most serious crimes, imprisonment in the bishop's prison or ecclesiastical prison for life or for a lesser amount of time could be imposed. Dismissal or degradation in the ministry or church rank was also used. In the cases of heresy, apostasy, and sorcery, the secular courts were brought in to impose the death penalty, which was generally burning at the stake. The fourth Lateran Council in 1215 relegated incorrigible offenders to secular courts, which usually meant death. The most serious *censure*, of course, was excommunication.

In England, the beginnings of law enforcement can be traced back to the Anglo-Saxon period from 600 A.D. to 1066 A.D. For purposes of security and mutual economic benefit, the tribes and clans were replaced by "tuns" and the "hundreds." Ten families made up a tun (town) and ten tuns made up a hundred. The hundred was roughly congruent with the shire or county in subsequent political subdivisions. The hue and cry of the night watchman or old lamplighter set up a community chase against any thief or other offender. Generally, the offender was branded for purposes of punishment and for identification.

## FROM VENGEANCE TO JUSTICE

While primitive peoples had a wide variety of responses to offending behavior, from ceremonial singing and other approaches to resolving conflict in a consensus model to death inflicted by the victim or his family, the concept of compensation and vengeance in proportion to the offense ultimately emerged (see Exodus, Chapters 19–22). *Lex talionis* became a limitation of retaliation to make the punishment fit the crime. This concept is embodied in the Law of Moses and has been expressed in both the Old Testament and the New Testament, as follows:

Deuteronomy 19:21 (650 B.C.)—"And thine eye shall not pity; but life shall go for life, eye for eye, tooth for tooth, hand for hand, foot for foot."

Leviticus 24:20 (570 B.C.)—"Breach for breach, eye for eye, tooth for tooth: as he has caused a blemish in a man, so shall it be done to him again."

Matthew 5:38, 39 (65 A.D.)—"Ye have heard that it hath been said, An eye for an eye, and a tooth for a tooth: But I say unto you, That ye resist not evil: but whosoever shall smite thee on thy right cheek, turn to him the other also."

Although ancient cultures developed this idea of justice relating to vengeance, retribution, and compensation, after the rise of the great religions and the concept that sin and crime were offenses against God, punishments became more severe because these offenses were over and above damage to society; they were now infractions of divine law and God's will. Around the tenth century, the king became strong enough to extend his power and protection, and the mitigation of the blood feud resulted in other agencies' taking responsibility for law and order.[7] By the sixteenth century, punishments had become severe and bloody, completely out of proportion to the seriousness of offenses. Common penalties were flogging, public boiling, mutilation, stocks and pillory (persons placed in public view with head and hands secured so the public could pelt them with stones and other missiles), blinding, cutting out tongues, the rack (stretching a person by binding ankles and shoulders and pulling in opposite directions), cropping (cutting off the ears), disemboweling alive, drawing and quartering, burning, and similar tortures.[8]

The death penalty was used frequently, and several ingenious devices were employed. Visitors to the Scandinavian countries reported seeing the remains of offenders still dangling from the wheel at the gates of the cities. Although the idea of "natural rights" was introduced into the theological milieu in an attempt to lessen the harshness of criminal disposition, punishments remained severe. Offenders were given horrendous types of punishment until as late as the sixteenth and seventeenth centuries.

Convict ships were built during this period that sailed the seas, sometimes aimlessly, with a cargo of felons. Torture equipment was incorporated in the ship's equipment. One of the most grotesque devices was the iron maiden, which was a container attached to the mainmast. Half of this was stationary and the other half was hinged like a door so that a person

[7] Harry Elmer Barnes, *The Story of Punishment: A Record of Man's Inhumanity to Man* (New York: The Stratford Co., 1930), pp. 52–54. Republished by Patterson Smith (Montclair, N.J., 1972).

[8] *Ibid.*, p. 63.

could be placed inside. When the door was shut, protruding spikes, both back and front, entered the body of the victim. Needless to say, many convicts died on these ships. These vessels may have been offshoots of the "hulks" or nonseaworthy vessels that had been anchored in the Thames River and elsewhere as places of confinement. Later, when major offenders began to be transported to distant lands as punishment, these convict ships became unnecessary. They had been an expensive torture luxury.

Reaction against this type of treatment appeared in the writings of social philosophers in the sixteenth to eighteenth centuries. Grotius (1583–1645), Hobbes (1588–1679), and Locke (1632–1755) expounded the concept of government at the consent of the governed. This paved the way for Montesquieu (1689–1755), Voltaire (1694–1778), and Rousseau (1712–1778) to bring the philosophy down to the individual citizen. Justice had replaced vengeance.

## THE EMERGENCE OF CRIMINAL LAW

The beginnings of law enforcement and the administration of justice as it is known today were in the eleventh and twelfth centuries. When William the Conqueror invaded England in 1066 and established Norman control over the Anglo-Saxons, a new phase of social control began. England was divided into fifty-five military districts, or shires, and a trusted lieutenant, known as a reeve, was placed in each district. A *comes tabuli* assisted the reeve by keeping the stables, a position that eventually evolved into that of constable. The position of *shire reeve* eventually became that of the sheriff.

Soon after William's arrival in England, a census was taken, including an assessment of wealth for tax purposes. This information was included in the *Doomsday Book*, the first record of such a census and taxation on this basis.

The many references to "prison" in the Old Testament and New Testament and other religious books were there long before the modern concept of prison evolved. They referred, then, to confinement in rooms and facilities not originally designed for the purpose, such as old cellars, dens for animals, and other makeshift resources, not unlike sending an errant child to his room for punishment or detention. In fact, long-term confinement was not to be used as punishment for crime, according to the ancient codes, including the Justinian Code, and they were followed. The Church first made use of long-term confinement of offenders by locking them into the gatehouse of the abbey during the Middle Ages as a humane gesture to replace execution. The jail, authorized in 1166 A.D. at the Assize of Clarendon, was the first group of facilities built officially for purposes of confinement.

Some private prisons were built in the twelfth century and after. A person with sufficient power and influence could build his own prison and incarcerate those who interfered with his political ambitions or personal inclinations.[9] Brian Fitzcourt built a special facility, called "Cloere Brien," to accommodate the famous William Martel in 1128,[10] the same year Rennulf Flambard was the first prisoner to die in the Tower of London, originally built as a fortress for the defense of London in 1066 by William the Conqueror. Other famous private prisons were the Castle of Spielberg, the Conciergerie and Bastille in Paris, the *pozzi* or wells of the Ducal Palace in Venice, and the Seven Towers of Constantinople. The last private prison appears to have been built in 1785 by Sir Thomas Beever at Wymondham in Norfolk, England.

The Assize of Clarendon (Constitutions of Clarendon), called by Henry II in 1166 A.D., formalized court procedure. The jury system, including the grand jury and the petit jury, was structured essentially as it remains today. The sheriff was recognized as an officer of the law and his responsibilities were delineated. The construction of jails was authorized. Certain "offenses against the king's peace" were defined, including arson, robbery, murder, false coinage, and crimes of violence. The beginnings of classification of crimes as felonies and misdemeanors appeared.

In 1215, King John issued the Magna Carta under compulsion from his barons. It became a symbol of a general movement toward civil and constitutional rights, although in itself it was not intrinsically so significant. The king's court had become more powerful, and the barons' courts were losing business to it. Increasing oppression and demands for armies, fines for barons who did not accompany the king on campaigns, increased demands in a losing fight for Normandy and the final defeat in 1214, and the king's alienation of the Church by placing its property into lay hands and sending the revenues into the royal treasury finally led to the barons' action in June 1215. Administrative reform and a growing philosophy concerning "government at the consent of the governed" were intertwined in the Magna Carta. Nevertheless, it was a symbolic document that seemed to mark the beginning of civil and constitutional rights in English-speaking countries.

The Westminster period (1285–1500) refers to the effects of the Statutes of Westminster, passed during the reign of Edward I. The first, passed in 1275, held that all persons shall be treated alike before the law, whether rich or poor, and without respect for persons and, further, that all elections shall be free and no man shall disturb them. The second, passed in 1285, remodeled the institutions of justice to eliminate some abuses, enabled a curfew to be imposed, and established a bailiff or night watch. Statutes of treason were passed in 1352. The office of justice of the peace was instituted in 1361. Local government and its regulations were inaugurated in 1370. Courts of the Star Chamber or *ex parte* proceedings were instituted in 1487

[9] Leslie Fairweather, "The Evolution of the Prison," in Guiseppe de Gennaro and Sergio Lenci, eds., *Prison Architecture* (London: United Nations Social Defence Research Institute, The Architectural Press, Ltd.), 1975, pp. 13–14.

[10] P.N. Walker, *Punishment: An Illustrated History* (Newton, England: David Abbott, 1972), p. 35.

to try offenders against the State. Testimony could be coerced in these proceedings. During this period, the security of the State was being consolidated, and social control methods to accomplish this consolidation were being legitimatized and formalized.

Parliamentary government began in England in the fourteenth and fifteenth centuries, and legislation was introduced to secure the social order. Laws forbidding war against the king, forbidding serfs to leave the land in search of work, and forbidding dogs from being kept by persons not owning property were involved in an effort to maintain the social status quo. Persons guilty of murder at this time were sentenced to short imprisonment or fines. During the sixteenth and seventeenth centuries, legislation was aimed at consolidation of Church and State. Treason and heresy became capital crimes, as did swearing, adultery, and witchcraft. During the eighteenth and nineteenth centuries, piracy, forgery, and banking offenses were made crimes. In the twentieth century, white-collar and commercial crimes resulted from the changing social order.

In 1764, Beccaria published his *Essay on Crimes and Punishments,* which was a reaction against the harsh penalties of the time and a call for punishments to fit the crimes. He said that the basis of all action should be utilitarian, that crime should be considered to be an injury to society, and that prevention is more important than punishment. Beccaria supported fair and speedy trials, and imprisonment and deterrence. He thought, with Bentham, that man was hedonistic in that he sought pleasure and avoided pain, and that he could choose his behavior. An important result of Beccaria's ideas was that crimes became codified and well-delineated in the statutes. Before that time, there was no criminal law as it is now known. Wrongs were heard on their own merit and punishments meted out according to the judgment of the court. The feeling expressed by Beccaria was central to social thinking of the time, even though he first published his book anonymously to avoid reprisal. William Blackstone and Jeremy Bentham of England, as well as others, joined in the contention. Blackstone recodified English criminal law and defined specific crimes, formulating the punishments that would result from different offenses. For the first time, definitions of crime and criminal procedure were formulated in law. By 1800, English criminal procedure had a basis in statutory law. It was at this time (1789) and under these influences that the American Constitution was written and adopted. (Edward Livingston [1764–1836] was central in codifying American criminal law and procedure.) The criminal law had now come to focus primarily on the seriousness of the offense rather than on the welfare of society.

After the downfall of the feudal system, the mercenary armies were disbanded and persons without skills congregated in the cities. This condition, combined with the suppression of the monasteries and the decline of the craft guilds, resulted in mass unemployment and pauperism. The city of London established a workhouse at St. Brigit's Well, called Bridewell, in 1557. A similar workhouse was opened in Amsterdam in 1596. The use of workhouses as institutions to hold minor offenders and beggars became widespread throughout Europe. In America, the colonial jail served the same purpose. At that time, the serious offenders were transported into banishment or exile.

The replacement of the feudal system by the developing capitalistic system was a gradual process that was completed with the Industrial Revolution, generally considered to be around 1750. The invention of the steam engine, the importation of gunpowder from China, and increased commerce, particularly the seeking of spices in the absence of refrigeration, all contributed to this change. Slavery was no longer profitable, either on land or in the galleys by sea. Consequently, criminals had to be exported. Russia sent hers to Siberia. Spain and Portugal sent theirs to Africa. France sent hers to South America, and her last penal colony, the infamous Devil's Island, was not closed until 1944. The destruction of the Spanish Armada in 1588 made the seas safe for England. Consequently, England sent her criminals to America.

In 1717, the British Parliament formally designated the American colonies as England's penal colony. The first prisoners had been shipped in 1650. By 1776, there had been an estimated 100,000 (some estimates are as low as 11,000) prisoners shipped in chains to the American colonies. (In 1776, *after* the battles of Lexington and Concord on April 19, 1775, 2,000 serious offenders were sent to the American colonies.) Stories in *The London Times* in the late 1700s indicate that persons convicted of murder and other serious crimes were frequently sentenced to service beyond the seas in the American colonies. At the beginning of the American Revolution in 1776, however, the American colonies were closed to English prisoners because the government did not want to risk shipping more able-bodied Englishmen who would take up arms against the mother country. Subsequently, convicted prisoners were sent to Australia until 1879, when that practice was informally terminated.

Prisons were eventually seen as the substitute for banishment and for capital punishment. England had used capital punishment extensively for more than 200 years. During the reign of Queen Elizabeth alone, for example, there were about 72,000 executions.

The Penitentiary Law of 1775 was passed by the British Parliament under the sponsorship of John Howard and Sir William Eden, but prisons as such were not constructed in England until later. Newgate Prison was constructed in London in 1769 as a large holding operation with little or no control inside and no attempt at program. It was demolished in 1902. A workhouse opened in Ghent, Belgium, in 1773, which made the first known attempt at programming for its inmates. Thus, some have referred to this workhouse as the first prison in the modern sense; others dispute this claim.

The Western Hemisphere was first settled by the Spanish and Portuguese, and all territories south of the United States are referred to as Latin America. A large minority of America's poor, in the cities, on the farms, and as migrant workers, are Spanish-speaking—and they contribute disproportionately to the prison populations. The first city settled by white

The famous Newgate Prison, built in London in 1769 and demolished in 1902, was not a prison in the modern sense. There were no programs or discipline inside until well into the nineteenth century.
By courtesy of Sir John Soane's Museum, London.

Europeans was Santo Domingo in 1496, just four years after the voyage of Columbus, and it is now the capital of the Dominican Republic. San Juan, now capital of Puerto Rico, was established in 1508. On what is now the continental United States, Pensacola was settled in 1559, but the first major city was St. Augustine, established in 1564.

Despite the fact that these first settlers were Spanish and Portuguese, the cultural heritage of the United States came from England. The language and social institutions that evolved were basically English, and other ethnic and racial groups had to adapt to English traditions.

The early history of the United States guided the direction of its culture and, with it, its criminal justice system. The early humanitarian penitentiary movement was an American contribution that European observers came to inspect, including Alexis de Tocqueville in 1831. Combining the religious concepts of sin with the protection of the rights of citizen-offenders, the American system became unique. But the emergence of a corrections system in America had a harsh beginning. Early colonists became increasingly intolerant of differences in established religion to the extent that Roger Williams, a minister, had to leave the original colony in 1636. (He then established Rhode Island.) The famous witchcraft trials in 1692 were probably prompted by the fervor of the Rev. Mr. Parrish, who depicted Satan and Christ fighting for supremacy. The American ethic was formed out of temper and hard work, and rooted in the religious literature, particularly Genesis, Exodus, and Deuteronomy. Even the celebration of Christmas was considered to be sacrilegious and was outlawed by a General Court statute of 1659. (It was repealed in 1681.) Extremely severe criminal codes were derived from England and made applicable to Pennsylvania from 1676 until 1683, when William Penn's First Assembly passed "The Great Law." The comparatively humane Quaker criminal code functioned until 1718, when it was repealed and the colony reverted to the former system. (Coincidentally, the former system became operative the day after William Penn died.)

The first prison in the United States was Newgate of Connecticut, in an old abandoned mine at Simsbury. Administration buildings were constructed over the shaft in 1773. Three parallel excavated caverns about 800 feet long, with one pool of fresh water, constituted the prison. The first known prison riot was there in 1774. The condition of prisons at this time was terrible. Men and women, adults and children, sick and well, were all placed together.

Many jails and prisons were housed near taverns for convenience. In fact, one at Hartford, Connecticut, shared the same roof with the tavern. There too, the food was minimal, sanitary conditions were deplorable, and discipline was nonexistent. Newgate Prison in New York City was built in 1796 in what is now Greenwich Village.

The Philadelphia Society for Alleviating the Miseries of the Public Prisons, a Quaker organization under the leadership of Dr. Benjamin Rush and including Benjamin Franklin in its membership, was organized in 1787. By 1790, this organization had established the first penitentiary in the world at the Walnut Street jail. Here the women and men were housed in separate facilities. It is interesting to note that after the separation, the average daily female population was three or four as compared with thirty-five or forty before the separation. Cells were constructed to provide solitary confinement in order to eliminate moral contamination from other prisoners and to force the prisoner to meditate on the evil of his ways. The religious motivation created a humane prison aimed at treatment by solitary confinement, religious instruction and Bible reading, and work in the cells. A small exercise yard was attached to each cell. An excellent history of the beginnings and early years of American prisons was published in 1922 by the Prison Association of New York, and reprinted in 1967.[11]

In 1815, New York established a prison at Auburn that imposed a silent system, individual confinement at night, congregate work during the day. Harsh discipline and strong security measures were taken at Auburn. European penologists came to America to examine both the Philadelphia and the New York prison, and generally considered the Pennsylvania system as being the most humane and treatment-oriented. On the other hand, most American states adopted the Auburn plan as being more economical and administratively feasible. Vestiges of the Auburn plan are seen in most of the large penitentiaries and prisons in the United States today.

*Parole* is a form of release under supervision after a prisoner has served some time in an institution. Captain Alexander Maconochie used it on Norfolk Island in 1840 when he thought inmates who had been banished from England could safely return home. They were given a ticket-of-leave to cover their return. Maconochie was dismissed in 1849 for being too radi-

---

[11] Orlando F. Lewis, *The Development of American Prisons and Prison Customs, 1776–1845* (Montclair, N.J.: Patterson Smith, 1967), p. 350.

cal. Subsequently, his ideas became central to the Irish system introduced by Sir Walter Crofton in Dublin in 1854 and were central to the discussions in the first meeting in Cincinnati in 1870 of what is now known as the American Correctional Association. Maconochie and the Irish system had a profound influence on American corrections following 1870.

As early as 1832, Richard Whately, Archbishop of Dublin, advocated the indeterminate sentence with release back to the community following incarceration. In the United States, Michigan was the first state to take legislative action on the indeterminate sentence in 1867, due to the efforts of Zebulon R. Brockway, then superintendent of the Detroit House of Correction. Parole, in its true meaning, including supervision, was first used at the Elmira Reformatory in New York in 1876, when Brockway was hired as superintendent of that institution. All states now have some form of parole.

*Probation* and the suspended sentence have been practiced since ancient times, although not according to the modern meanings of these terms. Probation today means supervision of a convicted offender by court personnel without sending him to prison. Historically, probably the oldest type of mitigation was the "right to sanctuary" in ancient times, by which certain places were designated as places where an offender might go to escape punishment. Holy places were frequently used for this purpose. A later concept was the "benefit of clergy," which first applied only to the clergy, but was then extended to persons who could read a test verse in Psalms 51 beginning, "Have mercy upon me." The beginnings of probation as we know it started in Boston when a cobbler, John Augustus, introduced the practice when he visited the courts in 1841 and requested the judge to let him pay the fines and give him supervision of minor offenders. By 1858, he had bailed out 1,152 men and 794 women and girls. In addition, he had helped thousands of others. He died in 1859 and his supporters continued his work. The first probation law was passed in Massachusetts in 1878 to enable the city of Boston to appoint a probation officer. All states now use some form of probation, although their probation laws may differ.

The first *police department* in its modern concept was established in London in 1829 as a result of riots in several English cities.[12] These disturbances assisted Sir Robert Peel in introducing and passing legislation creating a municipal police department. Police departments were established in New York, Baltimore, and Boston soon after. The United States Secret Service and other treasury agents of law enforcement were established with the beginning of the country as a measure against counterfeiting, smuggling, and tax evasion. The Federal Bureau of Investigation was established in 1908, and subsequent governmental agencies for law enforcement were established later.

The *juvenile court* was inaugurated in 1899 in Illinois, thus completing the pattern of major correctional services in existence today.

[12] H. Melville Lee, *A History of Police* (London: Methuen, 1902).

In review, the penitentiary movement began in Philadelphia in 1790. Parole began with the ticket-of-leave system by which the British let deserving offenders return to England from their penal colonies and was part of the Irish system of reduced custody in stages throughout the period of imprisonment. Probation began informally in 1841 with John Augustus in Boston and was formally recognized by the Massachusetts legislature in 1878. Juvenile institutions began privately in 1825 in New York and publicly in 1847 in New York and Massachusetts. The reformatory movement was implemented at Elmira, New York, in 1876, following the first meeting of what became the American Correctional Association in 1870 in Cincinnati. The juvenile court began in 1899. These form our basic correctional services.

## THE CONSTITUTION OF THE UNITED STATES

At the time of the writing of the United States Constitution, the population of the United States was approximately 3 million people. The heavy influence of America's history as England's penal colony seems to have had its effect on the political thinking of the newly emerging country. The Constitution of the United States was written to protect the individual citizen against the tyranny of government, whether implemented through law enforcement or military action.

The Constitution of the United States was ratified in 1789 with the understanding among the states that the Bill of Rights would follow. Accordingly, the first ten amendments were proposed on September 25, 1789, and were ratified when the state legislatures next met in 1791. The Constitution was a product of compromise at a time when the Constitutional Convention, held in 1787, faced many issues. There were problems with Spain about free navigation on the Mississippi River; Shays' Rebellion was under way, led by former Revolutionary soldiers resisting high taxes. Other problems included representation of blacks as citizens, concerns of business about the tyranny of government, and many other pressures, including the legacy as a penal colony for England. The colonists followed the thinking of Locke and introduced a new concept in government: they saw those "rights that belonged to them as men" as "inherent and inalienable rights."[13]

The Constitution is of prime importance to the field of corrections because it provides the framework for the American system of administration of justice, which includes the correctional field. Citizens may lose some civil rights, but their constitutional guarantees are always present. In addition, Title 18 and Title 42 of the United States Code also include civil rights sections. This should be well known by correctional workers over and above the Constitution. The civil rights sections spell out some specific areas to be honored by all correctional workers.

[13] Edward Elliott, *Biographical Story of the Constitution: A Study of the Growth of the American Union* (New York and London: G. P. Putnam's Sons, 1910), Chap. 1, pp. 1–26.

The sections of the Constitution of the United States that are of primary interest to the criminologist and the corrections worker are as follows:

## Articles

I.  8. The Congress shall have power

   To provide for the punishment of counterfeiting the securities and current coin of the United States.

   To constitute tribunals inferior to the Supreme Court.

   To define and punish piracies and felonies committed on the high seas, and offenses against the law of nations.

   9. The privilege of the writ of habeus corpus shall not be suspended, unless when in cases of rebellion or invasion the public safety may require it.

   No bill of attainder or ex post facto law shall be passed.

   No title of nobility shall be granted by the United States: and no person holding any office of profit or trust under them shall, without the consent of the Congress, accept of any present, emolument, office, or title, of any kind whatever, from any king, prince, or foreign state.

   10. No State shall enter into any treaty, alliance, or confederation; grant letters of marque and reprisal; coin money; emit bills of credit; make anything but gold and silver coin a tender in payment of debts; pass any bill of attainder, ex post facto law, or law impairing the obligation of contracts, or grant any title of nobility.

II.  2. The President ... shall have power to grant reprieves and pardons for offenses against the United States, except in cases of impeachment.

   4. The President, Vice-President, and all civil officers of the United States, shall be removed from office on impeachment for, and conviction of, treason, bribery, or other high crimes and misdemeanors.

III.  2. The trial of all crimes, except in cases of impeachment, shall be by jury; and such trial shall be held in the State where the said crimes shall have been committed; but when not committed within any State, the trial shall be at such place or places as the Congress may by law have directed.

   3. Treason against the United States shall consist only in levying war against them, or in adhering to their enemies, giving them aid and comfort. No person shall be convicted of treason unless on the testimony of two witnesses to the same overt act, or on confession in open court.

   The Congress shall have power to declare the punishment of treason, but no attainder of treason shall work corruption of blood, or forfeiture except during the life of the person attainted.

IV. 2. A person charged in any State with treason, felony, or other crime, who shall flee from justice, and be found in another State, shall on demand of the Executive authority of the State from which he fled, be delivered up, to be removed to the State having jurisdiction of the crime.

## Amendments

I. Congress shall make no law respecting an establishment of religion, or prohibiting the free exercise thereof; or abridging the freedom of speech, or of the press; or the right of the people peaceably to assemble, and to petition the Government for a redress of grievances.

II. A well-regulated militia, being necessary to the security of a free State, the right of the people to keep and bear arms, shall not be infringed.

III. No soldier shall, in time of peace, be quartered in any house, without the consent of the owner, nor in time of war, but in a manner to be prescribed by law.

IV. The right of the people to be secure in their persons, houses, papers, and effects, against unreasonable searches and seizures, shall not be violated, and no warrants shall issue, but upon probable cause, supported by oath or affirmation, and particularly describing the place to be searched, and the persons or things to be seized.

V. No person shall be held to answer for a capital, or otherwise infamous crime, unless on a presentment or indictment of a Grand Jury, except in cases arising in the land or naval forces, or in the militia, when in actual service in time of war or public danger; nor shall any person be subject for the same offense to be twice in jeopardy of life or limb; nor shall be compelled in any criminal case to be a witness against himself, nor be deprived of life, liberty, or property, without due process of law; nor shall private property be taken for public use without just compensation.

VI. In all criminal prosecutions, the accused shall enjoy the right to a speedy and public trial, by an impartial jury of the State and district wherein the crime shall have been committed, which district shall have been previously ascertained by law, and to be informed of the nature and cause of the accusation; to be confronted with the witnesses against him; to have compulsory process for obtaining witnesses in his favor, and to have the assistance of counsel for his defense.

VII. In suits at common law, where the value in controversy shall exceed twenty dollars, the right of trial by jury shall be preserved, and no fact tried by a jury shall be otherwise reexamined in any court of the United States, then according to the rules of the common law.

VIII. Excessive bail shall not be required, nor excessive fines imposed, nor cruel and unusual punishment inflicted.

IX. The enumeration in the Constitution, of certain rights, shall not be construed to deny or disparage others retained by the people.

X. The powers not delegated to the United States by the Constitution nor prohibited by it to the States, are reserved to the States respectively, or to the people.

XIII. 1. Neither slavery nor involuntary servitude, except as a punishment for crime whereof the party shall have been duly convicted, shall exist within the United States or any place subject to their jurisdiction.

XIV. 1. All persons born or naturalized in the United States, and subject to the jurisdiction thereof, are citizens of the United States and of the State wherein they reside. No State shall make or enforce any law which shall abridge the privileges or immunities of citizens of the United States; nor shall any State deprive any person of life, liberty, or property, without due process of law; nor deny to any person within its jurisdiction the equal protection of the laws.

The right to a charge and to face one's accuser is guaranteed. The Fourteenth Amendment had the effect of applying the constitutional guarantees to all the states.

The American philosophy of law enforcement and the control of crime in free society apparently functions on three principles. First, there is greater concern for the preservation of individual liberty than for the pursuit of justice. One often hears the slogan, "We would rather let nine guilty men go free than convict an innocent man." The cases which law enforcement agencies bring in for prosecution and subsequently lose because of errors in due process are many and frequent. New trials after an original conviction on the basis of error in due process are also common. As a matter of fact, it has often been observed that whether a person committed the crime or not is frequently not really the only central issue. Another issue is whether or not there is sufficient admissible evidence to convict the offender under the American system of justice and rules of procedure. Former attorney General Richard Kleindienst articulated this best in response to questioning by the famed committee headed by Senator Sam Ervin investigating the Watergate situation in July 1973: "But the Constitution is not designed to protect society—it is designed to protect the individual." To repeat our earlier statement, an important facet of the American philosophy of law enforcement is that we are more concerned with the preservation of individual liberty than with the pursuit of justice.

Second, Americans have confidence in law to a greater extent than most peoples. Legislation is a major governmental activity. There are many laws within the jurisdiction of the United States of America, including states, counties, and cities. Cartoons with the headline, "There ought to be a law," point up this confidence in law. A popular slogan is that America is a "government of laws—not men." There are laws covering almost every type of behavior and condition.

Third, selective enforcement of these laws is desired in order to maintain a reasonable amount of law and order. Frequently, laws are found to accomplish a given public objective. Further, it would be utterly impossible to enforce *all* laws. Consequently, laws are enforced on the basis of complaints by citizens or to preserve order and sometimes when a flagrant violation is observed by law enforcement officers. Selective enforcement to get a specific job done and to maintain law and order is thus part of the American philosophy of law enforcement.

Despite the idealistic intentions and approaches, the application of criminal justice has sometimes been lacking; however, frequently it has been right. Into the twentieth century, the corruption in American corrections, particularly in pardons and paroles, had become flagrant. Few correctional workers were willing to testify, however, generally for fear of political or other retaliation. In many systems of public service where corruption may have existed, a worker had either to go along with the system or fail to be promoted at best, or be dismissed at worst. One of the few persons who was willing to put some of these practices into documentation was Howard B. Gill, who wrote:

> In the great Commonwealth of Massachusetts, the sale of paroles during the 1930's was a matter of public documentation. In 1934, I stated at a public meeting in Roxbury that the sale of paroles reached right into the State House and I was prepared to back up the statement with facts. The Governor, Joseph B. Ely, said next morning, "Fire that man." . . . In 1939 under the governorship of Leverett Saltonstall, a legislative committee stated in a report to the legislature, "Never in the history of the Commonwealth of Massachusetts has there been so flagrant a sale of pardons and paroles as under the administration of Governor Joseph B. Ely." (Roland D. Sawyer, Secretary of the Pardon and Parole Commission, *Report to the Massachusetts State Legislature,* Boston, 1940.) The report listed numerous cases involving such activities and quoted the price paid for them. At least one member of the parole board was forced to resign and left the state.[14]

With increased court interest in the correctional process, investigative news reporting, increased sensitivity to public scandal like the Watergate situation, and internal controls, these situations have been either eliminated or drastically reduced since World War II. Most variations between intent and practice today involve lack of resources, underfunding, understaffing, and other logistic concerns.

## WHY KEEP CRIMINALS?

When a destructive riot damages a prison, or when a famous or infamous offender is released on work release or parole, there are many people who invariably ask publicly why their tax dollars have to go to support "crimi-

[14] "Community-Based Corrections," *Proceedings of the One Hundredth Annual Congress of Corrections of the American Correctional Association, Cincinnati, 1970* (College Park, Md.: American Correctional Association, 1971), p. 109.

nals." And why, these people ask, must they support the sick and the poor as well? The answers to these questions involve many factors that go into public policy. And public policy is a tradeoff between economic goals and social goals—a balance between economics and humanitarian values. In fact, primitive, ancient, and medieval man kept neither his serious offenders nor his nonproductive members. An Indian tribe in Labrador maintained a custom that the eldest son would kill his parents in a respectful and ritualistic manner when they began to consume more than they produced. The Eskimo before the coming of the white man had a practice in which the aging parents would kiss their families goodbye and go sit on the ice and wait to die. When such groups were observed by "civilized" people, these practices were thought of as inhumane.

Famine has plagued humanity from primitive times to the modern day in various parts of the world. In 436 B.C., thousands of starving Romans threw themselves into the Tiber. The Great Famine of 42 A.D., the universal famine throughout Europe in 101 A.D., and other famines indicated that primitive, ancient, and medieval people just did not have enough to eat and simply could not afford to keep nonproductive or dangerous people. In difficult economic situations, humanitarian values take second place. Even for modern people, the value system tends to lose its holding power in the face of immediate and tangible reward or punishment or when survival is threatened.

But with the increase in knowledge and improvement in technology, modern people have become more productive than their predecessors, with the sixteenth and seventeenth centuries leading to the Industrial Revolution in the eighteenth century. Social programs began to appear in England then, with the Elizabethan Poor Law of 1601 consolidating the beginning fragmented programs a half-century before. Workhouses for minor offenders were built and subsequently were constructed throughout England and the Continent, beginning in the Netherlands. It is obvious that at this juncture of man's productivity, he could begin to afford to keep his nonproductive, dangerous, and ill people and try to help them. Humanitarian values and social goals had become a viable part of public policy. In an affluent society, moral values can support "human rights," minimum welfare payments, protection of children, and minimum standards for offenders. This is simply a matter of public policy.

## BACKGROUND IN THEORY AND RESEARCH

When the criminal law emerged, the thinking of Beccaria and his contemporaries was that man was reasonable and behaved of his own free choice. This approach was known as the Classical school of criminology, and the key to its practical application was the statement, "Let the punishment fit the crime." A century later, in 1876, Lombroso published his book on the criminal man in which he held that the criminal was born as an atavistic individual, not civilized.[15] Lombroso was the first to classify offenders into types. The Positivistic school of criminology, as it was known, was the first to view crime and criminal from an objective and scientific approach. While the "born criminal" is the key phrase identifying Lombroso and his followers, further study swayed Lombroso in his later years away from the theory of strictly inherited criminal characteristics to the idea that only a few criminals should be so identified. Garofalo divided offenders into murderers, violent criminals, criminals deficient in probity, and lascivious criminals.[16] In 1912, Tarde introduced the Law of Imitation to explain crime.[17] Ferri in 1881 wanted to eliminate social causes of crime by providing better housing, sanitation, street lighting, and improved conditions of living.[18]

During the early part of the twentieth century, significant moves were made relating to the field of corrections. In 1908, England began the Borstal institutions, which were minimum security schools for delinquent youth. Belgium began classifying prisoners about the same time, a practice that was adopted in New Jersey in 1928 and in Illinois during the early 1930s.

The first large-scale significant research in criminology and its application to corrections developed at the University of Chicago in the late 1920s under the leadership of Ernest Burgess, Henry D. McKay, and Clifford Shaw. While Sam Warner had previously done the first study of parole prediction in Massachusetts, most subsequent studies on this topic came from Illinois.[19] The Chicago Area Project was initiated in 1926 by Clifford R. Shaw and his associates in the Institute of Juvenile Research. Twelve Chicago neighborhoods had projects by 1959 under a central civic board. The Illinois Youth Commission then expanded the projects to other cities in Illinois.

The New York City Youth Board, established in 1947, functioned in a manner similar to the Chicago Area Projects. The New York City Youth Board was practically eliminated in 1967 by Mayor John Lindsay, who instituted the New York Youth Services as a service organization. The Youth Board was reinstated in 1975 by Mayor Beame as a policy-making board, leaving Youth Services operational. The New York State Youth Commission, established in 1945, aided other cities in New York State to offer youth services. The Mobilization for Youth Project in New York City's Lower East Side was financed by a large grant from the federal government and began operations in 1962. Similar projects have been established in many other cities.

[15] See Gina Lombroso Ferero, *Criminal Man, According to the Classification of Cesare Lombroso* (New York: Putnam's, 1911).

[16] Raffaele Garofalo, *Criminology* (Boston: Little, Brown, 1914). Original in 1885.

[17] Gabriel Tarde, *Penal Philosophy,* Boston: Little, Brown, 1912.

[18] Enrico Ferri, *Criminal Sociology* (Boston: Little, Brown, 1917). Original in 1881.

[19] Sam B. Warner, "Factors Determining Parole from the Massachusetts Reformatory," *Journal of Criminal Law and Criminology,* 14 (1923), 4–14.

In 1935, the Cambridge-Somerville Youth Study was begun under the leadership of Dr. Richard C. Cabot to prevent delinquency and to develop stable elements in children. Cambridge and Somerville, in the metropolitan Boston area, were industrialized and deteriorated. First evaluations failed to show any significant differences between the participating groups and others with regard to delinquency. Subsequent and more intense evaluations also yielded discouraging results.[20] More recent examinations of the data, however, have indicated that there are encouraging possibilities for such projects in providing sound research for good social policy in the field of corrections.[21]

Edwin H. Sutherland presented the first important modern theory of crime in 1937 when he offered his theory of differential association. Simply stated, the theory maintains that one learns delinquent behavior from his associates—a "bad company" theory. Sutherland's students have elaborated on the theory, with Daniel Glaser proposing a theory of differential identification, and Matza and Sykes a theory of neutralization, among other spinoff considerations from the basic theory of differential association. Walter C. Reckless, originally from the Chicago School, has proposed a theory of containment based on inner self-concept and controls and outer containment in terms of social pressures and opportunities for crime. Merton has revived the concepts of Durkheim's anomie and applied the idea to criminal and delinquent behavior. *Anomie* refers to the situation in which the values and frame of reference of the individual do not fit the culture or society in which he lives. The nonbelonging, the rootlessness, the goallessness of the individual make him unable to adjust to the expectations of his society. This anomie or alienation results in crime and delinquency. Cohen based an interpretation of delinquent behavior on the delinquent subculture.[22]

Cloward and Ohlin attempted to combine and synthesize these theories into a theory of opportunity.[23] The basic idea, borrowed from Merton, was that legitimate goals or the "good things in life" were available to middle- and upper-class youth, but the means by which they are attained were not available to lower-class youth. Delinquency results from association with other have-nots who devise illegitimate means to achieve these goals, a theory which makes use of Sutherland's differential association.

The first national survey of the correctional field was made by the Wickersham Commission, or the National Commission on Law Observance and Law Enforcement. Appointed by President Herbert Hoover in

---

[20] Edwin Powers and Helen Witmer, *An Experiment in the Prevention of Delinquency* (New York: Columbia University Press, 1951).

[21] William McCord and Joan McCord, *Origins of Crime* (New York: Columbia University Press, 1959).

[22] Albert K. Cohen, *Delinquent Boys* (New York: Free Press, 1955), p. 198.

[23] Richard F. Cloward and Lloyd E. Ohlin, *Delinquency and Opportunity: A Theory of Delinquent Gangs* (New York: Free Press, 1960).

1929 and headed by George W. Wickersham, the commission was charged with studying the entire question of law enforcement and organization of justice. While the survey was initiated primarily because of the controversy over prohibition, the twelve commission reports that were published in 1931 provide an idea as to the status of law enforcement and, to a lesser extent, corrections at that time. The second major survey in this field was under the auspices of the WPA (Works Progress Administration) during the later stages of the Great Depression. The Attorney General's *Survey of Release Procedures* was published in five volumes 1939–40, covering work begun in 1935. Concentrating on probation, parole, pardon, executive clemency, good-time (for good behavior) deductions, prisons, and expiration of sentence, it came much closer to the correctional field than did the Wickersham Report. The third broad survey was the report of the Kefauver Committee, or the Special Committee to Investigate Organized Crime, during 1950–51. The most important current survey of American corrections, as well as the entire system of criminal justice, is The President's Commission on Law Enforcement and Administration of Justice, which did most of its work in 1966 and issued its publications in 1967.[24] The Joint Commission on Correctional Manpower and Training, comprising 95 private and public organizations, was made possible by the Correctional Rehabilitation Study Act of 1965, which was administered by the Social and Rehabilitative Service, Department of Health, Education and Welfare, with the aid of grants and donations from private sources. The Advisory Commission on Criminal Justice Standards and Goals published its report in 1973, but it has been challenged by the American Correctional Association in some areas. In conclusion, there appear to be three natural origins of punishment: (1) presence of a harsh environment with which man has to deal, (2) occurrence of natural disasters, and (3) religion.[25]

## SUMMARY

It took a long time for the regulatory system in society to move from the folkways and custom controls of primitive man to the laws of Greece and Rome. It took even longer to evolve the criminal law as it is known today. Pivotal in the history of man, the eighteenth century wrought many changes in technology, economics, and the social and political orders, including the development of the criminal law and the field of corrections.

The rise of complexity, or the advance of civilization, carries with it the need for stronger and more complex controls to protect the social order. As man gives up his freedom in exchange for security, each society finds its

[24] *The Challenge of Crime in a Free Society,* and the accompanying *Task Force Reports,* The President's Commission on Law Enforcement and Administration of Justice (Washington, D.C.: Government Printing Office, 1967).

[25] Graeme Newman, *The Punishment Response* (New York: J.B. Lippincott Company, 1978), p. 14.

own balance between these two mutually incompatible states of existence. The primitive, anarchical society had no formal controls. At the other extreme, in the modern totalitarian state in which holding opinions diverging from governmental policy is a crime, the security is severely controlled. In a democracy, where individual liberty is generally more important than the pursuit of justice, sometimes peculiar dilemmas and problems in law enforcement and corrections emerge.

## EXERCISES AND STUDY QUESTIONS

1. Trace briefly the development of social control from early times to the present day.
2. What is criminology?
3. What is corrections?
4. Why is the blood feud the matrix of law?
5. How does social control develop from folkways and customs of law?
6. What was the role of the ancient codes in developing law?
7. What was the importance of the Justinian Code?
8. Describe medieval law.
9. Describe the emergence of criminal law.
10. Describe the emergence of corrections.
11. What was the role of the American colonies in the English penal system in the eighteenth century, and how do you think it affected the formulation of American criminal procedure?
12. Describe the early development of prisons during the last quarter of the eighteenth century.
13. Describe the origins and early development of parole.
14. Describe the origins and early development of probation.
15. What guarantees does the Constitution of the United States provide the citizen in criminal procedure?
16. What is the American philosophy of law enforcement?
17. What was the Classical school of criminology?
18. What was the Positivistic school of criminology?
19. Why should criminals be maintained and provided programs with public funds?
20. Describe some twentieth-century research in criminology and corrections.

# 2

# THE CORRECTIONAL PROCESS

The correctional process begins formally with adults when the criminal court finds a defendant guilty of violating a criminal law. It begins less formally with children, when the juvenile court receives a complaint or a referral alleging delinquency, but becomes formal when an adjudication of delinquency is made. Actually, the correctional process is much broader than these demarcations suggest, since there are corrective and rehabilitative functions in many agencies whose primary function is noncorrective, such as the schools, child guidance clinics, and police departments.

Whether a person is treated as a child or an adult in the correctional process depends upon his age, and the age at which he is considered an adult varies in different jurisdictions. The statutes determine the jurisdictions of the courts. In most states, original jurisdiction for children resides with the juvenile court until the seventeenth birthdate. Most states permit the juvenile court to bind the child over to criminal court at its discretion at the fifteenth birthdate, some at the fourteenth birthdate. The minimum age for delinquency jurisdiction in most states is 12, but when the law is silent on minimum age, jurisdiction reverts to the customary seven years in English common law, such as in Florida. In the case of capital offenses (usually murder, rape, and kidnapping), it is conceivable, but improbable, that a 7-year-old *could* be tried in criminal court.

The resources available to the courts also affect the correctional process. The availability of specialized programs in the community, probation, various types of institutions, programs for the criminally insane, the defective delinquent, and the criminal sexual psychopath, the various available sentencing patterns, and other statutory restrictions and provisions all affect the correctional process. Some states have laws prohibiting narcotics and sex offenders from being placed outside the walls in minimum security installations. Many states identify certain types of offenders as not eligible for probation. )

It is very difficult to determine the amount of crime in the United States, because many victims do not call the police or even report crimes. It is estimated that there are about 13 million major or "Index" crimes, which constitute about 7 percent of all crimes, with misdemeanors and minor offenses making up about 93 percent. Only about 50 million of these lesser offenses are reported. On December 31, 1981, there were 369,009 prisoners in state and federal prisons and correctional institutions.[1] By March 3, 1982, there were 384,816 prisoners.[2] Of these, 16,702 (4.3 percent) were female. There were 47,642 children and youths in public facilities and 28,556 in private juvenile facilities in 1979.[3] Of these, 11,746 (24.7 percent) were female, about two-thirds being in private institutions. As of December 31, 1981, there were 1,222,824 adults on probation and 223,774 adults on parole.[4] There were 156,800 persons in jails.[5] The number of juveniles on unofficial and official probation today is not available, but there are surely more than the 235,421 in 1965.[6]

## TYPES OF CRIME

(There are many kinds of crimi. ~l behavior. They are classified in legal categories as (1) treason, (2) felonies, (3) misdemeanors, and (4) violation of ordinances. Treason, of course, is a national crime that involves providing aid and comfort to an enemy, which can take many forms, or levying war on the United States. Each state has laws against treason also, generally incorporated in the state constitution, but since there can hardly be a crime against a state without there also being a crime against the United States, treason is a federal crime for all practical purposes. A felony is defined in the statutes as the most serious conventional crime. In the *United States Code,*

---

[1] *Prisoners in State and Federal Institutions on December 31, 1980* (Washington, D.C.: U.S. Department of Justice, 1982), p. 27 (end-of-the-year listing).

[2] Table 1, *Corrections Digest,* Vol. 13, No. 15 (July 19, 1982), 3.

[3] *Children in Custody: Advance Report of the 1979 Census of Public Juvenile Facilities* (Washington, D.C.: U.S. Department of Justice, 1980), Tables 1 and 2.

[4] "Probation and Parole Numbers Increasing, BJS Study Shows," *Criminal Justice Newsletter,* Vol. 13, No. 17 (August 30, 1982), 6, from yet unavailable data from *Parole in the United States: 1980 and 1981,* and *Probation in the United States: 1980 and 1981,* to be published by the NCCD's San Francisco Office.

[5] *Ibid.,* p. 5.

[6] *Task Force Report: Corrections,* The President's Commission on Law Enforcement and Administration of Justice (Washington, D.C.: Government Printing Office, 1967), p. 1.

it is an offense for which one can be sentenced to prison for more than a year. In some states, it is an offense for which one can be sent to prison for five years or more, while in other states, one can be sent to prison only for a felony. The statutes define *felony* and *misdemeanor.* Misdemeanors are generally crimes punishable by state or federal law, but they are less serious than felonies. Ordinances are municipal laws; crimes in this category include such things as traffic and parking violations. The legal classifications of crime make differences not only in the law enforcement process, but also in the correctional process. |

( Conventional crimes, with which most prisons are primarily concerned, are street crimes such as robbery, burglary, homicide, larceny, rape, auto theft, and similar offenses. Dyssocial offenders show no personality disorganization but are products of lifelong environments that foster social values in conflict with the usual codes of society.[7] Gangsters, racketeers, and other professional criminals fall into this category. Organized crime, moonshining, prostitution, and similar offenses could be classified in this category. Public nuisance crime refers, in the main, to public drunkenness, possession of narcotics, and other "moral" crimes that do not hurt anyone but offend the public conscience. |

( Organized crime is big business. Goods and services are illegally provided on a massive scale, tax-free and without regulation. The Prohibition era from 1920 to 1933 gave rise to the illegal smuggling and manufacture of alcoholic beverages on a large scale, which, in turn, gave rise to illegal business organizations to serve the public. Outside the law, they had to provide their own protection, which resulted in the gangland activities that became famous during the 1920s in the larger cities. Organized crime soon branched out into prostitution, gambling, labor racketeering, loan-shark activities, narcotics and other drugs, "protection rackets," and other illicit activities promising profit. In recent years, organized crime has moved into legitimate business, such as vending machines, nightclubs and bars, and small loans, sometimes for profit and sometimes as a cover for illegal activities. Its operations are difficult to detect, and, as the *Illinois Crime Commission Report* pointedly notes, the situation is complicated by the "indiscriminate practices of some businesspeople."\

> There is a disturbing lack of interest on the part of some legitimate business concerns regarding the identity of the persons with whom they deal. This lackadaisical attitude is conducive to the perpetration of frauds and infiltration and subversion of legitimate businesses by the organized criminal element.[8]

\ Organized crime is the second largest business in America next to oil, which gained $365 billion in revenues in 1979, while organized crime

[7] James C. Coleman, *Abnormal Psychology and Modern Life,* 3rd ed. (Glenview, Ill.: Scott, Foresman, 1964), p. 346.

[8] *Task Force Report: Organized Crime,* The President's Commission on Law Enforcement and Administration of Justice (Washington, D.C.: Government Printing Office, 1967), p. 4. (After 1965 *Illinois Crime Investigating Commission's Report No. 11.*)

gained $150 billion.[9] By comparison, the automobile industry is estimated to have grossed about $125 billion. Of the total in organized crime, about $63 billion may have come from narcotics, $22 billion from gambling, and $8 billion from assorted other enterprises, such as arson, cigarette bootlegging, and prostitution. White-collar crime is estimated to have grossed about $100 billion. Street crime has been estimated as a loss of $3 to $4 billion, but it is the most visible and is feared by the public, and the majority of law enforcement effort has been focused on it.

( White-collar crime involves business practices, illegally raising or fixing prices in large corporations or groups of corporations, the "thumb-on-the-scales" types of offenses frequently difficult to detect, and computer crime. Computer crime is beginning to be a major part of white-collar crime. Sometimes, it involves "pillars of the community."* Traffic offenses are not "criminal" in the general sense, but they must be handled in courts at various levels. Regulatory crimes in the city involve offenses such as violations of zoning restrictions, building codes, and firearms laws. In rural areas, they include offenses such as exceeding allotted acreage in planning controlled crops and violations of livestock controls. All these offenses are committed by people who may be potential clients for the correctional process.

## EXTENT OF CRIME

The numbers of major crimes committed in the United States in 1979, estimated by law enforcement officials, is as follows:[10]

| | |
|---|---|
| Murder | 21,460 |
| Forcible rape | 75,990 |
| Robbery | 466,880 |
| Aggravated assault | 614,210 |
| Burglary | 3,299,500 |
| Larceny-theft ($50) | 6,577,500 |
| Motor vehicle theft | 1,097,200 |

The caseloads throughout the correctional systems tend to reflect the proportions shown in this table, with less serious or less numerous crimes making up the rest of the caseloads.

* "The toppling of a pillar of the community" was a headline in the *Tallahassee Democrat* that carried a Knight-Ridder News Service story of a popular man in Winter Haven, Florida who embezzled $3,679,157.13 from his employer by computer in 1981.

[9] James Cooke, "The Invisible Enterprise," *Forbes*, Vol. 126, No. 7 (September 29, 1980), 60–71.

[10] *Crime in the United States—1979, Uniform Crime Reports* (Washington, D.C.: Federal Bureau of Investigation, 1981), p. 41.

The numbers of arrests for lesser offenses in 1979 are as follows:[11]

| | | |
|---|---:|---:|
| Other assaults (simple) | | 485,500 |
| Forgery and counterfeiting | | 76,400 |
| Fraud | | 261,900 |
| Embezzlement | | 8,600 |
| Stolen property (receiving, buying, etc.) | | 115,800 |
| Vandalism | | 257,300 |
| Weapons (carrying, possessing, etc.) | | 64,200 |
| Prostitution and commercialized vice | | 89,400 |
| Sex offenses (except rape and prostitution) | | 67,400 |
| Drug abuse violations | | 558,500 |
|    Opium or cocaine | 68,100 | |
|    Marihuana | 391,600 | |
|    Synthetic | 18,400 | |
|    Other, nonnarcotic | 80,400 | |
| Gambling | | 54,800 |
|    Bookmaking | 4,600 | |
|    Numbers, lottery | 7,500 | |
|    Other gambling | 42,700 | |
| Offenses against family and children | | 57,400 |
| Driving under influence | | 1,324,800 |
| Liquor laws | | 416,200 |
| Drunkenness | | 1,172,700 |
| Disorderly conduct | | 765,500 |
| Vagrancy | | 37,200 |
| All other offenses (except traffic) | | 1,716,600 |
| Suspicion (not included in total) | | 19,600 |
| Curfew and loitering law violations | | 84,100 |
| Runaways | | 164,400 |

The majority of these lesser offenses are misdemeanors and would be handled at the local level, with the exception of felonies such as forgery, counterfeiting, arson, embezzlement, kidnapping, some sex offenses, stolen property, fraud, some weapons offenses, and other miscellaneous felonies. Arson was made an Index crime by Congress in 1980.

Although the statistics collected by the Federal Bureau of Investigation constitute the best information available, there is no way of knowing how much crime exists in the United States. There is even less reliable information from other countries. The Federal Bureau of Investigation says:

> ... there is no way of determining the total number of crimes which are committed. Many criminal acts occur which are not reported to official sources. In light of this fact, the best source for obtaining a count of crime is the next logical universe, namely, crimes which come to police attention. The crimes used in the Crime Index are those considered to be most con-

---

[11] *Ibid.*, p. 188.

sistently reported to police and the computations of crime trends and crime rates are prepared using this universe—crimes known to police.[12]

The Uniform Crime Reporting Program is voluntary, although jurisdictions have been consistently urged to participate since the 1930s when it was established. The Crime Index uses the seven crime classifications of murder, forcible rape, robbery, aggravated assault, burglary, larceny ($50 or over in value), and auto theft. There are various factors that distort the reported crime rates, the first and largest being the failure of citizens to report crimes. A second is whether the jurisdiction reports to the FBI. In addition, the FBI notes the influence of (1) the density and size of the community population; (2) composition of the population with reference to age, sex, and race; (3) economic status and mores of the population; (4) relative stability of the population, including commuters, tourists, and transients; (5) climate and seasonal weather conditions; (6) educational, religious, and recreational characteristics; (7) effective strength of the police force; (8) standards governing appointments to the police force; (9) policies of the prosecuting officials and the courts; (10) the attitude of the public toward law enforcement problems; and (11) the administrative and investigative efficiency of local law enforcement.[13]

There is now improved reporting of crime; in thirty-two states, reporting is mandatory by legislation, and the completed information is forwarded by a state agency to the FBI. Reports for at least some of the requested information came in 1975 from jurisdictions representing 94 percent of the population. It is apparent that reporting of arrests is better than that of court action and disposition.

Information on juvenile delinquency and juvenile courts is based on a national sample drawn from the Current Population Sample of the Bureau of the Census, United States Department of Commerce. This national sample includes 202 courts in urban areas, 170 courts in semi-urban areas, and 130 courts in rural areas. It is a considerable improvement over the old, small, and relatively unreliable sample used by the United States Children's Bureau beginning in 1926. The information in this sample indicates that the delinquency rate is 7 to 8 percent in urban areas, about 5 percent in semi-urban areas, and about 3 percent in rural areas, these percentages being drawn from the population between 7 and 17 years of age.

It is important to place such statistics in perspective. Statistics are a better measure of public policy than they are of criminal and delinquent behavior. A low crime rate or a high crime rate does not mean a healthy or unhealthy society. All other factors in that society must be evaluated, including economic, social, cultural, political, ethnic, psychological, technological, and other facets of the society, before valid judgments can be made.

---

[12] *Crime in the United States—Uniform Crime Reports—1968*, Federal Bureau of Investigation (Washington, D.C.: Government Printing Office, 1969), p. 115, and all issues since.

[13] *Ibid.*, p. vi.

Yet political policy rests on statistical information, and statistics are widely used in political campaigns.

Crime statistics must be used in the correctional process because they refer to the correctional caseload. Those persons represented in the crime statistics are not immediately potential clients, regardless of their behavior. Apparently, they are the hard-core crime problems that come to official attention, where the factor of visibility is highly important. They are also the offenders who are included in the correctional process.

The Crime Index (rate of crime for each 100,000 inhabitants) for each state in the United States is shown in Table 2-1.[14] It would be erroneous to draw many conclusions from these statistics. For example, the people living in Nevada, Arizona, Florida, California, and Hawaii are not four or more times as criminal as those living in West Virginia, Puerto Rico, North Dakota, Mississippi, or South Dakota! The more urban states *tend* to show a higher Crime Index than do more rural states because of greater opportunities for deviance, but there are several notable exceptions. As previously noted, crime statistics are a better measure of public policy than of human behavior and deviation.

## SCREENING FOR THE CORRECTIONAL CLIENT

The correctional client will have been through a long screening process by the time he or she arrives in a correctional caseload or correctional institution. The fact that there are an estimated 50 million felonies and misdemeanors committed by adults annually in the United States and yet there were 600,000 adults in correctional institutions and jails, or over 2.5 million in all correctional programs, in recent years, including probation, parole, and other community-based corrections, indicates that there must have been some intensive screening.

The first phase of the screening process for the correctional client is police knowledge of the crime. Police estimate that they know of considerably less than half, at best, of most major crimes and an even lesser proportion of the misdemeanors. Even homicide is significantly underreported. A visit to the morgue in any large city in the United States would reveal bodies showing signs of foul play that have been pulled out of rivers, culverts, alleys, and other places. Overworked law enforcement and the fact that many of these people are drifters or floaters without families to press complaints simply results in time going by and the case becoming less important than contemporary cases of homicide in which friends and family are present.

A survey of 10,000 households made by the National Opinion Research Center of the University of Chicago in 1965–1966 shows why crime is often not reported. The survey was made in the cities of Washington,

[14] Adapted from *Crime in the United States—1979*, pp. 48–59.

**Table 2-1   Rate of index (serious) crimes per 100,000 population, 1979**

| | |
|---|---|
| Nevada | 8,831.6 |
| Arizona | 7,857.3 |
| Florida | 7,688.1 |
| California | 7,468.8 |
| Hawaii | 7,247.5 |
| Colorado | 7,051.1 |
| Washington | 6,529.5 |
| Delaware | 6,525.8 |
| Oregon | 6,373.0 |
| **Standard Metropolitan Statistical Areas (urban)** | 6,313.1 |
| Maryland | 6,294.7 |
| New York | 6,205.1 |
| Alaska | 6,203.7 |
| Michigan | 6,147.0 |
| Texas | 5,925.3 |
| Massachusetts | 5,917.9 |
| New Jersey | 5,820.6 |
| New Mexico | 5,788.5 |
| Connecticut | 5,779.6 |
| Rhode Island | 5,769.5 |
| **U.S.A. (average)** | 5,521.5 |
| Utah | 5,492.0 |
| Georgia | 5,416.9 |
| Louisiana | 5,358.7 |
| Vermont | 5,299.2 |
| Illinois | 5,169.2 |
| Ohio | 5,129.8 |
| South Carolina | 5,066.2 |
| Missouri | 4,939.8 |
| **Other Cities (middle and smaller)** | 4,948.6 |
| Kansas | 4,895.8 |
| Wyoming | 4,824.0 |
| Oklahoma | 4,703.0 |
| Indiana | 4,601.4 |
| New Hampshire | 4,578.8 |
| Montana | 4,460.6 |
| Minnesota | 4,392.8 |
| Wisconsin | 4,388.0 |
| North Carolina | 4,372.5 |
| Virginia | 4,361.3 |
| Maine | 4,307.3 |
| Iowa | 4,301.7 |
| Alabama | 4,243.8 |
| Idaho | 4,240.8 |
| Tennessee | 4,013.4 |
| Nebraska | 3,993.1 |
| Arkansas | 3,620.8 |
| Pennsylvania | 3,495.4 |
| Kentucky | 3,183.9 |
| South Dakota | 2,959.6 |
| Mississippi | 2,960.6 |
| North Dakota | 2,755.9 |
| Puerto Rico | 2,330.4 |
| West Virginia | 2,325.5 |
| **Rural U.S.A.** | 2,167.5 |

Boston, and Chicago. The offenses in Washington ranged from three to ten times more than the number of offenses contained in the official statistics. Reasons for not notifying the police are reported in Table 2-2. There are several studies of hidden delinquency and unreported offenses which also support the fact that citizens generally do not report crime to police. There has arisen great concern about the accuracy of crime statistics.

( Other screenings occur in the process of the investigation and the court procedure. The system of guarantees afforded the citizen and due process tend to eliminate errors and cases without sufficient admissible evidence to warrant bringing the charge to court. Some arrested persons are screened out in the investigation, some are released without prosecution, some are booked, some are discharged after an initial appearance, others are discharged at the preliminary hearing, some are not indicted by the grand jury, some are dismissed at the arraignment, many are acquitted during the trial. Of 70,529 cases begun in the United States District Courts in 1968, only 8,031, or 11.8 percent, eventually reached trial,[15] a situation that continues today. Only a few, proportionately, get into the correctional caseload in prisons or on probation. In addition to the many cases of juvenile delinquency that are not reported, many cases are screened out by the police juvenile unit, in the hearing in the juvenile court, and in the adjudicatory hearing, and only a few, in proportion to the acts committed, get into the juvenile caseload. Visibility and social cohesion are important factors in deviation and what it does to social control. )

Some figures taken from the FBI *Uniform Crime Reports* suggest the approximate effectiveness of the American system of criminal justice (Table 2-3). It can be only an approximation. Since there is no point in refining the available poor statistics, although they are the best that can be obtained, this table is presented only to provide an approximation of the screening process.

In 1967, there were 26,344 convictions and 5,191 dismissed or acquitted cases in the United States District Courts. Of the total, 86.7 percent were disposed of without trial. People tried by the court without a jury constituted 4.6 percent, while 8.7 percent had jury trials.[16] Society could not and would not tolerate the prosecution of every person who violated even those laws which are perfectly clear.[17] The public attitude is the same today: It would be too expensive.

The *Uniform Crime Reports* no longer publish the dispositions of state and local courts, although they do publish the results of federal court dis-

---

[15] *Annual Report of the Director,* Administrative Office of the U.S. Courts (Washington, D.C.: U.S. Government Printing Office, 1969).

[16] *Federal Offenders in the United States District Courts, 1967,* Administrative Office of the U.S. Courts (Washington, D.C.: Government Printing Office, 1967), p. 7.

[17] Joseph L. Sax, *Law and Justice,* Public Affairs Pamphlet No. 433 (New York: Public Affairs Committee, 1969), p. 2.

**Table 2-2 Victims' most important reasons for not notifying police, by percentage—1979[a]**

| | Nothing Could Be Done | Not Important Enough | Police Would Not Want to Be Bothered | Did Not Want to Take the Time | Private Matter | Fear of Reprisal | Reported to Someone Else |
|---|---|---|---|---|---|---|---|
| Rape and attempted rape (91,624) | 13% | 11% | 6% | 0% | 27% | 12% | 10% |
| Robbery (471,464) | 18 | 20 | 12 | 4 | 16 | 5 | 7 |
| Assault (2,610,189) | 8 | 29 | 6 | 3 | 32 | 4 | 11 |
| Personal larceny with contact (1,457,071) | 7 | 34 | 7 | 3 | 29 | 3 | 14 |
| Personal larceny without contact (11,719,684) | 23 | 34 | 8 | 3 | 4 | 0 | 21 |
| Burglary (3,404,268) | 25 | 28 | 9 | 3 | 9 | 1 | 7 |
| Larceny (7,888,167) | 23 | 41 | 12 | 2 | 7 | 0 | 3 |
| Vehicle theft (420,061) | 19 | 14 | 9 | 3 | 13 | 0 | 3 |

[a] Timothy J. Flanagan, David J. van Alstyne, and Michael R. Gottfredson, *Sourcebook of Criminal Justice Statistics—1981* (Washington, D.C.: U.S. Department of Justice, 1982), pp. 242–43.

**Table 2-3  Approximate effectiveness of the American system of criminal justice in apprehending and convicting criminal offenders, 1974**

| Index (major) Crime | Estimated Number of Offenses[a] | Reported to Police[b] | Arrests[c] | Charged in Court[d] | Dispositions (in percentages)[e] | | | Percent Cleared to Satisfaction of Police[f] (%) |
| --- | --- | --- | --- | --- | --- | --- | --- | --- |
| | | | | | Guilty as Charged (%) | Lesser Offense (%) | Juvenile Court (%) | |
| Murder | 20,600 | 18,757 | 12,707 | 2,255 | 40.8 (920) | 18.5 (417) | 8.5 (192) | 79.9 |
| Negligent Homicide | — | 7,818 | 3,995 | 371 | 45.6 (169) | 12.9 (48) | 9.7 (36) | 78.0 |
| Forcible Rape | 55,210 | 50,997 | 37,847 | 2,948 | 28.0 (825) | 12.1 (357) | 22.8 (672) | 51.1 |
| Robbery | 441,290 | 419,072 | 371,750 | 15,921 | 31.2 (4,967) | 10.5 (1,672) | 33.6 (5,350) | 27.3 |
| Aggravated Assault | 452,720 | 412,608 | 328,039 | 28,810 | 40.9 (11,783) | 10.5 (3,025) | 14.8 (4,264) | 63.4 |
| Burglary | 3,020,700 | 2,716,136 | 2,006,532 | 72,367 | 24.3 (17,585) | 6.9 (4,993) | 56.0 (40,526) | 17.6 |
| Larceny-Theft | 5,227,700 | 4,786,184 | 3,682,285 | 198,544 | 43.8 (86,962) | 3.6 (7,148) | 38.0 (75,447) | 19.8 |
| Motor Vehicle Theft | 973,800 | 887,029 | 786,921 | 23,238 | 18.4 (4,276) | 4.8 (1,115) | 62.6 (14,547) | 14.6 |

[a] *Crime in the United States*, (see source below), p. 11.
[b] *Ibid.*, p. 153 (this reflects a much better reporting record than in previous years). (Population of 187,688,000.)
[c] *Ibid.*, p. 168 (5,582 cities, 120,601,000 population).
[d] *Ibid.*, p. 174 (2,440 cities, 41,773,000 population—not exactly comparable, but best information available).
[e] *Ibid.*, p. 174 (figures in parentheses computed from the percentages).
[f] *Ibid.*, p. 166.

Source: *Crime in the United States—Uniform Crime Reports—1974* (Washington, D.C.: Federal Bureau of Investigation, United States Department of Justice, released November 17, 1975).

positions. To see the general loss of cases in the courts, the 1974 figures have been retained in this edition.

Because of concern over the inadequacy of law enforcement crime statistics, a Panel for the Evaluation of Crime Surveys was established in 1974 by the National Academy of Sciences at the request of the U.S. Department of Justice. A new statistical series was initiated in cooperation with the Current Population Survey of the U.S. Bureau of the Census. The result was the obtaining of crime statistics based on victimization surveys.[18] A comparison of crime reported by the victimization surveys and by the law enforcement approach in the *Uniform Crime Reports* in 1979 is as follows:

| | Victimization Studies[a] | Uniform Crime Reports[b] | |
|---|---|---|---|
| | Estimated | Estimated | Known to Police |
| Murder | | 21,460 | 20,561 |
| Forcible rape | 191,739 | 75,990 | 71,935 |
| Robbery | 1,115,870 | 466,880 | 452,743 |
| Aggravated assault | 1,768,683 | 614,210 | 540,933 |
| Burglary | 3,666,796 | 3,299,500 | 3,143,796 |
| Larceny-theft ($50) | 6,684,018 | 6,577,500 | 6,259,041 |
| Motor vehicle theft | 1,392,837 | 963,163 | 154,500 |
| Arson | | | 19,800 |

[a] *Criminal Victimization in the U.S.: Summary Findings of 1978–1979 Changes in Crime and of Trends Since 1973—National Crime Survey Report SD-NCS-N-18* (Washington, D.C.: U.S. Department of Justice, 1980), Table 1.
[b] *Crime in the United States—1979, Uniform Crime Reports* (Washington, D.C.: Federal Bureau of Investigation, 1980), p. 188.

# THE TRIAL: GAINING THE AUTHORITY TO INTERVENE

In a democracy committed to the proposition that the preservation of individual liberty is more important than the pursuit of justice, the trial is society's mechanism to determine whether that society shall have the right to take responsibility for the individual because the individual has damaged that society. The laws, legal process, and administration of justice designed for a democratic society emphasizes the protection of the individual citizen. The laws, legal process, and administration of justice in a totalitarian society, on the other hand, emphasize the security of the State over the welfare of the individual. The Constitution of the United States of America represents the government of a free and democratic society. Thus, the emphasis in administration of justice is upon the protection of the individual.

[18] Panel for the Evaluation of Crime Surveys, Bettye K. Eidson Penick, ed., *Surveying Crime* (Washington, D.C.: National Academy of Sciences, 1976), 250 pp.

While the Constitution does not delineate due process, it indicates that due process must be observed and sets out the guarantees to be included in that due process. During nearly two hundred years of litigation, due process has been delineated by thousands of legal and judicial decisions at every level of the appellate system through the Supreme Court.

The first point of discretion is the arrest. At this time, the offender must be informed of his constitutional rights. Booking is the second point of discretion. This is an administrative record of arrest. Temporary release may be available, either on bail or on the offender's own recognizance. The initial appearance before a commissioner, a magistrate, or a justice of the peace is in the form of a notice of the charge with advice of the offender's rights. Minor offenses may be disposed of at this point.

The preliminary hearing held in a lower court is a testing of the evidence against the defendant. Depending upon the system, it may be held in the office of a justice of the peace or in a county or probate court. Bail is set at this time. In the case of a misdemeanor, the entire trial may be held at this point.

The formal charge is made in the form of an indictment by a grand jury or by an information or presentment by the prosecutor. It is at this point that the constitutional guarantees for trial by jury or the jury system enter into the criminal procedure. All capital or serious offenses must go through the grand jury. The prosecutor can present an information of lesser offenses.

The grand jury is an investigatory body appointed by a judge, usually a judge of the court of record or circuit court in the case of the states, or a district judge in the case of the federal courts. Jury members have to be qualified to serve as jurors, in most states property-owning and voting citizens. The usual practice is for the prosecutor, state's attorney, district attorney, or whatever his title may be, to present cases to the grand jury. The grand jury can return an indictment for prosecution or a presentment, which leaves more discretion to the prosecutor as to action to be taken.

After the indictment or information has been rendered, process on the indictment is taken by issuing summonses to witnesses and the defendant (offender). In an arraignment, the charges are read in open court to the defendant.

By this time, defense counsel will be appointed if this has not been done before. There are various systems of providing legal counsel: The defense can hire its own counsel, counsel can be appointed by the court, or a public defender defense can be assigned by rotation from the local bar association. It is very seldom that a defendant hires his own counsel, since many offenders come from the lower socioeconomic classes and cannot afford legal services.

The selection of a jury or the waiver of trial by jury becomes the next step. While each defendant has a right to trial by jury (Article VI of the Amendments), a minority of the trials are by jury. The majority are bench trials, the verdict being rendered by the judge upon hearing the case. Consensus among prisoners seems to be that if they are, in fact, guilty, then a trial by jury is desirable; if they are not guilty, they do not want to risk the more uncertain judgment of a jury. Plea bargaining is also involved.

The process of selecting a jury is a long one. A hundred persons or more who meet the requirements for jury service are called. The examining of the jury involves the judge's eliminating some as not being qualified to serve on that particular jury for various reasons. The challenging of the jury occurs when the prosecutors and the defense counsel examine each prospective juror to determine whether they want him or her to serve. There is no limit to the number of challenges for cause; the judge determines whether or not the cause is sufficient. Each has a prescribed number of peremptory challenges, however, which means that some jurors can be eliminated without cause. After the twelve citizens (and one or two alternates if the case may be a long one) are selected, they are "impaneled." When the jury members have been impaneled or are seated in the box, the judge swears them in.

The trial itself is made up of (1) the state represented by the prosecution, (2) the citizens represented by the defendant, and (3) the public represented by the judge. The adversary proceeding is a conflict in court in which the state prosecutes the defendant, who defends himself as best he can through counsel, within the rules of "due process" in law. The judge referees the conflict, making sure that the rules and due process are followed. From the opening statements to the closing statements, the pattern is that the state leads and the defense answers. Then, the jury or the judge decides the verdict.

In the case of a guilty verdict, the defendant may appeal for a new trial on certain grounds. If the verdict has been for acquittal, constitutional guarantees prevent a new trial on the same charge. The state has no appeal.

As can be seen from this summary, due process is cumbersome; this often results in plea bargaining, sometimes as a stalling measure to pick the right judge and sometimes in the hope that witnesses will disappear. Plea bargaining is the making of a "deal" between the prosecution and the defense with the consent of the judge for a lesser charge or a lesser sentence in exchange for a guilty plea, thereby avoiding a trial that might be lengthy. Because of this, the criminal justice system has sometimes been referred to as the "criminal negotiating system." There is a difference sometimes between actual guilt and legal guilt. Legal guilt gives society the opportunity to intervene in the lives of citizen-offenders.

## PRETRIAL INTERVENTION

Pretrial intervention involves the diversion of alleged offenders from the criminal justice system without subjecting them to trial. When a first offender or someone acting under mitigating circumstances is viewed by the judge, the prosecution, the victim, police, and other authorities as a good risk, he or she can be placed under voluntary supervision by a probation agent or other designated authority without being convicted. Eligibility, of course, means that everybody agrees that this person does not present a clear and present danger to society and that no constructive purpose would be served by conviction and sentence.

The American Bar Association has promoted the concept of pretrial intervention and has published a source book on the topic.[19] This volume listed 57 pretrial intervention programs in 24 states at the end of 1973. By June 1975, there were six states with legislation concerning pretrial intervention, two states were operating under court rule on a statewide basis, and 117 other identifiable programs were functioning in urban centers. The largest numbers of programs have been in California, Minnesota, Florida, Missouri, New Jersey, Massachusetts, Michigan, and Texas.[20] In the federal system and some states, this process is referred to as *deferred prosecution;* others call it *probation without adjudication,* and still others have a variety of names, such as Pennsylvania's ARD (*accelerated rehabilitative disposition*). Although the concept of this type of diversion has been traditional in juvenile court as unofficial probation, its application to adult offenders began slowly in the 1960s, was discussed in the President's Commission on Law Enforcement and Administration of Justice rreports in 1967,[21] and became an integral part of the justice system by the mid-1970s.

## SENTENCING

After the defendant has been convicted, the sentencing procedure determines the disposition by society's mechanism for the administration of justice. There is generally a lapse of time between conviction and sentencing, often two weeks to a month, although frequently more or less. During this time, a probation officer or agent gathers information and prepares a presentence investigation report for the judge to use for purposes of determining the sentence. Preparation of a presentence report does not occur in practice as frequently as correctional workers consider to be desirable. The judge imposes a sentence within the confines of the law covering the offense for which the defendant has been convicted and in consideration of the social information available.

Upon conviction, the offender-citizen becomes a ward of the state or jurisdiction and must function under certain legal handicaps. The correctional treatment must take into cognizance these handicaps. For example,

[19] National Pretrial Intervention Service Center, *Source Book in Pretrial Criminal Justice Intervention Techniques and Action Programs* (Washington, D.C.: American Bar Association's Commission on Correctional Facilities and Services, May 1974).

[20] *Ibid.,* pp. 2–11.

[21] *Task Force Report: The Courts* (Washington, D.C.: The President's Commission on Law Enforcement and Administration of Justice, 1967), pp. 97–107.

some state laws forbid sex offenders, narcotic addicts, or other offenders from being placed outside the walls of a minimum security setting, or they may forbid placement on probation.

The sentence imposed by the judge is determined by the statutes. The judge's discretion is bound by limits imposed by the law. For example, conviction for murder in the first degree without the recommendation by the jury for mercy leaves the judge no discretion—he or she must impose the death sentence. In the federal system, a crime may be punishable by ten years or $10,000 fine or both. The judge cannot give probation for some offenses in some jurisdictions. In the case of misdemeanors, the judge frequently can sentence for a certain number of days or, perhaps, months (less than a year).

Some of the dispositions the judge can make are (1) probation, (2) short-term confinement in a jail or workhouse, (3) fine, (4) suspended sentence for short-term confinement in a jail or workhouse, (5) capital punishment or the death penalty, (6) imprisonment for a period of years, (7) commitment under such laws as sexual psychopath laws, child molester laws, narcotic addict laws, or other special provisions, or (8) sentence under a youthful offender act. The sentence chosen is, of course, dependent upon the circumstances of the offender, the offense, and the discretion left by law to the judge.

The judge is a politician, whether appointed or elected, and has to be in tune with the desires of the people. The people have varying views, as can be seen in letters to the editor, editorials, barbership talk, and other means of expression. Sometimes the judge has to engage in "political sentencing" to meet the desires of the people represented, whether based on emotion or on wisdom. The corollary to this is that the judge can use the sentencing procedure and his/her discretion for public education by advising the news reporters and news media as to why the sentencing is being done in a certain manner. The judge must sentence in accordance with the fears and concerns of the constituency.

Dissatisfaction with disparity of sentences for similar offenses given by different judges has resulted in a move toward sentencing guidelines and presumptive sentencing. Fogel's "justice model" arranges offenses in categories of seriousness and suggests sentences accordingly.[21a] California adopted a Board of Prison Terms and Illinois adopted a Prisoner Review Board for that purpose in 1977. Minnesota adopted the Sentencing Guidelines Commission in 1980, which was also adopted by Florida in 1983. About 19 other states have implemented presumptive sentencing partially on violent, drug-related, and/or repeated offenses. Court discretion in sentencing has been severely restricted in California, Colorado, Florida, Minnesota, New Mexico, and North Carolina. Sentencing guidelines have been adopted less formally in several other jurisdictions.

[21a] David Fogel; " '. . . we are the living proof . . .' The Justice Model for Corrections, (Cincinnati: Anderson, 1975).

**Table 2-4  Fear of crime versus reality**

| Crime | Actual Crime Rate per 10,000 Population | Strong Fear of Being a Victim of 10,000 Population |
|---|---|---|
| Homicide | 3 | 3,000 |
| Rape | 7 | 4,300 |
| Robbery | 100 | 3,800 |
| Assault | 110 | 4,300 |
| Auto theft | 127 | 3,500 |
| Larceny | 137 | 3,400 |
| Burglary | 249 | 4,100 |

*Source:* Jack Rosenthal, "The Cage of Fear in Cities Beset by Crime," *Life,* 67, No. 2 (July 11, 1969), 16–23. Courtesy LIFE Magazine © 1969 Time Inc.

A Harris poll of reaction to crime in Baltimore, commissioned by *Life* magazine, was concerned with the reaction of the citizens to the crime problem. The poll found that the fear of crime is reshaping people's daily life in that major city, that the people least in danger are most afraid of crime, and that the principal victims think differently about crime than those who live in safety. Table 2-4 gives some of the information gathered in this poll. While whites consider America a peaceful society where crime can be eliminated, blacks are more willing to recognize that crime is a way of "making it" in a hostile environment. The less victimized whites consider crime a public issue, while the more victimized blacks consider it a personal problem.

One of the difficulties in the field of corrections is that the general public is not aware of what goes on behind the prison walls, in juvenile institutions and detention homes, in jails, or in the caseloads of probation and parole agents. Law enforcement, or the case-finding phase of the total correctional process, has greater social visibility. While in uniform, the policeman can find and arrest an offender, then "put him away." What happens after that is frequently left to the dark recesses of correctional caseloads and routine in which low visibility is desirable for effective treatment. The correctional process is long, is sometimes tedious, sometimes demands extreme patience, and is not very rewarding in terms of public acclaim.

A brief examination of objectives of corrections is in order. Punishment is the theme that appears as the objective of corrections in many public expressions in the mass media and by political candidates. According to the *National Prisoner Statistics Bulletin* of May 1975, only 3.2 per 1,000 prisoners died in prison in 1973 (0.32 percent), which means that nearly all prisoners are released to society. The average stay in prison is slightly under two and one-half years. In view of these figures and for many other reasons, punishment is impractical and undesirable as a correctional objective. If big resentments are made out of little ones through punishment in prison, the offender-victim is going to be worse when he comes out than he was when he arrived. The constructive advantage of punishment is that it permits the criminal out-group to absorb the hostility of "normal" citizenry, thereby permitting a general draining off of aggression by the public. On the other hand, punishment intensifies the individual's problem by adding frustration to frustration and reinforcing failure. In any case, it does not attack the basic problem of the individual.

At the other extreme, the sentimental approach has been advocated by several groups and championed by some literary greats and others who hold society to blame for individual deviation. These persons feel that society should accept its guilt and atone for it by kind and humane treatment of prisoners. This approach assumes that all have an equal chance for rehabilitation and that kindness will restore them as productive members of society, which is a highly unrealistic thesis. Even if the premise were true, compensatory kindness carries neurotic nuances that would interfere with therapy. The sentimental approach does not attack the problem for the individual, either. It is better than the punishment approach, however, because it does not create so many new problems.

The treatment approach appears to be the only practical approach to corrections. The objective in this approach is to prepare the inmate by therapy or conditioning so that his responses to stress will be socially acceptable responses. Because at least 97 percent of the inmates are released to society, it is a good idea to do something constructive with them while the opportunity exists. The treatment approach attacks the problem for the individual. It does nothing for society in terms of expressing aggression or atoning for guilt. The overall objective of protection of society, however, is better served in the long run by the treatment approach than by either of the other two approaches.

Certain civil rights may be lost when the offender is sentenced. Civil rights are personal and social privileges guaranteed by law. These privileges may be revoked as part of the administration of justice and the correctional process upon the conviction of crime. It is well to point out that no offender-citizen ever loses his or her constitutional rights—but the person can lose several civil rights. In most states, the right to vote is lost. Other civil rights that may be lost, depending upon the laws of the jurisdiction in which the conviction takes place, are the right to testify as a witness or serve as a juror, the right to hold office in most states, the right to enter into a contract, including installment buying, the right to marry, and the right to take some civil examinations, depending upon the rules and regulations of the jurisdiction giving the examination. The right to take a federal civil service examination has traditionally been denied, but with the increasing reintegration of the offender-citizen into society in recent years, some ex-offenders are now working for the federal government, including the United States Bureau of Prisons.

The restoration of these civil rights upon release is a matter of law.

Sometimes it is accomplished through a pardon board. Some states, such as Alabama and Nevada, require that restoration of citizenship be specifically expressed in the pardon, although the ex-offender's citizenship has never been lost—confusion in terminology in the law is not uncommon. Civil death has been used in the past more than it is at the present time. In some states, for example, an offender's marriage has been dissolved on the imposition of a life sentence for first-degree murder. If a prisoner were to be released for some reason later and wanted to live with the spouse, they would have to remarry.

The civil rights sections of Title 18 and of Title 42 of the *United States Code* have both been used frequently by prisoners to bring suit against the prison system. Generally, such cases involve unnecessary brutality, mistreatment, or denial of access to counsel.

## THE CORRECTIONAL CASELOAD

The correctional caseload on any given day in 1965 included 257,755 adults on probation, 224,948 juveniles on probation,[22] 221,597 adults in prisons and 141,303 in jails and county institutions, 62,773 juveniles in institutions and detention homes,[23] with another 10,000 in private juvenile institutions, 112,142 adults on parole, and 60,483 juveniles on after-care or juvenile parole.[24] (The 1965 data are presented because that was the last year when reliable data were available for probation and for juvenile parole or after-care. A decade later, the proportions appeared to be similar.[25]) The institutional population in 1979 can be broken down as shown in Table 2-5, and Table 2-6 presents the figures for 1965. While the 1978–79 numbers are greater than the 1965, the proportions remain similar.

Approximately 63 to 68 percent of the adults in the caseload are recidivists and have been in the correctional caseload before. There is little reliable information on repeaters among juveniles, but an estimate might be that about 40 percent return to juvenile institutions and 40 percent return at a later age to adult institutions.

On any given day, over 0.1 percent of the population is in state and federal prisons, and about 3.3 percent of the general population has spent some time in prison. The percentage of persons in jails is under 0.1 on any given day, but the number of persons who have experienced jail confinement is nearly ten times those who have experienced prison confinement.

[22] *Task Force Report: Corrections*, p. 27.

[23] *Ibid.*, p. 45.

[24] *Ibid.*, p. 60.

[25] See Michael J. Hindelang, Christopher S. Dunn, Alison L. Aumick, and L. Paul Sutton, *Sourcebook of Criminal Statistics—1974* (Washington, D.C.: National Criminal Justice Information and Statistics Service, LEAA, July 1975).

**Table 2-5  Institutional Population, 1979**

| Institutions Primarily for Adults | |
|---|---|
| Federal prisons | 26,371[a] |
| State prisons | 314,006[b] |
| Prisoners in jail because of overcrowding | 6,497[c] |
| Local jails | 158,394[d] |
| **Institutions Primarily for Juveniles** | |
| Juveniles in jail | 1,611[e] |
| Public training schools | 47,642[f] |
| Detention centers admissions (not population) | 564,875[g] |
| Private juvenile training schools | 28,556[h] |

[a] *Prisoners in State and Federal Institutions on December 31, 1979, National Prisoner Statistics Bulletin SD-NPS-PSF-7* (Washington, D.C.: U.S. Government Printing Office, 1981), p. 16.
[b] *Ibid.,* p. 16.
[c] *Ibid.,* p. 15.
[d] *Profile of Jail Inmates: Sociodemographic Findings from the 1978 Survey of Inmates of Local Jails* (Washington, D.C.: U.S. Government Printing Office, 1980), p. 42.
[e] *Census of Jails and Survey of Jail Inmates 1978, Preliminary Report* (Washington, D.C.: U.S. Government Printing Office, 1979), p. 3.
[f] *Children in Custody: Advance Report of the 1979 Census of Public Juvenile Facilities* (Washington, D.C.: U.S. Department of Justice), 1980, Table 1.
[g] *Ibid.,* Table 2.
[h] *Ibid.,* Table 1.

**Table 2-6  Institutional Population, 1965**

| Institutions Primarily for Adults | |
|---|---|
| Federal prisons | 20,377 |
| State prisons | 201,220 |
| Local jail and workhouses | 141,303 |
| Total | 362,900 |
| **Institutions Primarily for Juveniles** | |
| Public training schools | 43,636 |
| Local juvenile institutions | 6,024 |
| Detention homes | 13,113 |
| Total | 62,773 |
| Grand total | 425,673 |

*Source: The Challenge of Crime in a Free Society,* The President's Commission on Law Enforcement and Administration of Justice (Washington, D.C.: U.S. Government Printing Office, June 1974), p. 172.

**Table 2-7   Percent of repeaters by type of crime in 1972**

| Persons Released in 1972 and Rearrested within 3 Years | |
|---|---|
| Burglary | 76% |
| Robbery | 70% |
| Auto theft | 68% |
| Rape | 75% |
| Murder | 63% |
| Stolen property | 61% |
| Forgery | 60% |
| Assault | 60% |
| *Average* | 57.4% |
| Narcotics | 57% |
| Weapons | 55% |
| All other offenses | 54% |
| Fraud | 54% |
| Gambling | 40% |
| Embezzlement | 22% |

Source: *Crime in the United States—Uniform Crime Reports—1974*
(Washington, D.C.: Federal Bureau of Investigation, released November 17,
1975), p. 51.

**Table 2-8   Percent of persons rearrested within 3 years by type of release in
1972**

| | |
|---|---|
| Mandatory release[a] and pardons | 67% |
| Parole | 64% |
| Fine | 59% |
| Acquitted or dismissed | 59% |
| Suspended sentence and/or probation | 48% |

[a] *Mandatory release* refers to release at the expiration of sentence, or in some
jurisdictions, release a few months prior to expiration of sentence to get the
offender started on a job, although the supervision, if any, is generally
perfunctory.
Source: *Crime in the United States—Uniform Crime Reports—1974*
(Washington, D.C.: Federal Bureau of Investigation, released November 17,
1975), p. 52.

Some offenses are repeated more than others. Table 2-7 presents the
percentages of all persons released in 1972 who were arrested again within
three years. These are the last reliable figures.

Table 2-8 gives, by type of release, the percentage of persons released
in 1972 and rearrested within three years. These statistics do not mean that
one type of release is necessarily better than another in terms of all releases.
There is a selection process existing in which the better risks generally receive probation and the least favorable risks who have been convicted

do not receive parole but are subject to mandatory release at the expiration of sentence or some other related arrangement. In the American system of administration of justice, acquittal or dismissal after being brought to trial is frequently the result of the law enforcement officer's "making a poor case" because of technical infringements.

## CAPITAL PUNISHMENT

Capital punishment, or the death penalty, has endured since primitive and ancient times. Primitive people actually used it sparingly or, at least indirectly. It was seldom that an offender was killed for a crime. More frequently, a child or a maiden was sacrificed to the gods. The offender was usually banished from the tribe or exiled, which, in the absence of the protection of the group, presumably resulted in his death.

The ancients used capital punishment less for crime than for political or other deviant ideas that damaged or threatened to damage the society. Two significant early executions for crime were those of Socrates and Jesus of Nazareth, commonly known in the Christian world as Jesus Christ. Socrates was sentenced by the court to drink poisonous hemlock because the ideas he taught "corrupted the morals of youth" in Athens in that they varied from local custom and values. Jesus was sentenced by the ecclesiastical court to die by crucifixion, the penalty reserved for blasphemy, because he claimed to be the son of God. He was turned over to the Roman court by the Sanhedrin. The judge, Pontius Pilate, was torn between the wishes of the followers of Jesus and established Judaism, and his decision reflected what he considered to be the balance between orthodoxy and the modifications preached by Jesus, thereby evading violence in Jerusalem and a charge of maladministration from Rome.

Socrates' offense was political, having been based on close friendship with Critias, an extremist of the "terror" of 404 B.C., and the charge of educating Alcibiades, whose behavior had much to do with the downfall of the Athenian empire. In addition to having educated both these men, Socrates was also known as a critic of democracy, which was in the process of emerging. The hazy charge against him was "corruption of the young."

Conventional criminals were also put to death in ancient times, but the high point of capital punishment occurred in England during the reign of Queen Elizabeth (1533–1603), when about 72,000 persons were put to death.

In the United States, Maine, Rhode Island, Michigan, Wisconsin, Minnesota, and North Dakota have historically been known to be without capital punishment, although Rhode Island and North Dakota permitted death for an additional killing in prison, particularly the killing of a guard, under certain circumstances.

The electric chair.

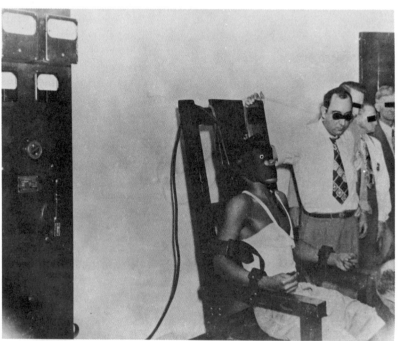

Strapping the executionee in the chair preparatory to electrocution.

Electricity going
through the person
being executed. Note
muscles being flexed
involuntarily.

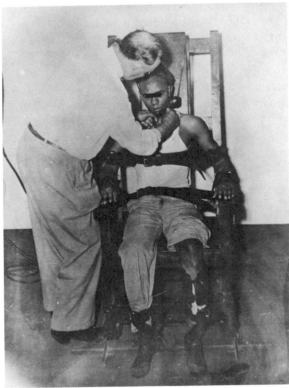

Prisoner being pro-
nounced dead.

Between 1930 and 1967, there were 3,859 people executed in the United States, of whom 32 were female.[26] Of the males, there were 1,731 white and 2,054 black. There were twenty white women and twelve black women executed during this period.

Capital punishment was abolished in the following states and jurisdictions in the years in parentheses:

Alaska (1957)
Hawaii (1957)
Iowa (1965)
Maine (1887)
Michigan (1847) (first to abolish the death penalty)
Minnesota (1911)
Oregon (1964)
Puerto Rico (1929)
Virgin Islands (1937)
West Virginia (1965)
Wisconsin (1853)

States that abolished punishment (and the years they did so) except for specified reasons include:

New York (1965)—death penalty for killing a peace officer in line of duty or for murder of a prison guard or inmate by a lifer while attempting to escape.

Vermont (1965)—death penalty for treason, kidnapping for ransom, conviction of a first-degree murder plus a second unrelated murder, murder by a convict of a prison employee, murder by a convict of a known law enforcement officer in line of duty.

North Dakota (1915)—death penalty for treason and for first-degree murder committed by a lifer serving a sentence for first-degree murder.

In the *Furman* v. *Georgia* case in 1972, the United States Supreme Court nullified existing death penalty laws because they were discretionary and therefore discriminating in their application. Immediately following this action, many states attempted to enact laws that were constitutional. By 1975, twenty-two states had reinstated the death penalty, Florida being the first on December 2, 1972.

Capital punishment is an emotional issue that polarizes people to extreme positions. Its proponents argue strongly that it is a deterrent to

[26] *Capital Punishment—1974* (Washington, D.C.: National Prisoner Statistics Bulletin, LEAA, November 1975), pp. 16, 56.

crime, but there is no evidence to support this argument. States with and without capital punishment which are located near each other and possess similar social, cultural, economic, and other characteristics have similar crime rates in which capital punishment might be inflicted. Examples in point are Maine and Vermont, Rhode Island and Connecticut, Michigan and Ohio, Wisconsin and Indiana, Minnesota and Nebraska, North Dakota and South Dakota, all with and without capital punishment. Conversely, there is no evidence available that capital punishment is completely useless. It may be a legitimate expression of aggression by collective society which, therefore, relieves some emotional pressure. If so, then the issue becomes one concerning how many people are expendable for this purpose.

Capital punishment has never been successfully argued on utilitarian or legitimate bases. It is useless as a deterrent to others, however effective it might be for the individual involved. Its legitimacy has been rejected by canon law, by the ancient Chinese *Book of Five Punishments*, and by Islamic law. It is nonutilitarian, illegitimate in most ethical systems, selectively used, and rarely imposed.[27]

Luis José Monge died in the gas chamber in Colorado on June 2, 1967. After that there was a ten-year period during which nobody was executed. On June 29, 1972, the United States Supreme Court found the death penalty to be unconstitutional in *Furman* v. *Georgia* (408 U.S. 228, 1972). There is nothing in the Constitution that prohibits the death penalty, but the application was adjudged discriminatory and constituted "cruel and unusual punishment" in violation of the Eighth Amendment.[28] There have been several arguments relating to this problem. If the philosophy is vengeance, the Old Testament idea of *lex talionis,* then the death penalty serves a purpose. On the other hand, if the philosophy is corrections, it is aimed at the wrong offenders, since the recidivism rate for murder is low. The charges for which the death penalty is imposed, such as murder and rape, have very low repeat records among those released—and most are released. On the other hand, the highest repeat records are among those not sentenced to death, those convicted of crimes of larceny, auto theft, forgery, and so on.

On the other hand, the presence of many inmates serving time in states that have the death penalty indicates that a conviction for death is harder to obtain. As we have indicated, there are many who believe that the death penalty serves no purpose for society other than vengeance.[29] It serves some groups, such as prosecutors, whose main interest lies in increasing conviction rates and furthering political careers by using the death penalty to obtain convictions on lesser offenses than murder. It is obvious that

[27] Thorsten Sellin, ed., *Capital Punishment* (New York: Harper & Row, 1967), p. 290.

[28] Edgar Smith, *Brief against Death* (New York: Knopf, 1968), p. 366.

[29] Hans Mattick, *The Unexamined Death: An Analysis of Capital Punishment* (Chicago: WCS Center for Community and Social Concern, 1972), p. 38.

the death penalty is irrelevant to the homicide rate, already presented, so it is indefensible on rational grounds, but it would be defensible in terms of a value system based on vengeance and retribution. In summary, the death penalty has never been argued successfully on empirical evidence or on the grounds that it is a deterrent to crime.[30] In fact, recent debates have centered on whether the burden of proof is on those who want to eliminate it or on those who want to keep it. Over two thousand years of argument, beginning with Cato in the Roman Senate in the second century B.C., has failed to produce statistics to support its efficacy, and retentionists hold that the statistics are inefficient anyway. It seems obvious that the death penalty does not accomplish its purpose in protecting society. It is equally obvious that the death penalty remains supported by a value system that emphasizes traditional beliefs and sentiments and has a function of relieving social anger in the collective aggression of the public. Whether it is used or not depends upon the balance of public opinion between these two views.

By 1976, 33 states had restored the death penalty, Florida being the first on December 2, 1972. By the end of 1982, 37 states had reinstated the death penalty.

On July 2, 1976, the Supreme Court of the United States held that the death penalty was not cruel and unusual punishment, as had been held in the Furman decision, essentially because of "society's endorsement." Justice Potter Stewart said that the death penalty for murder "has a long history of acceptance both in England and the United States." In two of the cases, *Woodson* v. *North Carolina* (44 U.S.L.W. 5267, 5274) and *Roberts* v. *Louisiana* (44 U.S.L.W. 5281), the Court struck down the statutes. In three other cases, *Gregg* v. *Georgia* (44 U.S.L.W. 5230), *Proffitt* v. *Florida* (44 U.S.L.W. 5256), and *Jurek* v. *Texas* (44 U.S.L.W. 5262), the death penalty laws were upheld. By the end of 1981, 36 states had reinstated the death penalty and there were 838 people on death rows, 41 percent of whom were black.[31] On December 31, 1981, there were 161 on Florida's death row, 144 in Texas, and 83 in California.

Figure 2-1 shows the number of persons executed through 1982. Since the resumption of executions, Gary Gilmore died in Utah on January 17, 1977; John Spinkelink in Florida on May 25, 1979; Jerome Potts in Nevada on October 22, 1979; Stephen D. Judy in Indiana on March 7, 1981; Frank J. Coppola in Virginia on August 10, 1982; Charlie Brooks in Texas, the first by lethal injection, on December 10, 1982; John Louis Evans, III, in Alabama on April 22, 1983; and Jimmy Lee Gray in Mississippi on September 2, 1983; for a total of eight executions from their reinstatement in

[30] Hugo Adams Bedau, "The Death Penalty as a Deterrent: Argument and Evidence," *Ethics*, 80, No. 3 (April 1970), 205–17.

[31] "Death-row Prisoners 1981," *Bureau of Justice Statistics Bulletin* (Washington, D.C.: Bureau of Justice Statistics, 1982), pp. 2–3.

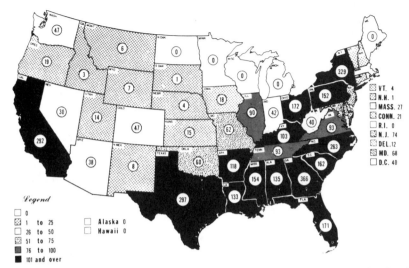

**Figure 2-1 Executions, 1930–82. Prisoners executed under civil authority in the United States, by state.***

* Excludes 33 federal executions carried out in the United States during the period covered.

*SOURCE: National Prisoner Statistics—Capital Punishment—1930–1968,* No. 45 (Washington, D.C.: United States Department of Justice, Bureau of Prisons, August 1969), p. 4. (Numbers of executions through 1982 added.)

1976 to October, 1983. By the end of 1982, there were 1,250 persons on death row in the United States, including 13 women. In addition, there were six on death row in the military services. This number on death row at the end of 1982 was the highest on record in the United States until that time.

## CORRECTIONAL PROCESSES
## IN NONCORRECTIONAL AGENCIES

The total correctional process is not limited to the courts, the correctional institutions, and the agencies for supervision in the community of offenders. Official corrections is society's last resort in an ongoing process of socialization. Legally, the correctional process for adults begins with the verdict of guilty and the correctional process for juveniles begins with referral to the juvenile court. Approximately half the referrals of juveniles never reach the stage of adjudication but are handled by counselors or probation officers on a semivoluntary or unofficial basis. Approximately half reach the legal phase of the court and may be adjudicated as delinquent.

Before all this, however, many agencies, including the family and recreation programs, have been "correcting" the developing individual. Discipline in the home and in the school, attention paid by public welfare departments, concern shown by the juvenile court in cases of dependency, private welfare and family service associations, child guidance clinics, and law enforcement rehabilitative and prevention programs have all preceded the official correctional procedure.

## The Family

Most correctional workers, police, and the general public consider that juveniles would not be delinquent if their families had not failed, nor would adults be offenders. It has long been popular to blame the parents for delinquent children. Prominent law enforcement administrators have publicly stated and written to advise a "back to the woodshed" policy for parents with children who show deviant behavior.

Scholars in the correctional field agree that the family is of basic importance to the development of deviant behavior. One view of the family's influence is seen in the Gluecks' Social Prediction Table, which is based on (1) discipline of the child by the father, (2) supervision of the child by the mother, (3) affection of the father for the child, (4) affection of the mother for the child, and (5) cohesiveness of the family.[32] Other researchers may use different approaches, but all emphasize the importance of the family in corrections.

## The School

The school has always been in the business of discipline and providing some correctional functions. Before World War II, it was common for schools to have truant officers and designated disciplinary officers. In some schools, the principal served as disciplinarian. The classroom teacher has always been on the "first line of defense" in terms of discipline and behavior of unruly students.

More recently, with the increasing size and better organization of school systems, other correctional methods have been used. The old truant officer is now a visiting teacher, whose role includes the function of the old truant officer but also involves much more in terms of working with families and beginning casework with problem children.

A dean of students or vice-principal has replaced the principal as the disciplinarian in many schools. Problem students are frequently referred to him or her. Liaison with the juvenile court and police department is frequently maintained by this person and the visiting teacher. In Ohio, Virginia, and some other places, the teacher probation officer (TPO) serves the juvenile court and the school by supervising delinquents in school. The TPO has full responsibility for the discipline of her/his caseload in school.

Another approach has been to develop a counseling program on a social problem basis in addition to or combined with the academic or voca-

[32] Sheldon Glueck and Eleanor T. Glueck, "Early Detection of Future Delinquents," *Journal of Criminal Law, Criminology, and Police Science*, 47 (1956), 175.

tional counseling program. Social service units have been established by some school systems, in which professional social workers with some background in and understanding of deliquency and other adjustment and mental health problems provide service.

In the larger cities, special schools have been established for problem students. In New York City, for example, the "600 Schools" serve problem students.[33]

## Child Guidance
## or Mental Health Clinics

Child guidance clinics, mental health clinics, and mental health programs are available in most areas of the country. The first child guidance clinic was established in Philadelphia in 1897 to work with behavioral disorders of children, and by 1913, there were 500 such clinics in the United States. Today, there are nearly 2,000 clinics that work with children and nearly half of these also work with adults.

## Welfare Programs

Public and private welfare programs have always concerned themselves with dependency and predeliquency problems. Some workers have said that the difference between a dependent child and a delinquent one is about ten years, the idea being that the underprivileged and deprived children are the ones who become delinquent more frequently than middle- and upper-class children. Therefore, the risk of delinquency would be higher among dependent children than among others. (*Dependent children* is a legal category in juvenile court and a child protective services in welfare departments that refers to children who are abandoned, abused, or neglected.)

Most departments of public welfare throughout the country have two divisions, the division of public assistance and the division of child welfare. Some are supplemented and complemented by county departments of welfare.

The divisions of child welfare services provide casework and foster home care, license and supervise private homes for children and private training schools for delinquents, and furnish homemaker and general protective services for children. The division works in liaison with the juvenile court. How closely it works with the juvenile court is sometimes determined by the personalities of the juvenile court judge and juvenile court counselors. Some units work so closely together that the judge views the welfare personnel as almost part of his/her staff. On the other hand, some judges do not want welfare departments attempting to tell them what to do, and, conversely, some welfare personnel want nothing to do with the juvenile

[33] Esther Rothman, *The Angel Inside Went Sour* (New York: David McKay Co., 1970).

court. In general, however, there is a working liaison between the child welfare services of the welfare department and the juvenile court.

The divisions of public assistance are just as much involved in the correctional process, but in a different way. When the breadwinners of families go to prison, the families are frequently left without support. The division of public assistance supervises the program, financed by the federal government with matched state funds known as categorical relief, which includes old-age assistance, aid to the blind, aid to families of dependent children, aid to the handicapped, and other types of relief. Aid to families of dependent children is most frequently called upon to support families that are without support by reason of imprisonment of the breadwinner. The caseworkers in these instances serve the family, both in casework and in income maintenance, and generally participate in the plan for receiving the parent back into the home after release.

Protective services, as part of the welfare function, have developed in many cities. Protective services serve as a welfare function, somewhat like the child welfare services previously discussed, but with greater emphasis on the predelinquent and problem child. This branch maintains a much closer relationship with the juvenile courts than do most child welfare programs.

Other programs were also available, such as vocational rehabilitation. Since 1965, when behavioral disabilities became eligible, vocational rehabilitation services have had close relationship with corrections.

## Police and Law Enforcement

The use of voluntary police supervision of juveniles is common throughout the United States.[34] In the major cities of some other countries, such as Rotterdam and London, there are special children's police. The pattern in the United States is similar, but the juvenile aid bureau is part of the police department. Even small cities have juvenile officers when they do not have a special unit. Sheriff's departments have junior deputies who frequently perform similar functions. Several sheriffs' associations support homes for dependent youngsters.

There are differing views on the correctional functions of police. The International Association of Chiefs of Police does not favor juvenile aid bureaus, on the basis that *every* officer should be competent in handling juveniles. The National Council on Crime and Deliquency feels that juvenile corrections is sufficiently different from adult corrections to make it necessary to have a juvenile aid bureau. The United States Children's Bureau has taken a view somewhere between these two.

One of the most important correctional functions in the area of law enforcement is the management of jails, stockades, and other detention fa-

[34] See John P. Kenney and Dan G. Pursuit, *Police Work with Juveniles* (Springfield, Ill.: Charles C. Thomas, 1954, 1959), p. 381.

cilities. In many areas of the world and in the United States' Canal Zone government, the main prison is the responsibility of the police. The jail is obviously a correctional responsibility of the police, although the diagnostic and rehabilitative function is rarely accomplished. Many such facilities in larger cities have a rehabilitation division or rehabilitation officer, whose functions are met in varying ways.

The stereotypes of antagonism and mutually exclusive functions between law enforcement and corrections are ill-founded and damaging. These stereotypes must be eliminated in order to promote effective working of law enforcement in the field of corrections.[35]

## CONFIDENTIALITY AND PRIVACY

Privacy of information was ensured by Congress for the first time in Public Law 93-830, commonly known as the Buckley Amendment, on August 6, 1973. Section 524 of that law provided that no officer or employee of the federal government or any recipient of assistance could use or reveal any research or statistical information identifiable to any specific person. Such information cannot be used for legal process and cannot be admitted as evidence in any action, suit, or judicial or administrative proceeding without consent of the individual citizen. All criminal history information shall maintain this position, and all must be kept current if used under due process. The security and privacy of all information is to be ensured by any administration, and its use in law enforcement and corrections purposes must be within a very narrow perspective.

On August 21, 1974, Congress passed into law the Family Educational Rights and Privacy Act (20 U.S.C.A., sec. 1232g, 1974) to provide citizens, including citizen-offenders, the right to examine their own files and have the opportunity to challenge and correct misleading information. While the Constitution does not guarantee or stipulate "privacy," the Fourth Amendment guarantees the right of people "to be secure in their persons, houses, papers, and effects, without consent of the owner. . . ," and this has been translated into privacy by law.

Some parts of the criminal justice system, including police, courts, and all phases of corrections, could encounter difficulty in these areas. The question has been asked about how much and what kind of information a criminal justice program can legitimately keep. With the increasing concern for privacy as described in the First, Fourth, Fifth, and Fourteenth Amendments, there is doubt as to what *can* be kept in permanent records that are subject to subpoenae. Because records in the criminal justice system may have a bearing on whether a person receives probation, or prison,

---

[35] Gary R. Perlstein, "Harmful Stereotypes in Law Enforcement and Corrections," *Lambda Alpha Epsilon Journal*, 33, No. 1 (March 1969), 9–10. Also, Gary R. Perlstein and Bernard C. Brannon, "Coordination in Criminal Justice Education," *Police*, 15, No. 4 (March–April 1971), 19–20.

or is denied parole, the use of records of any sort is coming more and more in view by the courts, particularly in view of the recent legislation concerning privacy and confidentiality. Information in computer data banks has been erroneous in some cases and has resulted in unfortunate dispositions regarding individuals, and the Code of Fair Information Practices has moved this privacy from the governmental sector into the private sector of society, such as regarding credit ratings.[36] The problem in corrections becomes one of what information can be kept in permanent files without violating the rights of the citizen-offender. It remains for the courts in the next few years to delineate that question. Protection of privacy in personal information systems has become important. The use of Social Security numbers in data banks has been challenged.[37] It is interesting to note that university attorneys have even interpreted these laws as preventing the posting of grades by professors, even using Social Security numbers or other codes, as an "invasion of privacy."

## SUMMARY

The correctional process extends from correcting minor behavioral deviations in preschool children to correcting the social ills that cause deviant behavior in adults. In the more narrow sense, the correctional process extends from the time an adult is found guilty of a crime or when a juvenile is referred to juvenile court until either is released from supervision, either from the institution or from parole or after-care supervision in the community. The discussion of the correctional process could include the family, school, recreational programs, and all social programs that assist the family to maintain itself. The official correctional process includes the juvenile court, adult probation, institutions and prisons, and parole and other release procedures. Several programs in the community, such as vocational rehabilitation, have special concerns for the offender. In the remainder of this book, we will be concerned with corrections in the narrow sense. In all cases, the rights of the citizen, whether offender or law-abiding, must be respected.

## EXERCISES AND STUDY QUESTIONS

1. *Describe briefly the correctional process.*

2. *What is the approximate volume of crime and delinquency in the United States?*

[36] R. Turn and W.H. Ware, "Privacy and Security in Computer Systems," January 1975, reported in *Selected Rand Abstracts*, 13, No. 2 (January–June 1975), 29.

[37] W.H. Ware, "Computer Privacy and Computer Security," October 1972, reported in *Selected Rand Abstracts*, 13, No. 2 (January–June 1975), 28.

3. What is pretrial intervention?

4. Differentiate between conventional crime, organized crime, and white-collar crime.

5. What crimes are committed most frequently, both serious and lesser offenses?

6. Describe the FBI Uniform Crime Reporting program.

7. Evaluate crime statistics in America.

8. What conclusions can be drawn regarding the difference in the Crime Index for the various states?

9. Describe the screening process, beginning from crime to arrest and through the verdict or adjudication that makes the offender a correctional client.

10. Why do people tend not to notify police about crimes even when they are the victims?

11. How does society gain the authority to intervene in the private lives of citizen-offenders?

12. Describe the sentencing procedure.

13. What factors enter into the sentence?

14. Discuss the relation between fear of crime and how frequently it occurs.

15. Evaluate the punishment approach, the sentimental approach, and the treatment approach to corrections.

16. What is the volume of the correctional caseload in America?

17. Which offenses are repeated most frequently, and which are repeated least frequently?

18. Evaluate capital punishment.

19. What are the restrictions in the correctional process with regard to privacy and confidentiality of information?

20. What agencies, organizations, units, and institutions are involved in the narrow concept of corrections?

# 3

# THE CORRECTIONAL CLIENT

There are several legally defined categories of clients who receive attention, assistance, treatment, and control through governmental agencies and institutions. With the exception of the population covered by compulsory education laws, welfare clients make up the largest of these groups. These people must be "eligible" under the laws of the programs that serve them. The eligibility of insane persons is determined in a civil proceeding in court so they can be committed to public hospitals for the insane. Crippled children, the aged, and the blind are covered under the law. Feebleminded or defective persons are generally referred to in statutes nd regulations as those with IQs below 70, and they can be institutionalized in public institutions and special schools. Epileptics in several jurisdictions have specialized treatment under the law. Persons with tuberculosis or venereal disease can be forced to accept treatment under the public health laws, whether they want such treatment or not. A public health officer is probably the only official under the American system of government who can force his way into a citizen's home when there is reason to believe that children are being endangered by illness and lack of treatment. Narcotic addicts can be committed to public hospitals. None of these clients have "willfully damaged society."

The correctional client is one who has damaged society and is legally responsible for his action. He has violated the law and, therefore, damaged the social order by his failure to conform to expected behavior. Welfare clients may have been poor managers, physically handicapped, inadequate, or for other reasons unable to deal effectively with their socioeconomic environment. Mental hospital clients may be mentally ill in a variety of ways, but they must meet the legal definition of "insane." Clients in general or charity hospitals are obviously physically ill and disabled. Clients of psychiatric clinics, marriage counseling clinics, and similar agencies of public health tend to have a high component of neuroses. The correctional client, however, differs from all the others, even though some of the others may be included in the correctional caseload. The correctional client has damaged society by violation of law.

There is no such thing as a "criminal personality." Crime and delinquency are definitions of a relationship between the individual and his society. By definition, crime is a sociopolitical event. It is important to remember the differentiation between mental illness and a social problem. Of course, mental illness could cause the social problem. Conversely, social and environmental conditions can cause mental illness. Crime and delinquency are social problems, and they are also mental health problems, since they are concerned with the adjustment of the individual in society. Any number of factors within the personality and within society may contribute to this dysfunctional relationship. Crime and delinquency are matters of adjustment of the individual to society.

## DEVELOPING THE CORRECTIONAL CLIENT

Some deviant behavioral patterns emerge in elementary school years, while, at the other extreme, some criminal behavior develops after middle adulthood.[1] The period of development has been charted by some researchers in definite stages. One comparison between normal development as supported by the sanctions of society and abnormal development in which positive social attitudes do not prevail is found in the work of Erik H. Erikson. His work is presented in Witmer and Kotinsky, *Personality in the Making,* edited by Helen Witmer and Ruth Kotinsky, which resulted from the mid-century White House Conference on Children and Youth. Erikson developed eight stages of man which could be of assistance in understanding some of the dynamics that generate delinquent and criminal behavior.[2] These stages are shown in Table 3-1.

The normal or desirable development and some of the deviations that are possible pose a considerable variety of possibilities with regard to personality development and the relationship of the individual to society. Emotional maturity or interpersonal maturity is a function of an individ-

[1] Bruno M. Cormier, Miriam Kennedy, Jadwiga Sangowicz, and Michael Trottier, "The Latecomer to Crime," *The Canadian Journal of Corrections,* 3, No. 1 (January–February 1966), 2–12.

[2] See Louis Tomaino, *Changing the Delinquent—A Practical Approach,* V. Hogg Foundation for Mental Health (Austin: University of Texas Press, 1969), pp. 24–25.

**Table 3-1**

| Age | Condition to Be Obtained | Opposite Condition |
|---|---|---|
| 0-6 | Trust—Autonomy | Mistrust<br>Shame—Doubt |
| 6-12 | Initiative, industry, identity | Guilt—Inferiority<br>Role confusion |
| 12-18 | Intimacy | Isolation |
| 20s | Generativity | Stagnation |
| Old age | Integrity | Despair |

*Source:* Helen Leland Witmer and Ruth Kotinsky, eds., *Personality in the Making: The Fact-Finding Report of the Mid-Century White House Conference on Children and Youth* (New York: Harper & Row, Publishers, Inc., 1952), pp. 6–28. Based on a presentation made to the Conference by Dr. Erik H. Erikson regarding his Eight Stages of Man.

ual's adjustment to society, the manner in which he copes with stress, and his general outlook and attitude.[3]

Human behavior, including criminal behavior, is broader than one discipline can handle. It is important in each case to know (1) personality, (2) society, and (3) culture. Personality is the primary focus of psychology and psychiatry. Society is the primary focus of sociology. Culture is the primary focus of anthropology, law, political science, and other areas of human endeavor. Crime and delinquency, as dysfunctional relationships between the individual and society, must be seen from all viewpoints.

Personality and modification of the behavior of the individual constitute the most significant phase of the correctional process, because it is the only area in which corrections can be effective. Moving the person from one environment to another is the only way to change his/her society and culture. Cutting off the individual from the ties he has developed seems to be a more realistic alternative than changing that person's environment—a difficult if not impossible task. Consequently, personality emerges as the most significant factor available to the correctional worker. Changes in attitude, self-concept, motivation, and goals are all within the personality.

Society involves the interaction between people and groups of people. Illustrations of social interaction or behavior might be seen in the various experiments which have dealt with the pecking order of chickens.[4] In one experiment, a flock of chickens was identified individually with leg tags and then observed. Chicken A pecked everybody else in the flock, but no-

[3] Clyde Sullivan, Marguerite Q. Grant, and J. Douglas Grant, "The Development of Interpersonal Maturity: Applications to Delinquency," *Psychiatry*, 20 (November 1957), 1–5.

[4] R.H. Masure and W.C. Allee, "The Social Order in Flocks of the Common Chicken and the Pigeon," *Auk*, 51 (1934), 306–27; "Flock Organization of the Shell Parakeet *Melopsittuacus Undulatus Shaw*," *Ecology*, 15 (1934), 388–98.

body pecked Chicken A. Chicken B pecked everybody in the flock except Chicken A, and Chicken A pecked Chicken B and the others. Chicken C pecked everybody in the flock except Chicken A and B, and so on through the flock until the pecking order was charted. The standing in the social order of any individual is a social function. Whether a legislator is a "heavyweight" or a "lightweight" determines his influence in political action. Similarly, social status in terms of individual stability and standing in the group is an influence in all social groupings. Even with chickens, mating receptivity is related to the hen's position in the flock hierarchy and will change if her relative position is changed by the flock size or membership.[5] Even elementary schoolchildren at recess exhibit a pecking order! In corrections, this approach can be used to identify inmate leadership in prisons and other institutions. Some youths at the lower end of the pecking order develop a self-perception of hopelessness to the extent that they will tattoo "Born to Lose" on their chests and arms.

Culture is man's way of doing things, including the system of distribution of goods and services, system of government, the legal structure, occupational patterns, religious attitudes and prejudices, and the rest of man's folkways, customs, ethical patterns, social institutions, and laws. It encompasses the rules, regulations, customs, procedures, and the "way of doing things" for man, independent of personality and society. The correctional client has difficulty in internalizing the values of the culture.

The correctional worker views his or her caseload as a group of people quite similar to other people who have not come into conflict with the law. The only common denominator among all offenders is their conflict with social authority. The only common motivating force among all offenders is to get out of jail, stay out, and to remain free from any sort of authoritative supervision. A common pattern among correctional clients is the projection of blame on society or "the system." Correctional clients, further, tend to refer to "the caught and the uncaught" and suggest that society and culture are unfair and that they were, in fact, "born to lose." The reality or unreality of these common attitudes does not matter. They exist. They reflect the way in which correctional clients tend to see their situation. The problem, as far as the relation of personality development to the correctional process is concerned, becomes one of how to understand the etiology of these attitudes and how to correct them.

The development of normal personality and its relationship to society and culture may give some clues as to what might have happened to cause a dysfunctional pattern of behavior defined as delinquency and crime. Throughout any discussion of human behavior, it must be remembered that all definitions are culture-bound. Culture establishes the expected norms and defines the deviations. This concept permeates all evaluation of human behavior. The Rorschach test, for example, considers the F+ (a

---

[5] A.M. Guhl, "The Social Order of Chickens," *Scientific American,* 194, No. 2 (1956), 42–46.

measure of ego strength) score as a measure of perception of reality. If a measurement drops below 70 percent, the psychologist looks for a psychosis. If it goes above 90 percent, the psychologists look for a neurosis. The normal range is between 70 and 90 percent perception reality, which provides intelligent identification with the environmental structure yet leaves some room for creative imagination and fantasy.

The development of a personality to fit a culture and to be able to interact appropriately with others takes a long time. Born with a rather complex physiological system, with the potential to develop, the infant's first stable relationship with others is established with its mother. During the first year and a half, the mother interacts with the child, eliciting smiles and other responses, providing comfort and nourishment, and generally providing the child with a secure relationship. As primitive people travel in tribes, rather than as "loners," and civilized people group themselves into political, religious, kinship, and other groupings, it appears obvious that human beings have a basic need to invest in others. The early nurturing of this need to invest emotionally in others occurs during infancy, when the mother provides security and comfort and nurtures the capacity to relate to others by eliciting responses.

Toilet training is the first imposition of social control over basic bodily functions. It is the first effort to induce conformity to expected behavioral norms. The manner in which toilet training is accomplished may set the tone for the imposition of other social controls. During the preschool years, further social controls are imposed and the child's span of participation with others is increasing. The child learns the expectations of culture concerning things such as property rights, customary dress, table manners, and eating habits. At the same time, the world has increased from the mother to siblings and people in the outside world.

By the time the growing child starts school, his or her value system has been fairly well internalized and systematized. In school, varying patterns of values learned by other children and, perhaps, the teacher, may be encountered. The child then goes through a period of modifying responses to fit the demands of expanded social relationships. Responses that do not work are discarded, responses that are reinforced are kept, and others are modified. Simultaneously, the span of social relationships has further expanded.

The child approaching puberty is increasingly more influenced by the father. Traditionally, the father's world has been out in the community, with the mother's world at home. It has been the function of the father to integrate the value system learned from the mother into the power structure and social relationships of the community. Even though this pattern seems to be undergoing important changes in contemporary Western society, the father still generally represents the authority of the society. In the traditional American family unit, a growing boy learns the tools of masculinity as defined in the culture from his father; the growing girl learns the feminine role from her mother. If the parents are adequate models as defined by the culture, the integrative function in adolescence will be done well. The absence of either mother or father in these formative years can have an important effect on the formation of the personality. Studies have shown that a missing father or father figure in particular vastly shapes a child's conception of his or her relationship to the society as a whole.

The importance of a culturally defined authority figure is most important in integrating the value system into the power structure of the community. Studying delinquent and nondelinquent white males, Newman and Denman found that children who lose their fathers before the age of 18 are more likely to be involved in felonies than are those whose fathers are present at that age.[6] This specific relationship of the loss of the father and criminal behavior could enable counselors and other helping persons in school and other programs for youth to identify potential problems and direct their efforts toward the more vulnerable population.

In summary, the family's influence on the development of children has traditionally placed greatest importance on the mother during the first year of life and the preschool years. The influence of the father is greatest immediately before and after puberty, perhaps between the ages of 10 and 15.

Comparisons of delinquents with nondelinquents have exposed some differences associated with the presence or absence of the mother in the family, but these differences are not statistically significant. Comparisons of delinquents and nondelinquents on the basis of the presence or absence of the father, however, have been significant.[7] The common denominator among offenders, as mentioned before, is conflict with authority. The father represents authority in the home, according to the culture. When the value systems are not functionally integrated into the power and social relationships structure of the community, difficulty in the form of crime and delinquency can be expected.

The social contacts and relationships of the developing personality are expanding throughout childhood and youth. During the first year of life and infancy, the family and the neighborhood children are important. When the internalized cultural values are strong enough to withstand conflict, the child goes to school and further broadens social relationships. By the time of puberty, the mother has ceased to be all-important in terms of personality development, and the focus of socialization is outside the home.

---

[6] Gustave Newman and Sidney B. Denman, "Felony and Paternal Deprivation: A Socio-Psychiatric View," *The International Journal of Social Psychiatry,* 17, No. 1 (1971), 65–71.

[7] See Thomas P. Monahan, "Family Status and the Delinquent Child: A Reappraisal and Some New Findings," *Social Forces,* 35 (1957), 250–58; Fritz Redl and David Wineman, *Children Who Hate* (Glencoe, Ill.: Free Press, 1951), pp. 55–56, 113, 121; Ruth S. Cavan, *Juvenile Delinquency* (Philadelphia: Lippincott, 1962), Chap. 10, "The Family Setting of Delinquency," 111–27.

The father becomes important, although neither the child nor the father generally knows it. The peer group determines the dress, behavior, and attitudes of most teenagers.

In terms of total development, the family is most important because it had first chance—the first dozen years. The peer group is a close second in importance in normal personality development. All other factors, such as school and church, are not significant in themselves, since their influence is determined by the family and later by the gang.

In families that produce deviant behavior in their children, the influence of family, gang, and other social units impinging on the developing personality deviate from the average. Some growing personalities have no family at all, and their entire development is influenced by the gang or by strong adults. On the other hand, some individuals develop in overprotective families where the gang or peer group never have a chance to influence the growing child. Each of these deviations in patterns of socialization produces deviations in behavior patterns. The absence of an adequate father is most important in producing susceptibility to criminal and delinquent behavior.

Development of the capacity for permanent and monogamous heterosexual personality also takes a long time. In the development of heterosexual interests about the time of puberty, simple physical attraction is paramount. This develops into a series of physical attractions to a same individual, so that a boy may be distracted from other matters by the girl in the front row. The girl may develop a crush on the teacher. In high school, boys and girls may go steady for two or three weeks or for a whole semester. This infatuation is a function of the gradual extension of the duration of heterosexual relationships. The next phase is one of viewing heterosexual relationships as a series of conquests. Boys and girls may go so far as to list the names of their conquests! This phase is referred to by some psychologists as the narcissistic stage.

The next phase comes some time in the early twenties, when suddenly the attention is focused on one person and a complete emotional investment is made in that person. In this stage of romantic love, all others are excluded, and the virtues and strengths of the object of love are exaggerated, while their weaknesses are considered insignificant. During this stage, love songs and possessive behavior flourish, and aggressive or suicidal behavior may result when one person attempts to withdraw from the relationship.

By the early middle twenties, the person considers himself or herself ready for a permanent, monogamous heterosexual relationship. Marriage counselors advise that a family not be started until a year after marriage in order to allow time for adjustment. Living with another person is considerably different from dating. Sometimes the faults and weaknesses become exaggerated and annoying, just as the strengths were exaggerated during courtship.

There are several problems in corrections that arise as a result of this development. For example, most boys and girls are sent to all-male or all-female juvenile training schools right in the middle of the narcissistic period. Placing a boy or a girl in a unisexual institution when sexual interests are intense may arrest or divert progress in the direction of permanent, monogamous heterosexuality. On the other hand, placing a 45-year-old man or woman in a unisexual population would not affect personality development. The age, race, and sex of this correctional client may provide a profile of his or her demographic characteristic.

Total arrests by age groups in 1979 are as follows:

| Age | Number | Percentage |
|---|---|---|
| 10 and under | 74,652 | 0.8 |
| 11 to 12 | 136,754 | 1.4 |
| 13 to 14 | 450,637 | 4.7 |
| 15 | 407,152 | 4.3 |
| 16 | 515,979 | 5.4 |
| 17 | 558,195 | 5.9 |
| 18 (largest single age group) | 595,798 | 6.3 |
| 19 | 550,079 | 5.8 |
| 20 | 504,901 | 5.3 |
| 21 | 466,326 | 4.9 |
| 22 | 425,099 | 4.5 |
| 23 | 382,882 | 4.0 |
| 24 | 253,421 | 3.7 |
| 25 to 29 | 1,279,025 | 13.5 |
| 30 to 34 | 827,300 | 8.7 |
| 35 to 39 | 564,716 | 5.9 |
| 40 to 44 | 418,477 | 4.4 |
| 45 to 49 | 329,217 | 3.5 |
| 50 to 54 | 271,102 | 2.9 |
| 55 to 59 | 186,336 | 2.0 |
| 60 to 64 | 104,507 | 1.1 |
| 65 and older | 94,264 | 1.0 |
| Not known | 9,528 | 0.1 |

Source: *Uniform Crime Reports for the United States, 1979* (Washington, D.C.: U.S. Government Printing Office, 1980), pp. 196–97.

### Increasing Female Crime

The number of females involved in major crime has risen sharply since 1960. The total increase of arrests in 1974 over 1960 for males was 23.7 percent, as compared with an increase for females over the same period of 108.8 percent.[8] During the same time, the increase in arrests for males *under*

[8] *Crime in the United States—Uniform Crime Reports—1974* (Washington, D.C.: Federal Bureau of Investigation, released November 17, 1975), 184.

*18* was 119.4 percent, while the increase for females under 18 was 245.1 percent. More significantly, the increase of major offenses (Index Crimes) for females was 383.2 percent, while this figure was 118.0 percent for arrests of males.

There were 2,665,339 males arrested in 1974 as compared with 540,987 females.[9] There were 121,511 males in state and federal correctional institutions in 1973 as compared with 6,175 females.[10] Females constitute about 16.9 percent of the arrests, 9.6 percent of the convictions,[11] and 4.8 percent of the prison population.

There is a tendency to treat women differently in the criminal justice system for a variety of reasons. Male judges and prosecutors tend to be easier on women. Many have families and are the sole support for their children, and imprisonment would create hardship. Too, judges regard women as not a clear and present danger to society. In 1972, for example, only one out of every 6.5 arrests was a woman; of every 9 convictions one was a woman; there was one woman in 30 sentenced to prison.[12]

There were 24,477 boys in public detention and correctional facilities for juveniles in 1971 as compared with 6,410 girls.[13] This means that 79.2 percent of juveniles in custody were boys, while girls constituted 20.8 percent of the public juvenile institution caseloads. But it is obvious from the arrest data and juvenile institutional data that younger females are being represented more in the criminal justice system in recent years than they have been in the past.

## THE OFFENDER

The offender develops under stress of some sort, and the patterns of his development vary with the patterns of socialization—or domestication—that shaped his characteristic responses to stress. The patterns of mothering lay the base of personality,[14] but the subsequent social stresses modify the hierarchy of social responses to stresses in society. Crime and delinquency are such responses. They constitute a mode of adaptation to stress for the individual. It is important for the correctional worker to know the general dy-

[9] *Ibid.*

[10] *Prisoners in State and Federal Institutions on December 13, 1971, 1972, and 1973* (Washington, D.C.: National Criminal Justice Information and Statistics Service, LEAA, May 1975), 21, 23.

[11] *Federal Offenders in the United States District Courts—1972* (Washington, D.C.: Administrative Office of the United States Courts, July 31, 1975), p. 7.

[12] Rita James Simon, *Contemporary Women and Crime* (Rockville, Md.: National Institute of Mental Health, Center for Studies of Crime and Delinquency, 1975), p. 87.

[13] *Children in Custody: Report of the Juvenile Detention and Correctional Facility Census, 1971* (Washington, D.C.: LEAA and Bureau of the Census, June 1974), pp. 34–35.

[14] See Sylvia Brody, *Patterns of Mothering* (New York: International Universities Press, 1956), p. 446.

namics of personality development in order to be successful in the art of changing people from deviant to adaptive social behavior patterns.

If the parents fail to nurture the capacity to relate during the first year of life, the growing child has to accommodate to nonrelating, which can become the base for psychopathy, sociopathy, or antisocial personality. Lack of affectionate interaction of parent and child can distort the transmission of cultural values. The chances for normal socialization of the child, then, are reduced.

Some studies have indicated that the direction in which the family deviates from the expected norm determines in part the area in which the child may experience difficulty in social adjustment.[15] For example, many aggressive delinquents come from homes in which they have always been rejected. Many "socialized delinquents," or those who are never in trouble alone but are sufficiently dependent that they go wherever the gang goes in order to be accepted, come from homes in which they were originally loved and given attention but subsequently replaced by other parental interests, such as a new baby. In any case, the influence of the family in normal homes is obvious, and the influence of families that do not fit the socially expected norms also seems apparent.

## BIOLOGICAL FACTORS

The field of modern corrections emerged around the time of the American Revolution, when the concepts of free will and individual responsibility prevailed. During the next century, however, the study of biology and evolution focused attention on constitutional factors, until Lombroso formulated his contentions concerning the "born criminal" and atavistic tendencies. The influence of the biology approaches remains with corrections today, particularly in Italy and Greece, and to a lesser extent in Scandinavia, France, and Belgium. European corrections tend to emphasize the Classical and the Positivistic schools of criminology in their programs by reliance on moral reeducation and interpretation of criminal behavior in terms of constitutional and biological factors. The Scandinavian countries use castration of offenders as treatment for some sexual offenses, on the basis that this neutralizes extreme sex drives.[16]

In America, most professional correctional workers today tend to reject these types of approaches as lacking adequate supportive evidence and as impractical from the standpoint of treatment. Habitual offender laws

[15] See E.S. Hewitt and Richard L. Jenkins, *Origins of Maladjustment* (Springfield, Ill.: Illinois State Department of Health, 1944).

[16] Georg Stürup, "Les delinquents sexuels et leur traitement au Danemark et dans les autres pays scandinaves," *Revue internationale de politique criminelle*, No. 4 (1953), 1–19. Also, Henri F. Ellenberger, "Aspects biologiques et psychiatriques de la criminalité," in Denis Szabo, ed., *Criminology in Criminologie—Action en Action* (Montreal: University of Montreal Press, 1968), pp. 45–82.

provide for increased penalties for offenders who have had previous felony convictions. Some of the thinking that went into these laws involved the biological predisposition to criminal behavior, at least during the nineteenth century. While such laws were passed in New York and Massachusetts as early as 1817, recent interest was stimulated by the passage of the "Baumes Act" in New York in 1926. While the Baumes laws have been passed in most states, the evidence indicates that they were passed only after many failures and justified as a means of protecting society rather than as a means of biological treatment.

The extent of biological determinism has not been agreed upon completely among scholars in the field of human behavior. Most sociologists and psychologists believe that all of man's behavior, within biological limits, is determined by experience and learning. On the other hand, many psychiatrists and neuropsychiatrists place more significance on biological determinism. The term "instinct," unacceptable to most sociologists and psychologists, appears in the psychiatric literature. There is a question as to what extent civilization has replaced basic drives and "instincts" in man.

The honeybee constructs a honeycomb in a perfect hexagon because it cannot help it—the bee was built to act in this way. One of Kinsey's early experiments with gull wasps involved his crushing a female wasp on a plank and brushing the remains away. The male gull wasps elicited sexual responses in that area in the complete absence of the female, which suggests reflex or "instinctual" behavior. Moving up the phylogenetic scale, dogs retain many characteristics that are apparently biologically determined, but they can be trained within limits. When the basset hound is given a bone and the bone is subsequently removed, the dog reacts with a sad-eyed hope that the bone will be given back to him sometime. When a bone is removed from a spitz, however, aggressive reaction may be expected. Some dogs are more easily trained for hunting, shepherding, and other functions than others. Nobody has ever heard of a chow shepherding a herd of cattle! German shepherds are used for sentry training because their temperament is appropriate for it. Regarding human beings, the question is raised as to just how much biological determinism is left in man and how much of his behavior is learned by experience or conditioning. Most social and behavioral scientists base their interpretations of behavior on learning and conditioning, while some others concerned with behavior, such as in neuropsychiatry, still include "instincts" in human behavior.

Body build has been conjectured as being related to crime.[17] Shakespeare, in *Julius Caesar,* had Caesar say, "Let me have men about me that are fat; sleek-headed men and such as sleep o'nights. Yond Cassius has a lean and hungry look; he thinks too much: such men are dangerous." It is known that some endocrinal situations will affect temperament. For exam-

---

[17] See Ernest A. Hooten, *Crime and Man* (Cambridge, Mass.: Harvard University Press, 1939); William H. Sheldon, Emil M. Hartl, and Eugene McDermott, *Varieties of Delinquent Youth* (New York: Harper & Row, 1949).

ple, a hypothyroid, or cretin, is obese and lethargic. On the other hand, a hyperthyroid is thin and nervous. These conditions involve problems of adjustment, however, and do not determine that the adjustment will be criminal or delinquent. The criticism studies in this area suggest, at the minimum, that the relationship of body type to criminality is not accepted by most professionals and scholars in the field of corrections today.[18]

Epilepsy is found more frequently in prison populations than in the general population. Periodic irritability preceding a seizure, may, of course, explain some quarrelsome behavior. It is more difficult for an epileptic than for the normal person to find a job if he acknowledges his disease on his application and more difficult for him to keep the job if he fails to record his affliction and then has a seizure. In general, social adjustment is more difficult. The side effects of his difficulty in social adjustment may be more responsible for criminal solutions to stress than the epilepsy itself.

Physical handicaps and disfigurements have been seen as factors in crime. Again, the social and self-concept problems caused by disfigurement are greater than those experienced by a normal person. Deviant compensatory behavior has been traced to physical appearance and disfigurement, but it is the social reaction to the disfigurement rather than the disfigurement itself which is involved. Many correctional programs include cosmetic surgery, such as straightening crossed eyes, removing tattoos, removing prominent facial scars, straightening noses, and correcting other physical problems.

There has been recent interest in the chromosomes of an individual and what their effect is on aggression or passivity. Ordinarily, the female chromosome makeup is 44A plus 2X, and the male is 44A plus XY, although all females are not really XX functionally, but XY, because one X is largely inactivated. Males are XY and are Barr-negative, leaving the difference between female and male as a little of the inactivated X and small y. As long as the individual has a y, he will be a male. Some females are XX, some are XO (lacking the extra A), and some are XXX (very female). One in 200 males is XXY and infertile, possessing a heavy component of female chromosomes and lacking full development of the testes. Some males are XYY or even XYYY, or supermales. Some individuals are mosaics, with uncommon combinations. The Russian "woman" who threw the hammer out of the Olympic stadium precipitated interest in the chromosomes, so that now, such international questions as who is a "man" and who is a "woman" are easily settled by examining Barr bodies present in cells from smears from the mouth. In any case, the chromosome problem has emerged in the field of corrections.[19]

[18] The many criticisms of the body-type approach can probably best be summarized by George Vold's statement in his *Theocritical Criminology* (New York: Oxford University Press, 1958), p. 74, in which he says, "There is no such present evidence at all of physical type, as such, having any consistent relationship to legal and sociologically defined crime."

[19] Norman G.B. McLetchie, "The Quality of Mercy," *The RCMP Quarterly*, The Royal Canadian Mounted Police, 34, No. 4 (April 1969), 6–12.

Recently, discussion has centered on the stability of the XYY chromosomes, or an extra male chromosome, being found more frequently in prisoners than in the general population. A British researcher reported that he found the XYY chromosome in 3 percent of the prison population but in only 0.5 percent of the general population. These findings have not resulted in any definitive conclusions. Criminal psychopaths over 184 cm tall may have a 47, XYY karyotype. Of 42 patients over 180 cm tall in a Danish institution for mentally abnormal criminals, two were found to have 47 chromosomes and six chromosomes XYY, an incidence rate which is 25 to 60 times as high as that in the general population.[20]

Of 34 prisoners between 69 and 82½ inches in height, 20 had normal chromosomes, three had 47 chromosomes with a XYY complement, and one was a XYY/YYY mosaic. The incidence of XYY in the general population is less than 0.2 percent.[21]

Karyotypic examination of 204 consecutive male admissions to a prison for psychiatric treatment revealed five abnormalities (2 XYY, 2 XXY, 1 XY, XYY mosaic), which represents a lower XYY incidence than reported in other surveys, but the same incidence for XXY. Those convicted of arson include the 2 XYY, 1 XYY, and 11 normals. Psychiatric evaluation revealed that both XYY males were homosexual with schizoid effect.[22]

Karyotypic analyses of 315 men at a special maximum security hospital indicated that sixteen (5.1 percent) had an abnormal chromosome complement. Nine men (2.9 percent) with XYY sex chromosomes were significantly taller than the average inmate; there was no difference in intelligence, but the men were noted to display more antisocial behavior. On the basis of this study, antisocial behavior was seen as possibly genetic, rather than environmental.[23]

The present status of the field indicates, however, that there is really no proof of a link between the XYY chromosome and crime at this time.[24] Sociological and legally defined crime is difficult to link with any biological factor, whether it be age, race, sex, disfigurement, or chromosomes. It may be, of course, just as in glandular deviations, that any deviation in chromosome structure results in more difficult social adjustment, but a chromosomal link to crime has not been demonstrated.

[20] Johannes Nielsen, Takayuki Tsubsi, Georg Stürup, and David Romano, "XYY Chromosomal Constitution in Criminal Psychopaths," *Lancet,* 2 (1968), 576.

[21] Saul Weiner, Grant Sutherland, Allen A. Bartholomew, and Brian Hudson, "XYY Inmates in a Melbourne Prison," *Lancet,* 1 (1968), 150.

[22] D.J. Bartlett, W.P. Hurley, C.R. Brand, and E.W. Poole, "Chromosomes of Male Patients in a Security Prison," *Nature,* 219 (1968), 315–54.

[23] Patricia A. Jacobs, W.H. Price, W.M. Court Brown, R.P. Brittain, and P.B. Whatmore, "Chromosome Studies on Men in a Maximum Security Hospital," *Annals of Human Genetics,* 31, No. 4 (1968), 339–58.

[24] "Link Between XYY Syndrome and Criminality Not Clear," *Public Health Reports,* 89, No. 10 (October 1969), 914.

# INTELLIGENCE

Intelligence may have a constitutional base, but it is greatly affected by environmental factors, cultural stimulation or deprivation, health, and other factors. For nearly a generation after intelligence testing was first brought to the United States in 1911 by Goddard, criminals and delinquents were still considered to be feebleminded or, at least, significantly lower than normals in intelligence. As intelligence testing became more refined and less bound to vocabulary and culture assimilation, the observed differences disappeared.

Recent studies indicate that intelligence does not significantly differ between offenders and the general population from which they were drawn. Even the early studies supported this contention. In 1926, Murchison said, "The criminal element of society, as will be shown by the facts reported in this book, does not possess a lower average intelligence than the adult civil population."[25] A study in Boston reported in 1928 indicated that the distribution of delinquent boys' IQs was a normal curve similar to that of the general population.[26] Prisoners have approximately the same average level of intelligence as that revealed for the adult population in the World War I army draft. The prisoner population presents a more heterogeneous distribution of intelligence than that of the general adult population, with the same proportion of superior and very superior individuals as in the general population.[27] In 1944, the intelligence of offenders was found to approximate the intelligence of the general population from which they were drawn.[28] The greater number of male juvenile delinquents are intelligent, at least as intelligent as the population from which they were drawn.[29] A 1950 study suggests that there is no need for further studies of intelligence and crime, since the review of a series of studies concludes that the distribution of prisoner and nonprisoner populations are almost completely superimposed.[30] There is no connection between intelligence and the seriousness of an offense and no reason to believe that recidivists will be drawn from the ranks of the least intelligent.[31] While the average intelli-

[25] Carl Murchison, *Criminal Intelligence* (Worcester, Mass.: Clark University, 1926), p. 37.

[26] William Healy and Augusta Bronner, *Delinquents and Criminals: Their Making and Unmaking* (New York: Macmillan, 1928).

[27] Andrew W. Brown and A. A. Hartman, "A Survey of the Intelligence of Illinois Prisoners," *Journal of Criminal Law and Criminology*, 28, No. 5 (January–Febraury 1938), 707–19.

[28] Herman R. Weiss and Robert Sampliner, "A Study of Adolescent Felony Offenders," *Journal of Criminal Law and Criminology*, 34, No. 6 (March–April 1944), 377–91.

[29] Lorena P. Wedeking, "A Note on the Intelligence of Delinquents at Indiana Boys School," *Journal of Consulting Psychology*, 12, No. 1 (January–February 1948), 58.

[30] Fabian L. Rouke, "Recent Contributions of Psychology to the Study of Criminogenesis," *Journal of Criminal Law and Criminology*, 41, No. 4 (November–December 1950), 446–55.

[31] B. Marcus, "Intelligence, Criminality, and the Expectation of Recidivism," *British Journal of Delinquency*, 6, No. 2 (September 1965), 147–51.

gence among delinquents is higher now than it has been reported in the past,[32] one reason for the lower past performance is that the tests used did not allow for the delinquents' handicap in verbal performance, because they have not assimilated the culture as have the nondelinquent population. Merrill compared 300 children referred to a child guidance clinic and 300 schoolchildren in a rural area in California and found that the problem or delinquent children had an average IQ of 86.7, while the schoolchildren averaged 89.3.[33] Sheldon and Eleanor Glueck compared 1,000 clinic-referred juvenile delinquents with 3,638 schoolchildren and found lower IQ scores for the delinquents.[34] Delinquents have done better on performance items of intelligence tests than on verbal items, but have balanced out to equal the general population.[35] It is difficult to find a valid comparison between offenders and nonoffenders because of the dependence of intelligence tests on the assimilation of culture, particularly verbal.[36] The "intelligence" tests are standardized on predominantly white schoolchildren.

Group testing is inadequate for children from culturally, socially, and economically deprived areas. Individual psychological examinations, nonverbal and performance testing, and subjective rating procedures are more effective.[37] Even if a culturally free intelligence test were devised, it is improbable that a true measure of intellectual potential of the delinquent population could be found.[38]

It has been found that the mentally retarded person may not experience any more frustration-induced aggression than the nonretarded, but may be deficient in controlling anger when it occurs.[39] A series of studies by Berg indicates that sex offenders may be lower than the remainder of the prison population, while car thieves may be higher than the average in intelligence.[40] It is apparent, then, that there is a tendency for some aggres-

[32] Nathan S. Kaplan, "Intellectual Functioning," in Herbert C. Quay, ed., *Juvenile Delinquency: Research and Theory* (Princeton: N.J.: Van Nostrand Reinhold, 1965), Chap. 4, pp. 100–38.

[33] Maud A. Merrill, *Problems of Child Delinquency* (Boston: Houghton Mifflin, 1947), p. 338.

[34] Sheldon Glueck and Eleanor Glueck, *Unraveling Juvenile Delinquency* (New York: The Commonwealth Fund, 1950).

[35] Leonard Blank, "The Intellectual Functioning of Delinquents," *Journal of Social Psychology,* 47 (1958), 9–14.

[36] William P. DeStephen, "Are Criminals Morons?" *Journal of Social Psychology,* 38 (1953), 187–99.

[37] Morris Krugman, "The Culturally Deprived Child in School," *NEA Journal,* 1 (April 1961), 23–24.

[38] David L. Haarer, "Gifted Delinquents," *Federal Probation* (March 1966), 43–46.

[39] David E. Silber and Thomas F. Courtless, "Measure of Fantasy Aggression Among Mentally Retarded Offenders," *American Journal of Mental Deficiency,* 72, No. 6 (1968), 918–23.

[40] Irwin A. Berg, "Mental Deterioration Among Sex Offenders," *Journal of Criminal Law and Criminology,* 34, No. 3 (September–October 1943), 184; "A Comparative Study of Car Thieves," *Journal of Criminal Law and Criminology,* 34, No. 6 (March–April 1944), 392–96.

sive crimes to be committed by persons with lower intelligence, and some other crimes, such as auto theft and forgery, to be committed by persons with higher intelligence. This intelligence differential manifests itself in the general population in occupational choices and other selective activities, including choices of entertainment. In summary, there is a selective process going on in the offender population and the general population as to what activities are attractive, and the intelligence of the offender population appears to be similar to that of the general population.

## Education

The correctional client is estimated to be about three grades retarded in school. In 1974, the average grades completed by persons over 25 years of age in the United States were 12.2 (whites completed 12.3 grades and nonwhites completed 10.3 grades), according to the U.S. Office of Education and the Bureau of the Census. At the same time, the grades completed by offenders were approximately 8, and performance on standardized tests on prisoners indicated 4.9 grades, according to the Law Enforcement Assistance Administration data. This means that half the correctional population is at the fifth-grade level or less in academic achievement, which is the limit generally accepted as functionally illiterate. Many of the correctional clients have failed in school for a variety of reasons and have dropped out. The chances for a dropout to be in the correctional caseload are significantly greater than they are for the high school graduate. In 1968, there were 5,417,000 high school graduates and 2,734,000 dropouts in the United States.[41]

The interpretation of educational data should not concentrate on education per se. Formal education is simply relatively easy to measure. The social values and other phases of culture have been missed by the correctional client also. As a matter of fact, he might be in a better position with respect to education than he is in regard to any other area, because that is an area in which he has been pressured by teachers and others to learn. Education in the correctional system has a contribution to make,[42] but it must be used as a vehicle to accomplish other objectives, such as work habits, a feeling of achievement that leads to self-respect, and the self-discipline it takes to acquire skills, as well as the skills themselves.

Poor work and study habits and lack of motivation appear to characterize the correctional client. The job-holding ability of gang members, school dropouts, and the unprepared is generally poor in relation to that of the regular work force.[43] They lack the staying power needed for participa-

[41] *Special Labor Force Report, No. 100,* U.S. Department of Labor, Bureau of Labor Statistics (Washington, D.C.: U.S. Government Printing Office, 1969).

[42] Paul A. Thomas, "Education and Its Contribution to Correctional Needs," *Journal of Correctional Education,* 19, No. 1 (1967), 4–5, 22–23.

[43] Samuel M. Burt and Herbert E. Striner, *Toward Greater Industry and Government Involvement in Manpower Development* (Kalamazoo, Mich.: W.E. Upjohn Institute, 1968).

tion in training programs, preferring a job *now* with money to spend *now*. Their expectations are often unrealistic in terms of the necessary background. Merely creating jobs will not correct their outlook. Prisoners have worked in occupations that require the least skill and have had the highest unemployment rates.[44] Labor unions can be of considerable assistance in vocational training and placement of delinquent and adult offenders.

## Development Rates

The rates at which individuals develop determine many school and social programs. As indicated in Figure 3-1, the *average* growing child develops rapidly during infancy and the preschool years, develops rather rapidly to puberty, and tends to level off in development around 15 to 17 years. Figure 3-1 assumes for purposes of demonstration that everyone represented will be the same at age 25. School programs are geared to the *average*. Girls develop faster than boys and are probably one and a half to two years ahead of them in the early teens. School tasks are considerably easier for girls in the eighth and ninth grades and more difficult for boys. The school honor rolls thus have disproportionately more girls than boys on them in junior high school. With boys beginning to close the maturation gap, the scholastic honors are more evenly distributed in the senior year of high school and the freshman year of college. Slow-developing girls and fast-developing boys have common interests through high school, but thereafter, the fast-developing boy reaches his plateau and the girl develops beyond him.

Most serious in the area of crime and delinquency are the fast-developing girls and the slow-developing boys. The fast-developing girls become interested in boys while the boys their age are still interested in cap pistols. Consequently, they go with older boys to find common interests. These girls tend to be shorter than average, and they "blossom" earlier and are likely to be involved in sexual difficulties. The slow-developing boy, on the other hand, has real difficulty in high school with academics and poor coordination, which handicaps him athletically. If he works hard and diligently, he will develop good work and study habits that remain with him as he matures, and he may eventually become outstanding in both academics and athletics, as well as in other areas. If he gives up, becomes frustrated and discouraged, he may drop out, in which case the chances of his becoming a correctional client are increased.

The implications for the field of corrections, both in diagnosing deviant behavior and in correcting it, are clear. Diagnosis and prognosis for treatment must account for developmental rates and the exigencies that come from deviation from the average. Correctional programs have to fit the individual. In many cases, the public schools that must gear their pro-

[44] Massachusetts State Labor Council, AFL-CIO, and The University of Massachusetts, *The Role of Organized Labor in the Vocational Training of Hard-Core Youth,* Office of Juvenile Delinquency and Youth Development, HEW (Washington, D.C.: U.S. Government Printing Office, 1968).

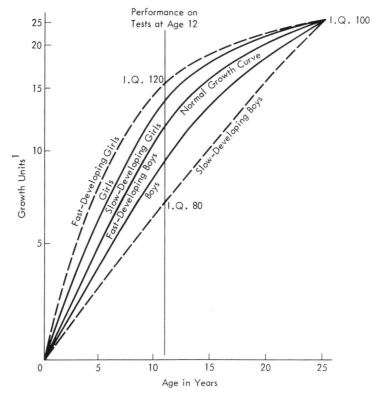

**Figure 3-1    Differential Developmental Rates.**

[1] Growth units, or Mental Growth Units, as they are called in intelligence testing, are vague concepts related to rate of growth as compared with average growth. Best demonstrated in intelligence testing, the original Binet-Simon intelligence scales and subsequent revisions, such as the Stanford-Binet, Form L and Form M, 1937, were based on the difficulty of the task being performed. A 10-year-old was expected to do the tasks generally performed by 10-year-olds. These "developmental tasks" were used to estimate the developmental growth rate of the individual as compared with other individuals the same age.

gram to the *average* have contributed to the delinquency of children. Correctional programming must account for all the developmental rates and provide individualized self-pacing programs to serve the correctional client.

## PERSONALITY PATTERNS

As one of the contributing factors to human behavior along with society and culture, *personality* refers to the characteristic responses of the individual to social stimuli, whether stress or otherwise. Reactions to stress that have been sufficiently pathological to bring individuals to the attention of psychiatrists, psychologists, and social workers have tended to pattern so clearly that the professional associations in these fields have developed manuals for the classification of the patterns.[45] The majority of correctional clients, both juvenile and adult, are normal people in terms of these clinical groupings. Deviant behavior may be called crime or be labeled as one of the clinical groupings only when it is sufficiently deviant to attract the law or the behavioral clinician.

The psychopath (sociopath, antisocial personality) is probably the largest single clinical group in the prison population, with estimates generally ranging around 20 percent. He does not relate to others, although may manipulate or "con" them. The "con artist" intellectually senses the feelings and moods of other people, but does not communicate emotionally or develop loyalty and empathy. He is described as lacking the deep emotional responses, having little or no anxiety and no guilt feelings, and being a dependent person who does not relate. He is dependent upon external control. He is most likely to be the person whose parents did not nurture the capacity to relate during infancy, and he has learned to deal with people at arm's length. Impulsive behavior is characteristic. He cannot postpone gratification. Some of these symptoms may show in all people at some time, thus hasty diagnosis is dangerous. Parsons warns:

> A person should be designated as an antisocial personality (sociopath or psychopath) only if he is grossly selfish, calloused, irresponsible, impulsive, and unable to feel guilt or learn from experience. A history of repeated legal or social offenses alone is not sufficient to justify this diagnosis. To justify the label he should also be incapable of significant loyalty to individuals, groups or social values. Certainly the diagnostician's own value judgments should not determine which individuals, groups, or social values are worthy of loyalty.[46]

The psychopath is a difficult correctional client. Unpredictable, he is likely to "con" the correctional worker out of his job. Treatment approaches must be firm, but ever-accepting, never rejecting or careless, and the worker must avoid letting provocative behavior create anger or the loss of his or her poise.

The neurotic has internalized many of his feelings, generates abundant guilt feelings, and lets his tensions manifest themselves in several types of symptoms. The obsessive-compulsive neurotic may steal cars or perform other acts compulsively, as opposed to the psychopath, who acts impulsively. Neurotically motivated delinquency has been reported more frequently in juvenile caseloads than in adult correctional caseloads, but it is present in both. Many correctional workers believe that the neurotic pattern is established early and that the client may grow out of it. The inadequate, guilt-ridden, dependent offender, juvenile or adult, may well continue to get into trouble because of internal pressures. "Normal" per-

[45] See *Diagnostic and Statistical Manual of Mental Disorders,* 2nd ed. (Washington, D.C.: American Psychiatric Association, 1968).

[46] Earl Parsons, "Recent Changes in Psychiatric Diagnoses in the Correctional Field," *Federal Probation,* 33, No. 3 (September 1969), 43.

sons experiencing this pressure and internalizing hostility bite their nails, develop ulcers, sweat in the palms, display tics, rely on alcohol, keep a full medicine cabinet, and find other types of acceptable pressure releases, but the offender acts out compulsively through an act such as stealing a car with the keys in it, and gets into trouble doing it. Treatment in this instance must be permissive and accepting so that internalized pressures aren't increased.

Psychotic offenders form perhaps the smallest clinical group in prison. Their contact with reality is so inadequate that they are unaware that social norms exist. The criminally insane group is made up mostly of psychotics, although not all fall into this category.

The defective delinquent is mentally retarded. Most institutions for defective delinquents are set up by law to accept persons with IQs of 70 or below, but in practice, the cutoff is frequently ten or fifteen points below 70. Some states, such as Pennsylvania, have established specialized institutions for the treatment of the defective delinquent, while others send him to institutions for the feebleminded (a legal classification) or to traditional state training schools.

Culture conflict has been considered to be a significant cause of crime. Such conflict can be best demonstrated in immigrant families, although it exists in varying degrees between neighborhoods, religions, families, and members within families. It has been observed that the immigrants themselves have a lower crime rate than the native whites. The children of immigrants, however, have a higher crime rate than do their counterparts among the native whites. These persons have the problem of conflicting cultures. For example, if Italian is taught in the home and old-world culture prevails there, the American school with English language and American customs can be shocking to the first-grade student who is the child of the immigrants. He spends some of his time trying to differentiate correct from erroneous values and customs and only part of his time learning subject matter. When competing with a native American student of similar capability who can spend all his energy on subject matter, the child of the immigrant is in a poor competitive position. With the same ability, the child raised in middle-class American culture can perform better than other children not so raised. This "culture conflict" appears in many areas, even among American children raised in different neighborhoods and at different socioeconomic levels.

Blacks have a higher crime rate throughout America than do whites. On the other hand, Oriental Americans, another minority, have a lower crime rate than native white Americans. The consensus is that these differences are related to cultural differences rather than racial differences. Blacks were brought to America involuntarily, without families; they were forced into developing a subculture in a white-dominated country. The Oriental, on the other hand, came to America voluntarily, bringing family and culture along. The social ties in the black culture, consequently, are not as strong as those in the Oriental culture.

The late Malcolm X, former leader of the Black Muslim group, had this to say:

> When you meet and talk with these good people, black or white, say to them that I am a Negro who signifies a new breed. I am a black man not born in the South. Although I am a product of the South's history, I did not come out of Mississippi or Alabama or Georgia. I came out of Michigan and Illinois. Say to these people—these good people—that I was one of those kids that nobody wanted to bother with. I was a nappy-headed nigger who smelled bad, who talked bad, and acted bad, who had bad grades in school. But despite all of this badness I knew that I had some ability. I told myself that, and because I could tell myself that, I reached out for some help.
>
> I reached out to the good people in every town. I lived in [hope] for some help. They said no. They couldn't see past my smell. They couldn't see past my language. They couldn't see past my raggedy clothes. They couldn't see me for looking and smelling and running.
>
> The people who helped me were the wrong people, from the point of view of the democratic society. The people who helped me, whose hands reached out to mine, whose hearts and heads touched mine, were the pimps, the prostitutes and hustlers, the thieves, and the murderers. The people who helped me through the high school of adolescence were the kids up in the reformatory. The people who helped me through the college of life were the people up in the prisons. And the people who helped me to get graduate training in the university of common sense were the people out on the streets, in the ghettos that were infested with crime and delinquency.
>
> Say this to them, because man there are a whole lot of kids on this street just like me. They smell bad, they act bad, they talk bad, and their report card says they're dumb. But you know something? These kids are smart. These kids are beautiful. These kids are great. They need to be seen and helped.[47]

Of the total prison population, 51.5 percent are white, 46.3 percent are black, and the rest are Native Americans (Indian or Eskimo) and Asian. The prison population per 100,000 of the racial representation in the total population, however, shows wider disparity, as seen in the following table:[48]

| Race or Ethnic Background | Number of Prisoners per 100,000 Population |
| --- | --- |
| White | 70.8 |
| Black | 600.0 |
| Hispanic | 182.0 |
| Native Americans | 280.0 |

[47] "Quoted by W. Ted Cobb in *Correctional Briefings,* Joint Commission on Correctional Manpower and Training (Washington, D.C.: U.S. Government Printing Office, 1969). p. 9.

[48] Adapted from "Incarceration Rates for Whites, Blacks, Hispanics, and Native

The number of Hispanics in America ranges in estimates from 12 to 20 million, and they are entering at a rate of a million a year, many illegally.[49] In 1981, there were 357,043 Hispanics in correctional facilities. They represent the following groups: (1) recent migrants and illegal aliens; (2) *jibaros,* or peon personalities from rural areas, generally committed for crimes of passion; (3) young first- or second-generation Hispanics, usually arrested for violent crimes; (4) older Hispanics who speak good English and are kingpins in drug rings or smaller rackets and burglary; and (5) mentally disturbed or retarded Hispanics arrested for fraticide, rape, or child molesting.[50]

## SOCIAL AND CULTURAL FACTORS

Social and cultural factors almost have to be considered together because the social factors (power, powerlessness, role, status, pecking order) are almost inseparable from the cultural factors (economic system, social system, laws). For example, there are "heavyweights" and "lightweights" in politics and legislatures (social), but they follow the rules of the political game (culture). If life is a game and money is a way of keeping score, then the hierarchy of social classes (power and powerlessness) is a function of society, and the means used (money) is a function of culture. Most frequently, attitudes emerge as personal responses to how the individual is faring in this "game." In the ghetto and in some other places, many people bitterly resent their position, together with all the social authority that thrusts that status upon them. On the other hand, there are approximately 40 million people in the American labor force who have police records.[51]

As was mentioned earlier, lower animals, completely devoid of culture, have been used to demonstrate experimentally the social processes and how these impinge on the behavior of individual animals. There is a "pecking order" in all groups and organizations. The responses of individuals in the system toward their statuses and roles in it are manifest in personality factors.

Neurosis can be experimentally induced in rats by using punishment in frustrating situations.[52] The neurotic rats display deviant behavior.[53] Rats develop hypertension and emotional disturbances when exposed over

---

[49] Agenor L. Castro, "The Case for the Bilingual Prison," *Corrections Today,* 44, No. 4 (August 1982), 72.

[50] *Ibid.,* p. 78.

[51] *A Study of the Number of Persons with Records of Arrest or Conviction in the Labor Force* (Washington, D.C.: U.S. Department of Labor, Office of the Assistant Secretary for Policy, Evaluation and Research, January 1979), p. 27.

[52] E. Stainbrook, "Experimentally Induced Conclusive Reactions of Laboratory Rats," *Journal of Comparative Psychology,* 39 (1946), 243–64.

[53] C.A. Hall, "A Comparative Psychologist's Approach to Problems in Abnormal Psychology," *Journal of Abnormal and Social Psychology,* 28 (1933), 1–5.

**Table 3-2**

| Sample Group | Socialization Scale[a] | Law Items[b] | Moral Judgment[a] |
|---|---|---|---|
| Ohio Penitentiary | 27.88 | 70.42 | 128.65 |
| Lebanon Reformatory | 28.63 | 67.89 | 123.95 |
| Dayton Probation | 30.82 | 58.52 | 137.47 |
| Labor Union | 35.82 | 53.61 | 148.12 |
| Mormons | 38.60 | 51.37 | 159.81 |

[a] The higher scores indicate more favorable direction.
[b] The higher scores indicate more unfavorable direction.
*Source:* Walter C. Reckless, "The Development of a Criminality Level Index," in Walter C. Reckless and Charles L. Newman, eds., *Interdisciplinary Problems of Criminology, 1964* (Columbus: Ohio State University, 1965), p. 75.

long periods of time to stress.[54] When an animal is surrounded by barriers and conflict is introduced, neurotic and deviant behavior results.[55] When transposed into cultural situations, this deviant behavior can be aggressive, withdrawn, or criminal, or may take any of a variety of forms.

It is apparent that the majority of criminals and delinquents are isolates in society who do not relate well to others. Of course, many scientists and scholars do not relate well to other people, either. Normal people and politicians do relate well to people, at least better than those who have problems. Francis Galton observed in 1833:

> There is yet a third peculiarity of the insane which is almost universal, that of gloomy segregation. Passengers nearing London by the Great West Railway must have frequently remarked on the unusual appearance of the crowd of lunatics who take their exercise in the large green enclosures in front of the Hanwell Asylum. They almost all, without exception, walk apart in moody isolation, each in his own way, buried in his own thoughts.[56]

Using scales developed at Ohio State, Reckless gave a socialization scale, attitude toward law items scale, and moral judgment scale to 335 inmates of the Ohio Penitentiary, 324 inmates of the Lebanon Reformatory, 344 cases on probation in Dayton, 195 labor union members, and 369 Mormons. The results appear in Table 3-2.

The results indicate that attitudes toward socialization, law, and

[54] E.J. Farris, E.H. Yeakel, and H.S. Medoff, "Development of Hypertension in Emotional Gray Norway Rats after Air Blasting," *American Journal of Physiology,* 144 (1945), 331–33.

[55] Norman R.F. Maier, N.M. Glaser, and J.B. Klee, "Studies of Abnormal Behavior in the Rat. III. The Development of Behavior Fixation through Frustration," *Journal of Experimental Psychology,* 26 (1940), 521–46.

[56] From James C. Coleman, *Abnormal Psychology and Modern Life,* 3rd ed. (Glenview, Ill.: Scott, Foresman & Co., 1964), p. 310.

moral judgments can be measured and can be differentiated between various groups of people exhibiting various patterns of adjustment to society. This knowledge could be used to provide initial "leads" in determining selection of cases for probation, conditional release, maximum or minimum security custody, and time of release, as well as other correctional procedures.

# RECIDIVISM

The problem of recidivism or repeaters involves probably less than half of all the persons who go to prison.[57] Of all the prisoners admitted in one year, however, 63 to 68 percent have been there before.[58] Over a ten-year period, there are probably more first-termers going through the prison system than recidivists, but the recidivists outnumber the first-termers in the prison population at any given time and in the number of admissions during a single year.

Recidivism, or repeated arrests, follows some pattern. With regard to crime committed, the percentages of persons released in 1972 and rearrested within three years were presented in Table 2-8 in Chapter 2.

It has been observed that the earlier a person gets involved with the criminal justice system, the longer he stays in it. For example, if a person has his first arrest before age 15, his chances for repeating are about 90 percent. Table 3-3 indicates the percentages a person has of coming back into the criminal justice system, by first arrest at various ages.

Recidivism as a syndrome may come primarily from two clinical patterns. First, the sociopath (or psychopath) may commit a series of offenses impulsively in an almost asocial manner. Secondly, the recidivist may be

**Table 3-3**

| Age | Percent |
|-----|---------|
| Under 20 | 72 |
| 20–24 | 69 |
| 25–29 | 67 |
| 30–39 | 63 |
| Average | 63 |
| 40–49 | 54 |
| 50 and over | 40 |

Source: Uniform Crime Reports—1968, pp. 38–39.

[57] Dan Glaser, *The Effectiveness of a Prison and Parole System,* abridged ed. (Indianapolis: Bobbs-Merrill, 1969), Chap. 1, "How Many Prisoners Come Back?" pp. 3–17.

[58] *Crime in the United States—Uniform Crime Reports—1968* (Washington, D.C.: FBI, 1969), pp. 38–39, reports 63 percent. Other years have been reported as high as 68 percent.

behaving compulsively in a pattern not unlike that shown in chronic neurosis. In either case, the recidivism cycle tends to be mutually reinforcing, resulting in repeated criminal behavior. A study of recidivism in England indicates that recidivists have a normal intelligence distribution and that low intelligence is not a contributing factor to recidivism.[59]

## CLASSIFICATION OF OFFENDERS

Delinquents have been classified into a number of different categories. In a community-treatment project between 1961 and 1967 in California, the diagnostic classification and percentages of representation shown in Table 3-4 were included.

Vold indicates that there are at least four offender groups, calling for broadly different treatment programs.[60] The deviant personality type involves intensive psychological, psychiatric, and social casework diagnosis and remedial work. The occasional, accidental offender type needs systematic training in some regular job specialty and opportunities for counseling and guidance. The ideational high-grade white-collar or political offender type, including those with intellectual or religious views contrary to the views predominant in present American society, needs a transformation of values. There is no technique known in American prisons to accomplish this. The established professional criminal type is difficult to change.

**Table 3-4**

| Delinquent Subtypes | Proportion of Population in Percentages |
|---|---|
| 1. Asocial, aggressive | 1 |
| 2. Asocial, passive | 5 |
| 3. Conformist, immature | 16 |
| 4. Conformist, cultural | 10 |
| 5. Manipulator | 14 |
| 6. Neurotic, acting out | 20 |
| 7. Neurotic, anxious | 26 |
| 8. Situational—emotional reaction | 3 |
| 9. Cultural identifier | 6 |

Source: P. B. Palmer, *Personality Characteristics and Professional Orientation of Five Groups of Community-Treatment-Project Workers: A Preliminary Report on Differences among Treaters*, Community-Treatment-Project Report Series Number One, 1967, from *The Annals: The Future of Corrections*, January 1969, p. 54.

[59] R.S. Taylor, "The Habitual Criminal," *British Journal of Criminology*, 1, No. 1 (July 1960), 21–36.

[60] George B. Vold, "Some Basic Problems in Criminological Research," *Federal Probation*, 17, No. 1 (March 1953), 37–42.

Gibbons and Garrity suggested eight types of property offenders: (1) professional thief, (2) professional "heavy," (3) nonprofessional property offender, (4) auto thief–joy rider, (5) naive check forger, (6) white-collar criminal, (7) embezzler, and (8) professional fringe violator.[61] Sex offenders are usually from broken homes and have shown poor relationship with their parents.[62]

Various studies report that 15 to 29 percent of offenders are intoxicated at the time of their crime.[63] Over one-third of police arrests in 1962 were for drunkenness, and if these are combined with disorderly conduct, drunken driving, and vagrancy offenses, they make up a clear majority of all arrests.

Glue-sniffing has been related to a youth's reaction to a situation in which he has been relegated to a passive state.[64] This is especially true in cases that involved young people from minority groups. The pressures of the environment have forced the youth to become inactive regarding his self-expression. Glue-sniffing can be seen as a socially significant problem, inasmuch as it is an indication of deeper problems.

The McGill Clinic in Forensic Psychiatry has identified the primary delinquent, an individual who is immature and unable to tolerate anxiety and depression; the secondary delinquent, a person who is generally not involved in difficulty until adolescence; and the late-comer to crime.[65] Approximately 40 percent of the late-comers could have been rehabilitated without imprisonment.

It is apparent that the role of society in the correctional process is to replace the original functions of the family and peer group. To accomplish these tasks, knowledge of human behavior in an accepting but strong environment that can apply external controls while in the treatment process is essential.

## SUMMARY

The correctional client is an acting-out person who has damaged society by his behavior. In general, he projects blame on others and "the system." Most clients do not feel or admit to feeling anxiety or guilt about their of-

[61] Don C. Gibbons and Donald L. Garrity, "Definition and Analysis of Certain Criminal Types," *Journal of Criminal Law, Criminology, and Police Science*, 53, No. 2 (March 1962), 27–35.

[62] Paul H. Gebhard and John H. Gagnon, "Male Sex Offenders Against Very Young Children," *American Journal of Psychiatry*, 121, No. 6 (1964), 576–79.

[63] Daniel Glaser and Vincent O'Leary, *The Alcoholic Offender* (Washington, D.C.: Office of Juvenile Delinquency and Youth Development, HEW, 1968).

[64] *Conference Proceedings—Inhalation of Glue Fumes and Other Substance Abuse Practices Among Adolescents* (Washington, D.C.: Office of Juvenile Delinquency and Youth Development, HEW, 1969), p. 140.

[65] McGill Clinic in Forensic Psychiatry, *Final Report, Federal Corrections*, 4, No. 2 (1965), 13–16.

fense. A missing father figure has been shown to be important in their experience. Their knowledge of authority has been aggressive, harsh, and not on their side. They need authority that is supportive and strong, but accepting. They have to view authority as accepting or liking them, personally, but not liking the criminal acts they commit and willing to invest resources into modifying their behavior.

The presence or absence of the mother is also important in the developing of normal socialization patterns. Traditionally, however, it is the father who has primarily shaped a child's attitude toward authority.[66] One study indicates that delinquency among blacks is higher when both parents are in the home than when one parent is there, suggesting that the absence of a parent is not significant in a subculture in which the one-parent family is the norm.[67]

The correctional client does not relate well to others and has not assimilated the cultural value system in a normal way. He has the same natural ability as the non-offender, but he has not assimilated academic content, has not developed good work habits, and sometimes relies on manipulation of others. Protecting himself, he projects blame on society and "the system," refers to "the caught and the uncaught," and rationalizes his behavior. Through a complex process, the offender has developed a "born to lose" outlook on life. There are numerous variations of this "typical" correctional client, but these characteristics are shared by many in correctional caseloads.

## EXERCISES AND STUDY QUESTIONS

1. *How does the correctional client differ from the other legal categories of clients who receive attention, assistance, treatment, and control through governmental agencies and institutions?*

2. *Define (1) personality, (2) society, and (3) culture; indicate how they interact to produce human behavior, including criminal behavior.*

3. *What is "pecking order," and how does it relate to the correctional client?*

4. *Describe the interaction of the mother and the father in the development of the personality from birth to the middle teens, and relate this development to delinquency.*

5. *From the standpoint of psychosexual development, why must sending a boy or girl to a unisexual institution be avoided if possible?*

[66] See Glueck and Glueck, *Unraveling Juvenile Delinquency*, pp. 88–89. Also see Thomas P. Monahan, "Family Status and the Delinquent Child," 250–58; and Ruth S. Cavan, *Juvenile Delinquency* (Philadelphia: J.B. Lippincott, 1969), pp. 116–26.

[67] Victor Eisner, "Effect of Parents in the Home on Juvenile Delinquency," *Public Health Reports*, U.S. Public Health Service, Washington, D.C., 81, No. 10 (Oct. 1966), 905–10.

6. What is the difference between the average age of arrest and the average age of institutionalization?

7. How does the racial distribution of persons arrested compare with the racial distribution of persons sent to prison?

8. How many males are arrested each year in comparison with females, and how many males are sent to institutions as compared with females? How would you explain the differences between the numbers of males and females involved?

9. How do you evaluate the biological causes of crime?

10. What is the relationship of intelligence to crime and delinquency?

11. What is the relationship between the number of high school graduates and the number of dropouts in the United States and their appearance in prison populations?

12. How should the lack of education be interpreted as far as the correctional client is concerned?

13. What significance to corrections can be found in developmental rates?

14. Describe the antisocial personality (psychopath, sociopath) in terms of his development, and explain why he appears more frequently than other clinical groups in prison populations.

15. Why do individuals from immigrant groups appear more frequently in prison populations than native-born people?

16. Why do blacks appear more frequently in prison populations than native-born whites?

17. How do neurotic patterns develop into criminal behavior?

18. Compare the attitudes of prison inmates and the general population toward law, moral judgment, and acceptance of socialization.

19. What is the amount of recidivism in the United States, and how does it relate to crime and age?

20. How can offenders be classified?

# 4

# JAILS AND MISDEMEANANTS

The jail is the oldest of existing institutions in the system of criminal justice, but its role in corrections has never been well defined. Realistically, the jail also holds juveniles and insane persons, sometimes houses homeless people overnight, and performs other functions that provide a service as a last resort where there are no other resources. Potentially the most effective of correctional institutions, the jail has been neglected in this area. In fact, many correctional administrators have difficulty in viewing the jail as a correctional institution. Simultaneously, many law enforcement administrators with responsibility for jails assign personnel there who cannot work effectively on the streets or "meet the public." The personnel assigned to jails are probably the most inadequate available. Responsibility for inspecting jails and holding them to minimum standards are assumed by many state correctional systems and the United States Bureau of Prisons.

At the 1943 meeting of the National Jail Association and American Prison Association held in New York City, the jail system was subjected to severe criticism. This criticism has persisted. A rather revealing account of the poorly defined relationship between jails and other parts of the correctional system was presented in 1965 by W.S. Brent, then Executive Secretary of the National Jail Association.[1] A revitalized National Jail Association met with the American Correctional Association in Miami

[1] The National Jail Association, Inc., *American Journal of Correction*, 27, No. 4 (July–August 1965), 43.

Beach in 1967.[2] It is apparent that it is in the jail that law enforcement fuses into corrections in the total system of criminal justice.

The literature on jails is almost nonexistent. The first significant book in the United States on jails was published in 1944.[3] Before that, Hastings H. Hart reported on jails in the Wickersham Report in 1930, saying that there were fully 3 million persons committed to jail each year, with some being committed several times.[4] (Considering the amount of vagrancy during the Great Depression, this figure was probably an accurate one.)

(All through history, the local jail has been denounced by social critics.[5] All sorts of suggestions for improvement have been made, including the avoidance of pretrial commitments, use of halfway houses and work release programs, and political suggestions concerning prisoners' voting and changing the often-used limited tenure for the sheriff who cannot succeed himself just when he is learning his job. However, the prospects for jail reform do not look hopeful. )

The jail as a place of detention is sometimes still not viewed as a correctional facility. But all the correctional clients in state and federal prisons have been processed through the jail. Estimates as to the number of jails in the United States have ranged from 15,000 to 41,000, depending upon what is termed a jail. Places of short-term and temporary confinement range from massive institutions in large open areas to small lockups in police stations. There are many city stockades that are used to house defendants awaiting trial. )

The jail serves four purposes. First, it is a place to hold accused persons while they are awaiting trial. Second, the jail holds convicted persons serving short-term sentences. Third, the jail holds convicted persons awaiting sentence or execution of the sentence. Fourth, material witnesses that have to be held are kept in the jail. In reality, the jail also serves other purposes for which it was not intended—in some cases, it holds juveniles, the mentally ill, and indigent transients. The majority of persons in jail are being held for short-term sentences, although the length of time persons can be sentenced to them varies. Many jails cannot hold persons for more than 30 days. At the other extreme, many jails can hold persons for as much as a year. In some cases, the jailed persons may be held for consecutive short-term sentences which, on occasion, can go beyond a year in total time. )

[2] R.A. Miller, "Jottings on Jails and Jailers," *American Correctional Association*, 29, No. 6 (November–December 1967), 16.

[3] Louis N. Robinson, *Jails: Care and Treatment of Misdemeanant Prisoners in the United States* (Philadelphia: Winston, 1944).

[4] *Report of the National Commission on Law Observance and Enforcement*, No. 9 (Washington, D.C.: U.S. Government Printing Office, 1951), p. 329.

[5] Hans W. Mattick and Alexander B. Aikman, "The Cloacal Region of American Corrections," *The Annals, The Future of Corrections*, 381 (January 1969), 109–18.

The jail processes more persons than any other correctional institution in the criminal justice system. Los Angeles, for example, has nearly half as many jail prisoners as the total prison population in the state of California. When the average sentence of about 30 days in jail is compared with the average sentence of nearly two and one-half years in prison, the turnover rate makes the number of persons with jail contacts far exceed those in adult correctional institutions and prisons.

## JAILS, LOCKUPS, STOCKADES, AND HOUSES OF CORRECTION

Jails are the traditional local institution used to detain accused prisoners and short-term offenders or misdemeanants. Their variation in size and design reflects the local conditions and needs they serve. The large city jails in New York, Chicago, and Los Angeles vary widely in size and level of service from those jails that serve the rural areas of Georgia, Kansas, and Nevada. Probably one of the best guides regarding design of jails is the *Handbook of Correctional Institution Design and Construction*, published by the United States Bureau of Prisons in 1949. It offers plans for one 25-inmate capacity jail, two 50-inmate capacity jails, and a 250-inmate capacity jail.[6] There is no design in this publication for the one-cell or two-cell jails frequently found in rural areas, the cage-type or "tank" jails sometimes found in smaller cities, or the large city jails, such as those in Chicago (4,150 males, 155 females), New York City (3,805 males, 415 females), or Los Angeles (8,536 males, 658 females).[7] The variation in needs and in populations served makes a "typical" or "ideal" jail difficult to depict. More recently, a complete set of standards covering all phases of the jail was published in December 1977 by the Commission on Accreditation for Corrections of the American Correctional Association.[8]

Lockups can be found in almost any police station. These are generally used for short-term interrogation of suspects, holding vagrants or suspicious persons while checking with their hometown police or other sources for clarifying information, or awaiting drunkometer, breathalyzer, or other tests for drunkenness. The number of these lockups cannot easily be determined.

Stockades are used in some parts of the country to hold untried prisoners. Others refer to confinement of misdemeanants or other minor offenders who can work on farms, roads, or other public works. Where some

---

[6] Washington, D.C.: Federal Prison Industries, 1949, pp. 168–87.

[7] These population figures were for 1974 and were derived from *The Directory of Correctional Institutions and Agencies*, American Correctional Association (Washington, D.C.: ACA, 1975).

[8] *Manual of Standards for Adult Local Detention Facilities* (Rockville, Md.: Commission on Accreditation for Corrections, American Correctional Association, December 1977), 89 pp.

An outdoor class at the New York City Correctional Institution on Rikers Island.
Courtesy of the New York City Department of Corrections.

jail populations work on maintaining public roads or other facilities, the stockade is sometimes used as a simple means of separating those who cannot be forced to work (untried) from those who can (convicted). Many counties and cities use separate wings of the jail to make this separation. Philadelphia constructed a detention center, opened in 1968, to house untried prisoners held on felony and misdemeanor charges (765 males in 1968).

The historical beginnings of houses of corrections were in England, when the workhouse was constructed at St. Bridget's Well, subsequently corrupted to Bridewell, in 1557. The majority of such institutions remain in the older colonial sections of America, particularly New York and Pennsylvania. The Westchester County Penitentiary, Albany County Penitentiary, New York City Reformatory on Rikers Island, and the New York City Correctional Institution for Men in Queens are examples in New York State. In Pennsylvania, the Allegheny County Workhouse, Allegheny County Prison, Bucks County Prison and Rehabilitation Center, Erie County Prison, and Lancaster County Prison are representative. In Michigan, the Detroit House of Correction is an outstanding example of this type of local institution. Other county institutions include county road prisons, found in many areas of the South, and separate penal farms, such as the Shelby County Penal Farm in Tennessee. There are many other county institutions that will not be mentioned here.

**Table 4-1  Local institutions and jails, by type of jurisdiction**

| Type | Number | Percent |
|------|--------|---------|
| County institutions | 2,547 | 73.3 |
| City institutions | 762 | 22.0 |
| City-county combined | 149 | 4.3 |
| Other | 15 | 0.4 |
| Total | 3,473 | 100.00 |

Source: Task Force Report: Corrections, The President's Commission on Law Enforcement and Administration of Justice (Washington, D.C.: U.S. Government Printing Office, 1967), p. 163.

The numbers of these jails, lockups, stockades, and houses of correction vary according to how they are counted. The number and types of local institutions reported by The President's Commission on Law Enforcement and Administration of Justice in 1965 are shown in Table 4-1. When including all jails, lockups, stockades, and houses of correction, the estimates have been much higher. One outstanding criminology text published in 1959 states, "There are over three thousand county jails in this country, in addition to some 10,000 city and town lock-ups. There are fewer workhouses, or 'houses of correction.'"[9]

The *1970 Jail Census*[10] reported 4,037 locally administered jails with authority to detain prisoners for 48 hours or longer, excluding the state-operated jail systems of Connecticut, Delaware, and Rhode Island. The surveyed jails held 160,863 inmates on March 15, 1970, of whom 7,800 were juveniles. About half (50.9 percent) of the adults had not been convicted and about two-thirds of the juveniles (66.1 percent) had not been adjudicated delinquent. Recreational facilities were reported by 13.6 percent of the jails, educational facilities by 10.8 percent, medical facilities by 51.0 percent, visiting facilities by 74.0 percent, and 98.6 percent of the jails reported having toilet facilities. It is noted that the jails operated by local units of government in 1972 decreased by 116, or 3 percent, under the number operated in 1970. By July 1, 1972, there were 141,588 inmates in these jails. This reduction is due to condemned jails not being reconstructed and the increased use of pretrial intervention discussed in Chapter 3. By 1978, the number of jails had been reduced to 3,493.[11]

Despite the apparent inability to get an exact count and to obtain accurate information about the operation of many of them, the local jails,

[9] Harry Elmer Barnes and Negley K. Teeters, *New Horizons in Criminology*, 3rd ed. (Englewood Cliffs, N.J.: Prentice-Hall, 1959), p. 387.

[10] *1970 National Jail Census* (Washington, D.C.: Law Enforcement Assistance Administration, February 1971), p. 19.

[11] *Census of Jails and Survey of Jail Inmates, 1978, Preliminary Report* (Washington D.C.: National Prisoner Statistics Bulletin, SD-NPS-J-6P, 1979), p. 3.

## Table 4-2 Number of jails, by state and size of jail

| State | All Jails | Jails with Fewer than 21 Inmates | Jails with 21–249 Inmates | Jails with 250 or More Inmates |
|---|---|---|---|---|
| Total | 3,921 | 2,901 | 907 | 113 |
| Alabama | 107 | 70 | 36 | 1 |
| Alaska | 7 | 6 | 1 | 0 |
| Arizona | 38 | 21 | 14 | 3 |
| Arkansas | 104 | 92 | 12 | 0 |
| California | 152 | 59 | 63 | 30 |
| Colorado | 76 | 65 | 10 | 1 |
| Connecticut[a] | — | — | — | — |
| Delaware[a] | — | — | — | — |
| District of Columbia | 6 | 0 | 2 | 4 |
| Florida | 164 | 97 | 59 | 8 |
| Georgia | 239 | 164 | 72 | 3 |
| Hawaii | 4 | 3 | 1 | 0 |
| Idaho | 59 | 51 | 8 | 0 |
| Illinois | 103 | 83 | 18 | 2 |
| Indiana | 90 | 72 | 17 | 1 |
| Iowa | 90 | 82 | 8 | 0 |
| Kansas | 123 | 110 | 13 | 0 |
| Kentucky | 137 | 117 | 19 | 1 |
| Louisiana | 98 | 63 | 33 | 2 |
| Maine | 14 | 9 | 5 | 0 |
| Maryland | 22 | 11 | 10 | 1 |
| Massachusetts | 16 | 1 | 13 | 2 |
| Michigan | 89 | 59 | 27 | 3 |
| Minnesota | 76 | 67 | 9 | 0 |
| Mississippi | 98 | 81 | 17 | 0 |
| Missouri | 141 | 126 | 12 | 3 |
| Montana | 66 | 63 | 3 | 0 |
| Nebraska | 100 | 95 | 5 | 0 |
| Nevada | 24 | 20 | 4 | 0 |
| New Hampshire | 11 | 7 | 4 | 0 |
| New Jersey | 33 | 6 | 24 | 3 |
| New Mexico | 39 | 27 | 12 | 0 |
| New York | 76 | 23 | 40 | 13 |
| North Carolina | 98 | 63 | 34 | 1 |
| North Dakota | 47 | 46 | 1 | 0 |
| Ohio | 161 | 114 | 42 | 5 |
| Oklahoma | 107 | 89 | 17 | 1 |
| Oregon | 65 | 52 | 12 | 1 |
| Pennsylvania | 77 | 41 | 31 | 5 |
| Rhode Island[a] | — | — | — | — |
| South Carolina | 97 | 59 | 38 | 0 |
| South Dakota | 57 | 55 | 2 | 0 |

continued

**Table 4-2** (*continued*)

| State | All Jails | Jails with Fewer than 21 Inmates | Jails with 21–249 Inmates | Jails with 250 or More Inmates |
|---|---|---|---|---|
| Tennessee | 115 | 82 | 30 | 3 |
| Texas | 318 | 259 | 52 | 7 |
| Utah | 33 | 30 | 2 | 1 |
| Vermont | 4 | 4 | 0 | 0 |
| Virginia | 96 | 64 | 30 | 2 |
| Washington | 76 | 56 | 16 | 4 |
| West Virginia | 59 | 45 | 14 | 0 |
| Wisconsin | 76 | 61 | 13 | 2 |
| Wyoming | 33 | 31 | 2 | 0 |

ᵃ No locally operated jails.
*Source: The Nation's Jails: A Report on the Census of Jails from the 1972 Survey of Inmates of Local Jails* (Washington, D.C.: National Criminal Justice Information and Statistics Service, LEAA, May 1975), p. 22.

lockups, stockades, and houses of correction emerge as the most important single group of institutions in the American system of criminal justice— and the most misunderstood.

## JAIL ADMINISTRATION AND OPERATION

In 1978, of 91,411 admissions to jail for alcohol and drug abuse, only about 61,346 were found to have actually abused these substances.[12] The remaining 30,065 persons were "under the influence" at the time of arrest, but later were determined not to have been "abusers." Of the 19,122 admitted for drug abuse, 3,659 had used heroin, 5,963 had used marihuana, 4,415 had used other drugs, and the rest were multiple drug users. There were 42,224 admissions for alcohol abuse, of whom 14,793 had consumed less than four ounces.

In 1978, there was an average of 158,394 persons in local jails.[13] Of these, 9,555 (6 percent) were female. There were 2,697 juveniles under 18 years of age (1.7 percent) in jails. By 1982, there were 208,000 persons daily in jail.

The typical American jail is a county institution supervised by the sheriff and his staff. In urban counties, the jail is delegated by the sheriff to a jail superintendent or warden. Most jail staff are relatively unskilled guards. On the average, the total staff numbers one to nine members, so that guards on duty are likely to be outnumbered by inmates by fifteen or

[12] *Profile of Jail Inmates: Sociodemographic Findings from the 1978 Survey of Inmates of Local Jails* (Washington, D.C.: Bureau of Justice Statistics, 1980), p. 23.

[13] *Ibid.*, p. 42.

Table 4-3  Number of jails, by type of drunk tank amenity and size of jail

| Type of Amenity | All Jails | Jails with Fewer than 21 Inmates | Jails with 21–249 Inmates | Jails with 250 or More Inmates |
|---|---|---|---|---|
| Total | 3,921 | 2,901 | 907 | 113 |
| Jails with a drunk tank | 1,711 | 1,207 | 472 | 31 |
| Beds or mattresses | 1,027 | 767 | 248 | 12 |
| Seating space (other than beds or mattresses) | 861 | 558 | 287 | 16 |
| Operating toilet(s) | 1,466 | 1,004 | 431 | 30 |
| Operating shower(s) | 642 | 457 | 177 | 8 |
| Drinking water always available | 1,369 | 939 | 400 | 30 |
| Heat | 1,585 | 1,116 | 438 | 31 |
| Light(s) | 1,594 | 1,115 | 447 | 31 |
| Air conditioning | 438 | 294 | 127 | 17 |
| Ventilation—windows and/or fan | 1,265 | 883 | 357 | 24 |
| None of the above | 19 | 13 | 6 | 0 |
| Not available | 15 | 13 | 2 | 0 |
| Jails without a drunk tank | 2,210 | 1,693 | 435 | 82 |

Note: Detail may not add to total shown because of rounding. The aggregate number of jails with specific drunk tank amenities exceeds the total number of jails having a drunk tank because a jail may have more than one type of amenity.
Source: The Nation's Jails, p. 27.

fifty to one. This ratio means that most jails are designed so that a small number of staff can insure confinement of a large number of inmates, a condition that emphasizes confinement and inactivity. Many guards are almost indifferent about what goes on inside the cages and cells as long as it does not generate mass disturbance or lead to public scandals.[14] The newly arrived inmate must negotiate to establish a status and his *modus vivendi* in the unit's social world. In this process, he may have to use such personal resources as his persuasive powers, aggressiveness, fighting skill, money, or attractiveness as a homosexual partner.[15] The old drunk is generally not faced with so serious a problem.

There is one quite unpleasant medical problem regarding some homosexuals in jails and prisons that is not usually discussed among the general public. This writer encountered it at the State Prison of Southern Michigan at Jackson in the 1940s through the prison's physician, Dr. William Huntley. Some fully committed homosexuals engage in anal intercourse, and the anal area sometimes becomes so distended that there is no

[14] Daniel Glaser, "Some Notes on Urban Jails," in Daniel Glaser, ed., *Crime in the City* (New York: Harper & Row, 1970), p. 239.

[15] *Ibid.*, p. 240.

**Table 4-4    Number of professional employees of local jails, by type of employee and state**

| State | Medical Doctor | Nurse | Psychiatrist | Psychologist | Social Worker | Teacher Academic | Teacher Vocational |
|---|---|---|---|---|---|---|---|
| Alabama | 27 | 8 | 2 | 2 | 5 | 2 | 1 |
| Alaska | 2 | 0 | 0 | 0 | 0 | 0 | 0 |
| Arizona | 7 | 7 | 2 | 6 | 6 | 1 | 1 |
| Arkansas | 4 | 0 | 1 | 1 | 2 | 0 | 0 |
| California | 74 | 177 | 9 | 7 | 38 | 42 | 21 |
| Colorado | 6 | 4 | 4 | 2 | 5 | 0 | 0 |
| Connecticut[a] | — | — | — | — | — | — | — |
| Delaware[a] | — | — | — | — | — | — | — |
| District of Columbia | 12 | 12 | 2 | 15 | 47 | 29 | 15 |
| Florida | 33 | 32 | 4 | 6 | 12 | 23 | 10 |
| Georgia | 56 | 10 | 3 | 1 | 15 | 22 | 8 |
| Hawaii | 2 | 1 | 1 | 1 | 1 | 0 | 0 |
| Idaho | 11 | 2 | 2 | 0 | 0 | 0 | 0 |
| Illinois | 48 | 50 | 7 | 11 | 28 | 24 | 16 |
| Indiana | 18 | 1 | 0 | 0 | 2 | 0 | 0 |
| Iowa | 12 | 1 | 1 | 1 | 3 | 0 | 0 |
| Kansas | 24 | 14 | 2 | 2 | 11 | 3 | 1 |
| Kentucky | 22 | 10 | 3 | 3 | 11 | 0 | 0 |
| Louisiana | 22 | 1 | 0 | 3 | 0 | 1 | 5 |
| Maine | 5 | 0 | 1 | 1 | 1 | 0 | 0 |
| Maryland | 12 | 18 | 1 | 0 | 1 | 5 | 2 |
| Massachusetts | 13 | 7 | 3 | 1 | 10 | 24 | 8 |
| Michigan | 18 | 8 | 3 | 6 | 24 | 12 | 11 |
| Minnesota | 11 | 4 | 2 | 1 | 10 | 3 | 0 |
| Mississippi | 7 | 1 | 0 | 0 | 2 | 0 | 17 |
| Missouri | 15 | 10 | 4 | 7 | 41 | 3 | 2 |
| Montana | 6 | 1 | 1 | 0 | 7 | 1 | 0 |
| Nebraska | 12 | 4 | 1 | 0 | 3 | 0 | 0 |
| Nevada | 6 | 15 | 0 | 0 | 0 | 0 | 0 |
| New Hampshire | 6 | 14 | 0 | 1 | 5 | 3 | 2 |
| New Jersey | 40 | 25 | 20 | 3 | 14 | 11 | 17 |
| New Mexico | 7 | 4 | 2 | 0 | 0 | 0 | 0 |
| New York | 178 | 145 | 45 | 27 | 43 | 50 | 10 |
| North Carolina | 18 | 1 | 1 | 0 | 2 | 0 | 0 |
| North Dakota | 7 | 1 | 0 | 0 | 3 | 0 | 0 |
| Ohio | 35 | 18 | 4 | 5 | 19 | 3 | 13 |
| Oklahoma | 25 | 11 | 6 | 0 | 0 | 1 | 2 |
| Oregon | 7 | 3 | 1 | 3 | 1 | 1 | 0 |
| Pennsylvania | 59 | 18 | 8 | 9 | 43 | 73 | 13 |
| Rhode Island[a] | — | — | — | — | — | — | — |
| South Carolina | 28 | 40 | 0 | 0 | 0 | 0 | 5 |
| South Dakota | 6 | 3 | 0 | 0 | 0 | 0 | 0 |
| Tennessee | 18 | 10 | 1 | 2 | 6 | 9 | 6 |

*continued*

**Table 4-4** (*continued*)

| State | Medical Doctor | Nurse | Psychiatrist | Psychologist | Social Worker | Teacher Academic | Teacher Vocational |
|-------|------|------|------|------|------|------|------|
| Texas | 55 | 31 | 6 | 1 | 23 | 11 | 5 |
| Utah | 6 | 6 | 2 | 1 | 3 | 0 | 0 |
| Vermont | 1 | 1 | 0 | 0 | 0 | 0 | 0 |
| Virginia | 44 | 3 | 5 | 2 | 1 | 1 | 1 |
| Washington | 12 | 5 | 2 | 2 | 12 | 3 | 2 |
| West Virginia | 6 | 0 | 2 | 1 | 3 | 0 | 0 |
| Wisconsin | 12 | 7 | 2 | 1 | 21 | 4 | 14 |
| Wyoming | 4 | 0 | 0 | 0 | 1 | 0 | 0 |

[a] No locally operated jails.
*Source: The Nation's Jails,* p. 38.

sphincter function.[16] Physicians in private practice who work with homosexuals have also reported this condition and have indicated that it must have begun early with child abuse, or even in infancy, to have developed to this state. A story appeared in a popular Sunday newspaper-magazine in 1982 about the 150,000 runaway children who disappear in America annually. The story stated that some pimps pick up these boys and girls for prostitution, and that a major cause of death among "runaway boys engaged in prostitution is rectal hemorrhage."[17] These unfortunate boys had not had the "advantage" of early childhood and/or infancy abuse! Physicians have indicated that excreta containment without sphincter function must be simply by pressure of the buttocks. A sanitary napkin might also be helpful. It is unfortunate that not enough effort has been exerted to find an adequate means or correction of this serious problem that is so widespread, yet so seldom discussed.

The population of all other penal institutions and many mental institutions have gone through the jail. The vast diversity of the offenses and mental conditions of the jail clients and the sparse resources available make the jailer's job most difficult.[18] Most jailers consider security to be of pri-

[16] Dr. Huntley had found an inmate who had inserted an electric light bulb into the anal area on a bet, and his report said, "To my surprise, it was a 150-watt light bulb." A former student, David A. Gantt of the Leon County Jail in Tallahassee, has told of an experience in another institution in 1981 when medical technicians showed him a similar case in the infirmary where a small bottle of nail polish could have been inserted into the anal orifice sufficiently distended at rest without touching the sphincter.

[17] Dotson Rader, "Who Will Help The Children?" *Parade,* Sunday, September 5, 1982, p. 5.

[18] *Let's Look at the Jailer's Job, Correspondence Course for Jailers,* Vol. 1 (Washington, D.C.: U.S. Bureau of Prisons, 1967).

**Table 4-5** Number of jail inmates and jail employees, by state—1972

| State | Number of Inmates | Inmates per 100,000 Population | Number of Employees | | | Ratio of Inmates to Employees | |
|---|---|---|---|---|---|---|---|
| | | | Total | Full-time | Part-time | Total Employees | Full-time Employees |
| Total | 141,588 | 68.0 | 44,298 | 39,627 | 4,671 | 3.2 | 3.6 |
| Alabama | 2,972 | 84.4 | 770 | 676 | 93 | 3.9 | 4.4 |
| Alaska | 87 | 26.8 | 53 | 42 | 11 | 1.6 | 2.1 |
| Arizona | 1,754 | 89.4 | 351 | 300 | 51 | 5.0 | 5.9 |
| Arkansas | 941 | 46.9 | 407 | 326 | 81 | 2.3 | 2.9 |
| California | 25,348 | 124.2 | 4,815 | 4,505 | 310 | 5.3 | 5.6 |
| Colorado | 1,427 | 60.4 | 532 | 479 | 52 | 2.7 | 3.0 |
| Connecticut[a] | — | — | — | — | — | — | — |
| Delaware[a] | — | — | — | — | — | — | — |
| District of Columbia | 4,215 | 560.5 | 1,131 | 1,122 | 9 | 3.7 | 3.8 |
| Florida | 8,104 | 110.3 | 2,202 | 2,028 | 174 | 3.7 | 4.0 |
| Georgia | 6,243 | 131.9 | 1,643 | 1,446 | 198 | 3.8 | 4.3 |
| Hawaii | 124 | 15.2 | 88 | 73 | 15 | 1.4 | 1.7 |
| Idaho | 411 | 54.4 | 271 | 202 | 69 | 1.5 | 2.0 |
| Illinois | 4,894 | 43.5 | 1,772 | 1,598 | 174 | 2.8 | 3.1 |
| Indiana | 2,017 | 38.2 | 647 | 599 | 48 | 3.1 | 3.4 |
| Iowa | 537 | 18.6 | 416 | 334 | 82 | 1.3 | 1.6 |
| Kansas | 870 | 38.4 | 587 | 454 | 133 | 1.5 | 1.9 |
| Kentucky | 1,896 | 57.4 | 589 | 488 | 101 | 3.2 | 3.9 |
| Louisiana | 3,340 | 89.4 | 839 | 778 | 61 | 4.0 | 4.3 |
| Maine | 247 | 24.1 | 110 | 92 | 18 | 2.2 | 2.7 |
| Maryland | 2,218 | 54.8 | 714 | 667 | 47 | 3.1 | 3.3 |
| Massachusetts | 1,847 | 31.9 | 977 | 926 | 50 | 1.9 | 2.0 |
| Michigan | 4,148 | 46.0 | 1,296 | 1,159 | 137 | 3.2 | 3.6 |
| Minnesota | 1,071 | 27.6 | 586 | 489 | 96 | 1.8 | 2.2 |
| Mississippi | 1,498 | 66.4 | 504 | 448 | 56 | 3.0 | 3.3 |
| Missouri | 2,246 | 47.3 | 1,092 | 1,010 | 82 | 2.1 | 2.2 |
| Montana | 281 | 39.2 | 231 | 191 | 40 | 1.2 | 1.5 |
| Nebraska | 742 | 48.6 | 443 | 351 | 92 | 1.7 | 2.1 |
| Nevada | 656 | 123.1 | 272 | 223 | 49 | 2.4 | 2.9 |
| New Hampshire | 283 | 36.6 | 160 | 126 | 34 | 1.8 | 2.3 |
| New Jersey | 3,517 | 47.9 | 2,043 | 1,914 | 129 | 1.7 | 1.8 |
| New Mexico | 899 | 83.6 | 279 | 255 | 24 | 3.2 | 3.5 |
| New York | 15,190 | 82.7 | 5,468 | 5,092 | 376 | 2.8 | 3.0 |
| North Carolina | 2,455 | 47.0 | 667 | 603 | 63 | 3.7 | 4.1 |
| North Dakota | 125 | 19.7 | 213 | 189 | 24 | 0.6 | 0.7 |
| Ohio | 4,804 | 44.8 | 1,898 | 1,592 | 306 | 2.5 | 3.0 |
| Oklahoma | 1,808 | 68.7 | 625 | 547 | 78 | 2.9 | 3.3 |
| Oregon | 1,185 | 54.2 | 486 | 398 | 88 | 2.4 | 3.0 |
| Pennsylvania | 6,274 | 52.7 | 2,169 | 1,932 | 236 | 2.9 | 3.2 |
| Rhode Island[a] | — | — | — | — | — | — | — |

continued

**Table 4-5** (*continued*)

| State | Number of Inmates | Inmates per 100,000 Population | Number of Employees | | | Ratio of Inmates to Employees | |
|---|---|---|---|---|---|---|---|
| | | | Total | Full-time | Part-time | Total Employees | Full-time Employees |
| South Carolina | 2,424 | 90.2 | 706 | 608 | 97 | 3.4 | 4.0 |
| South Dakota | 295 | 43.4 | 206 | 168 | 38 | 1.4 | 1.8 |
| Tennessee | 3,372 | 82.8 | 787 | 720 | 67 | 4.3 | 4.7 |
| Texas | 9,802 | 84.5 | 2,112 | 1,807 | 305 | 4.6 | 5.4 |
| Utah | 475 | 42.1 | 178 | 134 | 44 | 2.7 | 3.5 |
| Vermont | 4 | 0.9 | 21 | 5 | 16 | 0.2 | 0.8 |
| Virginia | 3,119 | 65.5 | 949 | 872 | 77 | 3.3 | 3.6 |
| Washington | 2,410 | 70.5 | 834 | 736 | 98 | 2.9 | 3.3 |
| West Virginia | 1,054 | 58.7 | 271 | 239 | 32 | 3.9 | 4.4 |
| Wisconsin | 1,767 | 39.0 | 697 | 532 | 165 | 2.5 | 3.3 |
| Wyoming | 192 | 55.5 | 193 | 150 | 43 | 1.0 | 1.3 |

Note: Detail may not add to total shown because of rounding. Ratio of inmates to population based on Bureau of the Census population estimates as of July 1, 1972.

[a] No locally operated jails.

*Source: The Nation's Jails, pp. 23–24.*

mary importance, and frequently they have little time or provision for anything else.

One of the best recent surveys of jails was made in Illinois.[19] Wide discrepancies were found within the state as to what or even whether records were kept in the jails. Two-thirds of the jails fingerprinted everyone. Some kept the prints within the jail, rather than sending them to the FBI for recording and reporting. The total jail population was 88.7 percent adult males, 5.2 percent adult females, and 6.1 percent juveniles. "Barn boss" and "kangaroo court" systems existed in many places because there were not enough civilian personnel to maintain control. The sheriffs recognized that their food allotments were insufficient. A quotation from the interview sheet of one interviewer on the survey team described the jail as follows:

> The jail is old, dirty, and poorly run. The inmates are surly and show no respect or even fear of jail personnel. Supervision of inmate activity is of the most minimal kind as is the staffing of the jail. Inmates were dirty and smelly as were their cells. I was not shown several sections of the jail which may have been worse. Inmate abuse of other inmates probably runs pretty much unchecked since at no time during the tour did I encounter any guards supervising or checking an area.[20]

[19] Hans W. Mattick and Ronald P. Sweet, *Illinois Jails: Challenge and Opportunity for the 1970's*, Center for Studies in Criminal Justice (Chicago: University of Chicago Press, 1969).

[20] *Ibid.*, p. 136.

One jail administrator said, "This ain't no hotel we're runnin'!" Another sheriff's response to "What would you like to see changed about the jail or its operation?" was "Everything torn down, start from scratch, the jail is a disgrace and unsanitary . . . it's condemned."

The modern sheriff and jailer must be aware of the basic legal duties and obligations they owe to the public and the prisoners.[21] Serious questions concerning the reliability of the sheriffs and jailers can arise from the custodial care of prisoners. The jail itself must be kept safe and fit for human habitation. Failure in this regard can result in charges of negligence. Fire protection, food, medical care, and other services generally known in public institutions and hospitals must be provided. If the inmates work, the sheriff has the same responsibility and duty as a private employer with respect to injury and harm by accident and to working men beyond their capacity. Injuries due to physical beatings by fellow prisoners are sources of trouble. When prisoners establish a "kangaroo court" or other similar systems to maintain their own order, the sheriff is liable for any injuries inflicted by the group. The sheriff or jailer is not an insurer of the safety of prisoners, but is accountable to prisoners and the general public for injuries that come about through intentional or negligent acts. The prisoner has the same constitutional rights as any other citizen.

> Inprisonment will bring further contempt for the system unless he [the prisoner] understands that he is still *human* and as such, still has enforceable rights and can successfully overcome abuse of over-zealous or over-cautious prison officials.[22]

Recruiting capable jail personnel is the beginning of good jail administration. Jail employees must be persons of good character and reputation in order to forestall many incipient jail problems.[23] Training of these good personnel is then necessary. Selective recruiting followed by a continuing in-service training program can result in an effective jail program, but the training must be supervised and considered by the administrator to be the most important part of the jail program. The training can be part of the administrator's job, or the administrator can recruit help from nearby high schools, vocational schools, junior colleges, and universities. In the 1970s, this kind of assistance was available throughout America.

Receiving prisoners is another important aspect of jail administration.[24] The attitude of the jailers and jail personnel during the receiving process sets the tone for the prisoner's attitude toward jail. Most jails have

---

[21] *Manual of Jail Administration*, The National Sheriff's Association (Washington, D.C.: NSA, 1970), p. 41.

[22] Comment 15, *Buffalo Law Review* 397 (1965), 419, quoted in *Manual of Jail Administration*, p. 64.

[23] Myrl Alexander, *Jail Administration* (Springfield, Ill.: Charles C. Thomas, 1957), p. 16.

[24] *Receiving Prisoners, Correspondence Course for Jailers*, Vol. 3 (Washington, D.C.: U.S. Bureau of Prisons, 1966), p. 8.

A new concept of detention emerged with the opening of the Metropolitan Correctional Center in San Diego. At a cost of $13 million, it is plush, carpeted, and has all the trappings of a nice hotel. Twenty-two stories high with narrow, four-inch windows, it was designed primarily for persons awaiting trial. It houses 500 offenders, 192 of whom are in open dormitories, the rest in private rooms. It can also be used for persons serving short sentences of six months or less.
Courtesy of the United States Bureau of Prisons.

an outside enclosure through which the police or sheriff's car transporting the prisoner is received. After the automobile is inside and the gate secured, the prisoner is transferred to the receiving area of the jail. The commitment papers must be checked carefully, since some legal problems can arise when a person is deprived of liberty without an adequate and completely legal commitment from a court.

Most jail personnel strip the prisoner, search newly admitted prisoners, carefully record all the valuables, place them in an envelope, and give the prisoner jail clothes. Some of the smaller jails do not have jail clothes, and the prisoner remains in his own clothes. Basic information is taken, such as his name, address, description, occupation, offense, date of com-

An inmate with the chief counselor in the Orange County Jail. The chief counselor coordinates all jail programs, which include the library program, high school General Education Development, drug rehabilitation, alcoholic rehabilitation, etc.
Courtesy of the Orange County Sheriff's Department, Orlando, Florida.

mitment and the authority for it, name and title of the officer making the commitment, name, address, and telephone number of person to be notified in case of emergency, name and address of the prisoner's attorney, names and addresses of relatives, minister, and other persons who may visit him, and as much of the inmate's personal history as the jail program can effectively use.

Proper handling of cash and property is important. All prisoners are photographed and fingerprinted in most jails. Complete fingerprints should be taken and sent to the FBI offices in Washington for checking and filing. The FBI, in turn, returns a "rap sheet,"which is a history of each inmate's criminal record based on the times he has been fingerprinted. Some jails use only a thumb print for their own use in release procedures.

The prisoner should then be given a shower and checked regarding items such as hair, dentures, artificial limbs, and braces. Body lice and vermin should be eliminated before placing him in the cells, tank, or other quarters. While it is important that all prisoners receive a medical examination at the time of admission or as soon as possible afterward, this is sometimes overlooked. Persons have died in jails for lack of medical attention. Some persons who have been arrested for drunkenness were later found to have had a fractured skull, diabetes, or other illness which actually caused their physical behavior, while the alcohol on their breath caused the arresting officer to interpret the behavior as drunkenness. Frequently, the behavior results from a combination of factors.

Supervision of prisoners is the jailer's special responsibility. A good quality of supervision can make any jail good, almost regardless of the physical plant. Conversely, poor supervision can make the best physical plant a bad jail.

Security is primarily dependent upon personnel. The good physical plant simply gives adequate time to personnel to be alerted and go into action. Weapons and keys should never be carried into the jail by any personnel, because the possibility of being overpowered by prisoners is real. It is important that shakedowns (searches of cells) be done in a manner that does not generate resentment on the part of the prisoners.[25] Institutions with good morale generally have fewer escapes and escape attempts than do institutions with poor morale. Morale can be controlled by the manner in which the jail is administered.

Escape attempts take many forms.[26] In one case, a telephone call from a probation officer requested the release of a prisoner, but a return call to the probation officer indicated that the officer had not called. The prisoner himself was discovered telephoning from the jail's pay telephone!

Control of inmates involves the day-to-day operation of the jail. Supervision of the cells, dormitory, or "tank" is always a problem because the interaction among prisoners is not always peaceful or healthy. Yet the low ratio of staff to prisoners in many jails results in inmate control by default. In such situations, a "kangaroo court" often takes place, with inmates being judged and punished by other inmates. Fights within the cellblock or dormitory, homosexual behavior, and similar interactions are more difficult to control. Riots and disturbances can be controlled in several ways. Some jail administrators uphold the use of gas and water hoses. Most progressive jail administrators hold to less harsh approaches, risking the accusation that they are "coddling" prisoners. Discipline is group order, not the technique by which it is achieved. Discipline can be achieved by good programs and by good relationships with clients. A jailer is indeed his brother's keeper.

It is dangerous to permit prisoners to supervise other prisoners.[27] In some small jails, however, the use of trusties to serve as work foreman is more frequent than good jail practice can support. In some jails, too, ruthless and aggressive prisoners extort money and other things from weaker prisoners. Much homosexual behavior begins in this manner. Insufficient

---

[25] *Jail Security, Correspondence Course for Jailers*, Vol. 2 (Washington, D.C.: U.S. Bureau of Prisons, 1967), p. 19.

[26] R.A. Miller, "Jottings on Jails and Jailers," *American Journal of Corrections*, 27, No. 5 (September–October 1965), 34.

[27] *Supervision of Prisoners, Correspondence Course for Jailers*, Vol. 4 (Washington, D.C.: U.S. Bureau of Prisons, 1966), p. 17.

supervision is behind many of the undesirable practices and conditions that occur in jails.

Visits must be controlled and a record made of who visits and when. Care must be taken not to delay visits from attorneys, since this could be interpreted as a denial of access to counsel and, therefore, serve as a basis for a civil rights suit. Mail should be controlled to ensure legitimate contacts and to reduce planning for escapes or other illegal activity. Packages have to be inspected to prevent the introduction of drugs, alcohol, hacksaw blades, and other contraband items. Medicines have to be controlled—issued by the doctor and taken in his presence. Inmates have "gummed" tablets, collected them, melted them down, and injected them intravenously after collecting a supply large enough for effect.

Raisin jack or pruno is made frequently in jails. Spud juice is made from potatoes or potato peelings. Canebuck is made in the South from sugar cane. All are alcoholic concoctions made with the assistance of yeast, raisins (or carrots), sugar, and the basic ingredient (raisins or prunes, potatoes, or sugar cane).

Inmates who work in the kitchen have copied keys left lying around by careless employees and have paid visits to the women's section of the jail. The handle of an aluminum cup has been used for a duplicate key that was fashioned with a fingernail file.

In situations of isolation and deprivation, bad influence and exploitation by "big shots" in the institution can occur. Situations where inmates try to improve their standard of life may result in bargaining, trading, and seeking favors from inmates who can help them. This procedure was well explained in a recent study of the Philadelphia House of Correction.[28]

Every jail should have a set of simple and reasonable rules for inmates. Prisoners cannot be controlled by rules and regulations, but the rules and regulations can be used as tools by sensitive and intelligent staff to achieve control and modification of behavior.

The food service program is of fundamental importance in the maintenance of good morale.[29] The history of jail feeding has been varied. Many jails have provided two meals a day as common custom. Since jailing is a temporary arrangement, menus have often been kept within the jail budget at the sacrifice of the prisoners. Some large-city jails have reports indicating that it costs about $5 to $8 a week for an inmate to supplement his diet (by sending officers or trusties out for hamburgers). On the other hand, in many rural jails the cooking is done by the sheriff's wife, and food is plentiful and wholesome, if simple and basic. Some jails that operate on a fee system—and they are declining in number—make money from the per diem allowed to feed prisoners. Most modern jails now provide three meals

---

[28] Menachem Amir, "Sociological Study of the House of Corrections," *American Journal of Correction*, 28, No. 2 (March–April 1966), 20–24.

[29] *Manual of Correctional Standards,* 3rd ed., American Correctional Association (Washington, D.C.: ACA, 1966, 4th printing 1969), p. 444.

a day, although the quantity and quality may vary a lot. Purchasing of food is important to the budget in terms of original cost and preparation time, as well as the amount of waste because it is not appealing.[30] One of the best jail diets in the nation is presented in Table 4-6. It should be regarded as an "ideal," far above the average.

Medical services are essential in a jail. It has been stated that "certainly no jail administrator has the right to impose the death sentence on a prisoner in his custody."[31] The jail can be a health hazard and can even endanger the surrounding community. Around 1750, for example, an epidemic of typhus fever, which was known as "jail fever" at that time, spread from the Old Bailey Prison in London to the adjoining courtrooms, with the result that an alderman, two judges, and several counsels died. A doctor should be available at all times. Physical examination should be made upon admission, including X-rays. Infectious diseases are not uncommon in the group of people most frequently brought into a jail, and treatment is far too rare out in the community. While society has these people in custody, it has an opportunity to provide diagnosis and as much medical treatment as possible. Dental care should be offered in the jail, also. It is probably the only place many of the jail clients ever receive any dental help. Eyeglasses should be provided. Unfortunately, although most jails have a physician available, few have a dentist or an eye specialist available.

Psychiatric service is more important in the jail than in most other places. Psychological counseling, social work, and other services are available in only a few jails, and these are generally in the larger cities. Sometimes these professional services are available on a contract or volunteer basis from community resources.

General cleanliness and sanitation need special attention in the jail, because the clientele it serves comes largely from poorer sections of the city, where rats and vermin are less well controlled than in some other areas. Good lighting, inordinate use of soap and detergents, and the maintenance of sanitary conditions are all highly important.

Providing special areas for unusually dangerous or contagious prisoners is helpful. Padded cells or cells in which psychiatric patients cannot hurt themselves should be available. The "drunk tank," of course, provides a place where the extreme inebriates can sober up. The area can be "hosed down" after the inmates have been transferred to regular cells.

It is important that a jail be well-ventilated and livable.[32] Bed linens should be changed on a regular basis. It is recommended that the temperature be maintained at 68 to 72 degrees in the daytime and not below 60 degrees at night. Drinking water and sewage from the housing units need to be handled in a sanitary manner. In states where jail inspectors are used,

[30] *Feeding Jail Prisoners, Correspondence Course for Jailers,* Vol. 5, p. 14.

[31] *Medical and Health Services, Correspondence Course for Jailers,* Vol. 7, p. 12.

[32] *Sanitation, Housekeeping and Safety, Correspondence Course for Jailers,* Vol. 6, p. 12.

**Table 4-6   One of the more adequate jail diets: Hillsborough County Jail,
Menus for the week of March 1, 1976**

|  | Breakfast | Dinner | Supper |
|---|---|---|---|
| **MONDAY** | Hot Griddle Cakes<br>Baked Sausage Links<br>Maple Syrup<br>Butter<br>Fresh Fruit<br>Hot Coffee | Barbecued Beef<br>  Chunks on Toast<br>French Fried<br>  Potatoes<br>Seasoned Greens<br>Bread<br>Beverage | Cold Platter of:<br>  Sliced Bologna,<br>  Salami and<br>  Headcheese<br>Cold Potato Salad<br>Baked Beans<br>Tossed Salad with<br>  Dressing<br>Bread<br>Beverage |
| **TUESDAY** | Fried Eggs<br>Hot Buttered Grits<br>Hot Buttered Toast<br>Jelly<br>Hot Coffee | Hot Pork Sandwich<br>  Pork Gravy<br>Baked Sweet Potato<br>Seasoned Squash<br>  with Tomatoes<br>Seasoned Blackeyed<br>  Peas<br>Bread<br>Beverage | Spanish Bean Soup<br>Saltine Crackers<br>Beef a Roni<br>Mexicorn<br>Cole Slaw<br>Bread<br>Beverage |
| **WEDNESDAY** | Plain Omelet with<br>  Spanish Sauce<br>Hash-Browned<br>  Potatoes<br>Hot Buttered Toast<br>Hot Coffee | Baked Stuffed Green<br>  Peppers in Tomato<br>  Sauce<br>O'Brien Potatoes<br>Seasoned Mixed<br>  Vegetables<br>Spiced Beets<br>Bread<br>Beverage | Chicken a la King on<br>  Hot Biscuit<br>Mashed Potatoes<br>Buttered Peas<br>Buttered Cabbage<br>Bread<br>Beverage |
| **THURSDAY** | French Toast<br>Hot Farina with Milk<br>  and Sugar<br>Maple Syrup<br>Butter<br>Fresh Fruit<br>Hot Coffee | Salisbury Steak in<br>  Creole Sauce<br>Parsleyed Potatoes<br>Seasoned Green<br>  Lima Beans<br>Seasoned Greens<br>Bread<br>Beverage | Vegetable Soup with<br>  Croutons<br>Tuna Salad<br>Cold Macaroni Salad<br>Tossed Salad with<br>  Dressing<br>Fresh Fruit<br>Bread<br>Beverage |
| **FRIDAY** | Creamed Ham on<br>  Toast<br>Hash-Browned<br>  Potatoes<br>Hot Buttered Toast<br>Jelly<br>Hot Coffee | Hungarian Goulash<br>  on Buttered<br>  Noodles<br>Savory Green Beans<br>Rutabagas<br>Cole Slaw<br>Bread<br>Beverage | Breaded Veal Patty<br>Brown Gravy<br>Mashed Potatoes<br>Cream Style Corn<br>Buttered Mixed<br>  Vegetables<br>Bread<br>Beverage |

continued

**Table 4-6** (continued)

| | Breakfast | Dinner | Supper |
|---|---|---|---|
| SATURDAY | Scrambled Eggs<br>Hot Buttered Grits<br>Hot Buttered Toast<br>Fresh Fruit<br>Hot Coffee | Fried Fillet of<br>  Whiting<br>Tartar Sauce<br>Creamed Potatoes<br>Buttered Peas<br>Stewed Okra and<br>  Tomatoes<br>Bread<br>Beverage | Black Beans<br>Steamed Rice<br>Baked Sausage Links<br>Chopped Onions<br>Mexican Cole Slaw<br>Bread<br>Beverage |
| SUNDAY | Hot Griddle Cakes<br>Broiled Spam Slice<br>Maple Syrup<br>Butter<br>Dry Cereal with Milk<br>  and Sugar<br>Hot Coffee | Country Fried Steak<br>  in Creamy Gravy<br>Parsleyed Potatoes<br>Buttered Corn<br>Seasoned Turnip<br>  Greens<br>Bread<br>Beverage | Beans and Franks<br>Cold Potato Salad<br>Pickled Beets<br>Tossed Salad with<br>  Dressing<br>Bread<br>Beverage |

Published in *The Tampa Tribune,* Thursday, March 11, 1976, p. 2-E.

the rating of the jail is too frequently based only or primarily on sanitation and cleanliness as an index of the total jail administration.

As a citizen, the inmate has a right to all the protections of the Constitution of the United States. He cannot be subjected to "cruel and unusual punishment" (Eighth Amendment) and he cannot be deprived of any rights "under color of law" (Civil rights section 242 of the United States Code, Title 18). He must be provided access to counsel at all times, not be held incommunicado, and be afforded the same protections that would be afforded an unconvicted citizen. Having been convicted of a misdemeanor, he loses none of the civil rights generally lost as a result of a felony conviction. He cannot be shot while attempting to escape, as can a felon. In short, he retains all his rights as a citizen but forfeits his freedom during the term of the sentence.

The constructive employment of prisoners is most difficult for the jail administrator, but it provides active occupation of time and can reduce the cost of jail management. One of the most frequent criticisms of the American jail is its enforced idleness.[33] Prisoner activities are basic to a jail program.[34] The jails should have reading materials available in a jail library, an active religious program, education through classes or any number of approaches, correspondence courses, handcraft activities or arts and crafts, recreational programs, group counseling, and individual counseling and casework.

[33] Alexander, *Jail Administration*, p. 185.

[34] *Ibid.*, pp. 208–25.

Warden John Case of the Bucks County Prison and Rehabilitation Center, Doylestown, Pennsylvania, decided that he was in the salvage business, rather than the junk business.[35] Consequently, he has required that all of his staff attend in-service and other types of training. Vocational training and an elementary school have been added to the program. An intensive treatment program for alcoholism has been included.

Many different problems appear in jails, such as (1) the juvenile offender, (2) the female offender, (3) the narcotic addict, (4) the alcoholic, (5) the mentally ill, (6) the escape-minded prisoner, (7) the suicide risk, (8) the handicapped prisoner, (9) the homosexual, (10) the epileptic, and (11) the diabetic.[36] All prisoners offer different and varied problems. It is obvious that no jailer can "treat everybody alike" and still operate a successful jail. Not only must different provisions be made for these individual types of offenders, but individualized treatment is necessary for each offender. Juveniles present a special case. Every year about 100,000 children under 18 are locked up in jails. The elimination of this practice has been strongly recommended.[37]

The physical plant varies widely from jail to jail.[38] There are many excellent physical plants in large cities and many more dilapidated and antiquated physical plants in rural areas of the country. The United States Bureau of Prisons has free consultation services through its jail inspection service. The needs of the population which passes through the jail or, in other words, the needs of the community should determine the physical plant and program of the jail.

Release of inmates must be by careful and meticulous procedure to avoid error. Not infrequently, incompetent or careless personnel have released the wrong person. As a matter of public relations, every attempt is generally made in these instances to keep the error out of the news media, but it is an embarrassing problem nonetheless. A convicted armed robber, for example, walked out of the Duval County Jail in Jacksonville on July 24, 1975, using identification of another prisoner who was supposed to have been released, but who was then held for aiding the escape.[39]

The jail administrator and staff are public employees.[40] As such, these people have an obligation to make the problems and programs of the jail available to the news media. When newspaper reporters and radio and television commentators are acquainted with the jailer and his staff and with

---

[35] Miller, "Jottings on Jails and Jailers," p. 34.

[36] *Unusual Prisoners in the Jail, Correspondence Course for Jailers,* Vol. 8, p. 12.

[37] "Why Children Are in Jail—and How to Keep Them Out," Office of Juvenile Delinquency and Youth Development (Washington, D.C.: U.S. Government Printing Office, 1970).

[38] *Plant and Equipment, Correspondence Course for Jailers,* Vol. 9, p. 13.

[39] "Wrong Man Gets Out of Jail," *Jacksonville Journal,* Friday, July 25, 1975, p. 7.

[40] *The Jailer's Public Responsibility in Relationships, Correspondence Course for Jailers,* Vol. 10, p. 9.

the jail, they are better able to interpret the problems before the county commission or the city budget agency when funding is needed to meet the needs. A jail administrator who tries to keep his jail secure by not talking with newsmen will have no support when he requests funds. The public (including prisoners) is entitled to the most courteous treatment possible in their contacts with him and his employees. Misdemeanants can vote, while felons cannot vote in most states. This may now be in question, since at least one court decision (*O'Brien* v. *New Jersey*, 1974) held that persons in prison cannot be disenfranchised solely for their incarceration if they are otherwise eligible to vote. Further, a prisoner in Massachusetts ran for public office in 1975. The jail administrator, as the public servant, must remember that he serves the general public, and especially that part of the public which he has in jail.

## BAIL REFORM, ROR, AND PREVENTIVE DETENTION

In 1961, there was concern for the problem of inidigent, legally innocent but accused people in jail awaiting trial who were there for probably needlessly long times. Justice William O. Douglas, in *Bandy* v. *Chambers* (82 S.Ct.

The jail in Kotzebue, an Eskimo village near Nome, Alaska.
Courtesy of Tia Schneider Denenberg.

11, 13, 1961), said that no man should be denied release because of indigence and that persons should be released on their own recognizance where other factors indicate that they will comply. In 1961, the Vera Foundation (reorganized as the Vera Institute of Justice in 1966) began the Manhattan Bail Projects, in which persons in jail awaiting trial were interviewed and investigated for purposes of release on their own recognizance, now commonly referred to as ROR. This project is now nationwide, and many persons awaiting trial are released on their own recognizance. In the federal system, ROR was covered in the Bail Reform Act of 1966 (Public Law 89-465). It was also recommended by the National Advisory Commission on Criminal Justice Standards and Goals in 1973.[41]

Preventive detention was authorized by the District of Columbia Court Reform and Criminal Procedure Act of 1970, whereby persons considered to be dangerous could be held without bail. An evaluation of this act has indicated that it is seldom used in the practical situation and does not provide any perceptible protection to the public.[42]

## THE MISDEMEANANTS

Misdemeanants are in a legal classification defined by statute, and therefore their offenses vary from state to state. A 1962 study of twelve states revealed that 93.5 pecent of persons arraigned for other than traffic offenses were charged with misdemeanors. The range is shown in Table 4-7, with Iowa having four times as many misdemeanants as felons and New Hampshire having thirty times as many misdemeanants as felons.

The number of times persons have been confined is indicated by the reports from the New York County penitentiaries as shown in Table 4-8. These figures indicate the frequency with which misdemeanants return to the same jail system.

The majority of persons in jail are short-term offenders or misdemeanants. Alcoholics probably represent the largest number of jail clients. Many misdemeanants are "steady customers" at the jail, well-known by the jailers and personnel. In some instances, the better-known inmates even establish and maintain loyalty to the jailer. They are frequently used to help maintain the jail, sometimes handling routine administrative procedures.

The frequency with which the most common misdemeanants are held in jail can be seen from the 1968 figures reported by the FBI. This information is shown in Table 4-9.

[41] "Standard 4.6-Pretrial Release," in *Courts* (Washington, D.C.: National Advisory Commission on Criminal Justice Standards and Goals, 1973), p. 83.

[42] Nan C. Bass and William F. McDonald, *Preventive Detention in the District of Columbia: The First Ten Months* (New York and Washington, D.C.: Vera Institute of Justice and Georgetown Institute of Criminal Law and Procedure, March 1972).

**Table 4-7  Misdemeanor and felony in 12 states, 1962**

| State | Misdemeanor Defendants | | Felony Defendants | |
|---|---|---|---|---|
| | Number | Percent | Number | Percent |
| Alaska | 8,098 | 93.2 | 587 | 6.8 |
| California | 505,521 | 93.6 | 34,767 | 6.4 |
| Connecticut | 53,009 | 96.8 | 1,769 | 3.2 |
| Iowa | 26,985 | 79.1 | 7,113 | 20.9 |
| Kansas | 66,516 | 95.0 | 3,502 | 5.0 |
| Massachusetts | 126,365 | 93.7 | 8,498 | 6.3 |
| New Hampshire | 31,348 | 97.0 | 955 | 3.0 |
| New Jersey | 122,398 | 91.4 | 11,566 | 8.6 |
| New York | 412,330 | 95.8 | 18,027 | 4.2 |
| North Carolina | 122,153 | 90.4 | 13,000 | 9.6 |
| Oregon | 62,111 | 94.4 | 3,676 | 5.6 |
| Wisconsin | 27,061 | 83.5 | 5,352 | 16.5 |
| Total | 1,563,895 | 93.5 | 108,812 | 6.5 |

Source: *Task Force Report: Corrections,* The President's Report on Law Enforcement and the Administration of Justice (Washington, D.C.: U.S. Government Printing Office, 1967), p. 72, after Lee Silverstein, *In Defense of the Poor* (Chicago: American Bar Association, 1965), p. 123.

Prostitution is often the major offense among women, but drunkenness, larceny, and assault also occur with some frequency.

The persons who commit these misdemeanors are generally indigent, inadequate in terms of personality, and ineffective in dealing with their environment. Many are homeless drifters, vagrants, and skid row inhabitants. (The term "skid row" originated in Seattle in the late 1800s, when that city was a shipping point for lumber from logging operations in the Northwest. Logs were skidded into the rivers and moved downstream for sawing and processing. The loggers would come into town on Saturday night and frequently get drunk.)

The largest single group of misdemeanants are those arrested for some form of drunkenness. Arrests vary according to the policy of the police, city, and system of justice. A comparison of the arrests for drunkenness in three cities appears in Table 4-10.

Public intoxication is a crime in almost every jurisdiction in the United States. Chronic drunkenness offenders are generally excessive drinkers who may or may not be alcoholics. There are no studies that clearly differentiate an alcoholic from the others in the chronic drunkenness offender group. Many persons, of course, are confirmed alcoholics. There are over 2 million arrests for drunkenness each year in the United States, and these place a heavy load on the court system and the jail. Some persons have been arrested for drunkenness more than a hundred times and have served ten to twenty years in jail on short-time sentences. One difficulty is that few jails have treatment facilities for this difficulty.

**Table 4-8  Number of times male prisoners committed have been confined in New York County Penitentiaries, 1963**

| Times | Individuals | Percent |
|---|---|---|
| 1st time | 3,568 | 49.62 |
| 2nd time | 693 | 9.64 |
| 3rd time | 408 | 5.67 |
| 4th time | 325 | 3.27 |
| 5th time | 207 | 2.88 |
| 6th time | 180 | 2.50 |
| 7th time | 156 | 2.17 |
| 8th time | 135 | 1.88 |
| 9th time | 105 | 1.46 |
| 10 times or over | 1,504 | 20.91 |

Source: *Task Force Report: Corrections*, p. 74, after the New York State Commission on Corrections, *Thirty-Seventh Annual Report*, 1963 (Albany: State Printing Office, 1964), p. 485.

**Table 4-9  Number of misdemeanants held in jail in 1968 by offense**

| Misdemeanor | Number |
|---|---|
| Drunkenness | 834,932 |
| Disorderly conduct | 237,552 |
| Larceny[a] | 195,672 |
| Driving under the influence of alcohol | 136,889 |
| Other assaults (simple assault, assault and battery) | 109,188 |
| Liquor laws | 107,084 |
| Narcotic drug laws | 44,935 |
| Vagrancy | 43,080 |
| Vandalism | 34,850 |
| Weapons; carrying, possessing, etc. | 33,724 |
| Gambling | 26,559 |
| Offenses against the family and children (nonsupport, etc.) | 21,741 |
| Prostitution and commercialized vice | 10,403 |
| All other (minor) offenses | 312,941 |

[a] There were 195,672 larcenies or thefts reported in 1968 from these 2,734 cities, of which some would be felonies but the majority would be misdemeanors. Depending upon state law, the offense may be a misdemeanor if it is under $50, $100, $25, or whatever the state sets as the distinction between petty and grand larceny.

Source: John Edgar Hoover, *Crime in the United States, Uniform Crime Report—1968* (Washington, D.C.: U.S. Government Printing Office, 1969), p. 105. These figures are based on the reports from 2,734 cities with an estimated population of 67,574,000 in 1968, so they represent only approximately one-third of the population.

**Table 4-10  Comparison of drunkenness arrests in three cities**

| City | Population (1965) | All Arrests | Drunk Arrests | Drunk, Disorderly, and Vagrancy Arrests |
|---|---|---|---|---|
| | | | Percentages | |
| Washington, D.C. | 802,000 | 86,464 | 51.8 | 76.5 |
| St. Louis, Mo. | 699,000 | 44,701 | 5.5 | 18.9 |
| Atlanta, Ga. | 522,000 | 92,965 | 52.5 | 76.6 |

Source: *Task Force Report: Drunkenness,* The President's Commission on Law Enforcement and Administration of Justice (Washington, D.C.: U.S. Government Printing Office, 1967), p. 2.

There is evidence that jail provides some alcoholics with a stable environment, a substitute social system, and a quasi-familial setting. They are dependent upon status jobs in jail, since they return frequently.[43]

The National Center for Prevention and Control of Alcoholism of the National Institute of Mental Health awards grants for the study of alcohol in many areas, including family, criminality, suicide, psychiatric illness, and alcohol usage patterns.[44] These studies are available to jails, universities, and others, but the jail is a "natural" point of entry to the study of the problem of alcoholism.

Treatment of the alcoholic in facilities designed to meet his peculiar deep-seated problems would probably remove 50 percent of the population in American jails today.[45] Alcoholics Anonymous developed as a mutual aid fellowship in 1935 and has grown to the point where it is believed to have been responsible for more successful cases of alcohol treatment than any other agency. The organization's Twelve Steps emphasize confession, religious interpretation, self-criticism, restitution for wrongs done, and service to other alcoholics. Hundreds of Alcoholics Anonymous chapters exist in penal institutions. It is generally agreed that before an alcoholic is amenable to treatment, he must "hit bottom" and suffer a severe shock because of the destruction resulting from his drinking. Compulsory treatment is apparently ineffective. There are probably 400,000 members of A.A. (Alcoholics Anonymous) in ninety groups throughout the world. But there are probably 5 million or more active alcoholics in the United States alone.

The Chicago Alcoholic Treatment Center began in the summer of 1957 on the basis of a multi-therapeutic approach. Milieu therapy is effective with alcoholics in maximizing peer relationships rather than parent-

[43] S. Sidlofsky, "The Role of the Prison Community in the Behavior of the Chronic Drunkenness Offender," Master's thesis, University of Toronto, 1961.

[44] "Research Grant for Alcoholism Studies," *Public Health Reports,* U.S. Public Health Service, Washington, D.C., 82, No. 9 (September 1967), 812.

[45] Alexander, *Jail Administration,* p. 312.

Plainclothes policemen working with drunks.
Courtesy of the Chicago Police Department.

child relationships.[46] Physical rehabilitation, use of antabuse (disulfiram) as a deterrent to further drinking, affiliation with Alcoholics Anonymous for the patient and Al-Anon for family groups, and group therapy are all needed to treat alcoholism.[47]

In 1966, two federal court decisions, *Easter* vs. *District of Columbia* and *Driver* vs. *Hinant,* held that conviction of alcoholics on charges of public intoxication was tantamount to conviction of sick persons for displaying symptoms of a disease and was unconstitutional,[48] although a subsequent Supreme Court decision brought these decisions into question. *Powell* vs. *Texas* indicated that chronic alcoholism is not a defense to criminal prosecution for public intoxication.[49] The Criminal Justice Coordinating Council of New York City and the Vera Institute of Justice initiated the Manhattan Bowery Project. In November 1967, the fifty-bed detoxification

[46] Vincent D. Pisani, "Milieu Therapy and C.A.T.C.: Reflections on the Development of a Therapeutic Milieu for Alcoholics," *Selected Papers,* Fifteenth Annual Meeting of the North American Alcoholism Programs, 1964, pp. 171–86.

[47] Ruth Fox, "Modification of Group Psychotherapy for Alcoholics," *American Journal of Orthopsychiatry,* 35, No. 2 (1965), 285–89.

[48] The Criminal Justice Coordinating Council of New York City and Vera Institute of Justice, "In Lieu of Arrest—The Manhattan Bowery Project—Treatment for Homeless Alcoholics" (New York: Vera Institute of Justice, 1969).

[49] *Powell* vs. *Texas,* 36 U.S.L.W. 4619 (U.S. June 17, 1968).

center was opened. Seven days a week, from 9:00 A.M. to 9:00 P.M., a two-man rescue team patrols the Bowery in unmarked police cars. The men are recovered alcoholics; one is a rescue aide, while the other is a plainclothes police officer. When a derelict is found in need of assistance, the aide approaches and offers to take him to the project to "dry out," an offer accepted 67 percent of the time. By October 1969, the detoxification center had over 5,000 admissions. The combination of detoxification and after-care service has offered some hope to the homeless alcoholic.

Detoxification units have been introduced in some of the larger jails. The possibility of separate facilities for alcoholics and offenders for drunkenness has received impetus from recent court decisions.[50] The federal appellate courts have questioned whether a person can be convicted and sentenced for such behavior. Most jailers, further, would like to "get rid of" or separate offenders for drunkenness from other offenders because they constitute a different problem and one of such magnitude that separate facilities are desirable in most of the larger jurisdictions. Some states have statewide rehabilitation services for alcoholics, which could be brought into a separate detoxification unit as part of or separate from the jail. The detoxification center or a "sobering-up station" is replacing the "drunk tank" in the jails of many larger cities. Some of the centers, such as those in St. Louis, consist of thirty beds, along with associated physical facilities and supportive medical, social, and rehabilitation services. Only the "drunk on the street" who is picked up by police is eligible for admission. Medical diagnoses and treatment, counseling and evaluation (social, vocational, and employment potential), group therapy, work therapy, didactic lectures, and films are incorporated into the program. The average length of stay is generally about seven days, during which time attention is focused upon the positive personality factors. The use of after-care services, such as halfway houses and field supervision, is part of the program.

High mobility characterizes the group of alcoholics to the extent that the homeless man stereotype focuses on the migratory patterns and social isolation of this group of misdemeanants. They are unable to assume responsibility or function in a stable capacity, yet most are intelligent and amiable. In 1967 in St. Louis, the addresses of alcoholics taken by police in the detoxification unit indicated that 765 were from St. Louis City, 34 from St. Louis County, 35 from Missouri outside St. Louis, 60 from other states, and 228 with no claimed address whatsoever.[51]

The success of the St. Louis detoxification and Diagnostic Evaluation Center is indicated by the figures in Table 4-11. Probably the fact that the police have acquired a better understanding of the alcoholism problem is one of the most favorable developments from the project.

[50] *Driver* vs. *Hinant*, 356 F. 2d 761, 4th Cir. (1966).

[51] *The St. Louis Detoxification and Diagnostic Evaluation Center,* Law Enforcement Assistance Administration Project Report (Washington, D.C.: U.S. Department of Justice, 1970), 98.

**Table 4-11   Improvement of cases by detoxification center**

| Factor | Markedly Improved | Percentages Remained Same | Deteriorated |
|---|---|---|---|
| Drinking | 47 | 50 | 3 |
| Employment | 18 | 76 | 6 |
| Income | 16 | 71 | 13 |
| Health | 49 | 42 | 9 |
| Housing | 15 | 82 | 3 |

*Source: The St. Louis Detoxification and Diagnostic Evaluation Center,* Law Enforcement and Administration Project Report, U.S. Department of Justice (Washington, D.C.: U.S. Government Printing Office, 1970), p. 18.

In summary, drunkenness is the primary problem of the misdemeanant and the primary problem of the jailer at this time. The establishment of detoxification centers in downtown and skid row areas would take approximately half the workload off the jail. The jail is not now prepared to handle this problem, anyway.

In recent years, the number of skid row areas has been declining, for a variety of reasons.[52] Probably most important are changes in the policies of departments of public welfare that permit homeless people better salaries and induce them to find new homes, often with families and relatives. Second, urban renewal projects and other improvments in the city prevalent in the last decade have changed the composition of the skid row population. Continued attention to the problem of the homeless is necessary, and the logical focal point is now the jail, where many of them come from time to time.

## LEGAL PROCESSES

The jail administrator and staff must be aware of constitutional and civil rights, as well as the legal processes by which they are implemented, in order to participate constructively in the system of criminal justice. For example, no prisoner can be held incommunicado. Some jails have adopted the policy of permitting one telephone call, which meets the letter of the law but not the intent of it. No person can be denied access to counsel at any time. Technically, then, a prisoner can call his lawyer at any time or the jailer may be subject to accusations of denying access to counsel.

Just across the street from almost any jail is the bail bondsman's office. Except under unusual circumstances in a capital offense, every citizen is entitled to bail, and the Eighth Amendment states that it shall not be ex-

[52] Howard M. Bahr, "The Gradual Disappearance of Skid Row," *Social Problems*, 15 (1967), 41–45.

cessive. Technically, a person is assigned bail at the time of the preliminary hearing. Practically, however, most law enforcement personnel have blanket coverage from their judges to act immediately; the preliminary hearing will be held as soon as possible. Consequently, the prisoner may arrive and find a bail bondsman virtually awaiting his arrival. The bail bondsman sells the prisoner an insurance policy for a premium and, therefore, "goes" his bail. In fact, the offender need not be locked up at all if he can afford the bail or the premium for the bail bondsman.

As mentioned earlier, there has been experimentation with releasing prisoners on their own recognizance without money. The majority of prisoners who go into jail cannot afford even the low premium that it takes to purchase a bail bond from a bail bondsman. There are enough, of course, who can afford it so that bail bondsmen stay in business. The trend is toward release on one's own recognizance.

Many law enforcement officers, including police, FBI agents, state law enforcement officers, sheriffs, and others, frequently want to interview jail inmates to learn about their case or other cases. Consequently, jails often have an interrogation room for interviews. Several lawyers have questioned the advisability of an interrogation room, on the basis that there may be a tendency to run afoul of recent Supreme Court decisions, such as the Miranda decision on warnings and the Escobedo decision on confessions. The interrogation room in the jail might be used as a place for intimidation. Upon seeing an interrogation room in one jail, an outstanding scholar and lawyer said he would like to defend a case in which information had been obtained from that interrogation room and added that it would be helpful if the prisoner fell downstairs a couple of times on the way to the room and could show the scars.[53] The point is that the jail should not represent one side or the other in an adversary proceeding. An "interrogation room" with a one-way mirror for observation purposes would seem to create a one-sided situation. The police officer should not be forced to "make a case," but to report what he saw and why he arrested the person. It is up to the prosecution and the defense to determine guilt or innocence.

## SUMMARY

Misdemeanants constitute the largest legal classification of offenders and receive the smallest amount of society's resources for treatment. Presentence information is almost completely absent for misdemeanants, which leaves the judge practically blind as far as treatment and disposition is concerned. The court is forced to operate in almost complete ignorance in terms of rehabilitative potential. The offender is simply penalized again in a similar fashion if he appears in court again within a specified time period.

[53] Conversation with Norval Morris, Director of the Center for the Study of Law, University of Chicago, 1969, now dean of the law school at the University of Chicago.

In ten states, there are no probation services for misdemeanants in any form. On the other hand, some probation services for misdemeanants are now appearing at the city, city-county, or court district levels, particularly in the larger metropolitan areas. Twenty states support some misdemeanant probation services.

Treatment programs in jails have been generally absent or, if present, fragmented and weak. Any program must have the support of the administrator. The use of detoxification programs and assistance in withdrawal from drugs can reduce suicides (and therefore improve the record of an administrator), according to a national study.[54]

Other studies have shown that children of jail inmates display extensive maladjustments in the school setting, meaning that some program within the schools might well be helpful.[55] The families are in immediate need of social services when a member is sentenced to jail. These services should be built into the process of misdemeanant justice and not be left to chance.

The National Conference on Adversaries in the United States in 1972 recommended decriminalizing behavior that does not involve (1) the threat or use of force against person, (2) fraud, (3) wanton destruction of property, or (4) violent attacks against the government.[56] This action would cut the jail population in half. It is also thought that a closer partnership between the jail and community human services could further reduce the jail population in the long run by providing assistance in solving the problems of jail inmates.[57]

In summary, the jail is probably the most important of the correctional facilities, because it receives nearly all the persons arrested for misdemeanors and felonies, as well as children, mental patients, and material witnesses. At the same time, the jail receives the barest of resources to perform its functions. The many misdemeanants, half of them alcoholics or heavy drinkers, need clinical services and other social programs. The jail is a natural place to gather information about people, to provide diagnostic services and the beginnings of treatment. Although the jail has the greatest potential of all correctional institutions, its performance to date has been the most disappointing phase of the correctional process.

[54] Charles L. Newman and Barbara R. Price, *National Jail Resources Study: Observation on the Delivery of Services for Drug Abusing Inmates in Local Jails* (State College, Pa.: Pennsylvania State University, 1975), p. 20.

[55] Sidney Friedman and T. Conway Esselstyn, "The Adjustment of Children of Jail Inmates," *Federal Probation*, 29, No. 4 (December 1965), 55–59.

[56] *A Program for Prison Reform: The Final Report* (Cambridge, Mass.: The Roscoe Pound–American Trial Lawyers Foundation, 1972), p. 10. Sponsored by LEAA, United States Department of Justice.

[57] Charles L. Newman, Barbara R. Price, Jacqueline B. Sobel, Sheldon Adelberg, Marque Bagshaw, and Dean Phillips, *Local Jails and Drug Treatment* (University Park, Pa.: Pennsylvania State University College of Human Development, February 1976), p. 300.

# EXERCISES AND STUDY QUESTIONS

1. What is the oldest existing institution in the system of criminal justice?
2. Discuss the place of the jail as a link between law enforcement and the correctional system, pointing out some of the problems that occur.
3. What are the four functions of jails?
4. How many people are detained in jails each year in the United States?
5. How many people are in jail on any given day?
6. Differentiate between jails, lockups, stockades, and houses of correction.
7. What are the responsibilities of the modern sheriff and jailer to prisoners?
8. Why is it difficult to recruit competent jail personnel?
9. What is the process of receiving prisoners in the jail?
10. What is a "kangaroo court"?
11. What is release on one's own recognizance (ROR)?
12. Why is medical service more important in jails than in many other institutions?
13. Describe the "drunk tank" found in most jails.
14. What are the constitutional rights of jail inmates?
15. What is the general ratio between misdemeanants and felons?
16. What are the six most frequent offenses for which persons are jailed?
17. How do drunkenness and public intoxication cases relate in terms of numbers and treatment to the total misdemeanant population?
18. Discuss the court decisions that hold that drunkenness should not be a public offense.
19. What is a detoxification unit?
20. Why must the jail administrator and staff be aware of the constitutional and civil rights of their charges?

# 5

# PROBATION

Probation is a judicial function in which the convicted offender is formally placed under the supervision of court personnel, usually a probation officer or probation agent. The time the offender serves under probation supervision averages about three years, although it may be shorter or longer. General practice is for the period of probation not to exceed five years. Special conditions of probation may be imposed, such as keeping reasonable hours, keeping employed, and supporting one's family, along with rules that apply to a particular individual, such as not drinking in public. There is a wider variation among probation rules than among parole rules, since the probation rules are set by the judge in most cases, rather than by a single state agency, as in the case of parole.

There were 1,222,024 adult persons on probation on December 31, 1981.[1] This means that 67.4 percent of the total adult correctional caseload, excluding jails, are on probation. If jails were included, it would still be 62.3 percent, so probation is really about two-thirds of the total adult correctional caseload.

John Augustus, the Boston shoemaker, is credited with beginning probation on a volunteer basis in 1841 (see Chapter 1), and his assistant, the jail chaplain, took over after his death in 1859. The first law establishing probation as a public office was in Massachusetts in 1878. The first "probation officer" was considered to be Lt. Henry C. Hemminway, but

[1] *Probation in the United States: 1980 and 1981* (San Francisco: Research Center West, National Council on Crime and Delinquency, 1982), Table 1. Also reported in *Criminal Justice Newsletter*, 13, No. 17 (August 30, 1982), 6.

the first probation officer with statutory status was police Captain E.H. Savage.[2]

The SEARCH Group, Inc., is an organization of the State Judicial Information Project funded by the Law Enforcement Assistance Administration (LEAA) to collect data in the judicial system, including probation. By mid-1974, 38 states were participating, but there was no uniformity, and data on probation were simply not available.[3]

It costs ten to thirteen times more to maintain a person in an institution than it does to supervise him in the community. Further, the total social situation can better be handled in the community, including working with the family. Other social relationships can be somewhat controlled, thus avoiding the "social surgery" of completely removing the person from his social setting. It is more effective to work with social relationships than to sever them when the objective is to assist the offender to adjust to his social environment.

The probation staffs in some larger cities and counties, such as Los Angeles and New York City, are large, well educated, and professional in their approach to the problems of offenders and the function of probation. Some courts, such as the Recorder's Court in Detroit, have their own clinics with psychiatric staff on a full-time basis. The majority of courts throughout the country, however, generally function with one or two probation officers. Most probation officers make good use of community resources. They generally know the community as well as anyone else other than the police. They are acquainted with employers with whom they can negotiate jobs for probationers. In some counties, of course, there is no probation service at all. In general, probation is available to misdemeanants only rarely, and then only in the larger cities.

With 2,238 probation agents in 1970, the Los Angeles County Probation Department has been considered by many to be one of the best in the field. Computed against the population of Los Angeles county, there are 87 probation agents per 100,000 population. At the other extreme, there are several rural states that have less than one officer per 100,000 population, and they handle parole supervision, also! Consequently, it is obvious that probation varies widely throughout the country in quality and quantity of service. Missouri and Nebraska law holds that where a probation officer is not present, the sheriff will assume probation functions as needed. All states have probation of some sort and to some extent. Many states have centralized this local function at the state level in order to bring some service to those counties that cannot afford a probation agent. In these states, the pattern is to have the state parole agent also assume the functions of a probation agent, generally limited to writing presentence investigation reports as requested by local judges.

[2] David Dressler, *Practice and Theory of Probation and Parole* (New York: Columbia University Press, 1969), pp. 16–33.

[3] "State Judicial Data System Surveyed," *Criminal Justice Newsletter*, 6, No. 23 (November 23, 1975), 3–4.

The two primary functions of the probation officer are (1) the presentence investigation and (2) supervision of probationers. The second generally follows from the first. The probation officer prepares the presentence investigation after interviewing the offender and assessing his social situation. During this process, the officer determines whether he can work with the offender in the community or whether the offender should be sent to the institution. There are many duties and activities carried out by the probation officer, but the primary functions are advising the judge on sentencing through the presentence investigation report and supervising the probation caseload.

For the vast majority of offenses, incarceration is not necessary. An advantage of probation is that it deals with problems in their social context, without removal from home and institutionalization of the offending person. The goals of reintegration into society in an acceptable form are easier achieved in the community. While probation has been characteristically understaffed and poorly administered, the summary analysis of success on probation ranges between 60 and 90 percent,[4] which compares very favorably with other correctional approaches.

The presentence investigation (PSI) is performed by the probation officer to learn the family and social background of the offender and to assess his strengths and weaknesses with a view toward working out a treatment program. The presentence investigation report is presented to the judge after the offender has been convicted but before sentencing, in order to guide the judge in the disposition procedure. It should include an evaluation of the offender's family background, social relationships, occupational strengths and weaknesses, school background, criminal background, and all other factors pertinent to the problem. There are several excellent sources that discuss the presentence investigation and the report in detail.[5]

The presentence investigation report serves five functions: (1) to aid the court in determining the appropriate sentence, (2) to assist institutions in planning their classification and treatment programs, (3) to furnish the parole board with information pertinent to the offender's release on parole, (4) to aid the probation officer in rehabilitative efforts during probation supervision, and (5) to serve as a source of information for systematic research.[6]

The presentence investigation is based on information gained by interviewing the offender, interviewing some members of his family, and interviewing or corresponding with previous employers, schools, and other

[4] Ralph W. England, Jr., "What Is Responsible for Satisfactory Probation and Post-Probation Outcome?" *Journal of Criminal Law, Criminology and Police Science*, 47 (March–April 1967), 667–76.

[5] Paul W. Keve, *The Probation Officer Investigates* (Minneapolis: University of Minnesota Press, 1960), is an outstanding example.

[6] Administrative Office of the United States Courts, "The Presentence Investigation Report," in Robert M. Carter and Leslie T. Wilkens, eds., *Probation and Parole: Selected Readings* (New York: John Wiley, 1970), p. 69.

social agencies, including the courts and police, who have had contact with the offender. Because of overworked staff and inadequate time, too many presentence investigation reports are based largely on interviews with the offender, with whatever corroborating documentary evidence that might be available. Consequently, the value and validity of the presentence investigation reports vary widely from court to court and, for that matter, from probation officer to probation officer.

The format of the presentence investigation report generally starts with the usual identifying information at the top of the sheet. The offender's name, birth date, offense, date of arrest and conviction, race, sex, and similar information may be abbreviated at the top of the page, depending upon the format in that particular court. Most presentence investigation reports then go into the facts dealing with that offense, divided into (1) the offender's version, and (2) the official version. Many probation officers see this section as a measure of the offender's contact with reality, the extent of his projection, and his attitude.

A brief social history generally follows, including significant members of the family, education, employment history, and general behavior pattern in terms of work habits and leisure time pursuits. The criminal history includes contacts with juvenile court, contacts with police, and previous contacts with adult courts. Generally, the FBI "rap sheet" is available, having been returned to the police after the original fingerprinting at the time of booking in the jail. This information sheet presents the individual's arrest record developed from the FBI's central file in Washington. The file contains records of each time a person has been fingerprinted after having been arrested.

An assessment of community attitudes toward the offender is generally included. Whether the offender could be retained in the community on probation or would have to be removed from it to an institution because of community attitudes is part of the total process in a democratic society. Parenthetically, the recording of the intensity of these community attitudes might be helpful in the future for planning, when parole from prison is being considered.

The closing paragraph of the presentence investigation report is generally a rough diagnosis of the problem—whether it is based in the family or the gang, or whatever the probation officer believes are the significant factors contributing to the offense. An assessment of the strengths available within the family, within the individual, within the community, or elsewhere is of assistance in developing a treatment program. Finally, a recommendation to the judge as to disposition is desired by most judges. If the probation officer believes he can work with the case in the community on the probation caseload, he so recommends.

Before pronouncing sentence, the judge should examine the case to determine whether the sentence (1) has been arrived at by procedures that were valid, thorough, and free of prejudice; (2) is consistent with the facts known about the offender; (3) makes the most productive use of the offender's capacities; (4) embodies a realistic treatment program for the offender which can achieve its purposes; and (5) protects the public from property loss and personal injury.[7] The presentence investigation can be significant in helping the judge answer these questions.

The probation officer and the defense attorney will undoubtedly develop a closer relationship in the future.[8] The recommendations by the probation officer generally have an effect on the liberty of the client. Also, the defense attorney can instruct his client to cooperate with the probation officer. It has been suggested that when the probation officer has reached the point in his investigation where he wants to make the recommendation, it might be well for him to contact the defense attorney and work out a recommendation mutually acceptable for the good of the client and society.[9]

The presentence investigation report has historically been considered confidential, its immediate purpose being to assist the judge in giving a "rehabilitative sentence." In Canada and some other places, however, the presentence investigation report is available to defense counsel and the defendant. There is some movement in the United States in the direction of stripping the report of its confidentiality because it relates directly to "life, liberty, and property" in the sentencing process. The recommendation of the probation officer is designed to influence the future freedom of the offender-citizen.

In the final analysis, there are no objective criteria for selection for probation, so the final decision becomes simply whether the probation officer thinks he can work with the offender. Sometimes, prison sentences are recommended because the probation officer does not think he can work with the offender in the community or because previous criminal history indicates that something stronger in terms of external controls—or prison—is required. Sometimes intense community attitudes hostile to the offender will prevent an otherwise tractable individual from being placed on probation. Sometimes the probation officer's caseload is already too heavy to add another case. Even though normal casework with the offender on probation would be more desirable and release under technical probation without real supervision would be undesirable, an otherwise tractable offender may have to be sent to prison because there is no more room left on the probation officer's caseload. He simply may not have the time to work with another offender.

---

[7] Advisory Council of Judges, *Guides for Sentencing* (New York: National Council on Crime and Deliquency, 1957), p. 53.

[8] John J. McHugh, "Some Comments on Natural Conflict between Counsel and Probation Officer," *American Journal of Correction*, 35, No. 6 (November–December 1973), 34–36.

[9] Alex K. Gigeroff, J.W. Mohr, and R.E. Turner, "Sex Offenders on Probation: The Exhibitionist," *Federal Probation*, 32, No. 3 (September 1968), 18–21. Also Morton B. Allenstein, "The Attorney–Probation Officer Relationship," *Crime and Delinquency*, 14, No. 2 (April 1970), 183.

**Table 5-1**

| Item | Percentage of Times Selected |
|------|------------------------------|
| Offense | 100.0 |
| Prior record | 100.0 |
| Psychological/psychiatric | 79.7 |
| Defendant's statement | 69.6 |
| Defendant's attitude | 62.3 |
| Employment history | 60.9 |
| Age | 53.6 |
| Family history | 52.2 |
| Marital status | 42.0 |
| Medical history | 29.0 |
| Education | 21.7 |
| Military history | 17.4 |
| Alcoholic involvement | 15.9 |
| Homosexuality | 15.9 |
| Drug usage | 13.0 |
| Interests and activities | 13.0 |
| Family criminality | 11.6 |
| Plea | 7.2 |
| Confinement status | 7.2 |
| Residence data | 4.3 |
| Religion | 4.3 |
| Legal representation | 0.0 |
| Place of birth | 0.0 |
| Race | 0.0 |

Source: Robert M. Carter, "The Presentence Report and the Decision Making Process," *Journal of Crime and Delinquency*, July 1967, p. 205.

Illinois law holds that probation may be granted if the following requirements are met:

1. A new offense is not likely to be committed.
2. Public interest does not require that the defendant receive a penalty.
3. Offender rehabilitation does not require penalty imposition.[10]

In making decisions regarding recommendations of probation, the items shown in Table 5-1 were considered in their order of importance in a California study.

Relatively few items actually seem to enter into the probation officer's decision to recommend probation or imprisonment. The items listed

[10] *Illinois Revised Statutes, 1969*, Chap. 28, Article 117-1.

**Table 5-2**

| Item | Percentage of First Three Times Selected |
|---|---|
| Offense | 97.1 |
| Prior record | 68.1 |
| Defendant's statement | 31.9 |
| Family history | 26.1 |
| Psychological/psychiatric | 21.7 |
| Plea | 7.2 |
| Defendant's attitude | 2.9 |
| Alcoholic involvement | 2.9 |
| Employment history | 1.4 |
| Marital status | 1.4 |

*Source:* R. M. Carter, "The Presentence Report," p. 207.

in Table 5-2 were among the first three selected by a group of probation officers.

The presentence investigation report is of immeasurable value to the judge in making disposition. Judges follow the probation officer's recommendation about 95 percent of the time. The probation officer works for the judge and is appointed by the judge. If the judge does not have confidence in the probation officer, he will probably get himself another. On some occasions, when the judge does not follow the recommendation of the probation officer, it might be a matter of differences in perspective. For example, the probation officer may place heavier emphasis on the basic rehabilitation of the individual over community attitudes. The judge, on the other hand, is generally an elected official, so he may place heavier emphasis upon community attitudes. In most cases, however, the judge follows the recommendations of the probation officer. If something goes wrong and the community objects, he can say that he followed the recommendation of his "professional." On the other hand, if he does not follow the recommendation of the probation officer and something serious goes wrong, the newspaper editorials and political opposition can say that he did not even follow the recommendation of his probation officer in significant cases! At any rate, the presentence investigation report provides the judge with greater sophistication when making a disposition of a criminal case.

Several states have laws making the presentence investigation mandatory. The majority of states leave it to the judge's discretion. In actual practice, a wide variety of patterns occur. Most judges like the presentence investigation report because it provides them with some information they otherwise would not have, thereby permitting them to feel more confident that they have made the best judgment possible. Naturally they feel more secure in meeting the awesome task of sentencing when they have all information available at hand when making the decision that involves the life and liberty of the offender-citizen. A few judges who possess a stern legalistic philosophy want no part of the presentence investigation, because they do not want to be influenced by anything other than "the merits of the case" as it was heard in court. A few judges of this type have gone so far as to tell the probation officer that he can make a presentence investigation report, but that they do not want to see it until after the sentence has been pronounced. In many cases where states have laws making the presentence investigation mandatory, it has been observed that between one-third and two-thirds of the convicted offenders still arrive in prison without presentence investigation reports. Regardless of what the law says, when the staff is not available, the presentence investigation just cannot be done.

The presentence investigation report will subsequently be used in the prison system, by the parole board, and by the supervising parole officer. Consequently, it is important that the information it contains be accurate and complete. A good presentence investigation report can be extremely helpful for a long period of time in the correctional process. On the other hand, a sloppy report can be a persistent impediment in the correctional process. General consensus is that the presentence investigation report should be about three pages long. Busy judges will look at the first and the second page, but most do not go beyond the third page except, perhaps, to read the last paragraph. Some presentence investigation reports made by trained social workers have run into a dozen or more pages. These are helpful to treatment people, but administrative people do not read them very often. Longer reports are most helpful in mental health and other agencies where the caseloads are controlled to a smaller size, but correctional caseloads are generally too large to warrant spending much time on an individual case, however worthy the objective. If further information is desirable, it can be submitted as an addendum to the presentence investigation report. A summarization of pertinent points without any wasted words on one to three pages has proved to be most useful.

## SUPERVISION OF PROBATIONERS

Supervision of probationers includes not only casework and counseling tasks and assistance in employment and personal planning, but enforcement functions as well. It is a type of treatment-supervision.[11] The probation officer must use the resources in the community skillfully to enhance his effectiveness in working with the probationer caseload.[12] The family

[11] See Charles L. Newman, "Concepts of Treatment in Probation and Parole Supervision," *Federal Probation*, 25 (March 1961), 11–18; see also Carter and Wilkens, eds., *Probation and Parole*, pp. 279–89.

[12] Howard W. Borsuk, "The Probation Worker and the Community," in Charles L. Newman, ed., *Sourcebook on Probation, Parole and Pardons* (Springfield, Ill.: Charles C. Thomas, 1958), pp. 141–48.

agency, child care or welfare agencies, child guidance clinic, mental hygiene clinic, vocational guidance agencies, and social group work agencies are all of potential auxiliary help to the probation officer.

Supervising probationers must be done on the basis of mutual trust, cooperation, and responsibility between the probation officer and the probationer. The probation officer has to find the balance between control and treatment that his probationer can best use. This balance will shift as the probationer responds favorably and needs less and less control. There are four general principles that are usually the basis for attaining this balance:

1. Change comes from within the person; therefore, a probationer must be a participant in any treatment program designed to help him.
2. The needs, problems, capacities, and limitations of the individual offender must be considered in planning a program with him.
3. Legally binding conditions of probation are essential and in the best interests of the offender and the community.
4. The goal of supervision is to help the offender understand his own problems and enable him to deal adequately with them.[13]

Probation's most important objective is not to control the offender, but to help the probationer understand himself and gain independent control over his own behavior.

Personal counseling for the offender is particularly important in cases of alcoholism, mental illness, or other deviation. On occasion, the probationer simply needs security or the implied presence of a supporting authority figure. Employment counseling and assistance in finding jobs is a major portion of the probation officer's work. Finding jobs is a major task, especially for the correctional client who does not have good work habits.

Investigation and information gathering regarding the activities of probationers is an important task. When a probationer is beginning to break contact with employment and family, it is important to know the peer group relationships he is developing. This break may be the beginning of a deteriorating social relationship. It may mean that the probationer should be returned to jail for a short time or, in extreme cases, that his probation should be revoked.

Casework methods are essential if the probation officer is going to provide more than simple surveillance. The police department could provide surveillance but should be careful not to provide undue harrassment in the process. A probation officer is supposed to provide more in terms of casework and counseling.

The use of the family to help supervise the probationer is indispensable. An interested family provides the "social ties" that assist in providing

[13] *Manual of Correctional Standards* (Washington, D.C.: American Correctional Association, 1966), p. 107.

the controls the probationer needs. As a matter of fact, if a probation officer had the choice of either working with the family or working with the individual, he would be better off working with the family. Fortunately, he is not faced with this type of alternative and can work with both.

The implied presence of the probation officer is sometimes more important than actual supervision. This implied presence means that the probation officer could appear at any time, and thus provide restraints on deviant behavior. Conversely, the implied presence of the probation officer means that the probationer has supportive authority available to him. The implied presence of the probation officer is helpful in either direction.

The counseling skills used by the probation officer in this type of day-to-day work and the auxiliary services relating to everyday problems are more a part of the probation officer's work than casework or the therapeutic process.[14] There is a tendency to overlook the practical services rendered by the probation officer in favor of the more "professional" casework services. In essence, most probation officers have time only for crisis intervention.

As in all casework procedures, exact duplications of how one person uses himself in a supervisory situation are difficult to accomplish. Each personality differs to some degree, although there are basic principles common to all casework or therapeutic relationships. The clients differ, also. There is no way to develop a single approach to probation supervision, since all people present different patterns.[15]

Local psychologists, social workers, physicians, clergy, marriage counselors, and others can be of considerable assistance to the probation officer in his work. A resident psychiatrist in a local university hospital or other facility is of utmost assistance to probation officers.[16]

Satisfaction by probation officers with psychological services seems to be based on (1) the psychologist's adaptability for work within the probation department, (2) ease of communication between probation workers and psychologists, and (3) the psychologist's promptness in returning meaningful evaluations to the probation department.[17]

The social worker as a probation officer has had to resolve the problem of self-determination in his work with offenders.[18] Some have held that the authoritarian setting of probation, as well as other phases of corrections, is inimical to the practice of casework. Properly conceived authority

[14] Eleanore Muhlmeyer, "A Probation Officer Looks at His Job," *Federal Probation*, 30 (March 1966), 5–10.

[15] Newman, "Concepts of Treatment in Probation," pp. 11–18.

[16] Wallace W. Wilkerson, "Psychiatric Consultation with Probationers and Parolees," *Federal Probation*, 33, No. 2 (June 1969), 45–50.

[17] Edward J. Fischer and Nathan Farber, "The Psychologist in the Probation Department," *Crime and Delinquency*, 12, No. 1 (January 1966), 55.

[18] Charles C. Lee, "The Concept of Authority in the Field of Probation and Parole," *American Journal of Correction*, 28, No. 2 (March–April 1966), 26–27.

demands that the probation officer be aware of his own feelings about authority. It is imperative that the probation officer conceive of authority and use it to the extent that the probationer is confronted with the reality that no man is an island unto himself.

The primary difficulty in the probation field is the problem of heavy caseloads. Probation officers have reported that they have had so many people on their caseloads that they could not keep the cards in alphabetical order in the office, much less provide casework services. The average size of caseloads in probation in 1966 was 103.8. Of these, 76.4 were probationers and the rest were other types of cases. The average stay on probation was 29 months. The range of caseloads on probation was between 12 and 800.[19] Of the 3,082 counties and districts in the fifty states and Puerto Rico, 91 percent have some probation service.[20] On the other hand, the adequacy of probation service in many areas is open to question. The Saginaw experiment indicated that a low caseload assigned to probation officers could result in excellent results, even though only 20 percent of the convicted persons were sentenced to prison.[21] On the other hand, the San Francisco Project on intensive supervision was considered to be a failure. The variables appear to be the amount of time spent in supervision and whether the focus was on surveillance that would increase technical violations or counseling that would improve adjustment.[22]

It is obvious that the fifty-unit caseload recommended by the National Council on Crime and Delinquency (NCCD), in which five points (measure of work load) are allowed for each presentence investigation per month and one point for each probationer under supervision, is not in practice in most places. This would mean that three presentence investigations per month would total fifteen points, leaving room for supervision of thirty-five probationers. In reality, most probation agents may do twelve or fifteen presentence investigations a month and supervise nearly a hundred probationers.

There has been some effort to get the probationer and parolee involved in his own supervision by paying for it. For example, Section 945.30 of the *Florida Statutes* provides that anyone on probation or parole shall be required to contribute $10 a month toward the cost of his supervision, beginning 60 days from the date he is free to seek employment. This has caused problems in collection and dilemmas as to whether to revoke probation or parole for nonpayment.

The factors used by the probation officer during supervision, of

---

[19] "Correction in the United States," *Crime and Delinquency* (Special Issue), 13, No. 1 (January 1967), 170.

[20] *Ibid.*, 164.

[21] *The Saginaw Probation Demonstration Project,* Michigan Crime and Delinquency Council (New York: National Council on Crime and Delinquency, 1963), reported in *Task Force Report: Corrections,* p. 28.

[22] M.G. Neithercutt and D.M. Gottfredson, *Case Load Size Variation and Differences in Probation Parole Performance* (Pittsburgh: National Center for Juvenile Justice, 1974).

**Table 5-3**

| Item | Percentages of Times Used |
|---|---|
| Employment history | 37.7 |
| Defendant's attitude | 34.8 |
| Psychological/psychiatric | 27.5 |
| Marital status | 26.1 |
| Defendant's statement | 24.6 |
| Medical history | 21.7 |
| Family history | 18.8 |
| Prior record | 18.8 |
| Age | 18.8 |
| Education | 15.9 |
| Interest and activities | 11.6 |
| Family criminality | 10.1 |
| Alcoholic involvement | 8.7 |
| Homosexuality | 8.7 |
| Drug usage | 5.8 |
| Confinement status | 5.8 |
| Military history | 5.8 |
| Religion | 5.8 |
| Residence | 4.3 |
| Offense | 2.9 |
| Plea | 0.0 |
| Legal representation | 0.0 |
| Place of birth | 0.0 |
| Race | 0.0 |

*Source:* R. M. Carter, "The Presentence Report," p. 207.

course, vary with the approach and situation in which supervision takes place and with the personalities of the client *and* the probation officer. Table 5-3 lists the factors used by a number of California probation officers in supervision.

Some cases are of particular concern to the probation officer because of their different nature, such as the public relations problems concerning sex offenders. Sex offenders on probation vary widely. The heterosexual pedophiles, who enjoy looking, showing, touching, kissing, and fondling young girls can be characterized in three main groups: (1) adolescents retarded in psychosexual development, (2) the middle-aged who have regressed owing to severe life stresses, and (3) the senescent or old-age group whose loneliness and social isolation may foster intimate contact with children. Since the recidivist rate is low in this category of offenses, most offenders are good risks for probation, but the chronic offender has problems too deep for the treatment the probation officer can provide.[23]

[23] Alex K. Gigeroff, J.W. Mohr, and R.E. Turner, "Sex Offenders on Probation: Heterosexual Pedophiles," *Federal Probation,* 32, No. 4 (December 1968), 17–21.

Homosexual behavior is more frequent than has generally been thought.[24] Homosexual cases appearing before the courts usually involve (1) adult homosexual acts in public places, (2) homosexual relations with youths, and (3) homosexual relations with children. It is important for the probation officer not to classify all persons involved in these cases as "homosexual," but to differentiate between them in terms of personality patterns. Psychiatric consultation can be of considerable assistance to the officer.

A probation officer is more likely to supervise an exhibitionist than any other type of sex offender. The peak period for sexual exhibitionism has been reported to be between the early and middle twenties. Since there is only a 10 percent recidivism rate, the exhibitionist is a good risk for probation.[25]

Supervision of casework services in a probation department is difficult. Presentence investigation reports are tangible and can be read, and constructive supervision in improving their quality is not a difficult professional task. Supervision of casework and treatment-supervision services between the probation officer and the probationer, on the other hand, is less tangible. This must entail reading of the progress reports in the cases handled by the probation officer to get a general factual background of what is happening, combined with professional conferences with each probation officer concerning his use of casework and treatment-supervision techniques. Observation of success or failure over a period of time is probably one of the best ways of evaluating the officer's work.

Studying cases in staff meetings tends to improve the probation officer's awareness of some of the problems and interpretations of the treatment-supervision process. This staffing means that on a weekly, biweekly, or monthly basis, the staff meets to hear one probation officer present a case in his caseload, including the problem, his diagnosis, and his method of treatment. Other members of the staff, including visiting clinical staff, such as psychiatrists, psychologists, and social workers, question him about his procedure. While such staffing may be initially threatening to the individual probation officer presenting the case, he soon learns that everybody is in the same situation and that the total procedure improves the professional level of the staff and each individual in it. Further, it is a good way for adjunct supervision of probation services. As a matter of fact, the staffing concept is a good idea in all correctional settings.

The Los Angeles County Probation Department has a citizen volunteer program known as VISTO (Volunteers in Service to Offenders) to assist in supervision.[26] During 1969, the program of 654 volunteers

[24] Alex K. Gigeroff, J.W. Mohr, and R.E. Turner, "Sex Offenders on Probation: Homosexuality," *Federal Probation*, 33, No. 1 (March 1969), 36–39.

[25] Alex K. Gigeroff, J.W. Mohr, and R.E. Turner; "Sex Offenders on Probation: The Exhibitionist," *Federal Probation*, 32, No. 3 (September 1968), 18–21.

[26] Philip Stein, "I'm Only One Person—What Can I Do?" *Federal Probation*, 34, No. 2 (June 1970), 7–11.

contributed 37,555 hours; 15,206 people attended 486 meetings designed to acquaint the community with the programs; 726 probationers were referred to manpower training programs; 757 probationers were placed on jobs; 43 probationers were provided temporary housing; 2,156 probationers were counseled; 818 probationers received tutorial and remedial educational instruction; 2,714 probationers were involved in special recreational activities; 2,215 probationers received miscellaneous services such as emergency transportation, babysitting, and clothing; 441 groups of probationers met for group counseling or discussions conducted by volunteers.

Overloading the caseloads appears to defeat the concept of probation. When the worker has to strain to even partially cover his caseload, he cannot apply professional techniques. Rather, he is forced to do the minimum supervision essential to keep the process going and then go to somebody else on his caseload. This situation means that everybody provides supervision in the same way, regardless of his education and qualifications. This is why, too, some correctional administrators have said that some uneducated people can do as good a job as some of the educated people can. The fact is that they *are* doing the same kind of job because of overwork and overload, but the professional people *can* do a better job, all else being equal.

## SHOCK PROBATION

Shock probation is the sending of a convicted offender to prison or jail for a part of his sentence and then placing him on probation within a short time.[27] The split sentence combines the advantages of probation with the use of the institution for evaluation purposes. This exists in modified forms in Sweden and Denmark, and in the United States in Maine, Ohio, California, Georgia, and Wisconsin; other states are now considering it. The Ohio law was enacted in October 1965, and a ten-year evaluation was sufficiently positive that a shock parole law became effective there in January 1974.[28]

## DISCHARGE AND REVOCATION

Persons on probation are released from supervision by discharge or by revocation. Discharge generally means that the probationer has successfully completed the period of probation, although some jurisdictions in recent years have developed the practice of discharging persons "not amenable to probation" rather than sending them to prison. In case of another conviction, these persons are not again placed on probation in that jurisdiction.

[27] Paul C. Friday, David M. Peterson, and Harry E. Allen, "Shock Probation: A New Approach to Crime Control," *Georgia Journal of Corrections*, 1 (1973), 1–3.

[28] Nick Gatz, "First Shock Probation: Now Shock Parole," *American Journal of Correction*, 37, No. 1 (January–February 1975), 20.

Revocation means that the probation has been revoked and that another disposition must be made of the case, generally incarceration.

After the period of probation has expired, the probation officer can recommend discharge. The court formalizes this discharge. Sometimes, the probation officer considers that the probationer could be discharged prior to the expiration of his probation term, which is within the discretion of the judge. On the other hand, an extension could be made for certain minor violations. In general, however, if a probationer has not violated within the first two years, the chances are good that he will not violate at all.

Revocation of probation can be recommended by the probation officer when the probationer is out of control. It is automatic, of course, when a new offense has been committed. The revocation hearing is a formal procedure in the court in which counsel for the defense is available.

The revocation hearing is generally held in the courtroom or the judge's chambers. The judge and the probationer hear the recommendations for revocation by the probation officer, and the judge makes the decision. The violation report provides the basic information. The Supreme Court decision in the case of *Mempa* v. *Rhay* (389 U.S. 128, 1967), on December 1, 1967, provides that the probationer must have counsel at the revocation hearing. Subsequently, the two most significant cases on revocation were *Morrissey* v. *Brewer* (408 U.S. 471, 1972), which provided for minimal due process protections for defendants in revocation proceedings, and *Gagnon* v. *Scarpelli* (411 U.S. 778, 1973), which provided for counsel when the outcome might require legal skills not possessed by the defendant. While these cases were originally concerned with parole, their principles have applied to revocation hearings in probation, as well. The practical result of these decisions has been a slowdown in revocations because the procedure has become more complex.

Just as disparities appear in sentencing, so do disparities appear in revocations of probation. Unrealistic conditions of probation invite violations. Violations of conditions of probation do not necessarily reflect poor probation adjustment. In too many cases, revocations have been automatic and routine, rather than being tempered by the use of discretion and considered judgment. Revocation and imprisonment should never be used for punishment, but for a constructive purpose.[29]

## DISCUSSION

While probation is a judicial function, there has been a trend in recent years to have it administered by the state, along with parole. The reason for this is simply that probation in rural and sparsely settled areas has been practically nonexistent. Making the state responsible for probation brings probation services in some measure to all sections of the state and, in addi-

[29] Eugene C. DiCerbo, "When Should Probation Be Revoked?" *Federal Probation*, 30, No. 2 (June 1966), 11–16.

tion, provides the vehicle for standardizing minimum requirements for probation officers. Where probation is a state responsibility, the probation officer still reports to the judge and works for the court.

The majority of probation services, and generally the better services, are provided by the larger courts that maintain their own staffs. Some of the larger county probation departments provide research services and in-service training, and demand professional-level services.

When the Federal Probation Service was established in 1930, all federal probation officers were required to have a minimum of a college degree. By 1933, some federal judges had brought pressure to eliminate the minimum requirement because it infringed on the discretion of the judges. Central control of probation services was simply not acceptable. It was not until February 1957, when the Federal Probation Officers Association held their annual meeting at Daytona Beach, Florida, that the Association adopted "recommended" standards, specifically the master's degree in Social Work or "equivalent," and brought some suggestion to their judges that the suggested minimum requirements be honored.

Centralization of policy, budget, and other matters was more difficult. Congress established the Administrative Office of the United States Courts on August 7, 1939, to assist the Judicial Conference in the following ways:

1. Prepare the annual budget for the judicial system.
2. Perform housekeeping tasks for the courts, such as assistance in providing personnel and facilities.
3. Collect and report judicial statistics, reporting from courts in a manner augmented by field trips for firsthand observation.
4. Assist in formulating and making effective plans for more efficient court operation.
5. Conduct studies to guide the Judicial Conference in its function of recommending new legislation to the Congress.

The Administrative Office of the United States Courts functions as administrator of the federal judiciary system, including planning, directing, and coordinating its efforts. This office also publishes *Federal Probation* as a service to the field of corrections.[30]

There has been interesting debate as to whether or not the probation services should be returned to the Department of Justice, from which it was separated in 1940. Those who favor this transfer take the position that federal corrections is now fragmented and that continuity of service would be better implemented if the prisons and the probation and parole services were in the same department.[31] Those who defend the present organiza-

[30] Administrative Office of the U.S. Courts, Supreme Court Building, Washington, D.C. 20544.

[31] Peter G. Fish, "The Status of the Federal Probation System," *Crime and Delinquency,* 12, No. 4 (October 1966), 365–70.

tion hold that 75 percent of the work of the American probation officer is done in the court and, as a judicial function, probation belongs in the courts.[32]

The probation officer's job can be depicted as follows:

> Investigation
> > Presentence investigation
> > Case writing
> > Custody investigation
>
> Counseling
> > Initial interview
> > Individual supervision
> > Family counseling
> > Employment counseling
> > Personal counseling
> > Financial counseling
>
> Enforcement
> > Probation violation
> > Probation revocation
> > Individual enforcement

As has been mentioned before, the quality of probation varies widely. Several ways have been explored to make probation uniform, such as placing it under state supervision. This can be done only with great difficulty, however, where local probation services have been well developed in the highly populated areas. California, for example, was unable to achieve this state supervision recently.

The probation subsidy is another idea for improving the quality of probation services. The Probation Subsidy Bill was passed by the California Legislature in 1965 to provide for a maximum payment of $4,000 to a county for every criminal adult or juvenile delinquent *not* committed to a state correctional institution, but whose incarceration was expected on the basis of past performance. The state of Washington passed a similar law in 1970. Subsidy of probation takes into account more than salary, but it must provide supporting services.[33] Reduction of workload is not sufficient to achieve maximum effectiveness unless there is a commitment to specific treatment programs by the administration of the department. Client-centered services are best. Subcultural delinquents often require practical assistance and extensive environmental manipulation. Neurotic delinquents require intensive one-to-one relationships. Classification must be continuously supported by adequate supervision and consultation. There is a ten-

[32] Albert Wahl, "Federal Probation Belongs with the Courts," *Crime and Delinquency*, 12, No. 4 (October 1966), 371–76.

[33] *Staff Recommendations on Subsidy,* 1964 Board of Corrections Probation Study, San Francisco, October 16, 1964.

dency for work patterns to persist, so probation officers need help through in-service training or other methods to make sure that work patterns do not become calcified.

A study of probation in fifteen selected counties in California reflected gross differences in the use of probation between counties.[34] Probation to felony defendants ranged from 56.9 percent in one county to 23.5 percent in another. The extent to which probation is used has its effect on state penal costs and workloads. Sixty separate probation departments in California maintain their independence. County and state efforts to reach agreement about ways to improve services have snagged over the issue of county independence. Subsidy is a possibility.

In the fifteen study counties in California, there were 30,833 superior court adult probationers under supervision at the end of 1963. There were 56,725 juveniles under formal supervision, of which 62.1 percent were for delinquency and 37.9 for dependency and neglect. There were 41,006 lower court probationers or misdemeanants under supervision, of which about 25 percent were for nonsupport. Of the total of 145,457 probationers under supervision, 66,064 adults and juveniles might be considered for commitment to institutions. This means that 4 percent of the total may be sent to institutions, depending upon the effectiveness of probation supervision. In 1956, superior court probation cases represented 43.6 percent of all jurisdictional cases under supervision. In 1963, these same cases constituted 42.9 percent of the caseload.

Many prison people have a misconception about the effectiveness of probation because they have experienced the presence of young offenders who have been on probation and failed.[35] In fact, probation is probably the most successful phase of the correctional process.

The greatest needs in probation are for more personnel, better education and training, and political action. Most good probation departments require at least a baccalaureate degree or a master's degree for entry into the service. Junior and community colleges can provide semiprofessional workers to do many of the jobs now left to the probation officer. Reformed offenders, indigenous aides, volunteers, and student workers can take many administrative duties from the probation officer, leaving him free to counsel his caseload.[36] One of the dangers is in specialization of the functions of probation; the probation agent needs to be aware of the entire spectrum of his job to be effective.[37]

Professional and in-service training in probation is one of the most

---

[34] *Probation Decisions and Practices,* California Board of Corrections, Sacramento, 1964.

[35] Daniel Glaser, *The Effectiveness of a Prison and Parole System,* abridged ed. (Indianapolis: Bobbs-Merrill, 1969), pp. 318–19.

[36] Donald E. Loughery, Jr., "Innovations in Probation Management," *Crime and Delinquency,* 15, No. 2 (April 1969), 247–58.

[37] Eugene H. Czajkoski, "Functional Specialization in Probation and Parole," *Crime and Delinquency,* 15, No. 2 (April 1969), 238–46.

Figure 5-1 **Adult probation: 23 Ohio counties currently serviced by state probation officers.***

* Shaded areas show counties currently being served.
From *The Annual Report—1969*, Ohio Adult Parole Authority, Columbus, Ohio, 1970.

urgent needs of the field.[38] The best approach to this in-service training is to work out an agreement with nearby colleges and universities for assistance and guidance. Some college courses would be appropriate.

The National Council on Crime and Delinquency Research Center has reviewed recent changes in the field of corrections supported by re-

[38] Edward H. Taylor and Alexander W. McEachern, "Needs and Directions in Probation Training," *Federal Probation*, 30, No. 1 (March 1966), 18–24.

search and political action.[39] Knowledge of the legislative process, lobbying procedures, the development of bills for action, and the whole political process is important for the probation officer and his administrator.

The general pattern is to vest administrative functions in a chief probation officer. He hires, promotes, and dismisses probation staff, subject to civil service or judiciary authority in the jurisdiction. He plans the program, supervises caseload management, provides in-service training, and carries on other duties related to the management of the probation office.

There appears to be a trend towards separating probation staff from the judicial appointment. Judicial control could be retained if the judge could select a probation officer from a list of eligible persons certified by a merit system. The constitutional doctrine of the separation of powers between executive and judicial branches would indicate that the primary responsibility should still remain in the judiciary.

The American Bar Association suggests that it is appropriate for probation services to be administered at either the state or local level, but that no control should be vested in any agency having prosecutorial functions.[40] Some jurisdictions, such as Ohio, have provided state probation service to some counties and not to others. The Ohio pattern as of 1969 is shown in Figure 5-1.

## SUMMARY

Probation is probably the most successful phase of the correctional process, because it involves supervision of persons in the community who have not entered very far into the criminal justice system. The presentence investigation report prepared by the probation officer can influence constructively all subsequent work with the offender, whether on probation, in prison, or on parole. There is a trend toward state control or subsidy of probation because most probation services tend to be in the large metropolitan areas. There is considerable need for more and better trained personnel in the area of probation.[41] Probation serves a larger number of people than prisons and parole combined.

## EXERCISES AND STUDY QUESTIONS

1. *What is probation?*
2. *How many offenders, both misdemeanants and felons, are on probation at any given time?*

[39] Leslie T. Wilkins and Don M. Gottfredson, *Research, Demonstration, and Social Action* (Davis, Calif.: NCCD Research Center, 1969).

[40] *Standards Relating to Probation*, American Bar Association (Chicago: ABA, 1970), p. 110.

[41] Herman Piven and Abraham Alcabes, *The Crisis of Qualified Manpower for Criminal Justice: An Analytic Assessment with Guidelines for New Policy*, Vol. 1, *Probation/Parole* (Washington, D.C.: Office of Juvenile Delinquency and Youth Development, n.d.).

3. What are the primary functions of the probation officer?

4. What is a presentence investigation?

5. What functions does the presentence investigation report serve?

6. How does the judge use the presentence investigation in the sentencing procedure?

7. How does the probation officer determine his recommendations for or against probation for a convicted offender?

8. What are the half-dozen or so factors used to determine whether a person should be recommended for probation?

9. Describe the process of supervision of probationers.

10. What are the four general principles frequently used by the probation officer to determine the balance between control and treatment of the probationer?

11. How can the family be used in the supervision process?

12. How does the probation officer resolve the problem of self-determination in his work with offenders?

13. What is shock probation?

14. What is the caseload size recommended by the National Council on Crime and Delinquency, and how can it be implemented?

15. What is the process of revocation in probation?

16. When is a probationer discharged from probation?

17. What are the functions of the Administrative Office of the United States Courts?

18. What is the significance of the cases of Mempa v. Rhay, Morrissey v. Brewer, and Gagnon v. Scarpelli in revocation hearings in probation and parole?

19. What is the intent of probation subsidy acts?

20. To what extent is probation actually being used in the United States?

# 6

# PRISONS AND CORRECTIONAL INSTITUTIONS

Prisons and correctional institutions form the hard-core base of the correctional process. Because they provide the external control needed to hold prisoners in any degree of custody, they are the resource used by the system of justice to control prisoners considered to be dangerous to society. Prisons and correctional institutions, because of their significance in the system and the historical development of corrections, tend to influence disproportionately the philosophy of the entire correctional system of which they are a part. As a matter of fact, the other correctional systems grew out of or were developed as complementary to the prison. The idea of parole developed in the old Norfolk Prison Colony and from the old Irish system when the administrators decided that prisoners could be returned on a ticket of leave or released from prison by stages of reduced security. Probation emerged almost as a "second chance" concept to prevent people from unnecessarily going to jail or prison. Juvenile institutions split off from prisons in the nineteenth century as a result of the "child-saving" movement. The prison staff and warden now make recommendations to the parole board for or against release of individual prisoners and control part of the gain time or "time off for good behavior" systems, thereby influencing other phases of the correctional systems. In short, the prison and correctional institution are a most significant segment of society's process of criminal justice.

On March 31, 1982, there were 384,316 inmates in state and federal correctional institutions, of whom 16,702 (4.3 percent) were female.[1] This

[1] Table 1, *Corrections Digest,* 13, No. 15 (July 19, 1982), p. 3.

143

means that, excluding jails, 19.5 percent of the adult correctional caseload were in institutions.

There were 172,753 persons received in state and federal institutions in 1979, of whom 131,047 were new court commitments and of whom 10,505 were female.[2] The number of institutions in the United States (not including the Federal Prison System) is shown in Table 6-1 for 1974 in the absence of more recent data. *Corrections Digest* has reported that there were 384,316 persons in prison in the United States on March 31, 1982. For a graphic review of prison populations in the United States from 1962 to 1976, drawn by the LEAA, and followed by figures for 1976 to March 31, 1982, drawn by the author, see Figure 6-1.

The maximum custody institution is the last and most remote phase of the correctional process. Some old-time prison wardens consider that personnel have not had correctional experience unless they have served in the maximum custody prison with the most hostile and difficult of prisoners. Certainly, the maximum custody prison is the place where the hard-core offender is found. Correctional institutions, of course, range from large maximum security prisons to smaller correctional institutions almost devoid of security.

## DEVELOPMENT OF PRISONS IN THE UNITED STATES

The development of prisons and correctional institutions in the United States has varied widely. The large, industrial, and more significant prisons developed in the areas of high population. The small, less secure forestry and road camps and the smaller prisons developed in more sparsely populated areas. Prisons and penitentiaries in the United States developed from the old workhouses begun in 1577 and London's Newgate Prison (1769), which was really a big jail with a strong perimeter and with neither program nor discipline inside. The workhouse at Ghent in Belgium, built in 1773, was the first large-scale penal institution architecturally constructed to accommodate a beginning treatment philosophy,[3] but the Cherry Hill institution, built in the 1830s in Pennsylvania, is considered to be the first large-scale "successful" prison with a program of any sort.[4]

Because the population of the United States has been disproportionately concentrated in the area from Boston to Washington and west to St. Louis, many of the first prisons developed in this great area. Well over one-half the population of the United States lives here. Nearly another 11 per-

[2] *Prisoners in State and Federal Institutions on December 31, 1979,* National Prisoner Statistics Bulletin SD-NPS-PSF-7 (Washington, D.C.: U.S. Government Printing Office, 1981), p. 20.

[3] Norman Johnston, *The Human Cage: A Brief History of Prison Architecture* (New York: Walker and Co., for The American Foundation, Inc., Institute of Corrections, Philadelphia, 1973), p. 13.

[4] *Ibid.,* p. 31.

cent of the nation's population is concentrated around Los Angeles and San Francisco in California. The majority of significant prisons were established in these areas of high population. The Pennsylvania system, which the Quakers implemented in the old Walnut Street Jail, was initiated in Philadelphia in 1790. The rival Auburn system was established in New York in 1815. This institution emphasized silence, harsh discipline, and congregate labor. In turn, the Auburn system was challenged by the Boston Prison Discipline Society and its leader, Louis Dwight, who had helped to obtain the adoption of the more humane treatment approach of the Pennsylvania system in Massachusetts. Large industrial prisons holding more than 4,000 prisoners were built within the areas of large population. The Ohio State Penitentiary at Columbus was established in 1834. The Illinois State Penitentiary at Joliet-Stateville was established in 1858. The California State Prison at San Quentin was built in 1852. The present State Prison of Southern Michigan at Jackson, the largest in America, was opened in 1926 to replace an older prison built in 1839.

Most of the prisons in the less populated western states generally developed from old territorial jails. Examples are found in Arizona, Montana, and elsewhere throughout the West. The same pattern appeared in Canada. The old territorial jails at Walla Walla and Calgary, for example, are now prisons. The major exception to this in the West is California, where the resources were available to develop an adequate correctional system in the eastern and midwestern pattern. If it were a separate nation today, California would rank twenty-seventh in population and eleventh in wealth, and would have the highest per capita income in the world.[5]

The Southern states developed correctional programs in still a different pattern, one of considerable interest. Because of the agricultural economy, based on a semifeudal system in which the landowners or planters maintained hired help and slaves on large tracts of land, people tended to assume responsibility for law and order within their own jurisdictions. Consequently, there was little need, except in the cities, for large central prisons and, for that matter, little need for jails. The Civil War, 1860–65, destroyed the old semifeudal system. Before the Civil War, Mississippi was the richest state in the Union, with Alabama second. Northern states were struggling, with government subsidies, to develop industry in competition with England. Mississippi built a small prison in Jackson in 1809 similar to the Auburn cellblock form. Built on the site of the present state capitol, it was called "The Walls."[6] It became a munitions factory in 1860, and the Union army destroyed it in 1863. After the Civil War, Mississippi went into the leasing of prisoners, as did the rest of the South. Georgia had begun a prison in 1817, but it was abolished by the legislature in 1830.[7] Tennessee

[5] *Business Week*, March 21, 1970, p. 61.

[6] "New Look at Old South—The History of Parchman," *The Mentor*, 14, No. 1 (June 1969), 1, 4.

[7] Orlando F. Lewis, *The Development of American Prisons and Prison Customs, 1776–1845* (Montclair, N.J.: Patterson Smith, 1967), p. 265. Originally published in 1922 by the Prison Association of New York.

**Table 6-1 Number of institutions and inmates, by state and type of institution, 1974**

| State | All Institutions | | Classification or Medical Centers | | Community Centers | | Prisons: All Prisons | | Prisons: Prison Farms | | Prisons: Road Camps | | Prisons: Forest Camps | | Prisons: Closed Prisons | | Prisons: Other Prisons | |
|---|---|---|---|---|---|---|---|---|---|---|---|---|---|---|---|---|---|---|
| | Institutions | Inmates | Institutions | Inmates | Institutions | Inmates | Institutions | Inmates | Institutions | Inmates | Institutions | Inmates | Institutions | Inmates | Institutions | Inmates | Institutions | Inmates |
| Total | 592 | 187,982 | 33 | 9,766 | 158 | 8,975 | 401 | 169,241 | 41 | 25,402 | 80 | 6,369 | 41 | 2,483 | 172 | 118,708 | 67 | 16,279 |
| Alabama | 20 | 3,995 | 1 | 503 | 2 | 64 | 17 | 3,428 | 3 | 1,187 | 10 | 469 | 0 | 0 | 3 | 1,670 | 1 | 102 |
| Alaska | 8 | 466 | 0 | 0 | 1 | 16 | 7 | 450 | 0 | 0 | 0 | 0 | 0 | 0 | 1 | 56 | 6 | 394 |
| Arizona | 6 | 1,756 | 0 | 0 | 4 | 208 | 2 | 1,548 | 0 | 0 | 0 | 0 | 0 | 0 | 1 | 1,417 | 1 | 131 |
| Arkansas | 3 | 1,755 | 0 | 0 | 0 | 0 | 3 | 1,755 | 1 | 1,287 | 0 | 0 | 0 | 0 | 2 | 468 | 0 | 0 |
| California | 35 | 22,927 | 2 | 604 | 4 | 160 | 29 | 22,163 | 0 | 0 | 1 | 67 | 15 | 933 | 11 | 19,224 | 2 | 1,939 |
| Colorado | 7 | 2,070 | 0 | 0 | 3 | 83 | 4 | 1,987 | 0 | 0 | 0 | 0 | 1 | 89 | 2 | 1,852 | 1 | 46 |
| Connecticut | 12 | 2,731 | 0 | 0 | 1 | 20 | 11 | 2,711 | 0 | 0 | 0 | 0 | 0 | 0 | 4 | 1,674 | 7 | 1,037 |
| Delaware | 4 | 683 | 0 | 0 | 1 | 26 | 3 | 657 | 0 | 0 | 0 | 0 | 0 | 0 | 3 | 657 | 0 | 0 |
| District of Columbia[a] | — | — | — | — | — | — | — | — | — | — | — | — | — | — | — | — | — | — |
| Florida | 46 | 10,334 | 1 | 1,025 | 19 | 895 | 26 | 8,414 | 0 | 0 | 13 | 812 | 0 | 0 | 8 | 6,466 | 5 | 1,136 |
| Georgia[b] | 30 | 7,593 | 2 | 1,027 | 3 | 137 | 25 | 6,429 | 0 | 0 | 13 | 957 | 0 | 0 | 8 | 3,950 | 4 | 1,522 |
| Hawaii | 5 | 303 | 0 | 0 | 3 | 46 | 2 | 257 | 0 | 0 | 0 | 0 | 0 | 0 | 1 | 200 | 1 | 57 |
| Idaho | 1 | 489 | 0 | 0 | 0 | 0 | 1 | 489 | 0 | 0 | 0 | 0 | 0 | 0 | 1 | 489 | 0 | 0 |
| Illinois | 15 | 5,843 | 2 | 470 | 6 | 133 | 7 | 5,240 | 0 | 0 | 0 | 0 | 0 | 0 | 7 | 5,240 | 0 | 0 |
| Indiana | 10 | 4,071 | 1 | 133 | 2 | 78 | 7 | 3,860 | 1 | 628 | 0 | 0 | 2 | 58 | 4 | 3,174 | 0 | 0 |
| Iowa | 9 | 1,462 | 1 | 93 | 4 | 140 | 4 | 1,229 | 0 | 0 | 0 | 0 | 1 | 26 | 3 | 1,203 | 0 | 0 |
| Kansas | 7 | 1,446 | 1 | 114 | 0 | 0 | 6 | 1,332 | 0 | 0 | 0 | 0 | 0 | 0 | 3 | 1,251 | 3 | 81 |
| Kentucky | 8 | 2,886 | 0 | 0 | 0 | 0 | 8 | 2,886 | 1 | 82 | 0 | 0 | 2 | 66 | 4 | 2,626 | 1 | 112 |
| Louisiana | 7 | 4,063 | 0 | 0 | 3 | 299 | 4 | 3,764 | 1 | 3,138 | 0 | 0 | 1 | 19 | 2 | 607 | 0 | 0 |
| Maine | 6 | 465 | 0 | 0 | 3 | 97 | 3 | 368 | 0 | 0 | 0 | 0 | 0 | 0 | 3 | 368 | 0 | 0 |
| Maryland | 12 | 6,489 | 1 | 462 | 4 | 749 | 7 | 5,278 | 0 | 0 | 1 | 135 | 0 | 0 | 4 | 3,879 | 2 | 1,264 |
| Massachusetts[c] | — | — | — | — | — | — | — | — | — | — | — | — | — | — | — | — | — | — |
| Michigan | 21 | 8,104 | 1 | 987 | 3 | 314 | 17 | 6,803 | 0 | 0 | 0 | 0 | 10 | 756 | 6 | 5,861 | 1 | 188 |

|  | | | | | | | | | | | | | | | | |
|---|---|---|---|---|---|---|---|---|---|---|---|---|---|---|---|---|
| Minnesota | 6 | 1,401 | 0 | 0 | 14 | 5 | 1,387 | 1 | 63 | 0 | 0 | 0 | 3 | 1,288 | 1 | 36 |
| Mississippi | 1 | 1,736 | 0 | 0 | 0 | 1 | 1,736 | 1 | 1,736 | 0 | 0 | 0 | 0 | 0 | 0 | 0 |
| Missouri | 9 | 3,449 | 1 | 174 | 32 | 7 | 3,243 | 2 | 322 | 0 | 0 | 0 | 2 | 1,579 | 3 | 1,342 |
| Montana | 1 | 336 | 0 | 0 | 0 | 1 | 336 | 0 | 0 | 0 | 0 | 0 | 1 | 336 | 0 | 0 |
| Nebraska | 4 | 1,010 | 0 | 0 | 34 | 3 | 976 | 0 | 0 | 0 | 0 | 0 | 1 | 647 | 2 | 329 |
| Nevada | 1 | 790 | 0 | 0 | 0 | 1 | 790 | 0 | 0 | 0 | 0 | 0 | 1 | 790 | 0 | 0 |
| New Hampshire | 2 | 279 | 0 | 0 | 8 | 1 | 271 | 0 | 0 | 0 | 0 | 0 | 1 | 271 | 0 | 0 |
| New Jersey | 13 | 5,655 | 0 | 0 | 74 | 11 | 5,581 | 0 | 0 | 0 | 2 | 91 | 4 | 3,587 | 5 | 1,903 |
| New Mexico | 2 | 775 | 0 | 0 | 0 | 2 | 775 | 1 | 72 | 0 | 0 | 0 | 1 | 703 | 0 | 0 |
| New York | 23 | 14,311 | 4 | 1,595 | 32 | 18 | 12,684 | 0 | 0 | 0 | 3 | 260 | 10 | 11,259 | 5 | 1,165 |
| North Carolina | 76 | 11,809 | 5 | 1,041 | 2,986 | 42 | 7,782 | 3 | 855 | 1,939 | 0 | 0 | 20 | 4,646 | 4 | 342 |
| North Dakota | 2 | 176 | 0 | 0 | 0 | 2 | 176 | 1 | 22 | 0 | 0 | 0 | 1 | 154 | 0 | 0 |
| Ohio | 11 | 7,873 | 2 | 201 | 0 | 9 | 7,672 | 1 | 257 | 0 | 0 | 0 | 6 | 7,237 | 2 | 178 |
| Oklahoma | 11 | 3,175 | 0 | 0 | 191 | 7 | 2,984 | 1 | 234 | 0 | 0 | 0 | 3 | 1,893 | 3 | 857 |
| Oregon | 12 | 1,686 | 0 | 0 | 139 | 5 | 1,547 | 1 | 71 | 0 | 1 | 33 | 3 | 1,443 | 0 | 0 |
| Pennsylvania | 22 | 6,065 | 1 | 122 | 434 | 8 | 5,509 | 0 | 0 | 0 | 0 | 0 | 7 | 4,845 | 1 | 664 |
| Rhode Island | 1 | 569 | 0 | 0 | 0 | 1 | 569 | 0 | 0 | 0 | 0 | 0 | 1 | 569 | 0 | 0 |
| South Carolina | 17 | 3,615 | 2 | 237 | 411 | 9 | 2,967 | 1 | 68 | 0 | 0 | 0 | 4 | 2,412 | 4 | 487 |
| South Dakota | 1 | 233 | 0 | 0 | 0 | 1 | 233 | 0 | 0 | 0 | 0 | 0 | 1 | 233 | 0 | 0 |
| Tennessee | 10 | 3,504 | 1 | 202 | 354 | 5 | 2,948 | 2 | 666 | 0 | 0 | 0 | 3 | 2,282 | 0 | 0 |
| Texas | 14 | 17,136 | 1 | 493 | 0 | 13 | 16,643 | 10 | 13,187 | 0 | 0 | 0 | 2 | 2,611 | 1 | 845 |
| Utah | 3 | 599 | 0 | 0 | 40 | 1 | 559 | 0 | 0 | 0 | 0 | 0 | 1 | 559 | 0 | 0 |
| Vermont | 7 | 368 | 1 | 43 | 240 | 1 | 85 | 0 | 0 | 0 | 0 | 0 | 1 | 85 | 0 | 0 |
| Virginia | 38 | 5,394 | 1 | 48 | 234 | 34 | 5,112 | 3 | 965 | 1,990 | 1 | 80 | 3 | 2,033 | 1 | 124 |
| Washington | 14 | 2,592 | 1 | 192 | 182 | 5 | 2,218 | 0 | 0 | 0 | 0 | 0 | 4 | 2,138 | 0 | 0 |
| West Virginia | 4 | 1,051 | 0 | 0 | 17 | 3 | 1,034 | 1 | 388 | 0 | 0 | 0 | 2 | 646 | 0 | 0 |
| Wisconsin | 12 | 2,183 | 0 | 0 | 73 | 10 | 2,110 | 4 | 163 | 0 | 2 | 72 | 4 | 1,875 | 0 | 0 |
| Wyoming | 3 | 281 | 0 | 0 | 15 | 2 | 266 | 1 | 11 | 0 | 0 | 0 | 1 | 255 | 0 | 0 |

[a] District of Columbia correctional facilities are considered to be local institutions.

[b] Excludes two institutions that did not submit data.

[c] No data are given for the 14 institutions in Massachusetts because of a lack of response from a majority of these institutions.

Source: Census of State Correctional Facilities—Advance Report—1974. National Prisoner Statistics Special Report, National Criminal Justice Information and Statistics Report, July 1975, pp. 18–19. Current data on types of institutions are not available, but populations have risen.

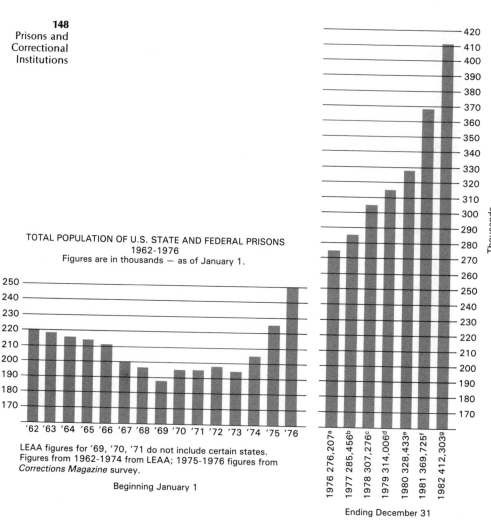

TOTAL POPULATION OF U.S. STATE AND FEDERAL PRISONS
1962-1976
Figures are in thousands — as of January 1.

LEAA figures for '69, '70, '71 do not include certain states.
Figures from 1962-1974 from LEAA; 1975-1976 figures from
*Corrections Magazine* survey.

Beginning January 1

Ending December 31

**Figure 6-1    Prison Population in the United States Annually between January 1, 1962, and December 31, 1982.**

From Steve Gettinger, "U.S. Prison Population Hits All-Time High," *Corrections Magazine.* 2, No. 3 (March 1976), 9.

[a] *Prisoners in State and Federal Institutions on December 31, 1976,* National Prisoner Statistics Bulletin, SD-NPS-PSF-4 (Washington, D.C.: U.S. Government Printing Office, 1978), p. 32.

[b] *Prisoners in State and Federal Institutions on December 31, 1978,* National Prisoner Statistics Bulletin, SD-NPS-PSF-6 (Washington, D.C.: U.S. Government Printing Office, 1980), p. 22.

[c] *Ibid.,* p. 23.

[d] *Prisoners in State and Federal Institutions on December 31, 1979,* National Prisoner Statistics Bulletin, SD-NPS-PSF-7 (Washington, D.C.: U.S. Government Printing Office, 1981), p. 11.

[e] "Bureau of Justice Statistics Prison Census as of 12/31/81," in Ralph Gardner, Jr., "Prison Population Jumps to 369,725," *Corrections Magazine,* VIII, No. 3 (June 1982), 6–11, 14, 46.

[f] *Ibid.,* p. 9.

[g] "Table 2. Prisoners under jurisdiction of State and Federal correctional authorities, by region and state, yearend 1981 and 1982," *Bureau of Justice Statistics Bulletin* (Washington, D.C.: Bureau of Justice Statistics, April 1983), p. 2.

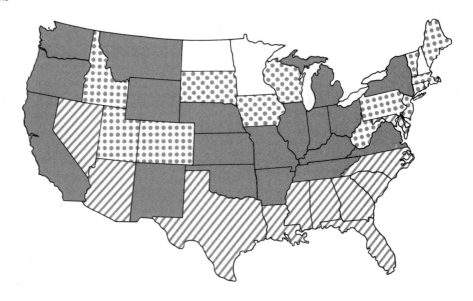

**Figure 6-2   Imprisonment rates at the end of 1981.**

*Source:* U.S. Department of Justice, Bureau of Justice Statistics, *Prisoners in 1980* (Washington, D.C.: U.S. Government Printing Office, May 1981). Taken from *Violent Crime in the United States* (Washington, D.C.: Bureau of Justice Statistics, September 1981, revised February 1982), p. 52.

**0-49**

| | |
|---|---|
| Federal system | 10 |
| North Dakota | 33 |
| New Hampshire | 42 |
| Minnesota | 49 |

**50-99**

| | |
|---|---|
| Massachusetts | 65 |
| Maine | 71 |
| Rhode Island | 72 |
| Utah | 73 |
| Vermont | 76 |
| Hawaii | 77 |
| Pennsylvania | 78 |
| West Virginia | 80 |
| Iowa | 88 |
| Colorado | 92 |
| New Jersey | 92 |
| Wisconsin | 93 |
| Connecticut | 95 |
| South Dakota | 97 |
| Idaho | 99 |

**100-174**

| | |
|---|---|
| New Mexico | 100 |
| Montana | 104 |
| Nebraska | 104 |
| Illinois | 113 |
| California | 114 |
| Kentucky | 114 |
| Kansas | 116 |
| Wyoming | 117 |
| Oregon | 124 |
| Washington | 125 |
| Missouri | 131 |
| Indiana | 138 |
| Ohio | 139 |
| Arkansas | 143 |
| New York | 145 |
| Michigan | 165 |
| Virginia | 165 |
| Oklahoma | 169 |
| Alaska | 170 |
| Tennessee | 171 |

**175 or more**

| | |
|---|---|
| Mississippi | 177 |
| Alabama | 183 |
| Arizona | 184 |
| Delaware | 208 |
| Texas | 210 |
| Louisiana | 216 |
| Maryland | 218 |
| Georgia | 220 |
| Florida | 224 |
| Nevada | 245 |
| North Carolina | 248 |
| South Carolina | 251 |
| D.C. | 467 |

State Prison of Southern Michigan at Jackson, the largest walled prison in the world.
Courtesy of the Michigan Department of Corrections.

built a prison in 1831. Alabama opened one in 1841, when Georgia began
one again.

The Civil War changed the economy and the penal system of the
South. Before this war, the South had been prosperous and was referred to
as the Southern "agricultural kingdom."[8] The South was confident with
the approach of the war because of its economic power,[9] even though it
never had more than 600,000 men under arms at any given time and the
Union had 3,000,000 in the army. Also, southern states could buy all the
equipment they needed from England. The Union naval blockade was effective, however. Ultimately, of course, the South was impoverished. When
Confederate money was made worthless and southerners who took part in
the war were disenfranchised by the Fourteenth Amendment of the Constitution,[10] economic and social chaos resulted. Landowners sold their
plantations at panic prices for United States currency in order to get a new
start. Slaves worth about $2,000 each had been freed without compensa-
tion to the owners. In short, the southern ruling class or power structure
was destroyed. It was the occupation armies from the North during Recon-

[8] William Warren Rogers, *Ante-Bellum Thomas County—1825–1861* (Tallahassee: Florida
State University Press, 1963), pp. 118–20.

[9] *Ibid.,* pp. 119–20.

[10] Article XIV, Section 3. Ratification proclaimed July 28, 1868.

struction who established the first real prisons in most southern states. By the time the occupation was over, northerners and blacks held positions of power and had gained wealth. The native disenfranchised southerners organized into secret societies such as the Ku Klux Klan and devised ways to frustrate the new power elite.

When the Union forces left the South in 1877, many of the formerly productive plantations had been taken out of production. They were now owned by northerners who had bought them to be used in the winter for hunting and other recreation. It should be noted here that it was the grandparents of contemporary southern adults who lost everything they had and whose antagonistic attitudes have been transmitted to their children and grandchildren. Not enough time had elapsed for the South to recover, either economically or culturally, and certainly not in terms of attitudes. And throughout all this drastic change, southern corrections systems reflected the economy and the culture.

There were not enough taxes to support adequate schools for the children, so it is not surprising that institutions for rehabilitation of offenders did not develop. There was simply not enough public money to spend on the schools, much less on prisoners. Consequently, arrangements were made in most southern states to lease the prisoners to the highest bidder. The bidders were generally large landowners or turpentine operators, frequently northerners who had come south after the war. The abuses and atrocities that developed in this system in the late 1800s form a sordid chapter in the exploitation of labor and human beings.[11]

Probably the worst American prison was the Confederate military prison in Andersonville, Georgia, where from February 1864 to March 1865 nearly 1,000 Union soldiers died each month.[12] The commander of the prison, Captain Henry Wirz, was executed after the war, and Andersonville has been preserved as a national park and cemetery.

Although little known, probably the most interesting and remote of America's prisons was Fort Jefferson, now a national monument, located on Garden Key in the Gulf of Mexico in the Dry Tortugas, 69 miles west of Key West.[13] As in Key West, there is no fresh water on the island. It has to be shipped in, rain has to be caught, or fresh water obtained through desalinization of ocean water. Among the many prisoners held there were Geronimo, the Apache Indian leader, and Dr. Samuel A. Mudd, who set the broken leg of John Wilkes Booth, assassin of Abraham Lincoln. It is interesting that Dr. Mudd was released in 1869 and went back to his home-

---

[11] The best documentary on this era seems to be J.C. Powell, *The American Siberia*, 1891, reprinted by Patterson Smith, Montclair, N.J., 1970.

[12] See *Andersonville: The Story of a Civil War Prison Camp* (Washington, D.C.: U.S. Government Printing Office, 1975). Also Peggy Sheppard, *Andersonville, Georgia, U.S.A.* (Leslie, Georgia: Sheppard Publications, 1973); and Ovid L. Futch, *History of Andersonville Prison* (Gainesville: University of Florida Press, 1968).

[13] Charles J. Eichman, "Florida's Historic Prison Fortress," *American Journal of Correction*, 29, No. 4 (July–August 1967), 24–26.

town in Maryland to renew his life, only to be rejected by all his former friends and neighbors, giving rise to the expression, "His name was mud." Started in 1846, Fort Jefferson was built by slaves from Key West as the "Gibraltar of the West," but the only military action it ever experienced was firing at a few passing Confederate ships. It was used as a prison from 1861 until about 1875, but it was too expensive to maintain for that purpose.

Around the beginning of the twentieth century, most southern states had begun effecting better controls over the leasing procedures. Most of the prison contracts were awarded by the Department of Agriculture, which had responsibility for prisons and prisoners because of the nature of the economy. Consequently, the first regulations involved sanitation and health.

As new railroads began to be built and new roads were needed for the automobile, there was a general trend away from the leasing of prisoners to private persons or companies and toward employing prisoners to build and maintain roads and railroads. This gave rise to the infamous chain gang. Some of the central prisons in the South were built to house women and infirm men who could neither be profitably leased nor do a good day's work on the roads. In fact, the presence of such people is why Florida built its first prison in 1913. Abuses continued, and criticism from other parts of the country helped to induce Southern legislators to consider other ways of handling prisoners. By World War I, central prisons and prison farms had been constructed in all southern states, and some, like those in Mississippi and Texas, were really large prison farms. Smaller camps or smaller institutions were geographically distributed throughout the states to provide labor for the maintenance of state highways. Criticism of southern penal systems continued into the 1950s. In 1929, Member of Parliament M. Leach introduced into the House of Commons a resolution attempting to find some way for the British government to investigate the Florida penal system. In 1950, a publication on international prison systems, published by the University of Paris Institute of Comparative Law, stated that the following southern states were among those with the most backward penal systems in the United States: *"les Etats du Sud—tels que la Floride, le Texas, et la Caroline du sud."*[14]

After World War II, however, the southern states began emulating the correctional programs found in the northern and western states. As a matter of fact, they assumed some leadership in the field, as evidenced by recent presidents of the American Correctional Association, including Ellis MacDougall of South Carolina, (1968–69); Dr. George Beto of Texas (1969–1970); Louie L. Wainwright of Florida (1970–71); Oliver J. Keller of Florida (1975–76); William D. Leeke of South Carolina (1976–77); and

[14] S. Grinberg-Vinaver, "Le Système Pénitentiaire des États-Unis," in Louis Hugueney, H. Donnedieu de Vabres, and Marc Ancel, eds., *Les Grand Systèmes Pénitentiaires Actuels* (Paris: Recueil Sirey, l'Institut de Droit Comparé de l'Université de Paris, 1950), p. 146.

Amos Reed of North Carolina (1981–82), who was terminated by a new conservative governor because he sent personnel to the American Correctional Association's Annual Congress of Corrections at San Diego in 1980 at state expense; Reed became secretary of the State of Washington Department of Corrections in 1980.

## TYPES OF INSTITUTIONS

The large institutions in the Midwest and California are products of the early twentieth century, although some were begun in the nineteenth century. The large, maximum security, industrial prisons, such as the California State Prison at San Quentin, Illinois State Penitentiary at Stateville, Ohio State Prison at Columbus, and the State Prison of Southern Michigan, have each held more than 4,000 prisoners for many years. At one time, the State Prison of Southern Michigan held 6,500 prisoners. At the other extreme, many road prisons in the South and conservation or forestry camps in other areas have held only about 50 prisoners each. Many prisons range between 800 and 2,000 prisoners. An average population for a major prison in the United States is around 2,000, although most prisons are

Iowa State Penitentiary, Fort Madison, Iowa, constructed in 1911.
Courtesy of Iowa Department of Social Services.

smaller. There were 559 correctional facilities in the United States in 1978, 38 of them federal and 521 state facilities.[15] Some of them were "conglomerates," in that road or camp systems may have several facilities under a single administration. On March 31, 1982, as has been mentioned, there were 384,316 inmates in these facilities. There were 153 maximum security, 224 medium security, and 182 minimum security facilities. There were 142,613 inmates in maximum security, 105,601 in medium, and 30,773 in minimum security in 1978.[16] Community-based facilities were apparently included in the minimum security figures. Another report indicated that there were 791 facilities for adult correctional confinement, of which 223 were community-based, in 1979.[17] At that time, they held 11,010 inmates in community-based programs.[18] The largest number in any state as listed in that report was 1,873 in Florida.

The following lists some prisons which are particularly influential because of their size:

| Prison | Maximum Inmate Population |
|--------|--------------------------|
| 1. State Prison of Southern Michigan, Jackson | 6,500 inmates |
| 2. Ohio State Penitentiary, Columbus | 4,900 inmates |
| 3. California State Penitentiary, San Quentin | 4,800 inmates |
| 4. Illinois Penitentiary, Joliet, Stateville | |
| 5. Louisiana State Penitentiary, Angola | 3,650 inmates |
| 6. Florida State Prison, Raiford | 3,600 inmates |
| 7. Missouri Penitentiary, Jefferson City | 3,050 inmates |
| 8. Eastern State Penitentiary, Philadelphia (recently closed as a state institution and opened as a detention facility for the City of Philadelphia in 1970) | 2,850 inmates |

Prisons and correctional institutions are classified for purposes of custody into three categories—maximum, medium, and minimum. A maximum custody institution generally has walls, cell blocks with inside cell construction or back-to-back construction with each cell facing a wall, armed guard towers, wall towers, and similar security measures. A medium custody institution usually has a fence (walls prevent visibility, but fences do not), a strong perimeter with guard towers, but with generally less restriction inside the fences or compound. A minimum custody institution

[15] Joan Mullen and Bradford Smith, *American Prisons and Jails, Volume III: Conditions and Costs of Confinement* (Washington, D.C.: National Institute of Justice, U.S. Department of Justice, 1980), p. 23.

[16] *Ibid.*, p. 243.

[17] *State Correctional Population and Facilities, 1979, Advance Report* (Washington, D.C.: U.S. Department of Justice, 1981), Table 5.

[18] *Ibid.*, Table 5.

frequently possesses a single fence or no fences, no towers, and no obvious security measures. Prisoners are then classified as to the degree of security they need and are sent to the appropriate institution within the system.

## THE PRISON POPULATION

The distribution of offenses in the prison population in state institutions might appear as shown in Table 6-2.

Federal prisons, unlike state prisons, hold offenders guilty of interstate commerce crimes, failure to pay taxes on required items, such as "moonshine" and income tax, and other federal offenses. About 8 percent of the federal prisoners are there for what would be state crimes, but these crimes have been committed on federal reservations, in post offices, banks covered by the Federal Deposit Insurance Corporation, and other areas geographically and legally within federal jurisdiction. Murder, for example, is not a federal offense, as was made widely known through the news media after the assassination of President John F. Kennedy in 1963.

Most military offenses represented in the correctional installations maintained by the United States Army, Air Force, and the Navy and Marine Corps are those that would not be crimes in civilian jurisdictions. Absence without leave (AWOL), desertion, disrespect for a superior officer, and similar offenses would result only in loss of job or other security in the

**Table 6-2**

| | |
|---|---|
| Burglary | 24.1% |
| Larceny | 16.1 |
| Robbery | 9.9 |
| Auto theft | 9.8 |
| Rapes | 7.1 |
| Other sex offenses | 6.2 |
| Forgery | 4.6 |
| Weapons offenses | 4.2 |
| Offenses against family | 2.9 |
| Homicide | 2.6 |
| Embezzlement | 2.3 |
| Escape from prison | 2.2 |
| Aggravated assault | 2.1 |
| Miscellaneous | 5.9 |

*Source:* Unpublished survey by the author of the State Prison of Southern Michigan at Jackson in 1950.

Note: The proportions of offenses tend to remain similar over time. In another study, this writer compared offenses in the same prison in 1850, 1875, 1900, 1925, and 1950 and found the proportions similar, with "auto theft" replacing "horse theft"!

Hawaii State Prison, Honolulu, Hawaii, had a population of 190 men in August 1970.
Courtesy of the Hawaii Department of Social Services and Housing.

civilian setting. Of course, there are conventional offenders, too, in the military installations. The primary objective in military corrections is the restoration of the offender to duty.

## INSTITUTIONAL OBJECTIVES

In many instances, it is difficult to determine what the objective of the institutional administration and program might be. As far as the public is concerned, the objective appears to be protection, as opposed to punishment or treatment. The general public is favorably disposed to education and religion, but there is little consensus about anything else. Riots and escapes produce apprehension for the safety of residents in the area of any prison.

Corporal punishment, such as whipping, was used through colonial days and into the twentieth century. Maryland repealed its corporal punishment law in 1937. Delaware still has corporal punishment on the books, indicating that "the punishment of whipping shall be inflicted publicly by strokes on the bare back well laid on."[19] It must be noted, however, that

[19] *Delaware Code Annotated*, Title 11, Sec. 3908.

Delaware's whipping post was put into storage with the construction of a new institution and is no longer in use.

An interesting event occurred in 1980, when Delaware's 78-year-old gallows narrowly missed being sold by the Department of Corrections to pay $21,650 in legal fees.[20] The hanging rope could not be sold because the law says it must stay in the commissioner's office. Delaware still has the death penalty, of course, but it has not been used since 1946.

The attitude of the public influences the type of administration which prevails at any institution, since it influences the political leadership that, in turn, appoints the prison administrator. This system of appointment, or influence, has resulted in three broad classifications of styles of prison administration. First, many prison administrators want to exert complete control, to be "on top of any situation," and leave no doubt as to who is in charge. Their need for control results in rigidly regimented prisons with strict rules and harsh discipline. Such a prison is known as a "tough" prison, in which tension and apprehension prevail.[21]

Second, many correctional administrators are political appointees without much knowledge of correctional procedures. This type of administrator tends to simplify procedures so that prison life may be as nearly "normal" as possible. The result is an institution in which discipline is used sparingly and only when it is necessary, and which lacks a significant treatment program. The prime objective is to run the institution as quietly as possible.

Third, the prison administration may be treatment-oriented, generally headed by administrators whose careers have been committed to the field of corrections. The type of "treatment" may vary widely, from programs placing a heavy emphasis on education and training, such as those found in many reformatories and smaller correctional institutions for youthful offenders, to the sophisticated treatment programs based on group living, guided group interaction (GGI), and group therapy, such as the program at Highfields in New Jersey.

A theory of corrections is necessary to provide the base for a correctional program.[22] Difficulties in prison organization include the alienation of the officer from policy making, the illusion of unlimited authority, and the fiction of official autonomy.

The implementation of the correctional objectives also varies in direction, intensity, and effectiveness. When asked what the objective of their program is, most correctional administrators focus on rehabilitation. Reha-

[20] "For Sale: One Gallows and Hanging Rope," in "News Briefs," *Corrections Magazine,* VI, No. 1 (February, 1980), 2.

[21] See Joseph Ragen and Charles Finston, *Inside the World's Toughest Prison* (Springfield, Ill.: Charles C. Thomas, 1962). (Referring to Stateville in Illinois.)

[22] Clarence Schrag, "Some Foundations for a Theory of Corrections," in Donald R. Cressey, ed., *The Prison: Studies in Institutional Organization and Change* (New York: Holt, Rinehart & Winston, 1961), pp. 309–57.

The Leesburg Medium Security Prison, Leesburg, New Jersey, houses more than 500 inmates. The prison comprises four zones. Referring to the aerial perspective (upper), three of these zones are enclosed by a security fence. They include a housing and dining zone, consisting of six doughnut-shaped housing units plus a dining hall, which encircle the central courtyard; a rehabilitation facilities zone arranged around the east arcade to the left of the dining hall; and a prison services and work areas zone, which consists of facilities arranged around the west arcade at the right of the dining hall and the two de-

tached industrial buildings above the athletic fields. The fourth zone is the building flanked by parking lots outside the fence. It contains offices for the administration and guard facilities, and serves as the main entrance of the prison.

The main entrance leads to the reception hall, which is connected to the inner security zone by a corridor terminating at the central security section. Focal point of the housing and dining zone is the two-story dining hall overlooking the central courtyard (lower).

bilitation is the goal, of course, almost the slogan, that most frequently permeates professional conferences in the field of corrections. In viewing various patterns in the United States, five broad types of philosophy emerge in correctional practice:

First, the punishment approach has been popular in the past and has been reported in newspaper editorials and in news commentaries on radio and television. Harsh discipline and punishment are the basic tools of the old Auburn system, which furnished the pattern for many of the larger prisons in America. The laws of some states still have vestiges of punishment.

A second approach emphasizes treatment. The basic reformatory idea emphasized education as a method of "treatment." Several institutions have been established with the central ideal of treatment from a clinical approach.

The third approach is a combination of treatment and punishment. Some of the programs in New Jersey, for example, have been viewed in this manner, comparing Highfields with the rather traditional Auburn-type philosophy at the New Jersey State Prison at Trenton. Illinois also offers good examples of this combined approach. This state has an excellent diagnostic depot at Joliet, where a concentration of professional workers make a good diagnosis and recommendation for treatment, and the Illinois State Penitentiary at Stateville, which has been called "America's toughest prison."

A fourth approach emphasizes custody. Some have called it "warehousing" or "deep freeze," the idea being neither punishment nor treatment, but to keep offenders "out of the public's hair."

The fifth observable approach has been to use prisoners as a labor force for the public works. This system has predominated in the southern states.

The objectives on a day-to-day basis can best be seen by determining what the correctional workers in institutions view as most important in their in-service training programs. Table 6-3 shows the preferences expressed for future training programs in a 1969 survey of 1,282 correctional personnel employed by the Illinois Department of Public Safety.

It is apparent that security is considered to be most important and that rehabilitation and treatment are seen on a par with riot control, institutional procedures, techniques of supervision, and institutional rules.

## ORGANIZATION AND ADMINISTRATION

The organization and administration of a prison or correctional institution may vary somewhat with the size, purpose, and degree of custody of the institution. The largest prison in America is the State Prison of Southern Michigan at Jackson, which held 6,500 prisoners in the early 1950s, but held fewer than 5,000 inmates in the early 1970s because of increased use of

**Table 6-3**

| | |
|---|---|
| Security measures | 86% |
| Riot control | 66 |
| Rehabilitation and treatment | 65 |
| Institutional procedures | 64 |
| Techniques of supervision | 64 |
| Institution rules | 60 |
| Working with groups | 51 |
| Inmate's personality, etc. | 36 |
| Counseling | 21 |
| Personnel code | 20 |
| Corrections law | 20 |
| Criminal justice system | 14 |

Source: *The Correctional Trainer—Newsletter for Illinois Corrections Staff Training,*
Southern Illinois University, Carbondale, 1, No. 3 (July 1969), 9.

probation and parole; it was back to maximum capacity in 1975. The smallest correctional institutions might be halfway houses that hold from ten to thirty persons. The road camps in the South and the forestry camps in the North and West frequently contain around 50 inmates. An "average" major prison might have about 2,000 inmates and be staffed by 400 personnel. The average ratio of prisoners to free personnel is 5 to 1, although there is a wide variation, from probably around 50 to 1 in Arkansas, Mississippi, and Louisiana to probably 3 to 1 in New York.

The chief administrator of the prison is the warden or superintendent. England refers to the chief administrator of the prison as "governor." The most commonly used terms in America are "warden" and "superintendent." Whatever his title, the chief administrator's function is complex. As a public relations man, he appears before civic groups, at conferences, and other places where it is advantageous for the work of the prison to be interpreted. The interpretations may range from image-making to honest and substantive discussion of problems and needs. Many prison administrators become defensive, particularly in time of trouble, and they may exclude reporters and issue no statements. Others open the gates of the prison to newspeople and let them have free access to everything. In any case, the warden or superintendent often determines public relations policy, although his superior in the central office, or the governor, may give him other directives.

The warden must present the budget to the budget commission, budget director, or other fiscal agents of the executive department. Subsequently, he may have to defend the budget before legislative committees. He may be responsible for personnel policies. He makes policy decisions when members or factions within his institution conflict over issues. Reporting to the warden or superintendent is the deputy warden or associate

Inside a cellblock at the California State Prison at San Quentin.
Courtesy of the California Department of Corrections.

warden. In the traditional prison, this deputy warden is primarily responsible for custody or the safety and security of the institution.

The political appointment of wardens has been a significant handicap in developing good correctional programs. The defense for it, of course, is that in a relatively primitive and turbulent political setting where the spoils and patronage system follows every election, it is important to know the political terrain. In such a setting, the administrator representing an institution had better know the politics and the political system within which he is dealing or he will be ineffectual in dealing with the legislature on whom he is dependent for appropriations. It has been demonstrated several times that when a career correctional expert is placed as administrator in a turbulent political system where he does not understand the politics, he is soon dismissed under fire. In only a few of the advanced and politically stable correctional systems, such as the one in New York, the United States Bureau of Prisons, and several others, can a career correctional administrator be hired without being primarily concerned with politics.

Correctional Training Facility at Soledad, California.
Courtesy of California Department of Corrections.

The best administrator, of course, is a career correctional administrator with political acumen.

Other important areas in the prison are (1) the school program, (2) the classification system, (3) the chaplain and the religious program, (4) the hospital and dental services, (5) industries, (6) the farm, (7) the chief engineer and maintenance departments, (8) the business management department (which generally also has charge of the kitchen and dining room, clothing issue and laundry), (9) psychiatric and mental health services, which sometimes includes a mental ward, (10) recreation, (11) the library, which is sometimes independent and sometimes under the school program, and (12) administrative services, such as an accounting, personnel, and record office where court papers and institutional reports are filed and where prison papers are signed.

The heads of the various departments may report to the deputy warden or they may wonder to whom they are supposed to report. In a maximum security institution, the department head knows that whenever any custodial personnel, from the lowest officer to the deputy warden, "suggests" something for the safety and security of the institution, he had better act on it. The custodial function is the most important function in the traditional prison.

Since World War II, there has been a trend toward establishing two deputy wardens or associate wardens, one for custody and one for treatment. The new organizational chart for prison, then, would have two deputy wardens reporting to the warden. Both have equal rank and attempt to

Cellblock in the California State Prison at Folsom.
Courtesy of California Department of Corrections.

work out problems and issues between them. The warden is consulted for decisions generally only when the two deputy wardens cannot resolve an issue. Also since World War II, the warden has increasingly become *the* administrator of the prison. The modern warden is generally an educated and sophisticated administrator who goes inside his prison, has staff meetings, and functions as any other administrator would function. The old political, traditional type of prison administration remains in only a few small prisons. All the progressive prisons have fused the functions of custody and treatment. As one administrator said, "It used to be *your* side and *my* side. Now it's *our* side."[23]

The maximum security prison can be compared to totalitarian societies.[24] While today's correctional programs are emphasizing rehabilitation and program, changes come slowly in the maximum security prison. The

[23] Conversation with Louie L. Wainwright, Director of Corrections, State of Florida, and president of the American Correctional Association, 1970.

[24] Henry Burns, Jr., "A Miniature Totalitarian State Maximum Security Prison," *The Canadian Journal of Corrections*, 11, No. 3 (July 1969), 153–54.

six features of a totalitarian regime appear in the maximum custody prison: (1) the totalitarian ideology focused on custody; (2) a single mass party headed by an authoritarian and totalitarian dictatorship; (3) a terroristic police control that includes a system of rewards and punishment to assure cohesiveness in implementing the ideology; (4) a communications monopoly to the public that includes public relations techniques and censorship; (5) a weapons monopoly, where the inside is free of anything that could be used in armed combat, but weapons in the hands of employees provide a strong perimeter and overlook the prison yard; and (6) a centrally controlled economy through bureaucratic coordination where expansion, conflicting staff, and in-fighting continues. Institutional procedures are expected to operate as they always have, and the deputy warden becomes concerned when he learns that one of the staff has discussed a point with the warden without informing him or going through channels. An authoritarian system reduces those upon whom it presses to a state of irresponsibility.

Good time, gain time, or time off for good behavior has several patterns. Generally, there is a regular gain time and a special gain time, the first frequently being two months off the first year and the second being an additional month for the first offender. Second (or more) offenders generally have a reduced amount of regular and special gain time. The gain time is graduated, so that the longer the prisoner serves, the more gain time he receives. A typical length of stay for a first offender with a 25-year sentence would be about 12.5 years.

By 1982, the average cost per day for adult prisons had more than quadrupled by inflation and by court-ordered improvements in programs. Fiscal information was provided in the American Correctional Association's 1982 *Directory,* published in 1983.[25] Information from 42 jurisdictions indicates that the average cost per day to keep inmates is $41.36, while the average yearly cost is $15,106.74, as computed from the figures reported in various forms. No information was available from ten jurisdictions, including the Federal Prison System, the Military Services, New York, Texas, and six other states. The proportionate costs were distributed similarly to the 1975 costs in Table 6-4.

The cost of building maximum security institutions and the cost of keeping people in prison has gone up considerably since 1975. The cost of building a maximum security facility is over $70,000 per bed in many jurisdictions as diverse as California, Minnesota, and Rhode Island.[26] Alaska spends $130,000 per cell for average prison construction. Medium

[25] *Directory: Juvenile and Adult Correctional Departments, Institutions, Agencies and Paroling Authorities,* 1982 Edition (College Park, Md.: American Correctional Association, 1983), p. 433.

[26] "Juveniles Tied to 23 Percent of Nation's Violent Crimes," *Juvenile Justice Digest,* 9, No. 17 (August 21, 1981), 7, reporting from the *Final Report of the Attorney General's Task Force on Violent Crime,* Washington, D.C., released August 17, 1981.

**Table 6-4    Cost per day of maintaining prisoners, by state and census regions, 1975**

| | Regions | Average Cost | States | Cost |
|---|---|---|---|---|
| **Northeast** | New England | $14.82 | Maine | $ 9.04 |
| | | | Vermont | 21.97 |
| | | | New Hampshire | 8.64 |
| | | | Massachusetts | 15.31 |
| | | | Connecticut | 15.07 |
| | | | Rhode Island | 18.87 |
| | Middle Atlantic | 10.49 | New York | 13.51 |
| | | | Pennsylvania | 7.00 |
| | | | New Jersey | 10.96 |
| **South** | South Atlantic | 8.60 | Delaware | 7.50 |
| | | | District of Columbia | 13.70 |
| | | | Maryland | 14.00 |
| | | | Virginia | 7.00 |
| | | | West Virginia | 9.32 |
| | | | North Carolina | 8.93 |
| | | | South Carolina | 5.17 |
| | | | Georgia | 5.68 |
| | | | Florida | 6.08 |
| | East South Central | 4.45 | Kentucky | 5.50 |
| | | | Tennessee | 5.48 |
| | | | Alabama | 4.93 |
| | | | Mississippi | 1.90 |
| | West South Central | 4.69 | Oklahoma | 4.33 |
| | | | Arkansas | 5.75 |
| | | | Louisiana | 5.50 |
| | | | Texas | 3.16 |
| **North Central** | East North Central | 11.97 | Wisconsin | 10.69 |
| | | | Michigan | 8.56 |
| | | | Ohio | 16.89 |
| | | | Indiana | 10.00 |
| | | | Illinois | 13.69 |
| | West North Central | 9.78 | North Dakota | 12.05 |
| | | | South Dakota | 8.90 |
| | | | Minnesota | 12.09 |
| | | | Iowa | 11.00 |
| | | | Nebraska | 8.25 |
| | | | Kansas | 9.75 |
| | | | Missouri | 6.44 |
| **West** | Pacific | 13.85 | Alaska | 17.50 |
| | | | Washington | 16.36 |
| | | | Oregon | 12.81 |
| | | | California | 2.60 |
| | | | Hawaii | 20.00 |
| | Mountain | 11.33 | Nevada | 10.96 |
| | | | Utah | 11.23 |
| | | | Arizona | 7.51 |
| | | | New Mexico | 7.32 |
| | | | Montana | 23.69 |
| | | | Idaho | 11.00 |
| | | | Wyoming | 7.67 |
| | | | Colorado | 11.23 |
| Average of all states' averages | | 9.99 | | |

*Source:* Kenneth J. Lenihan, "The Financial Condition of Released Prisoners," *Crime and Delinquency,* 21, No. 3 (July 1975), 277.

security institutional costs are about $50,000 per bed. New jail construction is costing $50,000 per cell in metropolitan areas. Expenditures for yearly operating costs range between $10,000 and $20,000 or higher. By 1983, the average cost was $23,000 per year.

Some departments have listed their operating costs in the 1982 *Directory* of the American Correctional Association.[27] They are about two-thirds to a half higher than the 1975 figures, but the proportions remain similar.

In summary, imprisonment is costly. You could go to the best universities in the land for what it costs to keep a person in a maximum custody prison. Ten to thirteen people could be well supervised in the community, whether on probation, parole, or in community-based programs, for what it costs to keep one person in prison. Some average costs of maintaining prisoners alone, on a daily basis, are shown in Table 6-4.

## WOMEN'S PRISONS

The 6,175 female offenders in federal and state correctional institutions in 1973 constituted 4.8 percent of the total prison population. Most states have a separate women's prison or a women's unit at the central prison, but some contract with neighboring states to care for the women because of the low population. For example, Idaho has a contract with Oregon to care for its women prisoners. Indiana was the first state to establish a separate women's prison in Indianapolis in 1873.

The Women's Prison Association, headquartered in New York City, in 1972 surveyed 153 correctional institutions, 40 halfway houses, and 70 private agencies which served women to determine the problems and needs of women prisoners.[28] Of the women prisoners, 78 percent were serving time for felonies, 43 percent were white, 45 percent were in the 22–30 age group, 24 percent were married, 46 percent had less than a tenth-grade education, and 67 percent had children dependent upon them. Most of the prisons were in remote areas, making visits from family and children difficult; for the states that have contracts with nearby states for incarceration, this is a further difficulty.

Recommendations of the survey by the Women's Prison Association included a first priority for jobs and job training, since women are the sole support of children in many cases. Supervised diversion from institutionalization was recommended so that women can maintain contact with their children and family, receive counseling, job training, job placement, medical assistance, and other services. Community-based corrections for women was emphasized, including work release and study release.

[27] *Directory: Juvenile and Adult Correctional Departments,* p. 393.

[28] Omar Hendrix, *A Study in Neglect: A Report on Women Prisoners, July 15–October 15, 1972* [New York: The Women's Prison Association, 1973 (mimeographed)], pp. 28–44.

## COEDUCATIONAL PRISONS

There have been several coeducational institutions for juveniles, one of the first being Kentucky Village at Ormsby in 1968, now closed. Several states and the United States Bureau of Prisons have coeducational prisons for juveniles. The first coeducational prison for adults was the Massachusetts Correctional Institution at Framingham, formerly the women's prison, which became coeducational in 1973. The former United States Public Health facility at Fort Worth, Texas, became a coeducational prison with the United States Bureau of Prisons in 1974. There are problems, of course, involved in coeducational prisons. According to Acting Superintendent Peter Bishop of Framingham, sexual activity is prohibited, but that is not to say it does not occur.[29] The general consensus among correctional personnel is that it is better to have that kind of problem occurring than what occurs in a unisexual or homosexual institution. Another problem that has been observed is that partners who may have spouses on the outside may "fall in love" with a person in the institution, and some officials have expressed fear that it may break up some existing marriages.

In the coeducational prison, inmates may eat together, study together, and associate with each other generally, except in sleeping arrangements. The men tend to behave better in the presence of women, have fewer fights, and take some pride in their appearance, and incidences of homosexuality are reduced. Denmark and Sweden both have coeducational prisons in which inmates are permitted to have sex on the theory that women "tame" men and make them more civilized.

## ORGANIZATION WITHIN PRISON SYSTEMS

Prison systems in the states and the United States Bureau of Prisons have a variety of institutions for different purposes and degrees of custody. Each has at least one maximum security unit that can hold anybody who needs to be held. At the other extreme, all systems now have minimum security units without much external control or regimentation. All systems also have medium security units at varying degrees between the extreme maximum and the minimum security units.

There are several types of organizations used by the states to supervise the prisons. The oldest and probably the most primitive type of organization features a board of trustees for each institution. Arkansas, Connecticut, New Hampshire, and New Mexico used boards of trustees recently, but they have now established departments of corrections. A second type of organization consists of an *ex officio* board made up of state officials who are on the board because of the positions they hold. The *ex officio* board is prob-

---

[29] "First Coed Prison Discounts 'Laymen Fantasies,'" *Corrections Digest,* 5, No. 19 (September 18, 1974), 2.

ably less desirable than other types of boards because the primary duties of its members are in other areas, and consequently, they may neglect the prison system. *Ex officio* boards are found in Montana, Nevada, and Wyoming. A third type of supervisory organization is a board of control, a part-time board of citizens appointed by the governor. Boards of this type tend to emphasize business phases, since that is what the members know best. Centralized boards (North Dakota, Colorado, Kansas, Idaho, South Dakota, Utah, Mississippi) represent a fourth type of supervisory organization and one which also tends to stress business.

The two most popular forms of state administration of correctional systems are to have corrections (1) a division within a larger department, and (2) a separate department of corrections or "offender rehabilitation." The division and department concepts seem to give corrections enough separate identity to allow centralization of budgetary matters and other concerns of administration and, simultaneously, provide sufficient framework for professional career service and staff development.

Divisions of corrections within larger departments fall into three categories: divisions in departments of justice, institutions, and public welfare. Corrections is a division of the Department of Justice in Pennsylvania and in the United States government. It is a division within a Department of Institutions in New Jersey, Tennessee, Vermont, and Washington. It is a division within the Department of Public Welfare or Social Welfare in Virginia, Kentucky, Rhode Island, and Wisconsin. Ohio has its Division of Corrections in the Department of Corrections and Mental Hygiene.

Separate departments of corrections exist in Alabama, Arizona, Arkansas, California, Colorado, District of Columbia, Connecticut, Florida, Georgia, Illinois, Indiana, Iowa, Kansas, Kentucky, Louisiana (institutions), Massachusetts, Michigan, Minnesota, Nebraska, New Mexico, New York, North Carolina, Oklahoma, Rhode Island, South Carolina, Tennessee, Texas, Vermont, and Virginia.

Vermont closed its prison in 1975 and negotiated a contract with the United States Bureau of Prisons to house forty inmates in federal facilities.[30]

The separate department of corrections is considered to be the best administrative setup by most correctional administrators. Advantages of centralization are that it provides better administration in terms of central purchasing, central accounting, central personnel policies, central classification, central statistical research and identification facilities, and central training facilities. Interdepartmental contracts are easier to negotiate and implement in a separate department. Frequently, the correctional system must enter into contracts with forestry and conservation departments, state police, sheriffs' groups, city police, prosecutors' associations, the judiciary, state and local boards of education, vocational rehabilitation programs,

---

[30] "Shutting Down Windsor Prison Creates Problems," *Corrections Magazine,* 2, No. 1 (September /October 1975), 36–37.

university dental and medical schools, and any of a number of other mutually beneficial relationships. The primary difficulty with having corrections as a division within a larger department is that this setup adds a significant additional office through which the correctional administration must go for action and policy decisions. An administrator of a separate department can go directly to the significant officers in state government, legislators and legislative committees, budget officers and commissions, and others without having to go through another administrator above him.

## INDUSTRIES AND PRISONER EMPLOYMENT

The employment of prisoners and the work they do have been central in the development of prisons and correctional institutions. The first workhouses in the sixteenth century were the forerunners of our modern prisons and correctional institutions. The Pennsylvania system placed a premium on hard labor, and the Auburn system emphasized congregate labor. Subsequent prison systems have emphasized work and, in many instances, the self-supporting prison. The New York prisons at Auburn and Sing Sing were paying for themselves by 1828. Large industrial prisons were also built in the Midwest and in California.

Prison industries have constituted an important part of the American prison since its inception. The Pennsylvania system begun in 1790 promoted "solitary confinement at hard labor" to reflect its founders' belief in isolation—to prevent moral contamination—combined with the dignity of labor. The Auburn system began with solitary confinement at night and congregate labor in silence by day. The early prisons in the Midwest and South were based on contracting or leasing prisoners to private industry or agriculture. The development of industrial prisons in California continued that pattern in the late nineteenth century.

Then, pressure from organized industry curtailed the industrial objective. The resulting restrictive legislation began in the early 1920s. The most serious federal legislation was the Hawes-Cooper Act of 1929, which divested prison-made goods of their interstate characteristics and went into effect on January 1, 1934. The effect was that they could not be used in interstate commerce—they could not be shipped across state lines. The Ashurst-Sumners Act of 1935 prohibited companies from accepting prison-made goods for transportation into any other state in violation of the laws of that state and required use of the "prison-made" label for any such goods involved in interstate commerce. The Walsh-Healy Act of October 14, 1940, excluded almost all prison-made products from interstate commerce. By 1940, every state had passed some similar sort of limitation on prison-made products. Some labor organizations have also made themselves felt in legislation against prison labor. For example, many states have statutes preventing the use of skilled labor on public highways or other public projects. The resulting enforced idleness in prisons has not been

Production of wooden furniture is a main area in the industries operation at Iowa State Penitentiary, Fort Madison, Iowa.
Courtesy of the Iowa Department of Social Services.

compensated for by corresponding programs in education or other activities.

The purposes of industries in the prison are (1) to provide productive work for the inmates, and (2) to perform work and produce goods for the state that would otherwise have to be purchased at high cost from private concerns. At the present time, idleness is one of the primary problems in American prisons. There are not enough teaching personnel, enough industry, or enough productive work of any kind to occupy the entire prison population to the fullest extent.

Systems of prisoner employment have always been part of the correctional program. From 1790 to 1800, the piece-price system was used at the Walnut Street Jail. Under this system, a private contractor furnished the raw material and received the finished product, and the work was done in the prison for an agreed price. From 1790 to about 1865, the contract system was widely used. The prisoners were let out to private contractors under supervision of prison personnel, while the contractor furnished the equipment and raw materials and supervised the work. From the Civil War to about 1936, the lease system was common throughout the South. All prisoners were leased to the highest bidder so that the system generated income, rather than having to be supported by tax funds.

There are three systems of prisoner employment currently in use by various prisons. One is the public or state account system in which goods are produced in prison and sold on the open market. A second is the state use system, in which goods are produced and used by other state agencies and offices or political subdivisions, frequently schools and jails. The third is the public works and ways system, which provides labor for construction and maintenance of roads, parks, conservation projects, and other public facilities.

Farming has been a special form of prison labor for many years, although with the development of advanced technology, some prison systems have found it unprofitable to maintain farms. Several juvenile institutions have hired farm manager corporations to operate their farms, and these corporations generally make it a stipulation that they do not have to use the boys or inmates but can hire their own labor. Experience seems to indicate that the farm manager corporations can make money for the institution over and above their fee, while the institution generally operates its own farms in the red when an adequate accounting system is used to assess the operation.

The most prevalent systems of prison labor today are the state use system, the public works and ways system, and farming. Farming seems to be the most acceptable system as far as special interest groups in the public are concerned. Farmers are traditionally independent, and their organizations have made no political objections aimed at restricting farm operations. Several large farm systems, including those in Arkansas, Texas, and Mississippi, consider their operations to be profitable.

The peak year for prison production in America was 1923, when $74,000,000 worth of materials was made in the prisons. Since then, despite that small amount when compared with the gross national product, lobbyists for special interest groups have successfully restricted prison industry.

Full employment of prisoners is essential, whether in industry or in educational processes.[31] It is a political matter as to how this employment should be financed and how much it costs the public in tax funds to cut off prison production and substitute private contracts. It could be that the interest groups who object to prison labor and products might want to pay for the programs to replace labor and production.

The primary goals of prison industry, as stated in the *Correctional Industries Association Newsletter,* are to provide useful and meaningful work, to provide trade training and practice, to instill self-discipline and inculcate work habits, and generally to prepare a person for release back to the community as a self-respecting, wage-earning citizen.[32]

[31] Ernest E. Means, *Prison Industries and Rehabilitative Programs* (Tallahassee: Florida Division of Corrections and Florida State University Institute of Governmental Research, March 1964).

[32] *Correctional Industries Association Newsletter,* 1, No. 2 (October 1968), 4.

A resurgence of support for prison industries began in the mid-1970s and reached recognizable proportions in 1982–1983. Minnesota has always had binder twine on the open market because it does not compete with in-state manufacturing. In addition, the Free Venture project funded by LEAA in 1975 promoted the transforming of traditional prison industries into profit-making businesses that benefit both the correctional system and participating inmates.[33] Since its founding, Colorado, Connecticut, Illinois, Iowa, South Carolina, and Washington have joined the effort. Kansas has begun a metal fabrication shop, called Zephyr Industries, in 1981 to make cabinets, carts, brackets, and other metal products.[34] Arizona has begun Resident Operated Business Enterprises (ROBE), in which the inmates have become the entrepreneurs and offer a bakery, auto body repair shop, photo-copying, belt buckle design and manufacture, and fishing lines and flies. Utah operates a graphics program in which the inmate employees have been granted the status of "employees of the state." Nevada has two projects based on free enterprise for inmates, the General Household Company that manufactures brooms, brushes, and mops, and the Satellite Video Technology Company of Las Vegas to manufacture Fiberglas disk antennae. When the Federal Prison Industries was created by Congress in 1934 as a corporation (18 USC 4121), it was recognized that there was a need to reduce idleness in prisons and to provide inmates with practical knowledge and skills necessary to obtain and retain employment after their release. This move received official support when Chief Justice Warren Burger said on June 11, 1983, and repeated many times afterward "prisons should be converted into factories," that inmates be paid and then pay their own way in prison, and gain the benefits of a normal work-a-day world.[35]

## INMATE SELF-GOVERNMENT

Many correctional administrators have said that most prisons are run by inmates. This contention stems from the fact that most of the clerical and technical skills come from the inmate body in many prisons whose budgets are too low to hire civilian clerical and technical skills. For example, most prisons rely on inmate carpenters, inmate plumbers, inmate typists, and inmate radio repairmen. Further, many prisons in the past have hired guards or correctional officers and sent them into the cell block or prison yards without recruiter in-service training, leaving them dependent upon

[33] *Improved Prison Work Programs Will Benefit Correctional Institutions and Inmates—Report to the Attorney General* (Washington, D.C.: General Accounting Office, June 29, 1982), 39.

[34] Ron Bertothy, "Prison Industries: Taking a Closer Look at the Seven State Pilot Projects," *Corrections Digest,* 14, No. 11 (May 18, 1983), 5.

[35] "Burger Again Calls for More Prison Industries," *Corrections Digest,* 14, No. 13, (June 15, 1983), 1.

friendly inmates to guide them as to their duties. In most prisons, then, there is a balance between inmate control and civilian control. Whether a particular prison emphasizes civilian control or inmate control is generally dependent upon the ratio of civilian employees to inmates.

Probably the extreme of inmate control could be found in some southern and southwestern states. Arkansas, Mississippi, and Louisiana still rely on inmate guards, and other states from Oklahoma to Florida historically employed them in the early twentieth century. Several states, such as South Carolina, still rely heavily on trusted inmates, or "trusties," for many routines, such as meeting visitors at the airport, delivering and picking up supplies and equipment, and bookkeeping and accounting.

In every prison there is an informal inmate control that makes the prison run smoothly. Inmates who have been placed in positions of responsibility have a "good go," so they have an investment in the system. They will take necessary steps to preserve that system and will help keep the other inmates in control. This type of informal social control imposed by the inmate body upon itself can help correctional administrators run their prisons without disturbance. In return for this healthy type of self-government, up through the years, privileges may be permitted to grow—for example, the conjugal visits allowed in Mississippi, which have received favorable attention recently. The work release program in North Carolina was initiated as an economic measure, but its social advantages were readily recognized. Inmates participating in it will guard the privilege and control other inmates whose behavior may threaten the system.

There have been several moves toward formalizing this inmate self-government. The first formal effort occurred at the Michigan State Prison, now the State Prison of Southern Michigan, at Jackson in 1885. Warden Hyram F. Atch devised the self-government, called "The Mutual Aid League."[36] It did not last long for a variety of reasons, some of them political. Thomas Mott Osborne established the Mutual Welfare League at Auburn during World War I, and it worked well for a few years. Failure of adequate protections and controls resulted in its abolition about 1928, when a few powerful inmate leaders were using it for their own purposes. Adequate administrative controls are necessary, just as they are necessary for student government in a school or university or for civilian government under military occupation. The most widely used system at present is the inmate council, well developed by the United States Bureau of Prisons, in which elected inmates discuss policies and complaints with the warden and/or associate warden. Some systems use inmate suggestion boxes.

Policies as to who goes to prison are not constant. There is considerable variation between states as to the proportion of people in prison. Table 6-5 shows the number of persons imprisoned per 100,000 population in 1973 in each state in the United States.

[36] Harold M. Helfman, "Antecedents of Thomas Mott Osborne's Mutual Welfare League in Michigan," *Journal of Criminal Law and Criminology*, 40, No. 5 (January–February 1950), 597–600.

**Table 6-5  Prisoners per 100,000 population, by region and state, 1979**

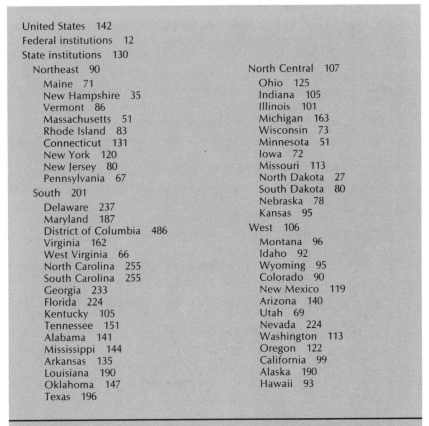

United States  142
Federal institutions  12
State institutions  130

| | |
|---|---|
| Northeast  90 | North Central  107 |
| Maine  71 | Ohio  125 |
| New Hampshire  35 | Indiana  105 |
| Vermont  86 | Illinois  101 |
| Massachusetts  51 | Michigan  163 |
| Rhode Island  83 | Wisconsin  73 |
| Connecticut  131 | Minnesota  51 |
| New York  120 | Iowa  72 |
| New Jersey  80 | Missouri  113 |
| Pennsylvania  67 | North Dakota  27 |
| South  201 | South Dakota  80 |
| Delaware  237 | Nebraska  78 |
| Maryland  187 | Kansas  95 |
| District of Columbia  486 | West  106 |
| Virginia  162 | Montana  96 |
| West Virginia  66 | Idaho  92 |
| North Carolina  255 | Wyoming  95 |
| South Carolina  255 | Colorado  90 |
| Georgia  233 | New Mexico  119 |
| Florida  224 | Arizona  140 |
| Kentucky  105 | Utah  69 |
| Tennessee  151 | Nevada  224 |
| Alabama  141 | Washington  113 |
| Mississippi  144 | Oregon  122 |
| Arkansas  135 | California  99 |
| Louisiana  190 | Alaska  190 |
| Oklahoma  147 | Hawaii  93 |
| Texas  196 | |

*Source: Prisoners in State and Federal Institutions,* National Prisoner Statistics Bulletin SD-NPS-PSF-7, p. 34. Adapted by *Sourcebook of Criminal Justice Statistics—1981* (Washington, D.C.: Bureau of Justice Statistics, 1982), p. 471.

## PROCESSING PRISONERS, OR CASE MANAGEMENT

The processing of prisoners is essentially similar in all prisons and prison systems, although the quality and effectiveness of this case management varies. There is an initial evaluation upon reception into the institution or system. It takes place either at a central reception or diagnostic center or in quarantine at the host institution. When the prisoner arrives at the institution, a file is set up in the record office. All departments are notified, such as the control room (custody), the deputy warden's office, the classification department, school, identification bureau (pictures and fingerprints), chaplain, inmate accounting office, medical officer, and all other departments whose services and procedures are affected by the arrival and presence of a prisoner.

Generally, this notification is done by consulting a daily roster of persons who have arrived at the prison from the courts. A much more effective notification technique is the use of an Addressograph machine with two plates. Within five minutes, the following information can be recorded on the plate:

| | |
|---|---|
| Name | Race (for identification) |
| Crime and sentence | Status (new, parole violator, etc.) |
| Dates of sentence and arrival | Birthdate |
| Sentencing court and judge | Religious preference |

Once these items are accurate on the metal plate, there are no typographical errors. If the appropriate forms from each department are stored in the record office or near the Addressograph machine, they can then immediately be imprinted with this information, a runner can deliver the imprinted forms to the departments, and the processing can begin easily.

After the classification study or social history has been completed, the lower plate can be completed and distributed, as follows:

| | |
|---|---|
| Sentence expiration computed with regular good time | Primary occupation (*Dictionary of Occupational Titles Code*) |
| Sentence expiration computed with special good time | Social Security number |
| Military history (branch, dates, type of discharge—coded) | Criminal history (by code—juvenile, adult, escapes) |
| IQ grade by test-grade completed | Medical history and status (by code) |
| Home address | Marital status and dependents |

This information, once correct, can be stamped on all forms used by all departments. In addition, the plates can be coded with tabs for selection purposes, although coding is more easily accomplished by computer. The use of machines makes personnel much more effective and is generally worth the expenditure, particularly in a large prison system.

After this information is gathered, the classification committee or treatment team makes assignments. During the incarceration, prisoners may be reclassified and assigned new jobs or programs any number of times.

As the date for expiration of a minimum sentence arrives, an evaluation is made for the parole board with a recommendation for or against parole, together with reasons. When a prisoner is released from the prison, even more care is taken than when he arrived. Careful rechecks of fingerprints and other identification are necessary to ascertain that the correct person is being released. Rigid release procedures are outlined in writing in most institutions.

# SUMMARY

The history of international corrections indicates that the United States took the lead in prison architecture from 1773 to 1811; England caught up with the construction of Millbank Prison on the Thames, which was opened in 1816; and France overtook them both with the telephone-pole type of architecture in 1898.[37]

Prisons and correctional facilities form the core of the correctional system. They range in security from maximum to minimum, and the systems range in size from 1,000 to 31,000 or more inmates. The programs they offer vary from specialized clinical services to virtually nothing. Security and custody remain primary concerns in American prisons, but education and treatment programs are now being developed. The current focus of new programs is on integration of the institution into the total correctional process.

## EXERCISES AND STUDY QUESTIONS

1. Why is the prison probably the most significant part of the correctional system?

2. How many persons are in prison and correctional institutions at any given time?

3. Discuss the early development of prisons in America, with particular attention to the Pennsylvania System and the Auburn System.

4. What was the pattern of development of prisons in various parts of the country?

5. Identify the classifications of custody.

6. What is the distribution of major crimes found among prison inmates?

7. How do federal prisoners differ from state prisoners?

8. How does the attitude of the public influence the administration of prisons?

9. Evaluate women's prisons in America.

10. Evaluate the punishment approach, the sentimental approach, and treatment approach in corrections.

11. Identify five broad types of philosophy that emerge throughout the country in corrections.

12. What are the functions of the warden or superintendent of a prison?

[37] Giuseppe di Gennaro et al., *Prison Architecture: An International Survey of Representative Closed Institutions and Analysis of Current Trends in Prison Design* (London: United Nations Social Defence Research Institute and The Architectural Press, Ltd., 1975), pp. 19–23.

13. What are the advantages and disadvantages of political appointments of wardens in different political situations?

14. How is a prison organized, and what departments are represented?

15. Evaluate the recent trend toward appointing two associate wardens or deputy wardens, one for custody and one for treatment.

16. Discuss the statewide organization of prisons and correctional institutions, and evaluate the advantages of a separate department of corrections.

17. What are the advantages and disadvantages of prison industries?

18. Evaluate informal and formal inmate self-government

19. Evaluate coeducational prisons.

20. What is the range of the number of prisoners per 100,000 population among states, and why does variation exist?

# 7

# INSTITUTIONAL PROCEDURES— CUSTODY

Institutions are designed to receive, to house and care for, and to release people sentenced or committed to their care. Custody, or the safety and security of the institution and the prevention of escapes, is of primary concern among correctional administrators. The institution cannot treat inmates if it does not have them. Further, the type of treatment that is best is sometimes a matter of debate, while security is not considered to be debatable. Any discussion of institutional procedures must include custody, treatment in terms of classification and other approaches, housekeeping, and administrative procedures.

Traditional custody involves well-known established procedures, such as counting, shaking down cells, tower duty, making disciplinary reports, and other procedures that can be taught easily and in which the correctional officer can be expert. The newer view of custody, however, is in the direction of "mass treatment." Correctional treatment is usually nonspecific and involves procedures that are only very broadly standardized, if at all. The shifts from the old type of guard to the new correctional worker or correctional office is a significant one. It involves communicating effectively, understanding (empathy), caring (respect), and a genuine relationship with the inmate so that the officer's level of tolerance can be increased significantly and he can be more effective in working with people.[1] The following discussion of custody covers the traditional and day-to-day custo-

[1] William L. Megathlin, *The Effects of Facilitation Training Provided Correctional Officers Stationed at the Atlanta Federal Penitentiary* (Athens, Ga.: U.S. Department of Justice and the University of Georgia, 1969).

dial functions and leads into the newer, treatment-oriented custodial procedures.

## FUNCTION OF CUSTODY

The long-range function of custody is to provide external controls for persons who have not internalized the social controls sufficiently well to get along without outside social forces. Enlightened custody attempts to provide only that amount of external control which is immediately necessary and to gradually reduce that external control as the individual is able to function in society on his own devices. This function really exists in the family, the school, the gang, organized and unorganized recreation, the church, and throughout all society. Custody in corrections is generally better organized, because it deals with more people whose behavior has to be more severely controlled to prevent them from damaging themselves or society.

The purposes of custody are (1) to prevent escape, (2) to maintain peace and order within the institution, and (3) to perform these two functions with the least possible hindrance to the primary objectives of the program, thereby promoting efficient functioning of the overall institutional

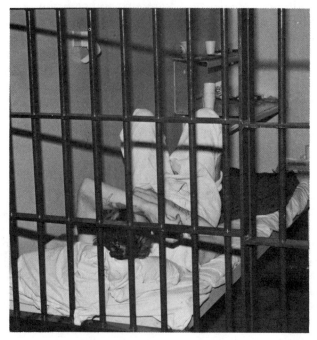

A typical cell at Iowa State Penitentiary. Each man is housed in an individual cell within the institution.
Courtesy of the Iowa Department of Social Services.

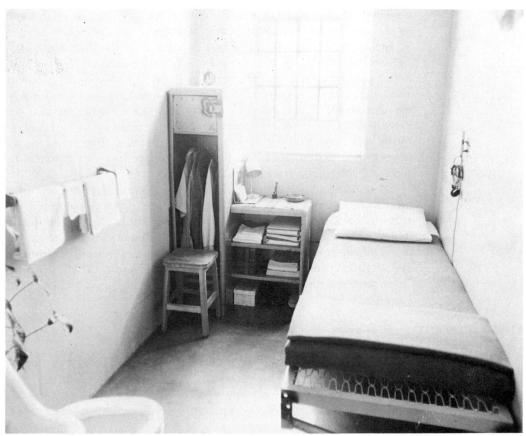

Living quarters (a cell) at the California Medical Facility at Vacaville.
Courtesy of the California Department of Corrections.

program. The primary objective of correctional institutions is to rehabilitate offenders so they can re-enter society as contributing citizens or, at least, not dangerous ones. Whether the institutional program is based on education, clinical services, or just a holding operation, custody must permit the program to function. The most secure institution might be one that keeps the inmates in their cells all the time, but it would be difficult to operate a school or any other program that way. Consequently, the institution is faced with finding the appropriate balance between program and security.

The techniques by which custody is maintained can be classified broadly as (1) segregation, and (2) controlled movement of inmates. In the most secure prisons, each inmate is in a separate cell. Some prisons have two or more inmates in a cell, while many correctional institutions use the dormitory concept. Each type of domicile has different custodial advantages and problems.

Segregation is used administratively for discipline and to isolate problems. All prisons have their troublemakers, agitators, or quarrelsome people who cannot get along with others. Some prisons isolate all these troublemakers in a single unit. Other prisons distribute them throughout the population and permit the informal inmate control to handle the problem. Most prison wardens seem to favor the diffusion of problems, rather than their concentration in one place, reserving the latter for those few who cannot be controlled by the other inmates. This isolation is generally reserved for (1) disciplinary purposes for inmates who have violated institutional rules and regulations, and (2) administrative segregation to prevent inmates from assaulting or being assaulted by other prisoners and to control extreme homosexual activities.

The controlled movement of inmates within the prison is an important feature in custody. Moving inmates from cell blocks to central dining halls and back must be worked out. Some maximum custody institutions march inmates in military-type companies. The majority use informal lines accompanied by correctional officers. Many minimum security institutions exercise little or no control, permitting the inmates to go from their domicile or work assignment to the dining hall at specific times.

## PHYSICAL PLANT

The interdependence of correctional philosophy and construction of the physical plant has been obvious since the beginning of prisons.[2] As mentioned in Chapter 4, institutions are classified as maximum, medium, and minimum security, depending upon the presence or absence of walls, towers, and other security measures.

The physical plant and equipment has an influence on custody. Maximum custody institutions generally have high walls, although some recent ones have fences and are well guarded from towers. Medium security institutions generally have fences. Minimum custody institutions may or may not have fences. The purpose of a wall or fence is to keep prisoners in and to prevent the passage of contraband. A general principle of wall and fence construction is that there should be a minimum of wall openings combined with remote control of the gate. The wall has been the most expensive item in security. Outside towers are sometimes built with bullet-proof glass, although usually with plain glass, and guards there are well armed and equipped with binoculars. Wall towers are generally less well equipped. The Illinois State Penitentiary at Stateville has inside towers in its circular cell blocks. Inside ground posts are generally located on the prison yard, unarmed, and are used as headquarters for the unarmed yard sergeant on duty.

Outside ground posts are generally unmanned and situated between

[2] See Chap. IV, "The Development and Interdependence of Correctional Philosophy and Construction," in *Handbook of Correctional Institution and Design* (Washington, D.C.: U.S. Bureau of Prisons, 1949).

Example of overcrowding at the State Prison of Southern Michigan at Jackson.
Courtesy of the Michigan Department of Corrections.

towers, to be manned at times of low visibility, such as during fogs or storms. Sally ports are generally equipped with a ground post and a wall tower. The gates are manipulated by the correctional officer in the wall tower, while search of vehicles and inspection of passes and credentials are made by the correctional officer in the ground post. The main gates are made secure by locks, and the passages of persons in and out of the prison is controlled by the correctional officer on duty there. Common practice is to search everybody except, perhaps, the chaplain. This search procedure varies from a superficial "frisk" to use of the expensive and sophisticated inspectoscope.

Based on the same principle as the fluoroscope, the inspectoscope can detect almost anything. It operates similarly to the equipment used to search baggage in airport security. Much more frequently used for reasons of economy and ease of operation is the gun detector, a metal arch that sets off an alarm when it detects metal. The difficulty with the gun detector is that a belt buckle or the foil on a pack of cigarettes can set off the alarm.

On the other hand, it will not detect plastic, glass vials of narcotics, and some other items. Many institutions with gun detectors have gone back to the hand-frisking procedure except in the case of large groups.

## COUNT PROCEDURES

Having exactly the right number of inmates in custody at any given time is most important to the prison or correctional institution. One or more fewer than there should be results in an escape alarm, notification of appropriate law enforcement agencies, and a manhunt. One or more in excess of what should be there could result in litigation and, certainly, the embarrassment of the administration.

The control room is the central headquarters of the custodial operation. The officers in the control room should know the location of all prisoners and be responsible for the count. Direct telephone lines from each tower and cell block go to the control room. Over these lines the cell blocks

Cellblock with electrically operated cell doors at Kentucky State Reformatory.
Courtesy of the Kentucky Department of Corrections.

report the counts, and the towers report any unusual occurrences. In the case of counts, correctional officers report inmates who are absent for work assignments and other reasons, and the control room checks passes and details to determine whether the inmate is absent or on a legitimate call. In the case of towers and posts, the correctional officers report routinely, probably every hour.

Counts are probably the most important single function of custody. Correctional officers are always counting inmates. In maximum security institutions, there are counts every two hours. In minimum security institutions, there may be counts at mealtime and at bed check. In either instance, the count is important. All counts are called in to the control room by telephone and are followed by the count slips. These are checked against passes and details that may account for an inmate's being away from where he is routinely supposed to be, in order to get an accurate count. Any count that does not match the number of inmates the prison is supposed to have, either over or under, results rapidly in a recheck and another count.

## CONTROL OF THE YARD AND THE INSTITUTION

Control of the yard and the institution as a whole is a custodial duty. All persons or articles going in and out of the prison should be controlled by custody, particularly in the maximum security institution. During the day, the inside of the institution is also supervised by custody, with at least one officer in every assignment, such as schools, factories, maintenance shop, and the yard. In the yard, the yard sergeant is responsible for control, including issuing passes to other areas of the prison, such as the infirmary, counseling offices, or elsewhere.

Control of gates is necessary for security. In maximum custody institutions there is generally a main gate, a freight gate for trucks, and sometimes a railroad spur. Adequate supervision is always provided when these gates are opened.

A system of passes and details group passes is used to control the movement of inmates inside the prison. For example, if an individual prisoner is to go from a work assignment to a counselor, the correctional officer writes a pass, including the time of departure, and signs it. The pass is then similarly signed by the correctional officer at the place of destination. When the inmate returns to his assignment, the correctional officer notes the time. All such passes are returned to the control room or the deputy warden's office at the end of the shift to be filed for future reference in case they are needed.

Custodial zoning refers to the time and space differentiations in the yard and physical plant in which inmates may be present. For example, inmates may have a wider range of movement between 8:00 A.M. and 4:30 P.M. After 4:30, factories and other areas may be closed off to inmates. The yard may be available until sundown, after which only the cellblocks may be open to inmates. Consequently, there is a time and space zoning which inmates must respect in the interests of yard control.

## SEARCHES AND SHAKEDOWNS

Searches of cell blocks or dormitories, generally referred to as "shakedowns," are regular routines in security-minded institutions. A maximum custody institution might have a shakedown once or twice a month and more frequently on an irregular basis, depending on the need. Shakedowns generally occur during the day when the inmates are at work or in school.

Contraband, or articles that are not permitted in the prison, vary widely, depending upon the type of security and the practices in the institution. For example, some prisons permit money in the prison, frequently making it a rule that a prisoner should not be in possession of more than $10 at any one time. At the opposite extreme, no money is permitted at all, and a check system, complete with signatures, is necessary to purchase items at the commissary or inmate store. Some institutions use metal tokens or a scrip system without the signatures. However, these items can be hijacked or stolen in the prison yard by other inmates. In the major institutions throughout the United States, the following items have been listed as contraband: matches, razor blades, broken spoons, metal objects, rocks, earth or sand (which may come from a tunnel being dug somewhere or be used for weight in a sock to make a blackjack), alcoholic beverages, narcotics, jail plants (marijuana), keys and key-making materials, cutting tools, gambling equipment, money, spices (particularly mace and nutmeg), buzzers, knives, and tools for breaks.

## TOOL AND KEY CONTROL

Tool control is important in the maximum security prison because stolen tools can be used in escape attempts and in making weapons. The basic factor in tool control is a rigid check system, with receipts for the tools available in the shop, and a classification system for different storage of tools. Class A tools, for example, are those which can cut steel, such as welding torches, parts of which must be stored in the arsenal overnight and checked out by the maintenance supervisor or vocational school instructor each morning for the day's work. Class B tools may be stored in the machine shop but under close scrutiny. Class C tools, such as screwdrivers and pliers, need observation, of course, but do not require unusual surveillance. While Class A tools are frequently stored in the arsenal at night, other tools must be accounted for in the tool crib.

Shadow boards are helpful. These are boards on which the tools are stored, with the outline of the tool painted on the board so that the tool crib operator can tell at the end of the day what tools are missing. When

A kitchen scene at a Florida prison.
Courtesy of the Florida Department of Offender Rehabilitation.

tools are checked out, each inmate using a tool surrenders a chit with his assigned number on it and signs a receipt for the tool.

Key control is of primary importance. Key rings are stored in the control room, arranged according to the tour of duty of each correctional officer. An officer may have twenty to twenty-five keys on a key ring or he may have only one or two, depending upon his duties. These key rings must be checked out and records kept in a rigid manner. If an officer takes a key ring home, he should be called and made to bring it back immediately to help him remember the next time. Keys inadvertently left on a table for only a moment have been pressed into a bar of soap for models. Inmates have even been known to observe keys and to manufacture replicas from visual recall. When a key is lost, there is no recourse but to change the locks and issue new keys to the affected areas.

It may seem paradoxical to discuss careful tool control to control the making of weapons and escape tools when, at the same time, knives and cleavers are available in the prison kitchen and butcher's shop! Inmates are frequently stabbed by other inmates in the tailor's shop with one blade of the large scissors used to cut cloth. To weed out quarrelsome and assaultive men, the attempt is made to classify inmates to work in the butcher's shop, the tailor's shop, or other areas where the tools used in routine operation may be dangerous. The expense of operating a large prison's kitchen using only civilian help would be prohibitive.

## SUPERVISION OF WORK ASSIGNMENTS

Supervision of work assignments is a primary task of the correctional officer. He is frequently in charge of the assignment himself, without a civilian foreman. In industrial situations, there is frequently a work foreman in addition to the correctional officer. In the case of outside assignments, the correctional officer must prohibit illegal contacts with outside persons and prevent acquisition of contraband while he is accomplishing the assigned detail. He must prevent a "trafficking service" in contraband items and underground mail and a "messenger service" between the outside and inside of the prison.

Many of the tasks that have fallen to the correctional officer informally involve counseling of inmates. The officer finds himself counseling because he is immediately available, while the professional counselors are not. Correctional administrations are beginning to recognize that the correctional officer is probably the most effective counselor in the prison, because he is with the inmates a greater length of time each day than are the professional counselors, such as social workers and psychologists. Inmates will discuss their problems on the job, making on-the-job counseling a significant part of the correctional officer's work.

## PROPERTY CONTROL

Property control is an important custodial function. In many prisons, the personnel "appropriate" more property than do the inmates. When inmates steal, it is primarily to obtain food, materials for escape (although they seldom make it from inside), or items for making a weapon. When employees steal, it is generally to obtain things to take home. Foodstuffs are the most difficult to control. Automobile heaters and parts, as well as gasoline, need constant scrutiny. Clothing, radio equipment, and office supplies "shrink." A rigid system of property inventory and control is important to the prison. While the business office has some responsibility for this, the custodial force has primary responsibility for implementing the control and the surveillance.

## VISITING AND CORRESPONDENCE

Visiting and correspondence have been traditionally under custody in most prisons. In many progressive prisons, they are handled by treatment personnel, but the correctional officers in most prisons supervise visits. Approved visiting lists and correspondence lists are made up for each inmate. The inmate's immediate family are generally almost automatically approved. Other relatives and friends need further corroboration in many cases. In the traditional prison, all incoming and outgoing mail is censored, and incoming and outgoing packages undergo thorough inspection. Contraband is confiscated and rejected articles are returned to the sender. In more progressive prisons, the censorship of mail is limited to a spot-check of a few inmates from whom trouble may be expected. Letters to attorneys and certain state and federal officials generally always go without censoring. The use of censorship of mail is rapidly declining, and its value is being questioned. Limiting visitors is going the same route. Both these trends emerged from the general trend away from the old objective of maximum security or banishment and toward the new goal of reintegrating the inmate into the community as part of the correctional process.

## RULES AND REGULATIONS

Rules and regulations of the institution are generally worked out as a result of experience as to where the problem areas are in the adjustment of inmates to institutional routine. They provide the guidelines for the correctional officer to maintain order within the prison. Most prisons print booklets containing these rules and regulations that are presented to the inmates as they arrive in the reception process. Because this reception process generally takes 30 to 45 days, the inmates have plenty of time to read the booklets.

The rules relate to the overall institution and each part of it, including the cell, the cellblock, the yard, the work assignment, the school, the chapel, the dining hall, and all other areas. A survey of a dozen rulebooks from various major institutions throughout the country revealed the following rules generally present in all institutions:

1. Address employees respectfully.
2. No insolence.
3. No fighting, suffering, or violence (suffering refers to masochistic behavior).
4. No attacking employees.
5. No forcing way through gate.
6. Remove cap when entering chapel, administration building, and other specified places.
7. No gambling.
8. No writing of notes or contacting other inmates.
9. Smoking only in designated places.
10. No profane use of language.
11. No contraband.

12. No trafficking, bartering, or trading.

13. All confiscated articles will be considered contraband and not returnable.

14. When wearing coat, at least two buttons shall be buttoned.

15. No staring, gesticulating, or speaking to outside visitors.

16. No running—walk!

17. No catcalls, whistling, hissing, or derisive shouting.

18. No sexual perversion.

19. No money.

20. Work on your own case only, making no legal writs for anybody else.

21. Prisoners are subject to search at any time.

There are other rules of a special nature, but the rules mentioned are found in many institutions. There were 76 rules at the Iowa State Penitentiary in the 1960s.[3]

The enforcement of regulations varies from institution to institution and sometimes from officer to officer. Some correctional officers have been nicknamed "P-38" by the inmates, because they "shoot everybody down." Others have been known to be too lax. It takes experience, some sensitivity, and some in-service training or other instruction to learn how to use these "tools of discipline," just as it takes practice and instruction to use any other kind of tool.

## DISCIPLINARY PROCEDURES

The enforcement of discipline by correctional officers must be reasonable. The officers must steer a middle course between severity and laxity. The development of a uniform and reasonable approach to discipline must result from in-service training, administrative orders and memoranda, and the action of the disciplinary committee (summary court, adjustment committee, or whatever its name might be). The officers must know the institution's disciplinary standards and methods and must know their limits and act within them. The officer must know the rules and regulations, just as an umpire does.

Punishment must be a last resort in most cases. The only justification for punishment is to hold the inmate in suspension long enough to get a good idea across. In the case of the sociopath or psychopath who learns by conditioning, punishment becomes part of a re-education process, but these

[3] Norman Johnston, Leonard Savitz, and Marvin E. Wolfgang, eds., "Rules for Inmates," in *The Sociology of Punishment & Correction*, 2nd ed. (New York: Wiley & Sons, 1970), pp. 387–92.

people represent a minority of the prison population. To be effective, the correctional officer must have an appreciation of the broadness of the concept of discipline, rather than the narrow concept of a method by which it is achieved.[4]

Disciplinary problems in prisons are frequently handled by a summary court within the prison. In the traditional prison, this has been composed of (1) the deputy warden for custody, generally, (2) a captain, and (3) another high-ranking custodial officer. In the more progressive prisons, the court is more frequently made up of (1) the deputy warden, (2) a custodial officer, and (3) a representative from treatment, probably the director of classification or a psychologist. In some institutions, the classification committee or the treatment team also handles the behavior problems.

Several court cases in the 1970s have determined that due process is required in institutional disciplinary hearings, just as it is in criminal court. *Landman* v. *Royster* (333 F. Supp. 621 E.D. Virginia, 1971) interjected minimum due process into those hearings. *Wolff* v. *McDonnell* (418 U.S. 539, 1974) established due process in federal prisons, including (1) advance written notice of the charges, (2) written statement of the decision as to evidence and reasons, (3) right of the inmate to call witnesses and present documentary evidence "when permitting him to do so will not be unduly hazardous to institutional safety or correctional goals," and (4) use of counsel or counsel substitute for illiterate accused persons or those who otherwise cannot understand the proceedings. Confrontation, cross-examination, and right to counsel are constitutionally mandated. *Clutchette* v. *Procunier* (497 F. 2nd 809, 1974) ordered full due process in disciplinary hearings.

Penalties vary widely in correctional institutions and prisons. Solitary confinement is general, combined with limited diet. The old bread and water diet is nearly gone. Many institutions now use a measured amount of unseasoned vegetables ground and mixed into a soup, without seasoning, and measured to 1,800 calories. The rationale for this is that the individual is inactive while in solitary. More progressive institutions provide full meals taken off the main line, the advantage being that a separate preparation does not have to be made and, more important, a punishment connotation is not attached to a basic necessity of life. Periods in solitary confinement vary from a few days to generally 30 days maximum, although there have been several cases in which the time ran much longer.

*Morris* v. *Travisono* (Civil Action 4192, United States District Court for the District of Rhode Island, 1970) held that conditions in the adult correctional institutions at Cranston, Rhode Island, constituted cruel and unusual punishment in violation of the Eighth Amendment and assumed supervision of Rhode Island's prisons for eighteen months to give time to

---

[4] Cornelius D. Hogan, Jr., "A Training Design: Discipline in the Correctional Institution," *American Journal of Corrections*, 32, No. 1 (January–February 1970), 14–18.

correct the conditions. *Landman* v. *Royster,* mentioned above, also held bread and water diets to be unconstitutional, as well as other conditions that constituted cruel and unusual punishment.

Solitary confinement is not necessarily unconstitutional, but may be, depending upon the circumstances, as in *Holt* v. *Sarver* (300 F. Supp. 825, E.D. Arkansas, 1969). This case came close to providing the inmates the "right to treatment" and indicated that mental abuse and corporal punishment are in violation of the cruel and unusual punishment clause of the Eighth Amendment. When the state has deprived an individual of his liberty, it has a constitutional duty to use ordinary care to protect his life and safety while in prison.

The adjustment center is the disciplinary unit in California prisons. A study of these centers has concluded that the persons who should be there are those who are dangerous to others, are dangerous to themselves, or need protective custody from other inmates.[5] They do not need adjustment center treatment for suspicion, "bad-mouthing" staff, or refusing to work.

The major violations in prisons involve gambling, sex, and fighting, although stealing and refusing to work also appear with some frequency. The fighting is often about the gambling and the sex. Assaults frequently occur against inmates who have testified against another prisoner back in the court of sentence.

The use of inmate tipsters in maintaining discipline has its proponents and opponents. Many correctional administrators indicate that a prison could not be operated without them. Other correctional administrators indicate that if they are used, the administrator abdicates his responsibilities. The arguments for using inmate tipsters are that (1) more effective custodial control is available when the inmates do not trust each other and the "inmate code" is broken, (2) fewer officers are needed to maintain the same discipline, and (3) a group of administrative-minded inmates can be developed for the informal self-government of the institution.

The arguments against using tipsters are that (1) the administration becomes dependent upon inmates in a matter of their own responsibility and (2) it builds up an artificial hierarchy of prestige-status or lack of it between the informers and the rest of the inmate body. It is apparent that better all-around custodial control can be maintained by attending to matters that come to official attention rather than by running down leads given by inmates with dubious motivation. An administrator or correctional officer can spend a great deal of his time chasing down rumors when he should be performing more important duties.

The constructive factors in prison discipline are that (1) it allows inmates to experience the desirable results of obedience to rules for the com-

[5] Robert E. Doran, *A Study of California Prison Adjustment Centers* (Washington, D.C.: LEAA Library, 1973), pp. 39–44.

mon good; (2) it permits various recreational and other pursuits which, through transfer training, may help teach inmates the advantages of cooperation with others; (3) it produces a general atmosphere of order and system that includes regular living habits; (4) it helps inmates to acquire recreational habits that can be transferred to the community later; and (5) it neutralizes the negative aspects of prison life as much as possible by controlling and reducing disturbing elements.

The irritating factors of prison discipline are (1) restrictions on individual behavior, (2) regimented movement of groups from place to place, (3) complete lack of privacy, (4) constant supervision by uniformed officers representing authority, and (5) limitations on social contacts with friends and relatives outside by limitations placed on correspondence and visits.

## REDUCTION OF CUSTODY

Prisons are always attempting to reduce the level of custody from maximum to close, from close to medium, from medium to minimum, and from minimum to community custody. The less the custody, the less expensive the institutional supervision and, simultaneously, the closer the correctional process is to reintegrating the prisoner into society.

Just as prisons and correctional institutions are classified as maximum, medium, minimum, and community security on the basis of their construction, so are the inmates classified as maximum, close, medium, minimum, or community custody, depending upon the estimate of the risk they manifest. A maximum custody prisoner is one who must be locked up at all times and be accompanied by an officer when moving from one place to another. A close custody prisoner is one who must be locked up at night and can work in gangs under supervision inside the walls during the day. A medium custody prisoner is one who locks (lives) inside the walls, can work in gangs under supervision outside the walls, and can work alone inside the walls—sometimes called on "inside trusty." A minimum security prisoner is one who can live outside the walls and work alone outside the walls—generally referred to as a full trusty. A community custody prisoner is one who can leave the institution during the day and work downtown or away from the institution in a work release or similar program. These classifications are important in terms of general reduction of custody in the treatment process.

The factors involved in selecting persons for reduced custody are varied. The best custody is a good relationship between the prisoner and the correctional administrator. In juvenile institutions, it has been observed that when one cottage has a high rate of runaways and a second cottage has a low rate, a shift of cottage parents will result in a shift of the runaway rates. It is difficult to include these personal relationships in a method of selecting inmates for outside placement in a prison setting.

There have been few objective studies of custody reduction and outside placement methods. In 1942, Pigeon indicated that the following factors raised the risk involved in reduction:

1. Long sentence or anticipated long sentence
2. Long criminal record
3. Bitter attitude
4. Psychopathic
5. Have warrants filed against them
6. Worry about families
7. Concerned about fidelity of wives and sweethearts
8. Young
9. No family ties
10. Afraid of assault
11. "Hoodlum" type who have received newspaper notoriety[6]

In 1945, Cochrane observed sixty cases of escapes from the Norfolk Prison Colony in Massachusetts.[7] He indicated that no inmate had escaped who was on congenial terms with his wife. Further favorable factors were:

1. Congenial family
2. Served half of entire term
3. Less than one year to parole hearing
4. Less than three years to the maximum sentence expiration
5. Over 35 years of age
6. Fair geographic stability
7. Occasional or first offender
8. Fair employment record
9. No detainers on file (legal notices that prisoners are wanted in other states or by federal authorities)
10. Generally cooperative attitude
11. Mild, unaggressive personality[8]

Conversely, unfavorable factors were:

1. Weak or nonexistent home ties
2. Served less than 40 percent of term

[6] Helen Pigeon, *Handbook of Correctional Procedures* (Harrisburg, Pa.: Pennsylvania Department of Corrections, 1942).

[7] Nelson N. Cochrane, "Escapes and Their Control," *The Prison World*, 10, No. 3 (May–June 1948), 3–5, 28–29.

[8] *Ibid.*, p. 29.

3. More than eighteen months to a parole hearing
4. More than four years to the maximum
5. Habitual offender
6. Under 30 years of age
7. Frequently transient
8. Poor employment record
9. Detainers on file
10. Uncooperative attitude
11. Daring, aggressive personality
12. Mental instability
13. Inferior intelligence[9]

Most institutions reduce custody on the basis of experience and judgment.

## ESCAPES

Escapes and disturbances are central to the task of custody. As indicated before, most escapes are "walkaways," generally after nine o'clock at night. All good institutions have escape-prevention plans they put into operation, depending upon their locale, the inmate's place of residence, whether he has had a recent disturbing letter or visit, and several other factors. Many institutions close down their operations while looking for escaped inmates, and everybody hunts them. Most progressive institutions today, however, do not close down their operations for long. Generally, if the escapee is not picked up by the time normal operations begin, a set of his prints are sent to the FBI in Washington, D.C., with a notation that he is wanted. If he is never heard from again, it means that he is either deceased or is getting along somewhere without being arrested, which was the original objective in the first place. Experience has indicated, however, that few escaped inmates stay away for very long.

Escapes vary widely from institution to institution and among the various types of programs. The majority of escapes are not escapes but "walkaways." There are very few escapes from inside the walls—and these make news. From juvenile institutions, the escape rate can be generally estimated at one-half the population but involving probably only one-fifth of the juveniles, since many who run away do it several times annually. In 1952, the national escape rate was 19.0 per 1,000 prisoners; in 1967, it dropped to 14.2 per 1,000. It is noted that prisons in the Northeast, with maximum cutody institutions and a high ratio of employees to prisoners, have the lowest escape rates. Conversely, the Southern prisons that make heavy use of road gangs and camps, together with a low ratio of employees

[9] *Ibid.,* p. 30.

**Table 7-1   Escapes in 1979 by region**

|  | Escapes | Escapes per 1,000 Prisoners |
|---|---|---|
| United States | 8,241 | 27.4 |
| Federal institutions | 643 | 28.5 |
| State institutions | 7,598 | 27.3 |
| Northeast | 603 | 14.6 |
| North Central | 1,749 | 28.3 |
| South | 14,551 | 40.8 |
| West | 1,304 | 31.0 |

*Source: Prisoners in State and Federal Institutions on December 31, 1979,* National Prisoner Statistics Bulletin SD-NPS-PSF-7 (Washington, D.C.: U.S. Government Printing Office, 1981), p. 21.

to prisoners, have the highest escape rates. The 1979 escape rates are shown in Table 7-1.

The first escape from a maximum custody prison by a helicopter was accomplished when Dale O. Remling was picked up from the yard of the State Prison of Southern Michigan at Jackson on June 6, 1975. He was apprehended thirty hours later.

The question as to whether a person should be brought back to prison after a long period of time on escape is questionable. An Associated Press release of November 19, 1969, reported that Leonard T. Fristoe had escaped from the Nevada State Prison in Carson City in 1923. At age 77, Fristoe was ordered by a judge in Los Angeles to be returned to Nevada authorities on November 28, 1969.[10] The issue is one of finding the optimum balance between the legalistic objectives and the correctional or rehabilitative objectives of the process of criminal justice. Many jurisdictions are now working out informal arrangements with other jurisdictions where long-term escapees have been found to reside, in order to satisfy both objectives and not uproot people. With Social Security, birth certificates needed for pension plans, drivers' licenses, credit cards, identification cards, and other documents that make up "the wallet card cage," the number of successful escapes is going down. This decline is reflected in the increased use of minimum custody institutions and community-based correctional programs.

## RIOTS AND DISTURBANCES

Riots and disturbances are as old as prisons themselves. There have been many efforts at explaining riots and describing how to control them. The American Correctional Association developed a manual on riots in 1953

[10] This Associated Press release was carried by many newspapers throughout the country, including the *Tallahassee Democrat,* November 29, 1969.

and a revision in 1970.[11] The conclusion was that it is not possible to identify a cause or set of causes, and simple explanations do not exist. Causes frequently mentioned have been understaffing, underbudgeting, inadequate food, dissatisfaction with parole board policies, and other general causes. These conditions exist in almost all prisons. There may be predisposing causes, with the precipitating one being an altercation between an inmate and an officer, a fight, or another "triggering" event. Riots have not been reported from Mississippi, Arkansas, and Louisiana, where budgets are low and inmate guards have been traditionally used. Many riots have been reported from reputedly relatively "good" prisons, such as in California, Michigan, Illinois, New York, Massachusetts, New Jersey, and elsewhere. It is apparent that they occur in settings where there is a tenuous balance between controlling behavior (custody) and changing behavior (treatment) and there may be a chance to tip the scales.

The pattern of riot appears to be (1) the initial explosion into violence, (2) organization into a pattern of leadership, both inmates and staff, (3) confrontation, whether by force or negotiation, (4) termination when custodial control is regained, and (5) explanation, which is designed for the public to assure them that the cause of the disturbance has been identified and corrected. Whether force is used or not depends upon the situation. Where there are no hostages, force can be used. Most progressive correctional administrators believe that it should be gas and nonlethal weapons, while some have held out for shooting. If there are hostages, then caution must prevail. Negotiation, or "keeping them talking," has saved many lives in dangerous prison riots. While negotiation may be politically unpopular, it is the most prudent course where lives of hostages are in danger. Police have learned to negotiate on a practical basis with gunmen holding hostages, as does the New York City Police Department's Psychological Service Unit.[12]

Inmates have never won a prison riot. Custodial control has always been restored. Riots are not planned, but are spontaneous. Planned disturbances end in the form of sit-downs and strikes. The inmates know who has the weapons and firepower. In such a situation, "negotiation" takes on connotations different from labor medication. Rather, it is a form of "keeping them talking" until group cohesion begins to break down and then offering an honorable and face-saving way out for the inmate leadership.

Disorders must be dealt with instantly and decisively, almost automatically. The ringleaders in a disturbance must be spotted immediately and then isolated. The conditions leading to the disorder must be investi-

[11] Committee on Riots and Disturbances, *Causes, Preventive Measures, and Methods of Controlling Riots and Disturbances in Correctional Institutions* (Washington, D.C.: American Correctional Association, October 1970).

[12] John A. Culley. "Defusing Human Bombs—Hostage Negotiations," *FBI Law Enforcement Bulletin*, 43, No. 10 (October 1974), 10.

gated and corrected if possible. If this initiative is lost, however, and hostages are held, discretion is imperative.

## MISCELLANEOUS CUSTODIAL TASKS

Transferring prisoners from one place to another is the responsibility of custody. When prisoners are taken home for funerals and sick visits, these trips must be well planned. The local police should verify the illness or time of funeral, the route should be planned and scheduled, police must be notified to provide protection, and upon return, the officer should make a full report. When taking inmates out on court orders and family visits for funerals and sickness, the prisoner should be taken only to the places specified in the instructions. In case of emergency of any sort, the institution should be notified. Contact with the public should be avoided as much as possible. If the prisoner is held overnight in a jail, an endorsement should be secured from the committing judge, a receipt obtained for the prisoner, and the commitment papers secured from the jailer; also, the new custodians should be informed of the nature of the case and appropriate precautions, and the prisoner should be searched thoroughly before leaving.

The use of inmate guards was traditional throughout the South where economy took precedence after the Civil War. Most southern states have replaced these inmate guards with civilian correctional officers. Arkansas, Louisiana, and Mississippi were the last to make extensive use of inmate guards. It is obvious that this practice saves money, but the presence of inmate guards intensifies the bitterness of the other inmates, and the inmate guard cannot participate in any of the programs within the institution.[13] The use of inmate guards has been ordered eliminated in *Finney* v. *Arkansas* (505 F. 2nd 194, 8th Cir. 1974), *Hamilton* v. *Landrieu* (357 F. Supp. 549, E. D. Louisiana, 1972), and several other cases. Federal Judge William C Keady of the Northern District of Mississippi at Greenville ordered Mississippi on October 20, 1972, to eliminate "shooter trusties and other trusties performing custodial duties," since they were in violation of the First, Sixth, Eighth, and Fourteenth Amendments.

Some religious groups have been involved in disturbances. For example, the Black Muslims were involved in the major racially oriented riot at the District of Columbia Youth Center at Lorton, Virginia, in 1972. A group that has caused some concern to custody in some prisons is the Church of the New Song (CONS). It was started by Harry W. Theriault at the United States Penitentiary at Atlanta in 1971. He had purchased a "Doctor of Divinity" for about $15 from a correspondence business in Modesto, California, and thereby had become ordained in the Universal Life

---

[13] Jack Wright, Jr., "Inmates, Convicts and the Inmate Guard" (Tallahassee: *Proceedings of the Fifteenth Annual Southern Conference on Corrections, February 25–27, 1970*), pp. 32–37.

Church. Immediately, he left that church and set up the Church of the New Song with himself as head or bishop. CONS became popular in prisons among inmates. The group was composed of some of the penitentiary's most disorderly prisoners, with the stated purpose of using First Amendment rights to organize against the prison administration. One of their first requests was for steak and wine. The courts have given this group full status as a religion in *Remmers* v. *Brewer* (361 F. Supp. 537, S.D. Iowa, July 24, 1973). Consequently, CONS chaplains may sit on institutional diagnostic and classification committees.

One way to reduce the possibility of riot and disturbance is the development of inmate grievance procedures. The first statewide inmate grievance commission made up of citizens not in the penal system was established in Maryland in 1970. Since that time, several states have established similar commissions, and many prison systems, including the United States Bureau of Prisons, have established grievance procedures. The procedures include legal services, inmate councils, and ombudsman programs.[14] Correctional administrators like these groups because they tend to reduce litigation initiated by inmates.

The role of uniforms and attire of officers has long been a matter of debate. In some poorer prisons, officers wore their own clothing for a long time, and much of it was unkempt. Providing uniforms tended to make a better appearance in these institutions. Today, some institutions are going to a rather informal blazer and slacks type of uniform. Fliegel studied the effectiveness of prerelease instruction by officers wearing different types of clothing in the Texas Department of Correction and found that officers wearing T-shirts and regular trousers received better attention than those in regular uniforms or those with shirt and tie and ordinary trousers.[15]

Restraint equipment for moving inmates is varied. Handcuffs are used frequently when moving groups, and a chain is passed through the handcuffs of several inmates in the groups for bus or other transportation. Belly belts with handcuffs are frequently used when an inmate is being transported alone. Leg irons of varying lengths are used to control the stride of an inmate and eliminate a foot race. Come-ons, or "wrist-breakers," as inmates sometimes call them, may be used to break up small disturbances and bring an unruly inmate into confinement.

The arsenal is generally staffed with one or two correctional officers who are experts in firearms. These experts keep the arms in working order, check them in and out, and supervise qualification by personnel on the firing range. The most popular weapons are the .38 caliber Smith and Wesson revolver or the .45 caliber Colt automatic pistol. Shotguns are part of

[14] V. McArthur, "Inmate Grievances Mechanism: A Survey of 209 American Prisons," *Federal Probation*, 38, No. 4 (December 1974), 41–47.

[15] Alan B. Fliegel, "Effects of Model Characteristics on Observation of Learning of Inmates in a Pre-Release Center by Correctional Officers in a Diagnostic Unit," unpublished Ph.D. dissertation, Sam Houston State University, Huntsville, Texas, 1975).

the arsenal. Carbines from World War II have also been popular. The rifle is probably the strongest and most effective of the weapons in the arsenal. A riot gun to shoot gas projectiles is also part of the arsenal.

Barbers are generally under the supervision of the custodial staff because of their peculiar situations in prisons. Barbers in prison are inmates, most of whom learned barbering in prison. There may be a barber in each cell block or dormitory, or all the barbers may be in a central location. The control of barter, tipping, or other considerations is very difficult and has resulted in the inmate barbers' being in an economic hierarchy above the other inmates in many prisons. For example, if an inmate wants a good haircut, it might be customary to give the barber a pack of cigarettes. While every inmate is entitled to, perhaps, a "state haircut" each month, the cuts, wedges, and generally poor haircuts make the inmates who did not tip the barber easily identified. It takes close watching and rigid supervision to prevent this problem from arising. Custody is further interested

In-Service Training Program at Hawaii State Prison, Honolulu, Hawaii.
Courtesy of the Hawaii Department of Social Services and Housing.

because the barbers have lotions that could be used for drinking and razors that could be used for cutting, and their location makes them an ideal contact point for inmates who would otherwise be kept apart.

Fire protection is generally a custodial matter, because fires can be used to express resentment or create confusion to cover escapes or other disorders. The famous fire at the Ohio State Penitentiary in 1931 that claimed the lives of 231 inmates was reportedly set to cover a mass escape. It is difficult to rely on official statements interpreting riots and disorders, because part of their function is to assure the public that the remaining power structure is competent and in control.

## THE TREATMENT FUNCTION OF CUSTODY

Custody should be used as part of treatment. Most correctional administrators indicate that their first task is to secure the inmate as much as he needs securing, and then treat him. Custody has the primary task of securing and can also contribute considerably to the treatment. The training of custodial officers ranges from security and firearms to understanding emotional and mental disturbances.[16]

The correctional officer should be given a central role in the treatment of inmates.[17] The role of the correctional officer is changing from that of guard to member of the treatment team.[18] He is in a better position than other staff members to relate to sociopaths.[19]

## SUMMARY

Every prison has custody at its central core. Some prisons emphasize virtually *all* custody. Generally, 60 to 65 percent of the personnel and budget in prisons and correctional institutions is allotted to custody. Consequently, custody is the backbone of the prison or correctional institution, regardless of idealistic professions of philosophy. This means that if the prison or correctional institution is to be really "corrective," the custodial personnel must support and augment that objective. They are becoming the mainstay of the treatment program in most progressive prisons. The correctional guard is not a "guard" any more—he is a "correctional officer." He will

[16] Committee on Personnel Standards and Training, *Correctional Officers' Training Guide* (New York: The American Correctional Association, 1952), p. 180.

[17] Herbert E. Thomas, "The Dynamics of the Interdisciplinary Team in the Adult Correctional Process," *Prison Journal*, 44, No. 2 (Autumn 1964), 21–27.

[18] *Perspective: The Changing Role of the Correctional Officer* (House organ of the Washington Department of Institutions), 12, No. 4 (Spring 1969), 33. State of Washington Department of Institutions, Olympia.

[19] Thomas, "The Dynamics of the Interdisciplinary Team," pp. 21–27.

soon be a "correctional counselor." As a matter of fact, leaders in the correctional field are currently talking in terms of "security and control," rather than in terms of "custody." Security and control would not be limited to institutions, but would also serve to conceptualize community-based correctional treatment.

## EXERCISES AND STUDY QUESTIONS

1. *Why is custody considered to be so important by correctional administrators and personnel?*

2. *What is involved in the shift from the old type of guard to the new correctional worker, correctional officer, or correctional counselor?*

3. *What are the three functions of custody?*

4. *By what general methods are the functions of custody achieved?*

5. *Why are the correctional philosophy and the construction of the physical plant of a prison interdependent?*

6. *Describe count procedure.*

7. *Discuss control of the yard and the institution.*

8. *How should searches and shakedowns be carried out, and what contraband should be confiscated?*

9. *Describe the procedures in tool and key control.*

10. *Why is supervision of work assignments a primary task of the correctional officer?*

11. *Why is property control an important custodial function?*

12. *What is the role of custody in visiting and correspondence?*

13. *Discuss the development and enforcement of rules and regulations.*

14. *What are the disciplinary procedures in many institutions?*

15. *What are the constructive factors in discipline, and what are the irritating factors?*

16. *How are inmates classified with regard to custody, and by what procedure does reduction of custody take place?*

17. *Why are escapes and disturbances a central task of custody, and how should they be handled?*

18. *Describe some of the miscellaneous custodial tasks, such as transfering prisoners from one place to another, taking prisoners home for funerals and sick leave visits, supervising barbers, fire protection, and other functions.*

19. *What do you consider to be the treatment function of custody?*

20. *Are escapes important in modern times? Why, or why not?*

# 8

# INSTITUTIONAL PROCEDURES– TREATMENT

Treatment in prisons and correctional institutions consists of those programs that bring socializing influences to bear on the inmate population. These programs are viewed broadly, since "treatment" in the narrow sense of psychotherapy and depth diagnosis and casework is almost nonexistent in American prisons. Consequently, *treatment* refers to those processes ordinarily found in the normal socialization of people in the free community, such as schools, religion, recreation, hospitals, and medical attention, as well as the psychological, psychiatric, and social work services that might be available. Treatment in prisons even includes industries and farms where work habits and skills might be learned.

Classification is the means by which inmates are assigned to different programs in an effort to provide the best available program to fit their individual needs. While the formalization of the classification procedures has been recent, all prisons have always had the classification function in some way. The decisions as to what job an inmate should have, his level of security, medical attention, and other differentiations between inmates and assignment of their programs have always been made by somebody. Even in some of the less progressive prison systems that use inmate guards, somebody must decide who should carry a gun and who should not. The newer classification systems simply formalize this decision-making function.

Treatment is considered by many persons to be the most important phase of the correctional process. This is the basic objective of the correctional process. More time and effort is devoted to it in the progressive prisons and correctional institutions than to any other phase. The legal responsibility of the prison, of course, is to the court's demand for security and custody of the prisoner. Society's protective demand is for the treatment and rehabilitation of the citizen-offender.

The treatment process is accomplished in several ways. Broadly, there is a period of reception and diagnosis, after which the inmate is placed in an appropriate program. Second, the period of incarceration, which averages slightly under two and one-half years, is characterized by job assignments, school programs, and treatment programs in individual and group therapy, depending upon the facilities within the institutions. The final phase is that of release by parole or discharge. Throughout this entire period, treatment personnel work with each prisoner. Their work may be in classification, education, medical and dental services, psychological or psychiatric assistance, individual counseling, group therapy, or any of the other services that come under the heading of treatment.

# CLASSIFICATION

Classification refers to the separation of offenders by a variety of criteria. While the modern concept of classification refers primarily to treatment potential, the early separations were basically custodial. Spain began to separate the men from the women—or the women from the men—in 1519. In the United States, the Quakers separated the sexes in the penitentiary movement in 1790. Children began to be separated from adults in the early part of the nineteenth century with the establishment of private Houses of Refuge (Danzig, Germany in 1824, New York in 1825), public training schools for juveniles (New York and Massachusetts in 1847), and the emergence of the educational program at the Elmira Reformatory in 1876.

Separation for treatment purposes began to appear in France when Binet and Simon were commissioned in 1904 to develop an intelligence test to determine which problem children were educable and could be sent to school and which might as well be sent to work. Their work resulted in the first intelligence test in 1905. The test was subsequently revised in 1908, translated into English in 1911, and brought to the Vineland Training School in New Jersey.

In the 1930s, the major state correctional systems in the United States adopted the classification concept. Before adoption of classification on a statewide basis, judges could sentence persons to any of a series of prisons or correctional institutions within the state, a type of classification being accomplished by the courts. During the 1930s, the Federal Bureau of Prisons was organized, and programs of individual treatment using classification were introduced.

The reception and diagnostic center idea has been popular in American corrections. The first and probably the best known of these installations was the Diagnostic Depot at Joliet, Illinois. Several states subsequently opened reception centers or diagnostic centers. The purpose of these centers is to place everyone who is sentenced by the courts in a jurisdiction under the authority of the Department of Corrections, Division of Corrections, or whatever the correctional system might be called, rather than under the authority of a single institution. )

( At the diagnostic center, the inmates are interviewed by professional persons, tested by psychologists, examined by psychiatrists, and evaluated educationally. A chaplain's report may be included. Routinely, questionnaires and letters of inquiry are sent to relatives, particularly immediate family, and to previous employers and schools. Frequently, the reception center is a member of the Social Service Index or Central Filing System for Social Service Agencies in the major cities within its jurisdiction. Consequently, when the Index or clearinghouse is notified that the person has arrived at the prison, that agency follows through by notifying the reception center of previous contacts other social service agencies in the city have had with the inmate's family. Follow-up of those contacts on a selective basis provides further information. )

( After all the information has been gathered, a social history is prepared. The staff meets as a classification committee to classify the inmate as to the institution in which he should be held and the general program or assignment he should have. In addition, the committee makes an estimate of his custody needs (generally close, medium, or minimum) and any special programs that might be advisable, such as programs in group therapy, alcoholic rehabilitation, psychiatric referral, or other specialized programs. The inmate is then sent from the reception center to the appropriate institution. The strength of the reception center is that a good diagnosis and plan of treatment can be involved in each case. One of the weaknesses of the reception center idea is that it tends to drain the institutions themselves of professional personnel to staff the reception center, thereby placing a premium on diagnosis rather than treatment. )

( Classification within institutions takes on essentially the same form as classification in the reception center, but with generally better follow-through. Sometimes the reception center is in one of the host institutions. In this case, the practices vary. Generally, when the reception center is in a host institution, the assumption is that the majority of prisoners will remain at that host institution or central prison, younger "reformatory" type offenders will go to a reformatory, and other obvious types of classification will be made. When this occurs, it is frequently the practice to send on inmates obviously bound to other institutions within the first week and to forward their files. The information that arrives at the central prison after they have been transferred to the receiving institution where the social history is prepared is forwarded when it arrives. )

The development of classification in American prisons has thus far gone through the following stages:

1. Pre-professional
2. Traditional
3. Integrated

4. Professional

5. Team treatment

6. Functional unit management

Most prisons that have introduced the formalized classification system have gone through these stages. In 1938, a committee to develop a handbook on classification was appointed by the American Correctional Association. The subsequent handbook was published in 1947[1] and has since been revised.

( When classification first began in prisons, the committees were large. The warden was frequently included, and the deputy warden was always included, together with the significant department heads, such as the farm superintendent, director of industries, chief steward, director of education, director of classification, the laundry superintendent, the chaplain, the director of education, and other staff members that made up a ten- to twelve-person classification committee. The practice was generally to meet twice a week for an afternoon to classify the inmates who had come in approximately thirty days before and about whom some information was available. Each member of the classification committee in turn would take a file and give a brief history and a recommendation, usually more directed toward needs of the institution than the benefit of the inmates. When the inmate came in to meet with the committee, the person with the appropriate file would tell the inmate what the committee had decided. This type of classification has been called the *pre-professional* type. |

\With the addition of a sociologist or other professional person to prepare a social history, the social history provided a beginning recommendation which could be accepted or changed by the rest of the classification committee. Everything in this second stage operated the same as it did in the pre-professional approach, with the exception that a professional person had been added to prepare the inmate's social history. This was generally referred to as the *traditional* classification system. )

| The third phase in the development of classification was the integrated committee. Before this, the classification committee's recommendations were simply recommendations. The deputy warden had to implement them because the controlled movement of inmates necessitated simultaneous job changes and cell changes. For example, custody did not want prisoners coming from all directions of the institution to the kitchen at 4:30 in the morning to prepare breakfast. Consequently, everyone who worked in the kitchen would be locked in one cellblock, everybody who worked in the laundry in another, and so on. )

( The implementation of the classification committee recommendation in the deputy warden's office left much to be desired, since many deputy wardens thought they could tell more about a prisoner than a classification

---

[1] *Handbook on Correctional Institutions* (New York: American Prison Association, 1947, 1968). Also, see Leonard J. Hippchen, ed., *Correctional Classification and Treatment* (Washington, D.C., and Cincinnati: American Correctional Association and W.H. Anderson Company, 1975).

committee could and paid no attention to the recommendations. As classification systems became stronger, correctional administrators insisted that the classification committee recommendation become an order, with a copy going to the central office, generally located in the state capital. This resulted in the classification committee's being integrated into the prison program as it had not been before. The deputy warden could still request the classification committee to reconsider a case for the safety and security of the institution. If he did so too frequently, however, he would be requested to send to the classification committee a custodial representative in whom he had greater confidence, since custody was already represented on the classification committee. This development was known as the *integrated* classification committee.

The fourth development was the *professional* classification committee. The previous classification committees, the pre-professional, the traditional, and the integrated, were made up of ten to twelve department heads and significant people in the institution. Consequently, the high-paid staff in the institution were tied up for two half-days a week. The reduction of those large and unwieldy classification committees was seen as a step toward efficiency. A small, three-man professional classification committee emerged. It was composed of the director of classification, a high-ranking custodial officer, and the counselor or sociologist who prepared the social history for the inmate. If there were five or ten sociologists or counselors, the classification committee meetings could be scheduled so that all those in the caseload of each counselor who were coming to classification that week would be scheduled at the same time. One of the disadvantages of that small committee was that it lost the function of educating and involving the department heads in the correctional process.

A fifth and more recent development in classification is the *treatment team* concept. This had its origin in 1958 and 1959 at the 3320th Retraining Group at Amarillo Air Force Base in Texas and at the Federal Correctional Institution at Ashland, Kentucky, under Warden John Galvin. In this system, three persons—generally a counselor, a custodial officer, and a school teacher—became the team for each individual prisoner. As implemented elsewhere, the same team may be assigned to all men in a specific dormitory or cellblock. The teams determine all the actions the classification committee formerly determined. When fully implemented, they also handle disciplinary problems. It has become apparent that involvement and participation in the correctional process in the team treatment concept has produced more treatment-oriented correctional officers, as well as educators and other correctional staff. Anybody can be on a treatment team, but it must include a custodial officer and a counselor.

*Functional unit management* was introduced into the United States Bureau of Prisons and several states in 1973–74.[2] A refinement of the treatment team concept, it is designed to decentralize treatment services. Each

---

[2] Martin J. Bohn, Richard A. Wazak, and Bill R. Storey, *Transition to Functional Unit, 1973–1974* (Tallahassee: Federal Correctional Institution Notes, 4, No. 1, 1974).

unit has a unit manager, one or two caseworkers, two counselors, and an administrative assistant. The unit is a living unit, such as a dormitory or cellblock. The unit manager serves as a "subwarden" and each unit is a "subinstitution." All problems of the inmates are handled in the unit, with the unit manager in charge.

The background of the personnel working in classification departments is quite varied. Social workers, psychologists, criminologists, and sociologists have been preferred in the past. Other and almost nonrelated persons have been included also, in the hope that they can learn on the job the basic tasks of the correctional process. Classification personnel, therefore, are frequently called "counselors." The better systems require degrees in social work, criminology, psychology, and other appropriate behavioral and social sciences. Even so, they are referred to as counselors in most places to eliminate the professional differentiations. For the same reason, social workers were not called "social workers" in most prisons until recently because of the reaction of inmates and correctional administrators to the stereotype of "social worker."

In some systems, the counselor approves visitors and correspondence and, in addition, special purpose mail. He or she receives and processes requests for job and program changes, taking them through the reclassification process or whatever the system might be.

Treatment programs available to the classification committee may emphasize individual or group counseling. There is wide variation in the manner in which the services are organized. The more recent counseling programs have assigned each inmate to a counselor as he arrives at the institution, and the counselor keeps him on the caseload throughout his entire incarceration.

Some prisons have a special psychiatric unit, and some also have a mental ward. These units can be used for referral of cases for special treatment.

Classification is based on various systems. A number of suggestions have been made to base it on criminal typology. The Oregon State Correctional Institution, opened in 1959, classified inmates according to the major source of their difficulties: (1) conflict with individual and societal values, (2) conflict stemming from relationships with others, (3) problems caused by need for material things, or (4) problems based in self-concept.[3] There is no satisfactory way of measuring the success of such a system. Morris has suggested that inmates be classified as (1) legalistic or technical offenders, (2) situational offenders, (3) pathological offenders, (4) avocational offenders, and (5) career offenders.[4]

Classification is helpful in managing large numbers of cases in social programs more efficiently than they could be handled by individuals on an

[3] Jean Long, "A Symbiotic Taxonomy for Corrections," *American Journal of Correction,* 27 (November–December 1965), 4–7.

[4] Albert Morris, "The Comprehensive Classification of Adult Offenders," *Journal of Criminal Law, Criminology, and Police Science,* 56 (June 1965), 197–202.

individual basis. Classification makes use of the patterns of problems and patterns of treatment. It is helpful even in the public schools. It permits better homogeneous grouping of offenders for purposes of programming focused on specific or more narrow targets and goals. These more homogeneous targets may be specific age groups, IQ or intelligence groups, alcoholics, or other specific groups. The goals could be more specific and homogeneous objectives, such as vocational training in auto mechanics, achieving functional literacy, and group therapy and group living techniques to achieve social understanding and adjustment. The methods of grouping have not been adequately researched.

In public schools, the most important factors in grouping have been reported as reading level, performance on standard academic achievement tests, and teachers' opinions. Social maturity, aptitude tests, age, and previous performance as shown by report cards are next in importance. All other criteria seem to be neglible.[5] If corrections can become better stabilized, at least as well stabilized as the public schools, research may assist in better classification.

In 1969, the United States Bureau of Prisons implemented a system of classification according to diagnoses that can be computerized.[6] On the basis of experience in placing offenders into the treatment categories of (a) intensive, (b) selective, or (c) minimal as to likelihood of change according to staff judgment, further systematization was considered to be logical. The new RAPS system can develop a code that can be translated into categories I, II, or III, dependent upon whether there should be a great, medium, or no expenditure of resources above the essential level of service. The $R$ (rehabilitation potential) in the code is based on the staff's professional opinion regarding the prospects of change. The $A$ refers to age, as under 30, 30 to 45, or over 45. The $P$ is the number of prior sentences, ranging from none to two or more. The $S$ refers to the nature of the sentence in terms of special classification (Federal Juvenile Delinquency Act, Youth Center Act, or Narcotic Addict Rehabilitation Act) or length of sentence.

The code combinations fed into the computer can elicit the categories of treatment. Category I inmates would be reviewed every 30 days and have first priority on assignments. The treatment team makes all assignment changes, and the caseworker sits in disciplinary action procedures. Category II persons are reviewed every six months and do not have first priority on assignments. The caseworker is advised regarding assignment changes and disciplinary actions. Category III persons are reviewed annually, have last priority on assignments, are routinely assigned to the labor pool, are used as needed to maintain the institution, and are processed by regular procedures in disciplinary actions.

[5] Joseph Lederer, "The Scope of the Practice," *The Urban Review,* 3, No. 1 (September 1968), 5.

[6] *United System Bureau of Prisons Policy Statement on the Case Management System* (Washington, D.C.: U.S. Bureau of Prisons, 1969).

As the inmate approaches the expiration of his sentence, perhaps 60 to 90 days before the end of his minimum sentence, a pre-parole progress report is developed, generally by the counselor and sometimes by a classification committee. This pre-parole progress report presents the original circumstances of the inmate's offense and sentence, evaluates his institutional record in school and work, his progress in counseling and therapy, his misconduct reports, work reports, and school reports, and summarizes all this information in a recommendation for or against parole, together with reasons. A parole plan, both residence and job, is included. This is sent to the parole board or other paroling authority.

## MUTUAL AGREEMENT PROGRAMMING

Mutual Agreement Programming (MAP) is a contract between the inmate, the institution, and the parole board that includes a definite parole date contingent on the completion by the inmate of specified rehabilitation goals. Initiated by the Parole-Corrections Project of the American Correctional Association and funded by the United States Department of Labor, the effort was designed to increase communication between agencies, cooperation in delivery of services, a definite parole date, and articulated parole criteria. Phase I was research and planning from September 1971 through August 1972. Phase II was implementation in Wisconsin, Arizona, and California between September 1972 and February 1974. Phase III was dissemination and technical assistance between March 1974 and April 1975. In the voucher system of MAP, inmates can draw up to $3,000 to purchase education and training services in the community. Problems most frequently expressed by officials involve whether available programs and services are sufficient, whether the contracts with inmates are legal, whether they could be sued by dissatisfied inmates who have lost parole dates, and whether the contract must include a definite release date.[7] The interpretations are that definite parole dates must be included and are binding, even if the institution does not provide the promised program. By the end of 1974, MAP programs were established in the District of Columbia, Alabama, Colorado, Florida, Maine, Massachusetts, New York, North Carolina, Tennessee, Virginia, and Michigan, in addition to the original three states. Evaluation of MAP indicates that observers believe it has good potential; the early results are good, but the potentially far-reaching effects are still unknown.[8]

The contract was used informally in some prisons, such as North Carolina, in the 1960s. The idea of contracts in social work practice outside

---

[7] *The Mutual Agreement Program* (College Park, Md.: American Correctional Association, 1973), p. 31.

[8] Anne H. Rosenfeld, *An Evaluative Summary of Research: MAP Program Outcome in the Initial Demonstration States* (College Park, Md.: American Correctional Association, 1975), p. 57.

corrections is gaining momentum. The more difficult involuntary client frequently found in corrections is no longer a target group in social work.[9] The danger of the contract is that performance may not meet the contract, which reduces the effect and increases resentment.

# EDUCATION

Education was the second major change in the correctional process after religion and moral education. The reformatory movement, based on academic and vocational education, began in Elmira in 1876. The movement was a direct result of the deliberations of the first American Correctional Association's annual congress at Cincinnati in 1870. It is well known that offenders, both juveniles and adults, are approximately three grades academically retarded, and an estimated average grade placement by tests would be approximately the fifth grade. Yet the offender appears equal in ability and intelligence to the population from which he is drawn. In the main, he has been a "nonlearner" in public school. He has also been a dropout or kickout, since few offenders in institutions have completed high school.

Schools in prisons have emphasized academic and vocational training, although many have commercial schools, agricultural schools, and special schools. Night study and cell study are available in many prisons and correctional institutions.

The academic schools in prisons and correctional institutions generally place considerable emphasis on the primary grades. Using an ungraded system, the tools of literacy are provided to help the many functional illiterates found in prisons. Textbooks are a real problem in prison education. A grown man returning to his cell with a *Run, Jane, Run* book under his arm is certain to be mocked by other inmates.[10]

Some prisons also have a high school in which considerable pride is taken. A number also offer the first year of college through extension courses from nearby universities. Recently, several prisons, such as Walla Walla, the United States Penitentiary at Marion, Illinois, and Florida State Prison at Raiford, have had inmates graduate from junior college. The justification for placing some emphasis on the high school diploma, despite the fact that about half the correctional clients are functionally illiterate, is that American culture makes the high school diploma a prerequisite for many jobs. When an inmate is close enough to it to earn the high school diploma through the General Education Development Test (GED), it is of sufficient social importance to provide this opportunity. The work-

[9] Brett A. Seabury, "The Contract: Uses, Abuses, and Limitations," *Social Work*, 21, No. 1 (January 1976), 16–21.

[10] E. Eugene Miller, "Education at Bucks County Prison," *American Journal of Correction*, 29, No. 2 (March–April 1967), 22–25.

School instruction in a Florida prison.
Courtesy of the Florida Division of Correction.

study program being developed by several jurisdictions would permit full college attendance for some inmates.

Vocational training is popular in correctional institutions and prisons. There is always an effort to find trades that are marketable in the local area. Automobile mechanics, welding, printing, and the construction trades have always been popular. In women's prisons, beauty culture is popular. Special schools for data processing and key punching have been rather popular recently.

Commercial schools are present in many prisons and correctional institutions to teach typing, stenography, business English, filing, bookkeeping, and business practices. In many of the maximum custody institutions, only long-termers go to the commercial school. While employability is reduced for them outside, they can staff the offices of the prison officials and classification department.

Agricultural schools are sometimes maintained during the winter in preparation for the "on-the-job" phase in the summer. The type of agriculture taught should fit the region in which the inmates live.

The Correctional Education Association has been active in finding new ways to teach nonlearners in prisons and correctional institutions.

Commissioner Benjamin J. Malcolm of the New York City Department of Correction addressing a graduating class in secretarial skills at the New York City Correctional Institute for Women at Rikers Island.
Courtesy of the New York City Department of Correction.

Computer-assisted instruction has been installed in some institutions. It is certain that the educational program must be a continuous one, with each inmate studying at his own rate, rather than a school year running from September to June. Inmates at various educational levels arrive continuously around the calendar. New approaches are needed in the correctional setting to motivate learning and to accomplish it. Basically, it must be noted that the subject matter is only a vehicle by which some other objectives are accomplished, such as work habits, feeling of achievement, and dealing with the environment effectively. Educational level offers the easiest way to measure many factors that may be an index of lack of cultural assimilation or of alienation from society. )

( The primary objectives of correctional education are to provide the inmates with (1) tools of literacy, (2) a trade with vocational training, and (3) valuable secondary advantages, such as good work habits, self-percep-

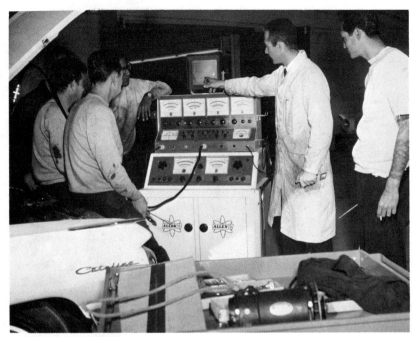

Vocational auto shop class at Arizona State Prison.
Courtesy of the Arizona Department of Correction.

tion of accomplishment, feelings of worthiness, a sense of the dignity of labor, and the rewards of successful competition. The high school diploma and the certificate of achievement assist in all these objectives. The school environment must be physically and emotionally safe to achieve them.

Prisoners are economically deprived, culturally disadvantaged, and educationally deficient, while having the same intellectual potential representative of the population from which they were drawn. This background makes educational programs in prisons and correctional institutions different from those in the public schools, of necessity, for the needed remedial work transcends the entire culture, not just education.

Programmed instruction, or Computer-Assisted Instruction (CAI), eliminates many of the deficiencies found in academic programs of correctional institutions.[11] It is self-pacing, presents material in short and easy steps, keeps the learner active by calling for responses based only on previous steps, and provides immediate feedback of results. Programs can be used at all grade levels. The shortage of prison educators is a problem everywhere, and the CAI system appears to be one of several ways to overcome this problem of education in prisons and correctional institutions.

Cooperative arrangements for college studies have been made be-

[11] Frank P. Belcastro, "The Use of Programmed Instruction in Canadian Correctional Institutions," *The Canadian Journal of Corrections,* 11, No. 4 (Oct. 1969), 233–39.

Vocational training in a machine shop on a metal lathe.
Courtesy of the Florida Division of Corrections.

tween several prisons and universities, in which professors go to the institutions and conduct extension courses. A cooperative arrangement was made in 1972 between the District of Columbia Department of Corrections and the Federal City College in Washington.[12] The freshman year is taken at the institution, and the residents are bused to the college for the sophomore through senior years. Approximately 750 residents have earned college credits, and one earned the master's degree.[13] South Carolina, without such an agreement, generally has twelve to twenty inmates in colleges and universities that will accept them. In 1970, LEAA funded a Manpower Program Project for Oregon, in which professors go to the institutions and teach college-level courses in the same manner they would on campus.

( Two major reasons for stressing education are that offenders are probably three grades retarded, on the average, and that educational attain-

[12] Kenneth L. Hardy and Harland Randolph, *Guidelines for the Administration and Implementation of the Federal City College Lorton Extension College* (Washington, D.C.: District of Columbia Department of Corrections and Federal City College, March 1972).

[13] "Lorton Resident Ready for Degree," *The Washington Afro-American*, April 12, 1975, p. 1.

ment is easy to measure. It may well be that the offenders are "three grades retarded" in *all* social and cultural areas, including the inculcation of society's value system. )

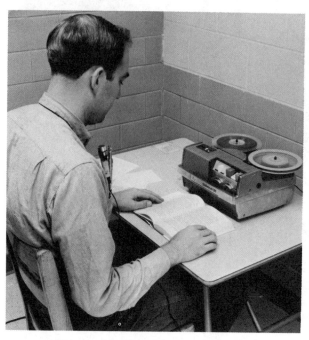

Tape recording books for use by the Iowa Blind Commission and the Library of Congress at Iowa State Penitentiary.
Courtesy of the Iowa Department of Social Services.

Vocational computer programming class.
Courtesy of the Arizona Department of Corrections.

# RELIGION

Religion has been central to the correctional process since the Quakers organized the first penitentiary at the Walnut Street Jail in Philadelphia in 1790. The chaplain has always had access to all parts of the prison. Historically, the chaplain was the first treatment man, and, in fact, he spearheaded other treatment programs in the prison. The chaplain is present in many prisons and other institutions today which have little or no educational program, classification procedure, or other treatment program.

While the chaplain has always been in the prisons, his acceptance there has never been complete and unreserved. The majority of inmates do not go to chapel or church. Most delinquents outside have not been known to the Sunday school teachers and pastors they claim to have known in reception center interviews. Church is considered by many prisoners as representative of the Establishment, constituted authority, and they are not part of it. Many inmates have taken the attitude, well expressed by a prisoner, "If there is a God, he sure as hell was not on my side!" Consequently, the chaplain is seen by many inmates as a person who is selling intangibles without much security.

On the other hand, inmates whose behavior problem is primarily neurotically based, with a heavy component of guilt and remorse, can make use of the chaplain and chapel programs for support and forgiveness. While their number in juvenile and adult correctional institutions is relatively small, they are sufficient in numbers to absorb the time of the one or two chaplains available to most institutions.

The custodial staff frequently looks upon the chaplain as an enigma. His job calls for him to be friendly with the inmates. The fact that he elected the clergy as his vocation means that he is a "do-gooder."

In a security-oriented institution, the chaplain must confront inmates' anxieties and administer to their religous needs and serve the administrative needs of agencies by whom he is appointed and sometimes paid. A conscientious chaplain is generally undertrained, underpaid and overworked, and receives little compensation besides personal spiritual reward. The New York City Board of Corrections studied the role of the chaplain and found that he is often the ombudsman of the system where no official ombudsman or inmate grievance committee exists. A strong recommendation was that part-time chaplains should be eliminated and only full-time chaplains should be appointed in prisons because of their unique services and the need for them.[14] From the custodial standpoint, the chaplain frequently poses a dilemma. Although he is not to be fully trusted, he cannot be searched or questioned as can other personnel. Even outside

---

[14] *Final Report: Task Force on the Role of the Chaplain in New York City Correctional Institutions* (New York: New York City Correction Board, 1972).

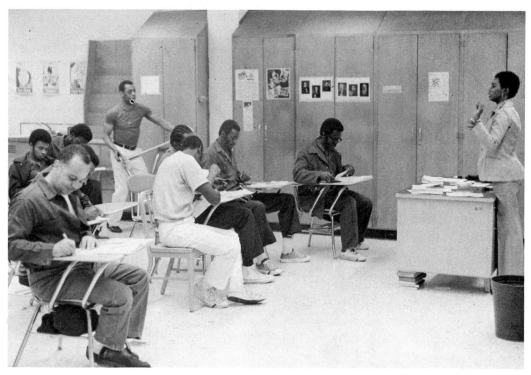

Students in a college class held by the John Jay College of Criminal Justice at the New York City Correctional Institution on Rikers Island.
Courtesy of the New York City Department of Correction.

clergy can get on inmates' correspondence and visiting lists more easily than other nonrelatives can.

The chaplain's contribution to treatment is primarily among the group of neurotically based personalities in the prison who have a high potential for guilt in the first place. Finding security in religion provides a large *number* of offenders, even though a small *percentage* of them, with the stability that permits them to make a successful adjustment in society. Many outside religious agencies, such as the Salvation Army, Youth for Christ, the Home Mission Board of the Southern Baptist Convention, the Society of Saint Vincent de Paul, and other religious groups support and reinforce this transformation.

In summary, the chaplain is an indispensable part of the correctional program. In the old prison of a century ago, his function was primarily to convince the inmates of the justness of their sentences. He has some of that function today, together with the important function of assuring inmates of a brighter future. As the oldest and most consistent treatment man in

Protestant chapel services at Iowa State Penitentiary. Volunteers from the community assist in the services almost weekly.
Courtesy of the Iowa Department of Social Services.

prison today, the chaplain has contributed more than any other position or role to the correctional process.

## COUNSELING, CASEWORK, AND CLINICAL SERVICES

Counseling, social casework, and psychological and psychiatric services do not exist in the majority of prisons and correctional institutions. Where they do exist, the patterns vary widely in terms of numbers of professional personnel and the manner in which their services are used. The fact that a sociologist, social worker, or psychologist works in a classification department does not mean that he is providing counseling, casework, or clinical services. Professional personnel in most classification departments are *processing* prisoners—not counseling them. That a history or business administration major could process a prisoner as well as a social worker points up some of the problems in manpower utilization in prisons and correctional institutions. The function of the psychiatrist in the correctional setting has frequently been misunderstood by correctional workers and administrators, with the result that he is either expected to perform miracles or his opinions are regarded as impractical. It is also misuse of professional time to require a psychiatrist to make routine reports.

Counseling is a relationship between the counselor and his client in an effort to understand the client's problems and help him solve them by mutual consent, rather than by giving advice or admonition.[15] Casework includes professional services in (1) obtaining case histories and description, (2) solving immediate problems involving family and personal relationships, (3) exploring long-range problems of social adjustment, (4) providing supportive guidance for inmates about to be released, and (5) providing supportive guidance and professional assistance to probationers and parolees.[16] Clinical services provide more intensive diagnostic and treatment services aimed at (1) discovering causes of individual maladjustments, (2) applying psychiatric techniques to effect improved behavior, and (3) providing guidance, support, and consultation to other staff members working with offenders.[17]

## GROUP METHODS

Group therapy, group counseling, guided group interaction (GGI), psychodrama, and other group methods found their way into the correctional field after World War II. The earliest significant uses of these methods were made at the Army facility at Ft. Knox, Kentucky, during the last phases of World War II. Subsequently, they were used by Dr. Lloyd McCorkle (who was at Ft. Knox) and Dr. F. Lovell Bixby in New Jersey in the late 1940s. New Jersey developed a professional group therapy program in several institutions.

California developed a program of group counseling in the late 1940s and 1950s. Under the leadership of Dr. Norman Fenton, training programs were established for volunteer personnel who would lead groups in the evening. Correctional officers, record clerks, and anybody else who was interested could participate. After the groups were started, the assessment was that they helped everybody, especially the group leaders. Wives of correctional officers who participated in the program indicated that their husbands were better fathers and more understanding of human behavior as a result of their experience in group counseling. Simultaneously, the understanding of behavior was improved throughout the entire correctional system.

[15] "Counseling, Casework, and Clinical Services," Chap. 25 in the *Manual of Correctional Standards,* 3rd ed. (Washington, D.C.: American Correctional Association, 1966, 1969), p. 422.

[16] *Ibid.,* p. 423.

[17] *Ibid.*

(In recent years, there has been some movement toward making the inmates themselves part of the group process. The idea of using peer pressure to promote improvement is a product of the 1960s and emanates from the Provo Experiment and other sources. In this process, the inmates participate in groups and provide the leadership that helps individuals improve themselves.)

( Group methods appear to be a coming phase in correctional treatment. They are economical, in that they allow one leader to handle more than one client at a time. Further, they dilute the threat of authority that occurs in a one-to-one relationship between a counselor and a client. The use of peer groups appears to be even more helpful. )

# RECREATION

( Recreational pursuits in prisons generally comprise individual or programmed athletics, either varsity or intramural. The majority of prisoners and correctional institutions have athletic teams in football, basketball, and baseball that play outside teams. Many of the teams they play are local teams from the industrial leagues or semipro teams. Some are fraternity or other teams from the local college or university. The individual sport that is the most popular in prison is boxing. Many of the leading contenders in this sport, as well as a champion or two, have been in prisons or training schools and many learned to fight there. One of the factors that leads to the popularity of boxing is that it is an individual sport, rather than a team sport, and thus appealing to people who do not relate well to others. Meaningful recreation may well be potentially the most rewarding program in a prison. People do not get into trouble while busily occupied. Trouble almost always starts during leisure time. )

# LIBRARY

The importance of the library has long been underestimated. Most prisons have a small library, and until recently, many used a vault type of library where books were stored but no inmate was permitted except the inmate who ran the library. Books could be ordered and delivered in two or three days. Most modern prisons and correctional institutions now have a library similar to the public library, where inmates can come and browse and check out books. Like other people, inmates steal books; however, some prisons have taken stealing books off the list of offenses for disciplinary action because then inmates do not feel the need to destroy the "evidence." Furthermore, regardless of how they have to get their books, the prime objective is to get these nonreaders to read.

A law library is an important part of the prison. It improves morale and reduces the number of suits for denial of access to counsel. At least one prison has assigned advanced commercial school students to the library as typists, provided legal forms for writs, and provided a good supply of law books relating to the state in which it is situated. Many prisons, however, have kept law books in the warden's office or in another inaccessible place, and have given them to the inmates only upon request. Technically, this is not a denial of access, but it is a hindrance. Morale can be improved by openly furnishing a law library. Experience has been that the library's initial few months or year may cause objections by the prosecutors' associations and may make some courts clean up their procedures, but the annoyance falls off after a year, while the benefits continue.

## MEDICAL AND DENTAL CARE

Medical facilities in the prison are important. An initial examination of all inmates and an evaluation of their medical condition must be made. In the group of people generally admitted to prison, there is a high incidence of venereal disease, tuberculosis, and epilepsy. In addition, approximately 5 percent have been estimated to be psychotics whom the court did not recognize as such or who were sent to the prison because there was no room for them at a state hospital.

Psychopharmacology has been used in some prisons to control violent behavior. Anectine has been used to reduce violence. Prolixin is a "supertranquilizer" more powerful than librium. Psychopharmacology has also encountered legal difficulties.

Cosmetic and plastic surgery is more important in prison and juvenile institutions than anyplace else. There are crossed eyes that need to be straightened. There are prominent facial scars, including gunshot wounds, that need to be removed. There are many disfigurements—congenital, the result of fights and accidents, and tattoos—that need to be removed. Beyond the regular dental attention needed by any population, dental surgery of the cosmetic variety is also important in a prison population.

## BEHAVIOR MODIFICATION

*Behavior modification* refers to conditioning by reward and punishment to change behavior. The use of a token economy, in which points are given for good behavior and taken away for misbehavior and which can be used to purchase privileges, has been used in many forms, particularly in juvenile institutions. Electric shock treatments were used in Connecticut for treatment of men serving time for molesting children, in which they went through a three-stage procedure aimed at making them desire women rather than children. California has used behavior modification extensively.

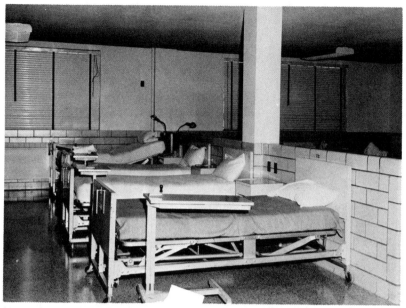

Hospital at Iowa State Penitentiary.
Courtesy of the Iowa Department of Social Services.

The Special Treatment and Rehabilitative Training (START) program at the Medical Center for Federal Prisoners at Springfield, Missouri, was based on behavior modification principles. Litigation by the Prison Project of ACLU and by several inmates has resulted in the elimination of behavior modification from most systems, however. The LEAA announced in 1975 that it would fund no behavior modification projects. In reality, some of the procedures referred to as behavior modification go beyond what was originally meant by the term. The legal problems it has encountered resulted in START's being eliminated from the United States Bureau of Prisons programs. Sufficient attention was brought to behavior modification that the *Criminal Law Bulletin* even published a symposium on it.[18]

## TREATMENT AND THE LAW

The right to treatment relates to an individual's potential dangerousness to himself or others. Birnbaum first referred to the right of treatment in 1960, referring to mentally ill persons.[19] The constitutional issues involved are

[18] See "Symposium—The Control of Behavior: Legal, Scientific, and Moral Dilemmas, Part I," *Criminal Law Bulletin,* 11, No. 5 (September–October 1975), 598–636.

[19] Morton Birnbaum, "Right to Treatment," *American Bar Association Journal,* 56 (1960), 499.

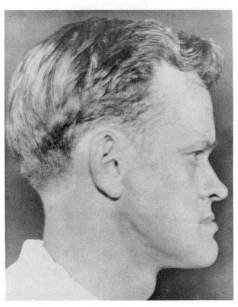

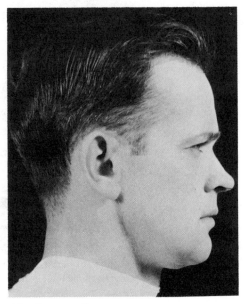

A simple operation setting back the jaw can change the facial features. This photo was taken before the operation.

After the operation.
Courtesy of the Michigan State Department of Corrections.

due process, equal protection, cruel and unusual punishment, and involuntary servitude. A 1966 decision by Judge Bazelon in the District of Columbia provided the initial recognition for the right of treatment on statutory grounds (*Rouse* v. *Cameron*, 373 F. 23 451, 1966). An earlier case involved the Patuxent Institution in Maryland and its failure to treat (*Sas* v. *State of Maryland*, 334 F. 2d 506, 1964). The case of *Holt* v. *Sarver* came close to the correctional field. It suggested that the absence of treatment might, in the future, be regarded as cruel and unusual punishment in violation of the Eighth Amendment.

The right to refuse treatment has also been upheld. This resulted from the wide use of psychosurgery and behavior modification techniques. Sol Rubin has suggested that such "treatment" is giving "humanitarianism" a bad name.[20] The First Amendment supports the right of an individual to freedom of the mind or privacy of the mind (*Stanley* v. *Georgia*, 394 U.S. 559, 1968). The use of drugs, specifically succinylcholine, used in aversive therapy, raised the serious question of impermissible "tinkering" with the mental processes (*Mackey* v. *Procunier*, 477 F. 2d 877, 1973).

[20] Sol Rubin, "The Concept of Treatment in Criminal Law," *South Carolina Law Review*, 21 (1968), 3.

Untreatables may be confined only on the basis of their need for treatment, but it must center on dangerousness (*Jackson* v. *Indiana,* 406 U.S. 715).

## PRISON AS A THERAPEUTIC COMMUNITY

The total treatment program and a treatment-oriented custodial staff can produce an institutional environment directed toward treatment. When the correctional officers participate in, support, and augment the total treatment program, the entire team is going in the same direction—this is a therapeutic community. When the objectives of the correctional program are known and accepted by all, the prison can be a therapeutic community.[21] A more sophisticated therapeutic community is one in which groups of inmates, the peer group, meet daily to work through problems. In this setting, the therapeutic community becomes helpful. Most prisons today, however, are simply "warehousing" operations.

## IMPACT OF THE "JUSTICE MODEL"

In 1975, David Fogel published a book that challenged the concept of treatment in prison and suggested that sentencing "fit the crime," rather than providing indeterminate sentencing to permit discretionary treatment of the offender.[22] As a consequence, many states considered going to determinate sentencing, even to the extent of abolishing parole, which some did, Maine being the first in 1976. (This will be discussed in Chapter 12.) Other states reduced emphasis on treatment, while others made treatment programs "voluntary." Debate about treatment and indeterminate sentencing as opposed to no emphasis on treatment combined with fixed sentencing went on for years and still continues. In a survey by *Corrections Magazine* in 1975, after the publication of Fogel's book and the beginning of the debate, 63 percent of correctional administrators in all fifty states supported rehabilitation, 90 percent supported it in community programs, 78 percent said that these community programs were effective in institutions, and an additional 14 percent said that there was not much evidence to scrap rehabilitation.[23] Most said that treatment programs had never really been tried, because they had not been adequately funded. Cullen and Gilbert wrote an excellent book in 1982 that reviewed the debate and trends, concluding that

[21] See Maxwell Jones, *Psychiatry in the Community, in Hospitals and in Prisons* (Springfield, Ill.: Charles C. Thomas, 1962).

[22] David Fogel, *". . . We Are the Living Proof . . .": The Justice Model for Corrections* (Cincinnati: W.H. Anderson, 1975).

[23] Michael S. Serrill, "Is Rehabilitation Dead?" *Corrections Magazine,* 1, No. 5 (May/June 1975), 3–7, 10–12, 21–32.

rehabilitation had been reaffirmed and was alive and well—that treatment programs should be continued.[24]

## SUMMARY

Since administrative and treatment decisions have come under judicial review, many prisons have backed away from mandatory programs. The United States Bureau of Prisons has deemphasized rehabilitation and attempted to expand pretrial diversion.[25] Requirements that all prisoners engage in educational, vocational, or other programs while incarcerated have been dropped. Participation in rehabilitative programs has become voluntary, leaving prisoners the option of not taking any program at all. If the inmate is motivated, he can take advantage of them.

On the other hand, the American Correctional Association promotes classification and rehabilitative programs. The use of classification techniques at the local and regional levels will assist the entire correctional process. The potential of classification and treatment programs has not reached their maximum contributions.[26]

## EXERCISES AND STUDY QUESTIONS

1. *To what programs in prisons does "treatment" refer?*
2. *What is classification?*
3. *Trace the development of classification.*
4. *What are the various forms and stages of classification in American prisons?*
5. *What is the treatment team concept?*
6. *What is the relationship between criminal typology and classification?*
7. *What is the RAPS system of classification?*
8. *What are the general trends in prison education today?*
9. *Evaluate vocational training in correctional institutions and prisons.*
10. *What are the objectives of correctional education?*
11. *How is programmed instruction, or Computer-Assisted Instruction (CAI), important in prisons?*

[24] Francis T. Cullin and Karen E. Gilbert, *Reaffirming Rehabilitation* (Cincinnati: W.H. Anderson Company, 1982).

[25] "The De-emphasis of Inmate Rehabilitation and Expansion of Pre-Trial Diversion," *Corrections Digest*, 6, No. 8 (April 16, 1975), 1.

[26] E. Preston Sharp, "Foreword," in Leonard J. Hippchen, ed., *Correctional Classification and Treatment* (Cincinnati: W.H. Anderson Co. for the American Correctional Association, 1975), p. xi.

12. *Evaluate mutual agreement programming.*

13. *Discuss the role of the chaplain in prisons today.*

14. *How are counseling, social casework, psychological, and psychiatric service implemented in correctional institutions?*

15. *What are the objectives of counseling for inmates?*

16. *Evaluate the use of group methods in prisons.*

17. *What is the role of recreation in prison treatment?*

18. *Evaluate behavior modification techniques in prisons.*

19. *Evaluate medical and dental approaches to prison treatment.*

20. *Can the prison become a therapeutic community?*

# 9

# THE EFFECTS OF INSTITUTIONAL LIFE

The effects of institutionalization are difficult to measure, but several observations can be made. One observation concerns the general recidivism rate or the number of repeaters coming back to the institution. Recidivism is difficult to measure also, because the records kept by 52 jurisdictions in the United States (fifty states, the District of Columbia, and the U.S. Bureau of Prisons) have not been centralized. There was an attempt to centralize these data beginning in 1970, when a Computerized Criminal History (CCH) program was added to the FBI's National Crime Information Center (NCIC) in 1968, but it became a center of controversy with the beginning of legislation regarding privacy. By 1976, it had received 800,000 criminal history records from eight states. In 1976 Attorney General Edward H. Levi requested that it be discontinued because of legal questions concerning wide dissemination of information that has no bearing on the guilt or innocence of an individual. Available statistics indicate that approximately 68 percent of all the prisoners who arrive in state and federal prisons each year have been there before, the estimate ranging from 63 percent to 70 percent over a period of years.[1] This does not mean that 68 percent of all persons who are admitted to prison each year return, of course, for many new admissions are first-timers. Probably less than half of all people who have served in prison are recidivists.[2] Recidivists make up

[1] *National Prisoner Statistics—1968* (Washington, D.C.: U.S. Bureau of Prisons, 1969).

[2] See Daniel Glaser, *The Effectiveness of a Prison and Parole System*, abridged ed. (Indianapolis: Bobbs-Merrill, 1964, 1969), p. 11.

between one-half and two-thirds of an average prison population. For further clarification, when 68 percent of incoming offenders to prison have been there before, they tend to be the same offenders, while the other approximately one-third are new first-termers each year. Consequently, repeaters make up about two-thirds of a prison population. Over a period of years, however, there is a large number of first-termers who do not come back.

Another serious problem in evaluating the results of institutions is presented by the wide diversity between institutional programs and their accompanying correctional programs. It is obvious that no two institutions are alike, even though they might be broadly classified similarly as to the type of program and the effectiveness of implementation. Supporting correctional programs, like parole, affect outcome. A poor parole program can make a good institution look bad, while a good parole program can make a poor institution look good, if the criterion for success is whether or not the released offender is involved in subsequent criminal behavior.

Information about the return of juveniles to institutions is even more difficult to obtain than information about adults. Different jurisdictions have different record systems, and they must all protect the general philosophy that juveniles do not have a "record." Many states have laws requiring the destruction of juveniles' records after a period of years. Informal discussions with the superintendents and other personnel of juvenile institutions suggest that, in general, two out of every five boys released will return, two others will later return to an adult institution, and only one out of the original five will never come in contact with the law again. The statistics from the Federal Juvenile Court Act reported in the *National Prisoner Statistics* show generally a 40 percent return of juveniles to the jurisdiction of the act, which supports the first half of the conjectured statement. In a study of the juvenile court system in Boston in the 1930s, the Gluecks indicated that about 22 percent of the juveniles there never come in contact with the law again.[3]

Recidivism apparently declines with age. For example, the highest recidivism rate is among juveniles; they have more time to return, and the risk is greater. Recidivism among young adults or reformatory age groups is almost as high as it is among juveniles. Those in adult prisons, with longer sentences and less time left to get into trouble, apparently have the lowest recidivism rate. In view of the rate of recidivism, it is clear that there should be much more extensive examination of the function of the institution and its effect on people.

Loyalty to the parental family prevails in an inmate culture, even though the loyalty may take the form of "protection" rather than "affection." Prisoners display a "halo" effect for parents, but this is apt to be absent when it comes to husbands or wives. Apparently, spouses have become

[3] Sheldon and Eleanor Glueck, *One Thousand Juvenile Delinquents* (Cambridge, Mass.: Harvard University Press, 1934), pp. 184–85.

associated with the disorganized personality (inmate) after it begins to conflict overtly with the legal norms. The separation by force intensifies the conflict and stigma without providing comfort. Inmates do not have the long-term association with spouses that they have had with parents, nor the close identification with them, so loyalty and resulting defensiveness are not present, at least to the extent as they are with parents.

The inmates run most prisons. They run them not because they have the authority to do so, but because there is not enough free help for outsiders to control everything. In addition, they obtain many jobs through default on the part of regular staff members. It is a rare prison that has enough clerical help. The majority of prisons have inmate clerks working in the office of the deputy warden, sometimes in the control room or elsewhere in the custodial force. There are inmate clerk-typists and other assistants in the classification department, in the school, where they also may teach, and in most of the factories, the maintenance department, the hospital, and elsewhere in the prison.

In this situation, the administration may issue an order, such as a classification committee recommendation or order to a certain job, which the inmate clerk in the deputy's office may implement. But there are problems involved with inmate staff. In those situations where a favored job might be involved, a card may get misfiled or lost until the inmate involved furnishes the inmate-clerk with a carton of cigarettes or other payment. Many standardized examinations are graded by inmate-clerks in the school. Grades or passing a test may be worth a certain number of packs or cartons of cigarettes. In the classification department, IQs have been "sold." In this world of "wheeling and dealing," the extent to which such arrangements exist is directly related to the amount of control the administration and custodial staff have over the prison.

In some prison systems, such as those of New York, California, and the United States Bureau of Prisons, most of the flagrant inmate control that existed in the past is gone. In some less fortunate systems, however, the warden's secretary may be an inmate, an inmate may operate the switchboard and central communications, and inmates may do all the teaching in the school and any testing that has to be done.

The inmate world is simple and sparse. Loss of self-determination and the process of "prisonization" involve acute psychological stress for the individual. Release to the outside transmutes bad times into bad memories, and civil reality takes hold firmly.[4] A primary component in prison life is homesickness.[5] Grief, mourning, and depression frequently lay the base for the immobilization and automation-like life style of many prisoners. In

[4] Irving Goffman, "On the Characteristics of Total Institutions: The Inmate World," in Donald R. Cressey, ed., *The Prison: Studies in Institutional Organization and Change* (New York: Holt, Rinehart & Winston, 1961), pp. 15–67.

[5] John Bowlby, *Separation Anxiety: A Critical Review of the Literature* (New York: Child Welfare League of America, 1962), reprinted from *Journal of Child Psychology and Psychiatry*, 1, 251–69.

children and in adults, the anxiety reaction to separation falls into three main phases: protest, despair, and detachment.

Lifers constitute a legal, rather than a sociological, group whose reactions to entering prison, socialization, time, religion, suicide, and rehabilitation vary widely.[6] Reaction to entering prison ranges from physical or mental rebellion to physical relaxation with abnormal hunger and capacity to sleep. Attitudes toward socialization range from never fully accepting the process to an immediate and complete acceptance of it. Attitudes toward rehabilitation also show wide diversion.

Assaults, homicides, and suicides occur with some frequency in maximum custody prisons. In 1973, there were 108 inmates officially killed by other inmates, as compared with 122 in 1972.[7] This writer's experience and observation suggest that the number has been considerably reduced since the 1950s! Former inmate Francis Marziani of the United States Penitentiary at Lewisburg, Pennsylvania, told U.S. District Judge Clarence Newcomer, "No big deal. With a population of 1,600, we get about 25 murders a year. With the going price for murder at two cartons of cigarettes, I guess that isn't bad."[8] Official statistics indicate that there were eight inmate murders at Lewisburg during the fifteen months ending May 1976. Warden Ken McKellar of South Carolina told the author about an incident in 1975 in which he chased an inmate who was chasing another inmate, and they went around the corner of a building. By the time McKellar arrived, one inmate was dead, other inmates in the area "never seen nothin'," which is standard, and there was no way to prove murder because "nobody seen nothin' "—not even the warden! There were 92 inmate suicides in 1973 as compared with 62 in 1972. The United States Bureau of Prisons had five homicides and eight suicides in 1973, as compared with nine homicides and five suicides in 1972, again an apparent reduction under the rates for the 1950s.

This type of prison society may not exist at all in a minimum security forestry camp or a treatment-oriented correctional institution. It does exist in most maximum custody prisons.

Under an authoritarian structure, the inmates treat some of their peers as scapegoats, rebel aggressively or passively, and sullenly bide their time until release. The type of prison and the attitudes of the prison staff will be reflected in the prisoner's adjustment. The inmate subculture will either conform to or reject the goals of the custodial staff. Riots are reported to be more common in custody-oriented prisons. Adjustment of the prisoner changes with the length of incarceration, with the poorest adjust-

[6] Charles M. Unkovic and Joseph L. Albini, "The Lifer Speaks for Himself—An Analysis of the Assumed Homogeneity of Life-Termers," *Crime and Delinquency*, January 1969, pp. 156–61.

[7] "Violence Figures Released," *Corrections Digest*, 5, No. 19 (September 18, 1974), 1.

[8] "Lewisburg Inmate Testifies on Widespread Prison Violence," *Corrections Digest*, 7, No. 12 (June 16, 1976), 7.

**Table 9-1   Deaths in 1979 by region**

|  | Prisoner Population | Number of Deaths | Deaths per 1,000 Prisoners |
|---|---|---|---|
| United States | 301,017 | 681 | 2.26 |
| Federal institutions | 22,588 | 66 | 2.92 |
| State institutions | 278,429 | 615 | 2.21 |
| Northeast | 41,337 | 71 | 1.72 |
| North Central | 61,698 | 160 | 2.59 |
| South | 133,351 | 293 | 2.20 |
| West | 42,043 | 91 | 2.17 |

*Source: Prisoners in State and Federal Institutions on December 31, 1979,* National Prisoner Statistics Bulletin SD-NPS-PSF-7 (Washington, D.C.: U.S. Government Printing Office, 1981), p. 21.

ment effected early in the prison term. Persistent lawbreakers habitually show poor adjustment both within the prison and outside. Except in the case of escapees, the man most likely to encounter disciplinary action is younger, nonwhite, with a history of previous violence in the institution and a criminal record. The escapee is more likely to be white, strongly isolated from and hostile toward his family, and having a poor relationship with his peers. In addition, he generally has an unsatisfactory sex life, suffers from severe depressions and a tendency toward hypochrondriasis, and rejects religion. Projective and perception tests both reflect the nonadjusted prisoner's tendency to behave violently.[9]

## THE INSTITUTIONALIZED PERSONALITY

The institutionalized personality is the victim of a process sometimes called "prisonization."[10] This process refers to the automaton-like behavior of the long-term prisoner who has become devoid of initiative, lives on a day-to-day basis, responds to the simple diversions of routine like the weekly movie and "store day" when scrip is issued, and has blocked off his past and his future. The institutionalized personality is an accommodation to a long-term control in which he "gets along" in a regimented society by "playing the nods" with his superiors, doing his own time with his peers, and has no outside family or friends. The late Tom Runyon said it took about five years for the average prisoner to reach this point.[11]

The social system within the prison community desocializes as well as

[9] Dorothy R. Jaman, *Behavior During the First Year in Prison: Reports 1 and 2—MMPI Scales and Behavior,* Research Report Number 34, California Department of Corrections (Sacramento: State Printing Office, 1969), pp. 83–84.

[10] See Donald Clemmer, *The Prison Community* (Boston: Christopher Press, 1940; reissued by Holt, Rinehart & Winston, 1958). The literature is replete with studies on this point.

[11] Tom Runyon, *In for Life* (New York: Norton, 1953).

resocializes individual inmates.[12] The desocialization process is caused by (1) the loss of personal and private property, (2) the loss of civil rights, (3) status deprivation, (4) experience in a state of helplessness, and (5) the redefinition of self-concept. The process results in the institutionalized personality. The resocialization process in prison is manifest in (1) the inmate's complete submission to authority of older inmates, guards, and other prison personnel to meet the expectations of the new social role in terms of submission, ignorance, awe for authority, and severe self-limitations; (2) the self-styled inmate who boasts about his deviant behavior, incarceration in other institutions, difficulty with the law, and crafty and sly deviant techniques; (3) the institutionalized person who accepts the norms and values considered socially acceptable to other inmates within the institution, including the use of vile language, disregard for the penal system and its authority figures, name-calling, distrust of fellow inmates and staff, and acceptance of the status quo; (4) the inmate who maintains a great degree of social distance from other inmates of the institution and is sneaky, secretive, irresponsible, unreliable, and untrustworthy; and (5) the loner who isolates himself from other prisoners and busies himself with his own affairs, maintaining distance from fellow inmates, although socially active with them. The role of the prison system in resocialization involves (1) development of the sense of worth through positive reinforcement, usable skills, and education; (2) development of the sense of status; and (3) change in self-concept.

Clemmer's classic work, first published in 1930 as *The Prison Community*, identified the process of prisonization and what prisons do to people.[13] Sykes's classic work, published in 1958, supported Clemmer's observation and suggested that it results from the "pains of imprisonment."[14] The pains of imprisonment are seen as (1) deprivation of goods and services; (2) deprivation of heterosexual relationships; (3) deprivation of autonomy; and (4) deprivation of security. A prison inmate can never feel safe, and at a deeper level lie his or her reactions to an unstable world filled with aggression, exploitation, and perceived injustice which has victimized the prisoner.

Authoritarian personalities abound in prison, among staff and inmates alike. These authoritarian personalities have intense feelings and attitudes, and are power-oriented and vindictive. They have been shown to appear among prison personnel and tend to characterize many prison inmates as well.[15] This provides a "pressure cooker" atmosphere that results

[12] Peter O. Peretti, "Desocialization-Resocialization; Process within the Prison Walls," *Canadian Journal of Corrections*, 12, No. 1 (January 1970), 59–66.

[13] Clemmer, *The Prison Community*.

[14] Gresham Sykes, *The Society of Captives* (Princeton, N.J.: Princeton University Press, 1958), pp. 65–78.

[15] T.W. Adorno, Else Frenkel-Brunswick, Daniel J. Levinson, and R. Nevitt Sanford, in collaboration with Betty Aron, Marcia Hertz Levinson, and William Morrow, *The Authoritarian Personality* (New York: Harper Brothers, 1950).

in stressful frustration, loss of hope, and identification with an inmate code that calls for doing one's own time on a day-to-day basis and not bothering anybody else, unless one is powerful enough to do it.

In most maximum custody prisons, the prisoners are subjected to strict regulation for the safety and the security of the institution. People respond to their environment. In prison, the inmates are taught to line up, are told that aggression will be met with aggression, and are ordered when to get up and when to go to bed. The lights never go out. Life is structured and well-regulated, generally far different from what most were accustomed to on the outside. The result has to be a dehumanizing environment where there are few individual decisions other than that of deciding whether to go along with the recommendations or to resist them. The resulting stereotyped pattern of behavior, moving like an automaton in response to stimuli, "institutionalizes" the behavior of people. This regulation allows inmates to "get into the routine" with a minimum of irritation and anxiety. However, it reinforces the futility of relating to others in a meaningful way, induces superficial courtesy to authority figures, and promotes flat emotional responses to others and their environment because it is dangerous to invest in others.

In maximum security prisons, there is a deprivation of meaningful emotional relationships and cultural experiences, and the minimal standard of living further drains life of meaning. Little things become important, such as the day's menu, a candy bar, or the weekly movie. Goals and aspirations become readjusted downward or given up completely. Lifers and long-timers learn to live from day to day.

Martinson's concept of social compression refers to social arrangements where communication, movement, and interaction are severely restricted.[16] This occurs in maximum custody prisons, and particularly in disciplinary units in these prisons. Inmate–staff stress in these situations generally establish stereotypes of inmates as troublemakers and dangerous management problems, while inmate–inmate relationships tend to fragmentize groups into factions. These factions are frequently related to minority groups, ethnic groups, or other identifiable entities. The result is that minor interactions become of major consequence. Some people react in this pressurized society by trying to remain alone, not risking involvement with others. Other people become aggressive in rebellion.

Many of the staff become institutionalized too. Many old correctional officers with 20 or 25 years of service sometimes see themselves as "doing time." Deputy wardens and other prison officials have seen their sons and daughters married, with the majority of the wedding guests being trusted long-term prisoners. In one case, wedding pictures were printed in the newspaper with the largest circulation in the state as part of the reporting of a political investigation of the prison system. For many of the staff, the

---

[16] Robert Martinson, "Social Interaction under Close Confinement," *Psychiatry*, 30, No. 2 (1967), 132–48.

prison is their world. They are "in the routine" and have become "institutionalized" themselves.

When anxiety and frustration become intolerable, the Ganser syndrome frequently appears. This is the technical term for what inmates and prison personnel call "stir bugs" or "stir-crazy." The symptoms are a general but mild confusion and flat emotional responses. A typical conversation by such a case might sound like this (from a real conversation):

> *Psychologist:* What can I do for you?
> *Joe:* Da parole board flopped me.
> *Psychologist:* Why did they flop you?
> *Joe:* Dey didn't tell me why dey flopped me.
> *Psychologist:* What did they say?
> *Joe:* Dey didn't say nuttin'.
> *Psychologist:* Did they give you any clue at all?
> *Joe:* No.
> *Psychologist:* Did they say anything else?
> *Joe:* Yeah, dey told me dat I was associatin' wid bums an' tramps an' no-
> goods.
> *Psychologist:* They told you that?
> *Joe:* Yeah, dey can't talk about me friends dat way.

Joe had done twelve years on a 15- to 30-year sentence and had lapsed into the Ganser syndrome after about five years. It is apparently a type of neurosis, rather than "prison psychosis," as it has been termed in some places. The only cure appears to be letting the person out. The Ganser syndrome suddenly disappears when an inmate is released, but it has never been successfully treated in a maximum security prison. Men who are going "stir-crazy" talk as though they are not in contact with reality and have to be separated in diagnosis from men with real psychotic problems. The "stir-crazy" men are simply accommodating to a more extreme and oppressive prison environment than they can tolerate, which leads to generally paranoid or persecutory reactions.[17]

After 17 years in prison, a lifer who expresses himself well wrote:

> ... I was hurt—frustrated, deprived of hope, regimented, humiliated, punished—I became worse, either deliberately or unconsciously. Each time I was helped—given some small hope or purpose, treated as an individual, given even a small reason to be grateful to authorities—I became, and behaved, better. Each time needless discipline has been relaxed, each time they have been allowed to relax and respect themselves, I've seen men in this prison become better prisoners and better risks as ex-convicts. Each time I've seen men really trusted—not partly trusted, as on the prison farms or other places with guards near—I've seen them try to deserve that trust.
>
> Today I am trusted, inside the walls to a large extent despite the fact that for over ten years I was the only man to escape from inside the walls after

---

[17] Cornelius C. Wholey, "Psychiatric Report on a Study of Psychopathic Inmates of a Penitentiary," *Journal of Criminal Law and Criminology,* 28 (May–June 1937), 55.

Warden Lainson took charge. He simply accepted my voluntary promise not to escape, and that fact made it impossible for me to let him down. If it wasn't for the federal detainer that has kept me on relentlessly nearly fifteen years, I'm reasonably certain I would as quickly be trusted outside the walls, and that belief alone makes me a better prisoner. More important, I have friends and relatives out there beyond the walls who believe in me. Allowed to come closer to emotional maturity as I have been, now I cannot let them down.

I believe my experiences and reactions to them have in many ways been the same as those of other convicts—that I have reacted much as any citizen thrown into an utterly unnatural environment might have. Today, treated like a man, I feel compelled to act like a man.[18]

First-termers without any previous institutional experience adjust better in prison than those with previous institutionalization. First-termers are more easily intimidated by other inmates and correctional officers and are more cautious and apprehensive of their behavior and records. Interviews with inmates with previous juvenile institutionalization support the contention that the highly emotionalized temper of the conditioning experience in juvenile institutionalization during adolescence makes it even more intense than adult imprisonment. More antisocial grudges are developed, feelings against inequalities and injustices in society and the personalization of social inequities leading to self-concepts of "born to lose" are all more intense in the young adolescent than in adults and shape the social attitudes for time to come. Conditioning during early adolescence is more indelible than conditioning at almost any other later developmental period of equal length.

The reformatory experience does not modify appreciably the effect of juvenile institutionalization, and those subjected to reformatory experience without juvenile experience have similar attitudinal conditioning, but it is less emotional and more based upon orientation and "learning the ropes." Here they learn the system of "inmate politics," where inmates in key clerical positions become influential with one or more civilian employees and use their influence to their own advantage with other inmates. While this system is suppressed by the custodial force whenever it is found, there is not enough custodial force to suppress all of it or even to keep up with it. The problem of getting along in prison with the "prison-wise" offender is one of institutional orientation and learning. The successful "conniver" is not caught and may elude detection.

## PRISONERS' ATTITUDES AND VALUES

The attitudes developed by inmates in this setting seem to grow in patterns. There are several books written by prison inmates over the years that are

---

[18] Tom Runyon, "Prison Shocks," Chap. 28 in Robert G. Caldwell, *Criminology* (New York: Ronald Press, 1956), p. 636.

excellent portrayals of the development of the inmate mind.[19] Authority is seen as aggressive and sometimes sadistic. Prison thus seems to reinforce the inmate's concept of authority as he has grown up with it in a lower-class home through the years. Authority has always been something to avoid because it was hostile and aggressive and bullying. The constant supervision in the prison society reinforces this concept. Very seldom does the inmate see authority in the treatment sense as supporting and protective. Correctional officers are referred to as "screws" throughout the prison world. There are "pencil-happy screws" in every prison who will write up an inmate for minor offenses. Consequently, the attitude toward authority by the prison inmate is one of resentment.

Inmates generally project blame for their situation upon society. As mentioned early in the book, the inmate may feel that being in prison is not his fault, but the fault of "the system." He sees himself against "the system" throughout life. He sees himself as "born to lose" in this social system. The pardon of President Richard Nixon by his successor, who simultaneously called for "stiffer penalties" for criminals, produced universal prisoner resentment, exemplified by cartoons captioned, "The big one got away."

Part of this attitude is reinforced by his concept of the social system as "the caught and the uncaught." Inmates know of and hear of persons who have commited offenses but who are never caught. Even more tangibly, when inmates see free personnel at the prison stealing gas or foodstuffs and "clipping" the system of right and wrong in a variety of services and goods, it frustrates them. They say, "They arrested *me.*"

Anxiety develops among many inmates until they accommodate to it. They are worried about their wives and sweethearts. They can do nothing about anything—they are utterly powerless. Disturbing letters from home leave them with no way to go and no way out.

Routinely, the inmate has a high anxiety level during the first few weeks and months of his incarceration, which lowers as he accommodates to the institution and then rises again as he is to be released. This changing experience provides a U-shaped anxiety curve, and helps to explain why some inmates escape or run away only a week or so before they are to be released on parole. Evaluation of an inmate's tolerance to anxiety is only one factor that has to be taken into consideration in predicting behavior. There is very little in the prison society to reduce anxiety. Those who do reduce it accommodate by doing their time "one day at a time." Wheeler also posited a U-curve in terms of early adherence to society's values, then adherence to prison values in the middle of a prison term, followed by adherence to society's values as release time comes for many inmates.[20]

The collective violence in correctional institutions can be attributed

[19] For example, see Victor F. Nelson, *Prison Days and Nights* (Boston: Little, Brown, 1932), and Tom Runyon's *In for Life*, cited above.

[20] Stanton Wheeler, "Socialization in Correctional Communities," *American Sociological Review*, 26 (1961), 697–712.

to "(a) the excessive reliance by staff on the acquiescence and cooperation of a pervasive inmate intrastructure, a practice which seems to derive from the very nature of large-scale, total institutions; (b) absent or restricted communication patterns which seriously impair the airing of legitimate inmate grievances and the detection of impending unrest; (c) failure to recognize the root causes of racial and political tensions which are reflections of tensions in society at large; (d) insufficient differentiation between militant and revolutionary prisoners, paired with the failure to physically separate these inmates; (e) insufficient awareness of the fact that ordinary criminal behavior is often rationalized and disguised as political activity; (f) failure to consider the effects of frustrations and the perception of deprivation in the light of promised prison reform; and (g) perpetuation of social and physical environments which are antithetical to the goals of correction and resocialization."[21]

## INMATE STORE AND PRISON BARTER

The inmate store or canteen is important in the life of the inmate. In his simplistic society, "store day" may be like "Saturday night." In some pris-

Fully stocked canteen at Iowa State Penitentiary.
Courtesy of the Iowa Department of Social Services.

[21] Edith Elisabeth Flynn, "Sources of Collective Violence in Correctional Institutions," in *Prevention of Violence in Correctional Institutions* (Washington, D.C.: National Institute of Law Enforcement and Criminal Justice, LEAA, U.S. Department of Justice, June 1973), p. 28.

ons, the commissary or inmate store is open daily. In other prisons, the commissary consists of a trailer that makes its rounds among various facilities once a week.

The economy among inmates is active in most prisons and correctional institutions. Cigarettes are the usual medium of exchange. They are used not only in gambling but also for favors and goods. In many maximum security prisons, where inmates handle clerical routines, certain jobs are worth a certain number of packs or cartons of cigarettes. As has been mentioned, where inmates score group tests and examinations for the schools, sometimes IQ scores and passing grades can be purchased. Barbers generally are relatively wealthy in the inmate hierarchy, because a good haircut is generally worth a pack of cigarettes despite the close supervision of custody. Only a few systems have close enough supervision of barbers to eliminate their hold over their fellow inmates.

Hijacking in the yard on store day is not unusual. Stealing and strong-arming is common in prisons. Custodial control of inmate property is a difficult objective to achieve.

## THE INFORMAL SOCIAL CONTROL

There is an informal social control within the prison. The prison administrator can use this informal control for his own ends, the maintenance of peace and tranquility, if he is sufficiently astute. Conflicts between specialized administrative units could result in fractional disputes and insoluble staff problems of contradictory purposes. Such conflicts impair the work of the staff and can also be manipulated by the inmates. The executive in a progressive institution, however, can formulate and communicate for the entire community a definition that transcends these narrow divisional lines based on different perspectives.[22]

Inmate organization is largely a response to institutional conditions. It emerges as a response to the deprivations of institutional living and the process by which individual inmates interact with institutional environments to produce the characteristic affiliations in inmate society. The recognition of the impact of inmate organization in the correctional endeavor is essential to successful correctional treatment. Inmate behavior may represent a subclass of behavior with organizational manifestations which are similar to those in a wide range of different environments.[23] The social organization in prison, then, is an expected and "natural" social phenomenon in that environment.

The disciplinary unit or the incorrigible unit in the prison is an integral part of the prison as a system of social control. It maximizes the vari-

[22] "The Governmental Process and Informal Social Control," in Cressey, ed., *The Prison*, pp. 149–88.

[23] Charles R. Tittle, "Inmate Organization: Sex Differentiation and the Influence of Criminal Subcultures," *American Sociological Review*, 34, No. 4 (August 1969), 492–505.

ables of external constraint as a system of social control and permits examination of the consequences. This unit also provides insight into both the attitudes and the process of extreme alienation, which is a relatively uncompromised culture of criminality.[24] Such isolation results in a disregard for appearances and decency and the spread of fantastic stories. The accompanying social degradation brings envy and hate, lying and boasting, together with the urge to dominate.

The informal social control held by inmates is based on the vested interests of the long-term inmates. When inmates have been around the institution long enough to know the routines and the power structure, the able men can gain power by gaining the trust of the warden, deputy wardens, and others from whom they take the "routine" tasks of day-to-day operation of the prison. When these able men develop a "good go" for themselves, they will protect it by preventing disruption from other, new or less able inmates. This system helps to explain why there are no riots or other disturbances reported from primarily inmate-operated prisons, such as some Southern prisons that have used inmate guards.

The official recognition and formalization of this informal inmate control is central to prison administration. Whether there should be an "inmate council," as is present in the United States Bureau of Prisons and some state prison systems, or whether the administration should remain in complete charge is a matter of debate in modern corrections.

The most famous experiment in inmate self-government replicated that experiment in New York, when Warden Thomas Mott Osborne initiated the Mutual Welfare League at Auburn and Sing Sing prisons in New York. He copied some of the program of the George Junior Republic at Freeville, New York, where the community organization comprised the inmates as *citizens* with responsibility for order within the community. In 1914, this experiment in prison democracy was inaugurated at Auburn. Discipline of the institution and the rules were left to a body of fifty delegates elected by the other prisoners on the basis of representation of several workshop gangs. The success of the experiment was watched with interest throughout correctional circles. The morale of the inmates rose and the institution functioned smoothly. As time went on, however, it was apparent that adequate supervision had not been applied, and some inmates were manipulating the program for their own self-service. By 1928, the plan was abandoned.

The problem of public relations and charges of "coddling" are always a problem in inmate self-government. Some criminologists have indicated that a primary weakness with this type of system is that it applies to the nonreformable as well as the reformable, which makes it unworkable.[25] Further, self-government without adequate supervision affords an opportu-

[24] Richard H. McCleery, "Authoritarianism and the Belief System of Incorrigibles," in Cressey, ed., *The Prison*, pp. 260–306.

[25] Harry Elmer Barnes and Negley K. Teeters, *New Horizons in Criminology*, 3rd ed. (Englewood Cliffs, N.J.: Prentice-Hall, 1959), p. 501.

nity for some inmates to exploit important offices for personal advantage, which is what happened with the Mutual Welfare League.

In 1927, Superintendent Howard B. Gill of the Norfolk Prison Colony in Massachusetts inaugurated a system in which an inmate council was established and inmates and all staff members discussed general policies. Joint responsibility was the keynote of the Norfolk plan.[26]

The inmate council idea is currently functioning in several prison systems, including the U.S. Bureau of Prisons. Elected representatives from dormitories or cellblocks within the institution meet with the warden and various members of the staff on a regular basis. They handle grievances from inmates, make suggestions with regard to general policy, identify certain problem areas, help work out unnecessary conflicts, and interpret some administrative problems and decisions to the inmate body. To say that the correctional administrators who are using the council have found it workable would constitute a self-fulfilling prophecy, but the consensus is that it reduces the dichotomy between administrative controllers and inmates who may consider themselves oppressed.

Conceivably, the most workable type of inmate government might include a basic constitution and bylaws similar to that of a civilian government in an occupied territory or student government in a university. Areas of primary concern could be delineated in a joint responsibility arrangement in which the inmates have an investment and involvement in the government of their institution. The advantages of this kind of government would be that inmates' involvement would foster the development of a therapeutic community with good atmosphere and morale. Its primary disadvantages would be its threat to correctional administrators, who might consider that such a program would essentially be an abandonment of administrative responsibilities to the inmates. In countries occupied by foreign military powers and in universities plagued by student unrest, however, involvement of the native or consumer population has been helpful in reducing problem areas.

## PRISONERS' UNIONS

The United Prisoners' Union was begun at the California State Prison at Folsom in 1970 to initiate collective bargaining with the administration and the legislature. It was a highly politicized group. A more moderate group, the Prisoners' Union, now active in the Bay area, split from it in 1972. The first labor union of prisoners was at the Green Haven State Prison in Stormville, New York, in early 1972, with the legal work done by the Prisoners' Rights Project of the Legal Aid Society. This Prisoners' Labor Union notified Commissioner Russell Oswald of New York that it wanted to be recognized as the exclusive bargaining agent for the inmates at Green Haven Prison.

[26] *Ibid.*, p. 502.

Since 1972, several prisoners' unions have been established in Minnesota, North Carolina, Wisconsin, and New England (Prisoners' Alliance—NEPA). The Washington State Prisoners' Union became defunct in 1975, but this group is attempting reorganization. There is a general movement in many states toward organizing prisoners' unions. Prisoners' unions became a major topic discussed as a viable and realistic movement at the Southern Conference on Corrections at Florida State University in February 1976. Prisoners' unions, of course, have been present in Europe for a long time (West Germany, Norway, Sweden, and other countries).

In 1976, the Prisoners' Union represented 20,000 convicts and exconvicts (terminology theirs) around the nation. The state of California considered the adoption of a policy that would recognize the Prisoners' Union as the bargaining agent to represent the inmates.[27] The Correctional Officers' Brotherhood threatened to strike if California recognized the Prisoners' Union as the bargaining agent for the prisoners. It should be noted here that the legal support for prisoners' unions comes from the First Amendment of the Constitution, giving citizens the right of peaceable assembly, further interpreted by some as the right to organize for redress of grievances.

Other inmate groups have organized to represent prisoners without calling themselves unions. The Incarcerated Veterans Assistance Organization (IVAO) was formed in July 1974 at the District of Columbia Reformatory at Lorton, Virginia, to assure that veterans obtain their maximum GI benefits and that offenders be permitted to serve their time in the military services with time credited toward parole.[28] The National Prison Reform Association was organized and is quartered at the Rhode Island Adult Correctional Institution, maximum custody section, in Cranston, Rhode Island, and this organization publishes the *NPRA News* to disseminate information regarding lawsuits by inmates and news stories regarding prison events.

## CONJUGAL AND FAMILY VISITING

Conjugal visiting has occurred in American prisons for a long time on an informal and haphazard basis, but Mississippi was first to make it public. Conjugal visiting has been part of the Mississippi State Penitentiary at Parchman since its beginning in 1900. An evaluation of the program by Hopper has been positive.[29]

[27] "California Considering Prisoners' Union," *Corrections Digest,* 7. No. 2 (January 28, 1976), 6.

[28] "Inmate Veterans Organize in D.C.," *Target* (Newsletter of Innovative Projects Funded by LEAA), 4, Issue 5 (May 1975), 4.

[29] Columbus B. Hopper, *Sex in Prison* (Baton Rouge, La.: Louisiana State University Press, 1968).

Minimum security family unit, used for family visiting, at the California Conservation Center at Susanville.
Courtesy of the California Department of Corrections.

Family visiting on an experimental basis began in California at Tehachapi in 1968. By 1972, this type of visiting was in effect in nearly all California correctional institutions.[30]

Many correctional administrators oppose the conjugal or family visit and are in favor of furloughs instead. More people are qualified for furloughs than for conjugal visits, because the majority of inmates are single or divorced. Further, the emphasis is on broader social reintegration and not focused on sex. Also important is the fact that children do not see their fathers in prison settings, but can see them at home.

Ordinary visits by the family are of importance to maintaining ties with the family members. Contacts with legally married wives of first-term inmates grow fewer in the second year of incarceration and later, indicating a gradual erosion of the marriage with the length of incarceration.[31] This has also been observed in women's institutions as the lesbian relationship replaces heterosexual relationships.

Many institutions are using telephone calls between inmates or residents and their families. Generally, the inmate can call his or her family collect or can pay for it. In a few cases, the families can call the inmates. The Kentucky Reformatory at LaGrange made 10,258 calls to families in 44 states between the initiation of the program in December 1973 and

[30] *Pattern of Change* (Sacramento: California Department of Corrections, 1972), p. 7.

[31] Norman Holt and Donald Miller, *Explorations in Inmate-Family Relationships* (Sacramento: California Department of Corrections, January 1972), p. vi.

Family visiting at the California Conservation Center at Susanville.
Courtesy of the California Department of Corrections.

mid-1974. The possibility of visual telephone equipment for this purpose is being explored by some private companies, such as Westinghouse.

## OTHER INMATE ACTIVITIES

Inmates may participate in a variety of other activities. Arts and crafts or hobbycraft is an activity found in almost every prison. Because of the materials purchased and the sale of items to the public, it must be closely supervised. There are several patterns of supervision. Probably one of the more successful approaches is to permit any prisoner to make anything that does not require contraband materials, have a selected inmate committee to control the prices, and have the hobbycraft store managed by a civilian paid from the profits of the store. Some prisons have a system in which a concession for any item, such as leather wallets, cedar chests, or ornate birdcages, is given to a single inmate. Anybody can make any item, but he must work through the inmate with the concession. Many other systems of control have also been used.

Other activities have been carried out by inmates in many ways. Some prisons have a radio program. The Texas system has a rodeo every

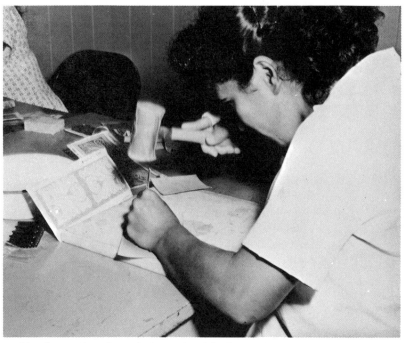

Hobby class at Hawaii Youth Correctional Facility, Kailua, Hawaii.
Courtesy of the Hawaii Department of Social Services and Housing.

Sunday in October. Several prisons have inmate teams that go out and talk before high school assemblies and civic clubs. Many institutions have varsity athletic teams that compete with neighboring community teams. It is interesting to note that most prisoner-spectators for these home games cheer for the outside team—not wanting anything to do with that "bunch of crooks" on the home team.

Alcoholics Anonymous (A.A.) chapters are present in most prisons. The establishment of chapters in prisons is explained in A.A. publications.[32] In prisons, an inmate general secretary is elected by the membership; this person corresponds with A.A.'s General Service Office. In jails, the population is too transient to have an inmate general secretary, so the jail A.A. is operated by an outside group. Some correctional workers have criticized A.A. in prisons on the basis that their objective is sobriety and prisoners "can't get alcohol anyway." This criticism really misses the point, since the A.A.'s quasi-religious approach to living through their Twelve Steps[33] program is a way of life, or a way of thinking.

The *Reader's Digest* has a special service for institutions. Each month,

[32] *A.A. in Prisons,* A.A., Box 459, Grand Central Post Office, New York, New York 10017.

[33] See *Alcoholics Anonymous* (the basic text), *Twelve Steps and Twelve Traditions, A.A. Comes of Age,* and *The A.A. Way of Life,* all available from the New York office.

the remaining unsold newstand copies of the *Reader's Digest* are reserved by the wholesale distributors and allocated to nearby charitable institutions, including correctional institutions. Because of union regulations, offsale issues cannot be delivered, so the magazines are picked up by the institution. Surplus volumes of the *Condensed Books* are mailed to selected institutions each year. The materials usually allocated on a population and age basis, generally one copy for each twenty adult readers and one copy for each ten young readers.

The Dale Carnegie courses are given frequently at prisons and correctional institutions. These courses are designed to promote self-improvement, the ability to speak, and the exercise of social leadership. They improve social effectiveness, develop a sense of worthiness, and generally improve the individual.

There are many other organizations represented in various prisons and correctional institutions. Toastmaster's Clubs and chapters of the Junior Chamber of Commerce, for example, can be found in many American correctional institutions.

The International Correspondence Schools has had a program for courses in prison. The original course has been paid for, but subsequent similar courses in the same prison have been given from the same materials, duplicated by the prison and graded by the inmates who completed previous courses.

Most prisons and correctional institutions have their own inmate publications. They range from sophisticated newspapers, such as *The Spectator* in Michigan, *The Mentor* in Massachusetts, and *The Presidio* in Iowa, to "slicks" primarily designed for public consumption, such as the *Raiford Record* in Florida, to the mimeographed publications issued by the majority of correctional institutions, such as *The Stretch* in Kansas. Each publication has its own inmate editor, staff of writers, and technicians. Many editors exchange publications and respond to articles and notices in other papers in their own columns devoted to this purpose, quite frequently called "penal press." The stories are primarily those of interest to the inmates, whether news inside the prison or statements and political action concerning prisons and prisoners from the outside.

The vilification or support of the prison administration in the penal press is frequently dependent upon the extent of censorship. The prisoners' unions really reflect inmate attitudes. One typical comment appeared in a prisoners' union paper as follows:

> The CDC [California Department of Corrections], though seemingly an organization of politically mature and publicly responsible officials, is nothing more than a group of silly dottering old fools who want to be seen as hard guys faced with an unsurmountable, extremely dangerous job of controlling the liberal urges of childless judges, the lawlessness of artistic lawyers, the rebellion of monstrous baby-eating, salivating captives, and the subversive sway of skirts. In an effort to find a scapegoat to cover for

their own impotence, these official dragoons have to look inside their own drawers! That would be the *manly* thing to do.[34]

For many years, a common prison rule was that no inmate could work on another inmate's case as a substitute lawyer because the resulting obligations established situations that had several undesirable consequences. Recent decisions, however, have held that inmates *can* prepare legal writs for other inmates (*Johnson* v. *Avery*, 393 U.S. 483, 1969; *Gilmore* v. *Lynch*, 319 F. Supp. 105, N.D., California, 1970; *Younger* v. *Gilmore*, 404 U.S. 15, 1971).

## RESULTS OF INSTITUTIONALIZATION

Institutional programs vary widely in philosophy and direction. The traditional maximum security prison is a regimented holding operation, in which inmates are "warehoused" for the duration imposed by the court. In only a few prisons has an honest attempt been made to introduce an adequate treatment program. The priorities of the prison system in the state's budgets, however, preclude much more than token programs in many institutions. In some of the smaller correctional institutions and specialized facilities, a clinical team, using the services of social workers and clinical psychologists together with psychiatric consultation, have produced varying results.

Recidivism, or repetition of crime, is one criterion that can be used to assess effectiveness, but recidivism itself is hard to measure. In a survey done in 1957,[35] the recidivism rates (based on the number of repeaters received annually, which is only a rough index) varied widely between jurisdictions that were spending money on treatment programs and those systems that were not. The average recidivism rate was 68 percent. New Jersey had the lowest rate, 41 percent. Other states with low rates were California with about 48 percent, Michigan, Minnesota, Massachusetts, and Wisconsin. All these states spend a higher proportion of their budget for treatment staff than the average. At the other extreme were states with recidivism rates running between 75 percent and 85 percent, according to their own reports, and in which virtually nothing was spent for treatment staff. When the average cost of maintaining a prisoner in these various states is computed, the higher expenditures per man result in substantial savings to the public in three to ten years, depending upon the jurisdictions, when prisoners do not return for second or third terms. Based on a

[34] Virginia L. Verrill, "Can't Get It Up!" *The Outlaw*, 3, No. 6 (October–November 1974), 5.

[35] This survey was done by the author and was reported in "Reputational Rankings of American Prison Systems," *Indian Journal of Social Research*, No. 3 (December 1964), pp. 279–88.

comparison of the top ten systems with the bottom ten systems, it is fair to conclude that if a good job is done the first time, then one-third to one-half of the persons sentenced for the first time will never return for another prison term.

One study compared two juvenile institutions, both equally reputable, really a comparison of two different types of philosophies with essentially the same expenditures.[36] One school had a philosophy of "education, hard work, and discipline." The second school had an orthopsychiatric philosophy in which clinical teams diagnosed emotional needs and unmet needs of the children in the institution. The orthopsychiatric approach was significantly superior in terms of reducing the number of boys who became involved in trouble again.

The most effective factors available in all records for estimating adjustment in prison without individually examining each inmate are as follows and in their order of significance:

1. Work reports (about twice as important as anything else)
2. Cellblock officers' report
3. Number of misconduct reports
4. Frequency of visits from the outside
5. Report from school
6. Type of misconduct reports (for example, assault as opposed to stealing food)
7. Frequency of correspondence with outside
8. Chaplain's evaluation
9. Personal financial budgeting in the prison
10. Steady work assignment
11. Steady school assignment[37]

Work reports are more important than any other single item. Cellblock officers' reports, number of misconduct reports, number of visits from outside (social ties), and evaluation of school performance are next in importance, each about half as important as the work reports. The remaining six items are of lesser importance, although still significant.

Custody does not appear to have much to do with rehabilitation. There is little relationship between the type of custody of a prisoner or how he is viewed as a security risk in the institution and his rehabilitation.[38]

[36] William McCord and Joan McCord, "Two Approaches to the Cure of Delinquents," *Journal of Criminal Law, Criminology and Police Science*, 44, No. 4 (November–December 1953), 442–67.

[37] These data were reported by the author in "The Effect of Counseling in Prison," *Social Forces*, 32 (1954), 285–89.

[38] Daniel Glaser, "Isolation Promotion and Custody Grading," Chap. 7 in his *Effectiveness of a Prison and Parole System*, pp. 149–71.

The damage done by institutionalization is generally in direct relation to the length of incarceration. Some stable personalities can endure institutionalization for a long time, while others "cave in." Human breakdown under prison stress was well documented by Hans Toch in 600 interviews dealing with the self-destructive acts of men and women in prison.[39]

Response to stress by attacks on others and abnormal interaction is far more frequent in prison than is self-destruction. Homosexual assaults on younger and weaker inmates in jails and prisons, among both men and women, occur frequently.

Lesbian relationships appear to be more troublesome because they tend to be more permanent than male homosexual relationships. The "butch" and her mate may have similar job assignments so they can be together constantly. In their free time, they are probably by themselves talking, sewing, playing cards, or dancing. Once they begin to hold hands, they have for all practical purposes announced to staff and inmates that they are lovers.[40] In female institutions, inmates frequently invent "families"; the value of family life is so firmly established in American culture that reformatory inmates frequently attempt to construct some facsimile of it.[41] Female inmates try to shake off the alienating and disorganizing experience of imprisonment by creating family structures. A letter from one partner in an institution to her mate already released on parole provides an interesting and informative picture of the situation:

Dear Darling:

I got your letter and was so glad to hear from you I could have shouted. I love you with all my heart and soul. But remember I'm going to slap your face for fooling around because you should have been a good little boy.

These women are so dizzy they really get on my nerves, so I stay in my room and think of you and what thoughts I have! You are a sweet black child and I love you. I love all your 5 ft. 5 in. and it is all mine. It is almost time for the lights to go out.

I want you to buy some pants so when we come out you can wear them. Don't do anything wrong. I don't want to have to kill you my first night out. I must close with love and kisses.[42]

Long-term confinement is not logical for "corrections," in that it is difficult to teach an offender to adjust to society by removing him from it. An institution devoted to treatment, however, can change a delinquent's perception of himself.[43]

---

[39] Hans Toch, *Men in Crisis: Human Breakdowns in Prison* (Chicago: Aldine, 1975).

[40] Clyde B. Vedder and Patricia G.. King, *Problems of Homosexuality in Corrections* (Springfield, Ill.: Charles C. Thomas, 1967), p. 30.

[41] *Ibid.*, p. 37.

[42] *Ibid.*, p. 36.

[43] Nick Bellizzi, "Self-Concepts of Delinquents Before and After Treatment," *Criminologica*, 55, No. 3 (November 1966), 27–31.

In a major study at the Ohio State Reformatory at Mansfield involving close examination of over 100 inmates over three years, the conclusion was reached that the amount of personality change among the inmates was slight.[44] Even in the absence of personality change, however, there was significant improvement in overt behavior. This means that people were learning to "get along," without much real change in personality. The significant improvement in overall social adjustment was not accompanied by the improvement in personal adjustment, which is considered by many to be necessary for long-range social adaption. (Test results indicated that people entering prisons do not improve in the course of their stay, but that a majority actually tend to deteriorate slightly.) Similar patterns of improved social adjustment unaccompanied by emotional integration have been observed in other prison populations and among brainwashed American prisoners in Korea. The better adjusted an inmate is on arrival, the more positive progress he or she tends to make during the prison stay. Conversely, maladjusted people become more maladjusted with long-term imprisonment.

## SUMMARY

Long-term institutionalization has a considerable impact on the person experiencing it. The younger the person is, the greater the impact, which is true of most experiences. Given equal institutional philosophy and procedure, the juvenile institution would have a greater impact than would an adult institution. Practice, however, is to keep juveniles in institutions for an average of about eight months, while adults are kept in prisons for an average of about 21 months. Further, juvenile institutions are generally minimum security cottage-type campuses, while significant adult prisons are large, maximum security, cellblock type.

An obvious conclusion is that a treatment program, which must involve correctional officers, has to be quite effective if it is going to counterbalance the dehumanizing effects of institutionalization. It has to be even more effective and comprehensive to be significant in going beyond merely counterbalancing the ill effects and providing constructive rehabilitation for the person whom society has taken responsibility for through its system of criminal justice.

Constructive changes in the present inmate system in a maximum custody institution could result from (1) reduction of deprivation, which accompanies confinement, (2) changes in the communication patterns between inmate and staff, and (3) programs of staff training designed to offset the patterns of accommodation through which the more negativistic inmates are supported in their positions of power and visibility.[45]

---

[44] Sheldon B. Peizer, "What Do Prisons Do, Anyway?" *Police* (November–December 1961), 6–10; and Clyde B. Vedder and Barbara A. Kay, eds., *Penology* (Springfield, Ill.: Charles C. Thomas, 1964), pp. 292–99.

[45] Stanton Wheeler, "Role Conflict in Correctional Communities," in Cressey, ed., *The Prison*, pp. 229–59.

Some observers question whether prison systems punish the right people. The criminal is not an island in society, but part of a family and social structure. The lives of many people are affected by the imprisonment of one person, and the social costs to the taxpayer in the form of welfare and other accommodations that accompany imprisonment are greater than the cost of imprisonment of the individual. Too many correctional workers consider the family as an external appendage to the correctional process, remote and irrelevant. A study of 800 prisoners and their families in British jails and prisons suggests that an alternative to imprisonment must be found.[46] A possibility is counseling to families in the community as part of the correctional program through the community services.

Institutionalization and the "prisonization" process affect personnel, too. The danger of being exposed to paranoid thinking is that one becomes involved in it. Few people in a democratic society are exposed to paranoid thinking more than correctional officers in a prison.[47] They are continually exposed to persecution and must resist the ever-present temptation to become persecutors themselves.

It is interesting to note that the longest time served by an inmate in America was 68 years, 8 months, served by Paul Geidel, who left Fishkill Correctional Facility in May 1980.[48] He had been sentenced in 1911 for murder. He was placed in a nursing home, which was cheaper than imprisonment. The oldest prisoner in America in 1980 was John Davis of South Carolina, at 103 years of age.[49] He was sentenced to life in 1922 for burglary. He had his own room in a prerelease center and was free to come and go as he pleased.

It is apparent that most prisons tend to "process" inmates without much treatment. It is difficult to avoid the conclusion that most of them damage the prisoner more than they help him, by concentrating him in a regimented situation with other persons having serious problems. This lowers the moral values of the prisoner. The moral values are bound to be lowered by association with others who do not reinforce the social norms. Even those institutions with treatment programs considered to be good have difficulty in demonstrating significant improvement in the inmates they serve. Some writers who question the idea of prisons suggest more community-based programs.[50] Certainly the impact of prisonization impedes the socialization process.[51]

[46] Pauline Morris, *Prisoners and Their Families* (New York: Hart Publishing Co., 1965).

[47] Bruno M. Cormier, *The Watcher and the Watched* (Montreal: Tundra Books, 1975), p. 12.

[48] "After 68 Years, Eight Months, Freedom," *Corrections Magazine,* VI, No. 4 (August 1980), 48.

[49] "Growing Old in Prison," *Corrections Magazine,* V, No. 1 (March 1979), 32.

[50] See Joseph Wilson, *Are Prisons Necessary?* (Philadelphia: Dorrance Press, 1950), John Barthlow Martin, *Break Down the Walls* (New York: Ballantine, 1954), and others.

[51] Matthew T. Zingraff, "Prisonization as an Inhibitor of Effective Resocialization," *Criminology,* 13, No. 3 (November 1975), 366–88.

## EXERCISES AND STUDY QUESTIONS

1. How would you evaluate the recidivism rate in American prisons?
2. How can the rate of return of juveniles to institutions be evaluated?
3. Discuss the concept that inmates run most prisons.
4. What are the broad characteristics of prison life?
5. Describe briefly the authoritarian structure of prisons as far as the inmate is concerned.
6. How does the prison social system desocialize people?
7. Describe the "institutionalized personality."
8. What is the Ganser syndrome?
9. How would you evaluate the reactions of long-term prisoners to prison life?
10. Evaluate conjugal visits, family visits, and furloughs.
11. How do most prisoners see authority and relate it to the correctional officer?
12. Why do prison inmates project blame for their predicament on society?
13. Why is the inmate store or canteen important in the life of an inmate?
14. Evaluate the informal social control that exists within the prison.
15. Evaluate formalized inmate self-government.
16. What is the role of arts and crafts or hobbycrafts in prisons?
17. Can Alcoholics Anonymous be effective in prison?
18. What classifications of offenders tend to come back to prison most frequently?
19. Can a person be kept in prison too long?
20. How would you evaluate the impact of long-term imprisonment?

# 10

# COMMUNITY-BASED CORRECTIONS

In recent years, community-based corrections has received considerable impetus from the realization that isolation in institutions does not accomplish the job of intensifying the social ties in the community for the correctional clients. The field of mental health and service to dependent and delinquent children deemphasized institutions in favor of community-based programs considerably earlier than did adult corrections. The effort has been to develop new work styles to reach into the community resources and relate them to the correctional client and correctional caseload. Community-based corrections encompasses community service centers, halfway houses and prerelease programs, vocational rehabilitation programs, neighborhood centers and projects, and all other community resources that can be used with correctional clients.

Constituting one of the earlier patterns of community-based corrections, the Chicago Area Projects were begun in the early 1930s. They developed as a result of studies by Shaw, McKay, Thrasher, and others of the "Chicago School" in the late 1920s and early 1930s. The importance of working with gangs and neighborhood youths had been emphasized. Subsequently, the idea was implemented in several other areas, such as Minneapolis and New York. The largest and most recent such neighborhood-type program is the Mobilization for Youth project in New York's lower East Side. Community-based corrections developed rapidly in the 1950s and became a major phase of corrections in the 1960s. In fact, it was the Federal Prisoner Rehabilitation Act of 1965 that gave official recognition and status to community-based corrections. While community-based corrections has existed in various forms for many years, it has until recently been looked upon in a condescending way as "unprofessional" and "meddling" by constituted correctional authorities.

## COMMUNITY SERVICES

The task of community services is to provide easy transition from prison to the community, by assisting the paroling authorities and coordinating the various agencies in the community to assist released prisoners. Community service activities involve education and relationships with the schools, assistance in finding jobs, bringing families to private agencies for assistance, helping the probation and parole officers, mediating difficulties within the family or with employers, or any other function that implements the maintenance of effective ties with the community from all correctional programs. Work release, study release, and other community programs can be managed from community-based residual treatment centers. Employment placement programs and technical assistance from residential treatment centers or from an office can be effective where the released prisoners live in the center, at home, or elsewhere in the community. The success of this function depends on the acceptance, involvement, and support of the community, which becomes the responsibility of the personnel in the community-based services office or facility. The use of the broadest range of community resources and services for corrections is the primary objective. A second objective is to provide technical consultation to other agencies and programs to assist in coordinating correctional program planning. Another objective is to assist in coordinating the efforts of colleges and universities and other educational programs to expand their services and resources toward becoming more effective in corrections. It must be noted that community-based corrections does not refer to the traditional services in the community. Although probation, jail, parole, and juvenile court are in the community, the modern meaning of community-based corrections does not include them but does include services and facilities that support and augment them.

The United States Bureau of Prisons established a Division of Community Services in 1967, which opened its first regional office in Atlanta. The idea has been adopted and modified by some state correctional services. The Community Services Office has no residential or domiciliary care, but provides assistance to offenders in terms of counseling, finding jobs, resolving problems of a social and legal nature, and otherwise assisting the correctional client in making a readjustment to the community. In this manner, the office assists and supplements the services of the parole officer. Establishment and maintenance of effective ties with the community is the primary objective directed toward facilitating the total correctional program.

It is interesting to note that private correctional agencies, such as

Prisoners Aid Societies, the John Howard Society, the Salvation Army, Volunteers of America, and others, have been providing this community service for a long time. Only recently have governmental correctional agencies invested resources in community-based programs.

In Iowa, the Des Moines project was planned in 1962 by the Halley Foundation and opened in 1964 to provide support for existing services. In 1970, the Polk County Jail was condemned, and there was no money for reconstruction; consequently, the Des Moines project assumed responsibility for local services, for all practical purposes. By 1970, this project included (1) pretrial release for carefully screened persons who appeared to be no risk for the community, (2) pretrial supervised release for defendants who failed to pass the screening, (3) county-based probation services, and (4) a community facility to serve as an alternative for a jail. Essentially, community-based corrections has become a substitute for traditional correctional procedures here.

# HALFWAY HOUSES

Halfway houses, prerelease guidance centers, or community treatment centers are residences where a few correctional clients about to be released live while they work in the community. The United States Bureau of Prisons has community treatment centers in Atlanta, Houston, Oakland, Los Angeles, Chicago, Detroit, Kansas City, and New York City. Their activities are coordinated by the Division of Community Services. Several states have implemented the idea to a lesser degree. There are also many halfway houses operated on a private basis throughout the country, such as Dismas House in St. Louis, St. Leonard's House in Chicago, and Talbert House in Cincinnati.

One of the best recent descriptions of halfway houses focuses on the use of peers in treatment of juveniles.[1] The methods involved have been field-tested in several places. Highfields in New Jersey began using them in 1960. Their use in the Provo Experiment in Utah was financed by the Ford Foundation from 1958 to 1964. California and New York have advanced programs in several places. Minnesota State Training School at Red Wing is probably the most advanced large institution using this program. Florida was the first to establish the approach on a statewide basis.

The patterns of group sessions in community-based halfway houses vary, but the central theme is social pressure from the peer group. Most patterns make use of the more responsible boys or girls to help guide or "pressure" the newer and less responsible participants toward conformity. There is frequently a group for the newer participants with one or two of the older participants leading it, another group for the older participants,

[1] Oliver J. Keller and Benedict S. Alper, *Halfway Houses* (Lexington, Mass.: Raytheon/ Heath, 1970).

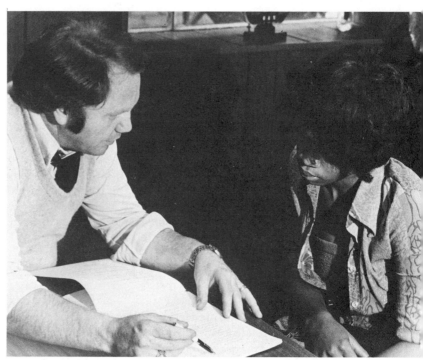

Counseling session in Talbert House in Cincinnati.
Courtesy of Talbert House.

and a third group for problem participants who are not making satisfactory progress. These groups frequently meet in the early evening, followed by evaluation sessions among the newer, older, and problem participants. Some programs are established so that "treatment teams" are made up of the more responsible boys and girls to assume peer supervision over the younger or less responsible participants.

The peer-take is frequently used as a screening device in which the participants evaluate the prospective new participant to determine whether or not he should become a member of the group. After the new participant is accepted, he becomes subject to the pressures of the peer group in the facility. The "crisis" group is frequently called immediately when a behavior aberration occurs on the part of any member of the group.

The key in this type of treatment is the pressure of peers, rather than evaluation and treatment by supervisors. The development of the therapeutic community is based on a preponderance of pro-social attitudes that can be developed in these therapeutic communities. To accomplish this, alert and competent leadership and supervision have to be present, while still leaving the "responsibility" with the group. The use of expectation of performance through leadership to the peer group is the primary control. Without this leadership and supervision, a halfway house can become a flophouse in short order, thereby defeating the whole purpose of the com-

Dinner at Talbert House.
Courtesy of Talbert House.

munity-based facility. While most of the groups are now in community-based correctional facilities, they can be and are also in institutional settings, such as the Minnesota State Training School at Red Wing.

# PAROLE CLINICS

The idea of parole clinics has been experimented with in several places, including Boston and Los Angeles. Under the auspices of the Massachusetts Division of Legal Medicine, a parole clinic directed by Dr. Stanley Kruger was established in the early 1950s. The Division of Legal Medicine still runs a parole clinic for offenders after their release. An offender can continue therapy with the same therapist he had in the institution. The purpose of this clinic is to provide intensive services to parolees and, in some cases, to persons sentenced to prison but not sent there, awaiting the success or failure of the parole clinic. This idea is similar to that used in mental health services. There are more than 1,600 mental hygiene and child guidance clinics throughout the country that have maintained persons with mental health problems without institutionalizing them. In the absence of the mental hygiene clinics, many more people would have had to be institutionalized. The idea of the parole clinic is similar to that of the mental health clinic in that a parole clinic may provide more intensive services outside and make sentence or commitment to an institution unnecessary for many offenders.

## WORK RELEASE

Work release is a program that allows persons to go from the institution into the community and work at civilian jobs, then return to the institution at night. Generally, transportation is provided by the institution, although it may charge the inmate $1 or $1.50 a day for the service, as well as a charge for room and board. A bus or station wagon may deliver the prisoners to their jobs in the morning and pick them up after the workday is over. Inmates can be delivered some distance to and from work. For example, the Federal Correctional Institution at Milan, Michigan, sends its inmates not only to Detroit and surrounding areas but also to Toleda, Ohio.

The Huber Law in Wisconsin, passed in 1913, provided work release for jails in Wisconsin. In the 1950s, North Carolina was faced with economic and budgetary problems, and experimentation with work release began as an economic measure. The advantages in social rehabilitation in involvement and ties with the community, however, quickly became obvious. Consequently, a majority of states have now passed work release laws.

Work release has been seen by some correctional leaders as a real advance, while other correctional administrators are not so enthusiastic.[2] In work release, the inmate is permitted to work for pay in the free community but spends his nonworking hours in the correctional institution. Work release is an alternative to total confinement and reshapes the conceptions of the prisoner while reducing the financial burden on the taxpayer and maintaining the labor force in the free community. It provides for the maintenance of family ties and assists in maintaining constructive attitudes and behavior on the part of the inmates.

Twenty-four states had work release of some sort in 1967, and nearly forty states had it by the end of 1969. By 1983, 44 states had community-based corrections in the form of work release or study release. Because of the problem of alcohol, some correctional administrators have indicated that Antabus, as a deterrent to alcohol, and work release go together. While there have been difficulties with persons not returning to the institution due to drunkenness or other problems, there is general consensus among correctional administrators that work release is worth the risk involved for the reintegration of the citizen-offender into society.

Work release is generally not difficult to get through a legislature because of its total merit. Conservatives like to see the economic saving. The

[2] Elmer H. Johnson, "Work Release: Conflicting Goals within a Promising Innovation," *The Canadian Journal of Corrections,* 12, No. 1 (January 1970), 67–77.

Work release in South Carolina.
Courtesy of the South Carolina Department of Corrections, Columbia, South Carolina.

prisoner contributes to his own maintenance at the prison and can support his family, thereby relieving the welfare rolls. In addition, he becomes a taxpayer and files income tax returns just like everyone else. Liberals like the rehabilitative aspects of work release, which provides prisoners with practice in living in society, while controlling their evening and night activities.

## STUDY RELEASE

Study-release programs operate in a manner similar to that of work-release programs. The difference is that inmates attend high schools, vocational and technical schools, junior colleges, or universities. At the United States

Penitentiary at Marion, Illinois, for example, inmates and correctional officers and other staff attend classes at Southern Illinois University together and as equals as far as the classroom situation is concerned. Where institutions do not have vocational training and other programs, community resources can be used in the work-study program. The NewGate project aims at university education. The NewGate program began in Oregon in 1967, funded by the office of Economic Opportunity. It is now in a half-dozen states and has been evaluated and further sponsored by the National Council on Crime and Delinquency (NCCD). Several study-release programs are now operative. South Carolina has about a dozen offenders housed in and attending colleges and universities that will accept them.

Student in the study release program at the University of South Carolina.
Courtesy of the South Carolina Department of Corrections, Columbia, South Carolina.

on the campus of the TEC Center (technical school).
South Carolina Department of Corrections, Columbia, South Carolina.

The STEP program in Cambridge, Massachusetts, also has a formalized study-release program.

## VOCATIONAL REHABILITATION

In the Vocational Rehabilitation Act of 1920, Congress authorized the creation of a federal vocational rehabilitation agency to fund state vocational rehabilitation programs for worthy persons with physical, emotional, and personality disorders. Under the original provisions of this act, a vocational rehabilitation counselor could interview prisoners to determine what type of disability was present and decide whether some of them qualified for help. In 1965, the act was amended, and under the new definitions, the majority of prisoners in an institution could be eligible for vocational rehabilitation services.

The federal vocational rehabilitation program operates in a decentralized manner, using federal funds to support state agencies. To qualify for funding, a state's plan must be approved by the national agency. The arrangement has been generally worked out in a contractual agreement.

The services provided under this federal-state plan take several forms. Additions to buildings have been constructed and counseling staffs provided. Generally, however, a vocational rehabilitation counselor interviews persons in institutions and may assist in planning programs and getting them started on vocational rehabilitation programs. In the case of paroled prisoners, the vocational rehabilitation counselor in the community can make plans for release if he is notified in reasonable time before the release. In this situation, the prisoner has to be interviewed in the institution, and the counselor develops a program in the community to provide follow-through with appropriate assistance.

The Vocational Rehabilitation Act placed emphasis on motivated, "worthy," physically and mentally disabled persons. The 1965 amendments provided for the rehabilitation of persons handicapped by cultural, economical, and social disadvantages. The interpretation has been broadened to mean that all persons who have been convicted of crime or adjudged delinquent are potentially eligible for vocational rehabilitation because of behavioral disorders. This does not mean that every person so convicted or adjudged is eligible, since eligibility is determined in part by a prognosis indicating that vocational rehabilitation can be of constructive service. The general approach to vocational rehabilitation is in twelve steps: (1) evaluation; (2) determination of eligibility for vocational rehabilitation on the basis of need and prognosis; (3) case analysis to determine strengths and weaknesses; (4) plan development; (5) treatment and counseling by a vocational rehabilitation officer; (6) training, whether vocational, academic, on-the-job, or other training approaches; (7) providing transportation where necessary; (8) providing maintenance when necessary; (9) purchasing tools and equipment when needed; (10) providing licenses and stock if the vocational rehabilitation includes the establishment of a business; (11) placement in a job; and (12) follow-up to determine whether or not the program has been successful.

Federal vocational rehabilitation help for prisoners having mental and behavioral disabilities has actually been permitted since 1943, but help has been limited in practice. It is necessary to show a history of unemployment, job instability, vagrancy, educational deficiency, and general need to be eligible for vocational rehabilitation. Work release and community services in connection with vocational rehabilitation were initiated in the federal system in September 1965.

Between 1963 and 1967, the number of cases closed in state vocational rehabilitation agencies rose from 148,000 to 218,000. Constituting about 1 percent of the caseload, drug addicts and persons referred by correctional institutions had the highest proportion of closures and the lowest percentage of rehabilitation rates. Table 10-1 shows the closures and the rehabilitation rates for the fiscal year 1967. It is noted that "Character, personality, and behavior disorders" constitute the category in which crime is committed, as well as "clients referred by correctional institutions."

Vocational rehabilitation projects for federal offenders have been carried out in Seattle, Denver, Atlanta, Tampa, Springfield, Pittsburgh, San Antonio, and Chicago. Of the total caseload, 46 percent were on probation and 2 percent were on parole. The rest were in institutions. Most frequent offenses were auto theft, larceny, forgery, and narcotic offenses. Thirty-four percent had been arrested once or twice, while 27

**Table 10-1**

| Selected Groups | Closures from Active Caseload | |
|---|---|---|
| | Total Number | Percent Rehabilitated |
| U.S. total | 218,415[a] | 79.5 |
| Blindness | 6,870 | 83.4 |
| Other visual impairments | 11,197 | 85.9 |
| Deafness | 5,694 | 88.0 |
| Other hearing impairments | 5,638 | 90.5 |
| Mental illness[b] | 37,534 | 70.3 |
| Alcoholism | 3,645 | 70.0 |
| Drug addiction | 225 | 60.4 |
| Character, personality, and behavior disorders | 9,968 | 70.9 |
| Mental retardation | 21,006 | 80.2 |
| Heart disease | 8,988 | 70.2 |
| Stroke | 1,668 | 67.8 |
| Epilepsy | 4,130 | 74.1 |
| Cancer | 916 | 78.2 |
| Speech impairments | 2,304 | 81.5 |
| Public assistance recipients | 26,824 | 73.0 |
| Clients 45 years old and older | 58,402 | 78.3 |
| Clients referred by correctional institutions | 2,142 | 59.5 |
| SSDI applicants | 33,139 | 66.2 |

[a] Sum of selected groups exceeds the U.S. total due to multiple counting.
[b] Includes psychotic and psychoneurotic disorders, alcoholism, drug addiction, and other character, personality, and behavior disorders.
*Source: Statistical Notes,* Rehabilitation Services Administration, U.S. Department of Health, Education and Welfare, October 1968, No. 2.

percent had been arrested more than eight times. Forty-one percent were below 30, while 21 percent were over 35. Sixty-seven percent had a high school education or more. Seventy-three percent were white. Ten percent were using narcotics when arrested, and 17 percent had alcohol problems. A sample expenditure, taken from the Pittsburgh project, is as follows:[3]

| | |
|---|---|
| Diagnostic procedures | $ 2,669 |
| Physical restoration | 4,180 |
| Training and materials | 17,230 |
| Maintenance and transportation | 5,403 |
| Rehabilitation centers | 1,717 |
| Innovative services | 5,131 |
| Total | $36,330 |

[3] Alfred W. Simpson, *Federal Offenders Rehabilitation Program, Denver, Colorado* (Denver: Colorado Department of Social Services Division of Rehabilitation, February 1969), p. 16.

The type of services used by clients of the vocational rehabilitation federal offenders projects is exemplified from the Denver project experience as follows.[4]

| | |
|---|---|
| Diagnostic procedures | 100% |
| Corrective (medical, dental, plastic etc.) | 15 |
| Psychiatric treatment | 20 |
| Training and training supplies | 40 |
| Maintenance and transportation | 65 |
| Guidance and counseling | 100 |

The Federal Offenders Rehabilitation Project (1965–69) was carried out by contract between the United States Probation Officers and the Board of Vocational Education and Rehabilitation, Division of Vocational Rehabilitation. The *Final Report*[5] of this project was disappointing in terms of success–failure statistics, but those close to the project believe that some of the disappointment derived from inadequate measuring instruments. The data are now being reviewed. It is interesting to note that the offender group members were particularly resistant to personality or psychovocational evaluation, and their counseling needs were high. The offender-client was quite often lacking in personal resources or family and friends to give assistance.

A study of released federal prisoners has indicated that they have a high rate of unemployment. A national sample survey shows that of the releases in the labor force, 63 percent have full-time jobs, 20 percent have part-time jobs, and 17 percent are generally unemployed. Factors associated with unemployment were color, marital status, age, education, prior criminal involvement, and prior employment experience. The type of institutional work assignment was not significantly related to employment status.[6]

While the caseloads of offenders have been disproportionately low in vocational rehabilitation programs, this resource is growing in scope and in knowledge to assist the correctional clients. The role of public vocational services and the rehabilitation of ex-prisoners can be expected to grow with the increasing recognition that they are one of the most vocationally handicapped groups in society. Their underutilization in employment is a loss to themselves and to the economy; this is compounded when the ex-prisoners

[4] Anthony M. Starr, *Pennsylvania Federal Offender Rehabilitation Project* (Pittsburgh, Pa.: State of Pennsylvania Bureau of Vocational Rehabilitation, April 1969), p. 24.

[5] *Federal Offenders Rehabilitation Project, Final Report, 1965–1969* (Springfield, Ill.: Division of Vocational Rehabilitation, 1970).

[6] George A. Pownell, *Employment Problems of Released Prisoners* (Washington, D.C.: U.S. Department of Labor, Manpower Administration, 1969), pp. 8–13.

return to prison.[7] Many correctional administrators have considered vocational rehabilitation one of the most underutilized of the major resources available to all segments of the correctional system. In 1973, however, the Division of Vocational Rehabilitation withdrew official support for working with offenders. Even so, many local and state vocational rehabilitation offices continued to work with offenders.

# NEW CAREERS

New Careers is a concept that has developed as a consequence of the governmental opportunity programs and the general thinking related to them.[8] While the concept originally related to impoverished areas, it has spread to the offender group, both juvenile and adult.[9] Despite considerable resistance from various sources, including private and political, the New Careers programs appear to constitute a potentially successful movement. Poverty is not inherent in the human condition, and the most effective way to turn the energy of the poor to productive use is to harness their available potential. Correcting deviant behavior is similar.

The New Careers Development Organization attempts to use offenders to reform other offenders. Dr. J. Douglas Grant of Oakland, California, president of New Careers, has achieved success by having prospective New Careerists selected by the offenders in an anonymous vote. In this way, inmate or offender leaders are identified. One function that this program can offer the field of corrections is training workshops for judges, probation officers, parole agents, parole board members, and attorneys. Preparation of resource material for in-service training programs would be most helpful, as has been indicated at the California State Prison at San Quentin. Inmates and ex-offenders can be used to staff openings in the field of research and innovation. They can staff data processing and computer programming components of information systems, such as has been done in Indiana, South Carolina, and elsewhere.

People develop communication in various frames of reference. Sometimes it is difficult to understand someone who is living in a frame of reference different from that of the observer. This is especially true when workers from the middle class attempt to work with delinquents or offenders from lower socioeconomic levels. Each may leave an interview or exchange wondering what the other person was talking about. The failure to communicate is generally a problem of not being in the same frame of ref-

[7] *Manpower Research Programs* (Washington, D.C.: U.S. Department of Labor, Manpower Administration, 1969), p. 97.

[8] Arthur Pearl and Frank Riessman, *New Careers for the Poor* (New York: Free Press, 1965).

[9] Robert Pruger and Harry Specht, "Establishing New Careers Programs: Organizational Barriers and Strategies," *Social Work*, 13, No. 4 (October 1968), 21–32.

| | Things Known by Probation Officer | Things Unknown to Probation Officer |
|---|---|---|
| **Things Known by Client** | I. The Arena (open area of the relationship where communication occurs) | II. The Blind Spot (realities not recognized) |
| **Things Unknown by Client** | III. The Facade (area of hidden defenses) | IV. The Unknown (unexplored realities) |

**Figure 10-1**

*Source:* Louis Tomaino, *Changing the Delinquent* (Austin: The Hogg Foundation, University of Texas, 1969), p. 61.

erence or on the same communication base. Joseph Luft and Harry Ingham developed a concept they call Johari's Window (Figure 10-1) to demonstrate some of the difficulties in communication. The middle-class worker knows the social norms expected but does not know the background of most offenders. The offenders do not appreciate the middle-class values. Breakdown in communication results. Effective communication occurs when both know the same things and can use that knowledge as a communication base. Communication occurs only in the Arena.

The New York State Division for Youth uses offenders as research assistants in its offices and also to conduct interviews with other youths. They can be used as liaison persons between the police and the family, peer group, and community. They can be used to establish community action programs, such as the Neighborhood Youth Corps projects. Ex-offenders can work exceptionally well at the grass-roots level. In institutions, ex-offenders can provide work supervision, custodial duties, reporting, data gathering, and many other functions performed jointly by inmates and the staff. In the community, parole agents and parolees can work together. In one instance, they helped move parolee residents of a halfway house into the community by finding jobs and residences. Many kinds of staff responsibilities can be provided. Milton Luger, former director of the New York Division of Youth, says that the Division wants offenders as part of the rehabilitative effort because they need them, not because they are sorry for them.[10]

Juveniles are frequently ambivalent about submitting to the direction and counsel of adults. Students' demands are frequently voiced in belligerent terms, and adults frequently become punitive. Using other juveniles or using juveniles as consultants to the adults can diminish negativism and resistance.[11]

[10] *Correctional Briefings,* No. 4 (Washington, D.C.: Joint Commission on Correctional Manpower Training, 1969).

[11] Herbert S. Steam, *Youth as Advisors to Adults and Vice Versa* (Washington, D.C.: Office of Juvenile Delinquency and Youth Development, 1970).

One of the earliest forms of federal financing was to aid cities. The Demonstration Cities and Metropolitan Development Act of 1966 (Title I, P.L. 89-754), administered by the Department of Housing and Urban Development (HUD), Model Cities Administration, provides grants and technical assistance to cities to develop and implement comprehensive plans to upgrade target areas within the cities. Law enforcement and correctional components, while incorporated in the original legislation, were specifically included in 1968.

One of the better model city plans is that of Woodlawn on Chicago's South Side. It comprises three operating systems: (1) core and outreach central structure, (2) an educational system, and (3) a Housing and Economic Development Corporation, which includes manpower training and employment.[12] The core includes programs for health and social service, environmental planning, and financial service. Outreach in this plan refers to the network of facilities, each serving a two- or three-block area of the community. These facilities are called "pads." The educational system includes work in (1) a preschool center, (2) primary schools, (3) middle schools, (4) Hyde Park High School, (5) a community cultural and language arts complex, and fluid schools to be located outside formal school buildings, so that a complete education can be obtained in the community at any level. The fluid schools could be located anywhere—in apartments, vacant buildings, factories, etc. The Housing and Economic Development Corporation refers to improved housing facilities and vocational training programs for upgrading the employability of persons in the areas.

Community service aides began working as part of the Chicago Police Department in February 1970 to implement the police part of the Model Cities Program. The program is designed to help the community by focusing on the problems the people consider to be significant, so the police department can call other departments, such as the health and welfare departments, to bear on resolving the problem. The centers under the Model Cities Program are staffed by seven veteran police officers and two to four community service aides to cover each of six centers strategically located in Chicago neighborhoods that need them.[13]

One difficulty for Model Cities has been political. When one area receives Model Cities' funds for a project, nearby neighborhoods want the same consideration and protest when it is not forthcoming. Model Cities as a program has been discontinued, but the Department of Housing and Urban Development (HUD) continues to support community projects generally related to housing on a lesser and more individual basis. HUD

[12] Eddie M. Williams, ed., *Delivery Systems for Model Cities,* Center of Policy Study and Center for Urban Studies (Chicago: University of Chicago Press, 1969).

[13] "On the Road to a Better Understanding of the Community," *Chicago Police Star,* July 21, 1970, pp. 60–70.

supports 13 programs, one of the most effective being Neighborhood Block Grants.

## MIGRANTS

The problem of migrant delinquency and crime has not been well defined. Migrants are not a recognized part of any community, so school, health, and other laws may not be so well enforced in relation to this group. The first extensive study of immigrant children was done by the Immigration Commission headed by Senator William P. Dillingham and was published in 1911. New reprints are now available.[14] Not much has since been done regarding migrants.

In many cases, migrants are singled out for special attention by police. They are locked up faster than the local citizens. The "floaters" who cannot stay on any job or with any crew are viewed as causing more trouble than the ones who stay in their own crew.

The three migrant streams in the United States are on the East Coast from Florida to New York and back; Texas to Colorado and Michigan and back; and California to Washington and Montana and back. In 1970, there were 93,000 workers below the age of 20 earning an average of $8.35 per day, and there were 103,000 workers 20 years of age and older making $13.10 per day.[15] Migrants view school problems as being economic, and teachers consider migrant parents to be uncooperative.[16] The school offers failure to migratory children, so they find their security with their families and in their own culture.

Migrants present a special situation for schools, health authorities, and other agencies of society.[17] They are generally economically inadequate, and the difficulties that bring them into court usually involve fights and drunkenness within their own group. Depending upon how delinquency is defined, the migrant population presents few problems unless a close check is kept on school attendance among children and younger adolescents of school age. Poor housing, lack of sanitary facilities, many unclaimed dogs, lack of occupational aspiration, and a kind of obedient docility characterize the migrant community. All their social ties are within the group, which is where their security lies, and these social ties also prevent breaking away and changing the life style of an individual born

[14] *The Children of Immigrants in Schools* (Metuchen, N.J.: Scarecrow Press, 1970), in five volumes.

[15] "No. 385. Farm Wage Workers—Characteristics and Earnings: 1969 and 1970," *Statistical Abstracts of the United States—1972* (Washington, D.C.: Bureau of the Census, 1973), p. 240.

[16] E. John Keinert and Robert W. Harner, *Migrant Children in Florida: The Phase II Report of the Florida Migratory Child Survey Project, 1968–1969,* Vol. I (Tallahassee: University of Miami and Florida Department of Education, undated, released 1971), pp. 510–19.

[17] See *Florida Health Notes—The Immokalee Story,* 50, No. 8 (October 1958), 172–90.

into this community. Yet when outside people, such as public health work-ers, come to the community and offer classes in the evening, the migrants respond enthusiastically and welcome the opportunity for the evening classes.

In one study, three traffic law violations, four jail sentences for drunk-enness, and one arrest for gambling were the total known violations of law by migrants during one year. In this study, it was concluded that it was impossible to confirm or deny the stereotype of the migrants as "lawless, good-for-nothing, shiftless, thieving, chicken-stealing rascals," a description volunteered by a county official.[18]

The Uniform Migrant Student Record Transfer System, financed under a special amendment to Title I making migrant children eligible for education, will assist in keeping track of more than 200,000 migrant chil-dren. Computer-generated records on each migrant student, with specific patterns of mobility, family, school attendance, health data, special test scores, information on the child's special interests, abilities, and needs, and general demographic data, will be fed into the system. The system began operation on July 1, 1970, with seven participating states (Arkansas, Colo-rado, Kansas, Missouri, New Mexico, Oklahoma, and Texas). When it is fully developed, the system will make background information on any mi-grant student available to any of the 48 mainland states within 24 hours.[19] After migrant children get into the school record system, the juvenile courts will soon be in a better position to provide services for them, not only in terms of delinquency and corrections, but also in terms of neglect, depend-ency, and need of supervision.

Migrants who have trouble with the law are very seldom an institu-tional problem. Rather, they are a problem for community-based correc-tions. They have undoubtedly been neglected in this area because they are not permanent residents of the community.

## PROBLEMS IN COMMUNITY-BASED CORRECTIONS

One of the problems in providing programs in communities is lack of coor-dination and jurisdictional disputes between agencies. In a single commu-nity, the agencies might include the day-care or nursery school association, the Family Service Association, Head Start, Job Corps, Job Fair, Job Op-portunity for Youth, Neighborhood Youth Corps, New Careers, Office of Economic Opportunity, Food Stamp Program, United Fund, Upward Bound, Volunteers in Service to America (VISTA), specialized school pro-grams, juvenile court services, juvenile aid bureaus and other programs of

[18] Earl Lomon Koos, *They Follow the Sun* (Jacksonville, Fla.: Florida State Board of Health, 1957).

[19] "Tracing Migrant Children," *Public Health Reports,* 85, No. 6 (June 1970), 502.

the police department, public welfare programs, church and other religious agencies, and a variety of other efforts devoted to general social development, improving the social conditions that generate deviant behavior, and direct assistance to the individuals who need it.

An example of a concerted effort toward community organization was the special Community Action Program in Harris County (Houston, Texas), which existed from the summer of 1968 to the spring of 1969. Because of jurisdictional disputes, the report of this program showed general failure to achieve its objectives of (1) improving the knowledge, use, and attitudes of the poor toward community agencies and programs; (2) involving the poor in community groups and activities; and (3) developing indigenous leadership among the poor.[20]

The magnitude of the problem of the city may be emphasized by the percentage of the population receiving public assistance in the 26 cities with a population of over 500,000 or in the counties where these cities are located (Table 10-2).

Public assistance payments, used as an index of social problems, are more easily measured than most other indices, such as crime and delinquency, because of financial accounting procedures and the central place income maintenance holds in American society. The need for correctional programs in cities becomes obvious.

The Neighborhood Youth Corps was inaugurated in January 1965 by the United States Department of Labor's Manpower Administration.[21] The purpose of the Corps is to bring to the poorest and most disadvantaged youth in the inner cities a chance to break the cycle of poverty and turn it into a cycle of opportunity. Regional offices are located in Boston, New York, Washington, Atlanta, Chicago, Kansas City, Dallas, and San Francisco, decentralized so that all regions of the country will be served. More than 1.5 million poverty-level youngsters have been enrolled in the program. In 1968, more than 620,000 youths, almost 48 percent of them from disadvantaged minority groups, were enrolled under supervision. They work at jobs. The Neighborhood Youth Corps, administered by the U.S. Department of Labor's Manpower Administration, reports that 70 percent of enrollees had improved themselves within five to fifteen months after termination of their project. Eighteen percent were back in school or training programs, 35 percent were in full-time jobs, 6 percent were in the armed forces, and 11 percent were housewives.[22]

Youth Involvement is a technique to motivate youth or to neutralize their opposition to program goals. It is a strategy to achieve a goal primarily aimed at socialization, which involves youth in decision-making re-

---

[20] Morris Kagan and Virginia Kennedy, *Special Community Action Program: Survey and Evaluation* (Houston: Harris County Community Action Association, 1969), pp. 15–16.

[21] *The Neighborhood Youth Corps: Hope and Help for Youth* (Washington, D.C.: U.S. Department of Labor, Manpower Administration, 1969).

[22] *Ibid.*, p. 6.

**Table 10-2  Percent of population receiving public assistance, February 1971**

| Cities and Counties | Percent of Recipients of Public Assistance |
|---|---|
| United States (total) | 6.9 |
| Large cities (or counties) total | 10.3 |
| Cities | |
| Baltimore | 15.2 |
| New York | 15.0 |
| New Orleans | 14.8 |
| Philadelphia | 14.8 |
| St. Louis | 14.7 |
| San Francisco | 14.2 |
| District of Columbia | 10.5 |
| Denver | 10.1 |
| Jacksonville | 7.5 |
| Counties in which large cities are located | |
| Suffolk (Boston) | 16.6 |
| Los Angeles (Los Angeles) | 12.7 |
| Shelby (Memphis) | 9.8 |
| Wayne (Detroit) | 9.1 |
| Cuyahoga (Cleveland) | 8.8 |
| Cook, DuPage (Chicago) | 8.1 |
| San Diego (San Diego) | 7.4 |
| Allegheny (Pittsburgh) | 7.0 |
| Bexar (San Antonio) | 6.7 |
| Franklin (Columbus) | 6.7 |
| Milwaukee, Washington (Milwaukee) | 6.2 |
| Clay, Jackson, Platte (Kansas City, Missouri) | 5.5 |
| King (Seattle) | 5.2 |
| Dallas (Dallas) | 5.0 |
| Fort Bend, Harris, Montgomery (Houston) | 4.2 |
| Maricopa (Phoenix) | 4.0 |
| Marion (Indianapolis) | 3.4 |

Source: *Public Assistance Statistics, February 1971,* Social and Rehabilitation Service (Washington, D.C.: United States Department of Health, Education and Welfare, 1971), p. 5.

garding policies and programs that have direct or indirect impact on them. It includes poverty groups, offender groups, students, or ghetto youngsters. It can be a youth council, a treatment model like Highfields in New Jersey, an action model like Mobilization for Youth in New York, or a job-training model like the Job Corps in many large cities and communities.[23]

[23] J. Robert Weber and Carson Custer, *Youth Involvement,* U.S. Department of Health, Education and Welfare (Washington, D.C.: U.S. Government Printing Office, 1970).

In many black neighborhoods, the Black Muslims have offered gang members a substitute ideology that permits them to reject the authority of all policemen as armed agents of the white society hired to keep the black in his place. In most neighborhoods, however, this ideology is missing, and gang members are confused and inarticulate about what lies behind their situation. They are perennial police suspects. Frustration frequently wells up into blind rage, making the policeman's position most difficult.[24] Knowing the men and youths on parole who have "been through the mill" and are the opinion-makers in the neighborhood is helpful.

There is general hostility between urban low-income and minority-group residents and their police that is dangerous and destructive. The contribution of the police to the field of corrections is direct. Poor police–community relations result in reduced morale and a heightened rate of crime and delinquency.[25] There is reduced community willingness to participate in the process of law enforcement, with consequent reduction in the success of preventive and investigative police work. This is accompanied by increased likelihood of abuse and injury to policemen, increased likelihood of infringement on rights and liberties of citizens, increased likelihood of large-scale violence, and reduction of funds for the rehabilitation of criminals and delinquents.[26] Violence is not power, but it is a method of seeking power when other alternatives are closed. More frequently, it is an expression of despair and frustration.[27] Crimes do not cause riots, but riots cause and are crimes.

Racial prejudice in both directions, lack of knowledge and understanding by each side about the other, and lack of communication and contact between the two groups motivate poor relations. The inverted power relationship, in which one group views the supposed master group as powerless to control it and in which the master group views the other group as dangerous, can generate violence and abuse.

The neighborhoods in which the majority of crime and delinquency is generated compare unfavorably in many aspects with the "average" in American society. The range of conditions and circumstances in which people live in this country is wider than most people realize, because most of us tend to come into contact with a relatively narrow frame of reference. In times of good jobs, high wages, and manpower shortages, the poor exist on an extremely small amount of money per month per person. The poor

---

[24] Carl Werthman and Irving Pillavin, *Gang Members and the Police,* Office of Juvenile Delinquency and Youth Development, HEW (Washington, D.C.: U.S. Government Printing Office, 1969).

[25] *Police–Community Relations in Urban Low-Income Areas,* Office of Juvenile Delinquency and Youth Development, HEW (Washington, D.C.: U.S. Government Printing Office, 1969).

[26] Marvin E. Wolfgang, "Violence, U.S.A.—Riots and Crime," *Crime and Delinquency,* October 1968, pp. 289–305.

[27] Bertram Beck, "Knowledge and Skills in Administration of an Anti-Poverty Program," *Social Work,* 11, No. 3 (October 1968), 102–6.

may average 7.8 grades of school while the "average" reported by the United States Office of Education in 1972 was 12.8 grades. Consequently, attitudes resulting from social class and perception of inequities emerge as more important.

Recruitment of indigenous staff is most important when working with people from the ghetto.[28] Constructive involvement is necessary for the community-based correctional agency. Almost any involvement of people begins with doubt and mistrust, goes into acceptance gradually, then to active participation, and finally to a feeling of growth.

The attitudes of boys in many ghetto neighborhoods are strongly anti-establishment, resentful, and hostile toward any type of authority, particularly the power structure. Some of the descriptions of their attitudes toward people who try to work with them indicate the difficulty community and governmental programs have in even communicating, much less working effectively with boys in that culture. One description was as follows:

> That Youth Commission and them cats—full of————————. Just like they never been. Who know them? Nobody. Who care to know them? Nobody. What they ever did for somebody? Nothing—nothing at all. They might interview a couple of peoples about they jobs on the line, but come down to cold facts, who they think about? Nobody but themselves. They pass some old exam for this job so the State decides to give it to them. They living the life of a King. What they got to do? Nothing. What makes their job so easy, the papers do most of they work. All they have to do is hop up and read the papers, ask a couple of questions, and write a report. They might not send it in for six (6) months. That's it. But for them to get down to real problems—no good. What I believe the caseworker should do if they was really out for the people is to be really true to they work. But you can't be a true caseworker with so many people who all got problems like in Lawndale, how many caseworkers do they got? About 50. Now how in hell can 50 caseworkers take care of damn near 4 or 5,000 boys all of who got problems? Half of them ain't got clothes to wear to school, and nowhere to get any from. Half of them are dropouts, and ain't nobody trying to get no jobs for them. And out of that 50 caseworkers, maybe about 10 is looking out for their job—they're looking out for the fellas—and the other 40 just there. They might as well not be there—just a way to spend money. It's sickening![29]

The hard-core multiple-problem family is an intense manifestation of all the problems that occur in the lower socioeconomic groups and provides in a single constellation an opportunity to study all the social, economic, cultural, and emotional problems of the acting-out disorders. Such families do not move in a wide radius but remain in a relatively permanent, familiar area. They tend to be large, so that adequate supervision, economically and emotionally, cannot be provided by the already inadequate parents.

[28] R. Lincoln Keiser, *The Vice Lords: Warriors of the Streets* (New York: Holt, Rinehart & Winston, 1969), p. 71.

[29] *Ibid.*, p. 71.

Mental illness does not appear as psychosis and neurosis very often in this type of family, but acting-out disorders appear frequently. Alcohol tends to flow freely in the family, which is typically disorganized, characterized by severe marital conflict and serious neglect or abuse of children.

The welfare department is best equipped to identify these families, because two-thirds of them receive continuous welfare, and the rest receive help sometimes. These problem families do not participate in Boy Scouts, Sunday school, or other middle-class activities, nor do they aspire to them. School attendance is spotty, and children drop out early. Sex experience comes early, but there is little evidence of sexual abnormality. Homosexuality is almost nonexistent in this group.

One of the greatest sources of chronic dependency is the repetitive out-of-wedlock birth that has its onset in the teenage years.[30] Of almost a million babies born during a nine-year period in North Carolina, a total of 22 percent had unmarried adolescent mothers, and 3,400 of the adolescent mothers were below the age of 15. For the United States as a whole, approximately 40 percent of out-of-wedlock babies are delivered by mothers 13 to 19 years of age.

## MAKING COMMUNITY-BASED CORRECTIONS WORK

The various driving forces and restraining forces in the balance of power in the community can be diagrammed as shown in Table 10-3.

Community action in the area of youth crime and juvenile delinquency is important, because the traditional methods of handling these

**Table 10-3**

| Restraining Force | M o r e | Community action programs | Good school system | Good police department | |
| --- | --- | --- | --- | --- | --- |
| Activity Level (Delinquency Rate in Community | | | | | |
| Driving Forces | L e s s | Understand correctional agency | Illegal sale of alcohol to juveniles | Slums and poverty | Broken homes |

*Source:* Jay Hall and Martha Williams, "The Correctional Worker as an Agent of Change" (training paper, Southwest Center for Law and the Behavioral Sciences, Austin, Texas, 1965), in Louis Tomaino, *Changing the Delinquent* (Austin: The Hogg Foundation, University of Texas, 1969), p. 51.

[30] Katherine Brownell Oettinger, *The School of Social Work's Responsibility in Family Planning Education,* U.S. Dept. of Health, Education and Welfare (Washington, D.C.: U.S. Government Printing Office, 1968).

problems have not been as effective as they should be.[31] A wide range of services to children and youth in the community has become important. Community-based programs, coping with the personnel shortage in this field, legal services for youth, community organization programs, and federal assistance are all needed.

Some reasons for lack of success in working with delinquents and offenders are (1) lack of diagnostic information, (2) inadequate family work, (3) inappropriate institutional atmosphere, (4) a specific limitation in time, (5) suppression of feelings and suppressive treatment in institutions, (6) weakness in professional services, (7) failure of the relationship to develop, and (8) lack of resources. Community-based treatment programs can use community resources and overcome, at least in part, most of these difficulties.[32]

Some of the issues in community organizations in regard to delinquency center on:

1. Reaching the target population
2. Service as compared to social action
3. The division of participating youth between upwardly mobile, success-oriented youngsters and unemployed, failure-oriented dropouts
4. The independence of constituent groups, in that government-supported projects cannot be used for militant demonstrations and public redress of grievances
5. The need to develop community-action strategies of powerlessness rather than influence to effect planning decisions, in order to bring about movement among civil rights groups, students, and trade unions
6. Obtaining full-fledged participation in decision-making by ensuring that the poor are allowed the same latitude for organizational inadequacies as is permitted the rest of the community
7. Community conflict between several projects
8. The role of governmental agencies, such as the Office of Juvenile Delinquency and Youth Development, which fund projects

Studies have indicated that community-based corrections can do all that the traditional correctional programs can do except hold dangerous offenders.[33] Johnson has written about Finland's penal system and how it

---

[31] John M. Martin, *Delinquency Today: A Guide for Community Action,* Office of Juvenile Delinquency and Youth Development, HEW (Washington, D.C.: U.S. Government Printing Office, 1969).

[32] Harland D. Daluge, "Group Homes in a Ranch Setting—A Deterrent to Delinquency," Proceedings of the American Correctional Association for 1969 in Minneapolis (Washington, D.C.: ACA, 1970), pp. 40–42.

[33] John O. Boone, *A Study of Community-Based Correctional Needs in Massachusetts* (Boston: Massachusetts Department of Corrections, 1972—mimeographed).

rests on community-based corrections.[34] The forbearant model in Finland's penal colonies has been suggested as a viable approach to community-based corrections in the United States. The rehabilitative model uses psychologists, psychiatrists, social workers, and other treatment people. The reintegration model directs all efforts toward preparing the offender for performance of legitimate roles in the community. The forbearant model, however, withholds custodial control or surveillance and relies on selected inmates to maintain discipline, such as first offenders with short sentences or recidivists nearing the end of their sentences and having enough equity in the sentence to be thought trustworthy. Finland introduced this plan in its penal colonies as a matter of economic necessity after World War II, when Finland joined with Germany against the USSR.

## SUMMARY

Community-based corrections appears to be the next major development in the correctional field. Already in existence in adult correctional programs and in juvenile correctional programs in several states, the value of community-based corrections is that it provides the more intensive services which the prison or correctional institution is supposed to provide while, at the same time, maintaining the social ties so important to successful adjustment in society. Certainly, the dangers of prisonization are considerably diminished in community-based corrections.[35]

## EXERCISES AND STUDY QUESTIONS

1. *What is community-based corrections?*
2. *What are some of the primary movements in the development of community-based corrections?*
3. *What is the task of community-based corrections?*
4. *What is the function of divisions of community services in prison systems?*
5. *Evaluate the use of halfway houses.*
6. *Evaluate work release.*
7. *How does vocational rehabilitation function in the correctional field?*
8. *Explain the New Careers program and evaluate its role in corrections.*

---

[34]Elmer H. Johnson, "Finland's Penal Colonies: The Forebearant Model and Community-Based Corrections," *Journal of Criminal Justice*, 1, No. 4 (Winter 1973), 327–38.

[35] Saleem A. Shah, *Graduated Release* (Rockville, Md.: National Institute of Mental Health, Center for Studies in Crime and Delinquency, 1971), p. 9.

9. Describe Johari's Window.

10. How is Housing and Urban Development involved in the field of corrections?

11. What is the "community service aide"?

12. Why are migrants a special problem in the correctional field?

13. Why is lack of coordination a difficulty in community-based corrections?

14. Evaluate the problem of jurisdictional disputes in community-based corrections.

15. What is the Neighborhood Youth Corps?

16. Evaluate the attitude of youth in many ghetto neighborhoods being served by community-based corrections.

17. How do you think the hard-core multiple-problem family can best be served in community-based corrections?

18. Why do community-based corrections appear to be the next major development in the correctional field?

19. Why are legal services important to community-based corrections?

20. What are some of the difficulties that result in lack of success in community-based corrections?

# 11

# SPECIAL AREAS IN CORRECTIONS

Correctional programs have to be built to serve the needs of the clients. Because the problems of the clients differ so widely, a single approach to treatment would be difficult to support. The variations within the group of conventional offenders is wide enough to tax most treatment programs. In addition, there are special problems in corrections that may merit special institutional facilities as well as treatment programs geared to their specific needs. Consider just a few of these special problems: the alcoholic, the narcotic addict, the criminal sexual psychopath, the criminally insane, the public official who violated trust, the moonshiner who makes and sells liquor unlawfully, the prostitute whose services are bought, the white-collar offender who fixed prices, or the "political" offender whose crimes involve labor activities, contempt of court, civil disturbance, or selective prosecution of cases because they are a part of a "previous" administration. It is difficult to formulate a program that would "rehabilitate" a conscientious objector or a 56-year-old county treasurer found to be $5,000 short. It is most difficult for the average prison or correctional agencies to successfully offer a treatment program to many of these people while simultaneously operating a program for a majority of conventional offenders.

The dyssocial offender is generally the product of a lifelong environment that has fostered social values in conflict with the usual codes of society.[1] Dyssocial offenders are part of a group which has a dysfunctional

[1] James C. Coleman, *Abnormal Psychology and Modern Life,* 2nd ed. (Glenview, Ill.: Scott, Foresman & Co., 1956), p. 346.

relationship with broader society. This group includes professional criminals, gangsters, racketeers, moonshiners, professional gamblers, and others who make their living in activities that are defined as criminal by the broader society but accepted in their subculture. Treatment of these offenders is very difficult. Most of them consider conviction and imprisonment as an occupational hazard. The moonshiner or bootlegger, for example, raises the price of his product in order to cover the costs of fines and other legal activities in case he is apprehended. In the prison, he tends to wait out his time until he can get back to work again. With his lack of motivation for change, the psychiatrist, psychologist, social worker, counselor, or other treatment staff member cannot easily make meaningful contact with this offender. He appears to be a cultural-anthropological enigma. He functions well in his own small culture, but his society violates the norms of the larger society. This situation is also characteristic of members of many small religious groups, such as rattlesnake-handlers and some who want to practice polygamy or violate selective service laws on the basis of freedom of religion.

The Bureau of Indian Affairs in the United States Department of Interior has special programs for Indians. The Offender Rehabilitation program for Indians, community treatment programs, financial aid to municipal and tribal institutions housing Indian prisoners, special services for alcoholism and narcotic addiction, and the development of Indian community resources to advise potential offenders, both juvenile and adult, are significant parts of the correctional program for Indians.

The white-collar offender is a person who has engaged in sharp business practices, price-fixing, antitrust violations, "thumb-on-the-scales" offenses, shady real estate transactions, and similar activities. These transactions are generally just within the criminal law, but occasionally far enough out so that the manipulators are convicted of some offense. Business and professional men, including some lawyers, are found in this group. Treatment of people who have run afoul of the law for relatively minor offenses is difficult to accomplish.

## POLITICAL OFFENDERS

In many other countries, where the political stability is precarious, political offenders threaten the stability of the government. As long as they pose a threat to the government's stability, they are just as dangerous as conventional criminals. Consequently, they may be placed in prison for criticizing the government or expressing views divergent to government policies. Political imprisonment occurs frequently in China, the Soviet Union, and other totalitarian states, as well as in Europe, Latin America, and elsewhere.

In America, the political offender is one who has violated selective service laws or engaged in civil disobedience and disruption that spills over into criminal activity at all levels, from trespassing to murder, violations of soil bank laws and other regulatory offenses, and similar laws that would not ordinarily be criminal except that they run counter to governmental stability and order. In some cases, these violations have been called "convictional" crimes because they are criminal behavior emerging from basic political and religious convictions.

Treatment of such offenders is seldom possible. Their personalities are generally well-integrated. Generally they do not recognize personal problems but continually criticize the social system. Consequently, working with these cases in a correctional program simply involves holding them until their time has expired.

## THE ALCOHOLIC

The incidence of alcoholism among prison inmates is high, although not as high as among misdemeanants in jails. This writer questioned incoming inmates at the State Prison of Southern Michigan for one year in 1942–43 regarding the contribution of alcohol to their offenses. Approximately 65 percent indicated that they had been drinking when they committed their crimes. Approximately 20 percent blamed the offense on alcohol. It is obvious that persons with problems may use alcohol for a variety of reasons. They may also commit crimes. Whether there is a causal relationship is doubtful. Rather, it would appear that crime and alcoholism are both symptoms of a deeper personality maladjustment.

Treatment of alcoholism must be based on the realization that drinking is more the result of problems than the cause of them, although the drinking causes other problems. The patient has to be strengthened psychologically so that he will not have to rely upon alcohol to meet responsibilities and problems and to relieve emotional tension. Institutional treatment is best, if on a short-term basis.

The Research Council on Problems of Alcohol has recommended that:

1. The general hospital should admit all alcoholics (most do not now), classify them, and route them as follows:
   a. The most seriously deteriorated alcoholics should be sent to farms or industrial colonies.
   b. The symptomatic problem drinkers—the psychotic, feeble-minded, etc.—should be sent to mental hospitals.
   c. The less serious cases not requiring special institutional facilities should be treated in the general hospital in either the out-patient or the in-patient clinic.
2. Custody and care of problem drinkers should be transferred from the police to the public health agencies, with custody ensured for a sufficient amount of time to permit effective rehabilitation.
3. Public agencies established to cope with problem drinkers should

be an integral part of existing state, county, and city health departments.

4. The many unknowns involved in the causes, method of treatment, prevention, and rehabilitation of problem drinkers call for continuous research—medical, psychological, sociological—if the facilities which government agencies are now establishing for problem drinkers are to be fairly effective. Existing medical schools and their affiliated hospitals should be encouraged to participate in publicly supported programs, so that along with treatment and education may go intensive research into causes, treatment, prevention, and rehabilitation of excessive drinkers. The treatment of alcoholism must include not only psychotherapy, but special diets to counteract vitamin deficiency and other treatment procedures focused on the alcoholic personality. Al-Anon Family Groups are group meetings for the families of alcoholics. While the emphasis is on men, there is also concern for the alcoholic wife. Generally, the literature and the discussions focus on living with the alcoholic for wives, parents, and sons and daughters of alcoholics. The National Council on Alcoholism is an excellent source of assistance.[2]

Studies have indicated that alcohol can be treated through counseling and vocational training with supportive gainful employment. In a study of 685 male alcoholics and 260 female alcoholics, one-third were found to respond favorably and were considered to have been successfully rehabilitated.[3] They had longer periods of sobriety, they consumed less alcohol when drinking, and alcoholic complications in employment appeared less frequently.

Alcohol has been used by man since the Neolithic Age (about 7000 B.C. in the Middle East and 3000 B.C. in Northern Europe); Rhazes, an Arabic physician, discovered distillation in the 11th century A.D., and distilled liquor become popular in the sixteenth century.[4] The American Medical Association classified alcoholism as a disease in 1947. From the medical viewpoint, alcoholism has (1) genetic, (2) sociological, and (3) psychological components.[5] Oral needs seem to have been frustrated early, resulting in frustration and rage to be diverted from those upon whom the child is dependent, leading to tense depression, guilt, and masochism, with a turning to alcohol that (1) physiologically reduces aggressive drives, (2) minimizes the effects of stress, and (3) affords a symbolic substitute for

[2] Research Council of the Problems of Alcohol, *The Scientific Approach to the Problems of Chronic Alcoholism* (New York: Research Council, n.d.).

[3] James H. Williams, *Florida Project on Follow-Up Adjustment of Alcoholic Referrals for Vocational Rehabilitation* (Avon Park: Florida Alcoholic Rehabilitation Program, 1967).

[4] Jean Kinney and Gwen Leaton, eds., *Loosening the Grip* (St. Louis: C.V. Mosby, 1978), pp. 4–14.

[5] Leland E. Hinsie and Robert Jean Campbell, *Psychiatric Dictionary,* 4th ed. (New York: Oxford University Press, 1970), p. 26. Also, Ray Oakley; *Drugs, Society & Human Behavior,* 3rd ed. (St. Louis: C.V. Mosby Co., 1983, p. 172.)

gratification, thereby giving temporary pleasure. Eventually, a pattern is established in which frustration brings anxiety and rage, and alcohol brings relief, but this is only temporary, and it leads to secondary frustration, anxiety, and rage, and more and more alcohol, in an almost never-ending cycle. Williams has suggested that alcoholism is a genetotrophic disease, in which the basis is genetotrophic and the sociological and psychological components are precipitating factors for the development of the clinical syndrome of alcoholism.[6] Medical treatment involves education regarding alcohol and alcoholism, individual counseling, group therapy, family involvement in the treatment process, and medical attention for physical problems.

Alcoholics Anonymous is a self-help group with chapters nationwide and in some other countries. It was started in Akron, Ohio, in 1935 by "Dr. Bob" (Dr. Robert Holbrook Smith) and "Bill" (William Griffith Wilson). They worked with other alcoholics, beginning with "Bill D.," and soon had a group of persons needing relief from alcohol. The first publication of "the Big Book"[7] was in 1936, with second and third editions in 1955 and 1976; it gave the general principles of Alcoholics Anonymous and contained personal stories of individuals who had recovered. These self-help groups are not analytical. They are not concerned with "causes." They view alcoholism as a personality defect and "causes" as excuses and rationalizations. As Glasser pointed out in one of the tenets of Reality Therapy, "Ask 'What,' not 'Why.' "[8]

There are many self-help groups in the United States that assist persons addicted to alcohol and drugs. There are Al-Anon Family Groups and Alateen groups for families of alcoholics; Friends of Sobriety, headquartered in Phoenix, Arizona; and many others. A central clearinghouse is available in New York City, National Self-Help Clearinghouse,[9] from which information can be obtained from almost any group. Such information is also available from the national headquarters of Alcoholics Anonymous.[10]

## THE NARCOTIC ADDICT AND DEALER

Narcotic addiction has become a problem of adolescence and young adulthood. Very few persons become addicted after the age of 50. The criteria

[6] *Ibid.,* p. 216. See R.J. Williams in E. Poldolsky, *Management of Addictions* (New York: Philosophical Library), 1955.

[7] *Alcoholics Anonymous,* 3rd ed. (New York: Alcoholics Anonymous World Services, 1976).

[8] William Glasser, *Reality Therapy; Another Approach to Psychiatry* (New York: Harper & Row, 1965), p. 30.

[9] National Self-Help Clearinghouse, Graduate School & University Center, CUNY, 33 West 42nd Street, Room 1227, New York, New York 10036.

[10] Alcoholics Anonymous General Service Office, Box 459, Grand Central Station, New York, New York 10163.

for addiction, according to the United States Public Health Service, are that the person (1) has to be physically dependent upon the drugs, (2) must have built up a physical tolerance that permits him to take large quantities of the drug, and (3) must have a mental dependency on the drug. The World Health Organization defines drug addiction as a state of periodic or chronic intoxication induced by repeated consumption of a drug, with characteristics including (1) an overpowering desire to need to continue taking the drug and to obtain it by any means, (2) a tendency to increase the dose, (3) a psychic and, generally, physical dependence on the effects of the drug, and (4) detrimental effect on the individual and on society. The major narcotic drugs are opium derivatives (morphine, heroin, paregoric, and codeine) and cocaine. Marihuana also presents a problem, although it does not meet the full definition of addiction in that it does not develop the physical dependence that leads to withdrawal symptoms when the supply is eliminated. General consensus is that people do not stay on marihuana for long periods of time for purposes of effect. Either they go on to the heavier drugs or they drop it. Narcotic addiction is a personality problem. Not everyone can be addicted, because many people do not have a psychological dependency upon drugs.

The extent of the problem is difficult to measure. A chart developed by the United States Bureau of Narcotics indicates that there were 200,000 addicts in the United States in 1914 when the Harrison Act for control of narcotics went into effect.[11] By use of suppressive methods, this figure was reduced to 60,000 in 1963 (one in 2,000). In 1945–46, the number dropped to 20,000 and a little below, but a sharp rise after World War II brought the number back to 60,000 in 1956. In 1960 the estimate was that there were 50,000 (one in 4,000) addicts in the United States. This chart has been questioned for its accuracy in several quarters, but it is the only real estimate available. There are no reliable statistics to count the amount of narcotic addiction—nor have there ever been. The 1970 estimates are based on various formulas, such as the national estimate on 200 times the overdose death rate, or one of New York City's borough's use of four times the arrest rate. Probably the estimates used by the news media are as close to reality as possible. These estimates were around 250,000 addicts in 1970 (*Time*, June 28, 1971 p. 18); the number had grown to 600,000 heroin addicts by 1975.[12]

Marihuana has been in use for at least 12,000 years.[13] A Chinese manuscript dated 3000 B.C. mentions that the plant was growing freely almost everywhere in the world except in the cold regions. It has long been known to man as a source of mind-affecting substances and of fibers for

[11] John B. Williams, ed., *Narcotics and Hallucinogenics—A Handbook*, rev. ed. (Beverly Hills, Cal.: Glencoe Press, 1967).

[12] Jerome H. Jaffe, "Drug Abuse: A Big Dirty War—The Treatment Side," *Justice*, 1, No. 10 (October 1972), 19.

[13] Ernest L. Abel, *Marihuana: The First Twelve Thousand Years* (New York: Plenum Publishing Co., 1980).

rope and cloth. Its use as a fiber was specifically mentioned in a 1200 B.C. manuscript. In 1848, Pope Innocent VIII issued a papal fiat condemning witchcraft and the use of hemp in the Satanic mass. Incidentally, "Mari-Juana" is the Spanish equivalent of "Mary Jane."

Marihuana is not an addicting drug, since it does not cause physical dependence, as do heroin and other narcotics. In the extreme, of course, almost all substances, such as coffee, would produce a nominal physical dependence, but, as in the case of marihuana and some other substances, the degree of dependence is not significant enough to be called an addiction.

Marihuana has been used as a pain reliever during surgery throughout history. Today other, more powerful drugs are used for this purpose. Marihuana was introduced into the United States in 1920, and estimates of its users today range from between 4 and 5 million to as high as 20 million users. Marihuana quickly enters the blood stream when smoked and acts on the nervous system and the brain. Because it causes hallucinations when taken in large doses, it can be called a mild hallucinogen. The obvious physical effects include increased heartbeat, lowered body temperature, and sometimes reddening of the eyes. Users may get talkative, loud, unsteady, or drowsy, and find it hard to coordinate movements. They find it more difficult to make decisions that require clear thinking. Marihuana is apparently an available drug that does not satisfy more serious anxiety problems, so the pathological user goes on to the heavier drugs. Many others reportedly stay on it for a few months to a year and abandon it unless socializing continues its use, as in some Latin American countries.[14]

*Narcotics* is a term that refers to opium and pain-killing drugs made from opium, such as heroin, morphine, paregoric, and codeine, as well as several synthetic drugs like Demerol, Dolophine or methadone, and cocaine, which is made from coca leaves. The effects of these drugs are to reduce tension, ease fears, or relieve worry.

The use of narcotic drugs usually begins with oral intake, since the smoking of opium is not a general practice any more. The second phase of the use of drugs occurs when the oral dose ceases to be effective and a "flesh pop," or injection into a muscle, eliminates the need for the oral dose to go through the mashed potatoes and hamburgers eaten by the individual. The third stage arrives when the drug has to be taken by injection directly into the vein so that the bloodstream receives it directly, without its going first through the capillaries. This injection involves the use of a tourniquet and hypodermic needle.

Heroin addiction is today found chiefly among young men of minority groups in the ghetto areas. More than 60,000 known addicts were listed by the Bureau of Narcotics and Dangerous Drugs in 1970, of whom more than half lived in New York State and most of them in New York City.

[14] Jules Saltman, *What About Marijuana?* Public Affairs Pamphlet No. 436 (New York: Public Affairs Committee, 1969), p. 3.

Marihuana smuggled in a surf board. It was discovered at an airport when a piece of the board broke off.
Courtesy of the Honolulu Police Department.

Once he is on narcotics, getting a supply becomes the main object of the addict's life. It takes probably $100 to buy the daily supply for a full-blown addict. Thus, most addicts must commit crimes to obtain money to support the habit. While very few addicts are convicted of crimes of passion, many are convicted of property crimes to obtain funds. It is apparent that the addict's life span may be shortened by fifteen to twenty years, during which time he is usually in trouble with his family and almost always in trouble with the law.

The Narcotic Addict Rehabilitation Act of 1966 gives some addicts a choice of treatment or imprisonment and for the first time provides a complete range of rehabilitation services. This act is administered by the National Institute of Mental Health and the Department of Justice. Under the act, an addict charged with a nonviolent federal offense who elects to be committed for treatment can be sent to the United States Public Health Hospital in Lexington, Kentucky. An addict already convicted of a crime can be committed to the Attorney General for treatment for not longer than ten years or for the maximum period of sentence that could be imposed because of his conviction. An addict not charged with an offense can be civilly committed to the Surgeon General for treatment upon his own application. The key aspect of the treatment program is the care of the addict after his release from the hospital. Clinical research centers are maintained at Lexington, Kentucky, and at Fort Worth, Texas. Research on drug usage, the effects of drug use, and antidotes for narcotic addiction are central. The success rate in these hospitals ranges around 2 percent.[15] The psychological dependency has to be eliminated before successful treatment can be achieved.

LSD, or lysergic acid diethylamide, was developed in 1938 from one of the ergot alkaloids, a fungus that grows as a rust on rye.[16] Reasons given for taking LSD include curiosity, "for kicks," "to understand myself better," or in quest of religious or philosophical insights. An average dose, amounting to a speck, can be taken in a sugar cube, cracker, or any other way, and its effects last for about eight to ten hours. It increases the pulse and heart rate, causes a rise in blood pressure and temperature, dilated eye pupils, shaking of hands and feet, cold sweaty palms, a flushed face or paleness, irregular breathing, and other physical symptoms. It is not physically addicting, since there are no withdrawal symptoms. There are sudden changes in physical senses, such as walls that appear to move, colors that taste, and many other variations. The user is insensitive to time, may become fascinated with an object in the room, may feel mystical and report a sense of rebirth or new insights, or other variations. LSD changes values and impairs the user's power of concentration and ability to think, which may lead to his "dropping out" of society. The dangers of LSD to the user are (1) panic for fear he is losing his mind, (2) paranoia in which he thinks somebody is trying to harm him or control his thinking, (3) recurrence in using the drug, and (4) accidental death, because the user may feel he can fly or float and may jump out of a high window. Also, later "flashes" may occur long after the LSD has been taken. The control of LSD is not well known, but research is continuing. Among LSD users, the primary reason for first usage is the belief that the experiences will be interesting and worthwhile.

The most widely employed methods of treating addicts are imprisonment, hospitalization, institutional counseling, community surveillance, casework in a community, and mutual aid organizations of addicts. The Supreme Court of the United States has indicated that narcotic addiction is essentially a medical problem, rather than criminal.[17]

California in 1961 and New York in 1962 passed laws providing for civil commitments of drug addicts to mental hospitals similar to those provided in the federal system at the United States Public Health Service Hospital in Lexington, Kentucky.

The nalline test involves injecting a person with Nallorphine. If he

[15] *The Up and Down Drugs: Amphetamines and Barbiturates,* National Institute of Mental Health, Public Health Service Publication No. 1830 (Washington, D.C.: U.S. Government Printing Office, 1969).

[16] *LSD: Some Questions and Answers,* National Institute of Mental Health, Public Health Service Publication No. 1828 (Washington, D.C.: U.S. Government Printing Office, 1969).

[17] *Robinson* v. *California,* 370 U.S. (1962).

has been using opiates, his eye pupils will be unchanged or enlarged, and if he has not been using opiates, his pupils will become smaller. This test has been accepted by the courts.[18]

Habituation as distinguished from addiction does not involve true compulsion or physical dependence, and there is little tendency to increase the dose.[19] The problems of narcotic drugs are (1) international, promoted by illicit drug traffic; (2) individual, caused by compulsion, a tendency to increase the dosage, and a psychological and physical dependency on the drugs; and (3) social, resulting from the addict's withdrawal from others and his need to steal to support his habit.

The California Narcotics Treatment-Control Project was begun in 1959 in Los Angeles and San Francisco.[20] The narcotics addicts were placed under specially trained parole agents dealing only with addicts, with caseloads of only thirty, while the usual adult caseload was 75. The parolees must have agreed to submit to one nalline test per week and one surprise test per month. Those found using drugs were returned for 90 days for special counseling at a prison. In the experimental narcotics group, 65 percent were detected using narcotics again within 18 months, while in the untested control group, only 47 percent were detected using drugs. The suspicion was that more of the untested group actually reverted to drugs than the figures suggest.

Special counseling programs for probationers and parolees with narcotics problems have been established in Philadelphia, New York, California, and elsewhere. A halfway house has been established in the Los Angeles area. In 1958, Synanon House at Santa Monica, California, was created as a mutual aid program for some fifty ex-addicts. Synanon House ceased operation in 1980 when its founder and director, Chuck Dederich, was arrested for attempted murder when a man was bitten by a rattlesnake that had been placed in his rural mailbox.

Daytop Lodge, subsequently Daytop Village, in New York is patterned somewhat after Synanon House in California.[21] The addict is initially told that he is an immature and irresponsible child and that the cause of his being an addict is his own stupidity. The "ungluing" sessions consist of group therapy in which the emphasis is on an emotional level of inter-

---

[18] *People* v. *Williams,* 164 C. A. Second supplement 858, 331 P. Second 251 (1958). Also see Thorvald T. Brown, "Narcotics and Nalline: Six Years of Testing," *Federal Probation,* 27, No. 2 (June 1963), 27–32.

[19] Ahmad M. Khalifa, "The Problem of Narcotic Drugs," *International Annals of Criminology, 1964.* Thirteenth International Course in Criminology, Cairo, June 22–July 10, 1963 (Paris, France), pp. 108–16.

[20] *Narcotic Treatment-Control Program, Phase I and Phase II,* California Dept. of Corrections Report No. 19 (Sacramento: State Printing Office, 1963).

[21] Joseph A. Shelly and Alexander Bassin, "Daytop Lodge: A New Treatment Approach for Drug Addicts," *Corrective Psychiatry and Journal for Social Therapy,* II, No. 4 (1965), 186–95.

The Synanon lifestyle was full of adventure for kids as well as for grownups. Here, some young Synanon residents perch atop a fire engine built from a government surplus truck to protect Synanon's property and that of its neighbors in rural Marin County, California. Courtesy of Synanon Foundation, Inc., Marshall, California.

action with discipline based on hard work, honesty, integrity, and concern for one's fellow man.

The provisions of the Narcotic Addict Rehabilitation Act of 1966 have been implemented by a series of contracts and agreements between the United States Bureau of Prisons, which has a particular concern in aftercare, the National Institute of Mental Health, and the United States Board of Parole. Under this act, the United States district courts may make commitments for examination to determine whether an eligible offender is an addict and whether he is likely to be rehabilitated through treatment. Under the federal statute, addictive drugs do not include alcohol, marihuana, barbiturates, LSD, amphetamines, and other drugs of this nature. A comprehensive psychiatric evaluation, physical examination for determination of overall health and evidence of addiction, and laboratory tests as indicated are part of the psychiatric and medical services provided the addict. The psychological services include the MMPI and the Lexington Per-

Here on Synanon's 3,400-acre ranch near Tomales Bay, California, youngsters who were once in trouble with drugs or alcohol, or who were headed for trouble with the law, lived in a community free of drugs, tobacco, alcohol, and violence—a community designed to instill character, morality, honesty, self-reliance, good manners, and respect for others.
Courtesy of Synanon Foundation, Inc., Marshall, California.

sonality Test items, the Revised Beta Test, other tests at the discretion of the psychologist, and psychological interviews as required.

Of 12,000 inmates in New York City jails in the early 1960s, 5,000 to 7,000 were estimated to be addicts.[22] Rehabilitation centers maintained by the Health Department of New York City are (1) the Central Harlem Center, (2) the West Side Rehabilitation Center, (3) a demonstration center to evaluate what effect compulsory treatment has on addicts, and (4) a rehabilitative center in Queens for counseling and service for young addicts who work.

An experiment to effect abstention from heroin was inaugurated in New York City by Mobilization for Youth, in which addicts were sent to a ward in Manhattan General Hospital for three weeks and summer camp

---

[22] The Quaker Committee on Social Rehabilitation, *Symposium on Treatment of Narcotic Addiction* (130 Christopher Street, New York, Oct. 28, 1964).

for six weeks, then returned home.[23] Back in the old neighborhoods, however, the old contacts were renewed and each boy returned to the use of heroin, so the project was terminated in January 1965.

Lindesmith states that the statistics published by federal narcotic officials indicating the decline in the number of addicts in the United States since the passage of the Harrison Act are inaccurate and that probably the number of addicts has increased.[24] For example, *Time* reported an estimated 250,000 addicts in the United States in 1970 (*Time,* June 28, 1971). This estimate is based on the "Jaffe formula" of 200 times the overdose death rate. Since World War II, the following trends have taken place in drug usage:

1. Increase in drug usage by younger persons
2. Increase in drug usage by persons of lower economic status
3. Concentration of drug usage in persons of minority racial and national groups
4. Concentration of usage in large cities
5. Widespread linkage of different types of drug use
6. Increased association of drug addiction with other types of criminalities to support the habit
7. Introduction of new types of drugs[25]

The community mental health approach to drug addiction is gaining favor.[26] A study of the lifestyle adaptation of 248 addicts, using median split points between high and low values, indicates that 23 percent were conformists, 21 percent were uninvolved, 25 percent were two-worlders (lived both conventionally and criminally), and 30 percent were hustlers (lived in criminal lifestyle).

Methadone maintenance is currently being used for treatment of narcotic addiction. This approach involves providing the addict with sufficient methadone, a synthetic drug invented in Germany during World War II, so that he can be maintained while psychiatric or other casework methods are employed to reduce his psychological dependence. Critics of the method suggest that it is merely trading one addiction for another. Supporters of the method contend that methadone can be more easily controlled by the doctor and that the amounts can be reduced as the addict's psychological dependence is reduced.

[23] Robert Rice, "A Reporter at Large: Junk," *The New Yorker,* March 27, 1965, pp. 50–142.

[24] Alfred R. Lindesmith, *The Addict and the Law* (Bloomington: Indiana University Press, 1965).

[25] Daniel Glaser and Vincent O'Leary, *The Control and Treatment of Narcotic Use,* Office of Juvenile Delinquency and Youth Development, HEW (Washington, D.C.: U.S. Government Printing Office, 1968).

[26] Richard Brotman and Alfred Freedman, *A Community Mental Health Approach to Drug Addiction,* Office of Juvenile Delinquency and Youth Development, HEW (Washington, D.C.: U.S. Government Printing Office, 1968).

Working at the Delancy Street Foundation in San Francisco.
Courtesy of Delancy Street Foundation, Inc.

The hallucinogens include LSD, mescaline, peyote, psilocybin, DMT, and a comparatively new drug, PCP (phencylclidine), commonly called "angel dust," that is dangerous. Its effects on different people are difficult to predict, and the risk of overdose is high enough to result in suicide and destructive behavior resulting from the drug's effect on the mind.[27] Tranquilizers most frequently used are Valium, Librium, and Miltown. Quaaludes (quads, methaqualone) have been popular. The number and assortment of natural and manufactured drugs are extensive.

The problem of marihuana is most widespread because the substance is more widespread than any drug (except nicotine). Some states have already "decriminalized" it for personal use, so there is no sanction against possessing an ounce or less for one's own use. This decriminalization as of 1980 extended to Alaska, California, Colorado, Maine, Minnesota, Mississippi, Nebraska, New York, North Carolina, Ohio, and Oregon.

In 1979, there were 160 drug programs serving 215 state prisons, and 29 drug treatment programs in the Federal Prison System.[28] About 21 percent of state prisoners need this treatment because of heroin addiction, but state programs treat only 10,000 inmates, or 4 percent of the total number,

[27] Peter B. Bensinger, "PCP—Its Rising Abuse—Rapid and Alarming," *LEAA Newsletter,* 7, No. 7 (September 1978), 2.

[28] *Drug Abuse Treatment in Prisons* (Washington, D.C.: U.S. National Institute on Drug Abuse, 1981). Department of Health and Human Services publication (ADM) 81-1149).

less than a quarter of those who need it. The federal programs treat 2,600 inmates. These programs involve drug education, vocational counseling, and family therapy.

Narcotics Anonymous (similar to Alcoholics Anonymous) is the largest self-help group that works with drug addicts and persons with drug problems. There are other less-well-organized groups around, such as Addicts Anonymous in some urban areas. Narcotics Anonymous will provide information and assistance in getting organized help for persons with narcotic involvement and addiction.[29]

## THE CRIMINAL SEXUAL PSYCHOPATH

Criminal sexual psychopath laws began in 1933 in Illinois and were adopted by 37 states. The purpose of the laws is to identify chronic sex offenders and commit them to state hospitals for treatment. The general practice is to commit them to the joint jurisdiction of the State Hospital Commission and the Department of Corrections or their respective counterparts. The laws generally identify criminal sexual psychopaths as those persons who are not insane, not epileptic, not feebleminded (and excluding other legal categories for which institutionalization is available), but have a "mental derangement" coupled with a propensity toward committing sex offenses. The phrase "propensity for the commission of sex offenses" is generally interpreted to refer to those who have committed at least two such offenses within a twelve-month period. Further, these acts usually indicate that no person shall be released until he shall have "completely and fully recovered from such psychopathy."

In practice, the fact that two sex offenses have to be committed within a year means that the most serious and dangerous sex offenders, such as those who murder after a rape, are not covered by the criminal sexual psychopath law. Rather, the minor sex offenders, voyeurs or "peeping Toms," exhibitionists, and some homosexual solicitors or similar relatively minor offenders, are covered by this act. Whether the law works well or not depends upon many factors. Apparently, the political stability or instability in a state may influence its effectiveness. For example, a psychiatrist must say that the criminal sexual psychopath has "fully and completely recovered from such psychopathy" in order for the person to be released, although no one can possibly testify in that manner within the body of psychiatric knowledge. Rather, testimony must be reinterpreted into legal terms in order to make progress within the system of criminal justice. The person who appears to be no longer a threat to society is most apt to be described by a psychiatrist as "fully and completely recovered from such psychopathy" and be released.

[29] World Service Office of Narcotics Anonymous, P.O. Box 622, Sun Valley, California 91352.

The criminal sexual psychopath laws have not been successful in integrating psychiatric knowledge and the legal framework in which these minor sex offenders are treated. The psychiatrist has had to compromise in order to fit the legal requirements.

Treatment of criminal sexual psychopaths in state hospitals has been almost negligible. Several jurisdictions have indicated that such cases get more attention in the prison than they do in the state hospital. The state hospital is primarily concerned with psychotics, while the prison will provide whatever professional help is available to assist the criminal sexual psychopath. Since there is very little psychiatric or psychological help in most prisons, the criminal sexual psychopath laws in most jurisdictions simply involve the prisons in a holding operation.

California's Sexual Psychopath Law was passed in 1937.[30] In 1963, the state enacted four major changes: (1) The term "mentally disordered sex offender" replaced "sexual psychopath," (2) eligibility for probation was provided, (3) reports were required to include a psychiatric opinion, and (4) credit was to be allowed for time in mental institutions if a prison sentence was subsequently given. Three-fourths of the offenders exposed to the revised procedures did not repeat their offenses in any way within a 5-year period.

Massachusetts sends sexually dangerous persons to the Center for the Diagnosis and Treatment of Sexually Dangerous Persons in Bridgewater, Massachusetts, for sixty days' observation.[31] Wisconsin has had a Sex Crimes Law since 1951,[32] and a special review board consisting of a psychiatrist, a social worker, and a lawyer make the decisions for release. Criminal sexual psychopaths have a recidivism rate significantly lower than offenders who pleaded not guilty by reason of insanity.[33] An accurate determination of sexual psychopathy is most difficult.[34] There are no positive criteria of sexual psychopathy except a history of repeated abnormal sexual acts. Potential violence is detectable by the use of projective techniques, but identification of the criminal sexual psychopath is elusive. Recent focus has been on the "dangerous sex offender," rather than the "criminal sexual psychopath," particularly in Europe and Canada.

[30] Louise Viets Frisbie, "Treated Sex Offenders Who Reverted to Sexually Deviant Behavior," *Federal Probation*, 29, No. 2 (June 1965), 25–27.

[31] Robert A. Serafian, "Treatment of the Criminally Dangerous Sex Offender," *Federal Probation*, 27, No. 1 (March 1963), 52–59.

[32] Leigh M. Roberts and Asher R. Pacht, "Termination of In-Patient for Sex Deviates: Psychiatric, Social, and Legal Factors," *The American Journal of Psychiatry*, 121, No. 9 (1965), 873–80.

[33] William R. Morrow and Donald B. Peterson, "Follow-up of Discharged Psychiatric Offenders—'Not Guilty by Reason of Insanity' and 'Criminal Sexual Psychopaths,'" *The Journal of Criminal Law, Criminology, and Police Science*, 57, No. 1 (1966), 31–38.

[34] Thomas J. Meyers, "Psychiatric Examination of the Sexual Psychopath," *The Journal of Criminal Law, Criminology, and Police Science*, 56, No. 1 (March 1965), 27–31.

Most states that once had laws covering the criminal sexual psycho-path are following California's lead and abolishing the criminal sexual psychopath as a legal category. Florida adopted the "mentally disordered sex offender" (MSDO) classification, similar to California, in 1979,[35] and other states have also eliminated the sexual psychopath legal status.

## THE CRIMINALLY INSANE

Many defendants enter pleas of not guilty by reason of insanity at their original trials. "Madness" has been a criminal defense since Edward I (1239–1307). *Insanity* is a legal term and status that is determined by a court. In any state hospital for the insane or mentally ill, there are many psychotics, many intense neurotics, some extreme psychopaths, some senile patients, and some normal people. They are all, however, "insane," having been sent there by a court. There are also many psychotics committed to prison through the regular procedures, but who have not been declared insane. The criminally insane, then, are persons who have committed crimes and have subsequently been declared insane.

The test of insanity today is known as the McNaghten Rule. In 1843, Daniel McNaghten was under the delusion that he was being persecuted unfairly by the then Prime Minister of England, Sir Robert Peel. McNaghten lay in wait and killed Peel's secretary by mistake. He was found not guilty by reason of insanity, and some furor resulted. To answer the question of insanity, fifteen judges from the House of Lords were appointed. They decided that civil insanity existed when a person did not know the nature and extent of his estate and could not handle his personal affairs, while criminal insanity occurred when a person did not know right from wrong (10 CL and F. 200, 1843). All states but New Hampshire adopted the McNaghten Rule; approximately one-third also adopted the "irresistible impulse" rule, which says that a person knows the difference between right and wrong but had an irresistible impulse that prevented him from acting on that knowledge. A jury decides the insanity status, generally with the assistance of expert witnesses, most frequently physicians. Since 1883, New Hampshire, under the leadership of a psychiatrist, Isaac Ray, has used the "product test" for insanity, in which the crime is considered a product of a mental condition. This was also adopted briefly in the District of Columbia in 1954 by Judge Bazelon under the name "Durham Rule," but now the District of Columbia goes by the McNaghten Rule.

The problem of identifying and treating the "criminally insane" is most difficult, because the terminology varies so widely that an adequate

[35] *Florida Statutes—1979,* Chap. 917, "Mentally Disordered Sex Offenders."

survey cannot be taken. The National Institute of Mental Health attempted in 1972 to identify the institutions that house offenders with mental disorders, but made no attempt to take a census.[36] The types of institutions that were identified were (1) security hospitals for which this type of activity may be a major function, (2) mental health facilities that have a definite program for this type of patient despite a more general mission of treating the mentally ill, and (3) correctional institutions that have established on-site psychiatric units for prisoners who become mentally ill in the course of serving their sentences. There were several known progressive programs that were omitted even from this survey.

The treatment of criminally insane persons also varies quite widely throughout the United States. Michigan was the first state to establish a hospital for the criminally insane at Ionia in 1847. At the other extreme, there are states that place their psychotic or criminally insane persons in the general prison population. Many states have mental wards within their prison system. Other states have special units for the criminally insane within the state hospital system. In all states, there is probably less treatment given to the criminally insane than to the civilly insane.

The numbers of criminally insane are difficult to determine. The difficulty is due to the fact that the policies and sophistication of the courts and the system of justice in the jurisdictions throughout the United States seem to be even less comparable than many crime statistics. One attempt to obtain the number of criminally insane in each state in 1966 appears in Table 11-1. This was the last known "brave attempt" to count the criminally insane! Terminology and definitions are so varied that an accurate count is obviously impossible. The 1966 prison and hospital populations were retained for whatever comparison with the available estimate that might be interesting.

The legal status of "criminally insane" is falling into disuse just as the "criminal sexual psychopath" did, and for the same reasons. Psychiatrists think it is strange terminology, alien to their medical training. Michigan adopted "guilty, but mentally ill" (GMBI) in 1979 and was followed by Indiana, Illinois, Georgia, and Kentucky. Idaho eliminated "criminally insane" in 1982. "Mentally disordered offender" and "guilty, but mentally ill" are the two categories that seem to be most acceptable, along with "mentally disordered dangerous offender."

The numbers of mentally disordered offenders entering prisons, as well as forensic units of hospitals, frequently amaze people. Dr. Dennis Jurczak, medical director for the Michigan Department of Corrections, has said that of *all* the inmates sent directly to the prison—that is, not including those sent to forensic units and hospitals—20 percent had serious men-

[36] William C. Eckerman, *A Nationwide Survey of Mental Health and Correctional Institutions for Adult Mentally Disordered Offenders* (Rockville, Md.: National Institute for Mental Health, 1972).

Table 11-1 Population of the criminally insane, 1966

| State | Prisons[a] | Mental Hospitals[b] | Criminally Insane[b] |
|---|---|---|---|
| Alabama | 4,056 | 7,725 | 69 |
| Alaska | — | 164 | 5 |
| Arizona | 1,627 | 1,138 | 65 |
| Arkansas | 1,864 | 89 | 71 |
| California | 27,467 | 23,127 | 1,329 |
| Colorado | 2,540 | 2,528 | 64 |
| Connecticut | 1,599 | 2,118 | 35 |
| Delaware | 270 | 1,172 | 25 |
| District of Columbia | 1,542 | 8,225 | 855 |
| Florida | 6,972 | 6,953 | 464 |
| Georgia | 5,385 | 11,134 | 280 |
| Hawaii | 423 | 715 | 20 |
| Idaho | 477 | — | — |
| Illinois | 7,491 | 2,276 | 570 |
| Indiana | 3,907 | 9,896 | 148 |
| Iowa | 1,885 | 76 | 69 |
| Kansas | 2,444 | 748 | 155 |
| Kentucky | 2,932 | 1,210 | 52 |
| Louisiana | 4,068 | 3,095 | 157 |
| Maine | 605 | 2,679 | 73 |
| Maryland | 5,117 | 188 | — |
| Massachusetts | 1,829 | 7,065 | 867 |
| Michigan | 6,754 | 964 | 750 |
| Minnesota | 1,620 | 143 | 74 |
| Mississippi | 1,829 | 4,264 | 103 |
| Missouri | 3,447 | 1,912 | 358 |
| Montana | 548 | 1,356 | 12 |
| Nebraska | 1,027 | 870 | 66 |
| Nevada | 651 | 535 | 5 |
| New Hampshire | 205 | 2,076 | 70 |
| New Jersey | 4,912 | 3,117 | 200 |
| New Mexico | 912 | 601 | 11 |
| New York | 15,760 | 1,105 | 1,105 |
| North Carolina | 5,295 | 8,691 | 606 |
| North Dakota | 199 | 1,413 | 21 |
| Ohio | 10,694 | 2,532 | 441 |
| Oklahoma | 2,776 | — | 12 |
| Oregon | 1,880 | 1,510 | 56 |
| Pennsylvania | 6,519 | 1,259 | 1,259 |
| Rhode Island | 329 | 1,950 | 23 |
| South Carolina | 2,248 | 5,976 | 117 |
| South Dakota | 555 | 1,497 | 8 |
| Tennessee | 2,968 | 1,873 | 206 |
| Texas | 12,392 | 17,441 | 817 |
| Utah | 659 | 550 | 5 |

continued

**Table 11-1 (continued)**

| State | Prisons[a] | Mental Hospitals[b] | Criminally Insane[b] |
|-------|-----------|---------------------|----------------------|
| Vermont | 233 | 1,094 | 23 |
| Virginia | 4,220 | 5,881 | 347 |
| Washington | 3,098 | 4,626 | 23 |
| West Virginia | 1,189 | 2,036 | 60 |
| Wisconsin | 2,709 | 1,668 | 975 |
| Wyoming | 279 | 569 | 9 |

[a] *National Prisoner Statistics—1966*, United States Bureau of Prisons (Washington, D.C.: U.S. Government Printing Office, 1968), pp. 34–35.
[b] Taken from a list compiled as of January 1, 1967, by Mrs. Donald D. Barry, Political Science Department, Muhlenburg College, Pennsylvania. Mrs. Barry corresponded with each state to request the information.

tal disorders.[37] It has been stated that "correctional psychiatry" is a contradiction in terms, almost like "capitalistic communism."[38]

In 1977, there were 574,226 patients in public mental hospitals and 184,189 in private mental hospitals.[39] How many had been in difficulty with the law, only a brave estimate such as that by Mrs. Barry in Table 11-1 can be made. In 1977, as indicated in Chapter 2, there were 285,456 persons in adult prisons in the United States. How many of those had serious mental disorders is for the professionals in the field to estimate, as Dr. Jurczak did for Michigan's prisoners. The Florida Department of Corrections estimated that 4,625 (23 percent) of their 20,000 prisoners in 1979 had serious mental disorders.[40] A summary of significant psychiatric evaluations of offenders in prisons from 1919 to 1970 by nine scholars in this field indicated that about 51 percent were "normal" and the rest needed psychiatric attention.[41] It is obvious that what used to be referred to as the "criminally insane" are really disturbed people who commit crimes and need more accurate and sophisticated treatment, both legally and psychiatrically, than they are getting today; society will continue to pay the price for this neglect and omission until the problem of the mentally disordered offender is addressed competently.

[37] Rob Wilson, "Who Will Care for the 'Mad and Bad,' " *Corrections Magazine*, VI, No. 1 (February 1980), 6.

[38] *Ibid.*, p. 8.

[39] "Patient Care Episodes in Mental Health Facilities," National Institute of Mental Health, Table in *The World Almanac & Book of Facts—1982* (New York: News Enterprise Association, Inc., 1982), p. 961.

[40] "Florida Moves to Improve Treatment of Inmates Suffering from Mental Illness," *Corrections Digest*, 10, No. 3 (February 2, 1979), 6.

[41] Lawrence A. Bennett, Thomas S. Rosenbaum, and Wayne R. McCullough, *Counseling in Correctional Environments* (New York: Human Sciences Press, 1978), p. 76.

## THE DEFECTIVE DELINQUENT

The defective delinquent or the mentally retarded offender is not separated in many systems. Pennsylvania has probably done more than other jurisdictions for defective delinquents by providing specialized institutions for them at Huntingdon and Dallas. The Illinois Youth Commission is attempting to have mentally retarded delinquents committed to schools for the mentally retarded, rather than schools for delinquents.[42]

The 1967 amendments to the Mental Retardation Act of 1963 authorized a dramatic increase in the construction of new facilities for research and direct service and expanding training programs so that there will be more professional people to serve the needs of mentally retarded persons in future years. The Commissioner of Education was granted authority through 1970 to continue and expand programs of training educational personnel to work with the handicapped. These provisions had considerable import to the field of corrections, particularly in the area of the defective delinquent.

## MILITARY CORRECTIONS

The United States Army operates the U.S. Disciplinary Barracks at Fort Leavenworth, Kansas, holding 1,250 prisoners, and the U.S. Correctional Training Facility at Fort Riley, Kansas, holding 1,968 prisoners. The Navy had the U.S. Naval Disciplinary Command at Portsmouth, New Hampshire, holding 997 men, but this installation was deactivated in 1974. It was replaced by a series of smaller correctional facilities distributed around the country. The Air Force has the 3320th Retraining Group at Lowry Air Force Base in Colorado, holding 132 men. In addition, all services have stockades and other confinement centers at every base and station.

A Uniform Code of Military Justice was approved May 5, 1950 (64 Stat. 107), for all the military services. Subsequently, procedures for the administration of justice in the military services have become uniform. Military jurisdiction comes from the Constitution and international law, including the law of war.

The general courts-martial can try an offense and impose the death penalty when authorized and may adjudge any punishment permitted by the law of war (Article 18). Special courts-martial can try offenses and adjudge any punishment except death, dishonorable discharge, dismissal, confinement in excess of six months, hard labor without confinement in excess of three months, forfeit pay exceeding two-thirds pay per month, or forfeit all pay for a period exceeding six months. Summary courts-martial try minor offenses and may not adjudge punishment of death, dismissal,

---

[42] Russel H. Levy, *Mental Retardation in Illinois,* Illinois Youth Commission, 2, No. 2 (1968), 22.

dishonorable or bad conduct discharge, confinement in excess of one month, hard labor without confinement in excess of 45 days, restriction to specified limits in excess of two months, or forfeit pay in excess of two-thirds of one month's pay (Article 20).

Trial is by a tribunal with a law officer and a panel of no less than five officers. Trial procedures follow due process similar to that in civilian courts, including the preliminary hearing, the arraignment, provision of defense counsel, and other, related guarantees. The U.S. Court of Military Appeals functions as the "supreme court" in military justice.

Confinement can be in any military installation or any penal or other facility under the control of or available to the United States government.[43] A punitive sentence of discharge or dismissal in a case involving an offense which demonstrates a degree of moral turpitude that disqualifies the individual for further military service shall not be suspended. Habeas corpus and appeal procedures are available, but it appears that the error must be more substantive and supported by more convincing proof than in civilian trials. Military offenses indicate the need for greater control than do civilian offenses. There are many AWOL and desertion offenses in the services which, in civilian life, would simply mean the loss of a job.

The services have been willing to experiment. For example, the Air Force developed the team treatment concept at the 3320th Retraining Group when it was at Amarillo Air Force Base. The Army has revised its approach at the Correctional Training Facility (CTF) at Ft. Riley, Kansas. Previously, men came to stockades with a bad attitude toward the Army that was reinforced by the manual work they had to perform in the stockades. The Army changed the stockade procedures, arming the prisoners with loaded weapons and continuing military training in the facility with support from social workers, chaplains, and lawyers from the Professional Services Division. The representatives from the Professional Services Division are referred to as "the problem-solvers."[44]

On July 5, 1968, the president signed a bill to amend Titles 10, 14, and 37 of the United States Code, the purpose being to provide confinement and treatment of offenders against the Uniform Code of Military Justice. Identified as Public Law 90-337, the act provides for uniformity among the services in the administration of military correctional facilities and the treatment of convicted persons. Before this, most impartial observers considered the Air Force to be the most advanced of the services in the correctional field, and the Navy the most retarded.

In October 1968, the Department of Defense published Instruction 1325.4 for the treatment of military prisoners and administration of military correctional facilities, thereby establishing uniform policies. The pri-

---

[43] *Manual for Courts-Martial, United States, 1951* (Washington, D.C.: U.S. Government Printing Office, 1966).

[44] SSG Paul D. Richard, Jr., "Crossroads to the Future?" *Army Digest,* 23, No. 11 (November 1968), 27–31.

Control Center, U.S. Air Force (3320th Retraining Group), Lowry Air Force Base, Colorado. Around-the-clock, seven-day-a-week monitorship and control of the prisoner and retrainee population is maintained by the Group Control Center. The status board on the wall shows the phase of training, custody status, privilege level, and other data on each prisoner. This center is the first place the prisoner sees on arrival and the last stop before departure.
Courtesy of the United States Air Force.

mary mission of the military correctional field has been seen as keeping secure the men placed in its charge and then attempting to bring about a change in the individual.[45] The Army's custodial and correctional program has been presented as a real opportunity for a young career officer with background in sociology, criminology, psychology, or the social sciences.[46] The thrust of the U.S. Army's correctional programs are (1) to return military offenders to duty as competent soldiers, (2) to provide efficient correctional management, (3) to improve the motivation of military offenders, and (4) to modernize the entire correctional field.[47]

At the correctional facility at Fort Riley, 92.7 offenders out of every 100 were confined for AWOL, while 7.3 were confined for other offenses during one recent year. At any given time, however, 95.7 are confined for

[45] See Col. John Morris Gray, "The Army Corrections Program," *Military Police Journal*, 18, No. 10 (May 1969), 9–12.

[46] See "Career Opportunities Unlimited," *Military Police Journal*, January 1968, p. 18.

[47] *Annual Report and Statistical Analysis, Fiscal Year 1969*, U.S. Army Correctional Training Facility, Fort Riley, Kansas, pp. 3–8.

AWOL and 4.3 are for other offenses.[48] This difference is caused by the fact that AWOL offenders serve less time than other offenders, thereby increasing their number over a year but reducing their number for any given day.

In 1969, there were sixty conscientious objectors in military custody at the United States disciplinary barracks at Fort Leavenworth. Specific charges, of course, involved AWOL, since these people had accepted induction into the military services hoping that they could endure their two-year requirement. The dilemma of the treatment staff at Ft. Leavenworth is how to "rehabilitate" a conscientious objector, since the AWOL in such cases is simply a symptom of the problem. Since the Peace Treaty in Vietnam was signed in 1973, there has been a change of attitude toward conscientious objectors and those who had opposed the Vietnam War. Public opinion had withdrawn support for the war, and political arguments began as to what extent amnesty should be afforded the persons formerly seen as offenders.

Army Regulation 190-47, dated 15 December 1975, and Change 1 provide the structure for the Army correctional system. The Disciplinary Barracks (USDB) is for serious offenders, and Army Retraining Brigades (USARB) are for persons serving six months or less. A Correctional Holding Detachment (CHD) has been established in conjunction with each confinement facility. Female offenders are confined only in facilities designed to house females, or contracts are made with local cities or counties. Release and return to duty is through the Army Clemency and Parole Board. Army disciplinary action meets all the constitutional requirements established by the United States Supreme Court, including due process, equal protection, and all other considerations.

The military offender, as mentioned previously, is predominantly noncriminal in the civilian sense. While around 5 percent of the offenders in custody of military corrections are conventional prisoners, about 95 percent are military offenders. The specific distribution of military offenses, civilian offenses, and their dispositions can be seen in the Navy's experience.[49] The Department of the Navy has 33 Navy and 13 Marine Corps correctional centers, or brigs. Unauthorized absences make up 81.8 percent of all the military offenses and 75.5 percent of all offenses. The average sentence in a Navy or Marine correctional program is three to six months. The number and types of military offenses during a six-month period are as follows:[50]

---

[48] *Ibid.,* p. 130.

[49] *Semi-Annual Statistical Report, 1 January–30 June, 1969,* Navy–Marine Corps Prisoners, Department of the Navy, Corrections Division (Washington, D.C.: U.S. Government Printing Office, 1969).

[50] *Ibid.,* p. 25.

| | |
|---|---|
| Unauthorized absence | 6,431 |
| Failure to obey lawful order or regulation | 424 |
| All other military offenses | 351 |
| Assault, disobey, show contempt to warrant officer or noncommissioned officer | 296 |
| Contempt, disrespect, strike commanding officer | 190 |
| Misbehavior of sentinel | 100 |
| Desertion | 74 |
| Escape, resist apprehension, break arrest | 37 |
| Misuse of government property | 35 |
| Missed ship or unit | 30 |
| False official statement | 25 |

The civil offenses for which sailors and marines were arrested during this period were as follows:[51]

| | |
|---|---|
| Larceny, robbery, wrongful appropriation | 275 |
| Narcotics possession | 184 |
| Assault | 139 |
| Riot, breach of peace, provoking speech or gestures | 24 |
| Forgery, bad checks | 13 |
| Drunkenness | 11 |
| Perjury, fraud against the United States | 6 |
| Murder | 4 |
| Burglary, housebreaking | 2 |
| Manslaughter | 1 |
| Maiming, arson, extortion | 1 |
| Sodomy | 1 |

The disposition of all Navy and Marine Corps prisoners released from correctional centers during the reporting period were:[52]

| | |
|---|---|
| Returned to duty | 7,964 |
| Bad conduct discharge | 295 |
| General discharge | 216 |
| Other (rehearing, hospitalized, etc.) | 149 |
| Undesirable discharge | 25 |
| Dishonorable discharge | 1 |

There is some literature on military prisons and their correctional procedures.[53]

[51] *Ibid.*, p. 26.

[52] *Ibid.*, p. 27.

[53] Stanley L. Brodsky and Thomas Eggleston, *The Military Prison: Theory, Research, and Practice* (Carbondale, Ill.: Southern Illinois University Press, 1970).

In 1981, there were 5,040 prisoners in military installations, including 38 females, all of whom were Army charges.[54] The Army had 3,075 prisoners, including the 38 females, with 1,450 men and 12 women at the U.S. Disciplinary Barracks at Ft. Leavenworth. The U.S. Army Retraining Brigade at Ft. Riley held 860 men and 12 women. The Navy held 1,147 men in brigs in 21 naval stations. The Marine Corps held 715 men in seven correctional facilities. The Air Force had 103 men in the 3320th Correction and Rehabilitation Squadron (formerly the 3320th Retraining Group) at Lowry Air Force Base, which is situated at Denver, Colorado. The purpose of corrections in the military services is restoration to active duty.

## THE FEMALE OFFENDER

The female offender is different from the male in many ways. Not only is her sex role defined differently from that of males in society, but the system of criminal justice screens out women more than men. While the ratio of arrests may be about 6.5 men for every woman, the rate of prison sentence is about 30 men to every woman. This means that women prisoners have been screened considerably more than men prisoners. In addition, cultural definitions, expectations of dependency and relationships, and physiological factors make correctional programs for women different from those for men.

Women are entering the criminal justice system in all areas. Comparisons of arrests in 1960 and 1979 reveal that arrests of females under 18 have shown an increase of 595.8 percent, while arrests of males under 18 have increased by 396.7 percent.[55] The *total* arrests for females between 1960 and 1979 increased 383.2 percent, while increasing 250.3 percent for males. In academic studies, 4 percent of all law degrees in the United States were awarded to women in 1967; women received 26 percent of the law degrees in 1978.[56] But even with these degrees, women still have difficulty in obtaining positions as judges and other administrators in criminal justice.[57] At the John Jay College of Criminal Justice of the City University of New York in 1973, 19 percent of the undergraduate student body were women; in 1980, 43 percent were women. In January 1981, a new class was sworn

[54] *Directory—Juvenile and Adult Correctional Departments, Institutions, Agencies & Paroling Authorities—1982* (College Park, Md.: American Correctional Association, 1982), pp. 314–19.

[55] *Uniform Crime Reports for the United States, 1979* (Washington, D.C.: Federal Bureau of Investigation, 1980), p. 195; similar data in 1960 reported from the *Uniform Crime Index for 1960* in *Woman Offender* (Lincoln, Neb.: CONtact, not dated but released in 1976), p. 2.

[56] Barbara Raffel Price and Natalie J. Sokoloff, *The Criminal Justice System and Women* (New York: Clark Boardman Co., 1982), p. 373.

[57] Clarice Feinman, *Women in the Criminal Justice System* (New York: Praeger, 1980), p. 102.

into the New York City Police Department; 184 of the 885 new recruits were women, which was most unusual.[58] The prison population, however, has remained about 5 percent women (4.3 percent in 1979) since the beginning of the penitentiary movement nearly two centuries ago, which reflects the reluctance of the courts to send women to prison.

Many of the women in prison today—about 70 to 80 percent—are responsible for children, and their incomes in the free community amount to about 57 to 60 percent those of men.[59] Yet the female offender has been called "the forgotten offender." A national survey of prisons by the *Yale Law Review* in 1973 found that there were about ten vocational programs in each men's institution and only 2.7 in women's institutions.

The prison school for women emphasizes secretarial work and beauty culture. Availability to a beauty shop seems to be much more important to women than access to a barbershop is to men. Domiciliary appointments, including pictures, embroidery, and other "feminine" articles are found more frequently in women's prisons. While weight-lifting tends to improve self-concept in men's prisons, it is beauty shop and charm school programs that improve self-concept in women's prisons.

Every institution for females has facilities to care for women and girls who are pregnant when they arrive. Some institutions want relatives to take care of the new babies, while others will permit the mothers to keep the children in the institutional nursery for as long as eighteen months.

Women prisoners appear to be more negative than male prisoners in their attitudes toward law and legal institutions.[60] The women express higher moral judgment than do the men. Women "need to be needed" more than men, have more intense homosexual relationships in prison, have more minor fights, and engage in gossip and agitating more than men do. While men have apparently learned to get along a little better, women are more emotional and "fly off the handle" more frequently, thereby causing more problems within the institution and on probation and parole.

Women's problems in prison are generally more serious than those of male prisoners, partially because of the greater selectivity given women so that only the most serious are incarcerated. While the male offender's family often remains intact, probably supported by public assistance, the woman's family is seriously disrupted when she is removed from the home. Consequently, more parole supervision or other assistance is needed when she is released.

Historically, society has viewed the female offender as a misguided,

[58] Price and Sokoloff, op. cit., p. 377.

[59] *Woman Offender*, p. 11.

[60] Barbara A. Kay, "Value Orientations as Reflected in Expressed Attitudes Are Associated with Active Social Sex Roles," *The Canadian Journal of Corrections*, July 1969, pp. 193–97.

sinful, pathetic person in need of protection and assistance to achieve sexual morality and sobriety so she can be a good mother and homemaker.[61] She was "more to be pitied than censured." In prison, women find adjustment more difficult than men do because they have less support from their spouses and sponsors than men do.[62] They fear that men will leave them and worry about their inability to cope with loneliness they might experience upon release. This is one reason homosexuality becomes a major adaptation employed by women in prison.[63]

A Women's Bureau study indicated that female prisoners are likely to be relatively young, poor, urban blacks in the larger states, and responsible for their children's support.[64] The majority of female offenders have children; many of them are the sole support of a family. The children are frequently indirect victims because of neglect or foster care during the incarceration of their mothers. Consequently, child protective offices of welfare departments, private child-care agencies, and other helping services become much more important as a result of incarceration of women than of men.

Ward and Kassebaum received the following distribution of answers in a study of what are the most difficult aspects of adjustment in prison for women:[65]

| | |
|---|---|
| Absence of home and family | 42 |
| Other inmates | 13 |
| More than one answer | 13 |
| Lack of privacy | 8 |
| Absence of social life and friends | 8 |
| Rules and regulations | 5 |
| Nothing, adjustment is easy | 4 |
| Other | 4 |
| Custodial officials | 3 |

Joy Eyman indicates that the sexual adjustment of women to imprisonment is strongly linked to the general goals to which most women are socialized in the larger society. She holds that the dynamics of psychosexual

[61] Rose Gialombardo, *Society of Women: A Study of a Women's Prison* (New York: John Wiley, 1969), p. 7.

[62] Kathryn Watterson Burkhart, *Women in Prison* (New York: Doubleday, 1973).

[63] David A. Ward and Gene G. Kassebaum, *Women's Prisons* (Chicago: Aldine, 1965), p. 102; Leonard H. Gross, "Lesbians in Prison," *Sexology,* 34, No. 7 (1968), 479.

[64] *Report of the Correctional Task Force* (Washington, D.C.: Women's Bureau, Office of Training Program Administration, Manpower Administration, U.S. Department of Labor, 1973), pp. 122–25.

[65] David A. Ward and Gene G. Kassebaum, "Homosexuality: A Mode of Adaptation in a Prison for Women," *Social Problems,* 12 (Fall 1964), 159–77.

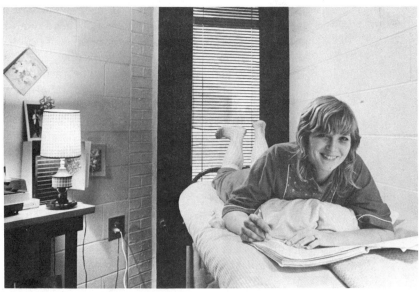

Studying at the Harbison Correctional Institution for Women, Irmo, South Carolina.
Courtesy of the South Carolina Department of Corrections, Columbia, South Carolina.

adaptation make the differences, and says, "Women are socialized in the language of love before they learn about sex, while men are socialized in the language of sex before they learn about love."[66]

Women offenders incarcerated in institutions are typically unaware of their legal rights. Consequently, they are often unable to make timely appeals or secure the relief to which they may be entitled. The Women's Prison Project at Bradford Hills Correctional Facility brings in female lawyers from New York University to teach women to handle their legal cases.[67]

Programming for women in prison has to be different from that for men. It is important that women in prisons be trained in occupations that will command salaries sufficient to maintain themselves and their families.[68] They should be trained in a field in which a felony record will not deter them from obtaining employment. Many states are in the process of removing these handicaps for beauticians and other occupations of interest to women. The District of Columbia Commission on the Status of Women

[66] Joy S. Eyman, *Prisons for Women: A Practical Guide to Administration Problems* (Springfield, Ill.: Charles C. Thomas, 1971), p. 135.

[67] Barbara Schwartz, "Legal Training for Women Inmates," *The Woman Offender Report*, No. 1 (March–April 1975), p. 5. Published by the National Resource Center on Women Offenders, Washington, D.C.

[68] Leon Leiberg and William Parker, "Mutual Agreement Programs with Vouchers: An Alternative for Institutionalized Female Offenders," *American Journal of Correction*, 37, No. 1 (January–February 1975), 11.

Learning automatic data processing at the Federal Reformatory for Women at Alderson, West Virginia.
Courtesy of the United States Bureau of Prisons.

has prepared materials to assist in programming for women.[69] Other groups are also interested in programming for the female offender. The National Association of Women in Criminal Justice was incorporated in January 1975 in Washington, D.C., to represent the interest and concern of women employed in the criminal justice system. The Female Offender Resources Center (FORC) was begun March 1, 1975, under the joint sponsorship of the American Bar Association's Corrections Commission and its Section on Criminal Justice. The National Congress for New Directions in Female Programming was sponsored by the Lewis University Special Services Center in Chicago, June 29 to July 2, 1975. With the increase in female crime, there has been an increase in interest in female programming in the correctional field.

There has been a recent effort at "co-corrections," or coeducational institutions that house and program for men and women together. Three institutions have considered themselves to be the first at this effort.[70] In the

[69] Virginia A. McArthur, *From Convict to Citizen: Programs for the Woman Offender* (Washington, D.C.: District of Columbia Commission on the Status of Women, June 1974).

[70] Charles Campbell, *Serving Time Together* (Forth Worth: Texas Christian University, 1980), p. 1.

juvenile field, Kentucky Village at Ormsby, which has since been closed, became coeducational in 1968. The Massachusetts Correctional Institution at Framingham has been considered by many to have been the first, having become coeducational in 1972. The Federal Correctional Institution at Fort Worth, Texas, has also been considered to be the first, having begun experimenting in 1971 with co-corrections. By 1981, there were about 16 adult institutions and many juvenile institutions functioning on a coeducational basis.

## THE VICTIM

The oldest concern for the victim, stated in several places in the Old Testament, is for compensation and restitution. Schafer has pointed out that the Middle Ages was the "Golden Age of the Victim"; at that time, criminal procedure, particularly under Germanic common law, emphasized compensation.[71] As the power of the king grew stronger and the State took responsibility for the protection of citizens, compensation to the victim ceased, but the same money or goods went to the State in the form of fines. In the modern day, compensation to victims of crime has existed in Switzerland since 1937, New Zealand since 1963, and the United Kingdom since 1964.

In the United States, California was the first state to legislate for compensation for victims in 1965, but only $100,000 was appropriated for the entire program. New York followed with legislation later in 1966 and began its program in early 1967, but only $500,000 was appropriated for the entire program. Other states that have compensation for victims are Alaska (1972), Georgia (1972), Hawaii (1967), Maryland (1968), Massachusetts (1967), Nevada (1969), New Jersey (1971), Rhode Island (1972), and Washington (1973).[72] New York's Victim Compensation Board is probably the most active, while many of the other programs are considered to be inadequate. The typical program in the United States to deal with compensation for loss lies in private insurance. The public efforts at compensation to victims of crime have not developed to a significant extent.

In any case, interest in the victim in the criminal justice system has increased in recent years. "Victimology" has emerged as a prominent concern in academic criminology and in the legal and political process within the criminal justice system. In fact, the first issue of a new journal, *Victimol-*

[71] Stephen Schafer, *The Victim and His Criminal* (New York: Random House, 1968), p. 3.

[72] Herbert Edelletz, Duncan Chappell, Gilbert Geis, and L. Paul Sulton, "Part I—Public Compensation of Victims of Crime: A Survey of the New York Experience," *Criminal Law Bulletin,* 9, No. 1 (January–February 1973), 5–48; and Lisa Brodyaga, Margaret Gates, Susan Singer, Marna Tucker, and Richardson White, *Rape and Its Victims: A Report for Citizens, Health Facilities, and Criminal Justice Agencies* (Washington, D.C.: Law Enforcement Assistance Administration, National Institute of Law Enforcement and Criminal Justice, November 1975), p. 223.

*ogy: An International Journal,* was published in Washington, D.C., in the spring of 1976. By 1980, 27 states had enacted crime victim compensation laws, and it has become apparent that many other states will follow their lead.[73]

## INTERNATIONAL CORRECTIONS

While a study of international corrections would require volumes, it is appropriate to take cognizance of the field around the world. During the early years of the United States, international relations usually involved force to correct injury done by one nation to another. For example, the United States sent an expedition of ships to eliminate piracy on the Barbary Coast in 1815, and Great Britain sent two later expeditions for the same purpose; piracy was finally eliminated only after the French conquest of Algiers in 1830. Treaties exist between nations today, generally concerning extradition of offenders[74] and agreements regarding border procedures or other means to reduce international traffic of narcotics or other contraband. The emergence of an international court, popularly referred to as the World Court, came when the League of Nations created the Permanent Court of International Justice at The Hague in The Netherlands, which opened on December 16, 1920, with 51 nations participating. The Hague Conferences of 1899 and 1907 had given precedence for this move by setting up a Permanent Court of Arbitration to serve nations which wanted to use it. Interrupted by World War II, the court was dissolved in the final session of the League of Nations, held in October 1945, as of April 1946. The United Nations established the International Court of Justice at The Hague in May 1946.

The patterns of law that permit society to take charge of the individual emerged as rather uniform by the twentieth century. While early tribes and ancient peoples had their own customs, primitive law, and codes, the growth of civilization tended to bring these rules of behavior together, a process similar to that which occurred in the development of the Justinian Code. The colonization of the world by European powers from the sixteenth to the twentieth centuries resulted in the two European stems of law being imposed and adopted throughout the world. Anglo-Saxon law influenced Northern Europe and the English-speaking world, while Roman law influenced the Mediterranean area, Eastern Europe, much of Asia, and Latin America. The major differences between the two systems are in the use of the jury or the tribunal, in the rules of evidence, and in the use of precedence or the merits of the immediate case. There have been some

[73] Randall A. Schmidt, "Crime Victim Compensation Legislation: A Comparative Study," *Victimology: An International Journal,* 5, Nos. 2–4 (1980), 401–20.

[74] United States Code, Supplement IV, 1965–1968, Washington, D.C., 1969, Chapter 209, Extradition, sec. 3181, Treaties of Extradition.

changes in patterns. For example, pre-Communist China tended to follow the English pattern, but Communist China has moved to the Soviet pattern. In any case, the procedures by which an offender becomes a correctional client follow some sort of due process.

Correctional systems vary more than do the legal systems. The earliest comprehensive study of international corrections was done by the Grolier Society in London in the early twentieth century in twelve volumes.[75] The second major contribution to international corrections was published by the Institute of Comparative Law of the University of Paris in 1950.[76] Rather complete reports were provided on the legal backgrounds and the correctional systems of Germany, Argentina, Belgium, Brazil, Chile, Spain, United States, France, Great Britain, Hungary, Italy. Mexico, the Netherlands, Portugal, Sweden, Switzerland, Czechoslovakia, the Union of Soviet Socialist Republics, and Uruguay. Extensive reviews of Soviet corrections can be found in several places.[77] Correctional systems in Latin America were explained well in the 1940s[78] and in various periodicals since that time. Correctional programs in Europe, particularly the northern regions, were well covered in the 1960s.[79] Current information from Communist China is probably most difficult to obtain, but a fair amount is available from several sources.[80] Since many correctional systems throughout the world are supervised by the police or the Ministry of Justice, the international police literature is helpful in understanding corrections on a worldwide basis.[81]

The English-speaking peoples generally have the same type of correctional programs. As a matter of fact, the annual directory of correctional institutions and programs published by the American Correctional Associ-

---

[75] *World's Famous Prisons,* 12 vols. (London: The Grolier Society, 1905–10, undated).

[76] Louis Hugueney, H. Donnedieu de Vabres, and Marc Ancel, eds., *Les Grands Systèmes Penitentiaries Actuels* (Paris: Recueil Sirey, 1950). Also see Dae H. Chang, *Criminology: A Cross-Cultural Perspective* (Durham, N.C.: Carolina Academic Press, 1976), Vols. I and II.

[77] For example, see "The USSR and the European Satellites," in Joseph Roucek, ed., *Sociology of Crime* (New York: Philosophical Library, 1961). The best available book on the USSR is Ilya Zeldes, *The Problems of Crime in the USSR* (Springfield, Ill.: Charles C. Thomas, 1981).

[78] Negley K. Teeters, *Penology from Panama to Cape Horn* (Philadelphia: University of Pennsylvania Press for Temple University, 1946).

[79] John P. Conrad, *Crime and Its Correction* (Berkeley: University of California Press, 1965).

[80] For example, Albert P. Blaustein, *Fundamental Legal Documents of Communist China* (Hackensack, N.J.: Fred B. Rothman and Co., 1962); the *White Book on Slave Labor in the Chinese People's Republic,* International Committee against Concentration Camps, Paris, April 30, 1956; Frank S.H. Yee, "Chinese Communist Police and Courts," *Journal of Criminal Law, Criminology and Police Science,* 48, No. 1 (May–June 1957), 83–92; and several other sources. A more complete bibliography is available in Tao-tai Hsia, *Guide to Selected Legal Sources on Mainland China* (Washington, D.C.: Library of Congress, 1967).

[81] For example, see James Cramer, *Police Systems of the World* (Springfield, Ill.: Charles C. Thomas, 1968).

ation includes the United States, Canada, and the United Kingdom. Programs in Western Europe and Israel are generally patterned similarly, with some heavier reliance on moral education. Latin American programs use the modified Pennsylvania system and generally permit conjugal visits. Africa is an emerging area, with governmental courts and corrections in the populated urban areas and native courts and tribal custom in the "bush." Poaching, for example, is a major crime problem in Tanzania. The Middle East and Northern Africa are reported by graduate students from that area as being harsh and limited in their corrections, but not much literature is available. The USSR, it satellites in Eastern Europe, and Communist China consider the security of the state over the welfare of the individual, so disagreement with the government is an offense. Law in these countries is an effective weapon in the class struggle.[82] Consequently, there are 800,-000 prisoners in China, for example, many of them in "Corrective Labor Camps."[83] Correctional programs in India and Australia are patterned after the British system. Programs in Japan and the Republic of China are patterned more after the American system, although they function under the Ministry of Justice along with police.

There are several international organizations contributing to the improvement of corrections on an international basis. The International Penal and Penitentiary Commission was begun at its first congress in 1872 as an intergovernment organization of official delegates with headquarters at Berne, Switzerland. Twelve congresses were held until 1950, when the commission's functions were taken over by the United Nations. The Section on Social Defense was created in the United Nations in 1948 under the Economic and Social Council (UNESCO), and it took over the functions of the commission in 1951. An International Penal and Penitentiary Foundation was then created to administer the trust fund left by the commission. The United Nations has done much toward assisting international corrections, including periodic publication of the *International Review of Criminal Policy,* which carries excellent articles regarding correctional problems from various countries. Other publications are issued singly. Standard minimum rules for the treatment of prisoners were adopted by the United Nations in 1956.[84] The International Society of Criminology, with headquarters in Paris, publishes a journal in English, French, and Spanish.[85] The Council of Europe, consisting of eighteen countries dedicated to the unity of Europe, contributes to the body of knowledge in corrections through confer-

[82] The Union Research Institute, *Communist China Problem Research Series, No. 37* (Kowloon, Hong Kong: The Union Research Institute, 1965), p. 153.

[83] Shu-Hua Kuo, *A Study of Chinese Communist Public Safety Organization and People's Police* (Taiwan, Republic of China: Yang Ming Shan Chan Press, 1957). (Published in Chinese.)

[84] *International Review of Criminal Policy, No. 26,* United Nations, New York, 1956.

[85] *International Annals of Criminology,* Centre National de la Recherche Scientifique de France, Paris.

ences and reports.[86] Finally, the State Department of the United States, through several agencies, particularly Aid to International Development (AID), has sent consultants abroad, brought officals from other countries to the United Nations for visits and training, and contracted with several universities for their assistance. Torture still exists in the world. The United States General Assembly passed Resolution 3218 on November 6, 1974, indicating that torture be forbidden and be made part of the *UN Standard Minimum Rules for the Treatment of Prisoners.*[87] The implementation of these minimum rules has not been uniform.[88]

Amnesty International is an organization in London that campaigns for the release of nonviolent political prisoners around the world. In its 150-page report, *Prisoners of Conscience in the USSR: Their Treatment and Conditions,* this group indicates that the Soviet Union so mistreats its 10,000 political prisoners that many are driven to suicide or self-mutilation.[89] There is a reported total of about 1 million prisoners in the USSR. Amnesty International also reports on existing slavery.

Although not much has been written on delinquency in the USSR, it is apparent from newspaper coverage and other indices that delinquency is similar in many aspects to that in industrialized societies.[90] It appears to be a problem of urban, lower-class male youth whose educational attainment and chances for upward mobility are low.

Correctional programs around the world are improving. Much of the improvement has been done through the United Nations. When governments want to improve programs themselves, they have guidelines and assistance from the United States and from international societies. The minimum standards for treatment of prisoners established by the United Nations have contributed significantly to the improvement of international corrections. Since the early 1950s, the United Nations Section on Social Defence has published the *International Review of Criminal Policy. The International Journal of Criminology and Penology* has been published since 1972. A new *International Journal of Comparative and Applied Criminal Justice* began publication in 1977, under the editorship of Dae H. Chang of Wichita State Uni-

---

[86] See *Fourth European Conference of Directors of Criminological Research Institutes,* November 22–25, 1966, I and II, Strasbourg, 1967; and *Fifth European Conference of Directors of Criminological Research Institutes,* November 21–23, 1967, I and II, Council of Europe, Strasbourg, 1968. Also see *International Exchange of Information on Current Criminological Research Projects in Member States,* Council of Europe, European Committee on Crime Problems, Strasbourg, 1969.

[87] "Fifth UN Crime Congress Banks Guidelines on Torture and Community Treatment," *Criminal Justice Newsletter,* 6, No. 22 (November 10, 1975), 6–7.

[88] See *World Implementation of the UN Standard Minimum Rules for the Treatment of Prisoners* (Washington, D.C.: American Bar Association, 1975).

[89] Associated Press release, November 26, 1975.

[90] Walter D. Connor, "Juvenile Delinquency in the U.S.S.R.: Some Quantitative and Qualitative Indicators," *American Sociological Review,* 35, No. 2 (April 1970), 283–97.

versity, to provide a forum for discussion of international problems in criminal justice.

## SUMMARY

The special problems in corrections involve persons with special needs and persons whose problems are social and anthropological in definition, rather than the personality problems to which psychotherapy and counseling are addressed. In the correctional process, it might be economical in the long run to separate some of these people and provide them with only the amount of security and the type of counseling that they will accept. The alcoholic, the narcotic addict, the criminally insane, and the criminal sexual psychopath have special problems which require special approaches to psychotherapy and counseling. The dyssocial offender, the white-collar offender, and the political offender, however, generally do not see themselves as needing treatment and are difficult to reach. In the latter case, reality therapy may help individuals to see the world as it is and to appraise the wider consequences of nonconformity beyond the immediate consequence of imprisonment.

In summary, these special cases in corrections present difficult problems in treatment not generally presented by the conventional criminal. Research and new methods of approaching these persons or, perhaps, of handling them in the system of criminal justice, are required, since very little is being accomplished with them in the present correctional systems.

## EXERCISES AND STUDY QUESTIONS

1. Why is the dyssocial offender difficult to treat in a correctional setting?
2. What special programs are available for the Indian offender?
3. What are political offenders, and how are they treated in correctional systems?
4. Evaluate the problem of alcoholism among offenders.
5. What are the major recommendations of the Research Council on Problems of Alcohol?
6. Evaluate the problem of the narcotic addict and the drug abuser.
7. Why should the dealer in narcotics be treated differently from the user?
8. Evaluate the Narcotic Addiction Rehabilitation Act of 1966.
9. What are the dangers of lysergic acid diethylamide (LSD)?

10. Evaluate the work of private organizations in the area of narcotic addiction and drug abuse, such as Synanon and Daytop Lodge.

11. Evaluate the problem of the criminal sexual psychopath and the laws relating to this offender.

12. Evaluate the treatment of the criminally insane and explain why there is so much difference between states concerning their treatment.

13. What is a defective delinquent, and how are some jurisdictions attempting to work with him?

14. What is the Uniform Code of Military Justice?

15. Evaluate the military correctional program.

16. Evaluate the differential roles in crime and the correction of the female offender.

17. Summarize briefly the status of corrections around the world.

18. How is the victim being treated in modern criminal justice, and what are his prospects?

19. How is the female offender handled differently from the male offender?

20. What would be the advantages and disadvantages of separating the special offender from the conventional offender?

# 12

# PAROLE AND OTHER RELEASE PROCEDURES

Parole is an executive function of government, as opposed to the judicial function of probation, and has been provided and controlled from each state's central office of corrections. Parole entails supervision, as opposed to other types of releases from prison. Releases by court order, death, escape, supervised mandatory release (conditional release, mandatory conditional release), expiration of sentence, and commutation of sentence do not involve parole.

Parole reporting and uniform parole practices have been difficult to achieve. Historically, about two-thirds of the releases from prison have been by parole, and approximately 80 percent of the parolees have successfully completed the period of parole supervision. There were 122,142 persons on parole in the United States in 1965,[1] of whom 102,000 were felons.[2] Of the 95,000 persons who leave state prisons each year, approximately two-thirds are released by parole or some type of conditional release.[3] Some states, such as New Hampshire and Washington,[4] have provided parole or conditional release for all persons leaving the prisons. More than 80 percent of the releases from prisons are by parole or conditional release in New

[1] *Task Force Report: Corrections*, The President's Commission on Law Enforcement and Administration of Justice (Washington, D.C.: U.S. Government Printing Office, 1967), p. 60.

[2] "Correction in the United States," *Crime and Delinquency*, 13, No. 1 (January 1967), 211.

[3] *Ibid.*, p. 213.

[4] *National Prisoner Statistics, 1966*, U.S. Bureau of Prisons (Washington, D.C.: U.S. Government Printing Office, 1968), pp. 28–29.

Hampshire, Washington, Kansas, Utah, Ohio, California, Wisconsin, Hawaii, New York, Michigan, Pennsylvania, Nevada, New Jersey, and Connecticut.[5] Less than 20 percent are so released from prisons in Delaware, Oregon, Tennessee, Texas, Maryland, Missouri, South Carolina, Nebraska, Oklahoma, and Wyoming.[6] All those not released by parole or some type of conditional release are simply discharged without any supervision. Consequently, about one-third of the correctional clients leaving prisons in America have no supervision upon their release.

After considerable discussion of a uniform parole reporting system at the 94th Congress of Correction in Kansas City, the system was implemented in 1970.[7] The reports, shown in Table 12-1, indicate that the success rate exceeds 80 percent. On June 30, 1974, there were 120,192 active parolees of whom 7,429, or 6.2 percent, were female, although two states were not in the count.[8]

The idea of parole began developing after the establishment of the penitentiary. Mirabeau (1749–91), a French statesman, suggested the function of parole in one of his last reports to the court in 1791. His suggestions were based on his observation of penal practices while he was imprisoned for espousing tax reform and other governmental changes. Captain Alexander Maconochie is generally credited with implementing the idea of parole for the first time when he provided a ticket of leave to each person in the Norfolk Island Prison Colony, beginning in 1843, so that they could earn their return to England. Sir Walter Crofton, in 1854, began using the idea as part of the grading system in Irish prisons. The Irish system had great impact on American corrections, as shown in the report of the first national conference in America devoted to the field of corrections.[9] Massachusetts was the first state to establish the parole service officially when, in 1846, an agent to assist released prisoners was appointed. Parole was an integral part of New York's Elmira Reformatory program, which opened in 1876. By 1910, 32 states and the federal government had parole systems.[10] Subsequently, all jurisdictions adopted parole.

Dr. S.G. Howe of Boston was the first person to use the term *parole* as a type of conditional release in a letter written in 1846 to the Prison Association of New York. The possibilities of parole were discussed in the Cincin-

[5] *Ibid.,* p. 9.

[6] *Ibid.*

[7] Don M. Gottfredson, Marcus G. Neithercutt, Peter S. Venezia, and Ernst A. Wenk, *A National Uniform Parole Reporting System* (Davis, Cal.: National Council on Crime and Delinquency Research Center, 1970).

[8] NCCD memorandum, *Number on Parole—1974,* p. 2.

[9] See E.C. Wines, ed., *Transactions of the National Congress on Penitentiary and Reformatory Discipline,* Cincinnati, October 12–18, 1870 (Albany, N.Y.: Weed, Parsons and Co., Printers, 1871).

[10] George G. Killinger, "Parole and Other Release Procedures," in Paul W. Tappan, ed., *Contemporary Corrections* (New York: McGraw-Hill, 1951), pp. 361–62.

**Table 12-1 Parole outcome in first year for males paroled in 1970–1972**

|  | Total Number Reported Paroled | | |
|---|---|---|---|
|  | **1970** | **1971** | **1972** |
| Continued on parole | 19235 | 20602 | 22359 |
|  | 75% | 79% | 81% |
| Absconded | 1517 | 1318 | 1297 |
|  | 6% | 5% | 5% |
| Returned to prison as technical violator | 3637 | 3063 | 2821 |
|  | 14% | 12% | 10% |
| Recommitted to prison with new major conviction(s) | 1201 | 1235 | 1073 |
|  | 5% | 5% | 4% |
| Total | 25590 | 26218 | 27553 |
| Percentage of total | 100% | 100% | 100% |

Source: "Probation, Parole," *Criminal Justice Newsletter*, 6, No. 12 (June 9, 1975), 5.

nati meeting of the ACA in 1870, tied into the use of the indeterminate sentence. Michigan was first to introduce the indeterminate sentence by legislative action in 1867. All states and jurisdictions now have some type of parole procedures. Some states parole nearly 100 percent of all first releases from prison. Other states parole as low as 8 percent of released prisoners. It is interesting to note that approximately 80 to 85 percent of all parolees successfully complete the parole period, regardless of the proportion of prisoners released on parole.

At that first national meeting of prison people, previously mentioned, Zebulon R. Brockway, who was superintendent of the Detroit House of Correction and responsible for Michigan's first indeterminate sentencing law, told the assembly that preemptory sentences should be replaced with indeterminate sentences so that prisoners could be released early after exhibiting some evidence that they had been reformed, rather than being released on mere lapse of time.[11] He suggested a "three-year law" that provided for some type of supervision for three years after release from prison. Brockway was subsequently selected by New York to be superintendent of the new Elmira Reformatory, where his concept of parole was first implemented in America in 1876.

Although many correctional administrators and parole boards have long referred to the "parole privilege," it has been held in court to be a right, rather than a privilege (*United States ex rel Bey* v. *Connecticut Board of Parole*, 443 F. 2nd 1079, 2d. Cir., 1971). The majority of corrections practitioners consider parole to be an integral part of the treatment process, as convalescence after hospitalization is a part of the treatment process.

Some legal problems have arisen concerning equality of sentencing

[11] John Lewis Gillin, *Criminology and Penology* (New York: D. Appleton-Century Co., 1915), p. 510.

and the clause in the Fourteenth Amendment guaranteeing equal protection of the laws. These general criteria of sentencing, however, go hand in hand with the equality of treatment, and it has long been established that aggravating and mitigating circumstances may be taken into consideration.[12] There have been other challenges to parole. As we shall discuss later in this chapter, for example, a move to abolish parole resulted in its disuse in five states between 1977 and 1980 and reduced its use in thirteen other states.

There were 223,774 persons on parole on December 31, 1981.[13] In regard to the proportions of persons under supervision in the community, the 1979 figures show that 84,287 (72.0 percent) were released on parole, 4,240 (3.6 percent) released on probation under shock probation laws, and 25,508 (21.8 percent) released on supervised mandatory release. Of the 26,754 (22.8 percent of all releases) released without supervision, 25,296 (94.6 percent) were released by expiration of sentence, 508 (1.9 percent) by commutation of sentence, and 950 (3.6 percent) by other methods.[14] These other methods included escape and death.

The primary parts of parole are (1) selection for parole, (2) preparole preparation, and (3) supervision of parolees. Selection for parole is the identification of the persons who should be released from prisons and correctional institutions, usually done by a parole board on the basis of good institutional records. Preparole preparation refers to a series of lectures, films, and other instruction to prepare persons who have been in the institutions for the decisions and self-discipline needed for resuming life in the free community. It is a kind of "debriefing" or "decompression" experience from the social viewpoint. Supervision of parolees is the long-term supervision-treatment in the home community by a parole agent or parole officer. All phases are needed for an adequate parole function.

## SELECTION FOR PAROLE

Many states before World War II had single parole commissioners appointed by the governor. These commissioners were frequently charged with corruption in selecting those who were released from prison on parole. At that time, many commutations of sentence and pardons were also questioned concerning political and/or financial motivation.

Since World War II, the vast majority of jurisdictions have improved

[12] Sol Rubin, *The Law of Criminal Correction*, 2nd ed. (St. Paul: West, 1973), p. 134. 15 Am. Jur. Criminal Law, par. 509, 1938.

[13] *Criminal Justice Newsletter*, 13, No. 17 (August 30, 1982), 6. Taken from *Parole in the United States: 1981 and 1982* (San Francisco: Research Center West, National Council on Crime and Delinquency, 1982).

[14] *Prisoners in State and Federal Institutions on December 31, 1979* (Washington, D.C.: U.S. Government Printing Office, 1981), p. 21. Also, *Sourcebook of Criminal Justice Statistics* (Washington, D.C.: Criminal Justice Research Center, 1982), p. 495.

their methods for selecting persons to be released from prison on parole. Two general approaches have been followed: (1) a parole board independent of the prison system, or (2) a parole board within a broader department of corrections that includes the prison system as well as the parole system. In both cases, a majority of states have full-time parole boards with three to eight members.

The procedures used by the boards also vary. In the past, one parole board member examined the institutional records and interviewed each inmate to be considered for parole. He recommended for or against parole, and the board ratified or modified his recommendations in executive session. Since the mid-1970s, however, the U.S. Board of Parole and many of the larger states have used hearing examiners, not members of the parole board; now the board acts on the recommendations of the hearing examiner in executive session. In almost all cases, the prison or correctional institution treatment staff will have already prepared a preparole progress report for the parole board. This report includes a summary of the inmate's basic problem, the institutional program through which he has progressed to alleviate it, a proposed plan for parole that includes employment and residence, and a recommendation by the institutional staff for or against parole, together with supporting reasons. Using this information and the interview with the inmate, the parole board member can later make a recommendation to the whole parole board sitting in executive session in central headquarters to review the recommendations of several of the parole board members. Generally, the parole board approves the recommendation of the individual member, but sometimes other information may arise to change it.

Some parole systems select prisoners for parole on the basis of records alone. In these systems, the inmate is not interviewed and may not even know that he is being considered. Under both systems, when the final decision is made in executive session, with or without the inmate's having been interviewed, the inmate is notified by letter or other appropriate means as to whether he has been favorably received or rejected for parole.

Many parole boards sit *en banc* while interviewing the inmate. In this case, a majority of the parole board visits each institution at scheduled times. The institutional records, together with the preparole progress reports, are reviewed, and each candidate for parole is interviewed by the parole board members. In many cases, an institutional representative also sits in to answer questions for the parole board as they arise. Frequently, the inmate is sent out of the room while discussion of his case takes place and then may be called back to hear the decision and a summary of the reasons for it.

Probably the most therapeutic approach to parole would be interviewing each inmate *en banc* and letting him participate in the discussion, rather than sending him out of the room. The reason that this procedure might be more desirable is simply that the inmate has an opportunity to hear his case discussed objectively, his strengths and weaknesses evaluated, and the prognosis for his success or failure assessed. With the knowledge o the way professional personnel view him, both institutional and parole, h has a better opportunity to modify his behavior and outlook. Further, ther is increased understanding, if not greater agreement, of the contribution o the parole board to the correctional process and, therefore, better inmat morale. This reduces the chances of the parole board's being verbally at tacked and accused of injustice and stupidity in the prison yard. The resul of this procedure, also, might well be in the pro and con debates in th prison yard where the parole board has an opportunity to be defended b other inmates who may see validity in what the inmate reported he hear in the parole board room. They are going to discuss the parole board, any way. They might as well have greater understanding of the process.

Parole prediction tables began in the 1920s with Warner (1923) an Burgess (1928). The parole prediction table by Burgess became the proto type for most parole prediction, using only existing records. Laune did prediction study based on analysis of the hunches of fellow inmates.[15]

In Laune's study, some of the statistical material involved in devel oping the "truth group" was done by "inmate X," who was reported to b Nathan Leopold. Ohlin has done probably the most significant parole pre diction study in recent years.[16] Wisconsin and Illinois are the only state who use the parole prediction tables to any extent. Wisconsin uses a Bas Expectancy type of table, while Illinois uses a synthesis of several tables

Most parole prediction studies indicate that the majority of parol violations occur shortly after release, 67.9 percent of them occurring withi six months and 89.4 percent during the first year. Statistical technique have been used successfully to identify more stable subjects among parolee as compared with parole violators.[17] The most successful groups release from prison were those with no arrests for five years or more in their arres records, while the least successful major release category were those wh were not able to avoid arrest for a period as long as five years in the fre community.[18] Parole violations drop as income rises.[19]

The fundamental criticism of most parole prediction tables is tha they are heavily based on factors present in the inmate's social situatio prior to the sentence. At the same time, of course, this basis could be thei chief strength. The social situation in which an inmate or anybody els

[15] Ferris Laune, *Predicting Criminality* (Evanston, Ill.: Northwestern University Press 1937).

[16] Lloyd E. Ohlin, *Selection for Parole* (New York: Russell Sage Foundation, 1951).

[17] Don M. Gottfredson and Kelly B. Ballard, "Association Analysis, Predictive Attrib ute Analysis, and Parole Behavior," paper presented at the Western Psychological Asso ciation, Portland, Oregon, April 1964 (mimeographed).

[18] Donald L. Garrity, "The Prison as a Rehabilitation Agency," in Donald R. Cressey ed., *The Prison: Studies in Institutional Organization and Change* (New York: Holt, Rinehart & Winston, 1961), pp. 358–92.

[19] *Training Needs in Correctional Institutions*, Manpower Research Bulletin #8, U.S. De partment of Labor, Manpower Administration, April 1966, p. 8.

lives will remain fairly stable. The correctional process must change the inmate's perception of it and his manner of dealing with stress situations or other situations that lead to crime. If the institution has done nothing to change the prisoner's self-concept, attitude, or outlook on life, then the social situation that produced him and in which he lives will remain the prime determinant of future behavior.

The parole prediction tables have a success rate of around 80 percent, which is also the success rate of parole systems not using parole prediction studies. (This is in the range of the accuracy of scientific weather prediction.) Eliminating human judgment and using only the prediction charts, on the one hand, and using judgment only, on the other, seem to yield essentially the same results. As a matter of fact, the release of about 1,200 prisoners without parole after the *Gideon* decision in 1963 resulted in about the same amount of recidivism as occurred among those released on parole in Florida.[20] Perhaps the prediction table might release some who would not be released on the basis of judgment alone following an interview. Conversely, individual judgment might release some persons considered to have changed in the institutional setting that the table would not have released. It seems likely that there are background factors in the prediction tables or in the experience of parole board members that serve as a general base from which judgment as to changed behavior and changed situations may result in a decision regarding parole.

Institutional recommendations to parole boards are reviewed in the parole selection process along with previous criminal record, work history, and social setting, as well as community attitude and future plans. The prison or correctional institution is inclined to give special weight to the inmate's prison record in its recommendations. Friction between prison wardens and parole boards is rather common because of these differences in viewpoint. Many prison wardens wonder why some people were paroled and not others, while many parole boards view some recommendations as favoring the "warden's pet," particularly if the parole candidate has been the warden's driver or has worked in his residence. At the same time, many parole board members place considerable weight on prison record, particularly the presence or absence of misconduct reports.

With a few notable exceptions, parole boards are not generally made up of persons with demonstrable knowledge of human behavior, such as advanced degrees in the behavioral sciences or helping professions. Consequently, some decisions to parole or not to parole have been based on factors held important by individual parole board members, such as attendance at chapel or Sunday school, hygienic habits like brushing teeth or taking baths, or similar factors not in the central theme of rehabilitation. Some parole boards refuse or are reluctant to parole a person who main-

[20] Charles J. Eichman, *Impact of the Gideon Decision upon Crime and Sentencing in Florida: A Study of Recidivism and Socio-Cultural Change* (Tallahassee: Florida Division of Corrections, 1965), taken from Eichman's master's thesis in Criminology, Florida State University, 1965.

tains that he was not guilty of the offense after having been convicted following a not-guilty plea.

On the other hand, there are several parole boards who base their decisions to parole or not to parole on criteria central to the rehabilitative or correctional approach. The inmate's attitude or favorable outlook toward society, combined with demonstrated change in work habits, self-improvement by education, and other manifestations of the capacity to adapt to society, govern their decisions. Some parole boards, feeling that a person should not be released, will release him on parole when the expiration of his sentence is approaching, since they feel it is preferable to release him under supervision than under no supervision at all.

The average time served by felony releases in each state in 1964 is shown in Table 12-2. It has not changed significantly since that time.

There is a public relations hazard in letting an offender out too early. There is no public relations hazard in keeping him in too long. These facts generally make for conservative parole board policy in politically unstable jurisdictions.

The parole board's dilemma with regard to releasing offenders who have committed violent crimes stems from extreme public concern with protection from violence. Homicide has clearly declined in the past few decades. Aggravated assault statistics have gone up, while tolerance to violence has decreased,[21] although the rise may reflect an increase of police intervention rather than an increase in violent behavior. The slight rise of recorded rape may similarly be accounted for in this manner. Homicide and assault are disproportionately high in the Southeast and low in New England. Rape and property offenses occur most frequently in the Far West. Murder occurs as frequently in rural areas as in urban areas. The most impoverished and poorly educated segments of the population show the highest rate of crimes of violence. Psychiatric advice may aid parole boards in deciding on cases involving strongly disadvantaged backgrounds.

Lifers have varying degrees of eligibility for parole.[22] In 80 percent of the states, official bodies responsible for parole are separate boards.[23] There are parole boards (20 states) or commissions on probation and parole (eleven states), boards or commissions on pardons and parole (nine states), and states where the board of pardons functions as the paroling authority (four states). In the remaining states, the paroling authority is the Adult Authority (California), Board of Correction (Idaho), Adult Corrections Commission (Minnesota), Board of Parole Commissioners (Nevada), Pro-

---

[21] Daniel Glaser, Donald Kenefick, and Vincent O'Leary, *The Violent Offender*, Office of Juvenile Delinquency and Youth Development, HEW (Washington, D.C.: U.S. Government Printing Office, 1969).

[22] Edwin Powers, *Parole Eligibility of Prisoners Serving a Life Sentence* (Boston: Massachusetts Correctional Association, 1969).

[23] *Ibid.*, p. 10.

**Table 12-2  Months served by average prisoner by state**

| State | Months Served in Prison | State | Months Served in Prison |
|---|---|---|---|
| Hawaii | 39 | Idaho | 19 |
| District of Columbia | 34 | Michigan | 18½ |
| Pennsylvania | 32½ | Alaska[a] | 18¼ |
| Minnesota | 31 | Massachusetts | 18 |
| California | 29½ | South Carolina | 18 |
| Illinois | 29 | Missouri | 17½ |
| New York | 27 | Rhode Island | 17 |
| West Virginia | 26 | Texas | 17 |
| Florida | 24 | Oregon | 17 |
| Ohio | 23½ | Arkansas | 16½ |
| Virginia | 23½ | Alabama | 16½ |
| Indiana | 23¼ | Oklahoma | 16 |
| Iowa | 23 | Delaware | 16 |
| Tennessee | 23 | Connecticut | 15½ |
| Kansas | 22½ | Wyoming | 15¼ |
| Louisiana | 22½ | Nebraska | 15¼ |
| Utah | 22½ | Maryland | 15 |
| Arizona | 22 | Wisconsin | 14 |
| New Mexico | 22 | North Dakota | 13 |
| Mississippi | 22 | South Dakota | 13 |
| Washington | 21½ | Colorado | 12 |
| United States average | 21 | Montana | 11 |
| Georgia | 20½ | Maine | 11 |
| North Carolina | 20¼ | Vermont | 11 |
| Kentucky | 19½ | New Hampshire | 11 |
| Nevada | 19 | | |

[a] Figure for Alaska from the state of Alaska, Department of Health and Welfare, August 9, 1971.
*Source: Statistical Abstracts of the United States,* 88th ed. (Washington, D.C.: U.S. Government Printing Office, 1967), p. 167, taken from *National Prisoner Statistics,* 1966, U.S. Bureau of Prisons, Washington, D.C., 1967.

bation, Parole, and Pardon Board (South Carolina), and Board of Prison Terms and Paroles (Washington). When the statutes require that a certain minimum time must be served, the "lifer" becomes eligible for parole. The minimum time ranges from a low of no time at all (after the 1971 legislative session) in Florida to a high of 25 years less credit for good behavior (Connecticut, Montana, New Jersey, and Tennessee).

Most correctionally oriented people in the field, as opposed to custodial and law enforcement–oriented people, hold that everybody should be paroled. It is not a question of "whether," but a question of "when." There is no dispute regarding the "convalescence" or "decompression" period in terms of the treatment process, but there are also other concerns. This writer experienced a case in which every treatment person in the prison, as well as others, predicted that the man involved would kill somebody. He was eligible for parole in eighteen months but was kept in prison for the maximum five years on his sentence. As his sentence expired, frantic calls were made to other state officials for a solution. He was not legally insane, so could not be committed to the state hospital. The attorney general ruled that the state could not follow him and keep him under surveillance "on suspicion," which would violate the Fourth Amendment. After his release, he killed three persons who served on the jury that had convicted him and was caught at the farmhouse of his intended fourth victim. Had he been paroled a year or any time before his release, he could have been under legitimate surveillance. Consequently, whether the orientation is treatment or custody and surveillance, parole is the most logical and sensible type of release.

Parole boards may not now be altogether in line with the new trends toward community involvement, continuity, and flexibility in getting offenders back into society, and with the need for legal and procedural norms. The "new parole board" may expand into a departmental division review board to hear complaints regarding classification, excessive or inappropriate punishments, denial of work release, and other actions which may affect the offenders' future prospects in important ways.[24]

Dissatisfaction with decisions and judgments by parole boards has resulted in a strong move toward having objective criteria incorporated in the law or otherwise firmly established. The U.S. Parole Commission went to objective criteria in the early 1970s called "Salient Factors," as shown in the table on the following page.

A perfect score of 11 would indicate parole, while 0 would not. Any range between would require consideration. There are some other factors considered, such as "dangerousness," but the court has already considered the seriousness of the offense. Any significant deviation from the objective criteria requires written reasons.

The legalistic directions taken by prison administration and the entire correctional system from the early 1960s into the 1980s has emphasized due process, definable standards, and defensible procedure and decision in the criminal justice system from constitutional and civil rights bases. By 1980, all parole boards except thirteen had written guidelines for the granting of parole.[25] In times of increased judicial accountability, thirteen is a surprisingly large number of jurisdictions *without* written guidelines.

The New York Parole Board has developed guidelines to determine its release procedures, prescribing a range of months, such as 18 to 24 months or 26 to 32 months, based on two major factors: (1) the seriousness of the current offense, and (2) the extensiveness of the prior criminal

---

[24] F. Lovell Bixby, "A New Role for Parole Boards," *Federal Probation*, June 1970, pp. 24–28.

[25] "Hitting the Boards," *Corrections Compendium*, V, No. 5 (November 1980), 1.

**Salient factor score**

Case name _____ Register No. _____

Item A ............................................................................................................ ☐
      No prior convictions (adult or juvenile) = 2
      One or two prior convictions = 1
      Three or more prior convictions = 0

Item B ............................................................................................................ ☐
      No prior incarcerations (adult or juvenile) = 2
      One or two prior incarcerations = 1
      Three or more prior incarcerations = 0

Item C ............................................................................................................ ☐
      Age at first commitment (adult or juvenile) 18 years or older = 1
      Otherwise = 0

Item D ............................................................................................................ ☐
      Commitment offense did not involve auto theft = 1
      Otherwise = 0

Item E ............................................................................................................ ☐
      Never had parole revoked or been committed for a new
        offense while on parole = 1
      Otherwise = 0

Item F ............................................................................................................ ☐
      No history of heroin or opiate dependence = 1
      Otherwise = 0

Item G ............................................................................................................ ☐
      Has completed 12th grade or received GED = 1
      Otherwise = 0

Item H ............................................................................................................ ☐
      Verified employment (or full-time school attendance) for a
        total of at least 6 months during the last 2 years in the
        community = 1
      Otherwise = 0

Item I ............................................................................................................ ☐
      Release plan to live with spouse and/or children = 1
      Otherwise = 0

Total score ...................................................................................................... ☐

record.[26] These guidelines were developed at a time when the abolition of the New York Parole Board was being discussed.[27]

    Reviewing the results of the guidelines, the factors to be viewed are (1) the increase or decrease in length of incarceration; (2) consistency in application of the guidelines; (3) consistency in terms of offense, offender, or both; and (4) other predictive factors that may affect the parole process and length of incarceration.[28] When reducing sentence disparity is a central correctional objective, parole commissions can play a major role in

[26] *New York Codes, Rules and Regulations*, Title 9, section 8001.3.

[27] Andrew von Hirsch and Jay S. Albanese, "Problems with Abolishing Parole Release: The New York Case," *Criminal Law Bulletin*, 15, No. 5 (September–October 1979), 423. Guidelines adopted in 1978.

[28] Michael R. Gottfredson, "Parole Board Decision Making—A Study of Disparity Reduction and the Impact of Institutional Behavior," *Journal of Criminal Law and Criminology*, 70 (Spring 1970).

"fairness" that focuses on "equal treatment" and "equally situated offenders."

## DECENTRALIZATION AND HEARING EXAMINERS

In recent years, the courts, prisoners' unions, and general opinion in the private sector have been concerned about parole policies. Some private groups and legislatures have seriously considered the abolition of parole. As a consequence, more frequent reviews have been imperative. To relieve the parole board of the heavy and almost impossible burden of reviewing large numbers of cases, a new position of hearing examiner has been created for the United States Board of Parole and many of the larger states. The United States Board of Parole has opened five regional offices to expedite parole action and ensure that decisions are considered in a manner that provides greater fairness to the inmates and to the public. Residents are told why paroles are denied, and they may appeal the decision to the full Board of Parole in Washington, D.C.[29] Regional offices have been opened in Philadelphia, Atlanta, Kansas City, Dallas, and Burlingame, California. Computer information in the central office also enters into the decision.[30]

In federal hearings, two hearing examiners interview inmates with an institutional caseworker. The interviews are taped and forwarded to the Board of Parole for their exclusive use. The board then bases the decision for or against parole on the recommendations of the hearing examiners and other factors. The general guidelines are (1) the severity of the offense, (2) the rehabilitative factor score or predictors of chances for success, referred to as "salient factors," and (3) institutional performance.[31] A notice of action is sent to each inmate considered, who can appeal to the regional director within thirty days of the notice.

## PRERELEASE PROGRAMS

Preparation for parole has taken several forms. Traditionally, the parole system maintains an office within the institution, and the institutional parole officer (IPO) reports to and is paid by the parole system. The purpose of the officer is to provide liaison between the paroling authority and the institution, particularly when certain problems arise concerning release of parolees. Sometimes the institutional parole officers and sometimes other

[29] *LEAA Newsletter*, 4, No. 3 (August–September 1974), 26.

[30] Don M. Gottfredson, Leslie T. Wilkins, Peter B. Hoffman, and Susan M. Singer, *The Utilization of Experience in Parole Decision-Making: Summary Report* (Washington, D.C.: LEAA National Institute of Law Enforcement and Criminal Justice, November 1974).

[31] *You and the Parole Board* (Washington, D.C.: United States Board of Parole, 1975), p. 4. Prepared for inmates of the United States Bureau of Prisons.

parole officers from the area hold preparole preparation schools. On occasion, outside employers, law enforcement officers, chamber of commerce representatives, and other persons from the community lecture and discuss problems of reentry into society. An approach often taken by employers or prospective employers is that they are less concerned with what the inmates have done in the past than with what they can do now. Reduction of institution-to-community disorientation, supportive peer associations, establishment of continuity between institutional and community vocational training programs and employers, and proposals to involve community leaders, influential employers, service agencies, and school officials are all important in improving the parole program.[32]

When a parolee takes a job, it is general practice that only the personnel officer of the company, the parolee, and the parole officer know that he is on parole. When he arrives at the shop or on the job, however, he frequently encounters other workers who have been in the prison whom he recognizes or who recognize him. The approach most employers take is that if anybody learns that he has served time or is an "ex-convict," it is generally not the fault of management, but the fault of the parolee himself or other parolees who work there. All are generally instructed not to conceal their parolee status from official records, but not to advertise it to the general public.

The parole officer generally points up the problems that previous parolees have had and, on the basis of experience, attempts to make prospective parolees aware of these problems.

Because they are suspicious of authority, many prisoners tend to consider all people dishonest. It is essential to orient inmates as to official action and reasons for it. After the parole board leaves, inmates talk in the cellblock and in the prison yard about what was done and why. They want to know why some people received parole and others were "flopped." Many parole officers holding preparole preparation schools find it difficult to explain all the nuances and minor factors that enter into parole decisions and simply indicate that the parole board thought that everybody in the group of parolees had intended to make good in the free world; further, it was their judgment that those chosen for parole had the ability to make good. Some of the inmates who were not paroled may also have intended to make good, but their capabilities of doing so were in doubt.

In the absence of solid and tangible evidence, the parole board must act on faith based on the evidence it has available. Consequently, as far as the parole board is concerned, the group of people who are favorably received by the parole board have simply "stood the test of faith." Intention to make good can be identified by attitudes favorable to society. Capacity to make good can be assessed by good work records, improved school achievement, reports from the counselors regarding progress in individual

[32] Elliot Studt, *Studies in Delinquency: The Reentry of the Offender into the Community*, Office of Juvenile Delinquency and Youth Development, HEW (Washington, D.C.: U.S. Government Printing Office, 1967).

counseling and group therapy, the presence of strong social ties outside, and other supporting factors. Reasons for paroling some people and not paroling others must be discussed in the preparole preparation sessions before realistic headway can be made in preparing people for release. Every effort should be made to eliminate the idea that selection for parole is based on chance—that some are "lucky," others "unlucky."

Nationally, there are more parole violations and revocations during the first month after release from prison than during any other single month of supervision. There are also more parole violations and revocations during the first six months after release from prison than during any other six-month period, and more parole violations and revocations during the first year of supervision than during the second year. Experience has indicated that, for purposes of practical supervision, there is generally not much need for close supervision after the parolee has successfully gone through two years after release from prison.

The parole board or the director of the field services, depending upon regulations or practice in each jurisdiction, must approve the residence and the job to which the parolee is going. Preference is generally given to the paroled person's own home, either parental family or married family. The reason for this is that parents or spouse and children are generally more interested in the person than anyone else is. When Saturday night comes, for example, and the parolee reports to his father that he is going down to the corner drugstore for a pack of cigarettes, the father knows full well that he had better accompany him, at least for the first few weekends. Knowing he is unwelcome in that situation, the father may still accompany him and prevent him from getting into situations that might lead into trouble. This is what is meant by social ties. One's own family provides more social ties than would a group of strangers.

Other residential arrangements may be necessary in the absence of a family or when the family situation is too undesirable to be helpful. The second choice would be the home of close relatives who would provide some of the same type of social ties. A parolee can rent his own apartment, but living alone is less desirable than living with members of his family, because there is less control over what would be going on in the apartment. Still less desirable would be the board-and-room or boardinghouse situation, since this places the parolee in a setting with other single men or "floaters" who have not accepted the social responsibilities as defined in American culture, such as maintaining a family and home. Temporary use of a hotel room has sometimes been approved. In the main, the homes of friends are not approved, since the parolee was probably not effective in choosing his friends before going to prison. Effective social ties in the home are one of the most important factors to be considered, together with economic adequacy and general stability.

The job must be approved, also. Most paroling authorities look for a job that places the parolee in the mainstream of living. An 8-to-5 o'clock job is generally better than a night job. There are some places, such as dance halls, bowling alleys, and taverns, where the paroling authorities are quite hesitant to permit parolees to work, because of the irregular times and some of the people with whom they may come in contact on these jobs. Jobs in music are generally not approved unless they are examined carefully. Exploitation by employers is always carefully watched by paroling authorities, and particularly by the supervising parole officer.

The two main trouble areas during the inmate's first few weeks out of prison involve alcohol and sex. When a person had been locked in prison for a matter of years, he has lost some of his tolerance for alcohol, or, as the alcoholics say, he has "dried out." Still, he remembers the taste of alcohol and is attracted to it by advertisements, memories, or other things. That is why many parolees who leave prison without family or officer supervision are picked up on the same day they are released. They may walk into a bar for a drink while waiting for the bus, and soon be arrested for public drunkenness. The "four Ds" are always a problem—"drink, drugs, debts, and dames."

Parolees are advised in prerelease school that the paroling authority knows it cannot control or supervise them 24 hours a day and at all times; this would, in itself, defeat the purpose of parole. It is well to remind the parolees that if they are going to drink, they should take a bottle of their favorite beverage home and test their tolerance in private. A general rule of thumb is not to attempt to drink in public for four weeks or a month after release from prison.

Getting acquainted with the "right" kind of people is a problem for many parolees. They have to be helped in the simple starting of conversation with neighbors they have not met before, fellow workers and supervisors, and other people considered to be desirable to know. While inmates often resist the idea of going to church, many will accept the concept of freedom of religion and the use of church to make social contacts. Using church for this purpose is a delicate issue and has to be handled carefully to avoid offending many outside clergy, but it is something the prison chaplains understand. Avoiding bars and poolrooms is generally stressed. This is done on the basis of social adjustment and avoiding areas and situations where the parolees may be vulnerable to a drink or two and subsequent criminal suggestion, and find themselves waking up in jail. While bars and poolrooms are legitimate business enterprises, many parolees have already demonstrated their inability to deal with these environments effectively.

In prison, there are many peculiar mannerisms, expressions, and words peculiar to the prison setting. These may vary from prison to prison. It is helpful to make a study of the prison jargon and customs so that they can be "unlearned" before release. Such expressions and mannerisms frequently identify "ex-cons" to other "ex-cons."

Parole rules are—or should be—reviewed and discussed thoroughly in the preparole preparation sessions. Most parole rules require behavior exhibited by most normal people, anyway, in their ordinary living. They include rules such as working steadily, supporting the family, meeting obligations, violating no laws, and keeping reasonable hours. Rules that are more restrictive than those imposed on free citizens are that parolees are not to leave the county of supervision without permission of the parole officer, not to leave the state without permission of the paroling authority, and not to marry or own and drive an automobile without consent of the parole officer. These parole rules refer to legal jurisdiction and some potential problem areas. Newly released parolees are impatient in their desire for an automobile or a spouse, and their impatience can lead to complications unless it is reasonably checked.

A common question asked by inmates concerns what they call "police harassment." The discussion generally involves the police role in society, the parolees' patterns of offenses already on record, and how well the police and the parole officers work together. If a burglary occurs at two o'clock in the morning and a parolee with a history of burglary is found within a block or two of the burglary, several miles from his home, it would appear to be reasonable for the police to ask questions. Emphasis should be on the fact that the parolee must not only *be* law-abiding, but also *look* law-abiding.

Generally, a preparole session or program might end with urging the parolees to know their parole officers and make sure that the parole officers know them. The emphasis is on a practical relationship. The parolee does not want to go back to prison because he does not want to lose his freedom. The parole officer does not want him to go back, either, because he does not

**Table 12-3  Subjects desired to be covered in prerelease preparation by 100 prisoners**

| | |
|---|---|
| Did not want to participate in a prerelease program at all | 47% |
| Would like to participate in the program | 53 |
| Parole agents to discuss problems of parole | 47 |
| Parole agents to discuss conditions of parole | 43 |
| Driving privileges on parole | 43 |
| Parolees to discuss parole problems | 36 |
| How to buy a used car | 36 |
| California Department of Employment representative | 32 |
| Labor union policies toward parolees | 30 |
| Applying for a job | 29 |
| Purchasing clothes | 27 |
| Income tax | 26 |
| Vocational rehabilitation | 25 |
| Social Security benefits | 23 |
| Family welfare aid | 22 |
| Certificate of rehabilitation | 20 |
| Budgeting your money | 20 |

*Source:* Norman Holt and Rudy Renteria, *Pre-Release Program Evaluation: How Effective Are Pre-Release Programs?* Research Report No. 30, California Department of Corrections, Sacramento, October 1968, p. 7.

like to have a high proportion of failures from his caseload. Consequently, regardless of how the officer and parolee might like each other personally, their common objective is to keep the parolee out of prison and discharge him from supervision successfully.

If the parolee makes sure that the parole officer knows him and has confidence in him through that knowledge, then the parole officer can protect the parolee or vouch for him when the police contact him in a case where the parolee might be a possible suspect in an offense. On the other hand, if the parole officer does not know the parolee, he has nothing on which to base protection. The result is that the parolee must consider the parole officer as a friend whether he thinks they like each other or not. A practical relationship based on knowledge of and confidence in the way each operates and functions becomes not only a protection for the parolee but a basic ingredient in the rehabilitation and correctional process.

In one study of California prerelease programs, 100 inmates were asked to select from a list of fifteen subjects usually covered in prerelease those topics that interested them most. The responses are shown in Table 12-3. These survey results may provide some idea as to the attitudes of prisoners being released and how they view the problem areas of return to the free community.

## SUPERVISION OF PAROLEES

Parolees are more difficult to supervise than are probationers, generally, if success in casework or treatment-supervision is the criterion. While probationers have been considered to be sufficiently hopeful that they do not have to be sent to prison, parolees have been sent to prison as poor risks for probation. In addition, they have been conditioned by an average of slightly less than two years of institutionalization in an adult prison or correctional institution. The parolee has learned to acquiesce to authority on a superficial basis while maintaining his basic behavior pattern essentially unchanged. Many parolees have learned to manipulate their way through social situations and official contacts with authority in the form of prison personnel, parole boards, and parole officers. They have already been selected as too difficult for probation, have subsequently been conditioned by the prison experience, and have learned the poker-faced, staid social veneer that makes diagnosis and evaluation difficult. They regard the parole officer as "another screw" (officer).

Successful parole supervision involves casework services with the parolee and his family, a good relationship with the police, and a thorough knowledge of all available employers in the area who will hire parolees. Consequently, parole supervision is an unusual mixture of roles for the parole officer.

For effective supervision, the parole officer should know the employers and the labor unions in the area. The labor unions can become most helpful in supervision. Some labor unions have suggested that since the Taft-Hartley Act went into effect, the closed shop is outlawed and unions are prohibited from having any say or setting standards for hiring. Consequently, they claim that juvenile delinquents and others have not been able to enter the working force because of extremely high standards set up by the employers.[33] The unions may also have shared responsibility for discrimination against ex-offenders at times.

The size of parole caseloads varies from around 20, in some experimental intensive supervision situations, to 200 and more in some backward areas where probationers and parolees are supervised together. One state has reported a probationer-parolee caseload of 314, with very few parolees. Each U.S. probation officer has a caseload of about 110, on the average, including probationers and parolees. The recommended caseload is 50 or less, but most progressive parole systems range around 80 under supervision by each parole officer.

Parole revocation is a formal procedure wherein the parole officer recommends to the parole board that a parolee be returned to prison. Certain violations of the parole rules are cited. Sometimes, the revocation is approved by the parole board in executive session. When requested by the parolee, a public hearing is held in which the parole board hears the parole officer, the parolee, and his counsel, and determines whether to revoke parole. The role of the attorney in parole revocations is becoming more and more important.

A good parole officer does not *enforce* the parole rules. Rather, he bases the progress of his case on the parolee's response to his treatment-supervision, whether casework, reality therapy, group counseling, or some other treatment technique is used. When it becomes obvious that the parolee is becoming unresponsive and in danger of getting into further trouble, the parole officer may recommend revocation of parole on the basis of violation of rules. He uses the rules as tools, rather than as limits. It is interesting to note that many decisions on the part of parole officers for recommending revocation of parole are dependent upon the visibility of the parolee's violation to the parole officer's supervisors. At times, the officer may have to place the parolee in jail for a week or so without recommending revocation if the use of authority is necessary to reestablish meaningful communication with the parolee.

Some parole systems maintain a policelike surveillance rather than treatment-supervision. This makes parole officers almost substitute law enforcement officers for a specialized caseload. In these systems, it is sometimes difficult to effect any real treatment.

Relationships with police are very important in parole supervision. Frequently, the parole officer may think that the police are harassing the

---

[33] *The Young Offender—Citizen or Outcast?* Community Services Activities Committee, Massachusetts State Labor Council, AFL-CIO, and Labor Relations and Research Center, University of Massachusetts, 1966.

people in his caseload. On the other hand, the police often think that the parole officer is hiding and protecting criminals. It is necessary for the parole officer to get acquainted with the police in his area so that they will develop a genuine understanding of the nature of each other's roles. A good relationship can be beneficial to the parole officer and to the police.

Parole supervision varies with the types of cases and with the environment. For example, a parole officer in a rural area can carry fewer cases than his counterpart in an urban area because of the geographical region he must cover. On the other hand, some urban cases require more supervision because of the unhealthy social pressures found in this environment.

Younger offenders have a greater violation rate on parole.[34] Lower violation rates have been consistently found for persons without prior criminal records, indicating that a behavioral pattern exists. The lower a person's age at first arrest, the higher his parole violation rate is likely to be at any subsequent age. Several clusters are observed as far as parole violation rates are concerned. Theft, burglary, and forgery have high violation rates. Average violation rates are found in narcotic offenses and robbery. The lowest violation rates are associated with crimes of violence, such as rape, assault, and homicide.

Some researchers have held that the high early violation rate is a function of supervision, in that parolees are supervised relatively heavily early, while supervision is relaxed as the parole period is extended.[35] The more closely people are supervised, the more likely violations will be detected. This position is challenged by many parole agents.

Revocation of parole is done by the parole board. The parole agent recommends revocation for technical violations of parole and for new offenses. The technical violations can be challenged, of course, more easily than can a new offense. New Supreme Court decisions have ensured due process requirements in parole revocations, just as they have in other sectors of the criminal justice system. *Morrissey* v. *Brewer* (408 U.S. 471, 1972) set out minimum due process procedures at two critical stages of revocation hearings, while *Gagnon* v. *Scarpelli* (411 U.S. 778, 1973) laid out rules concerning the necessity for counsel at parole revocation hearings. Due process according to *Morrissey* v. *Brewer* provides (1) written notices of the claimed violations, (2) disclosure to the parolee of the evidence against him, (3) opportunity to be heard in person and to present witnesses and documentary evidence, (4) the right to confront and cross-examine adverse witnesses, (5) a neutral and detached hearing body such as a traditional hearing

[34] Daniel Glaser and Vincent O'Leary, *Personal Characteristics and Parole Outcome*, Office of Juvenile Delinquency and Youth Development, HEW (Washington, D.C.: U.S. Government Printing Office, 1968).

[35] John E. Derecochea, Alfred N. Himelson, and Donald E. Miller, "The Risk of Failure During the Early Parole: A Mythological Note," *The Journal of Criminal Law, Criminology and Police Science*, 63, No. 1 (1972), 93–97.

board, and (6) a written statement by fact-finders as to the evidence relied upon and the reasons for revoking parole. The net effect has been to reduce the number of revocations, probably by eliminating the marginal cases.

Finding employment for parolees has been a particularly difficult problem, especially during times of high unemployment and minimum wage for young, unskilled parolees. Traditionally, many jobs have been denied ex-felons by state law, with many states having as high as 250 jobs not available, including barbers, beauticians, exterminators, some building trades, and other jobs. The move to remove arbitrary statutory restrictions on job opportunities for ex-offenders was first initiated in 1971 by "the pacesetting states of Florida and Illinois."[36] California followed suit in 1972. In 1973, Arkansas, Connecticut, Indiana, Oregon, and Washington passed laws alleviating restrictions, and bills were introduced in Colorado, Minnesota, Missouri, Nebraska, New Jersey, New York, and Wisconsin. A directory of agencies providing job assistance to ex-offenders was published by the American Bar Association.[37]

## MANDATORY CONDITIONAL RELEASE

Conditional release is a type of release of prisoners without parole but with certain conditions imposed. The releases may be under short-term supervision until they become settled in the community, either by parole personnel or by private correctional agencies. Several states have conditional mandatory release laws that provide for the release of all prisoners, or those prisoners designated by prison officials, six months or thereabouts before expiration of their sentences. This type of release affords a short period of supervision in the community. "Mandatory release" also occurs at expiration of sentence.

The states that used supervised conditional release most in 1979 were California (9,953), Michigan (3,234), New York (2,372), Florida (1,953), and Texas (1,117).[38] The states that permitted most prisoners to go out on expiration of sentence without supervision were Texas (2,693), Georgia (2,-215), North Dakota (1,438), Connecticut (1,399), Louisiana (1,394), Oklahoma (1,380), Florida (1,320), and South Carolina (1,081). In 1979, there were approximately 25,000 persons under supervision in mandatory conditional release.

---

[36] "Removing Offender Employment Restrictions: A Report on Legislative Developments," *Offender Employment Review* (Washington, D.C.: American Bar Association), No. 6 (September 1973), p. 1.

[37] *Directory—Organizations Providing Job Assistance to Ex-Offenders* (Washington, D.C.: Clearinghouse on Offender Employment Restrictions, 1976).

[38] *Prisoners in State and Federal Institutions on December 31, 1979,* National Prisoner Statistics Bulletin SD-NPS-PSF-7 (Washington, D.C.: U.S. Government Printing Office, 1981), p. 26.

## COMBINED PROBATION AND PAROLE SERVICES

More than half the states and the federal system have combined probation and parole services in the same officer. For example, a U.S. probation officer prepares presentence probation reports and supervises probationers and parolees. These systems have generally started in the more sparsely settled areas where probation services varied so widely that they were incorporated in the state parole system to provide some uniformity. In many cases, the combined system was a vehicle by which the state parole officers could be made available to perform presentence investigations and prepare the reports for the local judges.

Combined probation and parole services generally result in greater supervision of parolees, because this is where the greatest need is. The preparation of presentence reports became most important because it is a tangible service provided to local courts that can be counted, seen, used, and included in annual reports.

In 1979, there were 349,387 persons under probation supervision, 153,439 under conditional release, 34,199 supervised under the interstate compact, and 17,500 under other types of probation by parole agents in the United States.[39] These parole agents also prepared 148,489 presentence investigation reports, and 6,759 carried mixed caseloads, 770 carried parolees mixed with probationers, and 1,095 supervised only conditional releasees.[40] The average caseload in the United States was 62, with a high of 202 in Rhode Island and a low of 22 in Hawaii.[41]

## THE MOVE TO ABOLISH PAROLE

Based on interviews with parole officials and parolees and an extensive review of New York State parole statutes, the New York State Citizens Inquiry on Parole and Criminal Justice has recommended that parole be abolished in its present form and a more viable approach be adopted for reintegrating offenders back into society.[42] Parole as it is currently used was considered to be arbitrary, unfair, and self-defeating. It was called a tragic failure and a cruel hypocrisy that deceives the inmate looking for help and the public looking for protection. This group suggested that parole boards be dissolved and release decisions be made by a type of citizen review that would release offenders at the earliest possible date because long-term incarceration is counterproductive.

[39] "Cases Supervised and Supervision Staff, December 31, 1979," *Parole in the United States—1979* (San Francisco: Research Center West, National Council on Crime and Delinquency, December 1980), p. 36.

[40] *Ibid.,* p. 37.

[41] *Ibid.*

[42] "Citizens' Study Calls for End to Parole," *LEAA Newsletter,* 4, No. 2 (July 1974), 23.

**Control over the length of time a person serves in prison varies among jurisdictions as of January 1983**

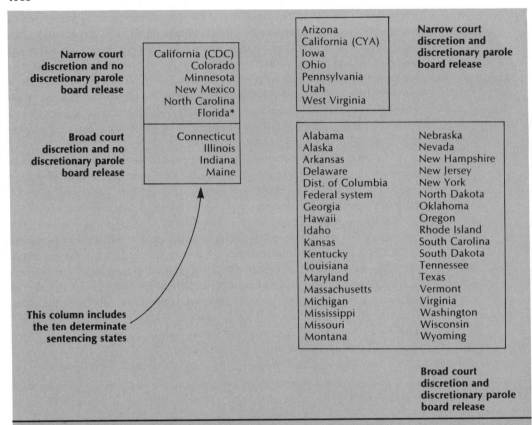

| | | | |
|---|---|---|---|
| **Narrow court discretion and no discretionary parole board release** | California (CDC)<br>Colorado<br>Minnesota<br>New Mexico<br>North Carolina<br>Florida* | Arizona<br>California (CYA)<br>Iowa<br>Ohio<br>Pennsylvania<br>Utah<br>West Virginia | **Narrow court discretion and discretionary parole board release** |
| **Broad court discretion and no discretionary parole board release** | Connecticut<br>Illinois<br>Indiana<br>Maine | | |

Alabama
Alaska
Arkansas
Delaware
Dist. of Columbia
Federal system
Georgia
Hawaii
Idaho
Kansas
Kentucky
Louisiana
Maryland
Massachusetts
Michigan
Mississippi
Missouri
Montana

Nebraska
Nevada
New Hampshire
New Jersey
New York
North Dakota
Oklahoma
Oregon
Rhode Island
South Carolina
South Dakota
Tennessee
Texas
Vermont
Virginia
Washington
Wisconsin
Wyoming

**This column includes the ten determinate sentencing states**

**Broad court discretion and discretionary parole board release**

\* Florida moved from "broad discretion" to "narrow discretion and no parole release as of October 1, 1983.
From *Setting Prison Terms* (Washington, D.C.: Bureau of Justice Statistics, Aug. 1983), p. 2.

Writing in the *Reader's Digest,* Herman Schwartz, a Buffalo lawyer and member of the Observer's Team at Attica during the famous riot of September 9–13, 1971, contends that the parole system is "bankrupt and capricious, providing neither security to the law-abiding nor fair treatment to offenders."[43] The premise that parole safeguards society by keeping criminals in prison until they are ready for release is viewed by Schwartz as nonsense. The premise that parole safeguards society through effective postrelease supervision is also nonsense, he says, considering that some caseloads reach 400 per parole officer. The third premise that parole safeguards society by fixing sensible parole rules and applying them impartially he regards as similarly unrealistic. Schwartz suggests that release

[43] "Let's Abolish Parole," *Reader's Digest,* August 1973, pp. 185–90.

should be decided by prison officials who know the offender, although within the limits of a minimum and maximum term established by the legislature and the court. Counseling should be separated from supervision in postrelease programs. Schwartz maintains that the criminal justice system can never be free of failures, but that parole has provided more than its share of them.

When Fogel published his book on the justice model in 1975,[44] there was considerable reaction politically to "let the punishment fit the crime," which was the old classical approach by Beccaria in 1764. Many legislatures considered eliminating the indeterminate sentence and parole, replacing that procedure with fixed sentencing and abolishing parole. Many legislatures concluded that it would be too costly, because the prison populations would rise. Some states did, however, abolish parole and go to fixed sentencing, while others did so on a selective basis, such as only for violent offenses. The first five states to eliminate parole were Maine (1976), California and Illinois (1977), Indiana (1978), and Minnesota (1980). By the end of 1983, ten states had abolished parole as seen in Table 12-4. California replaced the parole board with the Board of Prison Terms, which sets prison terms for adult prisoners. Illinois instituted the Prisoner Review Board, which sets release dates, although prisoners sentenced prior to the elimination of parole may reject the release date and maintain continued parole eligibility. All offenders sentenced in these states prior to elimination of parole continue in the parole process.

Studies of mandatory sentencing have shown that (1) laws designed to eliminate sentencing discretion displace that discretion in ways that might be counter to legislative intent, (2) attempts to anticipate and remedy these displacements are difficult, (3) to the extent that rigid controls are imposed, the effect may be to penalize some less serious offenders, while punishment for more serious offenders is postponed, reduced, or avoided, and (4) it is difficult to substantiate the popular claim that mandatory sentencing is an effective tool for reducing crime.[45]

Eighteen states enacted mandatory sentencing laws in 1979, and the five previously discussed adopted fixed-term statutes to limit the discretion of judges and parole boards.[46] Mandatory sentencing eliminates probation and parole, requiring fixed prison terms for some offenses, such as drug, violent, and repeat offenses. States adopting mandatory sentencing were Arizona (violent), Arkansas (violent), California (violent and drug), Florida (drug), Idaho (repeat), Illinois (violent), Iowa (repeat and violent), Kansas (violent), Louisiana (drug and violent), Maine (repeat), Montana

[44] David Fogel, "*. . . We Are the Living Proof . . .": The Justice Model for Corrections* (Cincinnati: W.H. Anderson, 1975).

[45] Kenneth Carlson, *Policy Briefs: Mandatory Sentencing: The Experience of Two States,* Washington, D.C.: National Institute of Justice, May, 1982, pp. 15–16.

[46] See listings in the *Directory—Juvenile and Adult Correctional Departments, Institutions, Agencies & Paroling Authorities 1982* (College Park, Md.: American Correctional Association, 1982).

(repeat and violent), Nevada (violent), New Mexico (repeat and violent), North Carolina (violent), Ohio (repeat and violent), Oregon (violent), Tennessee (drug, repeat, and violent), and West Virginia (repeat).[47]

## PARDONS

There are several types of executive clemency, including pardons, commutations, and amnesty. Pardons refer to a forgiveness on the part of the executive branch of government. A conditional pardon is dependent upon the performance of the recipient. A commutation is a reduction of sentence. For example, a frequent type of commutation is the substitution of a life sentence for the death sentence. Amnesty is a general pardon offered to groups of individuals, such as participants in an insurgency.

Although not a pardon, expungement of records accomplishes the same objective. The Ohio legislature in 1973 passed a law by which criminal records could be expunged. Applications for expungement can be made three years after release in the case of a felony and one year after release in the case of a misdemeanor. Expungement has the same effect as a pardon, in that civil rights are restored and the deleterious effect of conviction is eliminated.

The purpose of pardons varies widely. The first and original purpose was to undo miscarriages of justice. Pardons, sometimes called "technical pardons," have been used to avoid the deportation of persons under the Immigration Act as undesirable aliens. This pardon makes deportation unnecessary. Restoration of civil rights has also been accomplished by pardons.

## SUMMARY

Release from prison can be by parole, by discharge, by conditional or mandatory release, by pardon or general amnesty, by return on court order for a new trial, by death, or by escape. Parole has been a controversial topic since its inception in America in 1876, when the judgment of Zebulon R. Brockway, superintendent of the Elmira Reformatory in New York, was challenged for the persons he selected for parole. Parole policies have always been used as a reason for riots by prisoners, since the ones who were satisfied with the decisions of the parole board are out in the community and those who were turned down for parole are still in prison. Even so, most correctional people want a period of supervision in the community for the persons released from long-term confinement, to assist in their adjustment or to permit surveillance for the protection of society. Parole is still

---

[47] "Tougher Sentencing," *On The Line* (monthly by American Correctional Association), 3, No. 5 (1980), 1.

undoubtedly the best way to release people from prison.[48] Despite all the controversy, more people are released on parole today than ever before.

## EXERCISES AND STUDY QUESTIONS

1. What is parole?
2. How many persons are on parole in any given year?
3. How did parole develop?
4. What are the primary functions of parole?
5. What are the various methods by which parole boards consider inmates for parole?
6. What is meant by en banc interviewing of inmates by the parole board?
7. Briefly review parole prediction studies.
8. What is the average time spent in prison by inmates?
9. Discuss the variations of eligibility for parole for lifers.
10. Describe prerelease programs.
11. On what basis are paroles granted?
12. What might be considered to be a desirable parole plan with regard to residence, employment, and other matters?
13. What do you consider to be the reaction of prisoners to preparole programs?
14. What is involved in successful parole supervision?
15. What is the general size of parole caseloads?
16. What is the procedure for parole revocation, and why are paroles revoked?
17. Why should the parole officer maintain close communication with the police?
18. What is mandatory conditional release?
19. Discuss the reasons for and effectiveness of combined probation and parole services.
20. Why should all offenders who are released be released on parole, regardless of their offense?

[48] "Study Finds Parole Success Increasing," *Criminal Justice Newsletter*, 6, No. 12 (June 9, 1975), 5.

# 13

# TREATMENT APPROACHES IN CORRECTIONS

The treatment approach taken by any correction institution or agency may well reflect the personality and background of the administrator or, perhaps, the collective administration if selective hiring and policy decisions are employed. For example, an educator hired as a correctional administrator may favor education as the primary basis of correctional treatment, as is the case in many reformatories and correctional institutions. A social worker hired as a correctional administrator may emphasize the social work approach. Law enforcement persons have frequently been appointed as correctional administrators, and they often emphasize discipline, security, and orderly processes, and allow for only limited treatment. Consequently, there are many varieties of approaches to treatment in the correctional field.

When Schnur counted the number of prisoners in state and federal prisons and reformatories in the middle 1950s, he found 161,587 inmates and 17,280 prison personnel.[1] Of the 17,280 hired to keep the prisoners in prison, only 1,377, or 7.7 percent, were classified as people who were "there to get them ready to go out and stay out," and many of these were clerical. At that time, there were only 23 full-time psychiatrists in United States prisons and correctional institutions, a number that would provide an average of 82 seconds of psychiatric help each month per inmate, assuming an even distribution. There were 67 psychologists and psychometrists, a num-

---

[1] Alfred C. Schnur, "The New Penology: Fact or Fiction?" *The Journal of Criminal Law, Criminology and Police Science,* 49 (November–December 1958), 331–34.

ber that would provide about four minutes monthly for individual attention. These 96 institutional parole officers would have about six minutes for each man per month. The 155 chaplains in the same institutions would have less than ten minutes a month per inmate. The 257 caseworkers would have less than sixteen minutes per prisoner per month. The 739 academic, vocational, and trade teachers would have about 45 minutes per month for each inmate. These figures suggest that when "treatment" in prisons and correctional institutions is discussed, there is very little to discuss. When the routine procedures—such as social histories, admission summaries, and preparole progress reports—are prepared, there is virtually no time remaining for individual treatment or even group treatment. For example, it generally takes longer than sixteen minutes to gather the necessary information and to prepare a social history for a new prisoner arriving at the institution.

Since Schnur's study in the mid-1950s, more inmates and more staff have been added to correctional programs. By the mid-1960s, there were 210,895 prisoners (1965) and about 23,000 personnel, including 2,199 "treatment" persons.[2] Data from the *Directory* of the American Correctional Association for 1982 indicates that there were 412,303 inmates and 142,439 staff.[3] The ratio of inmates to staff remained at about 9.4 to one in the 1950s and 1960s, while the ratio had become about 2.9 to one by 1982, but the proportion of "treatment" personnel remained stable.

Nevertheless, there are attempts in some isolated places to carry out a treatment program. Probation, parole, and community-based programs apparently offer greater possibility and actual implementation of treatment programs than do institutions. In spite of the existing situation, however, it is important to discuss treatment and treatment potential in the correctional field.

## THE TRADITIONAL CORRECTIONAL PROGRAM

The traditional correctional program varies widely between institutions, on the one hand, and probation, parole, and community-based services on the other. While custody is foremost in the prison setting, treatment programs being limited, correctional programs outside the institutions are, of necessity, more casework-oriented, with some enforcement and surveillance functions. The traditional treatment programs in American prisons and correctional institutions involve custody, education, and the necessary counseling to process the prisoner through reception, job changes during his incarceration, and release procedures. Any "treatment" is generally a

[2] *Task Force Report: Corrections,* The President's Commission on Law Enforcement and Administration of Justice (Washington, D.C.: U.S. Government Printing Office, 1967), p. 97.

[3] *Directory: Juvenile and Adult Correctional Departments,* pp. xii–xiii and xviii–xix.

type of counseling offered by the correctional officer or job foreman, the chaplain, and the institutional classification personnel in case of special problems. Treatment becomes a process of helping a person adapt to the institutional environment with a minimum of irritation and anxiety.

In recent years, this type of habituation to regular living has been referred to as "operant conditioning." The term appears to be a new name for an old process. More formalized behavior modification, previously discussed in Chapter 8, is the use of punishment and reward in changing behavior.

## SOCIAL WORK

Social work has recently become interested again in corrections. Historically, social work and corrections were partners in the latter half of the nineteenth century and the early twentieth century. Associations of charities and reform at the national, state, and local levels were common. Wyoming still has a Board of Charities and Reform. With the development of the concept of self-determination, social work became "the art of helping people help themselves." Social work began pulling away from corrections before World War I. When the adoption of the doctrine of self-determination was formally included in a classic textbook in 1917,[4] the break was almost complete. Social workers then indicated that they could not work in an authoritarian setting. Corrections was forced to remain authoritative, however, because external controls were needed to manage the acting-out correctional clients. In the 1920s, social work focused on family service and, with impetus provided by the Commonwealth Fund, concentrated on child guidance clinics.

Since the Great Depression, dating from the stock market crash in October 1929 to probably the rise of the labor union movement in 1937 and the beginning of World War II in 1939, social work turned its attention to problems of income maintenance and economic relief. It is interesting to note that the change of focus in social work resulted in a shift in the composition of "the clinical team" as seen by psychiatrists. With the development of child guidance clinics in the early 1900s, psychiatrists selected social workers, rather than psychologists, as their primary assistants. After social work left corrections and the authoritarian setting and became interested in economic maintenance, the clinical psychologist became important to the psychiatrist, particularly during World War II in military and Veterans Administration hospitals and facilities.

At the National Conference of Social Work in Chicago in 1945, Dean Kenneth Pray of Pennsylvania began a controversy by stating that social work *could* be effective with correctional clients in an authoritarian setting. He pointed out that one additional step had to precede the orthodox social

---

[4] Mary Richmond, *Social Diagnosis* (New York: Russell Sage Foundation, 1917).

work approach in order for social work to be effective in corrections. Essentially, it was the process of talking people into wanting to help themselves. This offended many traditional social workers, who had based their entire concept on the doctrine of self-determination. The interchange was interesting and enlightening. Debates ensued in the social work profession and in the field of corrections through the 1950s as to whether or not social work could be effective in corrections. By 1959, the National Association of Social Workers developed a curriculum in which the profession indicated that it could work in corrections.[5] In the field of corrections, many correctional administrators, particularly in probation, decided that social work was the proper preparation for probation and, in some cases, for the entire correctional process.

The social work approach is through casework, group work, and community organization. The emphasis is more on adjustment with the environment than on depth psychotherapy. As stated by one correctional social worker, "My job is to zero in on what adolescence is all about, and to be a mediator with the adult world."[6]

Social workers and social work methods have become a part of the total field of corrections. The social work concept of the function and limitations of authority has been widely accepted, including the idea that the constructive use of authority is to withdraw services if the client does not remain eligible by circumstances or motivation. The use of social workers in corrections on a broad scale has been primarily limited to juvenile courts and adult probation. In some jurisdictions, such as New York State, the social work concept has been almost completely accepted in probation. For example, if a probationer does not respond to probation supervision, his probation is not revoked. Rather, he is discharged as unamenable to probation. If he gets into difficulty again, he will be sent directly to a prison or institution.

## PSYCHOLOGICAL APPROACHES

There are probably as many psychological approaches as there are psychologists, since psychological methods are not as structured as those of social work. The general consensus is that an aggressive psychologist cannot successfully work with an aggressive client. But whether this is true would appear to depend upon the personality pattern motivating the aggression on the part of the client. Many psychologists use the client-centered approach (formally called permissive and nondirective), which is similar to the social work approach. This approach is clearly indicated with the neurotic. In the

[5] Elliot Studt, *Corrections*, Vol. 5 of the *Curriculum Study Committee Report* (New York: Council on Social Work Education, 1959).

[6] Pete Hansen, in "What Is a Social Worker?" *Perspective*, State of Washington Department of Institutions, Olympia, 13, No. 1 (Summer 1969), 12.

case of psychosis, which characterizes a large number of the criminally insane, client-centered therapy is less desirable than directed intervention. A nondirective psychologist would make little headway with a severe catatonic patient, regardless of his crime. Treatment of the sociopath (psychopath, "antisocial personality") must be direct and authoritative.[7]

If the approach of the psychologist could be generalized, it would probably fall into four broad steps. In the first step, the psychologist and the client explore the problem and the total social and psychological situation together, developing common understanding. In the second step, the psychologist's acceptance of the client in a manner that is neither judgmental nor condoning of the criminal behavior tends to establish the relationship in which the client becomes dependent upon the psychologist—or "hooked" to him. In the third step, the psychologist confronts the client with the reality of his situation to generate awareness and insights that may be traumatic but necessary for working through the problem and restructuring defenses, or for reacting behavior to eliminate conflicts with social authority and lead the client to acceptance of both himself and society's expectations. The fourth and most important step is successful termination of the relationship, in which the client is no longer dependent upon the psychologist and can function on his own without help. It takes a long time to accomplish these four steps, but that is an essential part of the correctional process. Successful termination is the most important aspect of a counseling relationship. Almost anybody can establish rapport with a correctional client if he has average understanding and makes an effort to do so. Knowledge of personality dynamics can be learned. Successful termination requires exceptional skill.

Behavior modification is an approach based on the assumptions that criminal behavior is learned and can be altered, that desirable behavioral change can occur within the institution, and that offenders are not mentally ill.[8] A common criticism of behavior modification is that changes in behavior can hardly be attributed to experimental treatments because there have seldom been control groups of baseline data. There have been many attempts to discover effective reinforcers of approved behavior. Based on rewards and punishment or rewards and deprivation, this approach is essentially a learning type of therapy as compared with the more psychotherapeutic group therapy and individual counseling. The token economy being tried in some adult and juvenile institutions is a behavior modification approach. Another form of behavior modification has been the correctional contract, in which the administration and the inmate sign a contract that holds the administration to do certain things, such as outside placement, recommendation for parole, or other "favors," when the

[7] William H. Lyle, "A Psychotherapeutic Technique for the Sociopathic Offender," *Correctional Psychologist*, 3, No. 5 (May–June 1968), 6–8.

[8] Steven J. Zimberoff, "Behavior Modification with Delinquents," *Correctional Psychologist*, 3, No. 6 (September–October 1968), 11–25.

inmate completes his part of the bargain, such as completing trade training or other expectations. Behavior modification is closer to Sutherland's theory of differential association than it is to other theoretical frameworks.

Behavior modification has taken several forms, many of them involving brain surgery and other efforts that have gone beyond the original concept of behavior modification as reward and punishment for desirable and undesirable behavior. As previously discussed in Chapter 8, behavior modification has been extended in meaning to include surgery, which was not intended by B. F. Skinner when he introduced it. A report by the General Accounting Office in 1975 indicates that it had not been well handled by the United States Bureau of Prisons.[9] The original idea was to segregate prisoners displaying extreme behavior problems and apply the reward and punishment techniques. In practice, however, the techniques "turned into fiendish forms of punishment."[10] Electroshock and aversive therapy, use of drugs, psychosurgery, and similar methods have sufficiently alienated some prisoners that they have threatened to kill the officers rather than risk going to these behavior modification units.[11] As has been mentioned earlier in the book, in 1975 the LEAA refused to fund any further behavior modification projects after litigation had been brought by the Prison Project of the ACLU. The United States Bureau of Prisons halted these programs.

Testing of intelligence, aptitudes, and personality structure is traditionally a part of the psychologist's function. In prisons and correctional institutions, group tests are generally used, with individual tests reserved for special purposes. Some group personality tests, such as the MMPI, are given and can be scored by machine. More refined projective techniques are most helpful in critical cases. The Rorschach test can be used for guidance and in deciding for or against release on parole in questionable cases.[12]

Parenthetically, there has been discussion among correctional administrators as to the value of such tests as the Rorschach. Experience with this and other projective techniques has indicated that their value is dependent upon the competence of the examiner. Attempting to decide whether the test is worthwhile is like trying to decide whether a scalpel is good or bad—it depends on whether the scalpel is in the hands of a competent surgeon. A psychologist well trained in the use of projective techniques can be exceedingly helpful. On the other hand, a psychologist using these techniques without adequate training can bungle the diagnostic process. In summary, it is not the Rorschach test or other projective techniques that are good or bad, but the psychologists who employ them.

[9] "Behavior Modification Program Report Released by GAO," *Corrections Digest,* 6, No. 17 (August 20, 1975), 1–2.

[10] Wayne Sage, "Crime and Clockwork Lemon," *Human Behavior,* 3, No. 9 (September 1974), 16–25.

[11] *Ibid.,* p. 22.

[12] Robert Crosswaite, "Should Killers Be Paroled?" *Reader's Digest,* October 1963.

## PSYCHIATRIC AND PSYCHOANALYTIC APPROACHES

The psychiatric approaches to treatment in corrections are generally limited to consultation with the psychiatrist by psychologists, social workers, and other counselors and to diagnosis and prediction for treatment staff and the parole board. The small number of psychiatrists in the correctional field suggests that psychiatric approaches do not generally exist in prisons.

Psychoanalytic approaches have made even less progress. Dr. Robert Lindner (*Rebel Without a Cause, The Fifty-Minute Hour*) and Dr. Benjamin Karpman (*Case Studies in the Psychopathology of Crime*) stand almost alone in the use of psychoanalytic techniques in the treatment of criminal behavior. A good example of a full description of the psychoanalytic approach to delinquency may be found in *Searchlights on Delinquency: New Psychoanalytic Studies*.[13]

Psychiatric approaches to treatment of criminal behavior have been more popular than have psychoanalytic approaches, although some of the same conceptual framework is involved. On a private basis, the Association for the Psychiatric Treatment of Offenders (Dr. Melitta Schmideberg) and the Brooklyn Association for the Rehabilitation of Offenders (the late Dr. Ralph Banay) in New York City have contributed much to the understanding of criminal behavior and its modification.

There are very few psychiatrists in American prisons and correctional institutions. Most of the functions of those outside the institutions are used to determine whether a defendant is sufficiently legally responsible to stand trial.

Referrals for psychiatric hospital treatment for delinquents are frequently made by courts, law enforcement officers, and persons other than the family who do not know what psychiatry can and cannot do. A psychiatric hospital can evaluate and treat, but it cannot correct misbehavior and provide detention.[14] Referrals with real psychiatric difficulties can be successfully treated, but those without psychiatric problems are unaffected. The tendency to lump social problems and mental illness together confuses the issue as far as psychiatry is concerned.

The constructive function of psychiatric services would seem to be in training the staff, in working with the selection and weeding out of staff who are using inmates for their own emotional needs to the detriment of the program, and in fostering understanding of the overall correctional objective and how to achieve it. It is generally agreed that the treatment of the total person is necessary, not just the emotional areas.[15] Educational, vocational, psychotherapeutic, and other measures should be used. The

[13] K. R. Eissler, ed., *Searchlights on Delinquency: New Psychoanalytic Studies* (New York: International Universities Press, 1949, 1956).

[14] Robert B. Miller and Emmet Kenney, "Adolescent Delinquency and the Myth of Hospital Treatment," *Crime and Delinquency*, 12, No. 1 (January 1966), 38–48.

[15] Harold M. Boslow, "The Team Approach in a Psychiatrically Oriented Correctional Institution," *Prison Journal*, 44, No. 2 (Autumn 1964), 37–42.

team approach is essential. The correctional officer, therefore, will be the future vehicle for treatment, and he needs to be prepared for it.

## GROUP METHODS

Since World War II, group therapy and group counseling have been widely used in the correctional setting, both in institutions and in community correctional services. Probation, parole, and community-based halfway houses have used group methods effectively.

Group therapy has been used extensively in New Jersey and some other places on a professional basis. In its pure sense, group therapy is a treatment process by which a psychiatrist or clinical psychologist works with small groups, usually eight to twelve, for purposes of therapy. Structured group therapy and educational activities involving all inmates, professional staff, and correctional officers is needed to work with inmates.[16]

Group psychotherapy has several approaches and objectives. A review of some 300 articles in the literature on group therapy revealed nine general classifications that can be reduced to three primary factors.[17] First, the intellectual factor consists of universalization, intellectualization, and

Group at Daytop Village facility in the Catskills.
Courtesy of Daytop Village, Inc., New York City.

[16] Albert Elias, "Implementing an Interdisciplinary Treatment Program in a Correctional Institution," *Prison Journal,* 44, No. 2 (Autumn 1964), 28–36.

[17] Raymond J. Corsini and Bina Rosenbert, "Mechanisms of Group Psychotherapy: Processes and Dynamics," *The Journal of Abnormal and Social Psychology,* 6, No. 3 (November 1955), 406–11.

spectator therapy. Second, an emotional factor consists of reality testing, interaction, and ventilation. Thirdly, reinforcement by peer pressure renders it operational.

Group counseling, less demanding of professional personnel than group therapy, has been used extensively in California where it was developed. Correctional officers, administrative and service personnel, schoolteachers, and other personnel go through a period of training, sometimes four weeks, sometimes six weeks, in which some general principles of group counseling are examined. Then each employee becomes a leader with a group of inmates in the counseling sessions. Under supervision of the professional psychiatrist, psychologist, or social workers, the group counseling sessions proceed. The results among the inmates have been reported as optimistic.

A relatively new type of intensive group experience has been called the "sensitivity training group," the "T-group," or the "basic encounter group."[18] Sensitivity groups involving staff and inmates have been found to be valuable, especially in times of stress.[19]

"Sensitivity training" is used loosely to include a wide range of experiences in human relations that increase awareness—group dynamics, organizational development, and verbal and nonverbal experiences. Leaders in the development of sensitivity training include Leland Bradford, formerly director of the Adult Education Division of the National Education Association; Ronald Lippitt of the University of Michigan; and Kenneth Benne, now of the Boston University Human Relations Center. They based much of their work on the research of social psychologist Kurt Lewin. The T-group (training group) generally consists of a small group of people, from ten to sixteen in number, who meet in a residential setting for approximately two weeks. The objective of the T-group is to help individual participants become aware of why both they and others behave as they do in groups. The emotional component of the experience places it on the verge of therapy, although the T-group can also emphasize organizational change.

Encounter groups, confrontation sessions, and marathon labs are generally shorter, probably 24 hours or a weekend, and involve direct exposure of beliefs and feelings not usually on public display. These techniques offer great potential to the field of corrections for providing the bases for follow-up therapy and training. They could also be used to develop better understanding of the correctional process among all concerned groups, delinquents, correctional counselors, judges, correctional administrators, middle-class youth, and others.

Nonverbal exercises have also entered the training field, with tech-

[18] Carl Rogers, "Client-Centered Therapy," Chap. 13 in Silvano Arietti, ed., *American Handbook of Psychiatry*, 3 (New York: Basic Books, 1966), 183–200.

[19] Jerrold Lee Shapiro and Robert R. Ross, "Sensitivity Training for Staff in an Institution for Adolescent Offenders: A Preliminary Evaluation," *American Journal of Correction*, 32, No. 4 (July–August 1970), 14–19.

niques ranging from simple exercises with a minimum of body contact to physically intimate and emotionally involved designs. Probably dancing could be included among the techniques. The theoretical justification for these techniques comes from the possibility they present for achieving greater honesty and authenticity through bodily expression than can be achieved through verbal communication with its values and slogans. Each approach to sensitivity training can be directed to specific purposes.

Sensitivity training may be the opposite of role-playing. Whereas role-playing has a person assume the role of parent, inmate, probation officer, prison warden, or the like, sensitivity training has the participants divest themselves of their roles. Consequently, their interaction is as men and women, rather than as fathers, mothers, preachers, policemen, and so forth. The participants discuss their views toward issues and problems as people, rather than from the ascribed social role in which they have developed.

Sensitivity training hopes to produce improvement in the way people understand themselves. Participants in one sensitivity laboratory reported primary changes in the area of better listening, sensitivity to self, better understanding, and being more considerate.[20]

Group living in treatment centers and in halfway houses has become more prevalent (see Chapter 10). The first experimental project of significance was the Highfields experiment in New Jersey. Established soon after World War II, it was situated on the old Lindbergh estate and directed by Superintendent Albert Elias. Synanon in Los Angeles and Daytop Village in New York are examples of this approach applied to the treatment of narcotics addiction. Many halfway houses throughout the country, both juvenile and adult, are using this approach.

## REALITY THERAPY

Reality therapy is probably the most controversial approach to treatment in corrections. It receives generally favorable acceptance among the practitioners in the field but is viewed with suspicion among the professional community of psychiatrists and psychologists. It was developed by Dr. William Glasser, who became disenchanted with psychiatry and developed a system diametrically opposed to the approach in orthodox psychiatry.[21] Reality therapy takes the position that psychodiagnostic approaches and psychotherapy are used as excuses for deviant behavior. An example of this position is shown in the following statement:

> Plausible as it may seem, we must never delude ourselves into wrongly concluding that unhappiness led to the patient's behavior, the delinquent

[20] John E. Wilkinson, Donald P. Mullen, and Robert B. Morton, "Sensitivity Training for Individual Growth—Team Training for Organization Development?" *Training and Development Journal*, 22, No. 1 (1968), 47–53.

[21] William Glasser, *Reality Therapy* (New York: Harper & Row, 1965), pp. xxii, 166.

child broke the law because he was miserable, and that therefore our job is to make him happy.[22]

Reality therapy is based upon getting personally involved with the client, facing him with responsibility, and making him accept responsibility for his acts. Some of the key words in reality therapy are "responsibility," "involvement," "here and now," and "facing the consequences."

In discussing reality therapy, one author suggests that "in these days of wondrous alchemy it may be quite possible not only to make a silk purse out of a sow's ear but a revolutionary tool out of a pig's _____."[23] Reality therapy now has a restricted interpretation, discussing the client's current situation as one of his "own choosing" and making people feel loved and worthwhile. Under proper objective conditions, people *are* loved and worthwhile. Aggressive dealing with persons in a therapeutic frame of reference may result in people's loving themselves more, which has to be accomplished before they can love others. The "old make" of "reality" could provide social therapists with helpful models of therapy.

There are thirteen basic principles or steps in reality therapy that must be kept in mind:

1. Be warm, friendly, subjective
2. Reveal yourself (self-disclosure)
3. Be personal (I, me)
4. Concentrate on the present
5. Concentrate on behavior
6. Ask "What" not "Why"
7. Have client evaluate his own behavior
8. Work out plan
9. Negotiate contract
10. Accept *no* excuses
11. Work in groups as soon as possible
12. Praise, approve, reward, touch
13. Never give up—maintain relationship[24]

The strength of reality therapy is that it can be understood by correctional officer, staff, and inmates not trained in the behavioral and social sciences. Its weakness, on the other hand, may be in its oversimplification of

[22] *Ibid.,* p. 30.

[23] Norman Wicks, "Reality Therapy—Socialization: New Model, Old Make?" *Proceedings of the Ninth Annual Research Meeting,* State of Washington, Dept. of Institution Research Report, 2, No. 2 (April 1969), 135–38.

[24] Dr. Alexander Bassin, *13 Steps to Reality Therapy,* class handout in a course in group treatment (Tallahassee: Florida State University, School of Criminology, 1975).

human behavior and its failure to recognize some types of mental illness that may be worsened by too severe expectations.

Reality therapy has been successfully used in juvenile courts and in the probation setting. It has also been used in juvenile institutions, such as the Ventura School for Girls in California, the Minnesota State Training School at Red Wing, and elsewhere. It is obviously successful for a fairly large group of correctional clients who can take it. On the other hand, it may be too simplistic for some complex problems.

# ROLE-PLAYING, PSYCHODRAMA, AND SOCIOMETRICS

One of the group methods that has been occasionally used in corrections is role-playing. In the form of psychodrama, it emerges from the concept of sociometrics. The basic idea is that behavior is more of a reaction to other people than an action generated from within. Consequently, one must study groups, group interaction, and isolation to understand the behavior of individuals. J. L. Moreno, a New York psychiatrist originally from Vienna, posits the existence of bonds between people.[25] In a group, patterns of congeniality, rejection, and isolation can be diagrammed. When roles in society are introduced, relationships between the people involved accommodate. For example, some citizens may view a police officer as protective, while others may view him as hostile and suspicious, setting up congeniality or rejection feelings on the basis of how they view the role. Congeniality and rejection feelings can be modified as individuals become acquainted, thereby giving the citizen a new look at the police officer and, perhaps, the police officer a new version of that particular citizen.

In the correctional setting, there are all sorts of possibilities for role-playing and psychodrama to help the correctional client understand and appreciate the role of the correctional officer, the probation officer, the parole agent, the counselor, the administrator, the police officer, or other correctional clients. Role-playing has been used successfully to prepare prison inmates for parole status by playing roles in coming home to a stressful family situation, an alcoholic father, a potentially exploitative employer, or an unknown parole officer. The possibilities are limited only by the situations that can be replicated.

Sociometrics can be introduced for purposes of housing and other groupings. In a small institution, for example, inmates could be asked whom they would like to live with and whom they would like to avoid. Patterns can then be diagrammed so that congeniality groups can be identified, mutual rejections can be found, and the isolates in the social grouping can be identified. Inmate leadership can also be identified in this manner. In fact, use of sociometrics with staff can be helpful in grouping

[25] See J. L. Moreno, *Who Shall Survive?* (Boston: Beacon Press, 1934, 1953), Chap. 9.

and separating people for the effectiveness of the total effort. It is useful to identify staff members for promotion to supervisory positions who will elicit greatest support from the total staff, thereby avoiding a situation of one "faction's" winning over another. Many morale problems can be avoided in this manner.

## FAMILY THERAPY

Family therapy can include anything from marriage counseling to working with parent–child relationships. In the correctional context, however, it refers to working with the family in an attempt to promote the social adjustment and acceptance of an individual or group of individuals within the family who have been in trouble with the law. This type of therapy is complex but has greater potential than many other approaches. It takes into account the social ties in the primary group most permanently close to the individual offender, who is the ultimate object of treatment. Several case patterns serve as illustrations.

One pattern involves a family in which a mother uses other family members to maintain herself. In one such case, the father had never been in difficulty before his marriage. During the marriage, he began coming home later and later. The mother told her son about the father frequently. In the meantime, the son was growing. By the time he was 12 years old, his father was convicted of burglary and placed on probation. The mother reminded the son about that frequently, also. In about a year, the father burglarized another place and was sentenced to prison. The son, who had not been in trouble before, began showing behavior disorders within six months of the father's leaving home. Within a year, the son was in contact with the police and juvenile court. The court worker was able to see that the mother was a rigid, neurotic woman who drained those close to her to maintain her own equilibrium. She took pride in her honesty and good character and chastised others who fell below her standards. Family therapy was most appropriate in this case.

Another pattern can be seen in a study of the personality structure of the wives of men who have been convicted of rape.[26] Criminal behavior on the part of the husband has also been traced to marital situations (the wives of many sex offenders were found to come from mother-dominated parental homes, showing a pattern of cold and rigid manipulation of their husbands).[27] The literature is well supplied with information on family dynamics that can be applied therapeutically.[28]

Treatment in corrections is most helpful when the family is involved.

[26] Rose Palm and David Abrahamsen, "Some Rorschach Responses of the Wives of Sex Offenders," *Journal of Nervous and Mental Diseases* (January–June 1954), 119, 167–72.

[27] Bruno M. Cormier et al., "The Latecomer to Crime," *The Canadian Journal of Corrections*, 3, No. 1 (January–February 1966), 2–12.

[28] See Nathan W. Ackerman, *The Psychodynamics of Family Life* (New York: Basic Books, 1958).

If one has to determine whether to treat the individual *or* the family in cases of juvenile delinquency, it is obvious that more can be done through the family. With the counselor's guidance providing understanding and direction, the family's social ties with the juvenile and their constructive concern for him can be effective. The best arrangement, of course, is to have the worker work with the correctional client himself *and* the family.

The balance between family members is important. A case came into a clinic that was directed by this writer in which the mother thought the father needed marriage counseling because he was considered by their friends as a "perfect" husband, always considerate, never asserting himself as a male is expected to in our culture; she considered him inadequate and was bored with him. Asked whether she could get him into the clinic, she replied that all she had to do was tell him to come, which was part of the trouble. After he came in for several weeks, the woman came back and indicated that he was growing selfish and inconsiderate, and she wanted the treatment stopped. She said she had not realized what a fine situation she had had.

## SELF-HELP GROUPS

Self-help groups appear in all communities. Alcoholics Anonymous is probably the best known. There are also groups of ex-offenders who attempt to remain "anonymous" by operating in a low-key manner. There was a small group known as Convicts Anonymous for a while in Detroit. The advantage of self-help groups is the positive peer pressure gained by associating with other people with similar problems who help each other achieve "normalcy" in the particular area. The national headquarters for self-help groups needed most by offenders and ex-offenders are as follows:

> Alcoholics Anonymous World Services, Inc.
> Box 459
> Grand Central Station
> New York, New York 10163
>
> Narcotics Anonymous
> P.O. Box 622
> Sun Valley, California 91352
>
> Gamblers Anonymous National Service Office
> P.O. Box 17173
> Los Angeles, California 90017

The problem of alcohol and drugs relates to the chemical dependency of persons with problems and their need to "escape" from depression and anxiety. The problem of gambling comes from a group of underachievers who consider themselves to have been failures to the extent that some have tattooed "Born To Lose" on their chests and desperately hope to "strike it lucky with a throw of the dice" and win once, at least, by gambling. There are many other problems for which self-help groups have been organized. There are probably 500,000 local groups in which 15,000,000 participate annually. One of the outstanding benefits of these groups is that they are in prisons and in the community, and can serve as a "bridge" back to the mainstream of life for newly released ex-prisoners.

## MORAL REEDUCATION AND RELIGIOUS APPROACHES

Moral reeducation is the basis of treatment of delinquency in Europe, particularly in Belgium, France, Holland, Luxembourg, Portugal, and Spain. Its influence has spread throughout Europe, Latin America, and French Canada. It is a learning approach, stressing biblical and ethical precepts. In the United States, the moral reeducation approach is generally used by religious organizations that maintain juvenile institutions and community services, although some use the orthopsychiatric and clinical approaches.

Religious approaches are used by many organizations, also. The Home Mission Board of the Southern Baptist Convention has a broad program in delinquency rehabilitation. Youth for Christ is aimed at rehabilitation of juvenile delinquents. Many counselors in juvenile courts, police departments, and juvenile institutions come from religious backgrounds. Their approach to delinquency is quite broad and varied. Some institutions and agencies sponsored by sectarian groups do not "impose" religion on the delinquents in their case. Others go to the extreme in doing so, many using the counseling session to read biblical passages and to kneel and pray together.

Religious approaches are essentially similar, in that the minister or counselor is not considered to be effective himself but is a medium through whom spiritual power is transmitted to the client in trouble. Some quasi-religious and nonscientific approaches are based on "natural law" that emphasizes tolerance, responsibility of the individual, and nonviolence.[29] While psychiatrists, psychologists, and other behavioral and social scientists have different explanations, some inspirational-repressive and religious conversions *have* resulted in changed behavior.

Studies of religion and delinquency indicate that there is little relationship between the two. Some correctional administrators have indicated that they have never seen a delinquent who has gone to Sunday school—but delinquents would say the same thing! Whether or not one goes to Sunday school or is religious is an index of something deeper. Delinquency is also an index of something deeper. Making people go to Sunday school because they are delinquent misses the point.

Many religious approaches do good work because they recognize the value of clinical services, education, and forces other than the merely reli-

---

[29] Frank Coble, *Return to Responsibility: An Analysis of Social Problems and a Proposal for Action* (Pasadena, Cal.: Thomas Jefferson Research Center, 1969).

gious. Too many people try to treat the symptoms rather than the deeper cause. The difficulty is that one does not change the basic structure by imposing behavior that, in other cases, might be symptomatic of conformity.

A recent accelerated growth of church work with delinquency has involved personalities such as the Assemblies of God minister the Rev. David R. Wilkerson.[30] Even more recently, the religious movement has received impetus from the "way-out" youths themselves. The large numbers of street youth groups have been termed a "May–December wedding of conservative religion and rebellious counterculture."[31] The groups are referred to as "Jesus People," "Street Christians," or "Jesus Freaks," the movement having begun in San Francisco in 1967 and spread to most major urban centers. The Catholic Pentacosts also emerged in 1967 in essentially the same vein. The "straight" groups include Youth for Christ, which began with Billy Graham and is now in 2,700 high schools; Youth Life, which began in 1941 and now reaches 7,300 clubs; Campus Crusade for Christ; Inter-Varsity Christian Fellowship, and others. While all of these groups are concerned with working with delinquents, whether "way-out" or "straight," some have developed formal programs. It has become apparent that the role of church-related programs is growing in the field of corrections.

## MEDICAL APPROACHES

Tranquilizers have been considered by some correctional administrators as having been "made for prisons." Violent and unruly prisoners have been given sedatives in many prisons and correctional institutions, sometimes without much diagnosis. The administration of drugs as a substitute for treatment has been unfortunate but necessary in some areas, in the absence of adequate treatment personnel. Taken with treatment under psychiatric guidance, tranquilizers can be useful. Librium, Thorazine, and Prolin are used to help inmates adjust and accept the rehabilitation efforts.[32] Obviously, the use of tranquilizers would be to focus on personality disorders, rather than specifically on criminal behavior. Some brain surgery has occurred in prisons and correctional institutions. Prefrontal lobotomies and transorbital lobotomies have been performed. The results do not apparently relate to criminal behavior. Similarly, shock therapy using insulin, Metrozol, and electroshock may be useful in some emotional and mental disorders, but does not relate to criminal behavior.

Cosmetic surgery appears to be the most productive adjunct to other types of treatment in the prison and correctional institution (see Chapter 8). Removal of scars, straightening of eyes and noses, removal of tattoos,

[30] For example, see David R. Wilkerson with John and Elizabeth Sherrill, *The Cross and the Switchblade* (New York: B. Geis and Associates, 1963), p. 217.

[31] "The New Rebel Cry: Jesus Is Coming!" *Time*, June 21, 1971, p. 56.

[32] Wayne Sage, "Autism's Children," *Human Behavior*, September 1974, p. 19.

and correction of other types of characteristics that bring reactions from others appear to be helpful in the correctional procedure. A National Cooperative Data Bank to coordinate data collection and analysis from various correctional plastic surgery programs across the nation should be established. In December 1967, a Conference on Correctional Plastic Surgery at the Montefiore Hospital and Medical Center in New York City focused on this need. The rationale for the meeting was that physical disfigurement can contribute to antisocial behavior, and plastic surgery can be an effective rehabilitation source if supplemented by social and rehabilitative services.[33]

On the other hand, there has been no clear indication of a causal relationship to crime. A panel of experts convened by the National Institute of Mental Health's Center for Studies of Crime and Delinquency in Chevy Chase, Maryland, in 1969 indicated that the link between XYY male chromosome abnormality and criminal behavior was not clearly demonstrated at that time.[34]

By the 1980s, many correctional institutions, particularly the smaller ones, were contracting for medical services. In fact, they were contracting for several kinds of services, including food services, but medical services had become the most frequently contracted for among these institutions. Private companies specializing in correctional health care problems have become a permanent part of correctional institutional service.

## COUNSELING

Counseling can be considered a general approach used by almost everyone in the correctional setting. Correctional officers probably do more counseling than anybody, since they are closer to the inmates and stay with them longer than psychologists, probation officers, parole officers, wardens, or any other correctional personnel. Variations in the effectiveness of these counseling sessions are attributed to common sense, but closer evaluation brings out certain factors associated with successful counseling, regardless of the overall "commonsense" label.

Mutual understanding is basic in any counseling sessions. Too many middle-class persons with middle-class values completely fail to understand the values of other people with other backgrounds. Personality backgrounds may also enter into the situation. Matching cases with therapists for treatment purposes so that a better use of professional help can be obtained has been suggested in several places.[35]

[33] *Research and Demonstrations*, Research Utilization Branch, Social and Rehabilitation Services, HEW, II, No. 2 (1969), 1.

[34] "Link Between XYY Syndrome and Criminality Not Clear," *Public Health Reports*, HEW, 84, No. 10 (October 1969), 914.

[35] Marguerite Q. Warren, "The Case for Differential Treatment of Delinquents," *The Annals of the American Academy of Political and Social Science: The Future of Corrections*, 381 (January 1969), 47–59.

Differential treatment approaches by matching personalities of therapist and client or providing different programs for different types of problems have been offered by Herbert Quay[36] and by Marguerite Q. Warren and Ted Palmer.[37]

The behavior categories in Quay's Differential Treatment System are:

(inadequate-immature)
BC-1 is a daydreamer, inattentive, lazy, preoccupied, mildly neurotic, and generally shows a lack of interest.

(neurotic-conflicted)
BC-2 is anxious, withdrawn, hypersensitive, self-conscious, fearful, has feelings of inferiority, and lacks self-confidence.

(unsocialized-aggressive)
BC-3 is assaultive, cruel, defiant, and malicious.

(socialized or subcultural delinquency)
BC-4 has been involved in gang activities or group delinquent acts.

(subcultural-immature)
BC-5 is a mixture of BC-1 and BC-4 and is usually cooperative, quiet, and passive. His gang orientation arises from a need for direction.[38]

Each of these groups is to be treated differently according to its needs. Its primary use has been at the Robert F. Kennedy Youth Center at Morgantown, West Virginia.

Warren's approach and that used by Palmer are based on an Interpersonal Maturity scale, as follows:

|  |  | Percentage of Population |
|---|---|:---:|
| Level I₂ | Asocial, Aggressive | 1 |
|  | Asocial, Passive | 5 |
| Level I₃ | Conformist, Immature | 16 |
|  | Conformist, Cultural | 10 |
|  | Manipulator | 14 |
| Level I₄ | Neurotic, Acting-out | 20 |
|  | Neurotic, Anxious | 26 |
|  | Situational-Emotional Reaction | 3 |
|  | Cultural Identifier | 6 |

[36] Herbert C. Quay, "Personality Dimensions in Delinquent Males as Inferred from Factor Analysis of Behavior Ratings," *Journal of Research in Crime and Delinquency*, 1 (1964), 33–37.

[37] Warren, "The Case for Differential Treatment of Delinquents," pp. 47–59. Also, Ted Palmer, "The Youth Authority's Community Treatment Project," *Federal Probation*, 38, No. 1 (March 1974), 3–14.

[38] *Differential Treatment—A Way to Begin* (Washington, D.C.: United States Bureau of Prisons, 1970), pp. 3–12.

**High**

| Client-Centered Change | Change via Credibility |
|---|---|
| There is a natural trend toward personal growth once an individual is free to accept himself. The task of the change agent is to help the person accept his strengths and weaknesses without the judgmental pressures of others' values being introduced. Then he will be able to accept both society and its values. | Since behavior is learned, it may be modified through re-learning. The change agent's task is one of creating conditions under which people can learn the consequences of current behavior and explore the feasibility of new behaviors in realistic settings. Reality testing results in conformity based on commitment. |

**Charismatic Change**

People only accept suggestions from people they can respect. The change agent must be a "regular guy" if he is to gain enough prestige to influence. Changees will copy his behavior to win his respect and will then learn it is better.

| Custodial Change | Change via Compliance |
|---|---|
| No one person can really change another. People only conform or fail to conform if they want to. The task of the change agent necessarily is one of apprising the changee of the rules and then leaving it up to him to decide whether he wants to follow them and stay out of trouble or break them and suffer the consequences. At the same time, the change agent must keep those in authority informed as to how the changee is behaving. | It may not be possible to change a person's attitude, but one can change his behavior if he makes it clear what is expected of the changee and what can happen if the changee fails to conform. The change agent's task is to transmit this information clearly and then to follow up by keeping "tabs" on the changee to see that he conforms and knows that the change agent means business. |

*(vertical axis label)* Concern for Commitment

**Low**

**Low**      **Concern for Conformity**      **High**

**Figure 13-1 The Change Grid**

*Source:* Jay Hall, Martha Williams, and Louis Tomaino, "The Challenge of Correctional Change: The Interface of Conformity and Commitment." Reprinted by special permission of the *Journal of Criminal Law, Criminology and Police Science* (Northwestern University School of Law), Copyright © 1967, 57, Number 4, 497. After R. R. Blake and J. S. Mouton, *The Managerial Grid* (Houston: Gulf Publishing Co., 1964), p. 10.

It should be noted that the original format had seven levels, but the first level referred to persons too inadequate to be delinquent, and the levels above the fourth were too mature to be offenders. Its primary use has been at the Community Treatment Project of the California Youth Authority at Sacramento.

Neither system of differential treatment has been without problems. Most people do not fit into a system in a classic textbook style. Hans Toch has observed that classifying people "channelizes destinies and determines fate," because a person tends to live up to the labels placed upon him.[39]

As shown in Figure 13-1, "The Change Grid," there are various individual strategies of change that can be employed by the counselor. The low concerns for commitment and for conformity result in a strictly custodial view of the treatment process. The high concerns for commitment and for conformity result in deep concern and involvement with the client. The correctional worker may use any one or all of these approaches with different clients, depending upon his competence, flexibility, and sophistication. Change through compliance indicates that the caseworker is concerned with protection of society and cannot provide therapy for the delinquent, but places a premium on "getting along." The client-centered pattern, on the other hand, is less concerned with society than with the mental health of the client, so the caseworker does not "push" the client but helps him gain "insight." The custodial change pattern is a laissez-faire and "lock-em-up" approach in which the correctional worker's stance is "official" without getting involved. The change via credibility approach shows concern both for the client and for the protection of society, in which the correctional worker frequently enters into a compact or agreement/arrangement with the client and his family. In the charismatic change pattern, the correctional worker "goes halfway" with the client on the basis that people tend to resist being told what to do, so the agent of change has to be a person the client can respect and who "sets an example" for the client.

One useful interpretation of behavior is that people are continually faced with dilemmas. By the time they reach adolescence, they frequently have an established type of response. If the habit-based behavior is not effective and they use it anyway, the two ensuing responses are fight or flight. This is the situation delinquents face when they are confronted with their probation officer. The probation officer has to intervene in some way. If the delinquent is using a solution to a problem that does not work, the officer must expose him to other alternatives. The feedback is the officer's observation to determine whether his intervention worked and whether alternate courses of action were used. The resulting generalization becomes the product of the probation officer's intervention, whether positive or negative. This process is illustrated in Figure 13-2.

**Figure 13-2**

Source: Louis Tomaino, *Changing the Delinquent* (Austin: The Hogg Foundation, University of Texas, 1969), p. 57.

[39] Hans Toch, "The Care and Feeding of Typologies and Labels," *Federal Probation*, 34, No. 3 (September 1970), 15–19.

Counseling techniques suggested by one vocational rehabilitation project are as follows:

1. A significant number of public offenders can be rehabilitated, but more staff time is required than with physically disabled clients.
2. A team of individual personnel is apt to be more effective with public offenders than is individual counseling.
3. The typical public offender tends to behave in a generally inadequate manner. The inadequacies result from long-term socialization deficiencies.
4. A special philosophy and set of rehabilitation techniques are needed to rehabilitate the public offender.
5. A counselor must provide a protective setting for the client to have time and opportunity to function without disastrous punitive effects.
6. The rehabilitation counselor should verbalize and demonstrate that he has no punitive or police powers.
7. The counselor must be aware of the client's proficiency in manipulating authority figures and getting around agency regulations.
8. The counselor should use the dependency needs of certain clients to encourage continuation in the rehabilitation program.
9. The rehabilitation counselor should intercede with social and police authorities as an advocate of the client when a social crisis develops, but he should do so only when all parties are fully aware of the facts.
10. During a social crisis is probably the only time when insight counseling is effective, as the offender tends to show anxiety only at such a time.
11. Constant preventive counseling is necessary to prevent clients from committing transgressions which result in reincarceration or other severe social sanctions.
12. Personality characteristics and needs are more important as vocational determinants than intelligence, interests, or aptitudes.
13. The public offender tends to perform better in concrete, nonjudgmental jobs than in employment where abstract conceptualization is required.
14. Jobs which produce immediate satisfaction seem to be best suited for this type of client.
15. Long-term, high-level training goals do not usually lead to satisfactory job placement.
16. Job stability seems to be greatest in employment which enables the offender's hostility to be discharged in harmless fashion.
17. The counselor should realize that goals and plans developed while clients are institutionalized are usually modified or abandoned soon after release.

18. Young female offenders should be assigned to a female counselor or social worker. They tend to require a surrogate mother figure. Most male counselors will not have much success with them and should be aware of the seductive manipulation techniques used by female offenders.

19. Field counseling sessions create far better rapport with clients than across-the-desk contacts.

20. Home and family environmental factors tend to be closely related to the offender's chances of accepting services and their successful use.[40]

Inmates have been used in many institutions as facilitators in treatment, such as by putting an older multi-offender with good education and good communicative skills in an institution for younger inmates as a counselor. Outreach Minithons, a program in which inmates are selected to be used as case aides, have been inaugurated at the Correctional Institution for Women at Clinton, New Jersey.[41] These aides serve as inmate advocates and peer counselors, provide identification and referral of psychological problems, serve as liaison between staff and inmates, keep daily logs and monthly reports, and perform other duties as needed. They are paid a small salary. The program has been helpful, partially because it emphasizes preventive counseling rather than reactive approaches.

## SUMMARY

Treatment in the correctional field is almost nonexistent except in a few places where a valiant attempt has been made to organize it. In the maximum security prisons, it is almost completely missing. A few institutions for juveniles have made a creditable attempt at developing treatment programs. Most probation and parole and many juvenile court services must operate on a crisis basis because of the size of their caseloads. Consequently, any discussion of treatment in the correctional process must concentrate on the potential that is present. Group therapy has been most helpful in many places. Halfway houses and community centers have been helpful. In the main, however, there has not been enough treatment to counterbalance the ill effects of institutional living or the stigma of supervision by social authority in the community, much less to go forward and provide constructive treatment.

Punishment fails essentially because it increases frustrations, overwhelms the possibility for goal orientation, and forces more tension-reduc-

[40] S. Chandler and Bernard A. Sandick, *Rehabilitating Public Offenders*, South Carolina Vocational Rehabilitation Department, Social and Rehabilitation Service, HEW (Washington, D.C.: U.S. Government Printing Office, 1968), pp. 45–46.

[41] MaryLou Ramsey, "Outreach Minithons: An Antidote to Reactive Correctional Counseling," *Corrections Today*, 42, No. 4 (July–August 1980), 66–69.

ing actions[42] Treatment programs initiated by amateurs have sometimes worked. But an amateur trying to get his radio going may slap it until it starts, and where the difficulty is simply a loose connection, this approach can work. If it is continued over a long period of time, however, it results in a battered radio. Certainly, a radio repair shop could not be opened with that technique. Too many growing children have been treated this way.

Typologies based on treatment styles and types of offenders who can benefit from these styles have appeared to be hopeful.[43] It is generally agreed that therapy and counseling can assist in the adjustment of the offender to the institutional setting.[44] The management of the mentally abnormal offender is handled differently by different countries and by different disciplines.[45]

It is apparent, too, that no single type of treatment program is demonstrably superior to any other one. The detached worker or street worker who works in urban areas as an indigenous worker may use any of the types of treatment discussed, either by himself or by referral. His advantage is that he knows the area, knows the people, and lives with them, and this closeness may be more important in many cases than professional competence. In any case, the New York City Youth Board attests to his success. The counselor who nurtures "insight" in his client, regardless of the treatment approach, provides an intellectual backdrop that reduces guilt and anxiety. Some counselors not acquainted with the more sophisticated approaches have actually relied successfully on the four wishes of W.I. Thomas—security, response, new experience, and recognition.[46] Some have treated juvenile delinquency simply by keeping the mothers happy. Client-centered counselors have been as successful as aggressive and directive counselors, but with different people. The function of the counselor or caseworker appears to be to provide his client with (1) strength, (2) understanding, and (3) help. It is apparent that consistency in the relationship between the counselor and the client is important. Further, only a minority of correctional clients respond to one specific treatment approach. The correctional counselor must be sensitive enough to know the differences between the personality pattern and problems with which he is dealing and sufficiently flexible and competent to shift from one approach to another as the client's needs demand. Changing people's behavior results from a rela-

[42] Richard A. Ball, "Why Punishment Fails," *American Journal of Correction,* 31, No. 1 (January–February 1969), 19–21.

[43] Clyde E. Sullivan, "A Report of the Joint Seminars on the American Correctional Association and Large-Scale Research," *American Correctional Association Proceedings* (New York: ACA, 1963), pp. 145–53.

[44] Roy W. Parson, "Psychotherapy with Sociopathic Offenders, An Empirical Evaluation," *Journal of Clinical Psychology,* 21, No. 2 (1965), 205–7.

[45] A. V. S. DeRueck and Ruth Porter, eds., *The Mentally Abnormal Offenders* (Boston: Little, Brown and Company, 1968), p. 260.

[46] W. I. Thomas, *The Unadjusted Girl* (Boston: Little, Brown and Company, 1923, 1937), pp. 1–40.

tionship between two or more people and is apparently less dependent upon the system used than upon mutual awareness and responsiveness of those involved.

There are many different methods used in treating people. The orthodox psychotherapy practiced by psychiatrists and clinical psychologists, the casework and group work practiced by social workers, group therapy and group counseling performed by group therapists, and counseling done by many others, including the clergy, are the basic approaches to working with people. There have emerged in the past decade many other approaches proposed by professionals who have become "disenchanted" with the orthodox approaches. Some of these are Transactional Analysis,[47] Reality Therapy,[48] Emotional Maturity Instruction,[49] Primal Therapy,[50] and other approaches less well known. Harper has provided a long list of these "new psychotherapies" too numerous to list much less discuss, including multiple impact therapy, social network intervention, bio-energies, systematic desensitization, implosive therapy, and many others.[51] The Asklepieion approach to the treatment of character disorders was started by psychiatrist Martin Groder at the United States Penitentiary at Marion, Illinois, in 1968. A therapeutic community type of approach named after an ancient Greek god, it is used in Arizona, Arkansas, and Minnesota. There is some opinion among the professionals in working with people that the empathic ability of the therapist is much more important than the method he or she uses. This proliferation of approaches has resulted in some humorous satire appearing in the literature, such as *I'm OK—You're Not OK: An Impractical Guide to Transcendental Amnesia.*[52]

There are many approaches to treatment that work with some people, ranging from in-depth psychoanalysis to religious conversion, encounter groups to massage parlors, and Rogerian client-centered and nondirective therapy sessions to "Dutch Uncle" counseling. Even the Palmer School of Chiropractic reports success rates in mental health treatment that compare favorably with the psychiatrists. Not all these approaches work with everyone, but each seems to work with somebody. Each of these new therapies is aimed at a certain group representing a small segment of the correctional caseload, and none has the body of literature and

[47] Eric Berne, *Transactional Analysis in Psychotherapy* (New York: Grove Press, 1961).

[48] William Glasser, *Reality Therapy* (New York: Harper & Row, 1965).

[49] C. D. Warren, "A Promising New Approach to Rehabilitation," *American Correctional Association Congress on Correction—1969* (Washington, D.C.: American Correctional Association, 1970), pp. 121–25.

[50] Arthur Janov, *The Primal Scream—Primal Therapy: The Cure for Neurosis* (New York: G. P. Putnam's Sons, 1970), with six printings by Dell Publishing Co. by August 1975.

[51] Robert A. Harper, *The New Psychotherapies* (Englewood Cliffs, N.J.: Prentice-Hall, 1975).

[52] Dolph Sharp, *I'm OK—You're Not OK: An Impractical Guide to Transcendental Amnesia* (New York: Warner Paperbacks, 1974).

knowledge available in the orthodox approaches. While a treatment person would like to use them all as needed, he becomes limited in perspective and effectiveness when he identifies with one or two approaches and neglects the large body of knowledge in psychiatry, psychology, and social work.

After thirty-seven years of working with offenders, Harold F. Uehling, a psychologist, has indicated that experience in the correctional institution has proved to him to be the best teacher in the area of treatment, since this caseload is traditionally different from that in many public and private clinics where the helping professions educate and train their practitioners.[53] It is sometimes difficult to learn that an individual who is talking to the therapist about his problems in a correctional setting is neither ventilating, "getting it off his chest," nor engaging in emotional catharsis as he would in a clinic. Rather, he may well be "rehearsing." It is vital that the therapist be sensitive to know the difference.

A few trends can be observed in an overview of correctional treatment. First, it has become obvious that the correctional officer must be a full-fledged member of the treatment team. Educational and training programs are necessary to help him meet his new responsibility. Second, group therapy and group counseling are becoming more and more helpful in correctional institutions and agencies, both in handling large caseloads and in making constructive use of peer relationships among people who possess the common problem of conflicts with authority. Third, there is growing emphasis in corrections on contact with the community through various programs, rather than isolation from the larger society.

## EXERCISES AND STUDY QUESTIONS

1. *How does the administrator influence the treatment approach used in the correctional institution or agency?*

2. *What is the general proportion of "treatment" personnel to custodial, service, and administrative personnel in American prisons and correctional institutions?*

3. *Evaluate the traditional correctional program.*

4. *What has been the contribution of social work to corrections?*

5. *Evaluate the psychological approaches in the correctional program.*

6. *What is behavior modification? What is its current status?*

7. *How does psychological testing help in the correctional process?*

8. *Evaluate the psychiatric and psychoanalytic approaches in corrections.*

[53] *Correction of a Correctional Psychologist in Treatment of the Criminal Offender* (Springfield, Ill.: Charles C. Thomas, 1973).

9. What are the advantages and disadvantages of group methods?

10. How effective are encounter groups and similar approaches in corrections?

11. Evaluate reality therapy in corrections.

12. How can role-playing be helpful in the correctional process?

13. What is family therapy, and how does it enter the correctional field?

14. Evaluate moral reeducation and religious approaches to correctional treatment.

15. What contributions have been made by medicine and medical approaches to the field of corrections?

16. What is the role of counseling in corrections?

17. What are some basic counseling principles in the field of corrections?

18. Evaluate the relationship between custodial control and behavioral change in corrections.

19. Why have more treatment approaches appeared in community-based corrections than in institutions?

20. What are the current trends in correctional treatment approaches?

# 14

# JUVENILE
# CORRECTIONS

Juvenile corrections is probably the most misunderstood phase of the correctional field. Although the juvenile court is more than a half-century old, some persons still do not fully understand or accept the basic principles and objectives of juvenile court law.[1] The separate treatment of juveniles began long before the development of the juvenile court. Children were processed through the criminal courts and prosecution was frequently withheld so the child could be sent to a public or private training school without a conviction. Owing to litigation by resentful but uninformed parents, some of these children were returned to the court, tried and convicted, then sentenced to adult prisons. To prevent further cases of this nature and guarantee separate treatment of children, it was necessary to establish the juvenile court.

The concept of an age group between child and adult is not entirely new. Primitive man had a "rite of passage" when a boy passed through puberty and became a "man." Roman penal law recognized the *minor aetate,* older than the *proximus pubertati* but not yet a full adult.[2] The concept was revived in the nineteenth and early twentieth centuries after the Industrial Revolution and as correctional programs developed. In English common law, a child became an adult at age 7, when he could "make his own liv-

[1] William H. Sheridan and Pat O. Mancini, *On Becoming a Juvenile Court Judge,* U.S. Children's Bureau (Washington, D.C.: U.S. Government Printing Office, 1961).

[2] F. Farrarotti, "Les aspects sociologiques du problème," *Le statute légal et le traitement des jeunes adultes délinquants: Actes du VI*ᵉ *Congrès international de défense sociale Belgrade-Opatija, 22–28 mai 1961,* Belgrade, 1962, pp. 71–88.

ing" in the economy of England at the time. The expression "juvenile delinquency" is really inadequate, because it does not include the elements of crime as defined by criminologists in its original meanings. Juvenile delinquency was used as a concept long before the establishment of the juvenile court and before the concept became part of the criminal justice system. But although the term is inadequate, there is no other equally precise term to replace it, so it must continue to be used.[3]

The size of the juvenile caseload is increasing. In 1968, there were approximately 900,000 cases of delinquency[4] involving probably 774,000 children. In addition, there were 554,000 traffic cases[5] and 141,000 dependency and neglect cases referred to juvenile court.[6] It is estimated that the problems of dependency outnumber those of delinquency about two to one, but public welfare and private child-care agencies handle the majority of the children involved. A small proportion of other cases are also regularly handled by the juvenile court, such as adoption, custody of children, consent to marry, and other "special proceedings."[7] More than 500,000 runaways and other missing children are reported each year.[8] In 1972, there were 1,112,500 cases of delinquency, of which 827,500 were male and 285,000 were female.[9] It must be noted that the states of Alaska, Florida, Illinois, New Mexico, Wisconsin, and the District of Columbia did not report that year, which indicates that the delinquency rate was really much higher.[10] From reported data, there were 33.6 delinquents per 1,000 child population 10 through 17 years of age. There were 141,000 cases of dependency and neglect handled by courts in the states that reported in 1972, but many more are handled by the protective services unit of child welfare divisions and by private child-care agencies.

By 1978, there were 1,355,500 delinquency cases disposed of by courts with juvenile jurisdiction, of which 315,000 (24.4 percent) were female.[11] In

---

[3] "The Prevention of Juvenile Delinquency," *International Review of Criminal Policy* (New York: United Nations, Nos. 7–8 (January–July 1955), p. 12. Quoting from B. Parrin, *La minorité pénal en droit romain et dans les législations européennes antérieures au XIX$^e$ siècle*, Paris, 1947, pp. 28–34.

[4] *Juvenile Court Statistics—1968*, Office of Juvenile Delinquency and Youth Development, HEW, (Washington, D.C.: Government Printing Office, 1970), p. 3.

[5] *Ibid.*, p. 3.

[6] *Ibid.*

[7] *Ibid.*

[8] *The National Missing Youth Locator*, 1, No. 1 (Hayward, Cal.: N.M.Y.L. Publishing Co., January 1971), 3.

[9] *Juvenile Court Statistics—1972* (Washington, D.C.: Department of Health, Education and Welfare, Office of Youth Development, 1974), p. 11.

[10] *Ibid.*, pp. 11–12.

[11] Daniel D. Smith et al., *Delinquency 1978: United States Estimates of Cases Processed by Courts with Juvenile Jurisdiction* (Pittsburgh: National Center for Juvenile Justice, 1981), p. 55.

1979, there were 58,772 cases of child abuse, 111,162 cases of neglect, 42,-858 cases of abuse and neglect, and 21,135 other types of abuse cases reported.[12] The majority of delinquents (74.2 percent) are white.[13] There were 90,200 children reported for running away,[14] but the majority of runaways are never reported as missing by their parents.[15] About 80 percent of the runways are from white, middle-class families.[16] Over a million children are estimated to run away each year, and about 150,000 disappear completely, many through death.[17]

## THE JUVENILE COURT

A brief review of the development of the juvenile court might be appropriate. Throughout the nineteenth century, private juvenile institutions developed beginning in 1824, and public juvenile training schools began with the opening of the Lyman School in Massachusetts in 1847. Yet there were no juvenile courts. This led to litigation on the part of aggrieved parents when children were informally sent to a juvenile institution without having been convicted—the courts used this method to avoid conviction and sentence to prison. A juvenile court had to be found that was constitutional. It could be in the school system, with compulsory education laws providing jurisdiction; it could be in the child welfare sections of welfare departments; or it could be in the judiciary. Technically, the first juvenile court became effective in the school system in Denver on April 1, 1899, with Judge Ben Lindsey presiding, but Illinois has been given credit for the first juvenile court because it was in the judiciary, the pattern that other states subsequently followed. After the Illinois legislature passed laws in 1895 and 1897 establishing a juvenile court, only to have these laws declared unconstitutional, the Cook County Women's Clubs mobilized and were the driving force that motivated the Chicago Bar Association to write a law that was constitutional. It was passed in 1899, and the juvenile court became effective on July 1, 1899, as a voluntary court, in that the juvenile had to waive his constitutional rights as a criminal offender in order to be heard in this court as a juvenile. The juvenile court remains a choice court, either by signing of a waiver as under the Federal Juvenile Delinquency Act, review by a higher court, or a writ of certiorari.

[12] *Annual Statistical Report: National Analysis of Official Child Neglect and Abuse Reporting, 1979* (Denver: American Humane Association, 1980), p. 28.

[13] Smith et al., op. cit., p. 55.

[14] *Ibid.*, p. 58.

[15] Dotson Rader, "Who Will Help the Children?" *Parade*, September 5, 1982, p. 7.

[16] *Ibid.*, p. 5.

[17] *Ibid.*

In 1905, the famous case of *Commonwealth of Pennsylvania* v. *Fisher* (213 Pa. 48, 62 Atl. 198, 1905) established the principle of *parens patriae* in the juvenile court, meaning that the state has responsibility for the welfare of its children and should handle them as a wise parent would, without replacing the parent. Subsequent cases delineated the constitutional base of the juvenile court as a civil proceeding under the doctrine of *parens patriae*. Juvenile court proceedings, then, became "in the interests of the child," rather than the *State* v. *John Doe*. Precedence for the doctrine of *parens patriae* for juveniles was set in the Napoleonic Decree of 1811, indicating that the state was responsible for the welfare of its children, and the decision of the House of Lords in the Lord Wellesley case in 1828, when his nephew was taken from his custody and returned to his family. Consequently, the juvenile court was the culmination of a much broader social movement.

The misunderstanding of the juvenile court is not confined to law enforcement officers who resent the apparent leniency of the juvenile court when "the kid beat me home," but is pervasive in many areas. So many juvenile court judges are not acquainted with juvenile court philosophy and procedure that children under their supervision frequently get "the worst of two worlds"[18]—neither the protections guaranteed to adults in the criminal courts nor the rehabilitative treatment intended through the juvenile court.

The juvenile court has correctional as well as judicial functions. The basic philosophy underlying it, as stated in 1909, is that "erring children should be protected and rehabilitated rather than subjected to the harshness of the criminal system."[19]

The constitutionality of the juvenile court is based on (1) the voluntary nature of the court in cases involving what would be crimes if the child were an adult and which could result in deprivation of liberty, which ensures that the constitutional guarantees enjoyed by the citizen-offender in the case of felonies will not have been violated without consent; and (2) the principle of *parens patriae*. The concept of *non sui juris* has generally been considered to have been subsumed under *parens patriae*, in that juvenile court hearings are not a contest, but an effort to find equity in the interests of the child.

The juvenile court takes essentially four forms. The first is the separate juvenile court, which is probably responsible for a larger number of juveniles than any other court. The second is the part-time juvenile court, in which a probate or county judge is responsible for juveniles along with other duties, and which appears in the rural and sparsely settled areas. The third, the juvenile and domestic relations court, has broad jurisdiction over juveniles and some family matters, such as collecting money for child support. The fourth is the family court, which has broad responsibility that

[18] *Kent* v. *United States*, 383 U.S. 541, 556 (1966).

[19] Julian Mack, "The Juvenile Court," *Harvard Law Review*, 23 (1909), 104.

includes family counseling, divorce, and all matters concerned with family. There are other variations, such as the juvenile court which is a division of the court of record, making it equal to the criminal or circuit court.

In its simplest form, the juvenile court has a judge, a probation officer or juvenile court counselor, and whatever resources the community may offer. In some cases, the counselor is part-time. Many juvenile courts have several probation officers or juvenile court counselors. In the medium-sized cities, there may be two or three judges and a fairly large staff. The Jefferson County Juvenile Court in Louisville, Kentucky, for example, generally maintains between thirty-five and forty probation officers. In the major cities, such as Los Angeles, the probation staff becomes really large. The juvenile court generally handles delinquent children and dependent children, with the dependent children outnumbering the delinquent children about two to one, even though most dependent children are handled by public and private welfare agencies without going to juvenile court. Since the Gault decision in 1967, many states have added another case category, sometimes called "children [or persons] in need of supervision," covering children who were formerly referred to as delinquent because of incorrigibility, truancy, and other behavior that would not constitute an adult crime. The effect of this action is to limit the term "delinquency" to those acts which would be crimes had the offender been an adult and to move acts of truancy and incorrigibility into a new category of children or persons "in need of supervision" (PINS), (CINS), or (CHINS). The complications resulting from this limitation are exemplified by a New York case in which a minor girl was released to go back to living with two men in furnished rooms because no "crime" had been committed.[20]

The family court and the juvenile and domestic relations court, in various degrees, have jurisdiction over divorce, adoptions, marriage counseling, dependent and neglected children, delinquent children, wayward minors, psychiatric services for the family, protective facilities such as the detention home or parental home, and other matters concerning the family. There are a few juvenile courts at the level of the court of record or criminal court and circuit court. These courts provide for the possibility of bringing to trial parents who are accused of misdemeanors or felonies within the family. Further, they remove the question of review by a circuit court, bringing such review to the appellate level or, in the absence of the appellate level, to the state supreme court. The advantage of this setup is that juvenile court law is in equity or chancery, using civil rules of evidence and civil due process. When an equity proceeding in a lower court is reviewed by a circuit court accustomed to dealing in adversary proceedings, the decisions of the lower court are generally reversed. Then, when the case is appealed to a higher court with a broader perspective of law, the circuit court is frequently reversed and the juvenile court upheld.

[20] *In re Anonymous,* 42 Misc. 2nd 213, 250 N.Y.S. 2nd 395 (Family Court, 1964).

Qualifications for the juvenile court judge have not been stipulated in most jurisdictions. The judge handling juveniles frequently needs no other qualification than citizenship and the minimum age for election specified in the state constitution or statutes. In the larger jurisdictions where the vast majority of delinquents are processed, however, the judges are lawyers and will have been exposed to much more juvenile court law through appeals and practice, so that they generally become more sophisticated in the juvenile field than do most judges. On the other hand, some of the best judges in the field, including past presidents of the National Council of Juvenile Court Judges, have come from smaller jurisdictions. The trend in most states is for the judge to be a lawyer in order to ensure protection of civil rights and maintenance of due process. Many suggest that he should be a social worker or a psychologist. The question is whether he should be a social worker or psychologist and learn the law, or whether he should be a lawyer and learn the development and treatment of delinquent behavior. Usually the judge is a lawyer who leaves the probation staff to handle the treatment procedures.

The juvenile court probation officer and the juvenile court counselor in the larger metropolitan areas are from the fields of social work, psychology, or other related behavioral and social sciences. However, many counselors in rural areas have little background relating to behavior. Some estimates are that reasonably adequate probation programs exist in from less than one-tenth to approximately one-half of existing courts, depending upon the definition of "adequacy."

A crisis of confidence in the juvenile court developed after the *Gault* decision in 1967 and continued into the 1970s.[21] Many states moved services from the juvenile court to an administrative agency. Florida was one of the leaders in 1971, when these services were moved to Youth Services in the Department of Health and Rehabilitative Services. Sarri and Isenstadt placed a high priority on this question and lauded the move.[22] By 1981, 26 states and the District of Columbia had moved these services from the juvenile court to administrative agencies.

The numbers of juveniles under probation supervision by the juvenile courts in 1979 and the administrative agencies in 1981 are shown in Table 14-1. As can be seen, the reporting appears to be better among the administrative agencies than among the juvenile courts.

The reasons juveniles were referred to juvenile court in the United States in 1980 were as follows:

---

[21] John M. Pettibone, Robert G. Swisher, Kurt H. Weiland, Christine E. Wolf, and Joseph L. White, *Major Issues in Juvenile Justice Information and Training: Services to Children in Juvenile Courts: The Judicial-Executive Controversy* (Columbus, O.: Academy for Contemporary Problems, for the National Institute for Juvenile Justice and Delinquency Prevention, Washington, D.C., 1981), p. 16.

[22] Paul Isenstadt and Rosemary Sarri, "The Juvenile Court: Legal Context and Policy Issues," in Robert D. Vinter and Rosemary Sarri, eds., *Brought to Justice? Juveniles, the Courts, and the Law* (Ann Arbor: University of Michigan, National Assessment of Juvenile Corrections, 1976).

| Reason | Estimated Number | Percent |
|---|---|---|
| Criminal Homicide | 1,800 | 0.1% |
| Forcible Rape | 3,200 | 0.2% |
| Robbery | 26,500 | 2.0% |
| Aggravated Assault | 34,300 | 2.6% |
| Simple Assault | 82,100 | 6.1% |
| Burglary | 176,400 | 13.1% |
| Larceny | 278,100 | 20.7% |
| Motor Vehicle Theft | 51,000 | 3.8% |
| Arson & Vandalism | 84,300 | 6.3% |
| Stolen Property Offenses | 30,700 | 2.3% |
| Trespassing | 31,200 | 2.3% |
| Narcotics Offenses | 7,500 | 0.6% |
| Other Drug Offenses | 67,300 | 5.0% |
| Weapons Offenses | 17,000 | 1.3% |
| Sex Offenses | 12,500 | 0.9% |
| Drunkenness | 25,500 | 1.9% |
| Distrubing the Peace | 43,300 | 3.2% |
| Escape, Contempt, Probation, Parole | 27,300 | 2.0% |
| Other Delinquent Acts | 92,900 | 6.9% |
| Running Away | 68,700 | 5.1% |
| Truancy | 32,800 | 2.4% |
| Curfew Violations | 15,600 | 2.1% |
| Ungovernability | 50,700 | 3.8% |
| Liquor Violations | 56,300 | 4.2% |
| Other Status Offenses | 28,100 | 2.1% |
| Total All Offenses | 1,345,000 | 100.0% |

*Source:* Howard N. Snyder et al., *Delinquency 1980: A Description of Cases Processed by U.S. Courts with Juvenile Jurisudiction* (Pittsburgh: National Center for Juvenile Justice, 1981), p. 14.

Larcency and burglary constitute slightly over a third of all delinquencies.

## PROCEDURE

The procedure of the juvenile court begins with a complaint against a child. Complaints or referrals come most frequently from the police or other law enforcement agencies. School authorities concerned with truancy, vandalism, and other behavior refer many cases. Some cases are referred by other social agencies and some by other courts which either have adult jurisdiction or are not located in the state or county of the child's residence.

Upon receiving a complaint or referral, a juvenile court probation of-

**Table 14-1**

| State | Juvenile Court[a] 1979 | Other Agency[b] 1981 |
|---|---|---|
| Alabama | Not reported | |
| Alaska | 676 | |
| Arizona | | 3,504 |
| Arkansas | Not reported | |
| California | 57,058 | |
| Colorado | 3,336 | |
| Connecticut | Not reported | |
| Delaware | | 974 |
| Florida | | 8,915 |
| Georgia | | 2,253 |
| Hawaii | 378 | |
| Idaho | Not reported | |
| Illinois | 12,990 | |
| Indiana | 12,824 | |
| Iowa | Not reported | |
| Kansas | | 3,800 |
| Kentucky | | 10,490 |
| Louisiana | | 3,015 |
| Maine | | 625 |
| Maryland | | 4,257 |
| Massachusetts | | 381 |
| Michigan | Not reported | |
| Minnesota | | 67 |
| Mississippi | | 2,846 |
| Missouri | Not reported | |
| Montana | Not reported | |
| Nebraska | 1,216 | |
| Nevada | | 1,195 |
| New Hampshire | 1,386 | |
| New Jersey | 11,186 | |
| New Mexico | | 1,021 |
| New York | | 4,423 |
| North Carolina | Not reported | |
| North Dakota | Not reported | |
| Ohio | Not reported | |
| Oklahoma | | 655 |
| Oregon | Not reported | |
| Pennsylvania | Not reported | |
| Rhode Island | | 844 |
| South Carolina | | 2,920 |
| South Dakota | 821 | |
| Tennessee | | 2,003 |

continued

**Table 14-1** *(continued)*

| State | Juvenile Court[a] 1979 | Other Agency[b] 1981 |
|---|---|---|
| Texas | Not reported | |
| Utah | | 1,181 |
| Vermont | | 543 |
| Virginia | | 5,130 |
| Washington | Not reported | |
| West Virginia | | 818 |
| Wisconsin | 769 | |
| Wyoming | | 209 |
| Dist. of Columbia | | 1,391 |

[a] *Probation in the United States: 1979,* (Hackensack, New Jersey: National Council on Crime and Delinquency, 1980), p. 24.
[b] *Directory—Juvenile and Adult Correctional Departments—1982,* pp. xiv-xv.

ficer or counselor investigates the case. The circumstances of the complaint are recorded, the facts are verified and corrected if possible by interviewing the child, the parents, the victim of any offense, school personnel, and other people who might be able to contribute information. The probation officer or counselor then prepares a brief social history for use by the court.

If the circumstances warrant, the juvenile court probation officer or counselor places the child under informal supervision. In many jurisdictions, the child may already have been under voluntary police supervision by the juvenile aid bureau of the local police department. Probation officers, however, are sometimes reticent to accept the changing role of the police officer in delinquency control.[23]

In the treatment of juvenile delinquency, the juvenile court is really a "back-up" institution.[24] It provides informal court supervision, which is generally an unofficial probation type of supervision that does not call the case to the attention of the judge. The extent of this practice varies from court to court but, on a national basis, approximately half the juvenile delinquents under supervision are on unofficial probation, while the other half are on official probation. Some courts have approximately 85 percent of their caseload on unofficial probation, while some juvenile court judges want to see every child and place him on official probation if he is to be on probation at all. The reason that unofficial probation is used so much is that many cases can be corrected without going through official procedures. There is little or nothing to be accomplished in labeling a child delinquent if it is not necessary.

Many states have provisions for eliminating juvenile records, some-

[23] Peter G. Garabedian and Don C. Gibbons, *Becoming Delinquent: Young Offenders and the Correctional System* (Chicago: Aldine, 1970), p. 209.

[24] Robert M. Emerson, *Judging Delinquents: Context and Process in Juvenile Court* (Chicago: Aldine, 1969), p. 269.

times after ten years. Generally, the juvenile is not supposed to have a "record," but the military services and some other organizations are interested in the backgrounds of applicants. When a recruiting officer asks for information about a juvenile, it is sometimes difficult for the juvenile court to answer in a way that communicates realistically. The juvenile does not have a "record" in a sense that he has been convicted of a crime. On the other hand, he has been known by the juvenile court. Some juvenile court judges refuse to open the records for this purpose, but the information can be obtained from the police. The most successful arrangement appears to be for the judge or the chief probation officer to discuss openly with the recruiting officer or other interested persons the circumstances of the contact and the prognosis for the child's adjustment. In essence, the military services do not consider themselves to be rehabilitative agencies.

In cases where the child has been on unofficial probation and it becomes obvious that further control is desired, the juvenile court probation officer or counselor may prepare a petition. This petition requests that the child be declared delinquent because of the circumstances found in the original complaint or any other circumstances that might have arisen or have been discovered since that time.

A hearing before the judge is then set. Adequate notification of parents and counsel must be made. Before the hearing, the judge must explain to the child and his parents that he can have an attorney and that he does not have to be heard by the juvenile court in case of an offense which would be a felony if he were an adult. The *Kent* case of 1966 had the effect of requiring an attorney at the time of the waiver (*Kent* v. *United States*, 383 U.S. 541, 556 1966), which is the point at which the child consents to be heard by the juvenile court. Under the *Gault* decision, the child is entitled to counsel if he desires it (*In re Gault*, 387 U.S. 1, 18 L. Ed. 2nd 527 1967). A child has the right to a legal hearing in juvenile court when he is faced with the possibility of commitment to a detention facility for delinquents. Sometimes attorneys are appointed using procedures similar to those used in the adult courts. Some states have legal counsel provided for the child through a section or division of legal services made available to the juvenile courts.

Attorneys have always had a role in the juvenile courts, but until recently, they were most frequently hired by the parents of the child. The *Gault* decision in 1967 had the effect of providing counsel for every child who desired it. The full effect of the *Gault* decision was to (1) guarantee adequate notice in writing of the charge, (2) provide adequate notification of the child's right to counsel at the hearing unless intelligently waived, (3) guarantee the privilege against self-incrimination unless intelligently waived, and (4) guarantee in the absence of valid admission that determination of delinquency shall rest upon sworn testimony in open court.[25] While some judges were apprehensive about and resented the pressure of attorneys in the court representing the child, the majority of the better

[25] *In re Application of Gault*, 387 U.S. 1, 87 S. Ct. 1428 (1967).

judges tended to welcome the attorneys. Experience indicated that persons trained in the law knew the difference between criminal and civil proceedings and, after brief explanation of the function of the juvenile court, were able to understand and interpret to the parents what the juvenile court was doing and why.

The hearings by the juvenile court are divided into fact-finding and disposition. Consequently, there are generally two hearings or, at least, two parts to a hearing, although they may take place consecutively. If the child denies the allegations and desires an attorney, then there must be, in effect, three hearings. The first one takes place when the allegations are made and denied, the second one follows civil rules of evidence and procedure to establish the facts, and the third one is for the disposition of the case if the child is found delinquent. The state legislatures determine the alternative dispositions available to the courts.[26] Further, the courts cannot declare something to be an offense that the statutes do not make such. The *McKeiver* case in 1971 held that the right to trial by jury did not apply to juvenile court.[27]

At the disposition hearing, the judge is likely to place the child on official probation, which is more authoritative than unofficial probation, or he may commit the child to a state training school. There are generally six dispositions available to the juvenile court judge. The three most frequently used are probation, commitment to an institution, and placement in a foster home. A fourth, providing protective custody within the child's own home, is often used when the child has been abused by parents or other members of the household. A fifth disposition is to make the child a ward of the court and to order his parents to obtain medical treatment for him when the parents, by reason of religious belief or other basis, refuse to provide or permit medical help. This has frequently been used in cases of chronic illness in families whose religion objects to medical intervention and in the increasing number of cases involving abused and battered children. The sixth disposition available to the judge is severance of parental rights and adoption, which is used sparingly. Juvenile court judges indicate that the hardest part of their job is the severance of the rights of natural parents in the cases of children whose situations demand it.

The normal range of dispositions in juvenile court cases is shown in Table 14-2.

The criterion for determining disposition in the juvenile court and the statutes concerning juveniles is not what the child did, but rather what his best interests require.

In many states, the aftercare of children released from state training schools is also the responsibility of the juvenile court. Unfortunately, however, very few courts meet this aftercare responsibility. The average age for boys coming to the juvenile court is about 16.1, but the majority of them

---

[26] *In re Lewis,* 11 N.J. 217, 94 Atl. 2nd 328, 332 (1953).

[27] *McKeiver* v. *Pennsylvania,* 403, U.S. 528 (1971).

**Table 14-2   Dispositions of juvenile court cases**

### Delinquency Cases

| Disposition | Percentage |
|---|---|
| Warning or adjustment | 50 |
| Counselor to supervise on unofficial or official probation | 21 |
| Dismissed | 7 |
| Runaways returned home | 6 |
| State or private training schools | 5 |
| Referred to other courts, generally criminal, but some traffic | 4 |
| Other public or private institutions | 3 |
| Other dispositions | 3 |
| Public welfare department | 1 |

### Traffic Cases

| Disposition | Percentage |
|---|---|
| Warning | 37 |
| License revoked, suspended, or deferred | 28 |
| Traffic schools | 13 |
| Driving restricted | 7 |
| Referred to another court | 5 |
| Dismissed | 5 |
| Other dispositions | 3 |
| Supervision | 2 |
| Fine or bond | 1 |

### Dependency Cases

| Disposition | Percentage |
|---|---|
| Warning or adjustment | 27 |
| Dismissed | 20 |
| Change of custody | 16 |
| Support order only | 12 |
| Public welfare department | 10 |
| Referral to other courts | 5 |
| Referral to private agency | 4 |
| Counselor to supervise | 4 |
| Other dispositions | 2 |
| Public or private institutions | 1 |

Source: Computed from *Florida Juvenile Court Statistics, 1965, 1966, 1967* (Jacksonville: Florida State Department of Public Welfare, 1968), pp. 18, 19, 21.

first appear in court between ages 11 and 13. The average age of delinquent girls coming to juvenile court is 15.6. Ninety percent of these children had marked adjustment difficulty before the age of 11. Half have shown noticeable adjustment problems by the age of 8. Of the Gluecks' 500 delinquents, 44 percent have clearly shown the signs of antisocial behavior between the ages of 5 and 7.[28] Boys outnumber girls four to one in delinquency cases. The majority of boys are referred for stealing or malicious mischief such as vandalism. The majority of girls are referred for running away or for sexual

[28] *United States Senate Subcommittee Hearing*, 83rd Congress, Second Session, 1954.

offenses. Of over 1 million cases referred to the juvenile courts in America each year, about half are held open, dismissed, or adjusted. Of the remaining cases processed through the courts, more than half are placed on unofficial or official probation. Fewer than 50,000 children per year are committed to institutions.

There has been considerable debate as to whether the juvenile court is a court of law or a social agency. Some judges at conferences have stated seriously, if in a light vein, that the juvenile court is the product of an illicit relationship between social work and the law, and "nobody wants the bastard." Those who hold that the juvenile court is a social agency find that the majority of the court's work is done by juvenile probation officers and counselors in a casework or helping approach. Those who hold that the juvenile court is a court of law point out that it is obvious that the authority of the judge must be used for more serious cases. For the majority of juvenile court clients, the court has functioned as a social agency. For the more serious of the juvenile court clients, the social agency approach has had to have the authority of the court. Such arguments are merely semantic. There is no reason why the juvenile court must be either a court of law or a social agency. It can be both, simultaneously, having the function of the social agency backed by the authority of a court of law.

## JUVENILE TRAINING SCHOOLS

Delinquent children are received in public state training schools, private training schools, city and local training schools, and various types of forestry camps. The majority are received in state and private training schools. Probably 50,000 delinquents are in state training schools and fewer then 10,000 are in private training schools. The state training schools, of course, operate on state funds and are administered by the state in various ways. Many are within the Department of Public Welfare, while others are administered by specialized agencies dealing with juveniles and youth. All the private schools are licensed by the state, generally through the Department of Public Welfare's Division of Child Welfare, which inspects and generally supervises in terms of minimum standards of health, sanitation, care, and program. In 1960, there were 45,695 persons in custody of training schools for juvenile delinquents. Of that number, 38,359 were in public training schools, 7,336 were in private training schools, and 10,821 were in detention homes.[29] In 1971, there were 35,931 persons in public training schools, of whom 27,839 were boys and 8,092 were girls.[30]

In 1979, there were 30,948 juveniles in 933 public training facilities

[29] *Statistical Abstract of the United States, 1969,* U.S. Department of Commerce (Washington, D.C.: U.S. Government Printing Office, 1970).

[30] *Children in Custody: Report of the Juvenile Detention and Correctional Facility Census* (Washington, D.C.: U.S. Law Enforcement Assistance Administration and the U.S. Bureau of the Census, June 1974), p. 7.

and 27,945 juveniles in 1,558 private training facilities.[31] Of this total population, there were 3,861 girls (12.5 percent) in public facilities and 7,885 girls (28.5 percent) in private facilities. In 1979 also, there were 2,697 juveniles being held in adult jails and correctional facilities.[32] In 1978, there were 1,611 juveniles held under sentence in adult jails alone.[33] The cost of removing them by 1985 would be about $118.8 million.[34]

The private schools, generally supported by contributions and donations, have greater latitude in their operation than do the state schools in many cases. For example, they can be selective within limits with regard to the children they accept. One private school set its minimum intelligence at a rather high level and limited the intake to white children. Since the Supreme Court decisions and federal legislation regarding desegregation, such a school could keep the intelligence requirement but would have to drop the racial limitations. While it is a private school, it functions under license by the state and serves the public.

The state training schools must accept everybody committed to them. On occasion, there have been private agreements between the state training schools and the courts that a waiting list would be honored to avoid excessive overcrowding, but such agreements are rare and their implementation even more rare. The superintendent of an institution, whether public or private, is responsible for the institution. The superintendent of a private school is responsible to his board of trustees and the state licensing authorities. The administrator of a state training school must report to the state director of training schools or his counterpart in whatever administrative organization the state may maintain and, through him, to the legislature, the governor, and the budget director or commission.

The internal organizations of the training schools, whether private or public, are becoming more similar. The more progressive schools have a superintendent, an assistant superintendent, and three rather all-inclusive departments. (1) The department of cottage life has general supervision over all matrons, cottage fathers, or cottage parents, depending upon the organization and practice, in the living quarters. (2) The program director or clinical director generally has charge of social services, psychological services, and the general program aimed at the treatment of the children. (3) The educational director has charge of the schools and educational

---

[31] *Children in Custody: Advance Report on the 1979 Census of Public Juvenile Facilities* (Washington, D.C.: Office of Juvenile Justice and Delinquency Prevention, 1980), Table 2.

[32] Harvey D. Lowell, Margaret McNabb, and Anthony J. DeMarco, *Sentenced Prisoners Under 18 Years of Age in Adult Correctional Facilities: A National Survey* (Washington, D.C.: National Center on Institutions and Alternatives, 1980), p. 14.

[33] "Appendix 15; Profile of Jail Inmates—Survey Methodology and Definitions of Terms," *Sourcebook on Criminal Justice Statistics—1981* (Washington, D.C.: Bureau of Justice Statistics, U.S. Department of Justice, 1982), p. 586.

[34] *Jail Removal Cost Study* (Washington, D.C.: Office of Juvenile Justice and Delinquency Prevention, May 1982), Vol. 2, pp. i, 258–65.

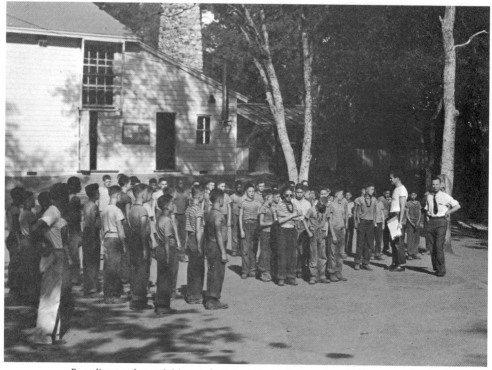

Boys line up for activities at the Fricot Ranch School, San Andreas, California.
Courtesy of the California Youth Authority.

procedures, frequently including the recreation program and interscholastic athletic competition. The kitchen, food services, clothing, and other administrative affairs, such as accounting, are generally left to the business manager. The superintendent is frequently away from campus in his public relations capacity. The superintendent of a state training school meets with legislative delegations frequently and the superintendent of a private institution is frequently speaking to women's clubs or other groups in the process of raising money.

Private and public training schools have developed side by side since the early nineteenth century. Judges send children or adolescents to private institutions when, for a variety of reasons relating to pressures, a particular private institution is deemed to be more desirable than the state training school. The number of applications to private institutions exceed by far the number that can be received. Consequently, the courts and the private institutions have developed procedures to provide a selective caseload to the private institutions. The private institution is thus able to gear its program to the type of boy or girl it can best serve.

The state institution, on the other hand, has no selection process. Without intervening reasons or pressures to do otherwise, all delinquents would be sent to the state training school. The state training school is geared to the "average" delinquent child, while the private training school can be selective and deal with special types of delinquent children.

Most state training schools maintain academic educational programs through the eighth grade. A few have high school programs, but the ages of their clients and the short time they stay seldom permit high school graduation. Also, some may be school dropouts. Consequently, a major focus is generally on vocational training. The type of vocational training offered is dependent upon the economy of the state and the market for trade. For example, in industrial areas, there may be an emphasis on machine shop trades. There is generally a printing shop, where the school prints its own forms and its own newspaper. Welding and auto mechanics are popular among juveniles. Many state training schools, as well as private schools, have farms. Farms are primarily used for production of food and providing employment for the boys. There is a trend toward eliminating the farms, however, both at the juvenile and adult level, because they have proved over a period of years to be unprofitable.

Juvenile institutions are operated on several types of philosophies. Many sectarian private training schools operate on an inspirational-repressive philosophy with a religious and moral reeducation theme. Probably the most common type of philosophy is the operant conditioning approach in which an effort is made to provide normal living. In some cases, it takes the form of just "getting along." In others, it takes the form of little

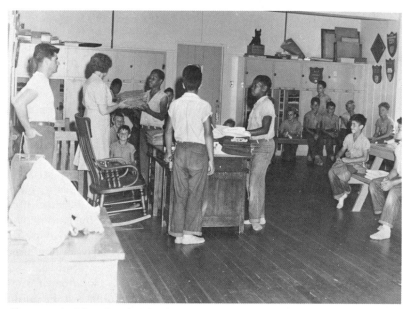

Classroom in Fricot Ranch School.
Courtesy of the California Youth Authority.

communities, such as Father Flanagan's Boys' Home in Nebraska, formerly called Boys Town, where the boys elect their own mayor and other representatives of government, have their own monetary system, and, in essence, replicate in miniature the community.

Education, hard work, and discipline is an approach employed in many state training schools. In a few state training schools, particularly in New York and California, and several outstanding private training schools, the orthopsychiatric approach to treatment, including psychiatric, psychological, and social work services, is the philosophy. Comparisons between these systems suggest that the orthopsychiatric approach is best, even though it costs more than any of the other approaches.

Institutional behavioral problems in training schools impair the peace and order within the institution and the institutional regimen. The population reinforces negative values for the juveniles themselves. Runaways are a serious problem primarily in terms of public relations. State training schools may have a runaway rate of nearly half the population per year, but involving about 20 percent of the children, since many run away several times a year. That rate would be considerably lower in training schools situated in rural states with a single main highway going through the area. The runaway rate would be higher in an institution situated in urban areas with traffic going by on all sides. Runaways also vary with the cottage parents and their relationships. There are more runaways at Christmas than at other times during the year.

Stealing is a predominant problem. Many insecure boys want to acquire things, whether they are utilitarian or not, because the acquisition of property provides them with some security they are not getting any other way. A boy who was a client of this writer had stolen a bushel basket full of belt buckles. The late Dr. Ralph Banay, a psychiatrist with a European degree who had to obtain American credentials, collected door knobs, a symbol of "opening doors," sometimes with this writer's assistance.

Sexual problems prevail in all unisexual populations. While they may involve a minority of boys or girls, they are always present and everyone is aware of them. Such problems exist in boys' institutions, but tend to be more intense in girls' institutions. Girls need to be needed. This dependency creates a need for someone in some way. Girls will carve or scratch the initials of their girlfriends on their arms and other parts of their body, similar to tattoos. Boys do not get that involved. Institutional personnel and aftercare workers must take into account the emotional results of living with a close relationship in the institution and breaking the relationship when one of the friends is released, particularly among girls.

Fighting is frequent in boys' institutions and less frequent in girls' schools. Smoking is almost always a violation of rules in juvenile institutions because of state laws and the opinion of the public. Smoking has been a source of debate among superintendents of juvenile institutions. Most of the juveniles smoked before they arrived at the institution and the withdrawal of cigarettes simply adds to the problem of institutional adjustment. Smoking is legal for adults and is not a crime, yet it is not permitted in many juvenile training school populations, a situation many superintendents of juvenile institutions consider to be a dilemma.

Many of the problems in juvenile institutions stem from the parents. There are many four-parent children. When the natural mother and stepfather visit on one Sunday and the natural father and stepmother visit on another Sunday, the child may remain in emotional turmoil.

Problems the child faces upon institutionalization include lack of privacy. Remaining on the defensive because authority has placed him there, he experiences a lack of freedom and lack of normal contact with the opposite sex. A child must reconcile his adjustment with the peer group with whom he lives and the institutional officials upon whom he depends for release. Sometimes these are difficult to accommodate.

## DETENTION

There are approximately 250 detention homes in the United States to serve approximately 3,000 counties. This means that less than 10 percent of the courts have detention facilities. They are the courts, however, which serve probably 85 percent of the delinquent children, since the detention facilities are in the larger and middle-sized population centers. The local detention home serving a county or urban area is most frequent. Rural and sparsely populated areas sometimes have contract detention homes, where the county contracts with a farmer to use his home as the detention home, or the county may contract for approved foster homes on a standby basis. Regional detention homes have been proposed on occasion, but several counties trying to build a single detention home have had difficulty in reaching agreement as to where it should be located. The use of regional detention homes actually resulted from counties' contracting for detention services with neighboring, larger counties already having detention homes.

The detention home is the first institution to which the child is generally exposed. Because this exposure could be a traumatic experience, it is important that the detention home be staffed by people who like and can live with children. Because juveniles' perception of time is different from that of adults, they need to be oriented at all times. A full and beneficial program of diagnosis, education, and treatment must be maintained in the detention home to achieve full benefit of the opportunity for correction. This program will counterbalance the frequent protest on the part of some that the correctional client in a detention home or facility for short-time detention is not there long enough to take advantage of a program.

Testing and other diagnostic procedures are commonplace in progressive detention homes. While the child is in the detention home, there is an opportunity to learn as much as possible about him. Intelligence, aptitude, and personality testing can be achieved. Information from schools, from other social agencies that have been interested in the family, and from families and relatives can be sythesized into a social history that will subsequently be useful in the treatment process, both on probation and in the institution.

Educational programs are essential for short-term detention homes so that the correctional client, probably already two or three years retarded academically, will not be further retarded. Special and remedial educational procedures can be instituted. Contracts can be entered into with the local school system to provide specialized education, as well as extension education such as that generally provided for homebound students in the public school systems.

Computer-Assisted Instruction (CAI) is available in almost every region. In fact, some universities and school systems already have centers in neighboring counties with terminals running back to central headquarters where a library of courses of instruction is available. Much can be accomplished in one hour, one day, or one week with this type of instruction.

Recreational programs are important. A professional recreation director should be hired or contracted for with the city for service in the detention home. Because many of the correctional clients are isolates, handicapped by inferiority feelings, and have never successfully competed anywhere, much of the recreational program should be creative rather than competitive or athletic. Arts and crafts, documentary films, television, radio, opportunity for music lessons, and many other activities should be available without reducing available athletic competition and play. Lessons in chess and other games should be made available.

Religious programs must be realistic and serve the needs of the children in the detention home. Many adolescents in difficulty with police and in the hands of the juvenile court confined in the detention home do not accept religion on faith. Rather, they frequently sit through a service and tolerate it because they have to, not because they are getting anything out of it. Since religion is an important part of American culture and individual life, a religious program must be carefully selected and supervised so that the greatest communication with the least "turning off" can be achieved.

Relationships with outsiders, particularly with the parents of the correctional clients, must be supportive. Regardless of hostility expressed by the children or their parents, the detention home staff must maintain assurance of the court's constructive interest in the children. On the other hand, the complainant in many cases must be assured that something is being done.

Shelter care is a type of domiciliary care for dependent children. In many places, this is accomplished in the detention home. In larger areas, a separate "parental home" or a shelter for dependent children is provided. The same programs described for detention homes, of course, should be present in these shelters for dependent children.

There are several alternatives to detention of juveniles.[35] Intensive probation service provides "relationship surveillance" that helps the parent and child assume responsibility for behavior pending court action. Emergency shelter care is sometimes important, but secure custody is seldom important. In fact, Michigan, Florida, New York, and some other states use shelter care successfully for delinquent children pending court disposition. Special group homes, mental hospitals, or other facilities for juveniles with severe emotional disturbances provide more effective help than detention homes do. The major problems with detention homes are (1) misuse and long stays, (2) substandard care, (3) insufficient community resources, and (4) lack of state responsibility. Before the building of a detention facility, needs should be studied and analyzed carefully.

## COMMUNITY PROGRAMS

Foster homes, halfway houses, and other community programs are becoming more prevalent in delinquency services. Halfway houses with their community-based type of treatment are considered to be the most important breakthrough in the correctional field in the past fifty years.[36] The use of group processes in group foster homes, prerelease guidance centers, halfway houses, institutions, and probation and parole is apparently one way of inducing peer group reinforcement in a therapeutic community.

The agency-operated group home is usually a single dwelling or apartment owned or rented by an agency or institution to care for four to twelve children.[37] The group home reaches out to the community for many of its activities and resources. Staff are employed as counselors or houseparents rather than as foster parents. The group residence serves thirteen to twenty-five children or youths. It generally has two or more groups of children, each with its own child-care staff, and provides more agency services than community services.

The traditional foster home usually cares for one or two children, sometimes three or four. Foster parents are reimbursed for their part of the cost in caring for a child. The specialized or professional foster home has foster parents selected because of their professional background or special capacity for working with agencies of a specific type. Foster family group homes care for four to six children with special needs. In many place, $5 per day is provided foster parents for each child in their care.

---

[35] *Think Twice Before You Build or Enlarge a Detention Center,* National Council on Crime and Delinquency (New York: The Council, 1968).

[36] Oliver J. Keller, Jr., and Benedict S. Alper, *Halfway Houses: Community-Centered Corrections and Treatment* (Lexington, Mass.: Raytheon/Heath, 1970), p. 174.

[37] Martin Gula, *Agency-Operated Group Homes,* U.S. Children's Bureau (Washington, D.C.: U.S. Government Printing Office, 1964), p. 35.

The group home can be used for dependents or delinquents as well as children with many problems, including psychiatric and emotional disturbances. Its advantage is that it provides small group living in the community without severing the social ties so important to emotional security.

## AFTERCARE PROGRAMS

Throughout the United States, there are three patterns of follow-up or aftercare of children after they leave the training schools. The most prevalent, and probably the least effective because of lack of staff and the ages of released children, is placing the responsibility for aftercare on the juvenile court that committed them in the first place. The majority of juvenile courts spend their available time on new cases coming to the attention of the court rather than on old cases of juveniles who, by reason of age, are beyond their jurisdiction if they commit another offense.

A second pattern is making another agency whose primary duty is not in this field furnish supervision for children released from training school. For example, the Department of Public Welfare, or whatever its name might be in a particular state, becomes responsible for aftercare services to juveniles released from the training school. These agencies generally devote their available time to the income maintenance or relief services, which are the primary reason for their existence.

Probably the best state system is the parental agency, in which the training schools and the aftercare services are in the same department, such as in California, Minnesota, Massachusetts, Florida, and several other states. Some of the better programs are in private training schools in the New York City area, such as Children's Village at Dobbs Ferry, Berkshire Farms, and Wiltwyck School. In these programs, the caseworker has offices in the institution and downtown. He or she may spend two days working in one office and three in the other. He or she works with children in the institution and their families outside, and assists in the transition from the institution to home again, continuing supervision, and thereby maintaining the continuity of relationship and security in that relationship. This plan appears to be best for the child but does not seem to be administratively feasible in large state programs where the training schools may be hundreds of miles from the urban centers.

The problem in all areas of corrections is trying to make developmental principles administratively feasible, rather than trying to make administrative principles developmentally sound.

Historically, aftercare was handled by the court of commitment. Unfortunately, juvenile courts were overloaded, and their attention focused on new and younger cases. Consequently, the juvenile courts offered very little aftercare. Some agencies, such as welfare departments, provided some aftercare in a few states. California in 1944 introduced the Youth Authority, which had an office for this service, and this pattern of a "parent agency" providing aftercare appeared to be feasible and was followed by other states. For example, the Ohio Youth Commission, Massachusetts Department of Youth Services, and other administrative agencies handled aftercare. By 1981, many states had aftercare services provided by these administrative agencies. Aftercare services data are not available from juvenile courts, but the aftercare provided by statewide administrative agencies are shown as follows:[38]

## Juvenile Aftercare

| State | Aftercare Cases |
|-------|-----------------|
| Arizona | 483 |
| Arkansas | 470 |
| California | 6,833 |
| Colorado | 302 |
| Connecticut | 731 |
| Delaware | 87 |
| Dist. of Columbia | 404 |
| Florida | 2,278 |
| Georgia | 1,036 |
| Hawaii | 24 |
| Illinois | 1,043 |
| Indiana | 943 |
| Iowa | 300 |
| Kentucky | 3,133 |
| Louisiana | 449 |
| Maine | 364 |
| Maryland | 1,721 |
| Massachusetts | 523 |
| Minnesota | 548 |
| Missouri | 498 |
| Montana | 217 |
| Nebraska | 105 |
| Nevada | 299 |
| New Hampshire | 159 |
| New Jersey | 322 |
| New Mexico | 198 |
| New York | 1,531 |
| Ohio | 2,326 |
| Oklahoma | 428 |
| Oregon | 577 |
| Rhode Island | 132 |

*continued*

[38] *Directory—Juvenile and Adult Correctional Departments—1982,* pp. xiv–xv.

**Juvenile Aftercare** (*continued*)

| State | Aftercare Cases |
| --- | --- |
| South Carolina | 362 |
| South Dakota | 162 |
| Tennessee | 2,220 |
| Texas | 2,627 |
| Utah | 85 |
| Vermont | 125 |
| Virginia | 1,011 |
| Wisconsin | 229 |
| Wyoming | 111 |

States not listed still have aftercare as the responsibility of the local courts, and those data are not available for aftercare.

## STATUS OFFENSES

After the *Gault* case in 1967 (387 U.S. 1, 87 S. Ct. 1428), delinquency cases arising from criminal offense were considered to be different from "misbehavior just by reason of age," such as truancy from school, incorrigibility, and other, similar offenses that were put into a category of "in need of supervision" rather than delinquency. These were "status offenses" because of the age status of the juvenile and would not have been crimes had the offender been an adult. Since that time, various states have referred to them as persons (or children) in need of supervision"—PINS, CINS, or CHINS.

There has been a strong movement to separate juveniles from adults and to separate delinquents from status offenders. The Juvenile Justice and Delinquency Prevention Act of 1974 (P.L. 94-415) was the first instance of making juvenile justice a congressional priority for the purpose of making major reforms in its administration. Failure to accomplish compliance in several areas would result in loss of eligibility for some grant funds. With regard to "separation," 33 states were in general compliance by 1980.[39] Many states moved status offenders completely out of the juvenile court jurisdiction. In Florida, for example, status offenses are the responsibility of the Children, Youth, and Families section of the Department of Health and Rehabilitative Services.

[39] *Juvenile Justice: Before and After the Onset of Delinquency—United States Discussion Paper for the Sixth United Nations Congress on the Prevention of Crime and the Treament of Offenders* (Washington, D.C.: Office of Juvenile Justice and Delinquency Prevention, 1980), p. 7.

# YOUTHFUL OFFENDER PROGRAMS

Special programs for youths, generally between their seventeenth and twenty-first birthdates, have been developed in several states to provide special attention to those offenders who are beyond juvenile court age but who should not be treated as adults. Probably the first such idea was the Wayward Minor Act in New York in 1886, which was implemented by several other states, for youthful persons not delinquent or criminal, but whose behavior or situation place them "in danger of becoming morally depraved." The Wayward Minor programs are gone now, and the Youthful Offender programs seem to be taking their place.

Most states, of course, have youth centers, special institutions, or camps in their correctional systems for the treatment of youthful offenders, whether or not this provision has been formalized under a Youthful Offender Act. California has a Youth Authority Act, probably the most well-developed program. Massachusetts has a Division of Youth Services and Minnesota has a Division of Youth Conservation, both well developed. New York has a Division of Correctional Camps for Youth. Vermont has a center for youthful offenders. Several states, such as Illinois, Michigan, Ohio, Tennessee, and Texas, have youth commissions that include juveniles, rather than separate programs for youthful offenders. As previously

Recreation room in a California Youth Authority institution.
Courtesy of the California Youth Authority.

stated, nearly all states have separate programs for youthful offenders, regardless of their designation.

The Federal Youth Correction Act, passed by Congress in 1950, was implemented in January 1954 and extended to all federal court districts in 1956. Its purpose was to provide services for those who are beyond the jurisdiction of the juvenile court yet still not to be treated as adults.

Youthful Offender programs are in the adult correctional systems of many states and are either administratively initiated and administered or are legislatively mandated. Their focus is generally on offenders between their seventeenth and twenty-fourth birthdates. States with Youthful Offender laws are Alabama, Arkansas, California, District of Columbia, Florida, Georgia, Massachusetts, New York, North Carolina, Pennsylvania, South Carolina, Virginia, and the Federal Prison System. Minnesota and Wisconsin had had laws covering Youthful Offenders, but Minnesota repealed its in 1981 and Wisconsin repealed its in 1978, indicating that the needs of the youthful offender were not seen as substantially different from other prisoners. In most correctional systems, there is some special consideration, however, of the youthful offender who is older than the juvenile and still not in the more hardened adult group, generally from the mid-teens to the mid-20s in age, with special focus on first-offenders.

## SUMMARY

Two major problems in juvenile corrections lie in the institutional program and aftercare. In the process of socialization, it takes a long time for the growing personality to achieve permanent and stable heterosexual adaptation. It is in middle adolescence that heterosexual contacts begin to lengthen from a single date to "going steady," subsequently to lengthening relationships and engagement to marriage. When the average age of appearance in juvenile court and commitment to unisexual institutions is about 16 for boys and about 14½ for girls, it is obvious that many youth are being sent to unisexual institutions right in the middle of this developmental process. Consequently, training schools have been called breeding places for abnormal behavioral patterns of all sorts, from homosexuality to crime, because of the concentration of many delinquents who see life as socially unjust in the first place, and have their negative values reinforced by their peers in an environment lacking adequate treatment. The need to counterbalance these values explains why the orthopsychiatric approach appears to be one of the most hopeful approaches now being used in institutions and why continuity of follow-up aftercare is vitally important.

A problem emerging from the *Gault* decisions is what to do with "status offenses," those that would not be offenses were the individual an adult. These include truancy, smoking and drinking under age, violation of curfew laws, and other offenses that are offenses simply because the individual is under the age of majority. Some states have created the PINS (persons in need of supervision) and CINS or CHINS (children in need of supervision) programs and placed these juveniles under juvenile court supervision. Some states, such as Florida, have placed them under supervision of the protective services section of the Child Welfare Units in the Department of Public Welfare. Certainly, the problem of "status offenses" needs further examination.[40]

The future of the juvenile court appears to be assured. Juvenile courts should be sources of information on children in trouble and should provide assistance for them. Simultaneously, children's legal guarantees will be watched, and their effectiveness will be assessed more in the future than it has been in the past.[41] While the *Gault* decision attacked due process as it existed in some juvenile courts, it did not attack the principle of *parens patriae*. The *Gault* decision applies when the result may be a finding of delinquency and the commitment of the child to a state institution.

> The observance of due process standards, intelligently and not ruthlessly administered, will not compel the States to abandon or displace any of the substantive benefits of the juvenile process.[42]

There was litigation for nearly a century on the principle of *parens patriae* before the creation of the juvenile court. Statutes concerning juveniles have involved the principle of *parens patriae* for the past 200 years, and "it is very late to call their constitutionality into question."[43]

> That the law, when administered by courts wanting in wisdom and wide judicial discretion, may sometimes be wrongfully applied and thereby work injustice to the accused, is not sufficient to vitiate it.[44]

# EXERCISES AND STUDY QUESTIONS

1. *What is the philosophy of the juvenile court?*
2. *What are the constitutional bases of the juvenile court?*
3. *What is the size of the juvenile court caseload?*
4. *What general forms does the juvenile court take?*
5. *Delineate the procedure of the juvenile court.*

[40] John Dineen, *Juvenile Court Organization and Status Offenses—A Statutory Profile* (Pittsburgh: National Center for Juvenile Justice, University of Pittsburgh, 1974).

[41] Ted Rubin and Jack F. Smith, *The Future of the Juvenile Court: Implication for Correctional Manpower and Training,* Joint Commission on Correctional Manpower and Training (Washington, D.C.: U.S. Government Printing Office, 1968).

[42] *In re Application of Gault,* 387 U.S. L, 87 S. Ct. 1428 (1967).

[43] *Reynolds* v. *Howe,* 51 Conn. 472, 473 (1884).

[44] *Ex Parte Januszewski,* 196 Fed. 123, 131 (C.C.S.D. Ohio, 1911).

6. What is the role of the attorney in the juvenile court?

7. Describe the adjudication hearing.

8. Describe the disposition hearing.

9. What are the majority of dispositions of delinquency cases?

10. What are the dispositions in traffic cases?

11. What are the dispositions in dependency cases?

12. How many children are in juvenile training schools?

13. How is the training school organized?

14. How many children per 100,000 child population 10 through 17 years of age are in public institutions for juvenile delinquents?

15. What are some of the behavioral problems encountered in juvenile institutions?

16. Evaluate the detention home and its programs.

17. What are the primary problems with detention homes?

18. Describe alternatives to detention, such as foster homes, halfway houses, and other community programs.

19. Evaluate aftercare programs in America.

20. Has the doctrine of parens patriae been successfully challenged in the courts?

# 15

# PRIVATE CORRECTIONS

Private individuals and groups have always played a major role in the field of corrections. The early blood feud and trial by combat in which the "offender" was killed were private matters. In the feudal system, the lord of the manor maintained arbitration courts for the serfs under his control as part of his private enterprise. The first permanent home for wandering children was built by the Society of St. Vincent de Paul in 1648. The church had ecclesiastical prisons during the Middle Ages until the seventeenth century. The first House of Refuge for delinquent and dependent children was created through private efforts in Danzig in 1824, and the first in America was built in New York in 1825. The first municipal policing organization was the private Bow Street Runners in London around 1750. In the United States today, private policing is used twice as frequently as governmental policing. The first probation services were the efforts of one man, John Augustus, in Boston around 1843.

John Howard, high sheriff of Bedford and a wealthy man in his own right, used his own resources to travel throughout Europe in the late 1700s to examine the condition of jails. He produced a document which resulted in the reform of the English penal system. The modern penitentiary, first established in Philadelphia in 1790, was created through the efforts of a private society. The Philadelphia Society for Alleviating the Miseries of the Public Prisons was a Quaker organization under the leadership of Dr. Benjamin Rush. In 1899, the modern juvenile court was started in Chicago as a result of pressure by the Chicago Women's Clubs. These are only a few examples of the influential efforts of the private sector in the field of corrections.

The pattern of social action in all fields, whether mental health, public health, control of business and commerce, policies of government, or corrections, has been that private efforts initiate programs. First, private groups supply the needed services. Second, the government begins to provide those services when a problem becomes too great to be handled by private individuals and groups. Third, governmental agencies subsidize or take over the entire function of the services. Fourth, the governmental agency providing the services many request assistance from private sources in terms of volunteer services, contractual services, or public relations eventually aimed at legislative appropriations.

Private corrections, then, is always in the process of filling gaps in governmental services as the need is seen. At the present time, private corrections may be most active in juvenile institutional services, legal aid services, and care for dependent children to prevent development into delinquency, although they augment, support, and complement governmental correctional programs in many other areas as well. Private organizations also serve as watchdogs over the governmental function in corrections and criminal justice. They bring political weight to move agencies of government in desired directions.

## RELIGIOUS GROUPS

Religious groups have been active in corrections for a long time. As previously stated, the Society of St. Vincent de Paul established a permanent home for wandering children in 1648. Pope Clement XI built the Hospice di San Michele in Rome for delinquent children in 1704, and it is still being used for its original purpose. The Quakers were instrumental in establishing the penitentiary concept.

The Salvation Army has a Corrections Division. This division provides material assistance in the form of residential homes, food, and clothing. In addition, it offers help in finding jobs, legal assistance when appropriate, and counseling.

The Volunteers of America have also been active in corrections. They have served in much the same way as the Salvation Army since they split off from that organization in 1896.

Both the Salvation Army and the Volunteers of America work in the slums and ghettos, in bars and skid rows, wherever the people who need assistance live. As well stated by MacLeod, "Jesus was not crucified in a cathedral between two candles, but on a cross between two thieves."[1]

Many private religious organizations are working primarily in the area of juvenile delinquency. Youth for Christ has been active throughout the country. The Juvenile Rehabilitation Ministry of the Home Mission Board of the Southern Baptist Convention has been quite active in the

[1] George MacLeod, *Only One Way Left* (Glasgow: The Iona Community, 1956), p. 38.

Southeast.[2] This approach is purely religious, not psychological, custodial, psychiatric, or sociological. It rests on the view that godlessness is a basic cause of crime, and religion is the basic cure. Members believe that the church and religious people should be where Jesus was, mingling with the publicans and sinners, the diseased, outcasts, and broken. The material and legal services they provide, however, are as significant as the spiritual contributions, since the stomach must be full and the body sheltered before spiritual or other counseling can be effective.

A recent religious group interested in jails, prisons, and ex-offender groups grew out of the Watergate scandals. One of the conspirators found religion in prison and began the Prison Fellowship after his release, using his newly written book as a guideline.[3] It is now a well-organized group, with the states divided into areas in which the local directors organize groups as the opportunities permit. Beginning in 1975, this Prison Fellowship, led by Charles W. Colson, had become popular.

## JOHN HOWARD SOCIETIES

It is appropriate to discuss the societies named for John Howard (1726–1790), since he was the first famous prison reformer. Howard's interest in prisons began when he was on his way to Portugal in 1754; his ship was captured by a French privateer, and those on board were treated with great severity in confinement at Brest. He was permitted to return to England on parole to negotiate an exchange. In 1773, he became high sheriff of Bedford and visited the jail, where people were detained for months until they paid their own fees for the jail. His first act was to apply for a salary for the jailer. From that time on, he devoted himself to penal reform. In 1774, he helped obtain passage of legislation liberating all prisoners on whom the grand jury had failed to find a true bill, and compensating the jailer for his fees. He also worked for another act requiring justices of the peace to see that walls and ceilings of jails were scraped and whitewashed once a year, that rooms were regularly cleaned and ventilated, that underground dungeons should be used as little as possible, and that measures should be taken to preserve the health of the prisoners. Howard printed the new legislation and distributed it at his own cost.

In 1775, Howard toured prisons in Scotland and Ireland, France, the Low Countries, and Germany. Two years later he wrote *The State of the Prisons in England and Wales with Preliminary Observations and an Account of Some Foreign Prisons,* and as a consequence of this work, a bill was drafted for the establishment of penitentiary houses for solitary confinement, labor, and religious instruction. In 1781, Howard went to Denmark, Sweden, and Russia, and in 1783, to Spain and Portugal. In 1789, he made his last jour-

---

[2] William S. Garmon, *Who Are the Criminals?* (Nashville, Tenn.: Broadman Press, 1968).

[3] Charles W. Colson, *Born Again* (Old Tappan, N.J.: Chosen Books, 1976).

Part of the Salvation Army's rehabilitation of homeless men who restore articles for sale. Courtesy of the Salvation Army.

ney, visiting St. Petersburg and Moscow. He died on January 20, 1790, of camp fever and was buried on the road to St. Nicholas.

During his imprisonment in France, Howard gained sufficient evidence to show that hundreds of English prisoners had perished because of poor treatment. Thirty-six were buried in a hole in Dinan in one day.[4] While he was not an advocate of luxury in prison (he would have had no meat for criminals except, possibly, on Sundays), he felt that every prisoner should have a pound and a half of good household bread a day and a quart of good beer.[5]

Several John Howard Societies have been organized in the English-speaking world. They are particularly prominent in England and Canada, and there is a significant organization in Chicago. The first Howard Association was founded in 1866.

Elizabeth Fry (1780–1845) was the chief promoter of prison reform in Europe after Howard. The result was that Elizabeth Fry Societies grew in the English-speaking world to serve women prisoners.

Currently, the John Howard League and the Elizabeth Fry Association have enjoyed a special relationship with the Home Office in England, especially with the prison commissioner. The result has been a vast improvement in prison conditions in England.

[4] D. L. Howard, *John Howard: Prison Reformer* (London: Christopher Johnson, 1958), p. 25.

[5] John Howard, *The State of the Prisons* (London: J. M. Dent, 1929), p. 41.

England still imprisons people for debts. In 1962, a special open prison, Drake Hall, was established for debtors. The majority of these people had not kept up with installment payments. There are between 5,000 and 6,000 persons in prison as debtors in England, Canada, and elsewhere.

## PRISONERS' AID AND STATE SOCIETIES

Prisoners' aid associations have been prominent in assisting discharged prisoners in readjusting to society. Their primary help is in counseling and job-finding, and some financial aid is also generally available. Several state societies perform the functions of prisoners' aid societies, but most focus on improvement of corrections from the public and political standpoint. hese voluntary correctional services agencies have contributed much to the improvement of corrections in America.

The Correctional Service Federation—U.S.A. was established in 1963 with headquarters in Milwaukee; it is composed of approximately 25 voluntary correctional services agencies.[6] It is an affiliate of the American Correctional Association and a member of the International Prisoners' Aid Association, which has consultative status with the Section on Social Defense of the United Nations. A brief summary of some of the voluntary agencies working within the states might be helpful.

### California

The Jewish Committee for Personal Services was established in 1921 in Los Angeles to maintain contact with the Jewish offender and his family and the Jewish community. The agency is involved with prison and parole officials and helps with realistic release plans. After the ex-offender's release to the community, the agency provides counseling, group therapy, and clinical services, and makes referrals for vocational counseling and job-finding.

The Northern California Service League was established in 1948 in San Francisco to serve the northern part of California. Receiving 80 percent of its budget from the United Bay Area Crusade, the league focuses mainly on the San Francisco County Jail. Its services are broader, however, and include casework and therapeutic services. Direct financial aid is limited.

### Delaware

The Correctional Council of Delaware has operated in Wilmington since 1920. Funded by the United Community Fund of Northern Delaware, it is staffed by professionals in the field of corrections. The council provides direct service to persons awaiting trial while serving in prison, to persons on

[6] Correction Service Federation—U.S.A., Room 300, 311 S. Juniper Street, Philadelphia, Pa. 19107. International Prisoners' Aid Association, University of Louisville, Louisville, Kentucky 40292.

probation and parole, and to those who are released from custody without supervision. A halfway house (308 West Residence) is maintained for ex-offenders to provide individual and group treatment. The council takes positions on legislative bills and provides information to interested political leaders.

### District of Columbia

The Bureau of Rehabilitation of the National Capital Area was established in Washington, D.C., in 1930 to provide service to persons in conflict with the law. Its primary source of funds is the United Giver's Fund, private foundations, and some governmental funds. The bureau provides casework services to juveniles and adults, and its prerelease planning, follow-up casework, and related services after release to the community have been most significant. Originally, the bureau prepared case histories and reports for the governmental agencies, including the United States Board of Parole, but this function was later taken over by governmental programs. The bureau also operates three halfway houses.

Efforts from Ex-Convicts (EFEC), opened in 1968 in Washington, D.C., develops self-help programs for ex-convicts and juveniles. Its work is directed toward helping ex-offenders find satisfactory jobs and solve problems accompanying re-entry into society. The organization provides counseling in budgeting, holding jobs, and other matters.

### Georgia

The Brotherhood of New Hope was started in 1966 by an ex-inmate and a group of interested businesspeople to help offenders being released from prison. In 1967, the Salvation Army assumed charge of the service. Located in Atlanta, the agency is approved by the Georgia Board of Pardons and Parole to assist men and women in planning and assisting in their release.

### Hawaii

The John Howard Association of Hawaii was founded in 1958. Supported by Aloha United Fund, the association works primarily in the preparole area of corrections.

### Illinois

The John Howard Association of Illinois was begun in 1901 and is headquartered in Chicago. In 1969, it became statewide with a professional staff in the correctional field. Ex-offenders Anonymous was established, and many research programs have been completed recently.

P-A-C-E, Inc., which stands for Public Action in Correctional Effort, was organized in 1960 in Indianapolis, supported by the United Fund of Greater Indianapolis. It provides extensive direct service programs for inmates, ex-inmates, and their families. A prime goal of the organization is the improvement of institutions and better treatment of prisoners in the entire Indiana Correctional System. Volunteer task forces meet with inmates at the Indiana State Reformatory once a week for programmed periods of twelve weeks before their appearance before the parole board or their release from confinement. P-A-C-E initiated an Inmate-Outmate program in 1967 with volunteers to assist inmates in reintegration into the community. The organization has arranged for Dale Carnegie courses in the institutions.

**Maryland**

The Prisoners' Aid Association of Maryland was organized in 1869, but its history goes back to 1829 when the rector of St. Paul's Episcopal Church in downtown Baltimore provided food, clothing, and shelter to men leaving the penitentiary. Supported by the United Appeal, it is located in Baltimore and provides assistance to offenders who apply for it. The association is concerned with legislation, inspects the jails as an official function for the state of Maryland, maintains a halfway house, and provides professional casework services. It established TARGET (Toward a Rightful Goal, Employment Together) as a self-help organization composed of ex-offenders and nonoffenders working jointly to solve problems facing releasees. Among the residences it maintains are Dismas House, a halfway house; Christian Outreach of Maryland, a resident treatment center for alcoholics and drug addicts; Friends House, a halfway house for problem cases; and St. Bernardine's Youth Center, an organization sponsored by parents to serve unemployed dropouts and problem youth.

**Massachusetts**

The Massachusetts Correctional Association was established in 1889 as the John Howard Industrial Home; later it became the John Howard Association, and then the United Prison Association of Massachusetts in 1940. Its name was changed to the Massachusetts Correctional Association in 1967. In 1976 it became the Crime and Justice Foundation, with new offices at 31 St. James in Boston. One of the most active correctional associations in the country, this organization provides services to inmates and ex-inmates, produces excellent publications on current issues in the field of corrections, has a legal service program, and is active in promoting legislation.

## Minnesota

The Correctional Service of Minnesota is active in promoting legislation and in developing juvenile and adult correctional programs in Minnesota. Most of the service it provides is advisory rather than direct service to inmates or ex-offenders.

## Missouri

The St. Louis Bureau for Men was organized in 1925 to work with the problems of nonfamily and transient men. It has also been involved in recommending reform legislation.

## New Jersey

The Morrow Association on Correction was originally organized in Trenton to provide rehabilitative service for inmates in and those released from the Middlesex County Workhouse and the Mercer County Workhouse, although its purpose now includes the entire state of New Jersey. It offers direct service to inmates, including plans for economic and social adjustment after release, aid to the offender and his family in carrying out the plan, and a visiting and counseling service. Research and informational activities are a part of the program. The staff includes professional social workers and case aides.

## New York

The Correctional Association of New York was founded in 1844 as the Prison Association of New York, and its present name was adopted in 1961. The association's main purposes are to aid and assist individuals being detained for trial, to assist discharged inmates, to improve conditions existing within prisons, and to improve the administration of criminal justice with the state. The original women's division was headed by Isaac T. Hopper, who left the association before the Civil War. The women's division continues as the Women's Assistance to Prisons Association. Under the direction of Dr. E. C. Wines as corresponding secretary, the organization initiated and promoted the first national congress on penology, which met in Cincinnati in 1870. This congress is now organized as the American Correctional Association, the name having been changed from the American Prison Association in 1954 at the Philadelphia meeting. Since 1846, the Correctional Association of New York has made legislative recommendations and has influenced New York law regarding corrections. Incorporated in the Association is a direct services employment and release bureau, a family service bureau, and other services.

The Osborne Association, Inc., was founded in 1916. Its Bureau of Institutional Services is directed toward making prisons and other correctional institutions more effective. Its Bureau of Vocational Placement assists in placing ex-prisoners into the community.

The Quaker Committee on Social Rehabilitation began in 1956 to offer a program for women at the New York City House of Detention through prerelease services, counseling, group discussion, and other services. In December 1966, the committee opened Baird House as a therapeutic community for twenty female narcotic addicts.

Special Social Services began in 1943 to serve the children, wives, and mothers of offenders. Individuals in very poor financial circumstances became the caseload of Special Social Services.

## Ohio

The Correctional Association of Ohio was founded in 1954, originally as a prisoners' aid society. It provides casework services, employment counseling, and emergency relief.

## Pennsylvania

The Pennsylvania Prison Society was founded in 1787, originally as the Philadelphia Society for Alleviating the Miseries of the Public Prisons. The name was changed to the Pennsylvania Prison Society in 1887. This society initiated the first penitentiary in the world in 1790. Its members then included Dr. Benjamin Rush and Benjamin Franklin. The association has been active in legislative procedure and publishes *The Prison Journal.*

The Personal Aid Bureau of Jewish Family Service of Philadelphia provides assistance for released prisoners.

## South Carolina

The Alston Wilkes Society was founded in 1962. It operates in about twelve of the state's 46 counties to assist inmates released from prison to reintegrate into the community. It operates a halfway house in Columbia. With 6,000 paid members generating 2,000 volunteers working throughout South Carolina, the Alston Wilkes Society is the largest "prisoners' aid" society in the world.

## Virginia

The Offender Aid and Restoration (OAR) program was started in 1971 to bring assistance to the jail in Richmond. It has since gone statewide and works with jails, prisons, and ex-offenders in the community throughout Virginia.

## NATIONAL SOCIETIES

The American Correctional Association was an outgrowth of the National Congress on Penitentiary and Reformatory Discipline held in Cincinnati, Ohio, in 1870. For a long time it was called the American Prison Association, but the group's name was changed at the Philadelphia meeting in 1954 to the American Correctional Association to reflect broader correctional interests than just institutions. It represents generally the power structure in American corrections today, primarily the long-term adult institutional corrections in the United States. It publishes the *American Journal of Corrections.*

The National Council on Crime and Delinquency, formerly the National Parole and Probation Association, is headquartered in Hackensack, New Jersey. It is generally considered to be the professional organization, as opposed to the power structure, in the field of corrections. It publishes *Crime and Delinquency, NCCD News,* and the *Journal of Delinquency Research.* The NCCD has a system of Citizen's Councils in eighteen states which provide leadership for corrections. There are state councils in California, Connecticut, Georgia, Hawaii, Illinois, Indiana, Iowa, Maryland, Massachusetts, Michigan, New Mexico, New York, Oklahoma, Oregon, Pennsylvania, Texas, Washington, and West Virginia. Ohio has an Ohio Committee on Crime and Delinquency which cooperates closely with the councils. The National Council maintains an NCCD Information Center in Hackensack, New Jersey, and an NCCD Research Center at the University of California at Davis.

The American Society of Criminology was founded originally as the California Correctional Association in 1946, but became the American Society of Criminology in 1956. A small organization, it has attempted to attract university professors and met with the American Association for the Advancement of Science in the late 1950s to the middle 1960s. It publishes *Criminology: An Interdisciplinary Journal.*

## EX-OFFENDER GROUPS

In several places on the West Coast and some communities as far east as Kansas City, Kansas, Bill Sands has established centers manned by ex-prisoners to assist other ex-prisoners to adjust to society. Called the Seven Steps Program, it has many similarities to the Twelve Steps of Alcoholics Anonymous. The seven steps are these:

1. Facing the truth about ourselves and the world around us, we decided we needed to change.
2. Realizing there is a Power from which we can gain strength, we have decided to use that Power.

Ex-con Charles McGregor rapping with new ex-offenders needing help.
Courtesy of The Fortune Society.

3. **E**valuating ourselves by taking an honest self-appraisal, we examined both our strengths and our weaknesses.

4. **E**ndeavoring to help ourselves overcome our weaknesses, we enlisted the aid of that Power.

5. **D**eciding that our freedom is worth more than our resentments, we are using that Power to help free us from those resentments.

6. **O**bserving that daily progress is necessary, we set an attainable goal toward which we could work each day.

7. **M**aintaining our own freedom, we pledge ourselves to help others as we have been helped.[7]

The first letters of the steps spell FREEDOM.

In 1963, 93 inmates at the Kansas State Penitentiary organized the Seven Steps Program. Many independent organizations subsequently orga-

[7] See Bill Sands, *My Shadow Ran Fast* (Englewood Cliffs, N.J.: Prentice-Hall, 1964), p. 205.

nized similarly, such as the Seven Keys to Freedom in South Carolina in the late 1960s. Today, the Seventh Step Foundation has national headquarters in Cincinnati, operates outside facilities in fourteen states, and has 34 organizations with prisons throughout the country. Observers hold different views as to the effect of this program. Undoubtedly, many persons have been helped by it. On the other hand, some professional prerelease guidance center personnel have been identified with it, rather than with their own program, in places where both function.

The New Careers Development Center, under the direction of Prof. Frank Riesman of New York University, is developing a design for subprofessional or semiprofessional vocational employment for the poor in career patterns, many of them in the law enforcement and correctional areas. The Social Action Research Center in Oakland, California, was adopted as the new name for the New Careers Development Organization in that area.

The Fortune Society was established in 1967 to create a greater public awareness of prison systems in America today.[8] This society sends out teams of speakers (ex-convicts) to talk to school, church, and civic groups and make presentations on radio and television. Relating first-hand experience of prison life appears to be the best approach to creating public awareness of the needs involved. Direct services are provided for ex-offenders through counseling and assistance in finding jobs.

It is apparent that ex-offender groups for purposes of self-help have become a general social movement.[9] The intensive study in the Chicago area indicated that there were thirty to forty groups, although the percentage of ex-offenders joining these groups was relatively small.[10] The fundamental goals of all these groups have been (1) positive self-identity, (2) self-help, and (3) ultimate change of the social system.

Junior Chambers of Commerce and some other civic organizations have been interested in the correctional problems. Several prisons have chapters of the Junior Chamber of Commerce. Many civic clubs, such as Kiwanis, have projects concerned with juvenile institutions at the local or state level. The Exchange Club has a Crime Prevention Week each February, during which their noon programs concern crime, law enforcement, and corrections.

## LEGAL AID SOCIETIES

Private legal aid societies practice not only in the courts but also in the prisons, where cases may be reviewed with intent to request new trials. Some

---

[8] The Fortune Society, 29 E. 22nd Street, New York, N.Y. 10010.

[9] Patrick D. McAnany, Dennis Sullivan, William Kaplan, and Edward Tromanhauser, *Final Report: The Identification and Description of Ex-Offender Groups in the Chicago Area* (Chicago: University of Illinois at Chicago Circle Center for Research in Criminal Justice, August 1974), p. 59 (mimeographed).

[10] *Ibid.*, p. 63.

prison administrators and prison personnel have seen cases returned to court and prisoners released because due process had not been followed even though they were convinced on the basis of other evidence that the offender had, in fact, committed a crime. The concern of legal aid associations, of course, is with due process.

Probably the most important decision concerning prisoners already institutionalized was the *Gideon* v. *Wainwright* decision of March 18, 1963, in which the right to counsel was guaranteed to everyone. Before this, the Betts Rule had prevailed, by which counsel was guaranteed only in capital cases and in noncapital cases involving special circumstances. The Sixth Amendment had been interpreted only as the right to procure counsel, but groups of concerned citizens and lawyers gradually moved this interpretation toward the direction of guarantee of counsel. It is probably true that legal aid on a private basis has existed in this country since the first law office was set up in the colonies. Charitable organizations were started in early colonial times that attempted to provide legal services to the poor, but their services were sketchy. One of the earliest was the German Society, which provided legal protection for German immigrants, who were often targets for unscrupulous and illegal business practices.[11]

By 1910, a Legal Aid Society was in operation in every major city in the eastern United States. The Boston Bar, the University of Pennsylvania, the Jewish Federated Charities in Cleveland, a law school in Denver, and other programs had been started. In 1910, the Board of Public Welfare in Kansas City was created to supervise probationers and parolees, and a full-time attorney and several assistants were appointed to look after the legal needs of the poor. In 1911, thirteen legal aid societies met in Pittsburgh to discuss common problems, and they created a liaison with the European Legal Aid Society. In 1912, the National Alliance of Legal Aid Societies was formed in New York City with the support of the Carnegie Foundation. The Legal Aid Societies met in Philadelphia in 1922 and created a National Committee on Legal Aid Work. The following year in Cleveland, representatives of 23 legal aid associations formed the National Association of Legal Aid Organizations. The present National Legal Aid and Defenders Association has its headquarters in Chicago.

## THE AMERICAN CIVIL LIBERTIES UNION

The American Civil Liberties Union was not created as a new organization but grew from a philosophy of groups organized to fight militarism at the beginning of World War I. In the fall of 1914, Jane Addams, founder of Hull House in Chicago; Paul Kellogg, editor of *The Survey;* Oswald Villard, editor of the *New York Evening Post* and *The Nation;* and Nicholas Murray

---

[11] Reginald Herbert Smith, *Justice and the Poor* (Boston: Merrymount Press, 1919), p. 3.

Dr. Karl Menninger, famed psychiatrist, and David Rothenberg, founder and Executive Director of The Fortune Society, New York City.
Courtesy of The Fortune Society.

Butler, president of Columbia University, created the American League for Limitation of Armaments to oppose American involvement in World War I. By the end of 1915, they invited several groups to unite in the Anti-Preparedness Committee, which changed its name within a short time to The American Union against Militarism, with a membership of 1,500. The organization's work was successful, but when Germany announced she was resuming unrestricted submarine warfare in February 1917, the United States broke off diplomatic relations. The organization was quickly activated as the Bureau for the Maintenance of Civil Liberties, replacing the Bureau of Conscientious Objectors, which had been a special committee within the American Union against Militarism. Roger Baldwin, a graduate of Harvard and a probation officer in St. Louis, headed the Bureau of Conscientious Objectors and the subsequent Bureau for the Maintenance of Civil Liberties. He continued to work with the organization even though the United States went to war with Germany in 1917, and continued working with it for another 52 years. In 1917, the organization renamed itself the Civil Liberties Bureau and concerned itself primarily with the freedom to think and speak, as well as pacifism. The worst effect of World War I on the United States, according to this group, was its official legitimatization of persecution of the different, which became the primary concern of the organization.[12] In 1920, the Civil Liberties Bureau changed its name to the American Civil Liberties Union and declared as its primary goal the release of state and federal wartime prisoners.

At the present time, the American Civil Liberties Union is a private organization chartered by the state of New York with headquarters at 156 Fifth Avenue, New York City. By 1966, its membership was 95,000 and it had an operating budget of $1.4 million. The American Civil Liberties Union works in all states except Maine, New Hampshire, West Virginia, South Carolina, Montana, North Dakota, South Dakota, Colorado, and Idaho. It has assumed the task of defending the civil liberties of minority groups, communists, religious groups, and others in cases where defense of civil liberties seems especially important. For example, the American Civil Liberties Union defended John Thomas Scopes in the famous trial in which the Tennessee schoolteacher was tried for teaching evolution in a public school. The ACLU defended Sacco and Vanzetti, who were arrested for robbery and murder but who some thought may have been framed because of their political views. In the area of censorship, the ACLU waged a court battle that culminated in 1933, when Federal Judge John Woolsey of New York issued an anticensorship decision that admitted James Joyce's novel *Ulysses* to the United States. In 1938, the ACLU took Mayor Hague's denial of free speech and assembly in Jersey City to the Supreme Court, and the subsequent decision ended all municipal bans on peaceful public assembly. In 1943, the ACLU fought for the rights of Jehovah's Witnesses, so that the Supreme Court reversed its previous ruling that schoolchildren could be expelled for refusing to salute the flag. In 1952, President Truman attempted to seize the nation's steel plants in a dispute between the companies and the union, but the ACLU vigorously protested that it was an extremely dangerous interpretation of executive authority, and the Supreme Court ruled the attempted seizure illegal.

The ACLU has helped to bring about several important Supreme Court decisions in the area of criminology and corrections. *Gideon* v. *Wainwright,* in which Abe Fortas was the ACLU lawyer who presented the case to the Supreme Court, resulted in a decision that made counsel mandatory for indigent defendants in all felony cases (1963). In the *Kent* case, the Supreme Court indicated that juvenile court cannot transfer a youth to adult court for criminal trials without certain procedural safeguards. It had the effect of requiring attorney for the juvenile at the time of the waiver. In the *Gault* case, in which Justice Abe Fortas wrote the majority decision, the right of counsel was upheld in the juvenile court. The *Escobedo* decision

---

[12] Charles Lam Markman, *The Noblest City* (New York: St. Martin's Press, Inc., 1965), p. 16.

reinforced the right to counsel and ruled out confessions made without counsel. The *Miranda* case upheld the defendant's right to know and understand the proceedings; law enforcement officers now have to read to the defendant prior to questioning cards which warn him of all constitutional rights, and they must clearly warn him of his right to remain silent (Fifth Amendment).

In 1965, the ACLU committed itself to opposing the death penalty, and it has since brought several cases to court. In 1967, a case was brought in Jacksonville when then-Governor Kirk signed death warrants for fifteen prisoners at the Florida State Prison at Raiford. The case was brought on the basis that most court actions were against indigent blacks and, therefore, many death sentences are based on racial bias. Judge William McRea, Jr., indefinitely stayed the executions.

The ACLU has also attacked wiretapping, with the result that Rhode Island and Alaska have banned it. In some areas, chronic alcoholism has been considered to be a disease rather than a crime, and the ACLU has contended this view in North Carolina and Washington, D.C. The stop-and-frisk approach to law enforcement, according to the ACLU, violates constitutional protections against illegal search and seizure, and it won its cases against this approach in Michigan and Illinois.

Recently, the ACLU has questioned chaplaincy programs, not on the basis of the concept of the chaplain, but on the basis of the First Amendment that protects the free exercise of religion and bars efforts to establish religion. The support by the government of chaplains in the military or elsewhere is questioned.[13]

Other current concerns of the ACLU include religious freedom, strict gun control on the basis that the right to keep and bear arms refers to a well-regulated militia, welfare with respect to Aid to Families of Dependent Children where "unsuitable homes" exist, freedom of speech in universities and elsewhere, the fight against vagrancy statutes where "no visible means of support" becomes a crime, and gaining release of young male prisoners subject to sexual attacks by their cellmates on the basis of "cruel and unusual punishment." Probably the most dramatic relatively recent work is what the ACLU refers to as "Operation Southern Justice," a campaign to restructure the all-white system of justice in the Deep South. In 1964, the Lawyers Constitutional Defense Committee was developed to provide legal defense to civil rights movements and the black community.[14] In the 1970s, ACLU efforts were directed toward prisoners' rights, such as supporting prisoners' unions as the right to assemble and organize to redress grievances, and supporting prisoners' rights to organize new churches, such as the Church of the New Song (CONS), granted First Amendment

[13] "The Stakes Grow Higher," *44th Annual Report of the American Civil Liberties Union* (New York: ACLU, 1964), p. 39.

[14] Gertrude Samuels, "The Fight for Civil Liberties Never Stays Won," *New York Times Magazine*, June 19, 1966, pp. 14ff.

rights. The Church of the New Song has since disintegrated and disappeared.

## VOLUNTEERS

Volunteers can be used in corrections in many areas.[15] Frequent sources are (1) friends and acquaintances of staff or volunteers, (2) women, (3) the middle class, (4) churches and religious groups, (5) service organizations and volunteer bureaus, (6) well-educated people, and (7) "people-contact" occupations and professions, such as attorneys, teachers, insurance personnel and salespeople, and others who contact the public. A coordinator of volunteers is important for their effectiveness. The coordinator would assist in recruiting and selecting volunteers, make assignments, keep attendance and contact records, maintain the records, expedite communications, and supervise the assessment of the effectiveness of the volunteer program. Volunteers can render casework and group work services, and serve as probation officers, teachers, and sophisticated discussion group leaders.[16] Volunteers in criminal justice now have a national organization.[17]

## SPECIALIZED VOLUNTARY ORGANIZATIONS

There are several specialized voluntary organizations that are contributing significantly to the field of corrections. Some were discussed in Chapter 11, "Special Areas in Corrections," such as those concerned with alcohol and narcotics addiction.

The Association for the Psychiatric Treatment of Offenders, APTO, organized by Dr. Mellitta Schmideberg, has been active in New York City for several years and has now opened offices in London. The publication of APTO is *The Journal of Offender Therapy*.

The Brooklyn Association for the Rehabilitation of Offenders (BARO) was founded and headed by the late Dr. Ralph Banay. Its publication is titled *Corrective Psychiatry*, with the subtitle, *Journal of Social Therapy*.

The Stone-Brandel Center, 1439 South Michigan Avenue, Chicago, actively promotes art in prisons and among offenders in a community-based program. There are many other smaller but active private specialized voluntary organizations contributing to the field of corrections. In ad-

[15] Ivan H. Scheier and Leroy P. Goter, *Using Volunteers in Court Settings: A Manual for Volunteer Probation Programs*, Office of Juvenile Delinquency and Youth Development, HEW (Washington, D.C.: U.S. Government Printing Office, 1969).

[16] Philip Lichtenberg, *The Volunteer in Juvenile Delinquency and Youth Development Programs*, Office of Juvenile Delinquency and Youth Development, HEW (Washington, D.C.: U.S. Government Printing Office, 1967).

[17] National Association of Volunteers in Criminal Justice, P.O. Box 1000, University, Alabama 35486.

dition, several associations of homosexual persons are lobbying for their "civil rights." Their objective is legislation to remove from the criminal statutes any homosexual or other activity between consenting adults in private. One of the foremost such societies is the Mattachine Society, with headquarters in San Francisco.

## PRIVATE JUVENILE TRAINING SCHOOLS

There are approximately 28,000 juveniles in private faculties in America. Many of these schools are exceptionally well regarded, such as Berkshire Farms, Hawthorne Cedar Knolls, Wiltwyck School, Father Flanagan's Boys' Home, and Starr Commonwealth for Boys. These schools and some others provide special help for disturbed youth committed by the juvenile court. Most such facilities are located in the East, and only a few of them cater to severe behavior problems.

The Berkshire Farm for Boys, located in Canaan, New York, is considered to be an excellent school for delinquents and children with severe behavioral problems. Its major goal is to produce new ideas and concepts for the care and treatment of juvenile delinquents that can be used in public training schools. Berkshire Farms has community service caseworkers who work with the boy's family while the child is in the school. These community service workers continue to work with the family and the boy after the boy has returned to his home. Berkshire Farms makes extensive use of group therapy, psychodrama, and other treatment methods.

The Wiltwyck School for Boys, Inc., in Yorktown Heights, New York, is an excellent school in the New York City area for emotionally disturbed youth. This was the school with the orthopsychiatric approach incorporated in the study by McCord and McCord in which the orthopsychiatric approach was compared with the "education, hard work, and discipline" approach.[18] The Wiltwyck School was considered significantly superior.

Hawthorne Cedar Knolls School, Hawthorne, New York, is a good children's institution under the auspices of the Jewish Board of Guardians. The Children's Village, Dobbs Ferry, New York, is another good school for children with behavioral problems. Father Flanagan's Boys' Home, formerly Boys Town, at Boys Town, Nebraska, is a well-known school. Connecticut Junior Republic, Litchfield, Connecticut, accepts children from the juvenile courts. The Starr Commonwealth for Boys at Albion, Michigan, with a branch at Van Wert, Ohio, is an excellent school situated in the Midwest.

Probably one of the largest private training schools for delinquent girls is Villa Loretto School in Peekskill, New York. Opened in 1857, this

---

[18] William and Joan McCord, "Two Approaches to the Cure of Delinquency," *Journal of Criminal Law and Criminology*, 44, No. 4 (November–December 1973), 442–67.

school accepts girls from 16 to 19 years of age without concern for creed or color. After the girls leave Villa Loretto, they are supervised by aftercare workers, all of whom speak Spanish. A clinical services and casework staff serves the girls. The Salvation Army maintains the Wayside Home for Girls, Valley Stream, New York.

There are several private schools for neglected and dependent children in the United States. One of the oldest is the Leake and Watts Children's Home, Inc., in Yonkers, New York. The Leake and Watts Home was established in 1831 and now handles 75 children at any given time. An effort is made to place these children in foster homes with aftercare follow-up and intensive care for emotionally disturbed children. At present, 25 of the 75 children at the school are sufficiently emotionally disturbed so that they cannot use the public schools, which has resulted in the establishment of a campus school to serve these children.

These private schools are all supported by private donations, United Fund plans, and payments by parents or the committing court.

There are several private schools for emotionally disturbed children to which middle- and high-income parents can send their children. The Devereaux Schools, for example, were founded in 1912. They are organized in separate home-school units at Devon, Pennsylvania, and Santa Barbara, California. A summer camp is maintained in Maine. Another good school of this type is known as the Brown School for Exceptional Children in Austin, Texas. Some private military schools are also used for behavioral corrections if the behavioral problem is not based on serious emotional disturbance.

## PRIVATE CONTRACTORS

Contracting for correctional and correctional-related services is not new. Many of the older prisons in this country, including Sing Sing and Auburn, did not have their own food services, but contracted for them in the early 19th century. Some prisons around the world, such as in Saudi Arabia, still contract for food services today. Contracting with private vendors is popular today in the smaller jails and prisons where a cost-benefit analysis would show that maintenance of in-house services would be uneconomical. Advertisements appear in every issue of *Corrections Today*, the official journal of the American Correctional Association, for medical and health services for jails and prisons, food service, planning expansion or new facilities, private financing of new facilities, computer systems, counseling and rehabilitation services, laundry services, and other services, including new building, to be contracted with a private vendor.

Management and correctional services in their entirety have been privately contracted. Florida has contracted with the Jack and Ruth Eckerd Foundation for $2.4 million to operate Florida School at Okeechobee with an average population of 360 juvenile delinquents, as well as with the Florida Ocean Sciences Institute at Pompano Beach and the Marine Institute at several locations to handle juveniles. Misdemeanant probation in Florida and 16 other states is under contract with The Salvation Army. The Salvation Army's National Correctional Services are headquartered in New York (120 W. 14th Street), while the headquarters of the National Correctional Services of the Volunteers of America with many good drug programs is in Baton Rouge, Louisiana (918 North Boulevard). There are many other reputable organizations contracting with jails, prisons, and other correctional programs around the country.

There are private firms that will build and operate jails and prisons for states and other governmental units by contract. The Correctional Corporation of America, for example, headquartered in Nashville, Tennessee, contracts for the full construction and operation of these facilities. One of the officers of this corporation is Terrell Don Hutto, well-known correctional administrator from Texas and Virginia and president of the American Correctional Association for 1984–1986. The advantage a private firm has over a state-operated program is that they can build in accordance with zoning laws without having to concentrate on the political aspects of community resistance against prisons, they can negotiate with fewer restraints, and they can meet the objectives of their contract with fewer concerns about pressure from individual politicians. In summary, contracting with private vendors has always been a part of the correctional scene and, in many instances, it is cheaper and has better cost-benefit analysis when audited for effectiveness.

## SUMMARY

Nearly every progressive and human change in the justice stream has resulted from private pressure. In addition to seeking improvements, the voluntary correctional service organizations support, augment, and complement services offered by public correctional institutions and agencies. The voluntary agency represents unofficial and generous community interest, as opposed to the official authority of the public correctional agency.

A few examples of the contributions private agencies have made are as follows:

1. Helped introduce probation with minor offenders (John Augustus).
2. Fought for bail reform (Arthur L. Beeley).
3. Initiated and supported work release programs for inmates of jails and penitentiaries.
4. Developed halfway houses for paroled and discharged offenders.
5. Promoted release on recognizance programs in lieu of bail.

Recreation at a private boys' school. In the center is "Uncle Floyd" Starr, founder and president emeritus of Starr Commonwealth for Boys, Albion, Michigan. Dr. Larry Brendtro, also a former president, is at the right.
Courtesy of Starr Commonwealth for Boys.

6. Provided broad-scale services to offenders throughout the criminal justice system, including legal services, counseling, employment, and financial aid.

7. Served as law volunteers in many areas.

8. Assisted police departments in improving methods of handling public drunkenness cases and other problems.

9. Created and staffed local and state citizen action programs for improving the justice system.

10. Recommended and supported legislation and provided expert testimony on pending legislation.

11. Prepared and disseminated educational and research data to professionals and lay citizens.

12. Provided field work placement for students in social work, criminology, and other areas interested in corrections.

13. Participated in university classes, seminars, and educational and professional conferences to promote better corrections.

14. Recruited, selected, and trained staff for public and private agencies in the field of corrections.

The private sector of corrections has contributed much toward correctional services and their improvement. Probably one of the greatest contributions of private organizations is the political influence they can bring to bear in a field generally devoid of political advantage in appropriations, program improvement, and resources.

## EXERCISES AND STUDY QUESTIONS

1. *What role have private individuals and groups played in the development of corrections?*

2. *What are some of the outstanding religious organizations that offer correctional services?*

3. *Describe the function of the John Howard Society.*

4. *Describe the function of the Elizabeth Fry Society.*

5. *What are the primary contributions of prisoners' aid associations?*

6. *Identify the Correctional Service Federation.*

7. *What is the general function of voluntary agencies working within the states?*

8. *What contributions to corrections have been made by the Massachusetts Correctional Association?*

9. *How does the Correctional Association of New York function?*

10. *What has been the role of the Pennsylvania Prison Society in the penal field?*

11. *Identify the important national societies in the field of corrections.*

12. *What are some of the societies made up of ex-prisoners, and how do they function?*

13. *Describe the activity of the American Civil Liberties Union in the field of corrections.*

14. *What is the function of legal aid societies?*

15. *How can volunteers be used in corrections?*

16. *What contributions have been made by some of the specialized voluntary organizations?*

17. *What contributions have been made by the private juvenile training schools?*

18. How are private juvenile training schools financed?

19. What are some of the juvenile training schools for emotionally disturbed children of middle and high income?

20. Give some examples of the contributions of private agencies to the field of corrections.

# 16

# CORRECTIONAL ADMINISTRATION

*Administration* refers to the organization and management of the delivery system that brings goods and services to the consumer. Correctional administration refers to the organization and management of a system that brings the basic necessities and the treatment programs of the correctional institutions or agencies to the correctional clients. In all types of administration, the administrator is a facilitator who expedites action. There are systematic approaches to each phase of administration, such as budgeting, program supervision, planning, and many other facets, that are basic to an ongoing successful program. The primary objective of administration is the optimum allocation of resources.

A crucial aspect of any program is its delivery system. Delivery systems are the programs by which services are channeled to the people who need them. Many noble and laudable plans have been made in the field of corrections and in general social welfare, but their implementation has often been frustrated by poor organization, self-interest on the part of persons and groups, or inadequate administration. Good plans at the top frequently fail at the point of delivery. The correctional administrator who knows management and the objectives of the correctional function, and who is in tune with the power-oriented political structure, is in a strong position to effect the delivery of correctional services to the offenders in his charge.

The field of public administration has only recently focused on the internal functioning of administration, the delivery system. Early studies of public administration developed a concern with the structure and function of administrative institutions and the development of new "organs" of administration in response to social need.[1] As a reaction against the organic approach, an institutional approach emerged between World War I and World War II. The concept of POSDCORB (Planning, Staffing, Directing, Coordinating, Reporting, Budgeting) became popular in public administration.[2] The most recent development is the institutional-legal approach, which is concerned with the jurisdiction and functions of the administrative office and administrative officer. Remnants of the previous eras of public administration remain, but something more has been added to make them functional. Public administration has thus evolved through the organic and POSDCORB stages to its present legal-oriented state.[3]

All types of administration appear in modern public administration. Correctional administration differs from other public administration because of the emotional connotations held by many of the "publics" concerning crime and the treatment of criminals. These troublesome connotations do not present themselves to administrators in hospitals, schools, road departments, or other situations.

Public policy is always a tradeoff between social goals and economic goals. Public policy in the field of criminal justice, particularly corrections, is further complicated by the dilemma as to whether the public wants protection through better treatment programs producing fewer offenders or whether the public wants "a pound of flesh" that embitters people and makes them more dangerous.[4]

Organizing, dividing the work into separate bundles, and making use of specialized personnel is important. Assembling resources, including capital, budget, physical facilities, and personnel, such as volunteer help, can bring services to the correctional field faster. Supervising the day-to-day guidance of operations, "leading," and providing effective leadership are so important that many administrators have said that anything that is not inspected routinely does not get done. Controlling or enforcing policies is significant to making the operation conform to plans. The comparison of results against the expectations or standard is an ongoing process. In some cases, such evaluation is called research. In other cases, it is called a "non-delegated activity," one of the activities that the administrator must perform by himself. He must supervise staff meetings, present the budget

[1] Edward W. Bemis, "Local Government in Michigan and the Northwest," in *Johns Hopkins University Studies in Historical and Political Science,* Study V (Baltimore: Johns Hopkins University, 1883).

[2] Leonard B. White, *Introduction to the Study of Public Administration* (New York: Macmillan, 1926).

[3] See Gerald D. Nash, *Perspectives on Administration: The Vistas of History,* Institute of Governmental Studies (Berkeley: University of California Press, 1969).

[4] Joseph R. Rowan, "Progressive Corrections—A Must, Not a Which," *State Government* (Spring 1971), pp. 72–76.

before legislative and executive committees, serve as a public relations representative for the organization, and perform many other duties he cannot delegate to others.

## OBJECTIVES

Administration is the establishment and maintenance of the delivery system so that goods or services get to the consumer with a minimum of dissipation. In the field of corrections, these services consist of the treatment and supervision processes needed to change the behavior of the offender so that he can adjust in an orderly society. Sufficient external controls must be provided to protect society. Adequate internalized controls have to be provided so the external controls can be safely withdrawn.

The basic issue in correctional administration is whether the program should be designed to change behavior or to control behavior. This issue has been central in policy directions in many prisons and correctional institutions. Old-line custodial thinking has too frequently prevailed, with the philosophy of "lock them up and throw the key away!" More progressive institutions have developed the therapeutic community, such as the Minnesota State Training School at Red Wing, the Highfields Institution in New Jersey, and the District of Columbia Correctional Complex at Lorton, Virginia. While this issue of controlling or changing behavior is clearly evident in the case of institutions, it is also present in community-based programs, particularly in parole. The basic behavior of persons successfully discharged from parole and those returned as parole violators has been shown to be essentially similar, but the parole agent's visibility to the public and his supervisors tends to govern his decision making even more than the behavior of the offender. Thus, the parole officer or agent is often placed in the role of a controller rather than a changer.

## IMPLEMENTATION

To implement the objectives of corrections, organization and control through supervision are most important. Some of the basic principles of organization have been well defined by Wilson as follows: (1) similar or related tasks are grouped together, (2) lines between units are clearly defined to facilitate the placing of responsibility, (3) lines of control are clearly established so information is facilitated by regulations that cross lines of control, (4) lateral transmission of information within the organization and supervision by staff officers (those lacking the authority to command personnel engaged in tasks under consideration) should be facilitated by regulations so that the members will not be hampered in the performance of their duties by being required to adhere strictly to channels of command, (5) each individual, unit, and situation is under the immediate control of one person, (6) the span of control is held to manipulatable proportions (approximately six), (7) each task is the duty of some person, (8) supervision is always provided at the level of execution, (9) each assignment carries authority commensurate with the responsibility, and (10) persons to whom authority is delegated are invariably accountable for its use, misuse, or failure to be used (misfeasance, malfeasance, nonfeasance).[5] Excellent guides to management procedures and concepts are available.[6] Basic principles of administration include planning, clarifying objectives, establishing policies, scheduling, and other means of facilitating the operation of the organization.[7]

The American Correctional Association has a *Manual of Correctional Standards,* first published in 1946, covering all correctional programs.[8] Revised in 1959 and in 1966, it is under revision almost continually. Its treatment of the correctional process in the community includes the jail, detention, community correctional institutions, camps, adult probation, parole and other release procedures, and community correctional centers. Treatment of the central correctional administration includes organization, personnel, fiscal management, statistics and records, research, public relations and education, legal rights of all prisoners, community agencies, voluntary service agencies, and citizen participation in correctional programs. The coverage of correctional institutions includes the administrative organization, physical plant, classification, custody and security, employment, discipline, counseling, health and medical services, food services, inmate property control, chaplaincy, education, library services, recreation, inmate activities and privileges, and facilities and programs for youthful offenders. This manual is a useful tool for evaluating correctional programs.

A written administrative code or manual of policies and procedures for all phases of the institutional or agency operation is essential. The manual should set down the policies and the procedures by which they are implemented. All administrative, middle-management, and key personnel should have office copies and disseminate significant materials to the staff in each department. Such a manual assists in implementing the philosophy of corrections of the department or agency.

Computer technology can speed procedures and retrieve information almost instantaneously, thereby helping to make administration and administrative decisions much quicker. The state of Texas, for example, once had a six-week lag in notifying inmates of funds added to their accounts;

[5] O. W. Wilson, *Police Administration* (New York: McGraw-Hill, 1963), p. 35.

[6] See Robert T. Golembiewski, ed., *Perspective on Public Management: Cases and Learning Designs* (Itasca, Ill.: F.E. Peacock, Publishers, 1969).

[7] William H. Newman, *Administrative Action* (Englewood Cliffs, N.J.: Prentice-Hall, 1963), pp. 1–4.

[8] *Manual of Correctional Standards,* 3rd ed. (Washington, D.C.: The American Correctional Association, 1966).

new computer equipment now makes it possible to notify inmates the day after the funds are added to their accounts. Information on each inmate can be divided immediately. For purposes of selecting needed occupations, reducing custody to move inmates outside the walls, programmed budgeting, and performing many other functions, the information retrieval system makes administrative decision making easier because it gives the administrator more information on which to base his decision.

Computer use is not limited to basic data. Cards can be punched for the computer containing opinions and recommendations of counselors, psychologists, and other personnel that transcend the basic data. For example, the general policy in most systems is that anybody who has escaped previously will not be placed outside the walls, but a counselor who believes the policy should not apply in particular case may add his recommendation to the data bank so that the case can be individually considered when the occasion arises. The computer can be systemwide, with terminals at each institution or community office. It can even be nationwide, such as the NCIC (National Crime Information Center), which was established in the FBI in 1968.

Some of the types of computer use are as follows:

A-Computing—Administrative data processing

C-Computing—Calculational computing to work problems

V-Computing—Using the computer as a vehicle to support CAI-assisted instruction (and similar activities)

I-Computing—Supporting information systems, such as those needed for management decision applications or for library automation

T-Computing—Teaching the computer how to carry out processes, use of command and programming languages[9]

The increasing number of automated personal data files collected for different purposes, including the criminal justice system, is beginning to cause concern to correctional administrators.[10] Public Law 93–380, commonly known as the Buckley Amendment, restricts the dissemination of information as an "invasion of privacy," which has been interpreted in some universities as going as far as to prevent professors from posting grades, even by Social Security number. Other "invasion of privacy" laws are also causing concern. Many decisions in the criminal justice system reflect the person's record and result in shorter or longer stays in confinement, which deprives them of "life, liberty, and property without due process of law," in violation of the Fifth and Fourteenth Amendments.

[9] "Time-Sharing Grows at Dartmouth," *Edcom*, 5, No. 2 (March 1970), 4.

[10] W.H. Ware, "Data Banks, Privacy, and Society," abstracted in *Selected Rand Abstracts*, 12, No. 2 (January–June 1974), from the *Rand 25th Anniversary Volume*, November 1973, p. 11.

Correctional administrators now do not really know where they stand with regard to personal records of inmates, and it will take some court decisions to determine in case law what the legislated law means. These automated records can be linked together to obtain individual dossiers by using Social Security numbers. Most files are subject to court seizure, and personal information in public records is accessible to all. Individuals have little or no control, and maintaining privacy in the correctional system has posed a serious problem.

## SUPERVISION OF THE CORRECTIONAL PROCESS

Supervision of the correctional process is most difficult to accomplish and has seldom been adequately achieved. Extensive reports and paper work have been used as a substitute for supervision. The rationale for this is that the central office knows from the reports how many contacts, interviews, probation and parole revocations, institutional misconduct reports, and other statistics on the decision-making process have been done within the department or division.

Much more important is the knowledge of how a correctional worker is handling the cases for whom he is responsible. One of the better methods is to "staff" each case periodically. In mental hygiene clinics and state hospitals, for example, one case is presented to the rest of the staff by the psychologist or psychiatrist or social worker. During the procedure, his colleagues question the diagnosis and procedures step by step. Over a period of months or years, this procedure serves as an in-service training component and helps to determine how effectively the individual presenting the case is dealing with his entire caseload. It is mutually reinforcing, in that the caseworker can learn from the experience, improve his procedures, and be evaluated by the supervisor. Such a procedure is more effective than paperwork.

## PROTECTING THE ADMINISTRATION
## FROM LITIGATION

Writs drawn up by prisoners are a constant concern of institutional administrations. When any prisoner wants to challenge violation of constitutional rights, civil rights, or civil redress for damages, he may appeal to the courts. Whether such an appeal is in the form of a typewritten legal writ or a pencil scrawling on a piece of paper bag does not matter. All writs and appeals to constitutional and civil rights are legitimate. The majority of writs generally involve denial of access to counsel. Frequently they concern delays caused by mail censorship.

In any case, the administrator must take precautions to protect himself against civil suits. One way he can do this is to prepare directives and memoranda regarding legal issues, including denial of access to counsel, cruel and unusual punishments, violation of civil rights under color of law, and other areas. These notices and memoranda should be read at the roll call of each custodial shift and initialed, with the date read, by all department heads. If constitutional or civil rights are then violated, the administrator can show that he has taken reasonable measures to ensure that all persons should comply with the law. The administrator, of course, is still responsible for all activities within his jurisdiction, whether he knows about them or not. The best and safest way for him to avoid trouble is to ensure that he has taken all means possible to disseminate information and orders relating to constitutional and civil rights of prisoners to all his subordinates. Many correctional administrators have placed all their property in their wives' names so that they own nothing and cannot be sued for it. Business pursuit insurance in addition to the administrator's bond is also frequently used for the protection of the correctional administrator.

In many prisons and correctional institutions, the prisoners have had little access to counsel and little assistance by prison officials and personnel to provide legal aid. For too long, the agencies of corrections have been

Inmate mailbox within the Kentucky State Penitentiary for correspondence to the commissioner and governor.
Courtesy of the Kentucky Department of Corrections.

Law Library, State Prison of Southern Michigan at Jackson.
Courtesy of the Michigan Department of Corrections.

enammored of their own rhetoric, and for too long the agencies of law have succumbed to it.[11] In fact, the correctional client has moved from relatively no protection to full protection with new trials, revocations of probation and parole, and similar activities.[12]

In January 1970, the former superintendent of Tucker State Prison Farm in Arkansas, James L. Bruton, was fined $1,000 and given a one-year prison term by Federal Judge J. Smith Henley on charges of brutality against inmates. The prison term was suspended because it would have been a virtual death sentence to send him to the prison.[13] On February 18, 1970, Judge Henley ruled that the conditions in Cummins Prison Farm and Tucker Prison Farm were unconstitutional and he would close them down if they were not improved.

Because of their responsibilities and the money they control, the majority of administrators have to be bonded. Most insurance companies sell an administrator's bond that generally varies from $25,000 up. An admin-

[11] Fred Cohen, *The Legal Challenge to Corrections,* Joint Commission on Correctional Manpower and Training (Washington, D.C.: U.S. Government Printing Office, 1969), p. 105.

[12]*Ibid.,* p. 51.

[13] *NCCD News,* National Council on Crime and Delinquency, New York, 49, No. 2 (March–April 1970), 8.

istrator's bond or a business pursuit policy is desirable for any administrator or supervisor to have, even if he has to pay for it himself.

In the 1950s, the number of writs by prisoners processed through the federal courts ranged between 100 and 200 per year. By the mid-1970s, the number of writs so processed exceeded 13,000. It is not uncommon for a director of a middle-sized state to be under litigation for amounts of around $3 million. Only a few such suits are won by the prisoner-petitioner, but the effort at defense and those that are adjudicated in favor of the prisoner-petitioner are sufficient to place the correctional administrator under apprehension. Some papers critical of the prison systems have even run articles on how to bring a federal suit against prison administrators.[14] Most suits involve alleged violations of the First, Fourth, Fifth, Sixth, Eighth, Thirteenth, and Fourteenth Amendments of the Constitution, as well as civil rights laws. The civil rights laws used most frequently are Title 18, Section 242, of the United States Code, and the Civil Rights Act of 1871 (42 U.S.C. 1983).[15] Title 28, U.S.C., Section 2255, has also been used.

It is advisable for correctional administrators to familiarize themselves with the laws covering various areas. In prisons, the installation of an inmate grievance procedure, whether in-house or an inmate grievance commission on a statewide basis, such as in Maryland, would assist in identifying problems before they get to litigation. Also, it would be advantageous to be familiar with the Model Act for the Protection of Rights of Prisoners developed by the National Council on Crime and Delinquency (NCCD).[16] The focus of these suits and court decisions have been in the direction of ensuring (1) humane treatment, (2) due process, and (3) equal protection before the law.

There are several books on the law that would be of assistance to correctional administrators.[17] Occasionally juveniles, as well, institute suits against administrators of correctional institutions. Consequently, administrators of juvenile programs and institutions must also be acquainted with

[14] Brian Glick and the Prison Law Collective, "The Jail House Lawyer's Manual: How to Bring a Federal Suit against Abuses in Prison," *Prisoner's Digest International*, 3, No. 5 (October 1973), 5, 8.

[15] William D. Leeke, "Some Aspects of the Effects of Inmates' Suits on Correctional Systems," *FBI Law Enforcement Bulletin*, 43, No. 7 (July 1974), 10–15.

[16] NCCD, "A Model Act for the Protection of Rights of Prisoners," *Crime and Delinquency, 18, No. 1 (January 1972), 4–14.*

[17] See Sol Rubin, *The Law of Criminal Correction* (St. Paul: West Publishing Co., 1973); Editorial Staff of the Criminal Law Bulletin, *Criminal Law Digest* (Boston: Warren, Gorham & Lamont, 1970 and annually afterward), together with a subscription to the *Criminal Law Bulletin;* John W. Palmer, *Constitutional Rights of Prisoners* (Cincinnati: W.H. Anderson, 1973); Michele G. Harmann and Marilyn G. Haft, eds., *Prisoners' Rights Sourcebook: Theory, Litigation, Practice* (New York: Clark Boardman Co., 1973); Sheldon Krantz, Robert A. Bell, Jonathan Brandt, and Michael Magruder, *Model Rules and Regulations on Prisoners' Rights and Responsibilities* (St. Paul: West, 1973); Hazel B. Kerper and Janeen Kerper, *Legal Rights of the Convicted* (St. Paul: West Publishing Co., 1974).

the law regarding juveniles.[18] The South Carolina Department of Corrections received a grant from the LEAA to develop information concerning correctional law and released an excellent publication in 1975.[19]

## THE BUDGET PROCESS

The most important single function of administration is the preparation and management of the budget. Managing the budget is one of the most widely recognized means of controlling an organization. The budget is the phase of the total operation that incorporates the resources of the institution, agency, or program. It determines what emphasis will be placed on any part of the correctional process. Whether a budget emphasizes custody or clinical personnel, or provides a balance between the two, will determine the type of program that will be carried on in the correctional facility. Budget preparation emphasizes the realistic objectives of the organization and efficiency in implementing them.

Management people frequently associate the budget with Procrustes from ancient Greek mythology. He was a highwayman with an iron bedstead. People who fell into his hands were placed on the Procrustean bed. If they were too long for the bed, their legs were cut off to fit it, and if they were too short, they were stretched to fit it. Budget-cutting across the board almost indiscriminately by fiscal commissions and officers to make expenditures fit revenue is part of the existence of all public administrators. A well-prepared budget that can be defended on the basis of realistic and logical goals has a better chance of being passed without cutbacks than an idealistic one.

The budget is prepared by the correctional administrator, is sent to the budget director or budget commission, and is then sent to the governor. After each has made changes and the administrator has defended his budget in each instance, the governor presents the total budget to the legislature. Through the appropriation committees, ways and means committees, or whatever their respective names might be, the legislature passes the final budget. Again, the administrator must have defended his budget requests in the legislative committee meetings. The approved budget is then returned to the governor and the state's fiscal officer or budget commission, from where it is allocated to the various departments.

The budget package submitted by the correctional administrator should include (1) a letter of transmittal, (2) the proposed basic budget for the coming year, (3) proposed supplemental programs, and (4) a program

[18] See Samuel M. Davis, *Rights of Juveniles: The Juvenile Justice System* (New York: Clark Boardman Co., 1974); also, Douglas J. Besharov, *Juvenile Justice Advocacy: Practice in a Unique Court* (New York: Practising Law Institute, 1974).

[19] William T. Toal, *Recent Developments in Correctional Case Law* in *Resolution of Correctional Problems and Issues*, Special Issue, Vol. 1 (Summer 1975).

of performance statistics, cost–benefit analysis, or unit costs on the basis of previous experience.[20] Adequate planning to reduce the incidence of unforeseen problems will avoid criticism and subsequent difficulties. There is a tendency for budget directors and budget commissions to ignore asking budgets. Rather, they begin with existing budgetary structures and then consider the additions or improvements in the asking budget. This procedure presses the correctional administrator hard to defend changes in the program if they require additional funds.

The budget process is a long one that takes time and effort. The federal budget process begins when the Bureau of the Budget sends letters to each agency in the first quarter of the calendar year (January to March) identifying major program issues, and the agencies provide the bureau with analytic studies either under way or planned.[21] Between February 15 and July 15, agencies submit programs and financial plans that reflect programs in the president's budget. From March to August, the Bureau of the Budget works with the agencies to prepare program memoranda and analytic studies of finances. From July to September, the administrators of the agencies make final decisions on program. By September 30, the agencies submit to the bureau final programs and analytic studies, programs and financial plans, annual budget, and legislative programs. From October to December, the bureau studies the plans and budgets and submits recommendations to the president. The president presents the budget to Congress in January, and the agencies revise their requests by Febraury 15 to conform to the president's recommendations.

Appropriation requests are submitted to the House Committee on Appropriations, where they are considered and then sent to the Senate, where the Senate Committee on Appropriations considers them. Agency administrators defend the president's budget in these committee hearings. When the appropriation bill is agreed upon by the House and the Senate, it is submitted to the president. When the president signs it, it becomes law. All governmental units, including state, county, and municipal, have generally similar budget procedures.

In recent years, a computerized budget system has become popular. Called the planning-programming-budgeting system (PPBS), it is designed to provide preview and decision-making functions for several years in advance. While the federal government uses a five-year planning base, some businesses and governmental units use longer or shorter periods. The federal government has used PPBS since the Bureau of the Budget issued a directive to that effect in October 1965. It has several advantages, including immediate information for decision making, cost–benefit analysis to mea-

---

[20] Charles N. Kaufman, "The Budget Process: Dollarizing Law Enforcement Planning," *FBI Law Enforcement Bulletin,* September 1969, pp. 12–18.

[21] Ralph Bahn, "The Federal Budget Process," *Public Health Reports,* 84, No. 2 (February 1969), 149–55.

sure the effectiveness of alternative programs, and the ability to handle several alternative programs, one of which may be selected by the participating agency. There are several good references the correctional administrator can read to gain a broad perspective of program budgeting and benefit–cost (or cost–benefit) analysis.[22]

In summary, the budget is the best way for administrators to manage their organizations. Through the budgetary processes of matching revenues and expenditures and identifying the most effective ways to implement programs, the administrator gains control of his agency. It is in the budget that the realistic objectives of an organization are translated into programs and that "lip service" is eliminated. Within the correctional department, institution, or agency, a business manager or comptroller may do most of the work in fiscal management, but it is the administrator who is responsible for the organization and who contributes to the policy making that is reflected in the budget. Over a period of years, individual decisions by the administrator tend to shape the direction of the organization. They may show in a correctional institution, for example, either in an emphasis on custody, an emphasis on treatment, an emphasis on education and training of personnel, or in any other of a variety of policies.

## IMPROVING THE PROGRAM

Improving the program refers to recruitment, selection, training, performance ratings, and elimination of personnel. In correctional systems, 70 to 85 percent of the budget goes into personnel. Fifteen to 30 percent of the budget goes into physical facilities, with more going into these phases in institutions and less going into office space in community-based corrections. When 70 to 85 percent of the budget goes into personnel, then any improvement of program has to be based in personnel.

In 1968, the United States Employment Service in cooperation with the American Correctional Association established the National Registry for Corrections. This registry is an employment service for persons who want jobs in corrections and correctional administrators who need personnel. It operates through the state employment agencies.

Recruitment in the better correctional programs has been based on the establishment of minimum standards of education and both written and oral examinations. Existing staff can be encouraged to go to school. At the lower levels, correctional officers and operational staff attend junior colleges. Minimum standards of training can be established in any correctional system. A basic performance evaluation is important to effective administration. Personnel policies with regard to vacations, fringe benefits,

---

[22] For example, Harley H. Hinrichs and Graeme M. Taylor, *Program Budgeting and Benefit–Cost Analysis* (Pacific Palisades, Cal.: Goodyear Publishing Co., 1969), p. 420.

and dismissals are also important. The often-quoted statement by Austin MacCormick, "I can run a good correctional program in an old red barn," reflects the emphasis placed on personnel.

William Nagel wrote a book about *The New Red Barn,* which reported on new correctional institutions opened in the past decade, some of them in old stores and other buildings renovated for the purpose, but with the emphasis on good personnel.[23] Any administrator of programs has to make decisions as to whether to put his money into the horses or into the barn. While both are necessary, no barn ever won a horse race! This general principle is true whether the administrator is running a prison, a university, a military force, a football team, or a factory.

## Recruitment

After the basic policies of the correctional institution or agency have been established, recruitment of new personnel should proceed in accordance with the policy. The first screening must involve the candidates' paper credentials.

When a minimum educational level is set at high school graduation or the minimum requirements for a profession or specialty, then further screening is needed. Persons with greater emotional problems than the correctional clients with whom they are to work should be eliminated. A written examination can provide considerable information about prospective personnel. An objective true-false or multiple-choice test can provide an index of the candidate's basic knowledge of facts in society, the field of corrections, legal procedures, civil rights, and other factual information related to the field. An essay part of the examination can establish hypothetical situations with which the candidate might work, and the nature of his replies will provide information as to his social orientation and his ability to communicate in writing.

An oral examination for everybody is always desirable. Candidates may have physical handicaps, oral communication handicaps, and other factors that would prevent them from being effective in a correctional job. Some excellent people have mannerisms that arouse the suspicion of inmates, probationers, and parolees as to various qualities that may vary from the norm expected in American culture.

After this screening, a period of employment on probation may confirm or counter the decisions. The screenings can determine whether the candidate shall be made a permanent employee.

This screening process will sound unrealistic to many correctional administrators who have gone for months with vacant positions and no applicants. Experience in related fields, such as law enforcement, have indi-

[23] William G. Nagel, *The New Red Barn: A Critical Look at the Modern American Prison* (New York: Walker and Co., for the Institute of Corrections, The American Foundation, Philadelphia, 1973).

cated that when the requirements are raised, people are rejected. When the institution or agency is willing to search for applicants, a sufficient number of them can be recruited to keep the program going. Then, as the program improves, a moral factor and identification with an up-and-coming organization produces more and more applications. There is no need to operate a program with "warm bodies," because they do not contribute to the team effort.

### Retention

Retaining good staff is necessary over a long time in building an effective organization. Selective retention is necessary. While it is difficult to identify people who should be transferred or eliminated and then tell them the decision, this weeding-out process is basic to the building of effective organization. There are ways of accomplishing it that reduce the traumatic effects for the individual concerned. In many cases, a transfer to a job that better fits his capabilities might be the best way. In some cases, however, severance by retirement or dismissal is essential to the effective operation of the correctional institution or agency.

Salary increments should never be "across the board." Salary increments should be tied in with education, self-improvement, and longevity. Education and self-improvement are obvious. Longevity should be included because a person good enough to keep but not good enough to promote should be provided some incentive.

Retirement programs comparable with or superior to the Social Security program should be instituted. In this modern day, pension plans and Social Security are part of the fringe benefits of any job, and, in turn, assist in recruiting and in retention of good employees.

### In-Service Training

Initial training for new personnel is essential. As a matter of fact, not only correctional officers but teachers, psychologists, or whoever works at the institution should go through the initial training period. In this way, a knowledge of institutional procedures and the institution itself can be acquired and new probation or parole officers can be oriented regarding police procedures in their area, the employment situation, other social agencies and community resources, and the policies of their organization.

Academy programs generally train new personnel in larger systems, and short-term in-service training programs are provided in some systems, but most systems have no formal in-service training or academy at all. In these cases, the new employee simply learns by observation and responding to demand. The academy or staff college as in Canada is essential for moving new personnel into a functioning organization.

Community and junior colleges are potentially helpful. With 1,000 community and junior colleges in America, there are not many correctional institutions or agencies that are not within commuting distance of such an educational institution. In law enforcement, a related area, over half the junior colleges in America have educational and training programs. Nearly all also have educational programs in corrections. The American Association of Junior Colleges is actively supporting the development of education in corrections.[24] Some junior colleges teach courses in the institution for prison personnel, some teach courses for inmates, and some hold all courses on their own campuses. The use of these programs is essential for the correctional officer or semiprofessional or other staff in the correctional institution or agency. A project was begun in 1975 by the American Association of Community and Junior Colleges to use junior college programs as an alternative to prison sentences.

There were about 900 criminal justice programs in the United States by the mid-1970s in all colleges and universities, about 750 of which were funded by the LEAA. These funds were reduced in the 1976 budget, but interest in criminal justice has kept the programs going by other funding. The use of these programs or of programs that do not have specific correctional content contribute to the improvement of the correctional program by improving the personnel. Consequently, the number of criminal justice programs in American colleges and universities has remained stable through legislative and other support.

In-service training is becoming more and more important. A national survey in 1966 indicated greater support for training conferences, lectures and seminars, institutes and workshops, and general training programs in order to help correctional personnel keep pace with rapidly changing practices and philosophy in the field.[25]

A survey based on the responses of 1,870 correctional personnel in institutions and in probation and parole interviewed during April and May of 1968 indicated that correctional personnel do not think they are doing a good job with the convicted offender.[26] In-service training has the goal of enhancing the ability of the correctional worker to motivate the offender to change his behavior.[27]

Training should encompass *all* members of the staff and should be formulated as much as possible by all members of the staff. As a continuing operation, it should be repeatedly evaluated as to aims, effectiveness, and results.

---

[24] Vernon Fox, *Guidelines for Corrections Programs in Community and Junior Colleges* (Washington, D.C.: American Association of Junior Colleges, 1969).

[25] Charles J. Eichman, "In-Service Training: Corrections Stepchild?" *Public Personnel Review*, January 1969, pp. 21–24.

[26] *Correctional Briefings—Corrections 1968: A Climate for Change*, Joint Commission on Correctional Manpower and Training, Washington, D.C., August 1968.

[27] Elmer H. Johnson, "In-Service Training: A Key to Correctional Progress," *Criminologica*, 4, No. 3 (November 1966), 16–26.

# Work-Study Programs
# and Educational Leaves

Work-study programs are most generally informal arrangements by which an individual may make an agreement with his employers to go to school while working full-time. These arrangements can be referred to as work-study programs when there is time off given for school work.

The use of educational leave is much more general than are work-study programs. Educational leaves permit personnel to take a year or a specific amount of time off for advanced study at a college or university at full or part salary, generally with an agreement to stay with the same institution, agency, or system for a specified number of years after returning to work. In public welfare programs supported by federal funds, educational leaves are built into the system. Departments of corrections and juvenile courts are also beginning to use them more frequently. In fact, the LEEP (Law Enforcement Education Program) of the LEAA (Law Enforcement Assistance Administration) is funding in-service education and educational leaves for personnel in the criminal justice system.

## Conferences and Institutes

Conferences and institutes are helpful in disseminating recent information and in stimulating implementation of new programs. Conferences of one or two days on a regional basis are most effective in providing correctional administrators and top-level practitioners with an identification with the field and knowledge of its trends. Some of the national conferences, particularly the American Congress of Corrections and the National Institute on Crime and Delinquency, provide knowledge also, as well as helpful contacts in the field of corrections. Southern Illinois University at Carbondale has been systematically cataloging information on these conferences and institutes and distributing it to institutions and agencies.[28]

## Physical Plant and Equipment

About 25 percent of the improvement of correctional programs is in physical plant and equipment. Just as money for salary raises should not be "across the board," so should the purchase of equipment and construction of buildings be selective. In the past, some new institutions have been built as carbon copies of old ones because more room is needed. The fact that the old ones were not effective has too frequently been neglected. When an architect designs an institution, he wants to know the services to be provided so that he can build the institution around them. The correctional administrator's correctional philosophy, then, becomes translated into the building. The National Clearinghouse for Criminal Justice Planning and

---

[28] *Inscape*, Southern Illinois University, Carbondale.

This house on state property near the Iowa State Penitentiary was renewed and is used as a work release house for 20 men who work in the surrounding area.
Courtesy of the Iowa Department of Social Services.

Architecture at the University of Illinois was funded by the LEAA starting in 1968 in order to provide technical assistance in planning for the criminal justice system.

Equipment can be used to save time. Office equipment, such as dictating machines, electric typewriters, calculators, and other, similar and related equipment are timesavers. Paper is cheaper than time. Consequently, office supplies and services should be secondary to the time of personnel when budgets are submitted. In correctional institutions and agencies, the new uses of computers will save more time in all areas than many correctional administrators realize. They can be used for property control, accounting of inmates in jobs and other programs, classification and reduction of custody, accounting and payroll procedures, and many other areas. Research is important to assess and evaluate the results of programs. The military services put 15 percent of their budget into research. Operating a prison or correctional agency without research is like operating a business without bookkeeping. In neither case does the operator know his profits and losses, where he has been, or where he is going. Rather, he is operating on faith, hope, and some charity.

Improving correctional programs means education and training of personnel. Better personnel can be recruited, and poorer personnel can be transferred or dismissed. The remaining personnel must be provided in-service training, opportunity for junior college and university work, and exposure to conferences and institutes in order to achieve a meaningful identification with the profession of corrections. With this identification come involvement and good morale. Effective organizations are characterized by this type of identification, pride, and morale.

## CHANGING PROGRAMS

Reforming old-line administrative procedures and policies into newer and progressive ones takes careful and patient planning and execution so as not to destroy the morale of the line personnel.

Several guidelines to help the administrator accomplish such change are as follows:

1. He should not attempt everything at once.
2. He should avoid being a perfectionist.
3. He should not skip over necessary intermediary stages.
4. He should develop a healthy reform climate and a predisposition toward new forms of thinking and behavior.
5. He should restrict preventable harmful consequences.
6. He should avoid blind imitation by remembering that the world is always new.
7. He should accept what he can get, settling for something less rather than spoiling future opportunities or unduly antagonizing opponents.
8. He should use available institutions as far as possible.
9. He should plan each successive stage and evaluate the previous one before total commitment.
10. He should attempt a trial run or confine reforms to a small area before total commitment.
11. He should identify reforms with the familiar and known.
12. He should pay particular regard to feedback.
13. He should provide for self-continuing reforms and permit his original reforms to be superseded.
14. He should act on flexible plans without concealing motives.
15. He should establish a dependable reform administration, whether formal or informal, public or private, large-scale or small-scale.

16. He should balance gains and losses, and he should evaluate mixed results.[29]

An example of delicate administrative decisions might be the implementation of conjugal visits or home furloughs for social reasons. Many conservative correctional workers and citizens resent both. Yet, as has been mentioned earlier, the trend is toward less security and more community participation in corrections. Mississippi and California have formalized the conjugal visit, but many correctional administrators favor home furloughs over the conjugal visit because they focus on the broader social concerns rather than on the more narrow sexual objective. This problem may be the most delicate of recent issues, but there are many others of importance to the correctional administrator and the acceptance of his policies by his staff and the public. Work release, whether or not inmates should be used as teachers, and many other issues must be handled by the correctional administrator in a circumspect manner.

There are several ways to fail. Too frequently, administrators want to keep things calm rather than make progress. A peaceful prison or organization is not necessarily an effective one.

The two most important internal factors that impede progress are recalcitrant veteran staff who find change difficult and entrenched veteran leadership who may find change even more threatening and difficult. Too frequently, the administration wants to "keep the lid on." This is understandable in view of external pressures from a turbulent political climate. Political instability contributes to lack of progress. Scared people play it close to the vest. In the field of corrections, tradition has a way of becoming ingrained in procedure and policy. Precedence is always a good defense in a disturbed situation. Pleas of "too costly," "too time-consuming," "too different from previous practice," and demands for evidence of successful precedence have prevented many correctional programs from attempting innovative and progressive policies. The objective of corrections must be kept in focus for adequate and successful correctional progress. The means by which it is achieved may call for understanding and a broad perspective not previously achieved in a given organization. The correctional administrator needs to provide understanding to risk new policies and demonstrate that they can be based on tangible precedence from the correctional or other fields in order to progress.

To weld a group of people with different backgrounds and different immediate functions toward a single overall objective, such as corrections, requires sensitivity and concern for all the people that make up the organization. Communication with all members, factions, and interests in the organization must be maintained. Any person, faction, or interest not in communication with the administrator reduces the effectiveness of the

[29] Gerald E. Caiden, *Administrative Reform* (Chicago: Aldine Publishing Co., 1969), pp. 204–5. Copyright © 1969 by Gerald E. Caiden. Reprinted by permission of the author and Aldine, Atherton, Inc.

team effort. Conversely, ensuring good communications places considerable responsibility on the administrator.

The most important single factor in improving correctional programs is in selecting an administrator who knows the correctional field and who personifies the correctional philosophy. The administrator can then direct all his functions toward the development of a correctional treatment program.

## CORRECTIONAL EMPLOYEES' UNIONS

Unions of correctional workers, particularly guards' unions, have been strong in some states, like New York, since just before World War II. Although originally concerned with salaries and working conditions, they have become active in policy making beyond the original intent. By 1975, the largest union was the American Federation of State, County, and Municipal Employees (AFSCME), with about 700,000 members, of which more than 20,000 are correctional personnel.[30] This is not the only large union in corrections. Many prisons have several unions, including the prsioners' union. There are seven different unions, for example, at the Wisconsin Correctional Institution at Fox Lake, and Warden John Gagnon has to deal with unions of teachers, nurses, craftsmen, blue-collar and nonbuilding trades, social workers, and the clerical staff, organized in 1975. He anticipates more in the future.

The guards' unions have traditionally been the strongest. In New York, for example, the Correctional Officers' Union is part of the AFL-CIO and is quite popular among the personnel. In the 1950s, the members worked out an agreement with the Civil Service Department that nobody could be appointed warden in New York unless that person had come up through the uniformed service. During the tenure of Commissioner Tom McHugh and Governor Averill Harriman, there was an attempt to broaden the base of these appointments, but nevertheless the original agreement still appears to be stable.

Disputes between the unions and the administration are difficult to handle in the public services. Strikes are undesirable from all viewpoints, leaving binding arbitration the only way left. There are several agencies that deal with arbitration, such as the National Labor Mediation Board and some private arbitrators. The Rhode Island Brotherhood of Correctional Officers, for example, has an agreement with the state to use the American Arbitration Society, headquartered in Boston, which has representatives under contract to mediate in all parts of the country, frequently capable professors in schools of business administration in universities.[31]

[30] "Unionization in Corrections," *Corrections Digest*, 6, No. 18 (September 3, 1975), 6.

[31] *Agreement Between State of Rhode Island and the Rhode Island Brotherhood of Correctional Officers* (Providence: Rhode Island Brotherhood of Correctional Officers, 1973).

Unionization has been viewed as reducing the capacity of the administration to manage the system.[32] Higher salaries, time-and-a-half for overtime during escapes and other emergencies, compensation for call-in and standby time, protection against abuse of extra-duty requirements, scheduling, and many other areas have been affected. The traditional autocratic authority of the administrator in personnel matters has given way to a new system of government by shared decision-making power, negotiation, and review of management decisions.

## THE ADMINISTRATIVE CODE

Clear policy statements for treatment and other procedures are important. A manual of policy and procedures can be developed in looseleaf style under a variety of headings, to be used as a vehicle to communicate these policies and procedures to everyone in the organization. The policies and procedures could be coded with a digit designating the area of concern. For example, a manual of policies and procedures in an institution might be coded as follows:

    1- Administration
    2- Personnel
    3- Custody
    4- Classification
    5- Treatment Program
    6- Records
    7- Business and Accounting
    8- Medical
    9- Maintenance
    10- Industries
    11- Farms
    12- Research

In the community, regarding probation, parole, or other community services, such a manual of procedures might have areas classified as follows:

    1- General Probation or Parole Board Policies
    2- Probation or Preparole Preparation
    3- Probation or Parole Rules
    4- Relationships with Law Enforcement
    5- Relationships with Employers

[32] Hervey A. Juris and Peter Feuille, *The Impact of Police Unions—Summary Report* (Washington, D.C.: National Institute of Law Enforcement and Criminal Justice, LEAA, December 1973), p. 9.

6- Relationships with Other Social and Mental Health Services

7- Use of Jail

8- Revocation Policies and Procedures

9- Coordinating Community Services with Probation and Parole

These are merely suggestions as to possible classification of policies and procedures. The important factor in improving correctional programs is that they be written and be communicated with all members of the organization.

A clear policy must aim toward improving correctional programs. The objective is the treatment of the correctional clients for reentry into society. A hospital administrator does not operate a hospital for the benefit of the hospital, nor a school for the benefit of the school. Neither can a prison or correctional agency be successfully operated for the benefit of the prison staff or the correctional agency.

## SOURCES OF FUNDS

The primary source of funds for prisons and correctional institutions is the appropriation from the legislature or Congress. Generated funds or profits from agriculture and industry most frequently go into the state's General Fund, but sometimes arrangements may be made for the instition to be credited for those funds. Through the 1960s and into the 1970s, there were various acts by which the Department of Labor, the Department of Health, Education and Welfare, the Department of Housing and Urban Development, and other governmental agencies could grant funds to individuals or institutions for special projects. By the 1980s, many of these sources of funds had disappeared. The Department of Health, Education and Welfare was divided into the Department of Health and Human Services and the Department of Education. Private organizations, such as the Ford Foundation, the Stone Foundation, the Edna Connell Clark Foundation, and several others have shown an interest in the correctional field.

In 1980, the National Institute of Justice (NIJ) was created. The National Institute of Corrections (NIC) had been created in 1974. The Bureau of Justice Statistics (BJS) was also created in 1980 to assume the function of collecting statistics for the field of criminal justice, formerly left solely with the FBI. The National Jail Center (NJC) at Boulder, Colorado, was placed under the National Institute of Corrections in 1980. The Office of Justice Assistance, Research, and Statistics (OJARS) was developed in 1980 to serve as a means of transition of functions from the Law Enforcement Assistance Administration, then being phased out, to the newer agencies just mentioned. Technical assistance and some grant funds have become available from the National Institute of Justice and the National Institute of Corrections. Jails would seek such assistance from the National Jail Center.

For the juvenile field, the Office of Juvenile Justice and Delinquency Prevention, created by the Juvenile Justice and Delinquency Prevention Act of 1974, provides some funds and assistance. Private programs and facilities, of course, survive on private contributions and donations.

## INTERSTATE COMPACTS

Interstate compacts are mutual and reciprocal legislation between states that permits them to function together without the "states' rights" restrictions. For example, probationers and parolees who have been convicted in some states can be returned to their home states for purposes of supervision. There are interstate compacts for supervision of probationers and parolees, juveniles, runaways, the mentally disordered, persons on detainers, prisoners as witnesses, and other phases of the criminal justice system.

## PUBLIC RELATIONS

The correctional administrator is a public relations person. The administrator has to interpret the correctional program to the political leadership in various ways, to the news media, and to the general public through civic clubs and church groups. He must be sensitive to the pressures and the questions. Political, economic, and social pressures, in that order, must be accounted for before intrinsic issues in public policy, such as reform and progress in the field of corrections can be meaningfully engaged.

The criminal justice process is somewhat like a marriage in terms of visibility. During the courtship and the marriage ceremony, there is considerable social interest, which diminishes in the long marital adjustment. In criminal justice, the visibility is in the arrest and trial procedures that end with the verdict and the sentence, after which there is a tendency to forget the offender. Yet it is "after the ceremony" that the correctional function occurs. The long rehabilitative process that takes place then has low visibility and constitutes a public relations problem for the correctional administrator.

In no case can the administrator afford to offend the news media. Consequently, the correctional administrator who provides free access to newspeople in almost any way they desire short of impairing the entire operation generally has a more sympathetic press. Experience has demonstrated that a correctional administrator who discusses problems and limitations openly, together with an explanation of objectives, will get help from the news media.

The tenure of top correctional administrators has become quite short in recent years because of political "target practice." In 1971, a survey indicated that of the fifty state correctional directors, 80 percent serve at the pleasure of the governor, which has resulted in a growing class of "roving" correctional administrators who accept jobs in state prison management knowing that they will average 18 months to two years in tenure.[33]

## SUMMARY

The art of administration is dependent upon getting the facts, adjusting to individual personalities, and considering the whole situation. It involves more than a simple step-by-step manual of procedures and regard for "principles of administration." An administrator must have an understanding of people, recognize that colleagues and co-workers are people, and that the prisoners and offenders are people also, with all the feelings and emotions that people have. Most important, the correctional administrator must know and keep in mind the overall objectives of the correctional effort, rather than getting inextricably involved in mundane and immediate matters so that the trees block his view of the forest.

## EXERCISES AND STUDY QUESTIONS

1. *What is the function of administration, and how have the trends in administration patterns evolved?*

2. *What is the basic issue in correctional administration with regard to changing or controlling behavior?*

3. *What do you consider to be some of the principles of administration?*

4. *How can computers help correctional administration?*

5. *How can supervision of the correctional process, particularly casework in the institutions and the community, be supervised?*

6. *How can the administrator protect himself from successful litigation?*

7. *Why is the budget process probably the most important single function of administration?*

8. *Describe the budget process.*

9. *What are some of the problems in improving correctional programs?*

10. *How should correctional workers be recruited?*

11. *What is the role of in-service training and, thereby, junior colleges and universities in improving personnel?*

12. *What is the value of educational leaves in the correctional setting?*

---

[33] "Correctional Administrators Face Increasing Job Insecurity as the Positions Become Hot Seats," *Corrections Digest*, November 12, 1975, p. 1.

13. What is the value of conferences and institutes for the correctional worker and administrator?

14. What is an administrative code? Suggest a rough outline for such a code in an institution and in a community setting.

15. Where are primary sources of funds for correctional services?

16. What is the function of the Office of Justice Assistance, Research, and Statistics (OJARS)?

17. What is the role of the Office of Juvenile Justice and Delinquency Prevention (OJJDP)?

18. What are some supplemental sources of funds for the programs?

19. What is the function of the National Institute of Corrections (NIC) and the National Jail Center (NJC)?

20. Why is the correctional administrator a public relations person, and how does he or she implement this function?

# THE FUTURE OF CORRECTIONS

The future of corrections lies in an increased awareness of its function and its value to society. The rapid population growth of society, combined with its ever-increasing complexity in technological, economic, and social patterns, will necessitate greater and stronger controls. This increase in controls, together with the bringing of people closer together, must of necessity generate greater irritation and conflict. The resulting social problems, including crime and delinquency, must increase. Some of these problems were not defined as problems a generation ago, but were accepted as facts of life. Greater sophistication and social awareness, pressures from minority groups and civil liberties organizations, and the mass media have brought into social consciousness a new awareness of problems because of a new frame of reference and social viewpoint.

The spinoff of this total social and political situation is an increasing crime rate. As all law defines problem areas, the criminal law and juvenile court law define problem areas in deviant behavior that damages society. The very presence of laws, needed to implement an orderly society and orderly social change, points out the areas where deviation and the violation of laws are to be expected. Correctional programs must be able to accommodate to these changes and expansions.

Social and political opinion have gone in almost all directions. Legislators, governors, and other political leaders have called for "tougher" policies, "stiffer" sentences, and "once-and-for-all" solutions, such as Governor Rockefeller's 1973 drug legislation in New York and the strict mandatory sentencing proposed by President Ford in 1975. On the other hand, some correctional experts have questioned whether the government should be involved in much victimless crime.[1] Others have questioned the effectiveness of imprisonment.[2] A survey showed that 72 percent of correctional administrators in all fifty states were opposed to sentencing offenders to mandatory terms.[3] If prisons "get tougher," some felt, it will defeat the purpose of prison to deter the individual from repeated crime and nullify the efforts at correction.[4] These opinions are pervasive in correctional literature, and yet the emotional "get-tough" approach has popular appeal, ineffective as it has proved to be. Certainly, tough and hard-nosed police and prosecution policies must force liberal correctional policies, since there are only a limited number of spaces in prisons, and one must be released for every person sentenced to prison—unless society wants to put its resources into new prisons.

The size of the prisoner population makes it very difficult to isolate that large group from the rest of society. When inmates organize a prisoners' union, as they have in West Germany, Scandinavia, several systems in the United States previously mentioned, and elsewhere, it is only an index of a general emerging need that has to be met. A corollary is that it is more difficult to assist people to live in a society when they are isolated from it in correctional treatment. The work of the National College of State Trial Judges at the University of Nevada at Reno is an indication that these trends pervade the entire criminal justice system—not just corrections. The breaking of social ties and the complete isolation from society in an institution complicates the problem of treatment and rehabilitation in the correctional process. In fact, the Joint Commission on Correctional Manpower and Training has identified many areas in which the ex-offender can be used in the correctional process.[5] All these trends—social, political, and psychological or developmental—combine to point to new directions in correctional treatment.

Menninger has posed several questions regarding whether crime flourishes in our society because it is needed and enjoyed, and whether punishment is promulgated to serve society's desire for vengeance.[6] Crime is a social relationship in which neither the negative (criminality) nor the

---

[1] For example, see Gilberg Geis, *Not the Law's Business?* (Rockville, Md.: National Institute of Mental Health, Center for Studies of Crime and Delinquency, 1972); also, Louis P. Carney, *Introduction to Correctional Science* (New York: McGraw-Hill, 1974), p. 274.

[2] Gerhard O. W. Mueller, *Crime, Law and the Scholars* (Seattle: University of Washington Press, 1969).

[3] Corrections Professionals Opposed to Strict Mandatory Sentencing Rule as Proposed by President Ford," *Corrections Digest*, 6, No. 14 (July 9, 1972), 1–2.

[4] William R. Conte, ed., *Selected Writings of Garrett Heyns* (Olympia, Washington: The Sherwood Press, 1975), p. 98.

[5] *Offenders as a Correctional Manpower Resource*, Joint Commission on Correctional Manpower and Training (Washington, D.C.: U.S. Government Printing Office, 1968).

[6] Karl Menninger, *The Crime of Punishment* (New York: The Viking Press, Inc., 1968).

positive (lawabidingness) can exist in isolation or be treated in isolation. Criminality is seen as its own cause, and society its own detriment.

Over the past 150 years, Western civilization has moved gradually but steadily in the direction of more and more commitment to rehabilitation and resocialization of offenders. Implementation of these ideas has been slow and fragmented. The movement is now away from excessive use of imprisonment and more toward community-based programs making use of the social sciences.[7] Further, there is a trend toward making public services liable for insufficiently trained personnel and inadequate services.[8]

Even the issue of capital punishment became academic in the 1960s, but the practice has since returned. Although a large number of persons were executed in the 1930s and 1940s, the number had steadily declined after that. In a case before the Supreme Court in 1967, there was beginning speculation as to whether the death penalty might be "cruel and unusual punishment" in violation of the Eighth Amendment.[9] The death penalty is being eliminated by disuse throughout the Western world. In this country, executions began again with Gary Gilmore in 1977 in Utah.

The United States Supreme Court held in *Furman* v. *Georgia* (40 U.S.L.W. 4923, June 29, 1972) that the manner in which the death penalty was applied in the United States was discriminatory, since the black, indigent male was disproportionately sentenced to death, which was considered to be in violation of the "cruel and unusual punishment" clause of the Eighth Amendment. Consequently, 638 persons sentenced to death were commuted to life sentences. Since that time, many states have attempted to develop death penalty statutes that could meet the constitutional challenge by being mandatory and not discriminatory. In 1967, the Supreme Court had accepted five cases on appeal to determine whether they met the constitutional test. On July 2, 1976, the Supreme Court upheld the death penalty laws in Florida, Georgia, and Texas because sentencing was a joint consideration between the jury and the judge. At the same time, the Court struck down the death penalty laws of Louisiana and North Carolina because they were too mandatory. This gave other states the pattern of death penalty laws that would meet the constitutional test as of 1976. By the end of 1981, 36 states had the death penalty, and there were 838 persons on death rows in the United States. After a ten-year period of no executions, Gary Gilmore was killed by firing squad in Utah on January 17, 1977. By November 1983, there had been eight executions.

The philosophy of government is changing significantly in favor of the underprivileged, minority groups, low-income families, and the correctional client. Certainly it is far different from the philosophy of 1854, when

[7] Richard A. McGee, "What's Past Is Prologue," *The Annals: The Future of Corrections*, 381 (January 1969), 1–10.

[8] See James P. Murphy, *Is the Municipality Liable for Insufficiently Trained Police?* Bureau of Public Administration (Orono, Maine: University of Maine, 1968).

[9] *Trop* v. *Dulles*, 356 U.S. 86101 (1967).

President Pierce vetoed a bill providing government land for mental health purposes for the reason that the condition of the individual citizen is not the proper concern of government. When problems become of sufficient magnitude to threaten the general welfare, however, governmental assistance is traditionally provided.

The first "human" or "welfare" service headed by the government was the United States Public Health Service in 1797, simply because public sanitation and related matters had become of sufficient magnitude that they could not be handled by individuals or small groups and had to be handled by government. Federal aid to Northern industry to assist in competition with English manufacturing was one of the basic factors leading to the outbreak of the American Civil War. Federal support to agriculture had its massive beginnings in the 1930s. Massive federal assistance for welfare and income maintenance began in the 1930s, for mental health in the 1940s, and for education in the 1950s, especially after Sputnik was launched. Federal aid to law enforcement, corrections, and the system of criminal justice was inaugurated in the 1960s and will undoubtedly become a stable part of governmental procedure.

The Children's Bureau was established in 1912 and performed significant services for many years. The sample juvenile court statistics system was inaugurated in 1926, after which some estimates of juvenile court activity was available through the *Juvenile Court Statistics*. Many valuable publications in the juvenile field were produced. In 1969, the functions of the Children's Bureau were absorbed by the Social and Rehabilitation Services, HEW, since divided into the Departments of Health and Human Services and of Education, as of 1980. The old Children's Bureau is no more.

The first major national survey in the field of corrections was the Report of the National Commission on Law Observance, commonly known as the Wickersham Report, published in 1931. The second major survey was the Attorney General's Survey of Release Procedures, which was published in 1939. The third major release was the Kefauver Report, published in 1951. The report of the President's Commission on Law Enforcement and Administration of Justice, released in 1967, was the fourth major survey of the field of corrections in the United States. The Joint Commission on Correctional Manpower and Training, composed of 96 private organizations and public agencies, was funded under the 1965 Correctional Rehabilitation Study Act for three years, but was extended into 1969. Its publications are now distributed by the American Correctional Association. All these reports assessed the crime situation of the times and made recommendations for the future. The trend is obvious in the shift of philosophy from one of stronger laws and better law enforcement to one of correctional treatment and rehabilitation. The recommendations of the President's Commission involved all phases of society in the focus on the offender, including universities.

Fear has changed the way of life of residents in Washington, D.C., for everyone from the cab driver to the senator.[10] It has changed ways of doing things everywhere, from the schools to the embassies. It is apparently a pattern for future urban areas. "The nation's criminal justice system has been starved for resources for decades. Public officials at every level, and the public itself, must be prepared to expend large sums if they are serious about controlling crime."[11] Simultaneously, the inability to make treatment available to the majority of offenders remains the central failure of the correctional system. Future efforts must be focused on comprehensive correctional prevention and treatment programs.

## INSTITUTIONS

The large, centralized institution appears to be a thing of the past, at least in philosophy. Several organizations, including the United States Bureau of Prisons and the American Correctional Association, have indicated that no adult institution should contain more than 600 inmates. In 1972, the National Council on Crime and Delinquency called for a moratorium on further construction of prisons. Where there are a large number of institutions in a state, there is a tendency to transfer inmates to the institutions nearest their homes.

Following through the trend toward smaller prisons, feasibility studies have already been inaugurated to determine whether a complex of, perhaps, a half-dozen institutions around each urban area in the state might replace the central juvenile institution. The same idea, of course, could well be applied to adult institutions. In the South, the old road prisons are being viewed as ideal small institutions for specializing in problems. They could provide good treatment programs, with the activities of the inmates directed toward group living, group therapy, and specialized treatment procedures.

The correctional officer in adult institutions and the house parents in juvenile institutions are increasingly being considered as the real vehicles of treatment. Consequently, their education and training is becoming more and more important.

Most current efforts of prison reform are regarded as stopgap measures. Any major improvement of the prison's efficiency will require a fundamental overhaul of both the system of justice and the community's normative structure.[12]

Several authors have stated that the criminal justice system has become a moral busybody, unwisely extending beyond its proper role of protecting persons and property, attempting to enforce private morality with

[10] *The Wall Street Journal*, February 11, 1970, p. 1.

[11] *The Wall Street Journal*, February 4, 1970, p. 1.

[12] Clarence Shrag, "The Correctional System: Problems and Prospects," *The Annals: The Future of Corrections*, 381 (January 1969), 11–20.

regard to alcohol, gambling, drugs, and sex. There are ways, they say, to provide cheaper and more effective protection without disrupting family life and causing further suffering on the part of innocent dependents.[13]

The extent of recidivism observable among present populations in the United States points toward the need for the development of more effective methods of inducing conformity to acceptable social behavior in the various clinical groups that make up the group of repeaters in these present populations. In any one year, about two-thirds of the persons who come into prisons have been in prisons before, although, over a longer period, about two-fifths to one-half of the individuals involved are recidivists.

The longer and further an offender goes into the system of criminal justice, the more likely he is to repeat. While recidivism may result from a self-fulfilling prophecy, a selective process is taking place in which the most serious problems progressively associate with other people with similarly serious problems. This process would certainly reinforce and complicate the individual deviations from social norms. A conclusion might be that sending people to some prisons is worse for society than doing nothing at all with the offender. An optimum solution might be treatment-supervision in the community.

According to a 1957 study, there was similarity of objectives and procedures and enlightment among the "good" prisons. The "bad" prisons were rather consistently custodial, unenlightened in understanding and behavior, and defensive in their relations with the public and other agencies.[14] The factors associated with the "good" prisons were an emphasis on treatment, use of professional treatment personnel, existence of active support of in-service training for all personnel, expenditure of funds for professional personnel and inmate care, use of research projects and programmed evaluation, and a generally positive attitude toward contacts with other agencies, newspapers, and the public. On the other hand, the "bad" prisons had more people in punishment status, spent less money on professional treatment personnel and inmate care, did not encourage research and program evaluation, and held a generally negative attitude toward newsmen and contacts with other agencies.

There was evidence to suggest that the prison may be a good index of the advancement of the general culture it serves. The positive correlations between how prison systems rank in the judgment of professionals and other factors more easily measured suggest that the quality of correctional systems may be associated with or reflect the total culture.[15] For example, a 1957 study indicated that there was a correlation of reputational rankings

---

[13] Norval Morris and Gordon Hawkins, *The Honest Politicians' Guide to Crime Control* (Chicago: University of Chicago Press, 1970), p. 144.

[14] See Vernon Fox, "Reputational Ranking of American Prisons," *Sociologica Internationalis*, Berlin, 6, No. 1 (1968), 88–95.

[15] See Vernon Fox, "Reputational Rankings of American Prison Systems," *Indian Journal of Social Research*, No. 3 (December 1964), p. 282.

of American prison systems with the rate of illiteracy in the states of +0.50; of +0.68 with per capita incomes; and of +0.67 with the amount of money spent on each inmate annually. These findings indicate that the enlightenment of the people and the use of resources to build correctional programs seem to be related to the development of effective corrections.

An organization that knew nothing about corrections was brought into the federal correctional institutions at Ashland, Kentucky, and Petersburg, Virginia, for a businesslike evaluation. Its reports indicate that better information on inmate needs is essential, follow-up analyses of inmate successes and failures are necessary for accounting, restructured training environments are mandatory, and some outside assistance in the establishment of program objectives is necessary.[16]

Present forms of correctional treatment do little good and often more harm.[17] Alternatives to incarceration must be found, since the institution establishes an artificial type of banishment.[18] The search for alternatives to imprisonment appears to be a significant trend in corrections.

In the meantime, the current programs in prisons must be in a process of reform and improvement. Already, several suits brought by inmates have changed the procedures and conditions within institutions. A Rhode Island case indicates that litigation by inmates can change the conditions and procedures within the prison. Federal District Judge Pettine ruled that the court would take over jurisdiction of some of the conditions and procedures in the Adult Correctional Institution at Cranston, Rhode Island, particularly the Behavioral Control Unit (solitary confinement or the disciplinary facility). The original petition said that health conditions were so seriously deteriorated as to constitute a violation of the Eighth Amendment. The federal court ruled that it would take over jurisdiction of the facility and procedures for eighteen months until the situation was corrected. This ruling serves notice that conditions in American prisons will improve through corrective administrative measures or the courts will take action to force their improvement.

Simultaneously, there is increasing concern on the part of correctional administrators to hear prisoners' complaints on an "in-house" basis so they do not have to be taken to court. An ombudsman type of correctional worker within prisons and correctional agencies to receive complaints from prisoners and other correctional clients appears to be part of the future development of corrections in a democratic society. Maryland passed a law that became effective July 1, 1971, creating an official Inmate Grievance Commission consisting of five citizens appointed by the gover-

[16] *To Help Men Change, A Report by Sterling Institute on Optimizing Training Potential in Federal Reformatories*, prepared for the U.S. Bureau of Prisons, 1968.

[17] Stanton Wheeler and Leonard S. Cottrell, Jr., *Juvenile Delinquency: Its Prevention and Control* (New York: Russell Sage Foundation, 1969), pp. 22–27.

[18] LaMar T. Empey, *Studies in Delinquency: Alternatives to Incarceration*, Office of Juvenile Delinquency and Youth Development (Washington, D.C.: U.S. Government Printing Office, 1969).

nor. This commission will hear inmates' grievances and is expected to reduce the number of cases brought to court by prisoners. By 1982, inmate grievance procedures had been instituted in the major penal systems in America.

## COMMUNITY-BASED CORRECTIONS

The jail is the oldest of the community-based institutions and the most resistant to change. The jail has been criticized by correctional workers for centuries. Yet the jail has the greatest potential for contribution to the correctional process of all institutions and services. It comes into contact with ten times the number of people contacted by other correctional services.

Rather than being strictly a holding operation, the jail could be staffed with professional personnel and become a community residential treatment center. It could be divided into units for group living experiments. It could provide the place for diagnosis and identification of problem cases that could be referred to other agencies. Diagnosis and short-term instruction could both be computerized. Short-term education and group counseling are possible. The trends are apparently in this direction.

Another trend is toward the regional jail, which can provide better services for several rural counties or one urban region than can a number of small facilities. A small local lockup will always be needed for short-term detention. A detoxification unit will be needed for the drunks usually sent to the jail. In addition, a facility for untried prisoners would separate the legally innocent people from short-term offenders and others awaiting sentence or execution of sentence.

In addition, there is a trend toward releasing prisoners on their own recognizance rather than holding them in jail. The Vera Institute was founded in 1961 as an organization to work for improvements in the criminal justice system. Financed by foundation grants and some government funds, it has concentrated on the relationship of criminal justice and administration to the poor, primarily in New York City. Its main contribution has been its work for the release of arrested offenders on their own recognizance.[19]

The Criminal Justice Coordinating Council, established in New York City by Mayor John Lindsay in 1967, had a series of projects designed to implement specific reforms in the criminal justice system of New York City.[20] The Vera Institute of Justice is consultant to the council and has designed a series of pilot projects to develop comprehensive plans. Among the plans are the Bronx Sentencing Project, Burglary Demonstration Project, Calendar Control Project, Community Service Patrol Corps, Computerized Court Calendaring, Criminal Justice Information Bureau,

---

[19] Jameson W. Doig, "The Police in a Democratic Society," *Public Administration Review,* 28, No. 5 (September 1968).

[20] *Criminal Justice Coordinating Council, City of New York, Two-Year Report,* April 1969.

Detention Overcrowding, Family Court Law Office, Federal Crime Control Grants, Guidelines for Demonstrations, Investigation of Burglaries by Patrolmen, Manhattan Bowery Project, Manhattan Court Employment Project, Manhattan Summons Project, Master Calendar Office, Methadone Project, Manhattan Summons Project, Master Calendar Office, Methadone Project, Minority Recruitment, Operation Safe City, Police–Youth Dialogues, Pre-Arraignment Processing Facility, Rehabilitation Services, Traffic Court Alert, Youth Diversion Project, VISTA, Teacher Corps Project, and a work-release program.

Community-based institutions include work release, halfway houses, prerelease guidance centers, and community residential treatment centers. The future of corrections lies predominantly in community-based programs, with the most serious problems short of incarceration in the central prison requiring domiciliary care and treatment in the community. Community facilities can serve the centers. There will be more halfway houses, both for those on their way to institutions and for those on their way out of institutions. The prerelease guidance centers, of course, are designed for those coming out of more secure institutions. Many halfway houses for juveniles and youths serve those who have never been in a large training school. The community-based treatment center for all offenders will be used more in the future.

In addition, the parole clinic, or a "walk-in" center for those needing correctional treatment but not its residential aspect, can serve persons in difficulty who are living at home. This is over and above the general probation and parole services, more in line with the community services in corrections. It is needed for the additional help such an office can provide. It might be considered a "first-aid station" in the correctional field. In any case, the future of corrections lies in community-based programs.

## PROBATION

There has been a steady increase in the use of probation in recent years, and this trend will continue. Better-educated and more adequate probation staffs have developed in the larger urban centers, and statewide supervision of probation has assisted in upgrading probation services in the rural areas. The economy of using probation over institutionalization, combined with the more effective treatment of the offender possible when his social ties are maintained, makes this trend essential for correctional process.

Additional facilities may assist the probation process, so that marginal cases which had previously been sentenced to prison may be handled at the community level on probation. Probation recovery camps or probation diagnostic facilities may hold the prospective probationer in a secure setting for 30 to 60 days before supervision in the community. These periods of observation are primarily for diagnostic purposes and, simultaneously, are probably all the security that many offenders amenable to probation might need. The Johnson Amendment [Title 18, U.S.C., Sec.

4208 (b)] permits a federal judge to send an individual to a federal prison or correctional institution for a period not to exceed 90 days for purposes of diagnosis, after which he can be returned to the court and placed on probation. There are many possibilities for implementing this idea.

Probation without adjudication has been adopted in some states, such as Florida, California, Pennsylvania, Michigan, and many others. The accused waives trial in this case and accepts probation supervision. Not only does this procedure eliminate the court procedure for trial; it avoids the stigma of conviction of the offender who, in the judgment of the court, is a good risk. It really is an extension of the philosophy of the juvenile court, where voluntary supervision is one of the constitutional bases. Because this is a voluntary procedure, the trial can be held if the probation without adjudication does not work out satisfactorily. This appears to be a possible future trend in corrections.

Probation and parole clinics, similar to mental hygiene or child guidance clinics, may well serve probation and parole. The idea has been experimented with rather informally in the Massachusetts Division of Legal Medicine and is being tried with narcotic offenders in some of the larger cities.

The probation officer case aide has been developed by the University of Chicago and the Vera Institute, using ex-inmates and people indigenous to the ghettoes. The New York City Youth Board detached worker idea is being implemented. The mobilization of community services and the establishment of probation clinics may assist in increasing the number of offenders on probation and, therefore, reduce the number of people being sent to prison.

## PAROLE

Release under supervision is imperative to a successful treatment program, whether it be postoperative convalescence from a general hospital, supervised furlough from a mental hospital, or supervised release from a juvenile or adult correctional institution. Consequently, it is apparent that all persons released from prisons and juvenile institutions will be more frequently released under supervision. The parole officer will supervise the adult releases. The aftercare worker will supervise the juvenile releasees.

In such a setting, the task of the parole board must of necessity be shifted.[21] The institution is probably in a better position to determine when a person with whom it has been working is ready to go. This is the pattern established in mental hospitals, both private and public, where a "staffing" is held—a conference of doctors to determine the progress of a patient and whether or not the patient is ready to go home on furlough. Similarly, a

[21] See F. Lovell Bixby, "New Roles for Parole Boards," *Federal Probation*, 34, No. 2 (June 1970), 24–28.

staffing by correctional professionals in the prison or correctional institution should determine whether or not an inmate is ready to go home.

The function of the parole board would be as an appeal board and review board. If an inmate or, for that matter, a staff member wanted the action of the prison staff reviewed, he could appeal for a review. In this way, the parole board could spend more time on questionable or marginal cases than it could possibly have spent while being responsible for the release of every prisoner in the system. Since the question would be *when* to parole a person rather than *whether* to parole, the communication between institutional staff and the parole board would be mutually informative and helpful in working out issues.

Community services in corrections will become more and more important. Community organization has been brought to bear on welfare, mental health, and other problems. It is beginning to be brought to bear in the area of corrections, both juvenile and adult. The community services agents are coordinators and facilitators. They assist the official probation and parole officers, juvenile courts, jails, halfway houses, vocational rehabilitation services, and other community services as they relate to the field of corrections.

As indicated in Chapter 12, there have been some movements to eliminate parole. Probably the broadest and most effective, because it was considered by several legislatures in the mid-1970s, has been David Fogel's "Justice Model" that provides for flat sentences, with aggravating and mitigating factors making some differences, abolition eventually of the "fortress prison system," use of ombudsmen for overseeing fairness in prisons, legal aid within the prison, and abolition of parole.[22] Fogel has testified in several state legislatures considering its enactment into law.

As mentioned before, Maine abolished parole in 1976. By 1982, four other states had abolished parole and gone to determinate or fixed sentencing. Illinois and California abolished parole in 1977, Indiana in 1978, and Minnesota as of July 1, 1980. Eighteen other states abolished parole and introduced mandatory sentencing for particular categories, including violent crimes, drug offenses, and repeaters, or a combination of these. Even so, the parole caseload at the end of 1981 was the highest in history at 223,774, and there were more conditional releasees than ever before. Regardless of legislative action, it is apparent that correctional professionals desire some supervision after release from prison.

## EDUCATION AND PERSONNEL

Salaries for correctional personnel amount to 75 to 85 percent of the budget, depending upon whether the program is institutional or community-

[22] David Fogel, "*. . . We Are the Living Proof. . .*": *The Justice Model for Corrections* (Cincinnati: W. H. Anderson, 1975).

based. Therefore, improvement of correctional programs is best implemented through personnel and education of staff. Universities are central in the educational process. Their resources can be used in in-service training. There are at least four different categories of persons who can be trained: (1) the general correctional worker of the future; (2) the present custodial or correctional officer, who can develop into the general correctional worker; (3) the professionals—the psychiatrist, psychologist, sociologist, social workers, recreation specialists, and others—who already possess skills in their own areas but come to the field of corrections without any preparation for it and should undergo adaptive training before working in the prison; and (4) the administrators themselves, who must establish policy. The administrators should know more about the philosophy and concerns of the broad field than anyone else, and without their support, any correctional progress would be impossible.[23]

Cooperative education programs had been established in 141 colleges and universities in the United States by 1969. These programs have the objective of providing a balanced education where occupational experience is an integral part of the process. In addition to regular classroom and laboratory exercises, the students spend some of the time, probably a half day, in on-the-job situations, an arrangement that blends work experience with classroom theory. The field of corrections is especially well suited to this kind of program. Types of work in corrections that could be performed are record keeping and other clerical duties, counseling of juveniles, assisting in counts in adult prisons and correctional institutions, meeting and assisting in hosting visitors, assisting in controlling and supervising correspondence and visits with inmates, and a variety of other functions.

A number of universities have established curricula in criminology, criminal justice, law enforcement, and corrections. In 1968, there were 33 established programs in criminology and corrections, ten new programs, and twenty nondegree programs.[24] The patterns varied widely. Among the established programs, for example, four were in criminology, 21 were in sociology, and eight were in other departments. By 1976, there were about 900 programs in criminal justice, most including law enforcement and corrections, in American junior colleges, colleges, and universities, of which about 750 were initially funded through the Law Enforcement Assistance Administration of the United States Department of Justice. By 1976 also, this federal funding was being reduced. While some programs were, in turn, reduced, most were funded by the college budget and some other

---

[23] *Proceedings of the Conference on Specialized Education Planning for Personnel in Corrections*, Mohonk Lake, N.Y., sponsored by the National Institute of Mental Health, N.Y.S. Department of Mental Hygiene, N.Y.S. Department of Correction, New York School of Psychiatry, New York City Community Mental Health Board, and New York City Department of Correction, May 21–23, 1963.

[24] Loren Karacki and John J. Galvin, "Higher Education Programs in Criminology and Corrections," in *Criminology and Corrections*, Joint Commission on Correctional Manpower and Training (Washington, D.C.: U.S. Government Printing Office, 1968), pp. 10–27.

sources, reflecting the interest in crime and criminal justice in the general public and educators. In fact, there were in the mid-1970s five Ph.D. programs in criminal justice or criminology and several other programs that offered doctoral degrees with concentration in this area in sociology and public administration. Correctional administrators and some of their critics have begun to realize that the university has perpetuated a gap in the field of corrections because there has been little higher education in this field.[25] However, by 1982, criminal justice had become a standard department in many colleges and universities, and there were nine outstanding and well-attended Ph.D. programs in this important field.

Lejins has suggested that the curriculum of the undergraduate program should include (1) a general introductory survey course in criminology, (2) a general introductory course in juvenile deliquency, (3) an introductory course in institutional treatment, (4) an introductory course in community-based treatment, including probation and parole, (5) a survey course in prevention, and (6) a field training course or placement with a correctional or preventive institution or agency.[26] Existing educational models, especially the liberal arts model, cannot satisfy the requirements for trained and educated manpower for society generally and in the field of corrections specifically. Changes are needed in the theory and practice of corrections to replace present correctional programs, which seem to produce social cripples.[27]

There are various types of work-experience programs in the field of corrections. Internships, work-study programs, and cooperative education programs all integrate theory and practice in the educational process. They can be used in juvenile courts, adult probation, adult parole and juvenile aftercare, juvenile and adult institutions, halfway houses, treatment centers, jails, and many other settings.[28]

A primary difficulty in education in any professional field is that instructors lack practical experience in the area in which they are teaching, or, having had that experience, have not visited the field, either institutions or agencies, in recent years. As professors rise in rank and become more and more involved with graduate programs of the institutions, there is a tendency to get farther away from the field and to relate the subject matter to outdated frames of reference.[29] This loss of contact can be avoided by fre-

[25] John J. Galvin, "Issues for the Seminar," in *Criminology and Corrections*, pp. 1–9.

[26] Peter T. Lejins, "Content of the Curriculum and Its Relevance for Correctional Programs," in *Criminology and Corrections*, pp. 28–56.

[27] Kenneth Polk, *The University and Corrections: Potential for Collaborative Relationships*, Joint Commission on Correctional Manpower and Training (Washington, D.C.: U.S. Government Printing Office, 1969), p. 78.

[28] Jimmie C. Styles and Denny F. Pace, *Guidelines for Work Experience Programs in the Criminal Justice System* (Washington, D.C.: American Association of Junior Colleges, 1969).

[29] W. M. Perel and Philip V. Vario, "Professor, Is Your Experience Outdated?" *The Educational Forum*, 33, No. 1 (November 1968), 39–44.

quent field trips and the professor's working with the correctional institution, agency, or department on practical matters that involve program and assessment.

The increasing use of junior colleges for training of line and supervisory staff is important for the future of corrections. The American Association of Junior Colleges has published a set of guidelines for correctional curricula in community and junior colleges, which provides an outline of the competencies and skills needed in corrections. These are presented as follows:

> Many jobs in corrections have three general phases, (1) investigation, (2) counseling, and (3) enforcement. The emphasis in various jobs may differ and the tasks may vary, depending upon the setting and function of the correctional institution or agency. For example, the juvenile court counselor investigates complaints, counsels delinquent children and parents, and sets limits if necessary, even to the extent of removing children from their home.

> The institutional case worker investigates background to prepare the social history or admission summary, counsels on the basis of diagnosis, participates in enforcing institutional limits, and recommends release through reports to the parole board. All other correctional personnel have these three functions as a part of their jobs.

> There are certain basic characteristics and competencies that are pertinent to all correctional duties. These should be taken into consideration, both in planning the program and in counseling the students. These characteristics and competencies include:

> 1. Ability to understand and withstand provocative behavior without becoming punitive
> 2. Development of objectivity in accepting relationships with all clients in a nonjudgmental manner, without either punitive or sentimental emotional involvement
> 3. Competence to accept an inmate or person on the caseload without personal involvement with neither punitive nor sentimental views, much the same as a physician views a patient—this does not mean complete detachment
> 4. On-the-job counseling techniques
> 5. Ability to say "no"—with reasons when necessary—and to say "yes" with equal reason
> 6. Sensitivity to pathological behavior as compared with normal random behavior, sufficient to permit intelligent referral to professional staff
> 7. Ability to assess strengths of an individual, to determine what the treatment team has to build on in the treatment of an offender
> 8. Making referrals to all staff, community resources, and other specialties with some sophistication
> 9. Ability to use tact to avoid creating or aggravating problem situations
> 10. Ability to use tact to ameliorate developing problem situations
> 11. Willingness to augment and support the therapeutic community and the therapeutic process in the institution and the community programs

12. Ability to observe and accurately record:
    a. Individual behavior
       —Pathological behavior needing referral to professional staff
       —Escape, manipulation, or other suspicious behavior in which the safety and security of the institution or community may be concerned
    b. Group behavior
       —Beginning of disturbance
    c. Miscellaneous behavior
       —Incidents that might be recorded that may crescendo into major difficulty or be part of an organized illicit activity
13. Ability to assess the community-reintegration model, including attitudes toward the returning offender
14. Ability to constructively interpret administrative decisions, actions, and procedures to inmates, probationers, and parolees
15. Ability to serve as upward communicator from the inmate body to the administration and from the probation and parole caseload to the judge and field services supervisor with the view toward improving correctional services
16. Ability to maintain discreet silence on some critical issues and "classified" information to maintain (a) staff morale, (b) inmate and caseload morale, and (c) good public relations
17. Capability of exerting external controls on individuals who need containment with physical force or firearms when necessary without using more force than the situation actually requires
18. Knowledge of specific procedures that might be modified or elaborated in the in-service training program of the correctional agency or institution—such as classification procedure, preparole planning, probation and parole revocation hearings, and procedures at similar level
19. Knowledge of the civil and constitutional rights of prisoners, whatever their status, and the incorporation of that knowledge into the supervisory process
20. Knowledge to interpret the system of justice, including laws of arrest, judicial procedure—and the total correctional process of probation, prison, and parole, together with knowledge of revocation hearing procedure and pardon procedure[30]

To staff all state and adult juvenile correctional institutions, 79,000 positions have been authorized, although 5 percent of these remain vacant.[31] The annual turnover in institutions is 16 percent; therefore, 13,000 must be recruited every year just to replace those who leave their jobs. An increase of 34 percent of authorized personnel in rehabilitation and training and 6.8 percent in child care and line correctional staff employees is urgent. Approximately 1,000 doctoral degrees in psychology, about 600 master's degrees in vocational rehabilitation counseling, and 4,700 master's degrees in social work are awarded annually. Although there has been an

[30] Vernon Fox, *Guidelines for Corrections Programs in Community and Junior Colleges* (Washington, D.C.: American Association of Junior Colleges, 1969), pp. 18–19.

[31] *Fact Sheet*, Joint Commission on Correctional Manpower and Training, Washington, D.C., 1969.

increase in the number of criminology and corrections degrees programs, the number of correctional personnel graduating is almost negligible when compared with the demand for them. By 1975, 37,000 new persons were needed for corrections in California alone.[32]

The use of ex-inmates in some of these jobs is here already and will increase in the future.[33] Several states have high-ranking personnel who have served time. The United States Bureau of Prisons has experimented with this approach. Some states use selected inmates to counsel younger offenders. Careful selection of inmates is more easily accomplished than careful selection of civilian applicants! More is known about them, and there has been a better opportunity to observe their behavior. The legal status, convicted or not convicted, will be less and less the governing issue in the future in the correctional field.

The idea behind New Careers is based on the same principle as the highly successful Alcoholics Anonymous. A danger is that sloppy and inadequate preparation for implementing New Careers programs will lead to failure, but they have considerable promise if properly planned. New roles for semiprofessionals and nonprofessionals in probation, parole, and institutions and the integration of treatment of the offender with social welfare services in all areas and levels, including the use of inmates, has been suggested for the field of corrections.[34] Twenty-five former offenders are now working for the New York State Division of Youth, performing a variety of counseling and supervisory jobs in sensitive areas. The use of indigenous personnel, the ex-offender, and the person on parole or aftercare has been especially effective in the ghetto areas in the large cities. It is obvious that they will be even more useful in the future.

The use of teachers as juvenile probation officers, generally known as teacher-probation officers (TPO), has been made in several places. In rural and sparsely settled areas, it is not uncommon for a teacher to work part-time in the evenings and on weekends as a juvenile court counselor or probation officer. The TPO, however, is a more formalized arrangement, in which a teacher works also for the juvenile court, as well as for the school. With a reduced teaching load, the TPO also has a caseload of delinquents under supervision by the juvenile court. Disciplinary problems in this caseload become the responsibility of the TPO, rather than the principal or other designated school disciplinarian. The advantages of this arrangement are many, with the coordination of school and juvenile court functions being of primary importance. It is apparent that this arrangement, already in operation in Columbus, Ohio; Alexandria, Virginia; and some other

---

[32] Eugene O. Saha, *Mobilizing Correctional Manpower for California: Guideline for Action,* Final Report, OLEA Planning Grant #287, Sacramento, September 1968.

[33] See *Offenders as a Correctional Manpower Resource,* Joint Commission on Correctional Manpower and Training, Washington, D.C., 1968.

[34] Judith G. Benjamin, Marcia K. Freedman, and Edith W. Lynton, *Pros and Cons: New Roles for Nonprofessionals in Corrections* (Washington, D.C.: Office of Juvenile Delinquency and Youth Development, HEW, 1969).

places, will become more popular in the correctional field in the future.

Government at all levels and private organizations will make increasing contributions to the field of corrections. Significant federal legislation in the area of correctional education include the Junior College Act, the Vocational Education Amendments, and the Higher Education Act. The Council on Legal Education for Professional Responsibility, Inc. (CLEPR), is interested in promoting the concerns of law schools in clinical programs to make participants acutely aware of the need for justice for all citizens, rich and poor.[35]

The National College of State Trial Judges was established in Reno, Nevada, in 1964 by the National Conference of State Trial Judges in conjunction with the American Bar Association. It seems certain that the nationwide focus on criminal justice, including corrections, is significant and will accelerate in the future.

## RESEARCH, COMPUTERS, AND TECHNOLOGY

Research in the form of evaluating programs will be used more and more in the future. While the military services and industry budgeted about 15 percent and 5 percent, respectively, for research in recent years, the correctional services have moved from practically nothing to a few experimental programs generally financed by grants. In the future, research and evaluation will become increasingly prevalent as built-in components of correctional programs. A significant beginning has been made by the self-accreditation project funded by the Ford Foundation for the American Correctional Association to evaluate all correctional programs in a voluntary effort in 1971.

Research studies in the field of corrections have, in the past, consistently been evaluated as more effective when they are conducted by persons identified with the project than by outside evaluators. Research in corrections has a major objective of using the social and behavioral sciences to develop more effective and efficient programs to modify criminal and delinquent behavior. It will be even more so in the future. Correctional programs have operated on faith, hope, and charity, without adequate assessment and evaluation. If "experimental programs" scare correctional administrators, the present "trial-and-error" programs should scare them more.[36]

Adequate records need to be kept for adequate research. Input statistics on persons coming into the program or institution, diagnostic statistics from the evaluations of the offenders, and outcome statistics are all neces-

---

[35] *Council on Legal Education for Professional Responsibility, Inc.,* New York, 1, No. 1 (January 1969).

[36] Gordon P. Waldo, "The Dilemma of Correctional Research," *American Journal of Corrections,* 31, No. 6 (November–December 1969), 6–10.

sary for adequate research programs. With computer technology, achievement of such a program is within reach of most correctional institutions and agencies.

Computers have the potential to coordinate and connect so that an enormous single pool of information on individuals and systems can be available. Concern over the effects of such an information pool on the privacy and freedom of the individual has attracted attention.[37] The major concern has been the danger of disclosure of personal information, which involves the government's right to collect and store such information and to subsequently allow access to it. A solution might be a determination of "authorized" and "unauthorized" disclosure of information at the centralized computer filing system.

Computers can now be used to detect neurological disease[38] and to provide complicated education on an individual basis, such as medical education.[39] They could well be applied to diagnostic processes in corrections and to educational programs in correctional institutions and agencies at all levels. They are already being used successfully in some of the larger and more progressive correctional systems for administrative purposes in classification, reduction of custody, accounting and printing of checks for inmates and staff, and assessment of progress on probation and parole, as well as in institutions.

A proposal for a National Criminal Statistics Center was introduced into the House of Representatives (H90-38) in 1969. Such central data banks were designed to be available in the future throughout all phases of the criminal justice system, including corrections.

The National Crime Information Center (NCIC) was established by the FBI in early 1967, together with its related state computer systems, as a center for operational information to law enforcement agencies. It will probably include other information in the future, such as the criminal histories of individual offenders. The potential uses to which the NCIC can be put are almost unlimited.

## EVALUATION

Evaluating correctional programs is most difficult, because the many uncontrollable variables impinge on personality development, the environment, and the individual's total adaptation to the society in which he or she lives. The family and associates contribute much to an individual's

---

[37] *Computerization of Government Files—What Impact on the Individual?* Reprinted from the *UCLA Law Review*, 15, No. 5 (1968) (Chicago: American Bar Foundation, 1968).

[38] "Computers to Detect Neurological Disease," *Public Health Reports,* U.S. Public Health Service, 82, No. 6 (June 1967), 538.

[39] "Computers in Medical Education," *Public Health Reports,* U.S. Public Health Service, 84, No. 11 (November 1969), 984.

ability to perceive situations and handle crises appropriately. Glaser points out that only the highest-risk offenders go to prisons, many of the poorer risks who go to prison are released "on trial" by parole, a large number of parolees are returned for technical violations, and the high-risk community to which they are released encompasses highly criminogenic circumstances.[40] No matter how effective a program is, it has little chance of changing this situation. Further, attempts at evaluation have too often been formulated in noncomparable terms, have been reported from widely scattered populations, and have provided disconnected bits of knowledge that are not cumulative. Glaser suggests that evaluative research has to be routinized before conclusions can be drawn about any program.[41]

Bailey collected the results of 100 studies that attempted evaluation of correctional programs in the 1960s and concluded that there was no consistency.[42] About half the studies reported positive results to some degree, while the other half produced no effectiveness. Bailey suggested the possibility that reformative treatment is really ineffective, that little realistic rehabilitative work has been done in "treatment," and that there is a possibility that some types of treatment may be effective for some people in certain conditions.

In the late 1960s, a survey of 231 research projects between 1945 and 1967 was made for Gov. Nelson Rockefeller of New York.[43] Known as the "Martinson Report," this survey, which contained 285 separable findings, concluded essentially that nothing works. It was released to the public as a publication in 1975, in which the primary conclusion was, "While some treatment programs have had modest successes, it still must be concluded that the field of corrections has not as yet found satisfactory ways to reduce recidivism by significant amounts."[44] Martinson has subsequently said that if corrections is unable to correct, then society should stop holding young offenders for long periods of time; further, reformatories are justifiable only when society can deliver on its promises to correct.[45] It is unfortunate that his conclusions exceeded his findings.

---

[40] Daniel Glaser, *The Effectiveness of a Prison and Parole System* (Indianapolis: Bobbs-Merrill, 1964), p. 504.

[41] Daniel Glaser, *Routinizing Evaluation: Getting Feedback on Effectiveness of Crime and Delinquency Programs* (Rockville, Md.: National Institute of Mental Health, Center for Studies of Crime and Delinquency, 1973), p. 182.

[42] Walter C. Bailey, "An Evaluation of 100 Studies of Correctional Outcome," *Journal of Criminal Law, Criminology and Police Science*, 57, No. 2 (June 1966), 153–60.

[43] Robert Martinson, Judith Wilkes, and Douglas Lipton, *The Effectiveness of Correctional Treatment: A Survey of Treatment Evaluative Methods* (Albany, N.Y.: Office of the Governor, 1969).

[44] *Douglas Lipton, Robert Martinson, and Judith Wilkes, A Survey of Treatment Evaluation Studies* (New York: Praeger Publishers, 1975), p. 627.

[45] "Corrections Programs Don't Correct, Says Leading U.S. Criminologist," *Criminal Justice Newsletter*, 5, No. 19 (October 21, 1974), 1–2. Published by LEAA, Washington, D.C.

The problem with "hard" research in evaluating programs lies in its reliance on demographic factors, such as age, race, sex, prior convictions, and other data easily collected but not really very significant in people-changing programs. Empathy is vital in all the helping professions, but it has to be considered in the recruitment of personnel. It is very doubtful that it can be "taught" or "learned." The wrong person trained is still the wrong person. It may be possible to understand another human being intellectually without feeling with him or her, but true empathic skill and effectiveness in treatment includes an emotional response.[46]

The argument that rehabilitation does not work and that society should go to some other approach appears to be begging the question. In the first place, "rehabilitation" has never been tried, in that the resources for treatment have never been available to corrections. An outstanding psychiatrist, Benjamin Karpman, told this writer that a good psychiatrist "changes the lives" of about 125 to 135 people in a professional lifetime. Corrections has never had that kind of resources and apparently never will. An average 2,000-person prison with no psychiatrist and a few classification officers with varying backgrounds and bogged down with paperwork can hardly be called a "therapeutic community." People are changed by other people. They are not changed for the better by a "program" or a "system," although they can be changed for the worse by being regimented and dehumanized. The "system" is much less important than the people who breathe life into the system. Research that assumes that the *system* or *program* is the crucial factor misses the point.

A 1975 survey of the correctional administrators in all fifty states indicated that 63 percent held that some rehabilitation programs can change people for the better.[47] Further, 90 percent was more committed to community programs than they were to the maximum custody prison. Only about 23 percent were ready to give up on implementing new treatment programs. Certainly, correctional programs have to be evaluated on the basis of what (1) is most effective, (2) is most economical, and (3) causes the least damage.

There have been six evaluative research projects which, according to Stuart Adams, have had considerable impact on the field of corrections. They were (1) the Probation Subsidy Study in California in 1956, (2) the Preston Impact Study in 1959, (3) the California Youth Authority's Community Treatment Project in Sacramento in 1961–71, (4) the Parole Work Unit Program in 1965–74, (5) Pretrial Diversion: Project Crossroads in 1958–71, and (6) the Community-Based Management of Narcotics Offenders in 1969.[48] These high-impact studies were made with weak "hard-re-

[46] Thomas Keefe, "Empathy: The Critical Skill," *Social Work,* 21, No. 1 (January 1976), 10–13.

[47] Michael S. Serill, "Is Rehabilitation Dead?" *Corrections Magazine,* 1, No. 5 (May/June 1975), 3–7.

[48] Stuart Adams, *Evaluative Research in Corrections: A Practical Guide* (Washington, D.C.: Law Enforcement Assistance Administration, 1975).

search" designs, suggesting that clinical observation in the field of human behavior changing is better than with "hard" data easily collected. This is indicative of the people who work with people as compared with "hard researchers" who work with demographic data and return with "nothing-works" data. This writer is aligned with the practitioners who effect change.

## ACCREDITATION

Accreditation of correctional programs in the United States became a reality in 1974. The Voluntary Accreditation Program appears to (1) provide the best means for approving and ensuring quality in correctional services; (2) provide the best means of mobilizing and capitalizing on professional talent; (3) indicate that volunteer programs are better than legislative approaches for a variety of reasons; (4) provide the best means of infusing research findings into correctional practices; (5) facilitate cooperative efforts among various elements of corrections; (6) provide support for enlightened elected and appointed state and federal officials committed to improving corrections; (7) provide correctional administrators with a sound rationale when appropriation for correctional services are requested; (8) provide states and communities with measurement of quality of service; (9) provide interested citizens with factual measurements of the correctional services in their communities or states; (10) result in professionalization of correctional services.[49]

Accreditation is important in correctional services just as it is in hospital and medical services, schools and colleges, and other programs interested in maintaining some semblance of high standards. Not only does accreditation mean higher standards, but the standards against which programs are measured can be used to support budget requests. Beginning in 1968, 46 states entered into a self-accrediting project and voluntary reporting in 1970.

By 1974, funding had been obtained from LEAA, and a 20-person Accreditation Commission was accepted by the Board of the American Correctional Association, representing the following specialties in corrections:

1. Probation—adult
2. Probation—juvenile
3. Short-term institutions—adult
4. Citizens-at-large
5. Law enforcement—police
6. Business

[49] E. Preston Sharp, "Why Accreditation?" *Proceedings of the One Hundred and Fourth Annual Congress of Correction, Houston, Texas, August 18–22, 1974* (College Park, Md.: American Correctional Association, 1975), pp. 31–32.

7. Long-term institutions—juvenile

8. Parole—adult

9. Detention facilities—juvenile

10. Education and research—academic

11. Parole—juvenile

12. Juvenile court

13. Community residential centers—adult

14. Short-term institutions—juvenile

15. Education and research—operational

16. Criminal defense

17. Detention facilities—adult

18. Community residential centers—juvenile

19. Criminal court

20. Long-term institutions—adult

The standards against which accreditation will be measured are in the series of manuals of correctional standards that began publication in 1977 by the Commission on Accreditation for the American Correctional Association.[50] This commission is a group of twenty correctional and criminal justice administrators and professionals elected by the membership of the American Correctional Association. Each standard is weighted as to its essentiality, importance, and desirability. Each institution or agency applies for accreditation by filling in self-report forms and is then checked out by a series of steps, including on-site visits. Many institutions and agencies had been accredited by 1982. It is apparent that the accreditation process that had become a reality in 1974 after years of effort will improve considerably the professional level of corrections in America.

## A THERAPEUTIC SYSTEM OF CRIMINAL JUSTICE

It is obvious that a therapeutic system will permeate all social agencies concerned with criminal justice in the future. The police, the courts, and the correctional system are all centrally concerned with the control of crime, which includes the treatment of offenders, since only the few who die in prison do not return to society. It is apparent that a revolution is underway in national thinking about crime and delinquency. The emphasis on the individual offender is beginning to focus on the manner in which social institutions, including courts and correctional agencies, relate to him. This is the objective of the therapeutic community.[51]

[50] Commission on Accreditation for Corrections, 6110 Executive Boulevard, Suite 750, Rockville, Maryland 20852.

[51] Maxwell Jones, *Social Psychiatry in the Community, in Hospitals, and in Prisons* (Springfield, Ill.: Charles C. Thomas, 1962).

# SUMMARY

The maintaining of orderly social processes in society is critical. It becomes a matter of mental health. While any culture must be sufficiently flexible to allow the individual to adjust by preparing him and permitting him to make a meaningful contribution so that ultimately the culture will survive, the individual is more effective and happy if he "fits in" with a minimum of irritation and conflict. Social change comes in varying degrees of slowness. In the meantime, the individual has to adjust reasonably well to his culture and his society or receive the attention of private and governmental agencies designed to help him. The culture existed before the person within it was born; it will still exist when that person is gone. The problem of the individual is to get along in the culture while he is here. The problem of corrections is to help him get along with a minimum of damage to him or to society.

Some logical predictions for the future of corrections follow:

1. Fewer offenders will be confined for long periods in custodial institutions.
2. Institutional programs will place greater emphasis on preparation for release and less on escapes and economic production.
3. New correctional institutions will be smaller.
4. There will be less of a sharp dichotomy between incarceration and parole or probation supervision.
5. Probation services will be expanded to include hostels, group homes, training programs, job placements, sheltered workshops, psychiatric services, and specialized counseling.
6. Postinstitutional supervision or parole will exhibit changes coming closer to probation.
7. The character, composition, and function of parole boards will change to include better people for other decision-making tasks. As a matter of fact, they may disappear.
8. New forms of disposition from courts as substitutes for conventional sentencing will be developed.
9. Community-based programs will make more and more use of related community services, both public and private.
10. More and more attention will be given to developing information systems, making use of computer technology to assist in decision-making tasks.
11. Empirical research methods will be employed to assess the effectiveness of programs.
12. Professional competent assistants will be provided at all levels so that the long-term needs for public protection will be better served.[52]

[52] Richard A. McGee, "What's Past Is Prologue," pp. 9–10.

There is an increasing trend to eliminate walls and maximum security in adult prisons. There is an increasing trend toward the use of community services for both juveniles and adults in the correctional process. There is increasing recognition that the breaking of social ties—or social surgery—does not help to promote adjustment but creates new problems.

Beginning in the mid-1970s, however, this therapeutic approach encountered a shift toward the political determination of correctional policy, which emphasized due process and a return to Neo-Classical theory in which the crime became the focus of concern, rather than the offender. The constraints on the courts by presumptive sentencing and the abolition of parole in ten states by 1983 seemed to be a diversion from the therapeutic approach. Nevertheless, when the total releases from prison in 1981 reached 174, 955 and only 791 were by death, then 99.6 percent of the people in prison in any one year get out and are returned to society. This means that the political determination of policy will have to give way to economic concerns and social values to some extent. This is why Michigan led the way for other states in the early 1980s to reduce the prison population by early releases, and why Florida placed a limit in 1983 on the ratio of prisoners returned to the general population at 250 per 100,000 within five years to allow the reduction from the 1983 ratio. The therapeutic and reintegrative ideal will mitigate the political determination of policy in prisons dominant since the mid-1970s simply by weight of social requirements and a general "law of saturation" in the criminal justice system. Society is already beginning to react to the harsh penalties imposed by the recent political determination of penal policy and will require the better success of more humane and therapeutic treatment of people in the system.

Institutions and services are becoming decentralized. The work-release program has people going from prisons into the community during the daytime. Community-based services have arisen side by side with probation, parole, and juvenile court counseling. The use of all available services, including psychiatic, mental health, vocational rehabilitation, welfare, employment, and other services in the community and the state, has become important in the field of corrections. They all have a contribution to make. That contribution, coordinated by community service workers, can ensure an increasingly effective future in the total field of corrections.

Justice in society is becoming less important than treatment. Szasz has said that "justice may thus be consigned to the history books, as a relic of a barbarous age that valued individual freedom more highly than collective security. Or, it may be redefined, in the new speech of our times, as Treatment."[53]

One theme that runs through Dostoevsky's *The House of the Dead,*[54]

[53] Thomas S. Szasz, "Justice in the Therapeutic State," in *The Administration of Justice in America,* the 1968–69 E. Paul de Pont Lectures on Crime, Delinquency and Corrections (Newark, Del.: University of Delaware, 1970), pp. 75–92.

[54] Fyodor Dostoevsky, *The House of the Dead,* trans. from the Russian by Constance Garnett (New York: Macmillan, 1950).

first published in 1859, is that the prison is a reflection of the society it serves. He amplified this theme in some places, indicating that from his experience in a Russian prison and penal colony in Siberia he had found that there was not much difference between the people in prison and those outside prison.[55]

In 1910, Sir Winston Churchill told the House of Commons:

> The mood and temper of the public with regard to the treatment of crime and criminals is one of the most unfailing tests of the civilization of any country.[56]

This was said after he saw John Galsworthy's stirring play, *Justice*.

In 1967, Halleck wrote:

> A society can be judged by the manner in which it treats its deviant citizens. If it treats them as lesser beings who are to be systematically degraded and abused, it is not a great society. It is not even a decent society.[57]

The basis for all these themes lies in the doctrine of least eligibilities, which refers to the customary practice of all societies to refuse to provide their offenders with more than they do the least of their law-abiding citizens. Consequently, prison conditions can be considered as a baseline or point of departure from which the advance of a civilization or society can be measured.

The president and the Congress of the United States gave their endorsement to an enlightened program and increased resources for corrections in the 1970s. While the "law and order" slogans can be interpreted in a variety of ways, only a brief reading of the content of material coming from political and correctional leaders today gives hope for an enlightened, treatment-oriented correctional program with its primary focus in the community where the citizen-offender lives. Maximum custody institutions will remain for those who need extreme external control, but they will be small.

The United Nations has undertaken a project intended to suggest that any prison construction anywhere in the world be humane and not secure beyond that necessary for ordinary control, in hopes that "all men share a common existence as citizens not only of their own nation but also of the world."[58] Mutual assistance between nations, particularly in the area of criminal justice, is seen as a way to increase professionalism, effectiveness, and humane treatment to serve the needs of society.

[55] *Ibid.,* p. 63.

[56] See Harry Elmer Barnes and Negley K. Teeters, *New Horizons in Criminology,* 3rd ed. (Englewood Cliffs, N.J.: Prentice-Hall, 1959), p. 50, after Evelyn Ruggles-Brice, *The English Prison System* (London: Macmillan, 1910).

[57] Seymour Halleck, *Psychiatry and the Dilemma of Crime* (New York: Harper & Row, Publishers, 1967), p. 349.

[58] United Nations Social Defence Research Institute, Giuseppe di Gennaro, Project Director, *Prison Architecture: An International Survey of Representative Closed Institutions and Analysis of Current Trends in Prison Design* (London: The Architectural Press, Ltd., 1975), p. 225.

Prison reform groups have been organizing at an acceleratd pace since the late 1960s. A directory of these organizations published in 1975 included 490, and a supplement published in 1976 listed 110 more.[59]

Corrections as part of the criminal justice system has sometimes been confused. Public opinion and political leadership sometimes provide emotional reactions to crime and call for severe and simplistic solutions that load the corrections phase without providing the resources, which must result in litigation and liberal policies, either forced or chosen. Glueck said more than a quarter century ago that it is still true that too often in the administration of criminal justice, "the right hand not only knoweth not what the left is doing but too often is raised against it.[60]

The prison experiment began as a humane gesture, both in England and in America. The Quakers, who began the penitentiary movement in 1787, wrote nearly two centuries later:

> The horror that is the American prison system grew out of an eighteenth-century reform by the Pennsylvania Quakers and others against the cruelty and futility of capital and corporal punishment. This two-hundred-year-old experiment has failed.[61]

For adequate rehabilitation, the lawbreaker's problems are greater today, and the needs for remedial assistance are, too. This was no problem when the only alternatives open for punishing offenders were execution, banishment, or whipping, but when the humanitarian philosophy of John Howard and the Quakers developed the modern prison, a new setting emerged, and the philosophy of the new setting has never been implemented. "Too little and too late" loses battles and wars. Crime and further crime is the cost of neglect. Humanitarian philosophy without the resources to implement it has been inadvertently damaging to its clients and, consequently, either a failure or a nothing. Equal treatment to unequals is as great an injustice as is unequal treatment to equals. The modern prison and traditional correctional services do not have the resources to tell the difference.

## EXERCISES AND STUDY QUESTIONS

*1. Why is corrections important in society, and why will it become more important as society grows and becomes more complex?*

[59] Mary Lee Bundy and Kenneth R. Harmon, eds., *The National Prison Directory: Organizational Profiles of Prison Reform Groups in the United States,* Base Volume (College Park, Md.: Urban Information Interpreters, April 1975); and Mary Lee Bundy and Rebecca Glenn Whaley, eds., *The National Prison Directory: Organizational Profiles of Prison Reform Groups in the United States,* Supplement No. 1 (College Park, Md.: Urban Information Interpreters, 1976).

[60] Sheldon Glueck, *Crime and Correction: Selected Papers* (Cambridge, Mass.: Harvard University Press, 1952), p. 6.

[61] American Friends Service Committee, *Struggle for Justice* (New York: Hill & Wang, 1971), p. v.

2. Trace the development of governmental activities in general welfare programs. When did they begin to include correctional programs?

3. What are the major national surveys of the field of corrections?

4. Why is the large, centralized institution becoming obsolete?

5. Why is the correctional complex around an urban area considered to be more effective than the large, centralized institution?

6. Describe the changing role of the correctional officer as he becomes a correctional counselor.

7. Why do some scholars consider that sending offenders to some prisons is worse for society than doing nothing at all with them?

8. What role has litigation had in improving correctional systems?

9. Why is the regional jail considered to be beneficial?

10. Why are community-based institutions becoming more popular in the correctional field?

11. Why has there been an increase in the use of probation?

12. Why has there been an increase in the use of parole?

13. Suggest some new roles for parole boards.

14. What will be the effect of computers and technology in the correctional process?

15. Describe the growth of correctional programs in junior colleges and universities.

16. What are the three primary components for any correctional job?

17. What are some of the competencies needed by the correctional worker?

18. Explain how ex-inmates are being used in the field of corrections, and indicate what their future role may be.

19. What are the recommendations of the final reports of the Joint Commission on Correctional Manpower and Training?

20. What are some logical predictions for the future of corrections?

# SELECTED
# BIBLIOGRAPHY

ABEL, ERNEST, *Marihuana: The First Twelve Thousand Years.* New York: Plenum Publishing Co., 1980.

Advisory Council of Judges, *Guides for Sentencing.* New York: National Council on Crime and Delinquency, 1957.

*Alcoholics Anonymous,* 3rd ed. New York: Alcoholics Anonymous World Services, 1976.

ALEXANDER, MYRL, *Jail Administration.* Springfield, Ill.: Charles C. Thomas, 1957.

ALLEN, HARRY E., and CLIFFORD E. SIMONSEN, *Corrections in America: An Introduction.* Beverly Hills, Calif.: Glencoe Press, 1975.

ALPER, BENEDICT S., *Prisons Inside-Out: Alternatives in Correctional Reform.* Cambridge, Mass.: Ballinger Publishing, 1974.

American Assembly, *Prisoners in America,* ed. Lloyd E. Ohlin. Englewood Cliffs, N.J.: Prentice-Hall, 1973.

American Bar Association Commission on Correctional Facilities and Services and the Council of State Governments, *Compendium of Model Correctional Legislation and Standards,* 2nd ed. Washington, D.C.: U.S. Department of Justice, Law Enforcement Assistance Administration, June 1975.

American Correctional Association, *Proceedings of the Annual Congresses of Correction.* College Park, Md.: American Correctional Association, published annually since 1870.

ATKINS, BURTON, and HENRY R. GLICK, eds., *Prisons, Protest, and Politics.* Englewood Cliffs, N.J.: Prentice-Hall, 1972.

BARNES, HARRY ELMER, and NEGLEY K. TEETERS, *New Horizons in Criminology,* 3rd ed. Englewood Cliffs, N.J.: Prentice-Hall, 1959.

BEDAU, HUGO ADAM, and CHESTER M. PIERCE, eds., *Capital Punishment in the United States.* New York: AMS Press, for the American Orthopsychiatric Association, 1976.

BENJAMIN, JUDITH G., MARCIA K. FREEDMAN, and EDITH W. LYNTON, *Pros and Cons: New Roles for Nonprofessionals in Corrections.* Washington, D.C.: Office of Juvenile Delinquency and Youth Development of HEW, 1969.

BENNETT, LAWRENCE A., THOMAS S. ROSENBAUM, and WAYNE R. MCCULLOUGH, *Counseling in Correctional Environments.* New York: Human Sciences Press, 1978.

BESHAROV, DOUGLAS J., *Juvenile Justice Advocacy: Practice in a Unique Court.* New York: Practising Law Institute, 1974.

BOWKER, LEE H., *Prison Victimization.* New York: Elsevier, 1980.

BRODSKY, STANLEY L., and THOMAS EGGLESTON, *The Military Prison: Theory, Research, and Practice.* Carbondale, Ill.: Southern Illinois University Press, 1970.

BUNDY, MARY LEE, and KENNETH R. HARMON, eds., *The National Prison Directory: Organizational Profiles of Prison Reform Groups in the United States.* College Park, Md.: Urban Information Interpreters, April 1975.

BUNDY, MARY LEE, and REBECCA GLENN WHALEY, eds., *The National Prison Directory: Organizational Profiles of Prison Reform Groups in the United States.* College Park, Md.: Urban Information Interpreters, 1976.

BURNS, HENRY, JR., *Corrections: Organization and Administration.* St. Paul, Minn.: West Publishing, 1975.

CAMPBELL, CHARLES, *Serving Time Together.* Fort Worth: Texas Christian University, 1980.

CARLSON, KENNETH, *Policy Briefs: Mandatory Sentencing: The Experience of Two States.* Washington, D.C.: National Institute of Justice, May, 1982.

CARNEY, LOUIS P., *Introduction to Correctional Science.* New York: McGraw-Hill, 1974.

CARTER, ROBERT M., DANIEL GLASER, and LESLIE T. WILKINS, eds., *Corrections in America.* Philadelphia: J. B. Lippincott, 1975.

*Census of Jails and Survey of Jail Inmates, 1978, Preliminary Report.* Washington, D.C.: U.S. Government Printing Office, 1979.

*The Challenge of Crime in a Free Society* and the accompanying *Task Force Reports.* Washington, D.C.: The President's Commission on Law Enforcement and Administration of Justice, 1967.

CHANG, DAE H., and WARREN B. ARMSTRONG, eds., *The Prison—Voices from Inside.* Cambridge, Mass.: Schenkman Publishing, 1972.

*Children in Custody: Advance Report on the 1979 Census of Public Juvenile Facilities.* Washington, D.C.: Office of Juvenile Justice and Delinquency Prevention, 1980.

CLARE, PAUL K., and JOHN H. KRAMER, *Introduction to American Corrections.* Boston: Holbrook, 1976.

CLEMMER, DONALD, *The Prison Community.* Boston: Christopher Press, 1940; reissued by Holt, Rinehart & Winston, 1958.

CLOWARD, RICHARD F., and LLOYD E. OHLIN, *Delinquency and Opportunity: A Theory of Delinquent Gangs.* New York: Free Press, 1960.

COHEN, ALBERT K., *Delinquent Boys.* New York: Free Press, 1955.

COHEN, FRED, *The Legal Challenge to Corrections: Implications for Manpower and Training.* Washington, D.C.: Joint Commission on Correctional Manpower and Training, March 1969.

COLEMAN, JAMES C., *Abnormal Psychology and Modern Life*, 3rd ed. Glenview, Ill.: Scott, Foresman & Company, 1964.

COLSON, CHARLES W., *Born Again.* Old Tappan, N.J.: Chosen Books, 1976.

*Conference Proceedings—Inhalation of Glue Fumes and Other Substance Abuse Practices among Adolescents.* Washington, D.C.: Office of Juvenile Delinquency and Youth Development, HEW, 1969.

CONRAD, JOHN P., *Crime and Its Correction: An International Survey of Attitudes and Practices.* Berkeley, Calif.: University of California Press, 1965.

CONSTABLE, GEORGE, *The Neanderthals,* in *The Emergence of Man* series. New York: Time-Life Books, 1973.

CORMIER, BRUNO M., *The Watcher and the Watched.* Montreal: Tundra Books, 1975.

*Correctional Officer Resource Guide.* College Park, Maryland: American Correctional Association, 1983.

*Corrections.* Washington, D.C.: National Advisory Commission on Criminal Justice Standards and Goals, 1973.

CRAMER, JAMES, *Police Systems of the World.* Springfield, Ill.: Charles C. Thomas, 1968.

CRESSEY, DONALD R., ed., *The Prison: Studies in Institutional Organization and Change.* New York: Holt, Rinehart & Winston, 1961.

CRIMINAL LAW BULLETIN EDITORIAL STAFF, *Criminal Law Digest.* Boston: Warren, Gorham & Lamont, 1970 and subsequent supplements.

CULL, JOHN G., and RICHARD E. HARDY, eds., *Fundamentals of Criminal Behavior and Correctional Systems.* Springfield, Ill.: Charles C. Thomas, 1973.

CULLEN, FRANCIS T., and KAREN E. GILBERT, *Reaffirming Rehabilitation.* Cincinnati: W.H. Anderson Company, 1982.

DAVIS, SAMUEL M., *Rights of Juveniles: The Juvenile Justice System.* New York: Clark Boardman, 1974.

DI GENNARO, GIUSEPPE, Project Director, *Prison Architecture: An International Survey of Representative Closed Institutions and Analysis of Current Trends in*

*Prison Design.* London: The Architectural Press, Ltd., for the United Nations Social Defence Research Institute, 1975.

*Directory—Juvenile and Adult Correctional Departments, Institutions, Agencies & Paroling Authorities—1982.* College Park, Md.: American Correctional Association, 1982.

*Directory—Organizations Providing Job Assistance to Ex-Offenders.* Washington, D.C.: Clearinghouse on Offender Employment Restrictions, 1976.

DRESSLER, DAVID, *Practice and Theory of Probation and Parole.* New York: Columbia University Press, 1969.

*Drug Abuse Treatment in Prisons.* Washington, D.C.: U.S. National Institute on Drug Abuse, 1981.

DUFFEE, DAVID, and ROBERT FITCH, *An Introduction to Corrections: A Policy and Systems Approach.* Pacific Palisades, Calif.: Goodyear Publishing, 1976.

EMERSON, ROBERT M., *Judging Delinquents: Context and Process in Juvenile Court.* Chicago: Aldine, 1969.

EYMAN, JOY S., *Prisons for Women: A Practical Guide to Administration Problems.* Springfield, Ill.: Charles C. Thomas, 1971.

FAUST, FREDERIC L., and PAUL J. BRANTINGHAM, eds., *Juvenile Justice Philosophy: Readings, Cases and Comments.* St. Paul, Minn.: West Publishing, 1974.

*Federal Offenders Rehabilitation Project, Final Report, 1965–1969.* Springfield, Ill.: Division of Vocational Rehabilitation, 1970.

FEINMAN, CLARICE, *Women in the Criminal Justice System.* New York: Praeger, 1980.

FLANAGAN, TIMOTHY J., DAVID J. VAN ALSTYNE, and MICHAEL R. GOTTFREDSON, *Sourcebook of Criminal Justice Statistics—1981.* Washington, D.C.: Bureau of Justice Statistics, 1982.

FOGEL, DAVID, *". . . We Are the Living Proof . . .": The Justice Model for Corrections.* Cincinnati: W.H. Anderson, 1975.

FOX, VERNON, *Guidelines for Corrections Programs in Community and Junior Colleges.* Washington, D.C.: American Association of Junior Colleges, 1969.

———, *Violence behind Bars.* Westport, Conn.: Greenwood Press, 1974. Originally published in New York, 1956.

GARABEDIAN, PETER G., and DON C. GIBBONS, *Becoming Delinquent: Young Offenders and the Correctional System.* Chicago: Aldine, 1970.

GILLIN, JOHN LEWIS, *Criminology and Penology.* New York: D. Appleton-Century Co., 1915.

GLASER, DANIEL, *The Effectiveness of a Prison and Parole System,* abridged ed. Indianapolis: Bobbs-Merrill, 1964 and 1969.

———, ed., *Crime in the City.* New York: Harper & Row, 1970.

———, DONALD KENEFICK, and VINCENT O'LEARY, *The Violent Offender.* Washington, D.C.: Office of Juvenile Delinquency and Youth Development, HEW, 1969.

GLASER, DANIEL, and VINCENT O'LEARY, *The Alcoholic Offender*. Washington, D.C.: Office of Juvenile Delinquency and Youth Development, HEW, 1968.

————, *The Control and Treatment of Narcotic Use*. Washington, D.C.: Office of Juvenile Delinquency and Youth Development, HEW, 1968.

————, *Personal Characteristics and Parole Outcome*. Washington, D.C.: Office of Juvenile Delinquency and Youth Development, HEW, 1968.

GLASSER, WILLIAM, *Reality Therapy*. New York: Harper & Row, 1965.

GLUECK, SHELDON, and ELEANOR GLUECK, *Unraveling Juvenile Delinquency*. New York: The Commonwealth Fund, 1950.

HAHN, PAUL H., *Community Based Corrections and the Criminal Justice System*. Santa Cruz, Calif.: Davis Publishing, 1975.

————, *The Juvenile Offender and the Law*. Cincinnati: W.H. Anderson, 1971.

HALLECK, SEYMOUR, *Psychiatry and the Dilemma of Crime*. New York: Harper & Row, 1967.

*Handbook of Correctional Institution Design and Construction*. Washington, D.C.: United States Bureau of Prisons, 1949. Supplement, 1960.

HARPER, ROBERT A., *The New Psychotherapies*. Englewood Cliffs, N.J.: Prentice-Hall, 1975.

HARTINGER, WALTER, EDWARD ELDEFONSO, and ALAN COFFEY, *Corrections: A Component of the Criminal Justice System*. Pacific Palisades, Calif.: Goodyear Publishing, 1973.

HAZELRIGG, LAWRENCE E., ed., *Prison within Society: A Reader in Penology*. Garden City, N.Y.: Doubleday, 1968.

HERMAN, MICHELE G., and MARILYN G. HAFT, eds., *Prisoners' Rights Sourcebook: Therapy—Litigation—Practice*. New York: Clark Boardman, 1973.

HEWITT, E.S., and RICHARD L. JENKINS, *Origins of Maladjustment*. Springfield, Ill.: Illinois State Department of Health, 1944.

HEWITT, JOHN D., and TODD R. CLEAR, *The Impact of Sentencing Reform: From Indeterminate to Determinate Sentencing*. Lanham, Maryland: University Press of America, 1983.

HINDELANG, MICHAEL J., CHRISTOPHER S. DUNN, ALISON L. AUMICK, and L. PAUL SUTTON, *Sourcebook of Criminal Justice Statistics—1974*. Washington, D.C.: United States Law Enforcement Assistance Administration, National Criminal Justice Information and Statistics Service, 1975.

HINSIE, LELAND, and ROBERT JEAN CAMPBELL, *Psychiatric Dictionary*, 4th ed. New York: Oxford University Press, 1970.

HIPPCHEN, LEONARD J., ed., *Correctional Classification and Treatment*. Cincinnati: W.H. Anderson, 1975. Published for the American Correctional Association.

HOFFMAN, ETHAN (photography), and JOHN MCCOY, *Concrete Mama: Prison Profiles from Walla Walla*. Columbia, Mo.: University of Missouri Press, 1981.

HOWARD, D.L., *John Howard: Prison Reformer.* London: Christopher Johnson, 1958.

*Improved Prison Work Programs Will Benefit Correctional Institutions and Inmates—Report to the Attorney General.* Washington, D.C.: General Accounting Office, June 29, 1982.

*Jail Removal Cost Study,* Vols. 1 and 2. Washington, D.C.: Office of Juvenile Justice and Delinquency Prevention, May 1982.

JACOBS, JAMES B., *New Perspectives on Prisons and Imprisonment.* Ithaca, New York: Cornell University Press, 1983.

JACOBS, JAMES B., *Stateville: The Penitentiary in Mass Society.* Chicago: University of Chicago Press, 1977.

JAMAN, DOROTHY R., *Behavior during the First Year in Prison: Reports 1 and 2—MMPI Scales and Behavior.* Sacramento: Research Report Number 34, California Department of Corrections, 1969.

JOHNSTON, NORMAN, *The Human Cage: A Brief History of Prison Architecture.* New York: Walker and Co., published for The American Foundation of Philadelphia, 1973.

JONES, MAXWELL, *Psychiatry in the Community, in Hospitals and in Prisons.* Springfield, Ill.: Charles C. Thomas, 1962.

*Juvenile Justice: Before and After the Onset of Delinquency—United States Discussion Paper for the Sixth United Nations Congress on the Prevention of Crime and the Treatment of Offenders.* Washington, D.C.: Office of Juvenile Justice and Delinquency Prevention, 1980.

KADISH, SANFORD H., Editor-in-Chief, *Encyclopedia of Crime and Justice,* Vols. 1, 2, 3, and 4. New York: The Free Press, A Division of Macmillan, Inc., 1983.

KEISER, R. LINCOLN, *The Vice Lords: Warriors of the Streets.* New York: Holt, Rinehart & Winston, 1969.

KELLER, OLIVER J., and BENEDICT S. ALPER, *Halfway Houses.* Lexington, Mass.: D.C. Heath, 1970.

KEVE, PAUL W., *The Probation Officer Investigates.* Minneapolis: University of Minnesota Press, 1960.

KILLINGER, GEORGE G., and PAUL F. CROMWELL, JR., eds., *Corrections in the Community: Alternatives to Imprisonment—Selected Readings.* St. Paul, Minn.: West Publishing, 1974.

———, eds., *Penology: The Evolution of Corrections in America.* St. Paul, Minn.: West Publishing, 1973.

KINNEY, JEAN, and GWEN LEATON, eds., *Loosening the Grip.* St. Louis: C.V. Mosby, 1978.

KOOS, EARL LOMON, *They Follow the Sun.* Jacksonville, Fla.: Florida State Board of Health, 1957.

KRANTZ, SHELDON, ROBERT A. BELL, JONATHAN BRANDT, and MICHAEL MAGRUDER, *Model Rules and Regulations on Prisoners' Rights and Responsibilities.* St. Paul, Minn.: West Publishing, 1973.

LAUNE, FERRIS, *Predicting Criminality.* Evanston, Ill.: Northwestern University Press, 1937.

LEAKEY, RICHARD E., and ROGER LEWIN, *Origins.* London: Macdonald and Jane's, 1977.

LEJINS, PETER P., *Criminal Justice in the United States—1970–1975: An Overview.* College Park, Md.: American Correctional Association, September 1975. (Prepared for the Fifth United Nations Conference on the Prevention of Crime and Treatment of Offenders, Geneva, Switzerland, 1975.)

LEWIS, ORLANDO F., *The Development of American Prisons and Prison Customs, 1776–1845—With Special Reference to Early Institutions in the State of New York.* Montclair, N.J.: Patterson Smith, 1967. Originally published in 1922 by the Prison Association of New York.

LINDESMITH, ALFRED R., *The Addict and the Law.* Bloomington: Indiana University Press, 1965.

LIPTON, DOUGLAS, ROBERT MARTINSON, and JUDITH WILKS, *The Effectiveness of Correctional Treatment: A Survey of Treatment Evaluation Studies.* New York: Praeger, 1975. (Commonly known as "The Martinson Report.")

LOCKWOOD, DANIEL, *Prison Sexual Violence.* New York: Elsevier, 1979.

LOMBARDO, LUCIEN X., *Guards Imprisoned: Correctional Officers at Work.* New York, Elsevier, 1981.

LOWELL, HARVEY D., MARGARET MCNABB, and ANTHONY J. DEMARCO, *Sentenced Prisoners Under 18 Years of Age in Adult Correctional Facilities: A National Survey.* Washington, D.C.: National Center on Institutions and Alternatives, 1980.

MCCAFFERTY, JAMES A., ed., *Capital Punishment.* Chicago: Aldine-Atherton, 1972.

MCCARTT, JOHN M., and THOMAS J. MANGOGNA, *Guidelines and Standards for Halfway Houses and Community Treatment Centers.* Washington, D.C.: U.S. Department of Justice, Law Enforcement Assistance Administration, May 1973.

MCCORD, WILLIAM, and JOAN MCCORD, *Origins of Crime.* New York: Columbia University Press, 1959.

*Manual of Jail Administration.* Washington, D.C.: The National Sheriff's Association, 1970 and 1973.

*Manual of Standards for Adult Community Residential Services.* Rockville, Md.: Commission on Accreditation for Corrections, 1977.

*Manual of Standards for Adult Correctional Institutions.* Rockville, Md.: Commission on Accreditation for Corrections, 1977.

*Manual of Standards for Adult Local Detention Facilities.* Rockville, Md.: Commission on Accreditation for Corrections, 1977.

*Manual of Standards for Adult Parole Authorities.* Rockville, Md.: Commission on Accreditation for Corrections, 1976.

*Manual of Standards for Adult Probation and Parole Field Services.* Rockville, Md.: Commission on Accreditation for Corrections, 1977.

MARTIN, JOHN BARTHLOW, *Break Down the Walls.* New York: Ballantine, 1954.

MARTIN, JOHN M., *Delinquency Today: A Guide for Community Action.* Washington, D.C.: Office of Juvenile Delinquency and Youth Development, HEW, 1969.

————, JOSEPH P. FITZPATRICK, and ROBERT E. GOULD, *Analyzing Delinquent Behavior—A New Approach.* Washington, D.C.: Office of Juvenile Delinquency and Youth Development, HEW, 1968.

MEGATHLIN, WILLIAM L., *The Effects of Facilitation Training Provided Correctional Officers Stationed at the Atlanta Federal Penitentiary.* Athens, Ga.: U.S. Department of Justice and the University of Georgia, 1969.

MENNINGER, KARL, *The Crime of Punishment.* New York: Viking Press, 1968.

MILLER, EUGENE E., *Jail Management: Problems, Programs, and Perspectives.* Lexington, Mass.: Lexington Books, D.C. Heath Co., 1978.

MITFORD, JESSICA, *Kind and Usual Punishment: The Prison Business.* New York: Alfred A. Knopf, 1973.

MONAHAN, JOHN, and HENRY J. STEADMAN, eds., *Mentally Disordered Offenders: Perspectives from Law and Social Science.* New York: Plenum Press, 1983.

MORRIS, JOE ALEX, *First Offender: A Volunteer Program for Youth in Trouble with the Law.* Pleasantville, N.Y.: The Reader's Digest Association, 1970.

MORRIS, NORVAL, and GORDON HAWKINS, *The Honest Politicians' Guide to Crime Control.* Chicago: University of Chicago Press, 1970.

MORRIS, PAULINE, *Prisoners and Their Families.* New York: Hart Publishing, 1965.

MULLEN, JOAN, and BRADFORD SMITH, *American Prisons and Jails, Volume III: Conditions and Costs of Confinement.* Washington, D.C.: National Institute of Justice, 1980.

MURTON, TOM, and JOE HYAMS, *Accomplices to the Crime.* New York: Grove Press, 1969.

MURTON, THOMAS O., *The Dilemma of Prison Reform.* New York: Holt, Rinehart & Winston, 1976.

NAGEL, WILLIAM G., *The New Red Barn: A Critical Look at the Modern American Prison.* New York: Walker and Co., published for The American Foundation of Philadelphia, 1973.

NEWMAN, CHARLES L., BARBARA R. PRICE, JACQUELINE B. SOBEL, SHELDON ADELBERG, MARQUE BAGSHAW, and DEAN PHILLIPS, *Local Jails and Drug Treatment.* University Park, Pa.: College of Human Development, Pennsylvania State University, February 1976.

NEWMAN, GRAEME, *The Punishment Response.* New York: J.B. Lippincott, Co., 1978.

NUFER, HAROLD F., *American Servicemembers' Supreme Court: Impact of the U.S. Court of Military Appeals on Criminal Justice.* Lanham, Maryland: University Press of America, 1982.

New York State Special Commission on Attica, *Attica: The Official Report of the New York State Special Commission on Attica.* New York: Bantam Books, 1972.

OAKLEY, RAY, *Drugs, Society, & Human Behavior,* 3rd ed. St. Louis: C.V. Mosby Company, 1983.

OHLIN, LLOYD E., *Selection for Parole.* New York: Russell Sage Foundation, 1951.

OSWALD, RUSSELL G., *Attica—My Story,* ed. Rodney Campbell. Garden City, N.Y.: Doubleday, 1972.

PALMER, JOHN W., *Constitutional Rights of Prisoners.* Cincinnati: W.H. Anderson, 1973.

*Parole in the United States—1979.* San Francisco: Research Center West, National Council on Crime and Delinquency, December 1980.

PENICK, BETTYE K. EIDSON, ed., *Surveying Crime.* Washington, D.C.: National Academy of Sciences, 1976.

PEOPLES, EDWARD E., ed., *Readings in Correctional Casework and Counseling.* Pacific Palisades, Calif.: Goodyear Publishing, 1975.

PERLSTEIN, GARY R., and THOMAS R. PHELPS, eds., *Alternatives to Prison: Community-Based Corrections, A Reader.* Pacific Palisades, Calif.: Goodyear Publishing, 1975.

PETERSEN, DAVID M., and CHARLES W. THOMAS, eds., *Corrections: Problems and Prospects.* Englewood Cliffs, N.J.: Prentice-Hall, 1975.

PETTIBONE, JOHN M., ROBERT G. SWISHER, KURT H. WEILAND, CHRISTINE E. WOLF, and JOSEPH L. WHITE, *Major Issues in Juvenile Justice Information and Training: Services to Children in Juvenile Courts: The Judicial-Executive Controversy.* Columbus, Ohio: Academy for Contemporary Problems, 1981.

PHELPS, THOMAS R., *Juvenile Delinquency: A Contemporary View.* Pacific Palisades, Calif.: Goodyear Publishing, 1976.

PIGEON, HELEN, *Handbook of Correctional Procedures.* Harrisburg, Pa.: Pennsylvania Department of Corrections, 1942.

POWERS, EDWIN, *Parole Eligibility of Prisoners Serving a Life Sentence.* Boston: Massachusetts Correctional Association, 1969.

————, and HELEN WITMER, *An Experiment in the Prevention of Delinquency.* New York: Columbia University Press, 1951.

POWNELL, GEORGE A., *Employment Problems of Released Prisoners.* Washington, D.C.: U.S. Department of Labor, Manpower Administration, 1969.

PRICE, BARBARA RAFFEL, and NATALIE J. SOKOLOFF, *The Criminal Justice System and Women.* New York: Clark Boardman Co., 1982.

*Prisoners in State and Federal Institutions on December 31, 1979,* National Prisoner Statistics Bulletin SD-NPS-PSF-7. Washington, D.C.: U.S. Government Printing Office, 1981.

*Probation in the United States: 1980 and 1981.* San Francisco: Research Center West, National Council on Crime and Delinquency, 1982.

*Profile of Jail Inmates: Sociodemographic Findings from the 1978 Survey of Inmates of Local Jails.* Washington, D.C.: Bureau of Justice Statistics, 1980.

RAGEN, JOSEPH, and CHARLES FINSTON, *Inside the World's Toughest Prison.* Springfield, Ill.: Charles C. Thomas, 1962.

ROBERTS, ALBERT R., *Sourcebook on Prison Education—Past, Present, and Future.* Springfield, Ill.: Charles C. Thomas, 1971.

————, ed., *Correctional Treatment of the Offender.* Springfield, Ill.: Charles C. Thomas, 1974.

ROBINSON, LOUIS N., *Jails: Care and Treatment of Misdemeanant Prisoners in the United States.* Philadelphia: Winston, 1944.

RUBIN, SOL, *The Law of Criminal Correction,* 2nd ed. St. Paul, Minn.: West Publishing, 1973.

*The St. Louis Detoxification and Diagnostic Evaluation Center,* Law Enforcement Assistance Administration Project Report. Washington, D.C.: U.S. Department of Justice, 1970.

SANDS, BILL, *My Shadow Ran Fast.* Englewood Cliffs, N.J.: Prentice-Hall, 1964.

SCHEIER, IVAN H., and LEROY P. GOTER, *Using Volunteers in Court Settings: A Manual for Volunteer Probation Programs.* Washington, D.C.: Office of Juvenile Delinquency and Youth Development, HEW, 1969.

SELLIN, THORSTEN, *Capital Punishment.* New York: Harper & Row, 1967.

SHAFRITZ, JAY M., *Government Budgeting: Theory—Process—Politics.* Oak Park, Ill.: Moore Publishing Co., 1978.

SHEEHAN, SUSAN, *A Prison and a Prisoner.* Boston: Houghton Mifflin, 1978.

SLOVENKO, RALPH, ed., *Crime, Law and Corrections.* Springfield, Ill.: Charles C. Thomas, 1966.

SMITH, ALEXANDER B., and LOUIS BERLIN, *Introduction to Probation and Parole.* St. Paul, Minn.: West Publishing, 1976.

SMITH, EDGAR, *Brief against Death.* New York: Knopf, 1968.

STEAM, HERBERT S., *Youth as Advisors to Adults and Vice Versa.* Washington, D.C.: Office of Juvenile Delinquency and Youth Development, 1970.

STRUENING, ELMER L., and MARCIA GUTTENTAG, eds., *Handbook of Evaluation Research,* Vols. 1 and 2. Beverly Hills, Calif.: Sage Publications, 1975.

STUDT, ELLIOT, *Corrections,* Vol. 5 of the *Curriculum Study Committee Report:* New York: Council on Social Work Education, 1959.

*A Study of the Number of Persons with Records of Arrest or Conviction in the Labor Force.* Washington, D.C.: U.S. Department of Labor, 1979.

SYKES, GRESHAM M., *The Society of Captives: A Study of a Maximum Security Prison.* Princeton, N.J.: Princeton University Press, 1958.

TAPPAN, PAUL W., ed., *Contemporary Corrections.* New York: McGraw-Hill, 1951.

*Task Force Report: Corrections.* Washington, D.C.: The President's Commission on Law Enforcement and Administration of Justice, 1967.

THORNBERRY, TERENCE P., and JOSEPH E. JACOBY, *The Criminally Insane: A Community Follow-up of Mentally Ill Offenders.* Chicago: University of Chicago Press, 1979.

*A Time to Act,* Final Report of the Joint Commission on Correctional Manpower and Training. Washington, D.C., 1969.

TOAL, WILLIAM T., *Recent Developments in Correctional Case Law,* Vol. 1, Special Issue. Columbia, S.C.: South Carolina Department of Corrections, *Resolution of Correctional Problems and Issues,* Summer 1975.

TOCH, HANS, *Legal and Criminal Psychology.* New York: Holt, Rinehart & Winston, 1964.

TURPIN, JAMES E., ed., *In Prison: Writings and Poems about the Prison Experience.* New York: New American Library, 1975.

United Nations Social Defence Research Institute, *Prison Architecture: An International Survey of Representative Closed Institutions and Analysis of Current Trends in Prison Design,* Giuseppe de Gennaro, Project Director, and staff. London: The Architectural Press, 1975.

VAN DEN HAAG, ERNEST, *Punishing Criminals: Concerning a Very Old and Painful Question.* New York: Basic Books, 1975.

VEDDER, CLYDE B., and BARBARA A. KAY, eds., *Penology.* Springfield, Ill.: Charles C. Thomas, 1964.

VEDDER, CLYDE B., and DORA B. SOMERVILLE, *The Delinquent Girl,* 2nd ed. Springfield, Ill.: Charles C. Thomas, 1975.

VETTER, HAROLD J., and CLIFFORD E. SIMONSEN, *Criminal Justice in America: The System—The Process—The People.* Philadelphia: W.B. Saunders, 1976.

VINTER, ROBERT D., and ROSEMARY SARRI, eds., *Brought to Justice? Juveniles, the Courts, and the Law.* Ann Arbor: University of Michigan, National Assessment of Juvenile Corrections, 1976.

*Violent Crime in the United States.* Washington, D.C.: Bureau of Justice Statistics, September 1981, revised February 1982.

WALKER, P.N., *Punishment: An Illustrated History.* Newton, England: David Abbott, 1972.

WEBB, G.L., and DAVID G. MORRIS, *Prison Guards: The Culture and Perspective of an Occupational Group.* San Marcos, Tex.: Coker Books, 1978.

WILKERSON, DAVID R., with JOHN and ELIZABETH SHERRILL, *The Cross and the Switchblade.* New York: B. Geis and Associates, 1963.

WILLNER, WILLIAM, and PERRY B. HENDRICKS, JR., *Grants Administration.* Washington, D.C.: National Graduate University, 1972.

WILSON, JOSEPH, *Are Prisons Necessary?* Philadelphia: Dorrance Press, 1950.

WRIGHT, FRED, CHARLES BAHN, and ROBERT W. RIEBER, eds., *Forensic Psychology and Psychiatry.* New York: The New York Academy of Sciences, 1980.

ZELDES, ILYA, *The Problems of Crime in the USSR.* Springfield, Ill.: Charles C. Thomas, 1981.

ZIETZ, DOROTHY, *Women Who Embezzle or Defraud: A Study of Convicted Felons.* New York: Praeger, 1981.

# INDEX